DISCARD
B.C.H.E. – LIBRARY
00132953

GAINS AND LOSSES

GAINS AND LOSSES

NOVELS OF FAITH AND DOUBT IN VICTORIAN ENGLAND

BY ROBERT LEE WOLFF

JOHN MURRAY

1977

This edition published 1977 by John Murray
by arrangement with Garland Publishing, Inc., New York

Printed in the United States of America
0 7195 3388 0

"If a Victorian novel deals with Faith and Doubt urgently enough we put it on our literature list, even if it is a deadly novel."

Ruth apRoberts, *The Moral Trollope* (Ohio University Press, 1971), p. 29.

"Such is the universal charm of narrative, that the worst novel ever written will find some gentle reader content to yawn over it, rather than to open the pages of the historian, moralist, or poet. We have heard, indeed, of one work of fiction so immeasurably stupid, that the proprietor, diverted by the rarity of the incident, offered the book, which consisted of two volumes in duodecimo, handsomely bound, to any person who would declare, upon his honour, that he had read the whole from beginning to end. But, although this offer was made to the passengers on board an Indiaman, during a tedious outward voyage, the *Memoirs of Clegg the Clergyman* (such was the title . . .) completely baffled the most dull and determined student on board, and bid fair for an exception to the general rule above-mentioned, when the love of glory prevailed with the boatswain, a man of strong and solid parts, to hazard the attempt, and he actually conquered and carried off the prize!"

Sir Walter Scott, reviewing Jane Austen's *Emma* in the *Quarterly Review* XIV (1815-1816), reprinted in Ioan Williams, *Sir Walter Scott on Novelists and Fiction* (London: Routledge and Kegan Paul, 1968), pp. 225-236.

To all the boatswains among us,
and most especially to the students
in English 251r at Harvard in 1974 and 1975,
this book is dedicated.

CONTENTS

ILLUSTRATIONS

ACKNOWLEDGMENTS FOR ILLUSTRATIONS:

1. and 2. Meriol Trevor, *Newman, the Pillar and the Cloud* (New York: Doubleday, 1962).

3. *The New Monthly Magazine*, March, 1839, lithograph by J. Brown after a painting by Greatbach, frequently reproduced.

4. Christabel Coleridge, *Charlotte Mary Yonge. Her Life and Letters* (London: Macmillan, 1903), from a photograph by the Reverend Duke Yonge.
5. *Life and Letters of J. H. Shorthouse*, edited by his wife, Volume I (London: Macmillan, 1905), photograph by Emery Walker.
6. Arthur Symons, *A Study of Walter Pater* (London: Sawyer, 1932), photograph by Elliott and Fry.
7. J. W. Cross, ed., *George Eliot's Life as related in her Letters and Journals*, Volume II (Boston: Houghton Mifflin, 1909).
8. Olive J. Brose, *Frederick Denison Maurice. Rebellious Conformist.* (Athens, Ohio: Ohio University Press, 1971) from the original in the National Portrait Gallery.
9. *Charles Kingsley, His Letters and Memories of his Life*, ed. Mrs. Kingsley, Volume I (London: Macmillan, 1901).
10. Greville MacDonald, M. D., *George MacDonald and his Wife* (New York: Dial, 1924).
11. Mrs. Harry Coghill, ed. *The Autobiography and Letters of Mrs. M. O. W. Oliphant* (Edinburgh and London: Blackwood, 1899).
12. and 13. Catherine Macdonald Maclean, *Mark Rutherford. A Biography of William Hale White* (London: Macdonald, 1955).
14. G. S. Layard, *Mrs. Lynn Linton. Her Life, Letters and Opinions* (London: Methuen, 1901).
15. W. H. Dunn, *James Anthony Froude. A Biography.* Volume II (Oxford: Clarendon Press, 1963).
16. Janet Penrose Trevelyan, *The Life of Mrs. Humphry Ward* (New York: Dodd Mead, 1923).

ACKNOWLEDGMENTS

My greatest debt is to the Department of English at Harvard, which in 1972 showed its sporting instincts by inviting a mere historian (and not an English historian either) to give a course each spring term on some aspect of the Victorian novel. Intending at first to change the topic annually, I found in 1974 that the "Novels of Faith and Doubt" raised enough difficult and interesting questions to warrant a second round in 1975. To the students in those two years who explored the novels and the issues with me I have dedicated this book. It was Garland Publishing who suggested the reprinting of a large collection of the important religious novels. Instead of providing each of the 121 novels in the series with a brief introduction, it seemed best to treat the entire subject in a single volume.

Mrs. Elly Solmitz, Miss Nancy Cramer, and Miss Martha Fox have typed the manuscript uncomplainingly; Mrs. Madeleine Gleason has given it expert editorial attention.

The Harvard College Library, as always, has proved an ideal place in which to work. But even its resources would have been inadequate for this subject: no American institutional library has all or even most of the novels dealt with. My own general collection of Victorian fiction, in active formation since the late 1930's, provided more of these religious novels than any other source. For this I should like once more to thank the book dealers, who over the decades have found me these books, many of them once celebrated, now forgotten, and here resuscitated if not revived.

I should like to express my gratitude and appreciation to Elspeth Hart and Carol Irelan of Garland Publishing, Incorporated. Mrs. Hart has cheerfully made all the complicated arrangements necessary for the reprinting of the 121 novels in the series from a widely-scattered group of first editions, and has seen them into production. Miss Irelan has supervised the production of this volume from manuscript to galleys, to pages, to its finished form as a book, and has firmly and kindly borne with my idiosyncrasies. It has been a privilege to have Lance Hidy as the designer, not only of the Catalogue of the Series but of this introductory volume. His resourcefulness, taste, and judgment have contributed immeasurably to its final appearance.

INTRODUCTION

Religion and the Victorian Novel

"It takes two to communicate," a distinguished scholar of Victorian literature noted not so long ago, "and we have not yet sufficiently recognized, let alone explored, the crucial problem of the mental equipment, the store of information and established responses, which the Victorian reader brought to his perusal of the latest novel."[1] Innocently we read Victorian fiction for enjoyment, and fail to realize that often we are not understanding it. Though not very remote from us in time, the Victorian novelist wrote—in language that appears misleadingly like our own—for an audience who automatically understood his allusions, who did not need the explanations that we in fact need but usually do not even know we need. When we read Shakespeare we at least know we must be alert to what we may be missing. But when we read the Victorians we are usually not alert. As a result, we miss a great deal.

We miss not only topical references to news of the day—a parliamentary election, a scandal over the conditions of child-labor in the cotton-mills, a sensational murder, a gold-strike in Australia—but also allusions to whole worlds of opinion, of discourse, and of social relations that have now vanished. The relations between landlord and tenant on a large estate, the attitudes of farmers towards the passage of the local hunt over their ploughed fields, the difference between a prison (gaol) and a penitentiary, the varying social status of undergraduates at the universities, the purchase and sale of commissions in the army: all are foreign to the late twentieth century and make readers of Victorian novels cry out for footnotes. However, of all the subjects that interested Victorians, and therefore preoccupied their novelists, none—not love, or crime, or

1. Richard D. Altick, "Victorian Readers and the Sense of the Present," *Midway* 10 (1969-1970): 95.

war, or sport, or ancestry, or even money—held their attention as much as religion. And of all the subjects none is more obscure to the modern reader.

Not since the seventeenth century—the period of the Civil Wars, the Commonwealth, and the Restoration—had religious contention been the stuff of everyday English life. Again, families were bitterly divided. The Church of England was rent by party controversy, with "High-Church" partisans battling "Low-Church" partisans, and—by the 1850's—a small but vocal and influential "Broad-Church" group opposed to both and to the very existence of party spirit. Quarrels raged over a wide variety of doctrinal issues: what to believe; and of practical issues: how the service should be conducted. Except for a few at the extreme High-Church end of the spectrum, members of the Church of England were united in their opposition to Roman Catholicism, which often amounted to detestation. Except for some at the extreme Low-Church end of the spectrum, members of the Church of England were united against the Protestants outside the Church: the many sects of Nonconformists or Dissenters. Before long, the question broadened in the minds of many, if not most, Victorians. They were troubled not only about what to believe and how to practice their religion, but also about whether to believe at all, and how continued belief might be possible. Doubts were fostered by the advances of science, which rendered the Bible's account of creation suspect; by the advances of scholarship, which showed that the books of the Bible must have been written down at widely different times; by ethical qualms over certain Christian doctrines; by the impossibility of reconciling the concept of a wholly benevolent and all-powerful God with the doctrine of eternal punishment for sinners. There seem at times to have been as many varieties of doubt as there were human beings in Victorian England.

Hundreds, perhaps thousands, of novels reflect every aspect of the public religious controversies and the private religious agonies. It is one purpose of this book to serve as an introduction to a collection of 121 Victorian novels of religion, now reprinted and made available once again to readers, most of them for the first time in many years. John Henry Newman, George Eliot, Disraeli, Walter Pater, Cardinal Wiseman, William Hale White, Samuel Butler:

these well-known names are all represented in this series and discussed in the pages that follow. But so are dozens of novels by writers now forgotten or nearly forgotten, whose fiction dealt primarily with religion. This book, then, is also intended as a map of territories now unfamiliar, enabling readers to range at will among the rich variety of fiction that assumes a knowledge of this topography.

Moreover, almost all Victorian novels—even those dealing primarily with far different subjects—touch upon religious matters. Although Dickens, Thackeray, the Brontës, never wrote a novel that dealt chiefly with religion, modern readers will find it impossible to understand key passages in their novels without such a map as is here provided. Take, for example, *Great Expectations.* In one of its climactic scenes, just before Miss Havisham sets herself on fire, she is kneeling to Pip and begging his forgiveness for the way she had trained Estella. Pip reflects that he cannot comfort her:

> That she had done a grievous thing in taking an impressionable child to mould into the form that her wild resentment, spurned affection, and wounded pride found vengeance in, I knew full well. But that, in shutting out the light of day, she had shut out infinitely more; that, in seclusion, she had secluded herself from a thousand natural and healing influences; that her mind, brooding solitary, had grown diseased, *as all minds do and must and will that reverse the appointed order of their Maker*, I knew equally well. And could I look upon her without compassion, seeing her punishment in the ruin she was, in her profound unfitness for this earth on which she was placed, in the vanity of sorrow which had become a master mania, like the vanity of penitence, the vanity of remorse, the vanity of unworthiness, and other monstrous vanities that have been curses in the world?

A Victorian reader would have known at once that the passage, notably the words I have italicized, is comparing Miss Havisham's unnatural solitary spinsterhood (complete with rotting wedding cake and tattered bridal dress) to Catholic monasticism. Nuns' minds, says Dickens, reverse "the appointed order of their Maker," and so necessarily grow diseased. Just as Miss Havisham's "vanity" has been sorrow, which has become a mania, so the nun's vanity is "penitence . . . remorse . . . unworthiness," all of them "monstrous" and "curses to the world." Dickens had carefully laid the groundwork for this reflection earlier in the chapter, when Pip, on his way to Miss Havisham's, had passed the site of an ancient monastery: "The nooks of ruin where the old monks had once had their refectories and gardens, and where the strong walls were now pressed into the service of humble sheds and stables, were almost as silent as the old monks in their graves."

Dickens, the master hand at playing on all the sensibilities of his readers, knew in his bones that most of them shared in some degree the almost universal English suspicion of convents. Anti-Catholic feeling was endemic in England. It varied in intensity and in rationality. But even among people who were relatively tolerant of other aspects of Catholicism, the celibacy of the clergy, the practice of confession, and above all the revival after 1829 of convents aroused fierce Protestant suspicions. Innocent young girls led astray by designing clerics, usually Jesuits, abound in novels. They are despoiled of their fortunes and of their chastity. They cannot escape. The flames of popular sentiment were fed by the press, which reported alleged cases in real life. Light-years removed from the most sensational and loud-voiced anti-Catholics, Dickens yet shared their apprehension about convents and put it—as naturally as breathing—into *Great Expectations,* where his readers—as naturally as breathing—appreciated it. We no longer breathe the same air. The meaning of such a passage must be painstakingly pointed out to us.

In Thackeray's *Pendennis,* when Pendennis and George Warrington are chatting about the way of the world, Pendennis, open-minded and somewhat cynical, declares that he sees truth on both sides of every political question, among Conservatives, Radicals, "and even on the ministerial benches." He then goes on to religion:

> I see it in this man who worships by Act of Parliament, and is rewarded with a silk apron and five thousand a year [which is to say: a Bishop of the Church of England, who has of course subscribed to the Thirty-nine Articles of the Church "as established by law," and so has reached high preferment]; in that man who, driven fatally by the remorseless logic of his creed,

> gives up everything, friends, fame, dearest ties, closest vanities, the respect of an army of churchmen, the recognized position of a leader, and passes over, truth-impelled, to the enemy, in whose ranks he is ready to serve henceforth as a nameless private soldier:—I see the truth in that man, as I do in his brother, whose logic drives him to quite a different conclusion, and who, after having passed a life in vain endeavors to reconcile an irreconcilable book, flings it at last down in despair, and declares, with tearful eyes, and hands up to Heaven, his revolt and recantation.

Few modern readers will see in this passage what Thackeray's readers late in the year 1850 would have seen at once. Pendennis's man and his brother, who have taken such contrasting religious paths, are not impersonal abstractions, but sensitive descriptions of John Henry Newman and his younger brother, Francis. It was the elder Newman who had been the leader in the Church of England, "with the respect of an army of churchmen," and who had given up everything to join the Roman Catholic Church ("the enemy"). And Newman's anguish at leaving Oxford and saying farewell to friends and family he had himself described in a novel, *Loss and Gain* (1848, no. 6, discussed at length below), which Thackeray had probably read. Francis Newman, on the other hand, had joined the Plymouth Brethren, one of the strictest Calvinist sects among Dissenters, and eventually (after trying vainly to "reconcile an irreconcilable book"—the Bible, of course) became a Freethinker. His religious pilgrimage was by no means over, but in 1850, only a few months before this passage in *Pendennis* was written, he had published his own book, *Phases of Faith*, in which he told his own story. The dramatic contrast between the brothers' religious experiences had struck Thackeray, who almost casually alluded to them in his novel, where we miss the allusion.

Sometimes, of course, a modern reader is aware that he does not fully understand the novelist's intention. In *Agnes Grey*, for example, Anne Brontë carefully describes Mr. Hatfield, the rector, "with his rich silk gown flying behind him," who mounts the pulpit "like a conqueror ascending his triumphal car; then sinking on the velvet cushion in an attitude of studied grace." He gabbles through the

Lord's Prayer, draws off "one bright lavender glove to give the congregation the benefit of his sparkling rings," and passes his fingers "through his well-curled hair, flourishing a cambric handkerchief." When he preaches, it is about

> church discipline, rites and ceremonies, apostolical succession, the duty of reverence and obedience to the clergy, the atrocious criminality of dissent, the absolute necessity of observing all the forms of godliness, the reprehensible presumption of individuals who attempted to think for themselves in matters connected with religion, or to be guided by their own interpretations of Scripture, and, occasionally, (to please his wealthy parishioners,) the necessity of deferential obedience from the poor to the rich—supporting his maxims and exhortations throughout with quotations from the Fathers, with whom he appeared to be far better acquainted than with the Apostles and Evangelists, and whose importance he seemed to consider, at least, equal to theirs.

It is obvious that Anne Brontë thoroughly dislikes Mr. Hatfield, but probably not many modern readers can tell why.

To her audience in 1847 it would have been perfectly obvious that the rector is a "High Churchman," or "Tractarian" or "Anglo-Catholic" or "Puseyite," all words for the same thing. His elegance in dress, the traces of effeminacy, the velvet cushion, give that away at once. In a time of bitter, omnipresent controversy over religion—fought out in the press, in the pulpit of every village church in England, and in the drawing-rooms of every household—Mr. Hatfield is a strong partisan. He vigorously favors the Catholic revival launched in the early thirties by the young writers of *Tracts for the Times*—hence "Tractarians"—the "Oxford movement" of which John Henry Newman was the most prominent leader until his conversion in 1845 to the Church of Rome. Mr. Hatfield's sermon presses for the Tractarian platform. He insists on the authority of the Church of England, based on the direct succession of its bishops from the Apostles, and the laity's need to submit. He opposes all the "Protestant" features of the Church of England: the exercise of private judgment in reaching one's religious belief ("reprehensible presumption") and the careful reading and interpretation of the Bible by individual Christians. Dissent—that is, even more extreme Protestantism, whose adherents do not conform to the Church of England and are therefore outside it (Nonconformists or Dissenters)—is to Mr. Hatfield "atrocious criminality." He is a strong defender of the social order (the poor must be deferential to the rich), and he has a special veneration—as Roman Catholics do—for the Church Fathers, whom he seems to put on a level with the Bible itself, shocking the Protestant-minded.

But why does Anne Brontë dislike him? Because her father was a member of the opposition, staunchly anti-Tractarian, a "Low-Church" or "Evangelical" clergyman. Several times he had been harassed by having as subordinates in his parish young Tractarian curates. Readers of Charlotte Brontë's *Shirley* will find them charmingly satirized there. All three Brontë sisters were brought up by their Aunt Branwell, who was even "lower" than their father, with leanings towards Methodism. No wonder Anne Brontë caused Agnes Grey to scorn Mr. Hatfield and to prefer the Low-Church Mr. Weston: she is "decidedly pleased with the evangelical truth" of Mr. Weston's "doctrine, as well as the earnest simplicity of his manner, and the clearness and force of his style."

Similar passages, similar scenes, could be found in the novels of almost any great Victorian writer. The richness and complexity of George Eliot's own religious experiences are reflected in the much discussed but still often opaque philosophical development in her fiction. Without an easy familiarity with the contemporary religious struggles the reader of Trollope misses half the depth, half the fun. That Mr. Arabin and Archdeacon Grantly are High-Church, Bishop and Mrs. Proudie and Mr. Slope Low-Church, is not an accident but an essential aspect of their characters and of their behavior. But the mere label "High" or "Low" Trollope himself supplies: what he does not do, because he did not need to, is tell his readers what this party struggle meant, not only in religious doctrine but also in social position, social attitudes, educational background. Why are the contrasting personalities of Archdeacon Grantly's three young sons in *The Warden*—who play no important part in the story—given as full and detailed a description as if they were major characters? Because each son is a caricature of a well-known contemporary bishop, each with the same first name as the bishop whose attitudes and behavior he is intended to satirize. Who are the bishops, and what did they do in real life to deserve to appear, unrecognized except by experts, in a novel which still commands a large and appreciative public? Unless we know, we are handicapped, our appreciation of Trollope's intention incomplete. So with *Phineas Redux*, for example, where the growing madness of Robert Kennedy, Lady Laura's husband, is identifiable as a form of Calvinist mania only if the reader has learned to recognize the symptoms. And so with *The Bertrams*, where the hero's entire career (as most critics wholly fail to realize) is transformed into failure because the girl he loves makes fun of his desire to become a clergyman, and so turns him away from the profession that would best have suited him and condemns them both to unhappiness.

The Victorian Religious Spectrum: An Overview

Before turning to the novels themselves, then, it will be well to take the briefest possible glance at the complex Victorian religious scene. We deal here only with the varieties of belief, leaving the varieties of disbelief and doubt for the chapters on the novels themselves. A spectrum—a horizontal bar of rainbow colors—serves us as a metaphor. All the visible colors from violet at the extreme right to red at the extreme left represent the diverse gradations of religious opinion within the Church of England itself. Outside the spectrum to the right, outside the Church of England, in the ultraviolet, are the Roman Catholics. Outside the spectrum to the left, and also outside the Church of England, in the infrared, are the Dissenters or Nonconformists, Protestants of many varying sects, who dissent from the Church of England and do not conform to its usages.

Until the Reformation of the sixteenth century, every English Christian was a Roman Catholic. He worshipped in a church governed by a hierarchy of celibate priests, subject to bishops, who were in turn subject to the two Archbishops—of York and Canterbury—who were in turn subject to the Pope. The services were conducted in Latin. The Catholic believed in the efficacy of seven sacraments or holy acts. *Baptism*, conferred in infancy, cleansed the child of sin. The *Eucharist*, a ceremonial eating of the bread and drinking of the wine that represented—indeed miraculously *were*—Christ's body and blood, was the central act of the Catholic Mass, a Holy Communion to which children were admitted at the age of six. *Confirmation*, a third sacrament, followed, usually between the ages of ten and fourteen. An adult Catholic was expected before taking communion to confess his sins privately to a priest (by talking into his ear: hence "auricular confession"), who then absolved him of his sins and might ask him to perform *penance*, a fourth sacrament. *Marriage* was a fifth, and the last rites for the dying, known as *extreme unction*, a final anointing with holy oil, and frequently the receiving of a last communion, was a sixth. The seventh was *holy orders*, the act of becoming a priest, by the consecration of a bishop who laid his hands upon the head of the kneeling ordinand.

The "laying on of hands" symbolized the continuity of ordination since the time of Christ himself; each bishop was in direct succession to Christ's own Apostles. Each Catholic was enjoined to believe in the authority of the Church, as conveyed in the writings of the early Christian writers, the "fathers," as well as in the authority of the Bible, which, however, was not generally circulated among the laity, although passages from it were of course read to them in Latin at every service. Catholics had a special veneration for the Virgin Mary and invoked her or other saints to intercede with Christ to forgive them their sins. They believed that after death—except for the damned, who would go to hell to await the final judgment, and except for the supremely virtuous who would ascend at once to heaven and be "saved"—ordinary human beings would spend some time in purgatory before they could be accepted in heaven, the length of time varying according to the gravity of their sins on earth. The better a man behaved during his lifetime—the more "good works" he performed and the fewer sins he committed—the shorter would be his probationary period in purgatory. The entire hierarchy of the priesthood constituted the "secular" clergy, who lived in the world of daily affairs. But in England, as on the Continent, there were a large number of different orders of monks and nuns, living according to a rule in monasteries and convents and therefore called "regular" clergy.

The English Reformation of the sixteenth century changed all this. It was prompted, as everybody knows, by Henry VIII's determination to divorce his wife, and by the inability of the Pope—for political reasons—to oblige the king. But although this political crisis determined the moment of the break between England and Rome, no such action would have been possible had it not been for a deep reservoir of hostility in England to the papacy and to Catholicism. This went back to the Middle Ages; in some of its aspects it expressed English resentment against papal interference in English affairs, in others a distaste for clerical corruption and clerical wealth, in others a wish to have the Bible generally available in English. The continental reformers of the sixteenth century, particularly Martin Luther, had many contacts with English scholars, and Tyndale, who published an English Bible in 1526, had studied with Luther. By the Act of Supremacy of 1534, Henry VIII ended papal supremacy and declared himself as king to be the head of the English Church. Between 1535 and 1540, he closed the monasteries and confiscated and redistributed their properties, enormously enriching the crown itself and the class of landed gentry.

Of course, loyal Catholics bitterly opposed these measures. But the strongly Protestant-minded felt that they had not gone far enough. As an English Protestant wrote in 1546, "Our king has destroyed the Pope but not popery; idolatry is nowhere in greater vigor. The impious mass, the invocation of saints, auricular confession, superstitious abstinence from meats, clerical celibacy": all these were still in force. Once Henry VIII had thrown off papal supremacy and got the wife he wanted, he wished to make no more changes. But the Protestant momentum could not be halted. Henry's son Edward VI (1547-1553) tried to impose Protestantism by abolishing the Latin liturgy and clerical celibacy; his half-sister Mary Tudor (1553-1558) tried to restore Catholicism by force, and burned Protestant martyrs; their half-sister Elizabeth (1558-1603) swung back to Protestantism. After many intermediate stages and more than twenty years of debate, Parliament in 1571 voted thirty-nine articles setting forth the official position of the Church of England with respect to all the doctrinal disputes then raging in European Christianity.

These "Thirty-nine Articles" voted in 1571 were not, of course, a complete summary of the Christian faith. But they have remained the official theological platform of the Church of England. In Victorian days, before a man would be ordained in the Church of England, he had to "subscribe the Articles," declaring that he acknowledged "all and every" one to "be agreeable to the word of God," a formula somewhat softened in 1865 to read, "I believe the doctrine . . . therein set forth to be agreeable to the Word of God." The Elizabethan religious settlement made English the language of the liturgy, ended clerical celibacy as a requirement for holy orders, abolished auricular confession. In effect, the seven Catholic sacraments were reduced to two: baptism and the eucharist. Where the Catholics held that the sacramental bread and wine of the eucharist were miraculously transformed into the body and blood of Christ (transubstantiation), even though they remained chemically bread and wine (their "accidents" or physical properties were constant), the Thirty-nine Articles declared: "Transubstantiation cannot be proved by Holy Writ, is repugnant to the plain words of Scripture, overthroweth the nature of a sacrament, and hath given occasion to many superstitions. The Body of Christ is given, taken, and eaten in the Supper, only after an heavenly and spiritual manner." But the act was not merely symbolic, as the Swiss reformer Zwingli maintained, since "the bread which we break is a partaking of the Body of Christ and likewise the Cup of Blessing is a partaking of the Blood of Christ. . . . And the means whereby the Body of Christ is received and eaten in the Supper is faith."[2]

By the end of Queen Elizabeth's reign, the official Church of England had repudiated both Rome and the extreme Protestantism of Calvin, which reigned at Geneva. In England, there were many Catholics who mourned the change in the old ways and hoped for a restoration of Catholicism, and many Protestants who felt that the newly emerging Church of England was not Protestant enough,

2. Although confirmation was no longer a sacrament, it became the custom in the Church of England to postpone the first communion until *after* a child had been confirmed.

who opposed bishops, and who favored a Presbyterian organization and principles. Both of these groups would ultimately fail, and so remain outside the spectrum: in the ultraviolet or infrared. Yet it took more than a century after Elizabeth's death to make this outcome certain.

Every few years there occurred an episode that deepened the ordinary Englishman's suspicion and fear of Catholicism: Mary Tudor's persecutions in the 1550's, the Catholic support for Mary Queen of Scots and for the papal-backed Spanish Armada in the 1580's, the entry of the Jesuits into England and the beginnings of Elizabethan persecution of "Recusants" (Catholics who refused to attend Anglican services or who left the service without taking communion) in the 1590's. Under Elizabeth's successor, James I (1603-1625), came the Guy Fawkes gunpowder plot, hatched by Catholics in 1605, and the marriage of Charles I (1625-1649) to a French Catholic princess. After the Civil Wars, the execution of Charles I in 1649, and Cromwell's Puritan-dominated Commonwealth and Protectorate, the pro-Catholic Charles II was restored in 1660. His brother and successor, James II (1685-1688), *was* a Catholic. James's efforts to circumvent parliamentary opposition and decree the toleration of Catholicism precipitated the Glorious Revolution of 1688, a *coup d'état* that brought the throne to James's Anglican daughter Mary and her Dutch Calvinist husband, William III (1688-1702). The Act of Settlement of 1701 made it illegal for a Catholic ever again to become King of England. But twice—in 1715 and 1745—the Stuart Catholic pretenders launched invasions in an effort to seize the throne by force.

In 1780, when a bill relieving Catholic disabilities was passed by Parliament, Lord George Gordon incited the mob to violence in the so-called Gordon riots, and London suffered much disorder. It took the French Revolution, with its violent antireligious policies that sent waves of Catholic émigrés as refugees to England, to arouse English public opinion sufficiently to support in 1791 an Act of Parliament allowing Catholics to become lawyers and to have their own schools and churches. They were not admitted to Parliament, however, until the "Catholic Emancipation" Act of 1829, and then chiefly because the English Parliament in 1801 had by the Act of Union with Ireland become directly responsible for governing some five million Catholics across the narrow Irish Sea. Catholic emancipation was accomplished against the misgivings of many conservatives; Catholic members of Parliament had to swear a special oath "not to disturb or weaken the Protestant religion or Protestant government in the United Kingdom"; and anti-Catholic sentiment remained alive and vigorous throughout the nineteenth century.

The immigration of Irish laborers into England from the early years of the industrial revolution onwards added a large stratum of poor urban workers at the bottom of the social scale to a small stratum of old noble or untitled but landed Catholic families at the top, with very little in between. At the opening of the Victorian age, then, Catholics in England were emancipated but still suspect. "In the days of Henry VIII," wrote a virulently anti-Catholic Church of England clergyman as late as 1875, "the abbots, priors and monks kept as many women each as any lascivious Mohammedan could desire, and their crimes renewed the existence of Sodom and Gomorrah," while convents were "no better than brothels of the worst description." Only against this historical background, here merely sketched in, can we read the Victorian novels by Catholics and anti-Catholics.

At the other end of the spectrum, in the infrared, those who were more Protestant than the legally established Church of England had their own troubled history. Unlike the Catholics, they did not want to overthrow the Church, but they wanted to change it. They were never the suspect instruments of a foreign power, despite their enormous regard for Calvin and his principles and their respect for John Knox, who introduced Calvinism into Scotland. They wanted to abolish bishops and govern the church by elders (presbyters), who would give greater consideration than Anglican bishops to the opinions of laymen. Worship was to be stripped of vestments, ornaments, and ceremonies. The sign of the cross was to be omitted from the baptismal rite, the imposition of priestly hands from confirmation, the use of the ring from marriage. Hymn singing and organ music should go. These "Puritans" tried to ignore the bishops and govern themselves, and as early as the late sixteenth century some left the Church of England: the Brownists, who formed an "independent" congregation and became the forerunners of later Congregationalist churches, always called "Independent" even in Victorian days. Each congregation, in their view, should be self-governing. Strongly sabbatarian and Judaizing, assiduous readers of the English Bible, and so devotees of the Old Testament, they were opposed by James I, whose Declaration of Sports of 1618 specifically commended as Sunday pastimes the very activities (dancing and the like) which the Puritans most abhorred. The Pilgrims who left England for Holland in 1609 and for America in 1620 were driven from England by such opposition to their views.

But it was the Civil Wars and their aftermath that eventually drove many more Puritans out of the Church of England and turned them into "Dissenters." Through his autocratic archbishop Laud, Charles I challenged the Puritans, who also objected to the King's autocratic style in politics. The Puritan-dominated Long Parliament in 1640 denounced Laud as "the stye of all pestilential filth, the common enemy of all goodness and good men," and two years after the Civil Wars broke out Laud was executed (1645). Falsely charging Laud with Romanism, the Puritan parliament abolished the episcopacy and, in effect, ended the Church of England temporarily. Those members of the clergy who refused to sign the Puritan Solemn League and Covenant of 1644 (about a quarter of the entire body) were dismissed. But Presbyterian tyranny was no less distasteful than Laud's Anglican tyranny. Sects multiplied; Cromwell himself was an Independent. The execution of the king in 1649 produced a great revulsion; it was felt to be a horrible and unforgiveable crime. The Commonwealth and Protectorate proved unable to organize a church and were forced to tolerate all sects that were neither Catholic nor Anglican. And the Laudian Anglican clergy held together in exile or at home, determined to await the inevitable restoration of the monarchy.

When Charles II was restored in 1660, the Laudian Anglicans restored the bishops, re-established the Anglican Church, punished the regicides, and made only the slenderest doctrinal concessions to Puritan views. Instead, the Clarendon Code of the 1660's and the Test Act of 1673 required that all those who held civic office must be communicants of the Church of England, forbade anyone over the age of sixteen to attend any religious services except those of the Church of England, and prohibited any minister of a nonconforming sect from living within five miles of any place in which he had previously performed his functions. Some officeholders tried to circumvent the first provision by occasionally taking Anglican communion; but such "occasional conformity" was forbidden in 1711. Soon after the Glorious Revolution of 1688, most nonconformists were permitted to have their own houses of worship, provided they had duly notified the bishop of the diocese and never locked their doors. But their civil disabilities, though not always enforced, remained valid until 1828. Even after they had been repealed, the year before the Catholics were emancipated, nonconformists (Dissenters) were still barred from the universities.

During these years of partial outlawry, the sects multiplied. Presbyterians and Congregationalists (Independents) were joined by Baptists, who rejected infant baptism and the ordination of ministers. For them church membership depended upon a specific conversion, a moment at which the believer underwent a major personal religious experience and accepted Christianity as a result. The idea that such a conversion was necessary gained greater and greater currency among other nonconformists and within the Church of England. We shall meet it repeatedly in our Victorian novels. The only two remaining sacraments were dropped altogether by the Quakers, who did not baptize their members at any time in their lives and abandoned the eucharist as well. Sermons and singing went by the board, as the Quaker congregations sat in silence waiting for the Spirit of God to speak to individuals. And late in the seventeenth century also, Deism—an abandonment of all dogma and a clinging to a pure and simple faith—manifested itself. *Christianity not Mysterious* was the title of an important early Deist book. Deists rejected the doctrines of the incarnation and the atonement, disbelieved in revelation, and adhered to reason and a natural religion. The Unitarians (in England often called Socinians after the Italian Fausto Sozzini, 1539-1604) were Deists who wholly denied the divinity of Christ. They shared with the Catholics a unique disability: they were not even allowed houses of worship.

Within the Church of England the eighteenth century saw the development of Methodism. The term was first used by a group of young Anglicans at Oxford to describe the strict standards of discipline by which they sought to regulate their own spiritual lives. One of them, John Wesley (1703-1791), at the age of thirty-five underwent a "conversion." He was listening to a sermon on the Lutheran doctrine of "justification by faith," which had become part of the Thirty-nine Articles and which maintains that only through faith—belief in Christ—can a sinner be assured of pardon for his sins and salvation. Christ's crucifixion had truly atoned for the sins of all mankind. Christ's "righteousness," it was believed, was "imputed" to the believing sinner. Justification by faith alone, closely allied with the idea that each individual must experience his own "conversion," was the central Protestant tenet both inside the Church of England and among the nonconformists. Wesley's long ministry involved itinerant preaching throughout the country to audiences in the newly industrializing towns whom the complacent clergy of the comparatively stagnant eighteenth-century Church of England largely ignored. Wesley's energy and earnestness, his dependence on "the plain genuine gospel," the "enthusiasm" he inspired and shared, his fiery zeal, all became legends. "To attract and hold together a crowd of two or three thousand miners at five o'clock on a winter's morning in the open air to listen to a sermon of anything up to two hours on the subject of Justification by Faith is no mean achievement. And Wesley did something of that kind nearly every day."[3]

Wesley's insistence on Anglican communion taken frequently conflicted with the standard practice of infrequent communion among Anglicans. Bishops of the Church of England would not ordain Wesley's preachers. In the 1780's he began to ordain them himself, first for the flourishing Methodist movement in America, and later in England itself. Even his brother, Charles, objected in satirical verse to this interruption of the apostolic laying on of hands: "How easily are bishops made/ By man or woman's whim! / Wesley his hands on Coke hath laid,/ But who laid hands on him?" So it was that by the late eighteenth century, the Methodists overlapped the red line of the Anglican spectrum and the infrared of nonconformity. Before long they were outside the Church altogether and in the infrared with the Dissenters, though they

3. J. R. H. Moorman, *A History of the Church in England*, 2d edition (London: Adam and Charles Black, 1967), p. 299.

retained their own episcopal organization as well as baptism and the eucharist.

All the visible color bands between infrared and ultraviolet consist of the shadings of the nineteenth-century Church of England parties. The red, orange, and yellow bands are occupied by what we may call Low Churchmen, closest in outlook to the dissenting churches, many of them essentially Puritans still within the Church of England. Some shared the Calvinist belief in predestination and election: every individual's future salvation had been decided upon from the beginning, and no action of his during his earthly life could change the decision. Only the elect would be saved. All those not elect would be damned to eternal hellfire. So the only value of good works on earth is that a man who performs them can convince himself that he is behaving in a way appropriate for one of the elect, and therefore come to believe that he is one of the elect. Other Low Churchmen emphasized the Lutheran concept of justification by faith and the necessity of personal conversion. Almost all emphasized the importance of private judgment and the need for constant study of the Bible. Simplicity of church architecture, of church services, and of the garments worn by the clergy were all Low-Church preferences. The term Low Church itself was used by the party's opponents. Low Churchmen generally referred to themselves as Evangelicals.

Beginning in the late eighteenth century there took place a great Evangelical revival, stimulated in part by the success of the Wesleyan Methodists within and without the Church, and in part by the French Revolution. "The triumph of Atheism in France restored Christianity to England," as a Victorian commentator picturesquely declared. The Church of England—self-satisfied, inactive, stagnant, in many ways corrupt—was greatly changed. At first in a minority and exposed to the sneers and discrimination of their opponents, the Evangelicals speedily acquired influence in certain centers. In Cambridge, Charles Simeon (1759-1836) overcame the opposition by his learning and his devotion and raised large sums of money to buy up livings which could then be awarded to his disciples, "Simeonites" or "Sims." Around Hannah More (1745-1833) in the West of England, and especially in the London suburb of

Clapham, Evangelicals, often members of the wealthy merchant class, congregated. William Wilberforce, Henry Thornton, Zachary Macaulay, James Stephen led the battle for Christian social reforms: the abolition of the slave trade, prison reform, the mitigation of brutal penal laws, the prohibition of suttee (widow burning) in India, and, as time went on, improvement in factory conditions and in the education of poor children: "ragged schools," Sunday schools, lending libraries, lectures, benefit societies, clothing clubs. Foreign missions, the translation of the Bible into many languages (148, ultimately) and its dissemination throughout the world, were other aims of the Evangelicals. They are, then, to be credited with major social achievements in the half-century immediately before the opening of the Victorian age. Living an active rather than a contemplative life, their clergy were usually not intellectuals or scholars. Exeter Hall, a London auditorium, became the headquarters for Evangelical meetings. In the novels, we shall come to know intimately Evangelicals of all degrees of rigidity ranging from the righteous extremists of "exaggerated" type in the red band of the spectrum through the "normal" type in the orange band to a relatively relaxed or liberal variety in the yellow.

At the opposite end of the spectrum, occupying the violet, indigo, and blue bands, we find the High Churchmen, the right wing of a church that sought to embrace both the Protestant-minded and the Catholic-minded. From the late seventeenth century "High Church" stood for rigorous adherence to the observance of the church, support for the idea of the establishment, and dislike for dissent. These High Churchmen were buoyed up by the advance of scholarship on the Church Fathers during the sixteenth century, which tended to demonstrate the antiquity within the church of reverence for celibacy, acceptance of private confession, preference for an elaborate formal liturgy, and deep respect for episcopal office. All of this suited the High Churchmen, who did not repudiate the Reformation but were sacramentalists by temperament. The Civil Wars and the Cromwellian rule that followed made Charles I a martyr, identified Calvinism with treason, and rendered the Puritans inside the Church (Evangelicals) suspect. With regard to doctrine, the High Churchmen emphasized the necessity of good works as well as faith for salvation. Where Luther affirmed justification by faith alone as an antidote to sixteenth-century overemphasis on good deeds (and the Thirty-nine Articles echoed him), the seventeenth-century High Churchman tried to correct the implications that seemed to follow from excluding good works: that one's conduct on earth was irrelevant (antinomianism).

Left behind as defenders of the old ways by a powerful liberalizing ("latitudinarian") current during the eighteenth century, the High Churchmen by the early 1830's had characteristically become defenders of the status quo. Inequities in clerical income which made the bishops very rich men while the lower clergy suffered, plurality of benefice whereby lucky and well-connected clerics had multiple preferments, nepotism, absenteeism, and neglect of parish duties all cried out for reform. But many of the clergy of the Church of England remained unmoved, "high and dry," living the lives of country gentlemen and comfortably indifferent to the needs of their poorer parishioners, administering communion four times a year (though gingerly moving in some advanced regions towards monthly celebrations), clinging to psalms rather than adopting the hymns characteristic of Evangelical worship, allowing the fabric of many village churches to decay, and acting like minor officials of the state—which, in a way, they were—rather than like spiritual leaders. In the riots and disorders that preceded the passage of the political Reform Bill of 1832 extending the franchise, bishops were burned in effigy, and the palace of the Bishop of Bristol was burned by the mob. The Church of England as an institution was threatened. Alarm, heightened by the Revolution of 1830 in France, became general.

In response to the threat, and stimulated also by the great Evangelical revival of the previous half-century, the High-Church party found new voices in the Oxford movement, so called because its leaders were all young Oxford dons. Evangelical emphasis upon the necessity of conversion made High Churchmen the more anxious to remind Christians of the power of baptism to regenerate (cleanse from sin); Evangelical emphasis upon the Bible as the sole authority made High Churchmen lay renewed stress upon the authority of the Church. But Evangelical fervor, itself in part the result of Methodist fervor, created fervor in turn among High Churchmen and removed the dryness from the High-and-Dry school. High-Church principles remained the same, but their defenders found in their opponents a new emotionalism with which to enunciate them. Politically, the threat to disestablish the Church of England called for a ringing reassertion of the Church's divine origins and of its necessity for Christians, whatever its relationship might be to the government.

The story of the Oxford movement has often been told in detail: how John Keble, author of the sensationally successful book of verse, *The Christian Year*; John Henry Newman, himself until recently an Evangelical; R. Hurrell Froude; and other young men chiefly of Oriel College issued a call to English Christians to rally in defence of their Church and of High-Church principles. Newman himself always dated the movement from a sermon of Keble's delivered in July 1833 in Oxford on "National Apostasy," which scholars often still take as its beginning. But although impeccably High Church in its views of dissent and of the establishment, the sermon "collected no disciples, raised no party-standard, asserted nothing but what other high churchmen were saying throughout the country."[4] The real beginning came with Newman's launching later in 1833 of the famous *Tracts for the Times*, short pamphlets of which there were twenty by the end of 1833, fifty by the end of 1834, and sixty-six by the end of 1835. It was from these that the Oxford movement received the name "Tractarian." Calling for "reserve in communicating religious knowledge," the Tractarians maintained, against the Evangelicals, that promiscuous reading of the Bible had its dangers for the unlearned, and they emphasized the importance of Christian tradition—the writings of the Church Fathers—as a guide to the interpretation of Scripture and a source of additional guidance for proper worship. In the writings of Newman, a man of the keenest intellect but of overriding emotion, even mysticism, the movement found its profoundest if not its most typical expression. The *Apologia pro vita sua*—Newman's extraordinary account of his life written in the early 1860's as a piece of explicatory polemic against Charles Kingsley—is of course a classic. But his two novels, *Loss and Gain* and *Callista*, respectively sixteen and eight years earlier than the *Apologia*, are far less well known and yet are

4. Owen Chadwick, *The Mind of the Oxford Movement* (London: Adam and Charles Black, 1960), p. 34.

of critical importance for understanding him. Both are published in this series and discussed at length below.

Edward Bouverie Pusey—older than his fellow Tractarians, a man of means and high birth and of great intellectual eminence in Oxford—wrote some of the later, and much longer and more scholarly, Tracts. Many opponents of the Oxford movement called it by his name: "Puseyism." Pusey himself declared that "Puseyism" meant a "high estimate" of baptism and the eucharist, of the episcopacy, of the visible church, of church ordinances, of prayer and fasts and feasts, and of the decoration of churches; and "reverence for and deference to the ancient Church," whose authorities, the Fathers, rather than "the Reformers," were to be looked to as the "ultimate expounders" of the meaning of the Church of England. Tractarian attitudes toward church architecture and the vestments worn by the clergy will be found richly elaborated in our novels.

In 1841 Newman published Tract 90, declaring that the Thirty-nine Articles were not nearly so greatly at variance with the doctrines of the Roman Catholic Church as Protestant thinkers usually maintained. The Thirty-nine Articles were man-made documents issued in the sixteenth century in response to a crisis that had long since vanished. Others had interpreted them in later periods in accordance with their own preferences. Newman's effort to interpret them in a more Catholic direction was an effort to make them more palatable to men like himself who were distrustful of the Reformation and hated the sectarianism to which the Protestant reformers' ideas had led. Tract 90 caused a storm, and the Bishop of Oxford forbade the publication of further tracts. Pusey and many of the Tractarians agreed with Newman. But Newman, in the four succeeding years, went through an extraordinary religious travail, and eventually in 1845 became a Catholic, rocking the Oxford movement to its foundations. Some followed him into the Roman Church; others stayed behind. *Loss and Gain* and *Callista* tell his own story. The drama of the movement and of its leadership stimulated a flood of novels for and against the Tractarians. In the discussions of the novels, the development and influence of the movement after 1848 will unfold, and we shall encounter a range of High Churchmen running from deep violet Tractarians to pale blue Anglicans.

In the green band in the middle of the spectrum we find the last of the parties, the Broad Churchmen. Their indebtedness to certain profound religious thinkers—Coleridge, Julius Hare, Frederick Denison Maurice—and to Thomas Arnold will be fully expounded in Chapter 4 below. These were the moderate, liberal men, called latitudinarian or indifferent by their opponents, who found comfort precisely in a Church of England—full of contradictions—that troubled High Churchmen as not Catholic enough and Low Churchmen as too Catholic. Preferring balance and compromise, sometimes professing to see truth and goodness even in heretical or agnostic views, emphasizing those matters which all Church of England Christians held in common and not those that separated High from Low, the Broad Churchmen objected to Roman Catholicism not because of its theology but because they felt that it attributed "magic virtue to outward acts," and so verged upon idolatry. Believing with the Low Churchmen in the overweening importance of the Bible, they believed with the High Churchmen in the importance of good works. They put their emphasis on the idea of Christian brotherhood. In the middle period of the nineteenth century, Broad Churchmen took over the role of social reformers played in the earlier period by the Evangelicals, and included among their number many distinguished scholars. Their tolerance, their opponents from both sides charged with some truth, often degenerated into indifference and even into scepticism. We shall sometimes find Broad Churchmen inexplicably flippant and casual in the treatment of issues that seemed of utmost importance to the High and Low parties.

So hurried a glance at the Victorian religious spectrum only begins to convey the nuances of opinion and the individual shadings of religious belief that for many decades made England such a contentious country, so puzzling to modern eyes. Moreover, the Catholics, Dissenters, and adherents of the Church of England—Low, High, and Broad—represent only half the drama. To the men of all these churches we must add the men of "No Church," who for a bewildering variety of reasons—intellectual, emotional, psychological—embraced an even more bewildering variety of disbelief. For a deeper view of the issues of the drama and of typical persons who played their parts in it we turn directly to the novels.

In each of the chapters that follow, the major novels are treated in roughly chronological order, enabling us to follow the changes in outlook from the 1830's to the end of the Victorian age. For the novels in the Garland reprint series, each novel's number in the series is provided with the date of publication whenever the book is mentioned. The numbered list of novels will be found at the end of the text. The initials "NIS," standing for "not in series," are used after the date of publication for all other novels referred to.

PART I.

THE CHURCH OF ROME

CHAPTER 1.

THE CATHOLICS, AND THEIR FRIENDS AND ENEMIES

Popery and No Popery

In the autumn of 1850, when Thomas Hardy was ten years old, his father took him to the ancient Roman amphitheatre in the town of Dorchester, county seat of Dorset in England's rural West Country, to see an extraordinary sight. A throng of citizens had gathered to watch the riotous burning of effigies of the Pope and of Cardinal Wiseman—newly appointed as Catholic Archbishop of Westminster and the head of a restored Catholic hierarchy in England. The chief actors in the drama were a ghastly procession of townsmen disguised in monks' cowls—long hoods that covered their faces. As the little boy watched the lurid sight, one of the cowls blew aside for a moment and revealed to him the familiar face of one of his father's workmen. A sense of bewilderment swept over the child, combined with a terror that he never forgot. All over England, in fact, "No Popery" riots of protest were taking place. How great was the danger, really?

Numerically, the Roman Catholic population was almost negligible. Four or five months after the riots, a careful religious census recorded the numbers of all those who attended Church services of any denomination on Sunday, 30 March 1851. A mere 383,630 persons attended Roman Catholic services in England and Wales, on a day when more than 9,800,000 attended one form of Protestant service or another. More than twenty years after Catholic Emancipation and in spite of increased Irish Catholic immigration, the number of recorded Catholic worshippers, then, was only a little more than four percent of the total recorded Christian worshippers. No doubt the figure would have been a good deal higher had there been in the slums enough of those churches for which the

Catholic hierarchy continued to press: the *Times* pointed out that the known population of Irish immigrants alone was higher than the figure of worshippers in church on that Sunday and wondered aloud what—under the circumstances—all the excitement over the re-establishment of the Roman Catholic hierarchy had really been about. What it had been about, of course, as the *Times* well knew, was ancient anti-Catholic prejudice, impossible to eradicate among English non-Catholics, slow to diminish, and heightened rather than eliminated by the emancipation of 1829 and by a loud political controversy in 1845 over increasing the Parliamentary subsidy to the Catholic College of St. Patrick at Maynooth in Ireland.

Socially, most of the Catholics of England belonged to one of two widely contrasting groups: either to the old aristocratic—if often untitled—families of landowners, whether rich or impoverished, who had held out generation after generation against persecution, harassment, or mere disabilities; or to the Irish working class, which had immigrated into the country in ever-increasing numbers as the industrial towns of the Midlands grew in importance. There was not much of a Catholic middle class and, naturally enough, not much social contact between the old English families and the new Irish arrivals. Both Catholic and anti-Catholic novels usually concern themselves with the Catholic gentle folk; the Irish Catholic laborer in England hardly ever appears in fiction. As an exception, however, we may note the wholly forgotten novel *Poverty and the Baronet's Family; A Catholic Novel* (1845, NIS), published nine years after the death of the author, the learned and eccentric Catholic convert Henry Digby Beste (1768-1836).

On the title page, the editor hails Beste as "originator of the religious opinions of modern Oxford." As early as 1793, indeed, aged twenty-five, he preached a notable sermon to the University in favor of auricular confession. Many agreed with Beste that the power of absolution was indeed inherent in the clergy of the Church of England, but declared that the people would not submit to its exercise. Beste's mother's family, the Digbys, had long been Catholics, though ostensibly accepting Anglicanism in the early eighteenth century, and Beste himself had Catholic leanings from his boyhood on. Eventually he overcame his last scruple—with regard to the real presence of Christ in the eucharist—and entered the Roman Church in 1798.

Poverty and the Baronet's Family begins in the year 1805, with the arrival in Lincolnshire of the O'Mearas, a family of itinerant farm laborers from Ireland, whose father is accidentally drowned in saving the life of a Baronet's son. In gratitude, the Baronet provides housing and a minimum income for the widow, Bridget O'Meara, and her children. The saintly Bridget refuses any further charity. Alone among the Irish immigrants, she stays in England and works hard to support herself and her infant son, exerting her good influence upon the downtrodden English rural poor of the district. Her son Bryan becomes the protégé of a local French émigré priest. His ability, character, and behavior help him move rapidly upward. Well educated and cultivated, an Irish patriot, Bryan is soon socially accepted—though on sufferance—in the household of the Baronet himself, and eventually marries Arabella, the Baronet's daughter and sister of the heir whom O'Meara had died to save.

Neither the marriage itself, nor the conversion of Arabella to Catholicism which precedes it and arises from her own independent preference, arouses nearly as much opposition as one would have expected and as would surely have manifested itself in real life. For one thing, Bryan O'Meara is the descendant of Irish gentry deprived of their rightful estates after the Battle of the Boyne in 1690, and by the usual novelist's hanky-panky with title deeds he manages to get them back again. Then too, Arabella's father is a wholly sceptical Deist, who has no more religious objection to Roman Catholics than to Anglicans, and his social objections to Bryan are overcome by a combination of gratitude to the O'Meara family and an appreciation of Bryan's personal attractions.

Poverty and the Baronet's Family provides occasional flashes of insight into situations seldom explored in fiction. The son of an Anglican parson, who has been converted to Catholicism, explains that his final decision to join the Church was precipitated by reading a letter from the Duchess of York, wife of James II, who had remarked that "England would have been Catholic . . . but for the bigamy of Henry VIII, the infancy of Edward VI, and the illegitimacy of Elizabeth" and added, "It is very odd the bishops could not find out that the Catholic Church was in error, till the king or queen ordered them to make the discovery." This, says the convert, "led me to reconcile myself to our ancient mother, abjuring all heresy and schism." But he has noted, he adds, that the old Catholic families have not welcomed him:

> . . . though I am as well born, and better educated than they, there is not one of these Catholic gentry into whose country-house I have entrance, not one whom I could appoint as guardian to my children were I to leave an infant family; and this after thirty years profession of their faith, and some service rendered to their cause! . . . These people have been oppressed, and depressed, and compressed together, till they are incapable of sympathy for any who are not of their old coterie and connection; and they are as to their knowledge of the state of society, a century behind the rest of the world.

The exclusiveness of the old families and their unwillingness to be hospitable even to an equally well-born convert perhaps reflect Beste's own experience and in any case provide a notable comment on social history.

The degree of tolerance manifested by the Baronet's family, however, is altogether exceptional in the novels of the early Victorian period, as it was in the Victorian world itself. The prevalent popular anti-Catholic sentiment involved a whole complex of ideas and emotions, some of them deriving rather from instinct than from reason, and many of them going far back in English history. The English Protestant hated the Catholic claim that only a Catholic priest could mediate between the layman and God and the claim of papal supremacy. Evangelicals and Dissenters often interpreted the prophetic books of the Bible as predicting the inevitable destruction of the Catholic Church. Politically, many Protestants feared that any increase of Catholicism in power or influence threatened their own hard-won liberties. They doubted that any individual Catholic could be loyal to the English monarchy and the Parliamentary system. Morally, they suspected Catholics of paying only lip service to truth, of casuistry, of believing any deed justified if it advanced the Catholic cause.

They disliked a priesthood that was celibate, set apart from the rest of society, separately educated, and denied wives and families: could such men possibly be chaste? Of course not: and no accusation against the Catholics was surer of a hearing than the one charging priests with seducing nuns. Indeed, nunneries and the Catholic confessional—in which the woman confessed her sins privately to the priest and received the penance he imposed upon her—stimulated prurient anti-Catholic imaginings. How could the confessional as an institution be reconciled to the duty of the father of a family to keep his womenfolk undefiled and under his authority? And at the apex of Protestant anti-Catholic emotions stood the Jesuits, since Elizabethan days always suspect, often rightly, of involvement in all politically subversive movements. Jesuits lived under a discipline even more rigorous than the ordinary priest, were known to be particularly learned, were believed to be in constant mysterious contact with papal authorities, and stopped at nothing to carry out their dangerous missions, the very incarnation of the black-clad, sinister, sacerdotal enemy, who never walk but always glide.

Fathers Clement, Oswald, Eustace, and Other Jesuits

These stereotypes were to be met with in the dramas of the seventeenth and eighteenth centuries and in many an eighteenth-century novel. The Victorian novelist carried on and deepened the tradition. We begin with a novel written six years before Catholic emancipation, *Father Clement; A Roman Catholic Story* (1823, no. 1) by Grace Kennedy (1782-1825), a staunch Scotch Presbyterian, highly intellectual, personally retiring, but an agreeably cheerful companion, who in her short life wrote some half dozen novels, of which this was the most famous, achieving many editions and translations into the European languages. As an anti-Catholic novel, it breaks new ground in an attempt to be reasonable and persuasive rather than simply denunciatory.

The protagonists in *Father Clement* come from two families of landowning cousins, the Protestant Montagues and the Catholic Clarenhams, with adjacent estates in northern England near the Scotch border. The Montagues are not members of the Church of

England, but Presbyterians, with a resident Presbyterian minister, Dr. Lowther, as their chaplain. He is on good terms with the Church of England rector of the village, having convinced himself that a clergyman of that denomination "could really be zealous, steady, and laborious in fulfilling the duties of his parish." But the Church of England plays no part in the novel. The Clarenhams too have their resident chaplain, a Jesuit priest, Father Dennis (Mr. Elliston), who is being replaced by a younger man, Father Clement (Mr. Dormer), as the story opens. For years Dr. Lowther has been at war with Father Dennis, who is "indefatigable in making converts, and ingenious in evading the laws which were in force against the encroachments of his church."

The two families of young cousins are on affectionate personal terms, but each family is determined to convert the other. Their parents permit them to mingle, but worry about it, especially the Calvinist Sir Herbert Montague, who is sure that "Popish poison" emanates from the Jesuit chaplain at the Clarenhams'. The novel deals primarily with the controversies and debates between the young people, each family backed by its own chaplain. Its chief innovation is the highly agreeable (and not only agreeable-seeming) personalities of both the departing elderly Father Dennis and the arriving youthful Father Clement. Clement is attractive, gentle in manner (without being "suave," like so many fictional Jesuits), eager to discuss theology or any other religious question with the Protestants, never excitable in debate, and always reasonable.

Among the many issues discussed, some more than once, are: the Protestant insistence on the Bible as the only source of truth and on the right of each individual to reach a private judgment, as against the Catholic reliance upon the authority of the Church and reluctance to disseminate the Bible among the laity; the Protestant hatred for image worship and for Catholic veneration of sacred works of art, allegedly supported by a deliberate mistranslation of the text of the Ten Commandments; the conflicting doctrines about the attainment of salvation: the Catholic belief in the efficacy of good works, as against the Protestant insistence upon justification by faith and imputed righteousness; the Catholic belief in the Virgin, the saints, and angels as mediators for man with Christ, as against the Protestant belief in Christ as the sole mediator for man with God; the practice of confession; the Mass; the doctrine of purgatory; the date of the origin of the papacy; the use of Latin prayers.

Grace Kennedy was, of course, partisan, and Father Clement does not win in his frequent debates with young Ernest Montague, a grave, thoughtful, introspective, devout Calvinist. Passages of Scripture are duly brought into the fray by both parties. The cards are stacked against Father Clement, however, in several ways. The story is set just before and during the invasion of Scotland and northern England in 1715 by the Stuart "Pretender" to the throne. The Catholics are all supporters of the invasion, and young Basil Clarenham carries out a dangerous mission on its behalf; all this reminded the reader of 1823 that the Catholics had been associated with treasonable movements. Moreover, Father Clement's superior, Father Adrian (Mr. Warrenne), chaplain in a neighboring great house and head of the Jesuits in northern England, carries on an enormous correspondence with Rome, much of it in cipher, and is determined to hold on to the wealth of the local Catholics for the Church. As the Calvinist propaganda begins to tell upon the young Clarenhams, Warrenne arranges to have Basil, after completing his mission to the Continent, sent on to Rome, where he is interrogated and imprisoned by the Inquisition; he is rescued only by Ernest Montague's justifiable blackmail of Mr. Warrenne.

Gradually the dedicated Ernest Montague, with the help of Dr. Lowther and smuggled copies of the New Testament in English, saps the Catholic faith of two of his cousins, Maria and Basil Clarenham, despite all that Father Clement can do. Moreover, Father Clement himself—portrayed as a victim of the Catholic confidence in the efficacy of works, and so, in Protestant eyes, trying to be his own Savior—cannot believe that any of his actions are sufficient: fasts, penances, mortifications of the flesh. Under his hair shirt he wears a sharp metal crucifix that inflicts a livid wound on his heart; when his death approaches, he sleeps and prays in his future coffin, on a bed of ashes covered with a haircloth coverlet. These excesses would have served to counteract in the Protestant reader any sympathy previously aroused by Clement's delightful personality. Yet Clement has always been sensible: he has been unwilling to take at their face value the visions seen by the youngest

Clarenham girl, destined to be a nun, and stoutly declared by her to be miraculous ("If you listen to that child, you will hear of a miracle every day," he says). And in his optimism that he may win the Montagues to Catholicism, he ignores the advice of his senior: "There is no heresy so deep-rooted and insurmountable as that wrought in the mind by the free use of the Scriptures with the right of private judgment of their contents." Clement not only fails to win the Montagues but also loses the Clarenhams (except for the prospective nun, who founds a convent and becomes the Lady Abbess).

The crowning Protestant triumph is won over the faith of Father Clement himself. Ernest Montague convinces him that our own exertions do not justify our souls. Only perfect righteousness can do that; and Christ alone has that. The Bible too becomes Clement's subverter, as he preaches his last sermon altogether from it. While he does confess to Warrenne on his deathbed and receive absolution, he does *not*, when asked in what faith he is dying, reply, "the true and apostolic church of Rome," but says only "the Church of Christ." Looking back on her characters from her own time (1823), Grace Kennedy notes that "in Britain" the Roman Catholic Church is almost forgotten, and she expresses the hope that Christ may yet unite all Christians in one Church.

Nineteen years afterwards, an anonymous Catholic, seething with anger, answered Grace Kennedy directly in *Father Oswald. A Genuine Catholic Story* (1842, no. 1). Its only aim, he declares, is "to present an antidote to the baneful production of 'Father Clement.'" As a novel "this story . . . has little to recommend itself to the mere novel-reader, who seeks only for the passing excitement of the moment." All the objections to the Catholic faith, the author says, he has taken verbatim from Grace Kennedy's novel, and he has allowed his characters to answer them. Wisely, he sets his story in 1830, when there was no episode like the invasion of 1715 to remind readers of past Catholic disloyalty to the House of Hanover. But instead of repeating Grace Kennedy's theological clash between Presbyterians and Catholics, which enabled her to create an apparent tension between two ostensibly evenly matched defenders of extremely opposed views, the author of *Father Oswald* entrusts the Protestant case for the most part to Dr. Davison, a bumbling

Church of England rector of the high-and-dry type: too much interested in good dinners, in shooting, and in writing his "little work on angling" to give proper comfort to his dying parishioners, and hopelessly outclassed in argument by three chief Catholic spokesmen: Father Oswald, an experienced Jesuit priest; a well-read and argumentative Colonel; and an Italian monsignor in Rome. The articulate Protestants are all presented as incompetent and ridiculous: an Anglican bishop—married, of course, and with a large family of children—who regards his daily bedtime game of whist with his wife as the most important event of the day, and who is insolently rude in discussions with cultivated Catholics, and a pair of Swiss ministers, nominally Protestant but actually latitudinarian. In the very city of Calvin himself, it is clear, "rational Protestants" have now abandoned as "antiquated" the dogmas of the Trinity, the Incarnation, and the Atonement. It is not so much that Grace Kennedy was fairer as that she gave the appearance of being fair, while the author of *Father Oswald* was so angry that he did not even try to seem fair in allotting characteristics to his Protestants.

Edward Sefton, a strict Protestant, suffers agonies when his beloved wife, Emma—whose father had been a Catholic—is converted to Rome. The happiness and contentment brought to a dying man by Father Oswald's instructions and eventual bestowal of extreme unction (which Dr. Davison had refused) move Emma to inquiry. Convinced that she must partake of the eucharist as a Catholic and that there is no salvation outside that church, she must brave a forced separation from her husband and children: to Sefton she is an "idolatress." Once it is clear that Emma is irretrievably converted, Sefton goes abroad.

In France he falls in with Le Sage, a one-time émigré from the French Revolution, who had been a fellow student at Cambridge. Still a nominal Papist, Le Sage had imbibed at Cambridge dangerously "plausible principles," and the cynical corruption of Paris had completed his transformation into a doubter: neither a Deist nor an atheist, he treats all religion flippantly. He cannot become a Protestant because "No sooner do we French take leave of Notre Dame than we seek refuge in the temple of reason and universal philanthropy. . . . The English reject a *few* of the obsolete dogmas of Christianity, we reject them *all*. . . . We are better Protestants than you are." Caught up in the political discussions and social frivolities of this group, Sefton fights with them in the Revolution of 1830 against Charles X, who—he thinks—is some sort of Jesuit. Sefton's faith rests upon his own intellectual reasoning; "it tottered to the ground," and he has no answers when his French friends ask him what the "genius of Newton and La Place owes to Revelation? and yet what sublime mysteries of nature have they not uncovered?"; whereas, had he been a Catholic, he would have seen at once that all scientific discoveries are merely material and "do not advance one step into the spiritual world."

Badly wounded in the fighting, Sefton is nursed back to health by a Sister of Charity, an English woman, who learns his story, prevails upon him to write to Emma, lends him Thomas à Kempis's *Imitation of Christ*, and persuades him not only to look into the Catholic faith but even to wear for her sake a silver medal of the Virgin. In Switzerland he is appalled by the degenerate state of Protestantism, which, he had expected, would be at its most powerful in the citadel of Calvin. No rational Protestant, he is assured there, could possibly subscribe even to the Thirty-nine Articles of the English Church, which require a belief in the Trinity: there is to be no more belief in mystery or in miracles. "Sickened" by what he has heard, Sefton proceeds to Italy, hoping to receive evidence that miracles still do take place.

When he gives alms in Rome to a poor woman praying for succor at the feet of a statue of the Virgin, Sefton is astounded that she feels her prayers have been answered and that it was the Virgin who had brought her the money. He is more impressed when he is captured by banditti, and the silver medal of the Virgin which he wears turns aside the point of the stiletto of a would-be assassin and saves his life. He is convinced by his own eyes that the miracle of the liquefaction of the blood of San Gennaro (St. Januarius) at Naples is a genuine recurring miracle. And he gives full credit to the recent appearance of a luminous cross in the heavens at Migné, a French village. It was the very cross which Constantine had seen more than fifteen hundred years earlier and which had led to his conversion to Christianity; and it had appeared in 1830 to reassure the faithful that in the forthcoming revolution they would be divinely protected. At the Vatican, Sefton is amazed by the similarity between the Mass, which he has thought of as idolatrous, and an Anglican service: he does not yet believe in the real presence of Christ in the eucharist, but he can now understand that any person who does so believe would not, by kneeling, become an idolater. The final step is for Sefton to stop merely wishing that he believed and to become a believer by an act of faith. He can then return to England, and to his wife and family, and enter into the richness of life as a Catholic.

In the course of the novel, the author takes up the questions in dispute between the Catholic and the Protestant churches treated by Grace Kennedy, and others besides: questions of theology, of ritual, of interpretation of Scripture, and of history. The positions defended are extreme: there was never a time of corruption in the Catholic Church; purgatory is no recent doctrine but has the sanction of Scripture and of the early Church; the Inquisition is a necessary and benevolent institution; clerical celibacy and the use of Latin prayers are the only proper practices. The Protestants are forced to admit that indiscriminate Bible-reading leads only to the proliferation of sects. They have no answer when Father Oswald says, "The fundamental error of the Protestant system of justification . . . consists in this . . . you conceive that the stain of original and actual sin remains indelible on the soul of fallen man, and that man is justified by the righteousness of Christ ["imputed righteousness"] covering over as with a garment, not obliterating, the odious stain." So, for a Protestant, the best works a man can perform are "vitiated by the original canker of his soul." Judas's treachery is morally no different from Peter's faith, and so Protestants question the efficacy of the sacraments. But Catholics follow the Gospel of St. John and believe that the blood of Christ has cleansed mankind from all sin. His grace is to be obtained through the sacraments of baptism and penance, with the accompanying absolution. Since the Protestant believes that we cannot merit grace, that no exertion of ours (good works) can justify our souls, and that we cannot achieve perfect righteousness, it is only on the perfect righteousness of Christ that we can rest any hope for salvation. This is a great error.

So the author of *Father Oswald* vented his wrath at Grace Kennedy, and "set straight" what to him were her perverted ideas about Catholic doctrine and practice. For twentieth-century readers, it is useful to have in a novel so articulate and aggressive a statement of the Catholic position against the prevailing anti-Catholic ideas and sentiments of virtually all sects of English Protestantism. But it is by no means clear that *Father Oswald* would have been effective as counterpropaganda. Where Grace Kennedy was sweetly reasonable and stated the Calvinist case with every appearance of fairness to the Catholics—though with just as much actual bias as if she had been unfair—the author of *Father Oswald* was openly and intransigently contemptuous of Protestant misconceptions about Catholics, their own teachings, their intellects, and their character as Christians. His vinegar would probably have caught few flies.

Both *Father Clement* and *Father Oswald*—with varying degrees of skill, credibility, and prejudice—deal with the issues that divided Catholic from Protestant, and include long pages of serious intellectual conversation about disputed points, theological and otherwise. All such learned or semi-learned matter has vanished from the pages of *Father Eustace* (1847, no. 4), and only the stereotypes of prejudice remain. Frances Milton Trollope (1780-1863), mother of the famous novelist Anthony Trollope, is best remembered today for her adventurous trip to the United States, where she founded a "bazaar" in Cincinnati, which failed, and for her book on *The Domestic Manners of the Americans* (1832), in which she outspokenly revealed her dislike for the transatlantic barbarians. Year after year she indomitably produced readable novels—some forty in all—on a wide variety of subjects, and in *Father Eustace* she turned her ever-lively attention to the Jesuits.

Mrs. Trollope's de Morley family belong to the same rich Catholic landed class as Grace Kennedy's Clarenhams. However, with the death of Richard de Morley, who has married a Protestant and whose heir is an only daughter, Juliana, brought up as a Protestant, the Jesuits are threatened with loss of influence and money. Juliana's parents had come to regret their youthful marriage for love, her mother because she soon discovered that "the idol of her youth, who had taught her to find a passion as vehement as that which he himself displayed, was . . . a stern, narrow-minded bigot, the abject slave" of the Catholic Church, and her father because he had yielded to his love and married a heretic. "A puling penitent for life," de Morley is not just an ordinary Catholic landowner, with whom his neighbors in the countryside would have been glad to consort on terms of intimacy, but a Jesuit-educated tool of that Order, each of whose members has "more eyes than are fabled in the head of a spider, and who weave webs of more delicate and widespreading texture and of threads more nicely vibrative, than all the spiders in the world."

Juliana and her mother welcome the departure of de Morley's Jesuit confessor, Father Ambrose (they are tired of seeing him glide), but as the result of Father Ambrose's report to the General of the Jesuits in Rome (in his secret headquarters, with its labyrinth of secret passages and its back staircase that leads into a tobacco shop), Father Eustace is selected to go to England, to convert Juliana, to induce her to become a nun, and to prevail upon her to bestow her great property and fortune on the Order. Handsome, intellectual, musical, and poetical, Father Eustace sets off in mufti under his true name of Edward Stormont. When he plays a requiem for Juliana's father on the organ and suggests that she kneel and pray for his soul, the first phase of Stormont's mission is easily accomplished: Juliana feels herself to be a Catholic. But deep complexities arise when she and Stormont fall in love. The only reason she can think of for his not proposing is that he may not be as rich as she.

Mrs. Trollope dwells upon the complete obedience that Jesuits owe their superiors, their duty "to abdicate all individual will, all individual judgment, and to live, think, speak, and act" wholly in accordance with their instructions. Stormont, in anguish at his dilemma, which the General of the Jesuits had entirely foreseen, must call for help on the supervisor of Jesuit affairs in England, and on his cousin, a nasty nun, ambitious to be an abbess. Paying him a visit in civilian disguise in the house he has leased near the de Morleys', these two spy on everybody, this being "*one* of the most effectual means, by which the human race are brought under subjection" to the Jesuits. "It is . . . wicked and ignorant to suppose that all Jesuits are vicious. But the subjection of human hearts to a human rather than a divine law, is and must be evil." Yet Stormont's realization that his superiors had actually *intended* Juliana to fall in love with him, so that she would have to become a nun when she discovered that he could not marry her, makes him think he has been "made the tool of demons." He writes Juliana a letter telling her the truth. For his disobedience the punishment is . . . what, the reader must discover for himself. Readable as a novel, *Father Eustace* is arresting as a piece of popular pathology.

Mrs. Trollope's kindly remark that it is wicked to suppose that *all* Jesuits are vicious would never have passed muster with the savage-minded William Sewell (1804-1874), whose *Hawkstone* (1845, no. 2) lashes out at all forms of religious belief except that of the High Anglican Church. He had been a Tractarian until 1841, when Tract 90 frightened him and he broke with Newman, afraid of Romanizing tendencies. Sewell indeed reserved his deepest hatred for the Catholics ("absolutely rabid," said a contemporary critic, himself an anti-Catholic, "absurdly overdone and extravagant . . . volcanic"). Mrs. Trollope ironically promotes the male English Jesuit who had intervened to manage Father Eustace's affairs, but she causes his partner, the "Jesuitess," to die of eating too many walnuts (the woman had an incurably sweet tooth). But Sewell imagines a far more gruesome punishment for his Jesuit villain, who has inflicted dreadful emotional torture—including the kidnapping of an only son—on the high-born High-Anglican hero. The "vengeance of heaven"—the hero predicts—will "sooner or later, in some frightful shape, fall upon those miserable men who, under the name and garb of religion, are rending asunder . . . ties which God has joined, and tearing the children [of England] from their Father in the State and in the Church." This pious hope, however, extends to *all* the Jesuits: the particular villain of the novel has *already* met his reward: he has been gradually eaten by rats, in a stone cellar from which he has been trying to escape. "All over the pavement were traces of blood as if the wretched man had fled from place to place before his ferocious assailants; and there were marks of bloody hands upon the walls, on one place especially, where the stones were convulsively scrabbled over with gory fingers. . . . The extremities were wholly gone. The vitals must have been attacked last." This brief passage will perhaps indicate the degree of pathological terror that "anti-Popery" at its most virulent aroused in its victims.

More decorous and less repulsive but hardly less determined were the anti-Catholic sentiments of Catherine Sinclair (1800-

1884), a strongly Evangelical spinster and philanthropist, who wrote popular stories for children and novels for adults. In *Beatrice; or, the Unknown Relatives* (1852, no. 8), she took advantage of the anti-Catholic furor stimulated by Wiseman's arrival and the re-establishment of the Catholic hierarchy in Britain to make her own contribution to the literature of hatred. Nobody is eaten by rats in *Beatrice*, and the imagery is not disgusting; but the message is the same. A Catholic convert wants his Protestant wife to become a "nun of St. Ignatia" so that he may become a Jesuit priest. He takes his two little boys away from their mother and immures them in a Jesuit school, but they escape. Do they have to go back? the weeping children want to know: "Are we to kiss those nasty old bones, and to kneel before that doll with the muslin frock? I like my own religion best, mamma . . . I am not accustomed to lick the floor with my tongue." Hysterical with grief and with the thought of her children forced to commit idolatry, the mother has brain fever, only to discover when she recovers that the boys have been recaptured and will be "kept under Jesuit guidance forever." Beatrice, the heroine, finally escapes the toils of her Jesuit mentor: "I could not accommodate my mind to his elastic code of morals, which consists entirely in becoming an automaton, growing blinder every hour, with no idea but to serve Rome in a course of small morality, of cheap absolutions, and of idle empty mechanical ceremonies." Mind, body, and soul are all threatened: the Catholic Church is "not apostolical but 'apostate-ical'. . . . Romish principles are as out of place in an English drawing-room as an Italian organ-boy would be in a palace."

"It Takes Time": The Novels of John Henry Newman

The fatuous Anglican bishop in *Father Oswald*—having seen the low level to which Protestantism has sunk in Geneva—remarks,

> It only convinces me more of the wisdom of what some people are pleased to term a new sect of Protestants, to which Oxford has had the honour of giving birth, and to which I am

> rather inclined myself. . . . Pusey, Newman, and Keble . . . contend that the Church is the sole depository of divine truth, which is not merely in the Bible, but in tradition as handed down to us in the writings of the early Christian Fathers. . . . The Church and not the Bible, should be the guide in matters of faith and practice.

And—inasmuch as the Bishops are the successors of the Apostles—they are the ones whose interpretation of the Bible is to be sought. Promiscuous Bible reading should be put down, and the Church regarded as infallible in matters of faith. To the Catholic author of *Father Oswald*, of course, this new Anglican movement, while still in error, at least demonstrates a growing realization among Anglicans themselves that the Church of England had become woefully latitudinarian. Appearing in 1842, this paragraph is an early Catholic appreciation of the Tractarian movement.

The enemies of the Tractarians declared almost from the first that their doctrines logically led directly to Roman Catholicism, and loudly warned of the dangers. And, indeed, in the years after 1840 such conversions multiplied, never in a statistically significant number perhaps, but enough to cause great alarm in an anti-Catholic society, especially since the converts were often prominent clergymen. Before long, as was natural, both the converts and the opposition began to write novels elucidating their position. Two of the most remarkable of these, from the psychological if not from the literary standpoint, are *From Oxford to Rome, and How it Fared with Some Who Lately Made the Journey* and *Rest in the Church* (1847 and 1848, no. 5), by Elizabeth Furlong Shipton Harris, who wrote anonymously and as if she had been a man, but whose identity was quickly uncovered.

Having begun as a Dissenter ("one of the proudest and most distinct forms of Protestantism"), the hero of her first novel undergoes a course of "transcendentalism," reading Carlyle, Emerson, and French and German poets and theologians, after which he moves first to Anglo-Catholicism and finally to Rome. In his progress, he clearly refers to Newman as "the undoubted intellectual chief" of the movement, but is more directly influenced by Frederick Oakley, "the Preacher of Sympathy," a Fellow of Balliol, who, after Tract

90, had attacked the Reformation and became a convert to Rome in 1845 only a few weeks after Newman.

But the extraordinary thing about Miss Harris was that once she had been converted, she regretted it and used her novel to say so, in effect urging that all those comforts which Rome might popularly be supposed to bring to the Anglican were in fact to be found in the hero's own church. So she wrote as a warning to others not to be converted; as for herself, she felt that she had burned her bridges and that her sufferings were the punishment for her sin. Astonished reviewers pointed out that it was immoral for her not to revert to Anglicanism. Miss Harris then acknowledged that indeed it would be if she had actually meant what she was saying, but that she had only been writing a novel, and she asked pardon of the Church of Rome: it was suggested that Mr. Oakley had persuaded Miss Harris to make this rather unconvincing retraction.

Rest in the Church is an equally peculiar novel. The failure of a "High-and-Dry" rector to appear at the deathbed of one of his poor parishioners ("a poacher and a drunkard") resembles a situation in *Father Oswald*, and represents one of the charges of negligence frequently levelled against Anglicans of this older school. In a turgid and sometimes confusing story, the author's chief points seem to be that the clergy of the Church of England should reside in their livings, should not neglect the poor, and should not oppose ritualistic changes, including auricular confession. Roman Catholic piety is favorably contrasted with Anglican, and eventually a Tractarian curate, suspended by his bishop for refusing to abandon his liturgical practices, becomes a convert: he has "gone in pursuit of a perfect earthly Church." The heroine becomes a nun. Yet at the end, the unfortunate, confused, and possibly hysterical Miss Harris longingly reaches out toward the Church of England once again, unable to accept the idea that the Church of Rome is the only Catholic Church or that there can be no salvation ("no authority, no grace, no sacrament, no light, no life, no existence") outside it. Moreover, she cannot swallow the Catholic doctrines of indulgences or of the intercession of saints (both so well rationalized in *Father Oswald*).

Miss Harris would be best forgotten, perhaps, were it not for the fact that Newman himself read her earlier novel and determined to answer it. *Loss and Gain* (1848, no. 6) was the memorable result. It appeared anonymously with a prefatory "Advertisement," declaring that it was "not the history of any individual among the recent converts to the Catholic Church" and that "no proper representative is intended in this tale of the religious opinions which had lately so much influence in the University of Oxford." But nobody believed this at the time, nor was it quite possible that they should. In 1896, Newman said *Loss and Gain* had been written against a novel (he meant *From Oxford to Rome*) whose "contents were as wantonly and preposterously fanciful, as they were injurious to those whose motives and actions it professed to represent." But only Newman's closest friends could read his novel at the time with full appreciation of its autobiographical content.

Loss and Gain has many comic passages (Newman laughed aloud from time to time as he wrote it); it gives the reader a vivid series of portraits, some of them caricatures of the protagonists of the various schools of religious opinion at Oxford in the thirties and forties; and most important of all, it provides an unsparing account of Newman's own spiritual travails leading to his conversion, shortening the process—which actually took a dozen years or more—for art's sake into a mere six. Years later Newman declared in a letter, "I have written in *Loss and Gain* of persons and of things that I knew." The novel belongs, then, to those works of fiction to which—as Mrs. Humphry Ward said—"the future student of the nineteenth century will have to look for what is deepest, most intimate, and most real in its personal experience."

Charles Reding—the name is pronounced "Reeding," and Charles is a "reading man" in the Oxford vocabulary of the day—son of an Anglican clergyman, with a close-knit, affectionate family, is Newman himself. "Joshua Jennings," the Vice-Principal of Charles's Oxford college—who, as the result of "a system of espionage" devoted to ferreting out "papistically inclined" undergraduates, interrogates Charles severely upon his opinions and then refuses to allow him to continue residing in Oxford—is Edward Hawkins, Provost of Oriel, a liberal and a strenuous opponent of the Tractarians. Newman's old friend Henry Wilberforce, who was delighted with the novel, thought Newman had been far less harsh with Hawkins than might have been expected: if he had wanted to, said Wilberforce, Newman "could have pounded Hawkins" to bits in a mortar. Yet "Jennings'" inquisitorial conversation with Charles is a sardonic masterpiece. Trying his best to mollify the angry don, Reding innocently catches him in a mistake, which leads to the final denunciation; there could not be, says Jennings, "a clearer proof that your mind has been perverted . . . debauched by the sophistries and Jesuitries which unhappily have found entrance among us." Perhaps Newman's Carlton, the firm and wise Anglican teacher, is Keble; perhaps Sheffield is Newman's one-time intimate, Frederic Rogers. But the pursuit of originals takes us only a short distance. "I have laughed at nothing in my tale," wrote Newman himself, "which I did not laugh at when a Protestant." Bateman, for instance—about whose real identity a regular guessing game apparently arose among those who read *Loss and Gain*—was, Newman declared, "drawn from no one at all." Newman had created him as "an unmanly, unreal character," in an effort to poke fun at "antiquarian foppery, at affectation of dress, at unreality and inconsistency of conduct."

Charles Reding's family background, his powerful intellectual interests, his failure to obtain a "first-class" in the examinations for his degree, his love of music, and his growing conviction that he must live a celibate life—all reflect Newman's own personal history. When an old family friend urges Charles not to be "an old bachelor. . . . Marry, my dear boy; look out betimes for a virtuous young woman who will make you an attentive wife," and members of his family chime in with their own predictions as to his future wife and children, Charles blushes and begs to be spared: "How have I deserved this?" he asks, and the reader thinks at first that it may be only a bashful response to good-humored teasing. Not at all: in a later conversation, when Charles's friends are jokingly predicting that most of the young enthusiasts for clerical celibacy will soon marry, he rather reluctantly admits that he has "a kindness for clerical celibacy," and confides in Carlton that he has felt this way ever since he was a boy at school. Carlton argues against celibacy, inside the church or out: "the genius of Anglicanism is . . . utterly at variance with it." But Charles declares it is as much "a yoke of bondage to compel marriage as to compel celibacy." This conversation stimulates Charles to think that the Church of England is "a form of religion very unlike that of the Apostles." Of course, the implication must be that the Roman Church, with its enforced clerical celibacy, is far more like that of the Apostles, a point which Charles's sister Mary—drawn from Newman's own favorite sister—rightly interprets to mean that Charles is well on the way to Rome.

In fact, Charles is positively repelled by the idea of marriage. He loathes the Oxford system, where the clerical "Heads of Houses" (masters of the colleges) are married "ministers of Christ with large incomes, living in finely furnished houses, with wives and families . . . without anything to make them clergymen but a black coat and a white tie. And then Bishops or Deans come, with women tucked under their arm; and they can't enter church" without a footman to put a cushion down for them to sit on. One is convinced that it is not the wealth (which high Roman Catholic dignitaries also enjoyed) but the women that really underlie Charles's revulsion. In a bookshop Charles sees his old acquaintance White, once feverishly pro-Catholic, now an Anglican clergyman, come in with his newly married wife. "Love was in their eyes, joy in their gait and bearing. Charles had a faintish feeling come over him; somewhat such as might beset a man on hearing a call for pork-chops when he was sea-sick." The remainder of the scene is high comedy, as White vainly tries to remind his wife of the title of a book she has forgotten but wants to buy: "Is it 'The Catholic Parsonage?' . . . or 'Lays of the Apostles?' or 'Anglicanism of the Early Martyrs?' or 'Confessions of a Pervert?' or 'Eustace Beville?' or 'Modified Celibacy?' " Charles's distaste—and Newman's—for the female sex is, however, unmistakably clear, and it was in a sardonic spirit that Newman selected White—of all his characters—to be now so besotted with marital love.

Some modern biographers have argued that Newman was at least subconsciously a homosexual, and have emphasized his deep, even passionate, friendship for Hurrell Froude, the handsome ascetic Tractarian who died in 1836, and whose four volumes of *Remains*, complete with their accounts of self-scourging and other austerities, Newman and others published in 1838 and 1839. Such an interpretation overlooks the emotional language frequent in nineteenth-century friendships between persons of the same sex, which arouses thoughts in post-Freudian minds that sometimes were not present and sometimes were strictly suppressed in pre-

Freudian minds. Newman did reprove his bachelor friends as one by one they embarked upon marriage: "You surely are inconsiderate," he wrote to Henry Wilberforce, "you ask me to give you my heart when you give yours to another," but he never sent the letter, which made for more of a temporary estrangement than if he had done so. Had Newman been conscious that there was anything sexually perverse in his attitude toward women and marriage, he would hardly have proclaimed it in *Loss and Gain*, which was immediately attributed to him despite its anonymity.

Sexual abstinence, then, is one of the themes of *Loss and Gain* and is closely connected with its religious themes. At Oxford, Charles encounters men of every shade of Anglican opinion. There are the Evangelicals, whose leading spirit, Freeborn, thinks "theology itself a mistake, as substituting . . . worthless intellectual notions for the vital truths of religion." The Bible "said much of faith and holiness, but hardly a word about churches and forms." Nothing should be interposed between the human mind and God: "faith . . . firm belief that God had forgiven you, was the one thing needful," and if that be present, a man might be anything from a Catholic to a Unitarian and still be saved. When challenged, Freeborn points to the Articles: they "expressly say that we are justified by faith only." And indeed they do: Article XI—which proves to be of major importance for Charles Reding's intellectual development, though he does not yet know it—reads: "We are accounted righteous before God, only for the merit of our Lord and Saviour Jesus Christ by Faith, and not for our own works or deservings. Wherefore, that we are justified by faith only is a most wholesome doctrine, and very full of comfort, . . ." Newman did not need to quote this: every educated Anglican would have known the reference. The phraseology of Article XI is largely Lutheran, and the term "justified" means literally "acquitted" of our ill deeds before God the judge.

Freeborn gives "spiritual tea-parties," at which topics such as original sin or justification are discussed and the Bible read. But Reding wonders—as Newman in his own boyhood had wondered—"whether perhaps, after all, what is called Evangelical Religion was not the true Christianity." Freeborn discourses to him on faith, "a divine gift, and . . . the instrument of our justification in

God's sight." It is "like a hand, appropriating personally the merits of Christ, and God, to whom we are all initially by nature displeasing, justifies [acquits] us for Christ's sake because of our faith." It also regenerates us and so ensures that we are fit for God's favor. So true faith naturally produces good works.

But Charles's unsophisticated questions to Freeborn elicit contradictions, and soon Freeborn is asking, "What need . . . of knowing metaphysically what true faith is, if we have it and enjoy it?" And in the end, it turns out that to know what faith is, one must experience it: "Strangers need verbal descriptions; the heirs of the kingdom enjoy." Yet, says Charles, "we ought to act by reason." So why listen to Freeborn instead of to a Roman Catholic? To which Freeborn says, "Surely . . . you would not compare the spiritual Christian, such as Luther, holding his cardinal doctrine about justification, to any such formal, legal superstitious devotee as Popery can make, with its carnal rites and quack remedies. . . ?" And this runs counter to Charles's own boyhood experience (like Newman's) of a Catholic chapel where the worshippers were full of true devotion.

And when Charles goes to Freeborn's tea party, intellectual query gives way to farce, as obviously lower-class persons, not even named, but given numbers 1, 2, 3, and 4, declare absurdly that "Mr. O'Niggins, the agent for the Roman Priest Conversion Branch Tract Society" has successfully converted the late pope to Evangelical Christianity: the Holy Father, on his deathbed, heeded O'Niggins's warning to "receive the Bible, the whole Bible, and nothing but the Bible." In fact, the best way to convert Romanists is to begin by converting the pope. Charles regards the Evangelical promise of salvation without good works to the "worst of mankind" as a cruel thing, and he defends baptism as the source of regeneration, throwing the Evangelicals into consternation. Soon they are disputing furiously among themselves, chopping logic, and displaying casuistry of the sort which Protestants so often attributed to Catholics. For Charles, it is the end of Evangelical doctrines.

Somewhere between High and Low Church, in a vague indescribable confusion of doctrine, stands the Very Reverend Doctor Brownside, surely drawn at least in part from Renn Dickson Hampden (1793-1868), friend of Thomas Arnold and Professor of

Moral Philosophy at Oxford, whose nomination by the Whig Prime Minister, Lord Melbourne, as Regius Professor of Divinity had aroused the violent opposition of Newman and his Tractarian friends in 1836, and who later became Bishop of Hereford. Solemnly described in *Loss and Gain* as "one of the acutest if not the soundest academical thinkers of the day," Dr. Brownside is always "so clear or so shallow, that he saw to the bottom of all his thoughts. . . . Revelation to him, instead of being the abyss of God's counsels, with its dim outlines and broad shadows, was a flat sunny plain, laid out with straight macadamised roads." There is nothing mysterious in Revelation for Dr. Brownside; it is all practical; and the remarkable thing is that all men do not see it his way: obviously other people are mixed up.

Brownside preaches that there are few good reasoners in the world: and this is odd because man alone reasons: at least—and he examines the possibility at length—there is no documented instance of animals reasoning. This failure of mankind to reason well explains the multiplicity of religious beliefs, when everything could so easily be settled by verbal understanding. Actually, Brownside implies, "there was no truth or falsehood in received dogmas in theology . . . they were modes . . . in which the intellect reasoned upon the great truths of religion," and the trouble lies in people's insisting on other people's holding them. So the Anglican mode is only one way of expressing eternal truths, which can be just as well expressed in other ways. Praising three notorious heretics in Catholic history—Nestorius, Abelard, and Luther—Dr. Brownside concludes that God is just as pleased with the opposite of Anglican views as with Anglican views themselves. Brownside is a Broad Churchman before the term was coined. His contradictory latitudinarianism—felt as an outrage by Newman—seems to be reenforced by the widespread influence of an American named Coventry, who believes that religion is not based on dogma but on principle: a quick dig at Emerson, then much admired in England.

Then there are the various High-Church Anglicans. Bateman, who, we know, was intended as a mockery of the type, founds an "English Catholic" chapel at Oxford, to be dedicated to Charles I ("Why should we not have our St. Charles as well as the Romanists?"). It will be "sweet" to hear the vesper bell tolling;

Bateman is quite indifferent to the probability that nobody will attend services. Its fittings are sedulously imitated from those of mediaeval Catholic churches, but the candlesticks will have no lighted candles, lest the bishop object, and there can be no saints' images in the empty niches duly provided for them. Above the altar is a "beautifully wrought closet or recess" because "our sister churches of the Roman obedience always had a tabernacle for reserving the consecrated bread," but it too is empty. Bateman's "rood-lofts without roods, and piscinae without water, and niches without images, and candlesticks without lights, and masses without Popery" make a hollow stage-show of religion and fairly represent Newman's scorn for those who toyed with the external features of the Roman observance and let it go at that.

There are the two Miss Boltons, eager for Catholicism, ready to turn the Oxford Heads of Houses into "Abbots or Superiors," but surprised to hear that converts will have to confess. All this is "the reign of universal humbug," but Charles is still puzzled by Anglican clergymen's use of canonical vestments for preaching. Why not leave the reading of the liturgy to a simple parish boy? Can Bentham have been right? What is the relationship between the Church of England and the Church of Rome? Bateman says they are one "save for the corruptions of the Romish Church," while the Evangelical Freeborn insists that they are "two except when they agree." And so the undergraduates go on, turning the subject over and over, endlessly fascinated with its problems just as undergraduates of a century later would be with politics and with the quarrels among Marxists.

Then there is White, who keeps the "college authorities in a perpetual fidget lest he should some morning wake up a Papist," who declares that there is "no life or poetry in the Church of England; the Catholic Church alone is beautiful," and who urges that a visit to a foreign cathedral will show the visitor "true worship, far above reason." White, who talks the loudest, never goes the whole way to Rome: "He hasn't it in him. He's a coward," as the observant Sheffield remarks. And later, White explains lamely that while he has never "denied the claims of the Romish Church to be a branch of the Catholic Church . . . I have ever loved, and I shall ever venerate, my own Mother, the Church of my baptism." What has altered

White's views from those of "a playful kitten" to those of a dull "old Tabby"? Why, he is engaged to be married and has a good living waiting for him: he will be "settled, in every sense of the word, in mind, in life, in occupation." So Newman punished the faint-hearted, and added a further blow when he portrayed White in the bookshop as revoltingly in love with his new wife.

In contrast, there is Willis, White's "nice, modest" friend, his mere shadow ("*umbra*") as an undergraduate, who has a large ivory crucifix in his rooms and a picture of the Madonna and St. Dominic, with a rosary and various other "tokens of Catholicism." He actually attends services in the Catholic church in Oxford, so humble a building that Charles thinks it a Dissenters' chapel, and taxes Willis with being a Dissenter of a sort, and having broken the Oxford rule against attending any dissenting chapel or meeting. Firm in declaring that "Catholics are not Dissenters," Willis defends himself: everybody ignores the statutes, and he is drawn to the warmth of the Catholic service. After scolding Willis unmercifully for failing to promise never to return to the Catholic services, Charles wonders suddenly whether after all the Catholic Church may not be the true Church.

Before long, Willis tells Charles that he has been converted: he is happy; it is only what Charles should do, "and half Oxford besides." Willis has taken a trip abroad with a slightly older man, Morley, a Catholic; and a French priest has taken him into the Church. Shocked, Charles thinks it all a wayward gesture; but Morley, who has always been a Catholic, counterattacks: "No other Church has faith. The Church of England has no faith. You . . . have no faith," he says to Charles, who is only too keenly aware of his own doubts and tribulations. To Willis's adjurations that he "enter the great home of the soul . . . and adore," Charles urges that one must not act against reason, and Willis emphasizes the perils of doubt. "I have much to learn, I am conscious; but I wish to learn it" from the Church of England, says Charles; after which Willis pounces: Charles *has* no faith, he has just admitted it; now that he has listened to Willis and Morley, he is no longer "in invincible ignorance." Charles emphasizes the need for prudence, the two Catholics the need for precipitate action. Charles, as a Protestant, is bound to inquire, and the occasion passes.

It is later rumored that Willis is abandoning Rome to return to the Church of England: he has been abroad and seen the squalor of Italian cities and the depths of superstition there: it has alienated him. Of course this is a false rumor: but the argument is an interesting one. Both Catholics and anti-Catholics urged young men to travel abroad, the former in the belief that Continental Catholic piety would make for conversion, the latter in the belief that Continental Catholic poverty and "idolatry" would make for disillusionment. ("Their images are awful and their ignorance prodigious.") Not only is Willis still a staunch Catholic; he has also decided that "Romanism and Anglicanism were two religions; that you could not amalgamate them; that you must be Roman or Anglican, but could not be Anglo-Roman or Anglo-Catholic." Writing from within the Roman Church, Willis has found the "whole system of worship" very different; it was a whole new religion, and might discourage the new convert. Here, of course, Newman was referring to his own experience of the three years between his conversion and the writing of *Loss and Gain.*

On his next chance meeting with Willis a year or two later, Charles believes the rumor of reconversion true. Willis talks more freely; he has lost the bloom of youth and is sweeter, placid, lined of countenance. Before long, he is routing the quarrelsome Anglicans present by reiterating his view that the churches of England and of Rome are wholly separate. One enters the Catholic Church to learn, and accepts whatever one finds there. One must not speculate on how Catholic worship might be and then judge it, like a Protestant, by criticizing adversely the veneration of the Virgin; one must, like a Catholic, simply act. Not even the alleged falsity of certain relics can shake Willis, and he easily turns the earnest Anglicans' arguments against them. He is so plausible, so "demure," that the fatuous Bateman wonders whether he may not be a "concealed Jesuit," bugbear of all proper Anglicans. In a deeply emotional speech that ends the discussion, Willis makes clear the passionate depth of his faith: there is

> nothing so consoling, so piercing, so thrilling, so overcoming as the Mass. . . . It is not a mere form of words,—it is a great action, the greatest action that can be on earth. It is . . . the

> evocation of the Eternal. He becomes present on the altar in flesh and blood, before whom angels bow and devils tremble. . . . Words are necessary, but as means, not as ends . . . instruments of . . . consecration, of sacrifice. . . . It is wonderful! . . . quite wonderful!

And he prays that Charles shall have the faith that is needed to take the plunge. Charles is on the way but not yet there: from his heart he cries out, "O mighty Mother! I come; but I am far from home," and then suddenly realizes that this is "enthusiasm." Charles knows where his heart is, but he must go by reason.

Of course, the theme of *Loss and Gain* is Charles's own pilgrimage toward the Roman Church. Even after we have completed it with him, however, mystery remains: he has been slow, he has gone through many hesitations, we have followed him, but we cannot be sure *why* he has taken the final step or why he takes it when he does. He is not one of those, Newman tells us, who "fidget at intellectual difficulties and . . . are for ever trying to solve them . . . a new idea was not lost upon him, but it did not distress him if it was obscure, or conflicted with his habitual view of things. He let it work its way and find its place, and shape itself within him by the slow spontaneous action of the mind." He would have sped up the process if he could, and cleared up the perplexity sooner, but he could not. After a year of exposure to the conflicting religious opinions at Oxford, he knows he must discover what are the true opinions, and he knows that there must be "a principle of dogmatism" at the base of them. And he cannot "begin with faith, as Catholics do"; he must begin—and continue, and continue—with inquiry.

In this state, he gradually comes to wish that somebody he could trust would say to him, "This is true; this is not true." If he could only ask St. Paul, for example! And it would be a comfort to believe, with the Catholics, that the Church had "the inspiration of an Apostle." Then you would "know, beyond doubt, what to believe about God, and how to worship and please him!" He is already, his friend Sheffield sees, "on the road to Rome," since if he could only believe that the pope had "the *power* to decide this or that," he could then believe whatever it was the pope decided. He is altogether dissatisfied by those who tell him to eschew party, "Be true . . . be good . . . don't go too far, keep in the mean. . . . I want some practical advice, not abstract truths." When Charles embarks on a regular course of study of the Thirty-nine Articles, it only makes him more uncertain than he already was.

The articles prove to be "a patchwork of bits of orthodoxy, Lutheranism, Calvinism, and Zwinglism." It had been a mere "tossup" that the Church of England did not adhere to one or another of these schools of thought. How about private judgment? Charles wants to know if this is allowed. "Had he asked a Wesleyan or an Independent [Congregationalist]," they would have said yes; had he asked a Catholic, "he would have been told that we used our private judgment to find the Church, and then the Church superseded it." But his teacher, a High-Church Anglican, cannot answer him at all.

On the one hand we "*must* use our judgment in the determination of religious doctrine"; on the other, it is a sin to doubt the doctrine of the Blessed Trinity." But although that doubt is sinful, "our highest state" on earth is one of doubt. What about the anathemas in the Athanasian Creed? They were written against believers in heresies that no longer exist, his teacher assures him; but the fuzziness remains. How will sins committed after baptism be forgiven? The Articles do not say, and the Catholic doctrine of pardons and purgatory is false: better not inquire further. Is Christ really present in the bread and wine? An open question. Is the doctrine of eternal punishment actually in the Scriptures, actually in the Articles, actually part of the faith of the Church of England? No answer. The ineffable Bateman tells Charles to wait until the course is over and reminds him how many prominent men have signed the Articles in the past. Charles must sign them on faith, as Bateman had.

But the problem grows intense when the discussion turns to that article which the Evangelical Freeborn had already cited to Charles, Article XI, which declares in Lutheran fashion "that we are justified by faith only is a most wholesome doctrine." Now, many months later, Bateman readily concedes that "the Protestant sense of this statement is point blank," in contradiction to the most eminent divines of the Church of England, but that one does not have to take it in the Protestant sense; indeed, "we need not take the Articles in any sense at all." All we do is sign them "as articles of peace" and agree not to preach against them: a view which—Bateman concedes—would admit the Unitarians into the Church. If those in authority agreed on the import of the Articles, the Articles would mean what such men said they meant.

But those in authority disagree widely: "One clergyman denies Apostolical Succession, another maintains it; one denies the inspiration of Scripture, a second holds Calvin to be a saint, a third considers the doctrine of sacramental grace a superstition, a fourth takes part with Nestorius against the Church, a fifth is a Sabellian."[1] We do not even know exactly who wrote the Articles or the textual history of each; so actually—since the Anglican Church is part of the Church Catholic—its creed is the entire Catholic creed. But this argument only leads Charles to ask, what if the Articles contradict part of the rest of the Catholic creed? It doesn't happen, says Bateman; any apparent discrepancy can be reasoned away. Yet nobody in authority holds this apparently "plausible" view of Bateman's; in fact, it is nothing but Bateman's own view. Charles is left where he was, without authority and still in search of it.

It is only unconsciously—we would say subconsciously—that Charles's views take shape. After two years, he "had not yet given names to these opinions, much less had they taken a theological form," yet in "an hour's conversation with a friend," he finds himself professing "what really were the Catholic doctrines and usages, of penance, purgatory, counsels of perfection, mortification of self, and clerical celibacy." The "Catholic system comes home to his mind, fulfills his ideas of religion, satisfies his sympathies." He is using *private judgment* "in order ultimately to supersede it." This is neither absurd nor inconsistent. Charles will use private judgment until it brings him into the Church; then he will denounce its use and abandon it. Combined with his notions is the "shadow of Cath-

1. Nestorius, Patriarch of Constantinople (428-431), allegedly emphasized the humanity of Christ, as against his divinity, and separated the human and divine natures within Christ. This heresy, condemned at the Council of Chalcedon in 451, was probably not actually held by Nestorius, but it has always retained the name Nestorian. Sabellianism (late second century A.D.) made no distinction whatever between Father and Son; Christ is the Father incarnate; and so the divine nature is emphasized; it left no room for Christ's human life or suffering on the Cross.

olicism without." It was the earliest Christian faith; it was once the faith of all England; the faith of the present Church of England is held nowhere else; and it is difficult to say what that faith is. Charles is "growing towards the Church."

And having set aside his doubts about the Articles for two years, he finds them "like an unpaid bill." To take his degree at Oxford, he must sign them, and his discomfort at the prospect is increasing. The kindly-meant argument, "It happens every day," is of no weight with Charles, nor is the consolation that (except for the Jewish) no faith "came simply and directly from heaven." He cannot sacrifice his private judgment and subscribe. If papal "infallibility, transubstantiation, saint-worship" and the other tenets of Catholicism—apparently difficult to accept—came to Charles "on the same authority as the doctrine of the Blessed Trinity," he could accept them. The trouble is that the Articles rest on no authority, and "If I *must* give up private judgment, there *is* a Church which has a greater claim on me than the Church of England."

The Articles are inconsistent (and he mentions the inconsistencies); the Roman Church is consistent. Above all, justification by faith (Article XI) is still sticking in Charles's throat. He feels out of place in the Church of England, but he is still only inching toward Rome. Even though Newman shortened the length of his own preliminary period of hesitations when writing the story of Charles Reding, we feel the interminable pulling and hauling that preceded the big leap. In order to preserve the Anglican position, one must believe, with the sixteenth-century reformers, that Rome is seriously corrupt. And if one believes that, one simply cannot give in to Rome's attractions. When the time comes and he has taken his examinations (and got only a second-class—while Newman himself collapsed and barely passed), Charles defers taking the degree, and so postpones the decision about signing the Articles.

He is entering the final phase. It is only after more than two additional years that *fear* begins to work in Charles, fear that if he doesn't become a Catholic, he may die first "with a great duty unaccomplished" and hence, presumably, be damned for eternity. He cannot ride or bathe for fear of an accident (the same thing had happened to Newman). He cannot wait for absolute certainty; he must act: "our grounds must at best be imperfect; but if they appear to be sufficient after prayer, diligent search, obedience, waiting . . . they are His voice calling us on." And after heartrending farewells (also like Newman's own) to his family and to his beloved Oxford, Charles sets off for London to offer himself up to the Passionist Order. Before he can complete his intention, he has a series of final adventures. His "defection" is published in an Oxford newspaper: "Mr. Reding . . . son of a respectable clergyman of the Establishment . . . after eating the bread of the Church all his life, has at length avowed himself the subject and slave of an Italian Bishop." And so on.

There is another drawback, not previously discussed: Willis, a convert and an Oxonian like himself, is really the only Catholic Reding has known. His Anglican mentor Carlton warns him that he "will have much to bear with" when he does know others; they will seem to him "under-educated men . . . men of rude minds and vulgar manners." Charles will find himself "a fish out of water," his talents perhaps unappreciated, wasted. "An English clergyman is a gentleman," at least; and Charles is moving into a strange world. The views are by no means as prejudiced as those voiced by an old family friend, who calls the Catholics "a set of hypocrites and sharpers. . . . not to be trusted." But there is much in Carlton's warning, and it reflected Newman's own experience.

A scholarly upper-middle-class convert to the Catholic faith in England in 1845 would indeed find himself in an unfamiliar world. It was not to be expected that he would have much contact with the Old Catholic aristocracy or, except in rare cases, that he would have found them any more congenial than other sporting landowners. His duty might well lie chiefly among ill-educated Irishmen, whether in England or in Ireland. It was a real point of argument; but of course in Charles's case, it comes too late, and he pays it no attention. A conversation with a priest on the train to London alleviates one of the last troubles: it is possible before conversion to attain a moral conviction that the Catholic Church is the only voice of God, and no clearer evidence can be expected until afterwards. In the end it is still a gamble, faith "is a venture before a man is a Catholic; it is a grace after it." It is as Charles had felt earlier: first one uses one's reason to get oneself into the Church; then one abandons it and accepts authority.

The final few hours of Charles's life as a Protestant are punctuated by a fantastic series of visitors, who in uninterrupted succession besiege his room in London and try to win him over. First there appears a former Oxford kitchen boy as an envoy of the "Holy Catholic Church," which is to say a follower of Edward Irving (1792-1834), a Scotch Presbyterian minister who had preached Christ's imminent arrival on earth for a reign of one thousand years, and believed that his own disciples had received the gift of tongues. The year before Irving died, the Presbyterians had ousted him, and he had founded his own "Catholic Apostolic Church." Jack the kitchen boy and his companion, the Reverend Alexander Highfly, explain that their church has created an order of Apostles superior to all bishops, priests, and deacons. The Irvingites are "gentle, well-mannered animals" compared to what is coming.

Next there arrives a young woman, who wants to recruit Charles for the Plymouth Brethren, an extreme Evangelical sect which maintained that anyone might celebrate the Lord's Supper or preach, launched in Dublin in 1827 but after 1830 centered in Plymouth, where their leader, J. N. Darby, founded his own sub-sect of Darbyites or "Exclusive Brethren" in 1847, the year before *Loss and Gain* appeared. Charles has heard that every Plymouth Brother may "name one or two doctrines of his own," and his lady caller assures him that this is true: "I'm for election and assurance; our dearest friend is for perfection; and another sweet sister is for the second advent."[2] Just as she has taken three quarters of an hour of Charles's time, there rushes in the excitable "Zerubbabel"—it is his only name; he has no Christian name, and it is his "Jewish designation"—an ex-Anglican deacon converted to his own form of Judaism, who expects the new Anglican bishop of Jerusalem to restore the Jewish Church, and who is ready to begin by negotiating a loan

2. In view of the sharp treatment meted out by Newman to the Plymouth Brethren, it is worth noting that his younger brother, Francis (1805-1897), became a Plymouth Brother in the late twenties. He was greatly influenced by Darby himself, who appears in his book *Phases of Faith* (1850) as "the Irish clergyman." Later Francis Newman became a Baptist and eventually a Unitarian.

for the rebuilding of the Temple and issuing stock yielding four percent interest.

On Zerubbabel's heels follows the representative of the "Truth Society," which has already elected Charles on the strength of the newspaper article about his imminent conversion. The emblem on the diploma now handed to Charles is the emblem of Truth (!): the moon under total eclipse, surrounded, as by cherub faces, by the heads of Socrates, Cicero, Julian, Abelard, Luther, Benjamin Franklin, and Lord Brougham. The Emperor Julian the Apostate (361-363)—who attempted to destroy Christianity and restore paganism, and against whose patronage Charles ironically protests—is included because he had embraced "what *he* thought Truth." But since, in any case, one of the Society's twelve principles is that Truth can never be found, it really makes little difference.

Somewhat disconcerted, Charles faces his last and most appalling visitor, Dr. Kitchens, author of an eight-page tract entitled "Kitchens' Spiritual Elixir," which "has enlightened millions." It is a marvellous cure for popery: after a single reading, "all the trash about sacraments, saints, penance, purgatory, and good works is dislodged from the soul at once." One of its preachers defeated thirty Jesuits in simultaneous debate; the mere voice of another shattered glass in a neighboring house and crippled two priests a quarter of a mile away. When Dr. Kitchens proclaims that the sign of the beast in Revelation was the sign of the Cross, Charles can take no more. He seizes his own crucifix and literally exorcises the room of Dr. Kitchens, driving him in torment out of the house.

This procession of members of the lunatic fringe of mid-nineteenth-century English religion is funny, of course, even hilarious, and provides a bit of not unwelcome comic relief for those who have patiently followed Charles Reding's long conversion. But it is also a serious expression of Newman's intolerant disgust with the proliferating sects that were, in his view, sure to spring up like evil fungi so long as every man, no matter how illiterate or how crazy, indiscriminately exercised his reason and his private judgment, acknowledging no higher authority than his own. Newman believed in miracles, and he closes Charles Reding's secular life with a miracle: the driving out of a devil by the use of a crucifix. "Take it away, Mr. Reding, I beseech you. . . . Oh, oh! Spare me, spare me . . . an idol!—oh! you young antichrist, you devil!—'tis He, 'tis He—torments!—spare me, Mr. Reding!" cries the satanic Kitchens as he rushes from the room and leaps down the stairs two or three at a time to get away from the sacred cross.

After the turmoil comes peace at last, as Charles is admitted into the Catholic communion: there is "a rock under his feet; it was the *soliditas Cathedrae Petri*," the firm permanence of the throne of Peter. And his old friend Willis, now Father Aloysius, greets him with joy. When Reding reproaches himself with having delayed too long the moment of his conversion, Willis answers also with self-reproach: he himself had taken the step too soon and has had to pay for his rashness afterwards. The last thought that Newman leaves with the reader, as Charles Reding disappears into "his temporary cell," happy and at peace, is that these processes move at different speeds, and are punctuated by decisive actions at different moments, in the spiritual lives of all Christians.

Loss and Gain may, as some critics assert, be too intellectual a novel to offer deep psychological insights into the irrational. But since it is all that Newman in 1848 felt able to tell about himself, and perhaps all that he knew, it remains extraordinarily significant. God plays the major part in deciding the protagonist's actions and ultimate fate, and secularist critics cavil at the lack of literary verisimilitude. But since God *did*, Newman was convinced, play just such a part in his own development, the secularist would be well advised to reflect that there are obviously decisive forces in some men's lives that fail to prove decisive in others', and that the Charles Redings are as legitimate subjects for novels as any other men.

When he had finished *Loss and Gain*, Newman began almost at once on a new novel, *Callista* (1856, no. 6), to be set in North Africa in the mid-third century. By 1848, when he began it, the fashion of novels set in ancient or early Christian or mediaeval times had become almost a mania. Educated Englishmen had studied some Latin, Greek, and ancient history. And the early days of the Christian Church abounded in examples of individual suffering for the faith that provided an edifying lesson for nineteenth-century readers. Moreover, by setting a story ostensibly in the distant past, and by dressing up the characters in more or less authentic costumes against the backdrop of more or less authentically realized scenery and buildings, one might comment indirectly and effectively upon the issues of one's own day. Such novels were immensely popular, beginning about 1825: King Herod, the Wandering Jew, priests of Isis, Vestal Virgins, Goths, Huns, and other barbarians strode through their pages. Bulwer-Lytton, Wilkie Collins, and a host of other writers now less well remembered had tried their hands at these fictional returns to antiquity before Newman's book was actually completed. And the vogue was only beginning.

Newman set aside his manuscript in an early stage, but returned to it in the early fifties under new circumstances. In 1853 there appeared a remarkable novel of Alexandria, *Hypatia; or, New Foes with an Old Face* (no. 47), by a redoubtable foe of Catholicism, Charles Kingsley (1819-1875), a "Broad Churchman," disciple of Frederick Denison Maurice, one-time Christian Socialist and declared Chartist, and a passionate believer in conjugal love. Though he admired Newman in many ways, Kingsley was driven almost beside himself by clerical celibacy and by what he took to be Newman's lack of masculinity, and in an earlier novel (*Yeast*, 1848 serially, 1851 in book form, NIS) he had included an unflattering portrait of Newman, the first round in a long duel between the two men. As can be deduced from *Hypatia*'s subtitle, and as we shall see in further detail below, Kingsley used his novel of Egypt about the year 400 to attack his "new foes" in their old guise: and among the foes were the Catholics in general and celibacy in particular. Appearing when it did, *Hypatia* was another weapon in the "No Popery" agitation that followed the restoration of the Roman Catholic hierarchy in England in 1850 and the appointment, also in 1850, of Nicholas Patrick Stephen Wiseman (1802-1865) as Archbishop of Westminster and Cardinal.

In keeping with the fashion, Wiseman helped to plan a series of historical novels for Catholic and other interested laymen, to be called "The Catholic Popular Library," and designed to illustrate the "condition of the Church in different periods of her past existence." And Wiseman himself volunteered to write the very first in the series, *Fabiola; or, The Church of the Catacombs* (1854, no. 9). Working during the intervals of a busy life "in all sorts of places . . .

in scraps and fragments of time," he turned out *Fabiola* (pronounced Fa-*bée*-o-la or Fa-*býe*-o-la) within a year. And he enlisted Newman to produce a later volume in the series. So Newman completed *Callista*, which appeared in 1856 as Number 12 of the Catholic Popular Library. It was, as he wrote in a preface, "the nearest approach" he could make to a "more important work suggested to him from a high ecclesiastical quarter," which is to say, Cardinal Wiseman. Both *Fabiola* and *Callista*, then, were answers to Kingsley, which endeavored to restore the balance upset by his novel of the early church. *Callista*, it has been suggested, was also a veiled answer to Wiseman; for despite *Fabiola*'s enormous popularity, its multiple editions, and its translations into many foreign languages, it was nowhere near as good a novel as *Hypatia*. Whether or not Newman was consciously seeking to outdo his ecclesiastical superior, he certainly managed to do so: *Callista* is one of the best historical novels of the entire nineteenth century.

Cardinal Wiseman, who had lived in Rome for many years, put into *Fabiola* much archaeological and historical knowledge of the city and its ancient monuments, together with the fruits of intensive reading in the lives of early Christian martyrs. The twentieth-century reader must remind himself that Victorians enjoyed learning their history in the form of thinly disguised fiction. They were accustomed to long digressions (many pages in *Fabiola*, for example, deal with ancient Roman tomb inscriptions) and do not seem to have minded frequent interruptions of the story by direct addresses from the author, telling them what his intentions were. Once over these hurdles, one may appreciate, if no longer enjoy, Wiseman's earnest effort to edify while amusing.

Rich, intelligent, and haughty, the pagan Roman heiress Fabiola, living in Rome toward the end of the reign of Diocletian (284-305), just before the unleashing of the last and severest of the official Roman imperial persecutions of the Christians, is gradually converted to Christianity, largely through the agency of one of her slaves, Syra (or Miriam), a Christian girl from Antioch. Many of the personages are historic figures: notably the Emperor Maximian and a number of the martyrs. Having cruelly punished Syra for suggesting that though physically Fabiola's chattel she has an independent soul, Fabiola regrets her violence and finds it possible to love even a slave. She recognizes in Syra "disinterested love, affection that asked for no return," and realizes that "in her maid's mind there seemed to be some latent but infallible standard of truth," a secret that she must discover. Syra convinces her that reading a book about crimes and foul deeds—even if one would not commit such actions—is an offense against God, the one God of her own "system"—as yet unnamed. Fabiola longs to acknowledge such a single supreme being, and shows that she is learning humility, as she delights in her first consciousness "of a controlling, an approving, and a *rewarding* Power . . . standing by us when no other eye can see, or restrain, or encourage us." She begs forgiveness for her earlier violence. And she asks whether there is "no great act of acknowledgment, such as sacrifice is supposed to be, whereby He may be formally recognised and adored?" There is, of course. But what sacrifice can be worthy of such a God, "spotless in purity, matchless in greatness, unbounded in acceptableness"? The answer is, "Only Himself." But the idea of the eucharist is still too awe inspiring for Fabiola to pursue the mystery further.

By accident, Fabiola acquires a written fragment of the Gospel of Matthew (v.44), "I say to you, love your enemies, do good to them that hate you"; Syra explicates the text for her: this virtue, which seems heroic and transcendent, we must practice every day. Sebastian—a fine, upstanding member of the imperial guard—has ideas much like Syra's and, indeed, he shortly attains his celebrated martyrdom by being shot full of arrows. When she hears of it, Fabiola is astonished that he has been a Christian, a sect of which she has believed all the vicious stories current in Rome. Next, Fabiola's friend Agnes (St. Agnes) proves also to be a Christian, but after the case of Sebastian, Fabiola is not surprised: "She had found that faith existing in what she had considered the type of every manly virtue," and it was natural also "in her whom she had loved as the very symbol of womanly perfection."

Before Agnes's martyrdom Fabiola promises to inquire further into Christian doctrines: Agnes predicts that she will be converted. Although Fabiola admires the "more than earthly" virtue that Christian faith had conferred on Sebastian and Agnes, she is still ignorant of Christian doctrine, of the Trinity, of the Incarnation, of the Atonement. She is leaning toward Christianity, but without these teachings she cannot become a Christian. The reader of the novel may follow Fabiola's Christian education and her baptism and first communion. She lives on through the persecutions without attaining martyrdom (probably because she was not an historic personage, and Wiseman hesitated to invent a martyrdom for a figment of his own imagination).

No modern reader will fail to be surprised by the repeated detailed accounts of torture and death of martyrs. The martyrs seek and glory in their agonies; their persecutors enjoy inflicting pain as much as the holy men and women enjoy receiving it. A good deal of this, of course, reflects the language and the feeling in the original *Acts* of the various martyrs, which Wiseman was paraphrasing. But some of it, one grows quite certain, reflects his own pleasure in contemplating such scenes. We may be sure that he knew what he was doing: he writes, "It is far from our intention to harrow the feelings of our gentle readers, by our descriptions of the cruel and fiendish torments inflicted by the heathen torturers upon our Christian forefathers." Yet he immediately continues, "Few are more horrible, yet few better authenticated, than the torture practised on the martyr Cassianus." And instead of letting it go at that, and refraining from harrowing our feelings with further details, Wiseman does in fact gloatingly rehearse precisely the horrible torture he has pretended he wishes to spare us. And as with Cassianus, so with Caecilia, Sebastian, Agnes, Emeritiana, and others. Despite the repetition of the Christian message that one should love one's enemies, Wiseman thoroughly enjoys the gruesome details of their deaths. One may leave to psychologists the decision as to the relative elements of voyeurism, sadism, and masochism in Wiseman's personality and writings, but at the very least a modern reader will discover in *Fabiola* a large element of *grand guignol.*

By dwelling on the persecutions and the successful passage of the Church through those difficult years before the new tolerance ushered in by Constantine after 312, Wiseman probably intended to remind his Catholic readers of their own political sufferings in England, their recent Emancipation in 1829, and their further triumph of 1850, when Wiseman himself had arrived as the new visible chief of the restored hierarchy in England. Perhaps the episode of Torquatus, a Christian who turns traitor, may have been designed to remind the reader of Father Achilli, an unfrocked priest: Achilli capitalized on the "No Popery" public feeling of 1851 to publish various "revelations" about Catholic convents that helped to confirm popular irrational prejudices, and he then won a sensational libel suit against Newman for accusing him of sacrilege and sexual misconduct. *Fabiola* includes an occasional aside to the reader referring directly to nineteenth-century reality. But unlike *Hypatia*—and unlike *Callista*—it was no parable of nineteenth-century England in the form of an historical novel.

For the setting of *Callista* Newman chose the provincial town of Sicca in Roman Africa—modern Tunisia—in the year 250, about half a century before the Rome of *Fabiola*. It was a moment at which the Christian Church had for more than half a century remained free from persecution by the Roman authorities, but in 250 the Emperor Decius required all Roman subjects everywhere to render on pain of death the obligatory act of worship (perfunctory enough, a mere pinch of incense before a statue) to himself as a god. Adherents of all the many cults in the huge territory of the Empire were quite willing to make this gesture with untroubled conscience—except for the Jews, who were traditionally exempted from it, and the Christians, who were persecuted and sometimes sought martyrdom. Newman's story is the same as Wiseman's: the conversion of a beautiful and intelligent pagan woman to Christianity; but Newman's art and his passion infused it with life, his own life.

For Callista—the beautiful Greek girl employed by the amiable Jucundus (his very name means "pleasant") as an artist in his workshop that turns out images for pagan cults—is as much Newman himself as is Charles Reding in *Loss and Gain*. Just as Charles Reding (and Newman) had a loving sister who was distressed at his conversion, so Callista has a loving brother who is distressed at hers. When her friend, the Christian youth Agellius, seeks her in marriage, Callista is repelled because marriage is not what she has wanted of him:

> I hoped that from you I might have learned more of that strange strength which my nature needs. . . . but O my disappointment when first I saw in you indications that you were

> thinking of me only as others think, and felt towards me as others may feel; that you were aiming at me, not at your God; that you had much to tell me of yourself but nothing of Him! . . . Why do you come to me with your every-day gallantry? . . . You have nothing to give. You have thrown me back upon my dreary, dismal self, and the deep wounds of my memory.

Callista is as predisposed towards celibacy as Charles Reding himself. And Agellius is, one can see, more than half relieved. He has been egged on to proposing by his uncle Jucundus, who would like to see the two handsome young people happily married in a normal way. But "it is undeniably a solemn moment . . . and requires a strong heart, when any one deliberately surrenders himself, soul and body, to the keeping of another while life shall last. . . . so tremendous an undertaking that nature seems to sink under its responsibilities." True enough for Newman and his major fictional characters, even if not so true for "nature" in general. "You will recognize the author in the work," wrote Newman in dedicating *Callista* to Henry Wilberforce, that very friend whose marriage had once so distressed him, "and take pleasure in the recognition."

Having decided for celibacy, Callista, though she indignantly denies that she wants to be a Christian, is ready to begin the agonizing process of conversion. Newman, as he wrote in 1849, was seeking "to bring out the ethos of the Heathen from St. Paul's day down to St. Gregory [Pope 590-604], when under the process or the sight of the phenomenon, of conversion; what conversion was in those times, and what the sophistries and philosophies viewed as realities influencing men. But . . . *I don't think I could do it from history.* I despair of finding facts enough." When Newman actually came to finish the story seven years after this letter, he skillfully used what facts history afforded him, but turned inward for his account of Callista's conversion. The persecutions begin; the Bishop of Carthage, St. Cyprian (called in the Roman way by his second name Caecilius), takes temporary refuge with Agellius. Coming to warn Agellius of a mob that is seeking to kill him along with the other Christians, Callista meets Cyprian.

As soon as he sees that she is bent on saving Christians from the mob, Cyprian realizes that "she who is so tender of Christians . . . must herself have some sparks of the Christian flame in her own breast." No, says Callista: a person must be born a Christian. To which Cyprian replies that most of the Christians in Roman Africa "are converts in manhood, not the sons of Christians," while most of those who have become renegades to paganism were Christians by birth. "Such is my experience," says the future saint, "and I think the case is the same elsewhere." By "elsewhere" may we not understand nineteenth-century England, and by "Christians" Roman Catholics? Was not Newman saying that the most faithful sons of the Church were the converts like himself, so often slighted and allowed to rot with their energies and talents too little employed in the Church's service?

Callista thinks she can never believe in Christianity because "it seems too beautiful. . . . to be anything else than a dream." Its maxims, that is, are beautiful, but its dogmas are shocking and odious: she cannot believe that all her ancestors are condemned to eternal punishment. Instead of reassuring her with an argument about "invincible ignorance" serving to liberate the souls of those who can never have known about the true faith, Cyprian makes the personal attack at once: she really means, he says, that she will not believe that *she* will go to Hell forever. She admits it, and he divines her unhappiness, which is likely to continue all her life: if so, what is irrational about postulating eternal wretchedness in Hell? But

> if you have needs, desires, aims, aspirations, all of which demand an Object, and imply, by their very existence, that such an Object does exist also, and if there be a message which professes to come from that Object [i.e., the Gospel] . . . and to teach you about Him, and to bring the remedy you crave; and if those who try that remedy say with one voice that the remedy answers; are you not bound, Callista, at least to look that way, to inquire into what you hear about it, and to ask for His help, if He be, to help you to believe in Him?

Cyprian teaches her of the Incarnation and the Atonement, but she is wholly reluctant to abandon her own ancestral paganism. Cyprian tells her that he himself, an old man, "a proud stern Roman, a lover of pleasure, a man of letters, of political station, with formed habits, and long associations," had been converted: why should she not be? But she says she fears he may be as bad as the priests of Isis or Mithra. She wants a God to worship, not a sinner like herself and like Cyprian. And—just as the mob appears and they must escape—he gives her a manuscript of the Gospel of St. Luke.

When Callista is arrested, she declares quite truly that she is not a Christian, but neither can she render the required sacrifice of incense to the Emperor. She is still drawn to Christianity but knows too little about it. She reflects constantly about what she has been taught: it is in her heart. And the Christians she has known—notably Cyprian—clearly have "a simplicity, a truthfulness, a decision, an elevation, a calmness, and a sanctity to which she was a stranger." As the reader passes through Callista's prison experiences, and suffers with her, he feels the agonizing slowness of the process, although her whole conversion is a matter only of months, as against the years that Reding waited and the even longer years that Newman himself hesitated. Even after rejecting the well-meant advice of the leading pagan philosopher of the town, Callista "was neither a Christian, nor was she not. She was in the midway region of inquiry, which as surely takes time to pass over, except there be some almost miraculous interference, as it takes time to walk from place to place. You see a person coming towards you, and you say, impatiently, 'Why don't you come faster?—why are you not here already?' Why? Because it takes time." She has already seen that heathenism is false; but she has yet to see fully that Christianity is true. It is then, at last, that she turns to the Gospel of Luke, which Cyprian had given her. From it she learns to enter a new world, where, instead of enjoying the present and forgetting about the future, one must sacrifice the present for the future: "what is seen must give way to what is believed." Soon she is ready for baptism, for confirmation, and for her first communion. Cyprian offers her all three sacraments in her prison, one immediately after the other. And her first communion is also her last, as her martyrdom—a grim and brutal one indeed—follows almost at once.

Contemporaries of Newman pointed out—though never in detail—that his third-century pagan North Africa had much in common with nineteenth-century Protestant England. This was easier for them to see than for us, since his allusions are always cleverly masked and one can easily read the novel through attentively without seeing them. But if the shoe seems to fit, one must at least try it on: quite probably Newman would have denied most of the suggested resemblances that follow; he enjoyed both mystification and satire, as *Loss and Gain* abundantly shows, and it was not to be expected that he would have let slip an opportunity to bang away at his enemies from behind the screen provided by seventeen centuries of time. Whatever else Henry Wilberforce was supposed to enjoy in *Callista*, he would surely have been on the lookout for these parallels.

Take Sicca, for example: the name of the town, as Newman carefully explains, is Punic (Phoenician), the Semitic language still spoken in Carthage and its territories long after the Roman conquest; in Punic "Sicca" may have meant "Tents of the Daughters." But the word also has a Latin meaning, and that meaning is "dry." And since the opening pages of the novel emphasize the heights on which the town is built and by which it is surrounded, Sicca is literally "high and dry." And so is its religion. "There are so many fantastic religions nowadays," says a sober-minded pagan to Agellius the Christian, implying that Christianity is a mere freak, just as many Protestants in Victorian England regarded Catholicism as a freak, one of those "absurd superstitions which are as plentiful here as serpents." Christians are treated with contemptuous toleration at best; but the lower classes of society mock them and believe in all sorts of superstitions about them, just as the English lower classes did about "Papists." Yet "men of sense" were beginning to understand Christianity better, which led them "to scorn it less, but . . . to fear it more." So "the philosophical schools"—which we may interpret as the Anglican dons of Oxford, those very Tractarians whom Newman had been so instrumental in launching—"had . . . been employed in creating and systematizing a new intellectual basis for the received paganism." And the philosophers—whom Kingsley had overpraised in *Hypatia*—are savagely ridiculed by Newman in *Callista*, when Arnobius mocks the great Polemo (who solemnly discovers that "the egg comes first in relation to the causativity of the chick, and the chick comes first in relation to the causativity of the egg").

Yet at the same time, Christians—as Cyprian wrote—were

showing signs of dreadful laxity and shared in a general slackening of social morals. One amiable old bishop devotes himself exclusively to farming, and his deacon is a famous huntsman: here one need not even draw the parallels with "high-and-dry" Anglicans. The Tertullianists—named for the notable theologian Tertullian (*c.* 160-220) who had abandoned Catholicism for the heretic sect of the Montanists—have a "flourishing meeting-house" and declare that every Catholic is eternally damned; these are surely Dissenters. Perhaps the "various descriptions of Gnostics who had carried off the clever youths" referred to the Oxford "Noetics," the pre-Tractarian Oriel College intellectuals who were willing to be tolerant of those who doubted the precise accuracy of Scripture on every point. It is even possible that the shop that employs Callista and sells "idols, large and small, amulets and the like instruments of the established superstition" is intended to be an Evangelical establishment. Surely Newman's remark about Caracalla's edict of 212 which made inhabitants of the Roman provinces citizens of Rome, but largely in order that they might be taxed, has reference to the British overseas empire: like the modern British, the Romans are "an imperial people," to whose splendid capital are brought all the luxuries of the earth, to enable the Romans to live in ostentatious style and to inspire awe in lesser peoples.

Listen to Jucundus, Agellius's uncle, mildly in his cups: "give me the old weapons, the old maxims of Rome. . . . Do the soldiers march under the old ensigns? do they swear by the old gods? do they interchange the good old signals and watchwords? do they worship the fortune of Rome? then I say we are safe. But do we take to new ways? do we trifle with religion?" If so, nothing will do any good. Here is the good old Tory English gentleman. And when Jucundus talks of Christians (substitute nineteenth-century Catholics) we hear the authentic voice of "No Popery" as of the early 1850's: "Spread? . . . spread, they'll spread? Yes, they'll spread. Yes, grow, like scorpions, twenty at a birth. The country already swarms with them; they are as many as frogs or grasshoppers; they start up every where under one's nose, when one least expects them. The air breeds them like plague-flies; the wind drifts them like locusts." And they "feed on little boys' marrow and brains; worship the ass," engage in foul magic. It is William Sewell's vision of the Jesuits to the life. One can play this game with *Callista* at great length, and each reader should try his own hand at it.

But if *Callista* has passages of clever satire of Newman's world and represents a second effort to tell in fiction the story of his own conversion, this time through the experience of a sensitive woman, it is also a considerable work of art. It moves with a speed and certainty and power far more certain than the pace of *Loss and Gain.* Despite his having an eye on his own day, Newman concentrated his chief attention on a period he knew well and whose historic sources he had studied. His account of the plague of locusts and of the wild disorder of the hungry mob that follows is a splendid piece of writing. And most horrific of all, and all the more credible because Newman himself believed in witchcraft, is the episode in which Gurta, the wicked witch who is the mother of Agellius, throws a spell over her second son, Juba. He is possessed by a fiend and, even after exorcism by Cyprian himself, becomes an idiot. After ten years, he recovers his sanity only long enough to undergo the Christian baptism he has so long blasphemously postponed by exercising his private judgment—the real reason for his ghastly punishment—and then to die immediately. As for the gruesome cruelties of the period, dwelt upon by Wiseman, Newman may enjoy them less, but he emphasizes them as much. Juba's witch-poem is fine magic verse. For those who can put aside the twentieth-century suspicion of the historical novel and give Newman a fair reading, *Callista* is a memorable book.[3]

3. The brilliant theologian and literary critic, Richard Holt Hutton (1826-1897), several times praised *Callista* to the skies. He quoted at length the description of the plague of locusts and called the novel an "exquisite tale" ("Cardinal Newman," *Essays on Some Modern Guides to English Thought in Matters of Faith* [London: Macmillan, 1891], pp. 65, 66, 68). Elsewhere (*Cardinal Newman* [London: Methuen, 1891], p. 225) he calls it "the most completely characteristic of Newman's books." Except for *The Dream of Gerontius* none, he says, "expresses as this does the depth of his spiritual passion, the singular wholeness, unity, and steady concentration of purpose connecting all his thoughts, words, and deeds." For Hutton's almost equally enthusiastic view of *Loss and Gain* see *ibid.*, pp. 194 ff., and also his "Romanism, Protestantism, and Anglicanism," *Essays Theological and Literary*, 2d ed., 2 vols. (London: Macmillan, 1880), I, pp. 342-343.

After Newman: The Issues Popularized

Newman's novels, as we have seen, delighted his peers. But unquestionably they were too subtle, too intellectual, too profound, then as now, for the ordinary novel reader, and they elicited some sharp criticisms from those, for example, who did not see that Charles Reding's inconclusive conversations at sociable Oxford breakfasts were a fundamental part of his spiritual experience. "A book of jokes and gossip, of eating and drinking, of smartnesses, levities, and most probably personalities," wrote one reviewer, "appears a somewhat undignified vehicle for the opinions of one [Newman] who has long been revered as a prophet and a saint." How to fictionalize and still make credible and poignant to the general novel-reading public some of the major religious questions of the day: this was a problem that perhaps Newman was not best equipped to solve. It was, however, solved beyond question by a writer now virtually forgotten, Lady Georgiana Fullerton (1812-1885), three of whose half-dozen novels about her contemporary world (she also wrote historical tales) we have included in this series.

Granddaughter of the Duke of Devonshire and the Marquis of Stafford, Lady Georgiana belonged to the very highest Whig aristocracy. Her father, Granville Leveson-Gower, became Viscount Granville when Georgiana was four and first Earl of Granville when she was twenty-one, and so made her "Lady Georgiana." Lord Granville was a professional diplomat, who served for seventeen years as Ambassador to France. Seated on the lap of George IV at a children's party, Georgiana—aged perhaps seven—told him she must now climb down, as she was about to miss a dance; few ladies occupying that perch would have been so daring. When she was ten, the Duke of Wellington (a very poor shot) accidentally peppered her father with bird-shot and burst into tears, but he recovered his spirits in time to dress up as an old nurse in a charade party, with the wife of the Russian Ambassador in his arms as his baby (he did insist that the show could not go on until all junior officers had left). Married early to a Guards' officer and Irish landowner, Alexander Fullerton, Lady Georgiana was a deeply religious Anglican from early youth and was greatly drawn to Tractarian beliefs and practices. Her husband was converted to Catholicism in 1843, but did not tell her in advance despite their great mutual love; she heard the news with "an inexpressible mixture of joy and agony." She was engaged at the time in writing her first novel, *Ellen Middleton* (1844, no. 25), and completed it as a practicing Anglican.

As a girl, Lady Georgiana read Grace Kennedy's *Father Clement* (1823, no. 1), a novel intended, as we well know, "to expose the errors and corruptions of the Catholic religion." But Grace Kennedy was "tolerably fair," and as a result, Georgiana found "a wonderful charm in the description of the old Popish castle" and felt herself full of passionate sympathy for Father Clement himself. She disliked the Catholic Maria Clarenham who went over to Protestantism, and she sympathized with Catherine, the future nun. Georgiana actually knelt and asked the Virgin to pray for her. "I wished," she wrote, that "I could, like her, *have gone to confession to Father Dormer* [italics mine] and thought how exactly I would have obeyed him." Grace Kennedy would *not* have been pleased. Though written down in Lady Georgiana's old age, long after her own conversion to Catholicism, these reminiscences of *Father Clement* show how prominent a part the question of confession could play in the life of a sensitive and devout Anglican girl of the 1820's.

Indeed, forgiveness of sin, the Catholic sacrament of penance, and the practice of confession combined to form one of the most crucial single problems of the period. Article XXV of the Thirty-nine Articles declared that baptism and the supper of the Lord alone were sacraments; the other five Catholic sacraments, including specifically penance, were "not to be counted for Sacraments of the Gospels, being such as have grown partly of the corrupt following of the apostles. . . ." But—since the Church receives warrant in Scripture for judging the sins of its members and declaring their fitness to remain in the Church—penance is by no means wholly dropped in the Anglican Church. The Book of Common Prayer, in the Morning Prayer for every day of the year, prescribes that the congregation kneel, make a general public confession of their sins, and ask for forgiveness, whereupon the priest absolves them, since

Christ "hath given power and commandment to his Ministers to declare and pronounce to his people, being penitent, the Absolution and Remission of their sins." This penance is, of course, public.

In the Order for the Visitation of the Sick, the minister examines whether the sick person repents his sins, and "the sick person shall be moved to make a special Confession of his sins, if he feel his conscience troubled with any weighty matter," after which the priest absolves him by the authority of Christ "committed to me." And in the Ordering of Priests, the Bishop, having laid his hands upon the ordinand, says, "Receive the Holy Ghost for the Office and Work of a Priest in the Church of God, now committed to thee by the Imposition of our hands. Whose sins thou dost forgive, they are forgiven; and whose sins thou dost retain, they are retained." Forgiveness of sins is thus the foremost duty of an Anglican priest, and the wording used is that of Christ himself to the assembled church in John xx.23: "Receive ye the Holy Ghost: whosesoever sins ye forgive, they are forgiven unto them; whosesoever sins ye retain [i.e., ye do not forgive], they are retained." Finally, in the first exhortation to the congregation when an Anglican minister announces a communion service, he requires any sinner who cannot quiet his conscience by repenting his sins to "come to me or some other discreet and learned Minister of God's Word and open his grief; that by the ministry of God's holy Word he may receive the benefit of absolution. . . ."

Private confession, then, was intended by the Prayer Book to be practiced in the Church of England. Moreover, it was widely practiced before and after the Civil Wars of the seventeenth century. But it fell into disuse in the stagnant period of the eighteenth century. As we have seen, Henry Digby Beste—later as a Catholic the author of the novel *Poverty and the Baronet's Family*—when a young Anglican clergyman of twenty-five in 1793, preached a sermon in the University Church of St. Mary's at Oxford on the text just quoted from the Gospel according to St. John, urging that priestly absolution be recognized as that fundamental prerogative of Anglican clergymen which their own Prayer Book declared it to be. "The Church of England," said Beste, "asserts and exercises its power of remitting and retaining sins [i.e., denying the sacrament of eucharist to the hardened sinner]. . . . But is the power

. . . exercised to any effect by its clergy?" No, he answered: the clergy "tacitly recede" from exercising it; they are "in some measure guilty of betraying these rights of the Church"; in fact, they admit almost "all persons indifferently, and without inquiry, to the holy communion." And the reason is that the "power of retaining sins . . . has been considered by some as odious, by others as ridiculous," by some as "ecclesiastical tyranny" or "ecclesiastical fraud," a power "which a Popish priest might indeed pretend to, but to which a Protestant clergyman was supposed to be no longer entitled."

Urging that the Church of England "guard . . . against the corruptions of Rome," Beste demanded also that it return to the exercise of this unquestioned and abandoned aspect of its authority, even though the people are not at present "sufficiently instructed in the origin or nature of these powers of the clergy, nor sufficiently informed of the benefits to be derived upon themselves by the due exercise of them." This is no excuse for clerical "supineness and indolence," and these times of "open and avowed apostacy of a whole nation" (he meant the French Revolution, then raging, and frightening the English severely) are precisely the times in which to reassert the ancient duties of the English clergy.

Beste himself reports that the "leading members of the university were prodigal in praise of this discourse" and that the following Sunday a bishop preached from the same pulpit, asserting that Beste had been entirely right. Those who "cried out 'flat popery' were silenced by the prayer book directions for the Visitation of the Sick." One of the leading clergymen in Oxford told Beste that while his sermon clearly stated the doctrine of the Church of England, the "people will not submit to the exercise of the power." True, says Beste himself, writing of the entire episode long after his own conversion to Catholicism; but neither did the clergy as a usual thing make any effort to find out how their parishioners felt. In one case, where an Anglican clergyman preached on the subject and announced a time when he would be at home to hear such confessions, this "caused a mighty hubbub in the parish; people did not know what to make of it"; some people wondered whether he meant what he had said, and one old woman said she'd "see him damned if she would tell him all she knew." At the time, the current periodicals said of Beste's sermon that "ground was laid for an important controversy," while the Dissenters said that "if the Church of England had renounced popery, it had got something that would do as well."

It was not until the early days of the Tractarian movement, however, that the subject received widespread attention. Henry Manning (1808-1892)—who did not become a Catholic until 1851— declared in 1835 that the Church of England would be in schism if it repudiated private confession; he counted amongst the leading characteristics of a priest his "acute, affectionate, and universal sympathy with the sick, the suffering, and, without partaking of their contamination, even with the sinful." It was not until 1843 that George Dudley Ryder introduced the practice of confession in his own parish of Easton in the diocese of Winchester and asked Keble to become his own "spiritual director." Manning had by then come to believe that penance was indeed a sacrament and in 1837 wished to introduce confession; his friend Samuel Wilberforce—later Bishop of Oxford—told him it would be playing with fire, and wrote one of his grim little tales for children called "Confession," in which an inexperienced clergyman clumsily makes wreckage of his penitent's life. In 1839—six years before his own conversion—Newman told Manning that the lack of private confession was one of the reasons for widespread Anglican apostasy to Rome: "Our blanket is too small for our bed. . . . We are raising longings and tastes which we are not allowed to supply."

Reflecting on Jeremy Taylor (1613-1677), a leading seventeenth-century theologian, Manning lamented that though Taylor and "no doubt thousands of Anglican priests and people both received and made confessions, yet the practice has died out." Manning believed that the fanaticism of Dissenters and Wesleyans was a clear indication of the "mischief of neglecting to use the keys of the Church." Pusey believed that "nothing except an extensive system of confession can remedy our evils." Both Keble and Pusey received private confessions. But of course there were many even among the Tractarians who did not go so far. Among those who favored an effort to restore confession, there were many shades of eagerness. And in the mind of any one clergyman the subject might assume varying degrees of urgency at different times. Bishop Blomfield of London in 1842 flatly forbade confession, along with many other Tractarian practices, in his enormous diocese, but he could not fully enforce the decree, which was sometimes disregarded or even flouted.

It is only against this background that one can fully appreciate Lady Georgiana's first novel, *Ellen Middleton* (1844, no. 25), an engrossing melodrama, whose chief theme is that very confession which as a child the author had yearned to render to Grace Kennedy's fictional Father Clement, and which was so preoccupying the religious leaders of England in the early 1840's. The saintly canon of an unnamed English cathedral observes in his congregation a stranger, a young woman, obviously ill and wretchedly unhappy. Finding some verses she has scribbled, he puts their very wording into his next sermon, and as a result she invites him to visit her. He urges her to seek forgiveness: "laying aside all human pride, all human fears, in meek distrust of your own judgment, in deep humility of spirit, you must make, as the Church requires, a special confession of your sins to one who, if you truly repent and believe, can absolve you from them by the authority committed to him by the Lord Jesus Christ." By way of preparing him to hear her confession, she gives him a manuscript telling the story of her life; this forms the body of the novel. After reading it, he hears her confession, absolves her, and enables her to die in peace.

Ellen Middleton, the penitent, at the age of fifteen, in an effort to reprove a fractious eight-year-old girl cousin who regularly put herself into danger and teased Ellen unmercifully, had slapped the child, who had lost her balance, fallen down a flight of slippery stone steps, and been killed. Somebody has seen the whole thing: a nearby voice says, "She has killed her!" But Ellen does not know who her witness and later tormentor is, and her entire life is literally ruined by her "crime," which is compounded by the fact that it has made Ellen a great heiress. Sure that she is a murderess ("without thought, without intention, I had struck her—one hasty blow was given, and now my youth was blighted, my peace of mind was gone; the source of all pure joys, of all holy thoughts, was dried up in me"), Ellen cannot pray for forgiveness or take communion. When a suitor gives her Keble's *Christian Year* as a present, she is sure that the passages he has underlined mean that he knows she is guilty. When somebody at a house party tells of an Italian brigand's *fiancée* who had lost her lover through her act of killing the very policeman who was about to kill him, and adds "there is something dreadful in life destroyed, death dealt by the hand of a woman," Ellen thinks of her own crime.

Once she plans to confess to a benevolent parish clergyman ("I would open my heart to him . . . for once pour out the secret anguish of my soul to one . . . who would tell me what my guilt had been—who would promise me its pardon, and point out the path of duty to my blinded sight"). But before they can meet for this purpose he falls into agreeable everyday conversation with her, and "the more he talked . . . the more I felt to lose sight of the priest of God—of the messenger of Heaven, in the amiable, conversable, gentlemanlike man." When the time for their appointment comes, her impulse to confess to him has passed. She cannot do it. Yet she knows that if she could have followed the example of Mary Magdalene and "gone to one of those who, ministering at God's altar, and endowed with his commission, have authority from Him to pronounce words of pardon in His name; if the fatal barrier which habit and prejudice so often raise between the priest of God and the erring and overburthened souls committed to his charge, had not in my case existed; if from his lips, I might have heard the injunction to forsake all and follow Jesus, and he had added 'Do this, and be forgiven,' it might have changed my life." As it is, emotional blackmail ruins Ellen's engagement and afterwards her marriage. Expelled from her husband's house, sick to death, she finally seeks and obtains the absolution she would have sought in the first place, had it not been for those "fatal barriers" imposed by "habit and prejudice."

While writing her novel, Lady Georgiana consulted Lord Brougham (1778-1868), celebrated judge, politician, and man of letters, who told her that the scenes between Ellen and the canon of the cathedral were "rank popery," and that a priest of the Church of England had "absolutely no authority" to confer absolution. Deeply concerned that she might somehow have misread the Prayer Book, she sent Brougham's letter to Charles Greville (1794-1865), man of affairs and noted diarist, who retorted that far from being "rank popery" it was "rank Church of Englandism." When Brougham rhetorically demanded, "What authority has our liturgy to teach paganism?" Greville urged Lady Georgiana to tell him to "settle that with the liturgy."[4] In short, she was quite right in her view of Anglican doctrine. And despite his initial alarm Brougham, too, greatly admired the book.

When it was published, it was an extraordinary success, perhaps in part because of Lady Georgiana's high social position and the English fondness for the aristocracy, but also because the story was a wildly exciting one, dramatically written, and touching on a key issue in the contemporary religious debates. Harriet Martineau (1802-1870), prolific writer of useful books and pamphlets and already author of one successful novel, thought it "very fine," though she was, as a freethinker, wholly out of sympathy with its religious teachings. It carried her away in "a torrent of passion" and made her feel guilty for two days. Among the many reviewers was Mr. Gladstone himself, then only thirty-three and a member of Peel's Cabinet. Of all the religious novels he had ever read, he declared, *Ellen Middleton* had "the most pointed religious aim," and "the least direct religious preaching . . . the least effort and the greatest force." It was "the least didactic and the most instructive," had a "tremendous moral," and should have a mighty impact on the "dull and hardened state of the public mind." Lady Georgiana's attack on the public hostility to confession, said Gladstone, assailed "the master delusion of our own time and country." We simply must not "nurse our infant sins into giants" but should "strangle them by the painful acts and accessories of repentance." Lady Georgiana must continue to strike blows "for the sake of truth and human happiness." But beyond his wholehearted approval of *Ellen Middleton*'s doctrine, Gladstone deeply admired "its eloquence and pathos . . . the delicacy and fullness of its delineations of passion . . . its always powerful, and, we think, generally true, handling of human action and motive." It was also wonderfully true to life in its description of society. In short Lady Georgiana had "the mastery of all human gifts of authorship."

Nor, 131 years later, does this seem hyperbole. The most arresting aspect of *Ellen Middleton* to a post-Freudian, once he has

4. Greville himself was then engaged in writing his book, *The Past and Present Policy of England towards Ireland*, published anonymously in 1845, which favored the controversial government grant to the Catholic College at Maynooth.

absorbed the doctrinal lesson Lady Georgiana was teaching, is the modernity of its psychology: it is, indeed, a textbook Freudian case-history, which may well account for the conviction that contemporaries felt when they read it. Ellen Middleton has lost her parents before she ever knew them; her bachelor uncle, remote and uninterested, is responsible for her upbringing until she is six. Then he marries an affectionate and demonstrative woman; it is from this new aunt, who treats her as her own child, that Ellen first experiences love. When the uncle and the beloved aunt have a daughter of their own—Julia—Ellen, who, it must be remembered, is telling her own story throughout, is *not* jealous.

Julia proves an unattractive child, "cold, sluggish, selfish," and Julia's mother loves Ellen best. Julia, however, *is* jealous: or why should she scream whenever Ellen is in charge of her and tries to prevent her doing something dangerous? Moreover, just after Ellen has rescued Julia from a high parapet, Julia makes so effective a scene that Ellen hears Mrs. Middleton say, "The children must be separated"; Ellen must be sent away to school, since there is nothing so important as Julia's health. And immediately after the shock of hearing her beloved aunt reveal that after all she prefers her own daughter, Ellen is faced with Julia's next rebellion and the taunting remark that "you are to be sent away if you teaze me." The slap and the fatal fall follow. No twentieth-century reader could fail to agree with Ellen's conscience: she has indeed committed murder.

Ellen has two ardent suitors, and she marries Edward Middleton—stern, forbidding, in fact, paternal—the one she asserts that she truly loves. But the other, Henry Lovell, is reckless, with a dishonest secret of his own, impulsive, wildly passionate, gloomy and exuberant by turns. He is a genuine Brontë hero, given to the public three years before either *Jane Eyre* or *Wuthering Heights* was published. Like Mr. Rochester and Heathcliff, he stemmed directly from Byron, whose verse Lady Georgiana had greatly admired when she was a girl (the censorship practiced on her prose reading did not extend to verse), and of whom she wrote years later, "his poetry, his picture at the beginning of the volume, and the idea of his having been a wild, strange, and even bad man, took hold of my fancy, and I actually *fell in love* with him." Although Byron had been dead for some years (Georgiana was well into her adolescence at the time), she blushed whenever his name was mentioned, and her heart beat faster. She wished she might have been his wife and have had the chance to convert him before he died. It was a wild infatuation, and it lasted for a year. Henry Lovell's character and behavior are purely Byronic.

Henry Lovell knows Ellen's secret (he had seen her slap Julia), but he is not the blackmailer. Henry must intrigue with the blackmailer to protect Ellen. Ellen's and Henry's repeated intimate conferences look to a jealous husband like infidelity, and lead to Ellen's final catastrophe. But Henry actually does love Ellen; he keeps urging his claims on her even after they are both married to others, and Ellen is powerless to send him away. With part of her she loves him too: "Never," she writes, "did two people know each other as well as Henry and myself. I always read his motives through the veil which he flung over them. . . ." For his part, Henry declares in a letter to Ellen, "I alone know the secret of your wild beauty, of your fierce humility, of your transient joys, and of your lasting sorrows." Not even her husband can rob him of his "share" in Ellen's soul. It is, of course, Heathcliff and Cathy before Heathcliff and Cathy were thought of. And—amongst other highly significant dreams that Ellen has in the course of the novel—she dreams before her wedding day that instead of the marriage service, the clergyman reads the burial service, a coffin appears, and she expects it to contain the corpse of her victim, little Julia: not at all, the corpse is that of Henry's wife.

Ellen Middleton is not a Catholic novel, since confession was in fact available for Anglicans who insisted upon it. Yet—quite apart from her husband's conversion—one can easily see that Lady Georgiana Fullerton was on her way to Rome, where penance is a sacrament and auricular confession a recognized part of every communicant's religious life. Had Ellen Middleton been a Catholic, there would have been no such novel. By the time Lady Georgiana wrote her next novel, *Grantley Manor* (1847, no. 7), she had become a Catholic, after overcoming her deep reluctance to hurt her family's feelings, and managing to retain her close relationship with them. By then she had become acquainted with Newman, who advised her about sending her only son to a Catholic school. But though *Grantley Manor* is a novel about the human damage that can be wrought by religious prejudices, it is not direct propaganda for Catholicism.

Colonel Leslie, master of Grantley Manor, has been twice married and twice widowed. By his first, English, wife he has had a daughter, Margaret, brought up in England as an Anglican; by his second, Italian, wife, a daughter, Ginevra, two years younger, brought up in Italy as a Catholic. The girls do not meet until Ginevra comes to England at seventeen after her uncle has died, and her great-uncle, a priest, has had to go on a foreign mission. Both half-sisters are great beauties and grow instantly fond of one another. But Ginevra is highly secretive, and is under suspicion for her inexplicably close relationship with Edmund Neville, a young man fancied by Margaret herself. In fact, Ginevra has married Edmund in Italy but has agreed to conceal the marriage, because Edmund's father, an enormously rich Irish Protestant landowner, is a fierce antipapist. The concealment leads to enormous strain, increased when Neville senior dies, leaving a will that disinherits Edmund if he shall ever marry a Catholic. Deep in debt, Edmund must have his rich inheritance; so he tries, vainly of course, to force Ginevra to give up her religion. Selfish—and something of a Byronic figure like Henry Lovell—Edmund brings such great pressure to bear on Ginevra that he almost kills her. In his remorse at his own cruelty, he admits to his sister—who will inherit the estate if he has to forfeit it—that he has already married a Catholic and has taken possession of his property fraudulently. She then reveals a codicil to their father's will whereby Edmund is allowed to retain everything, provided he has *already* married the Catholic before his father's death. She has been bound not to mention this proviso until he acknowledges such a marriage. Margaret, whose fondness for Neville had been only a girlish whim, marries the man she has really loved all along, her father's old friend and her own childhood mentor, Walter Sydney.

The elements of the novel seem shopworn when bluntly summarized. But *Grantley Manor* is of great interest both for the prejudices discussed and for the moderation with which Lady Georgiana handles them. The senior Neville, a "fierce Orangeman," fought as an undergraduate debater against Catholic Emancipation; he will never even have a Catholic servant. The act of a Catholic madman who had tried to kill young Edmund has only re-enforced his father's bias. One of Neville's brothers-in-law, who has travelled in Italy, succeeds in winning his respect only by attending the Evangelical meetings at Exeter Hall (described for the benefit of the innocent Italian Ginevra as "a place, my fair signora, where we thank God that we are not as other men are—that is deluded Papists like yourself. . . . It was necessary to convince him that I had not fallen a prey to Popery, the phantom that haunts him by day and by night"). Neville is so anti-Catholic that he has "neglected claims which might have been established to considerable property, from a determination not to have any dealings with Catholics."

Despite the criminal deception to which his prejudices drive his son, and the almost fatal effects on her Catholic heroine, Lady Georgiana hardly condemns him. After the crisis, Neville's tolerant and wholly admirable Anglican daughter, Anne, tells Ginevra's great-uncle, the Italian priest, Father Francesco, the whole wretched story:

> Her voice shook when she adverted to the prejudices which had been the origin of all their trials; her cheeks glowed with shame, and her eyes were bent on the ground as she spoke of the want of moral courage . . . and the criminal silence which had . . . stained her brother's character; but when she alluded to the stern uncompromising Protestantism of her family, and to the upright character of him who had unconsciously inflicted upon others such fearful sufferings, her eyes were raised again, and her voice grew firm. She saw the fatal result of long-standing prejudices and hereditary hatreds, and deeply lamented them; but she did not blush for one whose convictions had been sincere, and whose motives had been conscientious and pure.

We may take these views as fairly representing the ones Lady Georgiana wished her readers to attribute to herself.

Less virulent than Mr. Neville's feelings but nastily insular are the prejudices of Colonel Leslie's own family—before Ginevra's arrival in England—against the Italian Catholic daughter they have never seen. Even Margaret makes careless anti-Catholic remarks, and her father—cold and hard like Ellen Middleton's uncle—lectures her against prejudice, of which "one drop will turn to gall the milk of human kindness." Mrs. Thornton, wife of the local parson and Margaret's maternal grandmother, is a silly woman who "could not admit the right of that foreign girl to be called Colonel Leslie's daughter in any sense, but that she happened to be his daughter, a fact which she would protest against as long as she lived." "But as it is a fact, grandmamma, [says Margaret] you must make the best of it." To which the old lady replies, "I will never bow to facts, my love, when they go against my conscience." She will meet Ginevra "as something that exists, but which ought never to have existed." And another old gentleman, Walter's father, writes little verses declaring that "English eyes" will never approve the newcomer, and "English hearts will never love" her. All this casual prejudice vanishes in the first overpowering impression made by Ginevra's own great charm of person and manner. But Lady Georgiana is obviously almost as distressed by trivial social anti-Catholicism as by Mr. Neville's more serious bias. People still repeat the "oft-repeated slander" that Catholicism is a "half-scenic, half romantic religion . . . which has nothing to do with morality, and . . . teaches that you can make up for every kind of sin by good works of easy description."

The tone of the Catholicism in *Grantley Manor* is gentle. When the Catholic Ginevra and her Protestant half-sister Margaret meet for the first time, they pray together the prayer that "they *may* say together . . . the one that God himself made," the Lord's Prayer. Towards Protestants Ginevra feels sympathy because they are Christians, and—because they are Protestants—hopes that God may send them true illumination. The dreadful sin—which only a Catholic can understand—is to fail to listen to such a divine revelation. "Ascetic in its discipline and uncompromising in its morality," Catholicism "deals with each human being according to his secret needs." In the moment of her harshest trials Ginevra's faith gives her fortitude to bear them.

When Edmund wants her to apostasize, she asks him how he will answer to God at the last judgment "for having tempted a human soul into destruction," and predicts that he will one day thank God for her refusal. And when he pleads his debts as "most sacred engagements," she denounces him for his failure to realize that his engagements to her and hers to God are more sacred. In anguish at his behavior, she determines to enter a convent for a retreat, which is what a Catholic does when in trouble. Conscience will speak to her there and prepare her to face the worst problems that may follow in the world. In view of the theme of *Ellen Middleton*, it is extraordinary to note that Ginevra does not seek the comfort of the confessional, available to her, of course, as to all Catholics. She postpones it until she is at the end of her rope emotionally and physically, partly because she keeps hoping that Father Francesco, her uncle, will return to England. By the time she has determined not to wait for him any longer, she is already far advanced in the throes of a mental breakdown and cannot summon up her resolution.

And Ginevra's charity to the poor is *real* charity: "the idea had never even occurred to her that it was possible to *visit the poor* in the spirit of harsh dictation and arrogant superiority which at one time seemed prevalent among us, as if their poverty gave us, in itself, a right to invade their houses, to examine into their concerns, and to comment and animadvert on their conduct in a manner which we would not ourselves endure from our best friends." Here Lady Georgiana hit out directly at the frequent haughtiness of the upper classes in England (mostly Anglican, of course) toward the poor whom they were seeking to help; Victorian fiction is as full of such cases—often put forward in all innocence as instances of true kindness—as was real life. She was also indirectly answering the frequent charge that "popery"—especially among high Anglicans—put all its emphasis on the externals of the church service and neglected charity. True Catholics, she was saying, "respect the poor, and count it an honour and a blessing to 'have them always with us,' . . . to cast aside our refinement, our sensitiveness, our delicacy, and our false shame, and perform real offices of love to the poor, not as a matter of display, or effort . . . but as the natural result of belief in Christ's words, and our trust in his promises." Ginevra takes the washerwoman's ragged children on her knee and kisses the sick daughter as naturally as she would have embraced a close friend of her own class. Even if the political barriers between classes should vanish, says Lady Georgiana with great prescience, "the social ones may remain in full force." So it is all the more important to exercise sympathy, "the real source of influence. . . . We may bestow alms without end and have societies without number, and see no results from our gifts and our labours till we reach the hearts of the poor." It is one of Lady Georgiana's few sermons, and an effective one, especially as she herself practiced what she preached, founding one order of Catholic sisters of charity and introducing a second into England.

Although Ginevra's sufferings parallel those of Ellen Middleton and harrow the heart of the reader in the same way, *Grantley Manor* is a much less fiery novel. It won general critical applause, however, partly because the public had expected more bitter polemic from a recent convert and were surprised, as one said, to find her "mild, tolerant, and unambitious." Fanny Kemble read it so attentively at dinner that she took a sip of mustard from the mustard pot instead of a sip of wine from her wine glass.

In Lady Georgiana's *Ladybird* (1852, NIS), a Catholic widow will not marry her own true love because her conscience tells her that she has already been unfaithful in thought to her weak and unstable husband during his lifetime; she relinquishes the other man, who dies as a Jesuit missionary in China. Arid and without propaganda for the faith (indeed its exceptionally strict moral might well have acted the other way), *Ladybird* was probably written chiefly to obtain funds for Lady Georgiana's charities, and it is not included in this series. Three years after it was written, her only son died, aged twenty-one; his parents never put off mourning, and their lives thereafter became wholly austere.

Twenty-two years after *Grantley Manor*, Lady Georgiana's *Mrs. Gerald's Niece* (1869, no. 10) provided a kind of sequel, in which some of the chief characters reappear. Ginevra Neville has died, and Edmund has become a Jesuit priest working in a poor Irish parish in London (how his father would have hated the idea!). Walter Sydney and Margaret have also become Catholics and are bringing up their large family of children in the Church. But the central figures in the novel are Anglicans, Edgar Derwent, a Tractarian clergyman; his cousin, the downright Annie, heiress to a splendid property; and the beautiful Ita, a foundling brought up in Italy and, though adopted by an Englishwoman, always drawn towards Catholicism. Seeing that Edgar really loves Ita, Annie turns him over to her; Annie—whose hands and feet are suspiciously large for a lady's in any case—proves after all to be the foundling, and Ita (winner take all) the heiress.

But the main interest of the novel lies in the long passages of dialogue between Edgar and Edmund Neville, debating the Anglican case as against the Roman case. It is all curiously like *Father Oswald* (1842, no. 1), and the same points are scored on the same issues: the "gabbling" of prayers by Catholics, the "invention" of the doctrine of purgatory, the Catholic offering of communion in one kind only to the laity (which Edgar regards as withholding the chalice), the proper veneration to be paid to the Virgin Mary. Edgar holds out staunchly for the "Church of his Baptism," which Neville declares to be heretical and schismatic: in this novel, Lady Georgiana took off the gloves. Neville understands Unitarians and Infidels better than Anglicans (as we shall find that Unitarians and Infidels often understood Catholic arguments better than Anglican ones).

Elements of comedy are introduced into the debate when an Evangelical Anglican clergyman, whom the Tractarian Edgar dislikes more than the Jesuit, joins the discussion, and the subject of promiscuous Bible reading is canvassed. Puseyites like Edgar receive a blast from a plain-speaking moderate: "Just because a set of young fellows at Oxford wanted to have a Catholic Church of their own, and would not make use of the long-established one which had served the purpose since St. Peter's time, they must needs try and turn our poor old respectable Protestant Church of England into something she never was . . . and never was meant to be." Lady Georgiana's views on confession, a quarter of a century earlier her main subject in the Anglican novel *Ellen Middleton*, had of course changed: "How can confession be safe in a Church in which it is not authorized?" she asks, and the answer is clear: it cannot be safe, since Anglicans "hear confession on their own authority," and "their fitness for it has not been tested and examined," as is, of course, the case with Catholic priests.

Mrs. Gerald's Niece reads like a survival from an earlier age. It takes far too long for Edgar Derwent (as usual the man is weaker than the woman in Lady Georgiana's novels) to make up his mind to follow his wife Ita into the Church. By the seventies, indeed, though individual Anglicans or Dissenters might dislike Catholics personally as much as ever, the fear of "Popery" had considerably abated. Yet while Catholics' grievances had diminished, they were still keenly felt. In Edward Heneage Dering's *Sherborne; or, The House at the Four Ways* (1875, no. 12), for example, told in the first person by Reginald Moreton, twenty-seven, son of an Anglican clergyman and himself a convert to Rome, the complaint is repeatedly voiced that although English Catholics have now been politically enfranchised for forty years and more, they are still never elected to Parliament. George Sherborne, a boyhood friend, is, Moreton remarks, happy enough to visit the "old Catholic" county family of the Ardens, but regards Moreton himself "from the standpoint of papal aggression." Catholics may be patronized, so long as they don't get into Parliament or demand justice for their poor in workhouses and jails: "A certain number is all very well, but they must be kept down like hares and rabbits."

The Church of England has monopolized "all the great old avenues of influence" in English public institutions, and, as for a convert, he "doesn't even enjoy that kind of mysterious respect shown to Catholics generally." An English Catholic "is like a man walking along an unfrequented public path over land which his ancestors planted and reclaimed from the waste, and where he now lives by sufferance. . . ." He is trespassing whenever he seeks "that share of influence, political or social, for which he has theoretically a right to compete on equal terms with Jews, Unitarians, and Atheists." Not elected to Parliament, Catholics "are warned off the inner circle of all public life by the respectful suspicion of the general public, and the prohibitory nature of the demands that would confront their consciences there." Sherborne himself—drawn to the Catholic Church—postpones his conversion as incompatible with the political career he wants, and so risks damnation by neglecting grace.

And in private life Catholics are so sure that they will be "misunderstood on everything that bears, even directly, upon any objective truth" that they feel obliged to talk banalities in the drawing room. "No-popery traditions and the accomplished fact of possessing all the old Catholic endowments, are the title-deeds of the Establishment." Partly as a result, Catholics—who were formerly notable for "their good breeding, unassuming dignity, and just instincts of position"—nowadays sometimes display instead "supercilious assumption . . . capricious exclusiveness, and . . . self-satisfied devotion to marketable successes in society." Here Dering wrote more as a whole-hearted social and political reactionary than as a mere Catholic. Son of an Anglican parson of ancient lineage, Dering, like his own Reginald Moreton, began his career as a Guardsman. In Rome about 1848 when he was twenty-one, the sight of the sacrament being solemnly carried through the streets to the house of a sick man impelled him to fall on his knees in the mud—like the Italians around him—as it passed by.

Invalided out of the army, Dering passed the rest of his life in study: theology, philosophy, music, and history. At thirty, he met and married a widow, Georgiana, Lady Chatterton (*not* to be confused with Lady Georgiana Fullerton), a well-known novelist more than twenty years older than he. Dering was received into the Catholic Church by Newman himself in 1865, and his wife—after reading *Sherborne*—followed ten years later. The Derings lived with her niece and nephew, Mr. and Mrs. Marmion Ferrers, at Baddesley Clinton, a late mediaeval country house in which twelve generations of Catholic Ferrers had lived. All four dressed in seventeenth-century costume, the men in black velvet jackets and knickerbockers, black silk stockings, and pointed black Charles I hats. They lived the lives of cultivated recluses. Through the financial contributions of Dering to the household, the estate was saved from ruin. After Dering lost his wife and Mrs. Ferrers her husband, they were married in 1885. By special permission of the pope, the sacrament was "reserved" at Baddesley Clinton in the domestic chapel, and masses were celebrated weekly. Obviously, then, *Sherborne*—only one of Dering's eight novels—was written from a highly individual point of view.

Its hero, Moreton, divides the history of Catholicism in England into five periods of differing degrees of persecution since the days of what he would never call the Reformation. The old prejudices survive in less cruel, but hardly less galling, forms. And the plot—for there is a most complex if somewhat traditional plot in *Sherborne*—springs from injustice done during the period of intolerance during the eighteenth century, when English Catholic gentry families sent their sons to the Continent to be educated under assumed names. Moreton is sensitive to every slight. When paying a sentimental visit to his father's old rectory he is infuriated when the harmless wife of the present incumbent seems to hint that he cannot be moved by his childhood home because he has left the Anglican Church: "Considering the unfathomable ignorance concerning the Catholic faith, practice, history, and habit of mind, in which Protestants . . . are carefully trained and instructed by means of histories, novels, poems, plays, operas, pictures, newspapers, periodicals, lectures, sermons, and conversational gossip of every sort . . . I am not surprised at your confusing Divine faith with natural affection." In moments like this, Moreton seems to forget his view that "if honest Protestants in this country could but perceive that in the matter of Catholicity, they never hear the whole truth, the days of the No-Popery tradition would be numbered," and he turns into a whiner.

A second major theme in the novel is what its author regards as the misplaced sympathy given by the English public to the Italian revolutionaries, who—to Catholics—seem nothing but a band of thieves. Moreton himself enlists in the Pontifical Zouaves, a papal regiment, and finds himself involved in the covert struggle against the Freemasons as well as in the combat against the revolutionary forces. He narrowly escapes assassination at the hands of the "scum" in the service of the revolution. We are suddenly far from peaceful rural England and the familiar arguments about the relative merits of the Anglican and Roman Churches, and face to face with the characteristic Italian (or French) clerical party's hatred for Freemasons, Jews, liberals, and radicals. These views Dering fully shared and, alone among our novelists, purveyed them to the English reading public, behind the facade of a novel ostensibly devoted to English country life, agreeable social conversation, and apparent *bonhomie.*

Lady Georgiana Fullerton by 1869 was sounding old-fashioned and Edward Dering by 1875 was voicing wholly reactionary views: he thought the mediaeval monasteries had done a far better job of charity than the modern Poor Law and its institutions, and he recommended the return to the ancient system of toll-pike roads, where a fee to the "pike-man" by each passerby kept the road in repair. Lady Gertrude Douglas—daughter of the Marquis of Queensberry—wrote as if the issues of the forties and fifties were still as burning as ever. In her *Linked Lives* (1876, no. 13), the misfortunes of Katie, a beautiful Irish Catholic Glasgow slum-girl, fallen among thieves at eight (she has never heard of God and wants to know where he lives), are "linked" with the fate of Mabel, a charming High-Church Anglican girl of the upper classes, who falls in love with her cousin Hugh, the Evangelical clergyman who replaces an elderly extreme Puseyite as Vicar in the chapel of her village. Mabel has had the "makings of a papist" since childhood, and she fully accepts the extreme Anglo-Catholic position on the real presence ("heresy" says her new lover) and on the duty of an Anglican clergyman to give absolution ("down-right Popish").

It takes a complete massacre of all the chief characters—except for the durable slum child, Katie—before Hugh joins Mabel in the Roman Church. Except for Lady Gertrude's own wish to harrow her readers, there seems no reason why Hugh has to be on his deathbed in Australia before he can finally become a Catholic, although perhaps his conversion could be made credible in no other way. His spiritual travail in his journey toward Rome is never discussed. And Mabel, already a Catholic and on her way out to join him in Australia—why does she have to die in a fire and shipwreck at sea? The fictional vein that had yielded so much ore in the forties was by 1876 played out. Perhaps novels had taught the public as much as novels could about the questions at issue between the Church of England and the Church of Rome, and about the psychological, emotional, and spiritual responses of individual human beings to them.

Fin de Siècle

So in the latest period of the Victorian Age, the Catholic novel changes its themes, as Catholics no longer feel the need to stay on the defensive. At first, in Father William Barry's *The New Antigone* (1887, no. 16), published anonymously, the reader thinks that the old themes will recur, as Lord Trelingham, the enormously rich extreme Tory and extreme Ritualist (a term that by now has replaced "Tractarian" and almost eliminated "Puseyite"), proves to be also an astrologer who is devoted to black velvet clothes. He is already supporting the "missionary efforts to explain to the Andaman and neighbouring islands the exact difference between a cope and a chasuble" and to prevail on the Eastern Churches to recognize Anglican orders. One wearily expects that he is on his way to Rome by the usual stages. But no: we are launched upon a wholly new and extremely daring theme for 1887.

As the tangled, absorbing, and often incredible plot of *The New Antigone* slowly unfolds, one realizes that the anonymous author is mounting a full-scale attack on the doctrine of free love and on the larger bundle of radical social and political ideas with which it was associated. Exactly why or by what steps Colonel Valence, Lord Trelingham's closest friend at school and at Cambridge, became an atheist while he was an undergraduate we never learn. But it leads him to embark upon a lifetime of revolutionary activity: in the 1830's he commands an anti-Carlist band of guerrillas in the Spanish wars, demolishing churches and killing priests and nuns; in the 1870's and '80's he has become a key member of a large secret society of Nihilists and Anarchists preparing and carrying out the assassination of Tsar Alexander II of Russia, which takes place (1881) late in the novel. Communicating with one another by cipher messages, punishing traitors to the cause, and meeting secretly in the capitals of Europe, the revolutionary conspirators include at least one English duke. He is the leader of the "Athenian" wing, disillusioned members of the upper classes who do not mean to lose their comforts in the cataclysm they foresee and intend to help precipitate. The "Spartan" wing, men of action, includes Colonel Valence.

In keeping with his political ideas, Colonel Valence has his two children brought up without religion and taught to despise the conventions of society. His son by a first marriage to Trelingham's sister is left in ignorance of his parentage. As "Ivor Mardol," he becomes a discriminating craftsman and a devoted member of the revolutionary brotherhood, until, on his own, he comes to the conclusion that assassinations are abominable and is "excommunicated" by his fellow Nihilists. Valence's younger child, the beautiful virginal

Hippolyta (whose mother was a Spanish working-class girl), simply offers herself to the man she loves and who loves her. Much to his horror, she refuses his insistent offers of marriage, which she regards as mere "Christian mythology"! Rupert Glanville, well born, rich, and a brilliant painter, must accept Hippolyta on her own terms. She reluctantly consents to be called "Mrs. Malcolm," as he becomes "Mr. Malcolm." The incongruity of pretending to be married and living under a false name, rather than actually marrying and living under a true one, seems not to have penetrated Hippolyta's rigid antimoral morality.

Only when she becomes involved in efforts to rescue a lower-class girl who has been seduced does she realize the importance of marriage as a social institution. From that step, it is only one more to the nearby Catholic Church. One sermon and a brief hysterical visit to the confessional convince Hippolyta that she has sinned so gravely that she must imitate the Magdalen: marriage to her beloved Rupert can never wipe out the deadly sin by which she has polluted herself, and her expiation lies in mysteriously disappearing (driving him first to join the anarchists in a hopeless effort to find her, and then to brain fever). Throughout the book, the Catholic Church is soft-pedalled; none of the characters is Catholic except for the worthy working-class family of the seducer's victim; it is only chance proximity to the church building that leads Hippolyta to it.

But the Church is, of course, the victim of the revolutionaries in Spain. Moreover, there is a long historical association between the Davenant family of Lord Trelingham and a certain Spanish convent, where a seventeenth-century painter had portrayed a nun of the Davenant family in his altarpiece of the Virgin's Assumption. Even Valence—engaged in looting as he is—saves this picture in the 1830's because of the family resemblance to the girl he loves—a collateral descendant two centuries later—and brings it back to England. It is damaged in a storm and in the 1870's it is restored by Glanville and (unwittingly) by "Mardol," Valence's own son. The symbolism is clear. At the end of the novel the forces of evil have been defeated, but Hippolyta will live out her life as a missionary nun in India, and much wreckage has been made of human life and happiness.

It is as lethally wicked, Father Barry was surely declaring, to bring up a girl in the principles of free love as it is to murder an emperor for the revolutionary cause. Moreover, the two forms of wickedness go together. Perhaps the reader of many Victorian novels of conversion should be grateful to find one in which the steps towards atheism (in the case of Valence) or away from it (in the case of his daughter) are left vague. But *The New Antigone* is flawed as a result. Even the title at first seems inept. In Sophocles' tragedy, Antigone honors ancient custom by defying the edict of the tyrant against giving her brother decent burial and so achieves martyrdom. But Barry's Hippolyta *defies* ancient custom (marriage) itself, instead of honoring it, and so destroys herself.

One must read (and translate) the four Greek lines from a chorus of the *Antigone* that Barry put on the title page as an epigraph before one sees what he meant: "You have rushed to the outermost limits of daring, child, and fallen grievously against the lofty throne of Justice: but you are surely expiating some sin of your father's." Antigone was punished for the sin of her father, Oedipus, and Hippolyta for that of her father, Colonel Valence. When she says, "My father did not teach me religion," Hippolyta is "not aggressive or defiant, but natural and innocent," as if she were saying, "I was born blind." An "ardent disciple of Shelley" (among others), Valence "preached the emancipation of the whole human race. . . . the two sexes equal and free." She assures Glanville that "the old world is dying; it is nearly dead," but in fact in the 1880's it was still sufficiently alive to make free love impossible.

The wicked seducer of the poor girl who commits suicide is also one of the Nihilist brethren, both a liberal and a libertine. In love, there can be no such thing as freedom "when Duty is cast out"; marriage requires a sense of duty. As Mardol, Valence's son, begins to lose his belief in the revolutionists' program, he still despises the contemporary world: "Church, State, family, profession, rank in the world—what are these but names of long-established, deeply-rooted servitudes . . . manifest or disguised slavery?" Socialism and Nihilism are "desperate remedies for the universal gangrene." Yet the real question is "what will you do with your anarchy after you've got it?" We cannot expect that revolution will produce an earthly paradise. After Church, state, and family have been abolished, "all three will spring up again." There is only one Anglican clergyman in *The New Antigone*: a slum priest, presented without bias. Secure now, Catholic novelists were ready to combat the forces that most troubled them, the forces that Moreton, in Dering's *Sherborne*, fought against in revolutionary Italy with one hand while reserving the other for his Protestant fellow countrymen. Both of Father Barry's hands were free.

If the preoccupation of *The New Antigone* with revolutionaries seems extraordinary and Father Barry's notion of their ways perhaps somewhat childish, the reader should remind himself that in 1887 Europe did seem to be menaced by a wave of terrorism. Electioneering as early as 1876, Disraeli as Prime Minister solemnly warned that the "secret societies . . . have regular agents everywhere . . . countenance assassination, and . . . if necessary could produce a massacre." The assassination of the Tsar in 1881, the Trafalgar Square riots of 1886, and the almost simultaneous and linked disorders in Chicago, together with a dozen other manifestations, seemed to demonstrate the truth of Disraeli's fears. Henry James, in *The Princess Casamassima* (1886, NIS), and W. H. Mallock, in *The Old Order Changes* (1886, no. 81: see below), were only two of the novelists who turned to the timely subject. James's notion of revolutionaries was even dimmer than Barry's. It was not for many decades that the strands of Nihilist, Populist, Terrorist, Anarchist, and various forms of Marxist socialist thought were disentangled: it was precisely the mystery of the terrorist movement that made it terrible.

By the nineties the immediate peril seemed to have diminished. In his second novel, Father Barry turned away from politics altogether—although militant feminism still comes in for its share of brickbats—and, in *The Two Standards* (1898, no. 20), produced a full-fledged attack on materialism generally, the worship of wealth, its ruinous effect upon the arts and all that makes civilization worthwhile, the marriage market, and, notably, the wicked fallacies of Evangelical religion as seen by a Catholic priest. Outright propaganda in favor of Catholicism is more vigorously voiced than in *The New Antigone*. Although it occupies only a few pages in a very long and intricate story, Catholic doctrine determines the actions of the leading characters at the greatest crisis of their lives, and provides an unmistakable moral.

For Marian Greystoke, daughter of an Anglican country parson with an aggressively Evangelical wife, the manuscript memoir of an adventurous eighteenth-century ancestor is an inspiration. Brought up as a Catholic in France, he had travelled throughout the Middle East; as a nominal Muslim, he had served a Persian ruler and eloped with a beautiful Syrian Christian slave. A talented actress and brilliant singer, Marian at twenty longs to escape from the stifling atmosphere of her home and her mother's domination. When Lucas Harland, the enormously rich businessman, proposes to her, she finds herself virtually compelled to accept him because her father—an inveterate and unlucky speculator—has embezzled parish funds and faces exposure unless he can replace the money.

Harland is himself an Evangelical (he sometimes appears on the platform at Exeter Hall), and he has organized as a business venture a "Great Missionary Syndicate, which was intended to put the propagation of the Gospel on a sound financial basis, and enable those who loved the heathen in his blindness to treat him with due regard as an investment for both worlds." Up to the time of the engagement, Marian's mother (who is unaware of her husband's dishonesty) has been mournfully certain that the girl is "neither 'called' nor 'chosen.' " But now "that High Calvinism which was her innermost nature" thawed a bit, since the bridegroom elect was so pious and so rich. One rubs one's eyes in amazement: can this really be a Catholic novelist, casually allowing an apparently harmless Anglican clergyman to be little better than a common thief, and hitting out with irony at everything Low Church as well? We are now at the end of the century, and no holds are barred.

Once in London, Marian finds herself socially meeting a divorced woman, the first in all the novels we have been considering and the only one in all 121 in this series. True: she is a South African married to an American: "They divorced in some Western State—Iowa or Illinois; had no trouble in Court; everything smooth; speeches complimentary on both sides, and . . . a divorce breakfast" with the lady's maiden name in icing around a wedding cake. Rich, fascinating, sophisticated, this woman takes Marian's own cousin as her second husband. Her first husband sends her a pair of gold bracelets as a present. "My first wedding day," says the lady, "was the happiest day of my life, and I do so want to compare it with my second." Marian's own husband does not mind when an elderly peer, one of his business associates, tries to make love to her. After her discovery—innocent girl—that her husband had formerly had a mistress, she makes an hysterical excursion to see London night life, is robbed by a policeman, and has a miscarriage. This upper-class world of money and elegance is wholly decadent; adultery is everywhere. The nineteenth century is almost past, Barry writes; but already we can see "what the twentieth century is likely to do and to be." Harland loves "houses, lands, pictures, jewels, books . . . horses, chariots, the finest eating and drinking," but he is "mad after power. And power, in a democratic age, went to money." Brilliant and devastating parallels are drawn between certain financial transactions and the Black Mass. "The commercial idea, allowed to reign, is an insanity. . . . It is the destruction of art, and reduces life to a monomania as vulgar as it is imbecile."

At sixteen, the Evangelical Harland had already known that he was saved. "And I am sure of it now." His past peccadilloes, his present shady dealings, make no difference: "A Christian is not saved by his works, 'Free grace and dying love'; isn't that the good news?" he sardonically asks Marian. Father Barry lashes out at these doctrines which for him are clearly linked directly to the prevalent immorality he so detests. Under the domination of the mother whom Marian has escaped, her younger sister, Rosie, is injured beyond recovery. At sixteen, says her mother, Rosie is "dutiful, and in an excellent way of becoming a Christian, though the happy day is not yet." The "conversion" that the Evangelicals thought necessary has not taken place.

Naturally furious at this attitude ("What conversion? . . . Would you wash the lily in snow-water?"), Marian nonetheless has to promise her mother that Rosie will be given the Reverend Edward Jonathan (Jonathan Edwards turned backwards?) as her spiritual guide when she comes to London to live with the Harlands. In a ghastly series of episodes Jonathan—whom the Dissenters had ousted in his youth—literally frightens the child into a fatal illness; he preaches election and predestination: "all preordained, not a hair's breadth left to chance or man's caprice; the number counted, the sum sealed up." Good works are of no avail. It is all "a train of logic, without remorse, haply without reason." Rosie simply cannot be sure that she is saved, and the thundering sermons of Mr. Jonathan prove too much for her. She succumbs to the "fangs of a merciless creed." It is murder. There is no irony here: only anger, pathos, and prejudice against Protestantism of the kind that the Protestants had so often shown against the Catholics.

The hero of *The Two Standards* is Gerard Elven, a German composer and dramatist modelled at least in part on Wagner. A man in his mid-forties, a widower, a Catholic, Gerard has a much-loved brother, Rudolph, who is a monk. Marian's marriage has become a marriage "in name only," and she is greatly drawn to Elven, who comes to England to stage his *Descent of Istar*—a great Wagnerian pageant—under the sponsorship of Harland. Harland hopes to turn Elven and his compositions into another profitable syndicate. Substituting for the prima donna with great success on opening night, Marian feels again the determination to follow her professional career: after all, like her ancestress, the Arab Christian girl, she has been sold in the slave market of women. She compares Elven with the hero of *Heinrich von Ofterdingen*, the celebrated romance by Novalis (Friedrich von Hardenberg, 1772-1801), who seeks the mysterious blue flower that became a symbol for the later Romantics. Elven and she plan to run off together to America. But on the train to catch the steamer, Elven's brother, Father Rudolph, decisively intervenes.

It is at this crisis of Marian's and Elven's lives that the Catholic propaganda of the novel is concentrated. What will happen to them, the monk asks, conceding that they love each other dearly? Marian will get a divorce, and Elven will marry her: this is not a good ending; she will be "lessening the power of goodness, helping the evil in the world." Rudolph himself had long ago killed a man in a duel because he was in love with the man's wife: they suffered a horrible vengeance, and Rudolph had become a monk. Marriage—it is suggested but never openly affirmed—is a sacrament. Grief-stricken, Marian goes to New York alone, but—when she hears that her husband is in difficulties with the law (the Missionary Syndicate, ironically, has failed)—she returns and faithfully sees him through his trial, imprisonment, and illness.

In despair, Elven briefly joins his brother in a Jesuit house of retreat, where Loyola's *Spiritual Exercises* is the subject. Gerard learns—or learns again—that "man was made that he may praise God, do Him reverent service, and thereby save his own self." To that end, he must "keep himself in a state of perfect indifference" toward everything else in life, following the ancient Stoic rule of abstinence and bearing his griefs. It is one of St. Ignatius's meditations that gives the novel its title: the "Meditation of the Two Standards," the standard or banner of Christ and the standard of Lucifer. Modern society by and large is tragically enlisted under the devil's standard, a prey to passions of all sorts, whereas the sole passion that cannot go astray is the "passion for righteousness embodied in Christ."

Here, perhaps, the novel should have ended. But Father Barry made his own concession to the novel-reading public who prefer a happy ending. The pair who have been deterred from pursuing their love illicitly are in the end rewarded by the opportunity to pursue it licitly: on his deathbed, Harland begs Elven to take care of Marian. When an articulate Catholic spoke his mind, just before the turn of the twentieth century, he linked the moral degeneracy of the age directly to those Protestant doctrines that disregarded good works and emphasized faith alone as necessary for salvation.

The last in our series of Catholic novels fall naturally into a group of four, two by Pearl Mary-Teresa Craigie (1867-1906), who wrote under the pseudonym "John Oliver Hobbes," and two by George Moore (1852-1933), her sometime collaborator and ardent suitor, whom she repulsed and who responded with typical gallantry by kicking her in the rump (so he claimed) in a London park. All four novels take us into the London world of Father Barry's *Two Standards*, but Pearl Craigie's pair focus on religion, politics, and sex, while George Moore's pair focus on religion, music, and sex much as Barry's novel had done. Moore's heroine is at least in part modelled on Pearl Craigie herself. Although Mrs. Craigie was a devout Catholic convert and Moore a lapsed Catholic and a sceptic, the Catholic faith triumphs over the claims of love in both pairs of novels; neither Mrs. Craigie's hero, Robert Orange, nor Moore's heroine, Evelyn Innes, manages to perform the feat of Barry's Marian Harland and Gerard Elven and eventually find happiness in earthly marriage.

Beautiful, rich (her father was an American who made his fortune out of patent medicines, including Bromo-Seltzer and Carter's Little Liver Pills), clever, and neurotic, Mrs. Craigie was married at nineteen to an Englishman of good family, whom she divorced ten years later after four years of separation. Her husband contested the suit (which charged him with adultery and cruelty), and the *Times* called the case "an extremely filthy one . . . unfit for publication in a newspaper." Although she won the case, scandal clung to Mrs. Craigie: she could not be as lighthearted as Father Barry's American divorcée in *The Two Standards*. She had many suitors, but she could not, as a Catholic convert, marry again. She did have a circle of admiring friends, mostly men, and she aroused enough antipathy among women to inspire several hostile lady novelists to portray her unfavorably in their pages. *The School for Saints* (1897, no. 17) was her seventh novel and by far her most serious work to date. Its sequel, *Robert Orange* (1900, no. 17), according to a recent critic, has been "generally acclaimed as the finest Catholic novel of the Victorian age,"[5] a judgment which we cannot share.

Robert Orange, hero of both books, active in English literary and political life from the 1860's to 1880, is a strange hybrid of Disraeli and Newman, all the stranger since Disraeli himself appears as a leading character in both novels and seems at times to be talking to his own mirror image. Orange's father had been a Catholic priest in a "beautiful white surplice," who (naturally) had "startled the whole Order of St. Dominic" by his apostasy in marrying a descendant of one of Cromwell's close companions. Half English "Puritan," half French Catholic aristocrat by ancestry, Orange as a boy falls in love with a beautiful older actress, modelled on Sarah Bernhardt. Her "false" representation of chivalrous romance on the stage and her stage make-up horrify him, but not so much as his discovery that she has a six-year-old daughter by a morganatic marriage with the Archduke of "Alberia," one of those

5. Margaret Maison, *The Victorian Vision* (New York: Sheed and Ward, 1961), p. 165.

tiresome mythical kingdoms so fashionable in the nineties. The decadence and intrigues of high continental society in *The School for Saints* have all the reality of *The Chocolate Soldier*, without the merits of its frivolity or the charm of a later master of froth like Firbank. Mrs. Craigie vainly insists that we believe in her hero, whom she herself takes with the utmost seriousness, and in the various exquisite noblewomen who love him unbearably.

Ten years as a successful novelist and man of the world in London preparing for a political career do not harden Orange sufficiently to enable him to swallow the marriage of the actress's little daughter (at sixteen, fresh from the convent) to a vile worldly man much older than she. (Bismarck calls him a "velvet buffoon," Disraeli "a goldfish with a soul," others "a baptised satyr.") Looking like a combination of Charles I and St. Bernard, Orange falls in love with this innocent child, Brigit, who still trusts "greatly in the Sacred Heart" and prays that Orange will yield to his inclination and become a Catholic. Disraeli himself, after an acquaintance of a few moments, predicts that Orange "will become a Roman Catholic because you will find nowhere out of Rome poetry and the spirit of democracy and a reverence for authority all linked together in one irrefragable chain." But of course (as Moreton in Dering's *Sherborne* was always complaining) Orange's conversion would, Disraeli warns, "prejudice your whole political career." Robert welcomes the paradox: if it were to cost him dearly, such a conversion would be all the more attractive. But Disraeli urges him not to commit himself to priestly celibacy: "What might be an act of splendid obedience, sublime self-renunciation in a Newman [Mrs. Craigie apparently did not know how eagerly Newman desired celibacy] would be presumption and folly in a lesser spirit." In fact, Disraeli is just about to write a novel called *Lothair* (1870, no. 32: see below)[6] on the whole subject. Stimulated by the thought that he may be committing political suicide, Orange is converted.

Separated from her appalling husband, whom the Archduke orders into exile for cheating at cards, Brigit refuses all idea of a divorce and takes refuge in a convent. Orange is so hopelessly in love with her that he has taken—despite Disraeli's advice against

6. *Lothair*'s whole point was to combat conversion, not to recommend it. Perhaps Mrs. Craigie had never read it.

mediaeval behavior—what amounts to a vow of celibacy, much to the disappointment of London society. ("These things," as one beauty writes to Disraeli, "make one quite HATE the Papists.") Instructed by her husband that she is to proceed to Spain, Brigit goes. It is the summer of 1869, and civil war breaks out. Orange rescues Brigit, and gets her safely to England. Despite his faith, he has won election to Parliament. The news of Brigit's husband's suicide reaches Orange and Brigit, and they are married. But the suicide has been faked, for "Alberian" political reasons. The reader knows this, but the young couple (twenty-eight and seventeen) do not, as the novel ends with a promise of a sequel.

Robert Orange begins with what we would call a "flashback" to the eve of Orange's wedding and recaptures for the reader the Newman-like strain of austerity in him. Much as he loves Brigit, it has been an idealized love—even after he has held her in his arms—and "the moral training of a lifetime, the unceasing, daily discipline of a mind . . . most severe with itself, had given him a self-mastery in impulse and desire. . . . His soul drew back from its new privileges. . . ." He was, then, an ascetic. (Mrs. Craigie makes the deliberate parallel with Newman, but again she fails to realize how easy Newman found sexual continence: she obviously had not read *Loss and Gain* or *Callista*.) Yet Orange is quite ready to abandon himself to marital bliss, when close friends learn that Brigit's husband is still alive and pursue the couple on their honeymoon, overtaking them, it is clear, before the marriage has been consummated. Orange and Brigit determine not to see one another for a year: annulment of the first marriage would be possible, but "idealists abhor lawsuits," as a friend of Robert's says. Orange will go back in silent misery to his political and scholarly life. He finds comfort in Loyola's *Spiritual Exercises*, the same book that—in Barry's *Two Standards*—had saved the reason of Gerard Elven in a similar plight. Orange is, as a friend soon says, in fact "a born R.C. ecclesiastic."

Robert Orange is cluttered with the marital and political problems of the very most top-lofty British aristocracy (so Mrs. Craigie keeps on assuring us). She heightens the verisimilitude by introducing historic episodes, notably the excitement caused by Gladstone's nomination of Frederic Temple—one of the contributors to the controversial *Essays and Reviews* in 1860—to be Bishop of Exeter. (Temple rode out the parliamentary storm and then, after confirmation as bishop, withdrew his essay, which had, in any case, been far less incendiary than those of several other contributors to the volume.) In the heated discussions over Temple, Orange maintains that "the system is at fault, not Dr. Temple. . . . The English can never deal with systems or ideas. They can only attack individuals." The attack on Temple is sure to fail because the public cannot take a real interest in Church government. But essentially Robert is a Catholic onlooker at the Anglican dilemma: what is the historical validity of Anglican orders? Why not have clergymen in the House of Commons as well as bishops in the House of Lords? It is Robert Orange's character that, despite all the often irritating digressions, remains the most interesting aspect of the novel.

Scandal gathers around his abortive marriage, but he ignores it, in keeping with "his own instincts and Newman's advice." Knowing the sinister details of Alberian politics that led to the whole affair, Disraeli warns Orange of the forthcoming publicity and counsels him to "depend entirely now on the might of your religious belief." (Modern readers, inclined to be contemptuous of the "mythical kingdom" aspects of Mrs. Craigie's novel, should remind themselves of the maneuvering in the 1870's and 1880's over the thrones of Rumania and Bulgaria, preposterous in modern eyes but historic fact all the same.) Political rivals (sometimes old friends) say, "Orange is a born ecclesiastic. Orange is a mystic. Orange is under the influence of Newman. Orange begins to see that marriage is not for him." Disraeli tells him, "I believe you will be a Jesuit yet," and adds extravagant praise for the Order.

But with all his natural austerity, Orange is also a finished man about town and an experienced duellist (all his duels as a young man had been fought over women). So, with his exquisite sense of honor, he challenges and kills a possible rival for the inaccessible Brigit. When Brigit's husband actually dies and she is about to reclaim Robert, she finds that he is about to become a priest. She believes that since Robert's father had been a lapsed Dominican, "the Church will have her own again," and she silently relinquishes him for the second time. Orange's father's sins and her own father's sins (the Archduke was married only morganatically to her mother) have made the outcome inevitable. At first the Church—Disraeli later reports—is cool to its new recruit, but Orange's family influence and talents soon win him approval. Within a decade Orange is dead of overwork: he had become a Monsignor.

The semipublic kick that George Moore later claimed he had administered to Mrs. Craigie's bottom by no means exhausted his wish for vengeance. In *Evelyn Innes* (1898, no. 18) and its sequel, *Sister Teresa* (1901, no. 19), he used Mrs. Craigie as inspiration for his story of a successful singer of Wagnerian opera, daughter of the Catholic organist of a London Jesuit church and herself a Catholic, who yields easily to her profound sexuality, is kept by a rich dilettante lover who arranges for her advanced musical training, takes a second lover full of Celtic mysticism (modelled on the young W. B. Yeats in the early versions of the novel and on AE in later ones), and eventually enters a convent. The name she chooses as a nun, Sister Teresa, was one of Mrs. Craigie's own names. The degree of direct portraiture is perhaps unimportant: it was frequent for novelists to portray a practitioner of one art in real life as a practitioner of another in fiction, so that a novelist could easily enough become a *diva.* In any case, Mrs. Craigie was profoundly distressed by *Evelyn Innes,* calling it "false . . . an abomination . . . revolting . . . corrupt in conception . . . false to nature and therefore false to morality." No amount of "cheap Cathedral effects and religious humbug at the end," she wrote, could save it.

Though Moore knew little about music and had to enlist the help of experts to help him, he did succeed—as Father Barry, for example, in his detailed accounts of Elven's Wagnerian performances did not—in conveying to a reader the inherent sensuality of Wagner's music. For Evelyn the playing of *Tristan* on the harpsichord by her admirer, Sir Owen, makes the flesh tingle and creep. And it is *Tristan* music, as played for her by her second lover, that makes her yield to him too: "that music, it gets on one's nerves," she says. Before she has drunk the love potion on stage, Evelyn is the virginal suburban girl she had been before she met Sir Owen; afterwards she is transformed into the passionate misled queen. And if there were two Isoldes in Tristan's myth, a fair and a dark, there are two Tristans in Evelyn's. Many of the chief incidents in her life are operatic echoes, deliberately sounded by Moore. Her sexuality is the most vividly described—often in musical language—of any woman character in English fiction down to the turn of the century: it needed only a few monosyllables for her to become Lady Chatterley.

But if Evelyn's passions and her life as a Wagnerian singer lead her into sin, her religion delivers her from all of that. To make herself lose her faith and therefore feel more secure in her unchastity, Evelyn had deliberately read Darwin and Huxley, not at all because she wanted scientific knowledge. Her confessor, Monsignor Mostyn, whom she learns to know only near the end of the book, tells her, "When a Catholic loses his faith, it is because he desires to lead a loose life." But Evelyn still believes in the real Presence and for her the "act of consecration did seem to . . . call down the spirit of God." Her sins of the flesh are less important for Father Mostyn than her sins against the faith. If she does not regain her faith, she will sin again. She emphasizes that in her sex relationships with her two lovers, she has not confined herself to ordinary sexual intercourse, but has committed all excesses. Moreover, she has practiced contraception, which is a greater sin. At first, Father Mostyn is about to refuse her absolution because she cannot declare her belief in a future life or promise absolutely to see neither of her lovers again. But "a light seemed to break under her brain," and she capitulates and wins absolution. She has decided to leave the stage; she goes into a convent for a retreat: "It is by the denial of the sexual instincts that we become religious."

Of course, "a life of prayer and chastity was not natural to her; her natural preferences were for lovers and worldly pleasures, but she was sacrificing all she liked for all she disliked." And in *Sister Teresa,* these tensions are played out, as Evelyn becomes a nun. Her sexual dreams, her temptations, her rebelliousness, her sufferings, her abnegation, and her loss of all traces of her past—even her beautiful voice—these form the theme of a distressing book, perhaps the more distressing because one knows that Moore was insincere in its writing. The two novels together, however, constitute an extraordinary tour de force of the imagination. Evelyn Innes—

Sister Teresa—is the last of the Victorian and the first of the wholly modern Catholics. It is an irony and a paradox that she should have been created by a lapsed Catholic.

A Summing Up

From 1823 to 1901, then, the English novel of Catholicism passed through a traceable development of its own. It began with detailed—often theological—explications of Catholic belief, designed primarily to demonstrate to Anglicans that Catholics were not the threat to the social order that they were charged with being, and only incidentally designed to win converts. It progressed to case histories—contemporary and historical—of conversions to Catholicism, in Newman's case autobiographical and moving and likely to be influential. The spiritual pilgrimage, so detailed in these novels, later became reduced almost to a brief summary or even a single episode emphasizing—as was normal in popular fiction—the impact of the conversion on the life of the convert in his social and emotional relationships with other fictional characters. Once they felt relatively secure from legal and educational discrimination (and from the strident voices of their enemies as expressed in fiction by William Sewell or Catherine Sinclair), Catholic novelists spoke out against the vestigial disabilities that still hampered them in English politics and society. By the late eighties they were able to carry the war into enemy territory by attacking contemporary free love, materialism, and social decadence, attributing many such ills to the Protestant (Evangelical) doctrine that regarded good works as of no avail. At the same time, they brought to English readers their horror of continental anticlericalism and the revolutionary outbursts to which they insisted it would inevitably lead. And, with Pearl Craigie and George Moore, they themselves joined the decadents and the sensualists, their Catholic protagonists ultimately retiring altogether from the worldly scene.

But from the anonymous author of *Father Oswald* to George Moore, writers of Catholic novels made their Catholic characters insist that nobody who was not a Catholic could ever possibly know the spiritual peace that came after one had entered the Church. This was something that no Protestant, however hostile, could effectively deny, since he could never have experienced it. Yet a sceptical critic might have asked why—if membership in the Church brought instant spiritual peace—so many of the converts in fiction did not stop with such membership but felt it necessary, sooner or later, to become priests, monks, or nuns. As propagandists, the enthusiastic Catholic novelists may well have done themselves a disservice. Even a very "High" Anglican layman, for example, with no spiritual summons to the priesthood, would presumably have asked himself—after reading, say, *Mrs. Gerald's Niece* or *Robert Orange*—whether, after all, conversion from the Anglican to the Catholic Church should perhaps not be confined chiefly to those whose original bent was towards the priesthood or towards monasticism. If one accepts Catholicism, does one have to die as a Jesuit missionary to Tibet?

Newman could have answered simply by emphasizing the meaning of the very words *Loss and Gain*: only those who were prepared to sacrifice greatly could win through to peace of soul. To which the retort—from the myriads of religious novel readers who were not Newman, or Lady Georgiana Fullerton, or even Pearl Craigie—would have voiced itself at once: the sacrifice is too great. And, they might have added, how is it that so many converts complain of their treatment by "birthright" Catholics, both clerical and lay? Why should I (if I wish to become a priest) have to come of a family as exalted as that of Robert Orange to have my talents properly appreciated and utilized? and (if I wish to remain a layman) why should I put up with virtual social ostracism from my fellow Catholics? Only for the strong, the exceptional, the deeply troubled, the blessed recipient of a personal revelation, could the gain outweigh the loss: for the ordinary merely aspiring human being, *moyen sensuel* and not in spiritual torment, the loss—at least in the novels that he read—must often have seemed to outweigh the gain.

PART II.

THE CHURCH OF ENGLAND

CHAPTER 2.

THE HIGH CHURCHMEN AND SOME OPPONENTS

"Shivering on the Brink"

The conversion of an Anglican to Roman Catholicism naturally suggested the metaphor of a river crossed, even jumped, from one bank to the other. And inevitably, the river that came to mind was the Rubicon, that little stream south of Ravenna which Julius Caesar crossed in 49 B.C., leaving his own province behind him and marching into Italian territory towards Rome: "the die is cast," as he said himself. Newman and his fellow converts—so the popular image had it—crossed the Rubicon and left their former fellow Tractarians "shivering on the brink," unable to make up their minds to take the leap. No doubt this was true for many, who could not summon up the courage that Newman eventually displayed after all his preliminary hesitations. Some, no doubt, like White in *Loss and Gain*, had taken out their superficial Roman Catholic sympathies in brave talk, and cheerfully let them wither away at the prospect of a suitable living in the Church of England and a wife. But many other Tractarians, of varying temperaments, never huddled shivering on the brink; they did not even approach the bank; they liked their side of the river best, and they knew why. For every sympathizer of Newman's who failed to take the leap because he was too timid or because he could not take the final gamble that Newman took, there must have been hundreds who were simply never tempted.

Among these, of course, was Pusey, who had given his name in popular usage to the entire Tractarian movement. The term "Puseyite" was felt to be a denigration. William Sewell, a Tractarian until the appearance of Tract 90 in 1841,—and, as we have seen, a most vituperative anti-Catholic—makes Villiers, the proud hero of *Hawkstone* (1845, no. 2), turn fiercely on a man who has said to him, "You are one, then . . . of the new Oxford school—the P—" and reprimand him: "Sir . . . I am afraid you are proceeding to apply to me an expression which I never permit." It not only "calumniates a good man as being the leader of a party in the Church"—and of course "party" is anathema, especially to passionate partisans—but it "condemns all who accept it as being followers of an individual teacher, instead of being followers of Him whom only we may recognize as our Master." The term "unchristianizes" and suggests schism. "To give nicknames . . . has done more harm to the Church, by forcing men into parties almost in spite of themselves, even than heresy itself. It is the fomenter of schism." To a Catholic abbé ("educated, well-informed, and conscientious" as distinguished from Sewell's fiendish Jesuits), who points out that despite this attitude the Church of England is indeed widely split into party, Villiers answers that Roman Catholics too often confuse the "sectarians who have gone out from among us"—that is, the Dissenters—with Anglicans, who are "as deeply interested in the cause of unity—as solemnly pledged to maintain it"—as the Catholics themselves.

When the government held its official religious census on Sunday, March 30, 1851, the number of Anglican churchgoers recorded was just under 5,300,000—roughly half of the churchgoers of England and Wales. Almost 1,000 of the more than 14,000 parish churches, however, failed to return a form properly filled out, despite two later efforts to obtain the information. Samuel Wilberforce, Bishop of Oxford, had risen in the House of Lords, warned that the results would be misleading, and suggested that Anglican clergymen not comply. Moreover, it is not possible to estimate what percentage of the Anglicans heard High, Low, or Broad views expounded from the pulpit on that day. It seems likely, however, that by far the greatest number heard a Low-Church—Evangelical—message. Although the High Churchmen were certainly fewer in number than the Low, they were more numerous than the Broad.[1]

1. In 1853, the Reverend W. J. Conybeare, in a famous article on "Church Parties," originally published in the *Edinburgh Review* and revised and reprinted in his *Essays Ecclesiastical and Social* (London: Longmans, 1855), pp. 57 ff., attempted to esti-

But sheer numbers have little to do with articulate expression in fiction. By their persistent writing of novels expressing their views, the High Anglicans more than made up for whatever numerical inferiority they suffered. They, after all, were now the aggressive reformers, against both the old high and dry and the old and new Evangelical persuasions. Most of them were young, Oxford men or their Oxford-influenced woman relatives or parishioners, and they took naturally to the novel as a means of spreading propaganda for their views.

These included insistence upon the Apostolic character of the Church of England and upon the need to surrender "private judgment" to its authority in all matters of faith. The Tractarians wanted to restore the church buildings of England to their original appearance, to sweep away the pews, the plaster, the various modern concealments of the mediaeval details, and to substitute choirs and proper church music for the fiddlers that so often squeaked away in the balcony. With varying degrees of emphasis they demanded, and instituted when they could, changes in the externals of the ritual, putting candles on the altar (though often not lighting them), mingling water with the wine in the chalice, using unleavened bread for the sacramental wafer, assuming the "eastward position," using incense. The clergymen wore surplices, and there was as much intoning or chanting instead of recitation as the congregation would tolerate. All these efforts to revive "earlier practices" were viewed, quite properly, as "Romanism," and were advocated, accepted, laughed at, disliked, or denounced with every conceivable degree of intensity, depending on one's preconceptions, one's studies, and one's temperament.

Early in the twentieth century, a learned American literary critic, Paul Elmer More, himself a "High" Episcopalian, declared that "no more inveterate and vicious display of parochialism [than this controversy] was ever enacted in this world." What was it all about,

mate the number of clergymen (*not* communicants) belonging to each party. He went through the Clergy List and, on the basis of 500 clergymen whose views he knew (out of 18,300!), arrived at a figure of 6,500 Low Church, 7,000 High Church, and 3,520 Broad Church. But Conybeare's method was wholly unreliable. His Evangelical acquaintance was not large. He surely underestimated the number of Low-Church clergy and overestimated the number of High-Church clergy. Moreover, parishioners often differed with their clergyman, sometimes violently.

really? he wondered, contrasting the high intellectual content of the French religious controversies at the time or "even of our own pet transcendental hubbub in Concord." If a single idea had been introduced into that "mad" English conflict of words, said More, it "would have been a phenomenon more appalling than the appearance of a naked body in a London drawing-room." Bagehot had said that the stupidity of the English is the salvation of their politics, and More was ready to add: and of their literature as well. But even More saw that the struggle was essentially one over the position of the Church in English society and that the Tractarians were fighting desperately not to allow the newly liberalized government and social outlook of the 1830's and the ensuing decades to secularize the Church of England. "If paltry in abstract thought," said More, the battle was "nonetheless rich in human character." While one can appreciate and enjoy More's intellectual impatience with the Tractarians and their opponents, one need not—indeed must not—adopt his extreme contempt for their views on religion. And one must wholly agree that "the richness of human character" displayed in the course of the struggle makes its study attractive and at times hypnotically exciting. Nowhere is this richness of character so well illustrated as in the novels which the controversy inspired.

Early Tractarians

Two Anglican clergymen, the Reverend William Gresley (1801-1876) and the Reverend Francis Edward Paget (1806-1882), were the "acknowledged fathers"—so a contemporary critic declared—of the "novels and story-books illustrating the doctrines and practices of the newly-risen 'ism.' " Gresley was solemn and didactic, Paget pungent and often funny (much later he wrote—in *Lucretia* [1868, NIS]—the best satire on the "sensation novel" of the 1860's). Neither had—or sought to have—depth as a novelist: their purpose was instruction. In Gresley's *Portrait of an English Churchman* (1838, no. 22), a young man shows himself well aware of the danger of "Romanism," and expounds at length the need for keeping to the proper Anglican "middle way." Dissenters, doubters, and loose-livers all come in for eloquent abuse.

Gathering steam in *Charles Lever* (1841, no. 22, *not* to be confused with the popular Irish novelist whose name was Charles Lever), Gresley gave his protagonist a Dissenter as a father and a Latitudinarian as a schoolmaster. Imbibing principles as vague as those we have heard Newman's Dr. Brownside preach at some length in the witty lampoon of Hampden in *Loss and Gain*, poor Charles Lever becomes addicted to radical politics and to sin, but he winds up safe as a member of a High Anglican church newly and properly restored according to the best Tractarian principles. In Gresley's *Church Clavering; or, The Schoolmaster* (1843, no. 22), once more the theme, as indicated by the subtitle, is education: the government should get out of the business of education altogether, casting "off the trammels of unworthy liberalism" and simply taking the advice of "those whom God Himself has ordained to rule His Church and 'teach' His people." Schoolmasters "should receive their authority to teach from the Bishops of the Church, and . . . the matter of their religious and moral teaching should be what is written in God's word." Of course, a teacher must not explain the Bible to the children "out of his own head"; that is what the Catechism is for. If it seems too hard to understand, this is no problem: "Christian doctrine is full of mysteries which we are not required to understand but to believe."

Paget's *St. Antholin's; or, Old Churches and New* (1841, no. 23) is equally narrowly a novel of purpose, but its wit makes it far more readable. Designed to further the favorite Tractarian practical precept that dilapidated Anglican churches need careful restoration, it tells the story of the village churchwarden, Mr. Ouzel, who for twenty-five or thirty years has reigned supreme in questions of maintenance of the beautiful mediaeval fabric of the Church of St. Antholin's, and has given great satisfaction to the parish by spending no money at all on repairs, despite warnings and admonitions from the Archdeacon. Whitewash covers the beautiful stone carvings; the Gothic stone font is painted blue; the spire has begun to lean dangerously. Down it comes, of course, wrecking the entire building during a windstorm, after Mr. Ouzel is safely dead. One of the new churchwardens is endowed with the sinister name Walter Tyler (Wat Tyler was one of the leaders of the Peasants' Revolt of 1381). The new Rector, a young man ignorant of ecclesiastical law, mishandles a meeting, and the necessary funds are not appropriated. The first disaster leads to a series of others, as the nasty cheap modern church that Mr. Compo the architect designs burns like tinder when its new patent stove fails to work properly. The original engravings of the two churches, the old and beautiful, the new and shoddy, should be carefully studied by all readers of *St. Antholin's.* Mr. Compo even wants to dispose of the stone font, eliciting from the usually mild Rector the sarcastic remark, "I suppose that registration is to supersede the Sacrament of Baptism. . . . the march of intellect is advancing. . . ."

Paget returned in the next year to the general subject of church maintenance in *Milford Malvoisin; or Pews and Penitents* (1842, no. 23) but confined himself to what he himself calls "a never-ending, still-beginning subject of animosity and ill-will," namely, pews. During the seventeenth and eighteenth centuries it had gradually become the fashion to build in Anglican churches high-walled pews for the gentry, resembling separate rooms, often furnished with comfortable chairs and sofas, with tables, and sometimes even with fireplaces. The poor worshipped in the body of the church on benches. One of the Tractarians' practical aims was the abolition of the pews, both for aesthetic and for social reasons. They did not fit in with the original design of the churches (the arrangement was "not Catholic"), and they separated the social classes at divine worship in a way that made church only a continuation of the discrimination of daily life: "The Pews of the wealthy few," says Paget, "have driven . . . the Poor from our Churches. One great box after another has been erected, till there is no longer room for the humbler ranks of worshippers." "Great unsightly packing-boxes" or "sleeping-chambers" must go. And Paget traces the development of the small village church of Milford Malvoisin from 1643—during the English Civil Wars, when the Puritans desecrate the services, accuse the Rector of "popery," and build the first pew—down to recent times and what happens in the railway age when the controversy over pews hits the village.

Charlotte Yonge

Paget's and Gresley's novels were in effect fictionalized tracts, short campaign documents with one or another Tractarian purpose in view and only the crudest attempts at characterization. While the pioneers were still active, in the early forties, the most prolific and most skillful of all Tractarian novelists, Charlotte M. Yonge (1823-1901), made her debut, beginning an astonishing literary career during which she would publish well over 150 books, perhaps half of them novels. Although she is sometimes still considered primarily as an author of books for children, in fact she intended many of her works for adults. Older people, especially girls in their teens, read her avidly. Not even the most careful parent would need to fear that any of her books would bring the proverbial blush to the cheek of the most sheltered proverbial Young Person. She has never been wholly forgotten, and she is perpetually being rediscovered with new appreciation.

Charlotte Yonge spent all her long life in the heart of rural southern England, in the village of Otterbourne, Hampshire. She never married. Her parents were country gentry, and her personal life was centered in her family and her church. Kind and loving, but exerting undisputed domestic authority, her father was one of the two most influential people in her life. The second was John Keble (1792-1866), who had been a Fellow of Oriel with Newman. His *Christian Year* (1827) was a book of poetry with a verse for every Sunday of the English church calendar. Though he himself had no very high opinion of it, the book aroused enormous enthusiasm, went through hundreds of editions, and remained a standard wedding present for Anglican couples throughout the century. On its first appearance, Robert Wilberforce (elder brother of Samuel and Henry) wrote to Hurrell Froude, "Nothing that has come out for this past hundred years can bear a moment's comparison," and found the poetic effect overpowering. Keble, he said, "seems to make his poems out of the common perceptions of all mankind."

In mid-July 1833 Keble preached the famous Oxford sermon on "National Apostasy," from which Newman himself dated the beginnings of the Oxford movement. Though elected a Fellow of Oriel for his scholarship, Keble chose to leave Oxford and in 1836 took the rural parish of Hursley, only a short distance from the Yonges, whose family friend and religious counsellor he became. While Keble lived, he read each of Charlotte Yonge's books before she sent it to her publishers, often suggesting alterations, which she always adopted. Keble instructed her in Tractarian ideas and practices; her father taught her Greek and mathematics (she learned French and Italian early). This intellectual and spiritual grounding lasted throughout her life.

Miss Yonge had an excellent mind and was naturally devout. She was gladly submissive, not only for herself, but as a woman who believed that submissiveness was a woman's proper attitude. In her novels, intellectual girls give up their own educational and scholarly ambition if family or church duties call them, and they yield to their brothers: when they do not (see below the discussion of her *Magnum Bonum* [1879, no. 74]), they are terribly punished for their presumption. Charlotte Yonge's life, then, was narrowly provincial, wrapped up in the duties of family and of parish, and she was content to have it so. She expended her enormous creative energy and power in her writing, which reveals her as a woman with a keen ear, a warm heart, and a cool realization of the foibles of human nature. Her novels are deceptive to most modern readers, who may miss the earnest Tractarian message embodied in each one, because Charlotte Yonge—unlike the Catholic and anti-Catholic novelists we have been considering, and unlike Gresley and Paget—usually did no direct preaching. Her lesson is taught by indirection, by flaws in character, and by the rewards and punishments that these flaws bring upon her personages. This technique she perfected slowly, and her earlier books are more didactic than her later ones.

It was entirely typical that her first publication (*Le Château de Melville*, 1838, NIS) was written in French for sale at a church bazaar. She was then fifteen. Six years later came the first of her long list of books in English, *Abbeychurch; or Self-Control and Self-Conceit* (1844, no. 24). Her subtitle in itself shows that she was still under the influence of an earlier generation of novelists: it consists of a pair of those abstract nouns like *Pride and Prejudice*, *Sense and Sen-*

sibility, that had been used as titles for so many pre-Victorian novels. *Abbeychurch* already reveals many of Charlotte Yonge's lasting preoccupations. Its major episode is the consecration of a new church, one of the most important events in Charlotte Yonge's own girlhood: when she was sixteen, in 1839, the new church at Ampthill near Otterbourne, in every stage of which her father had taken an intense interest and which he had largely financed, was finished and consecrated. Because the new railway has brought many retired London tradesmen to live in Abbeychurch, a new church is needed. In the novel, Anne Merton "had many a time built the church in her fancy; she knew from drawing and description nearly every window, every buttress, every cornice. . . ." And now, she feels, "I cannot fancy anything more than the Consecration of a Church for which Papa has done so much." The sight of the beautiful new spire (Abbeychurch, we may be sure, was *not* built by Paget's cheap designer, Mr. Compo!) delights her: without her father's solicitude, it would never have been there. And at the consecration service itself, when the officiating bishop reads out the name of Mr. Merton (i.e., Mr. Yonge) as the "first among those who petitioned the Bishop to set that building apart from all ordinary and common use," Anne joins in the Psalms with exultation, and her heart swells with joy as she follows the prayer for the blessing "of those families who had been the means of the building of that House." Five years after her own delight and daughterly pride in the consecration at Otterbourne, Miss Yonge put its record into *Abbeychurch*: this was how a Tractarian maiden actually felt.

Keble had warned Charlotte Yonge against "too much talk and discussion of Church matters, especially doctrines, and against the dangers of these things merely for the sake of their beauty and poetry, aesthetically, he would have said, only that he would have thought the word affected." Obediently, she disciplined her enthusiasm. No word of doctrine appears in her story, and very few about the appearance and embellishments of the new church beyond the fact that it had a spire. The second theme of *Abbeychurch*, and one that would also preoccupy Miss Yonge for her lifetime, was precisely the need for energetic and enthusiastic young women with ready tongues to learn self-discipline, something that she felt her father and Keble had had difficulty in teaching her. If Anne Merton is Charlotte as the rapt daughter of the new church's leading benefactor, Elizabeth Woodbourne—eldest daughter of the vicar—is Charlotte as the well-meaning but willful girl whose impulses need curbing.

Not realizing what a dreadful thing she is doing, Elizabeth, without permission from her parents, takes a group of young people to the local Mechanics' Institute, where a pushing young radical lectures on feudalism in a way hostile to the nobility. Although Lizzie does not know it, her father, Mr. Woodbourne, regards the new Mechanics' Institute as "part of a system of Chartism and Socialism and all that is horrible," full of "follies and mischiefs." In Elizabeth's absence, "two or three Socialist lectures" had actually been delivered there, but Mr. Woodbourne had intervened and "stopped them before they had time to do much harm." Their chief promoter had been Higgins, the editor of the local newspaper, a Dissenter, and so Mr. Woodbourne's natural enemy. Higgins had then attacked the vicar in print for "illiberality and bigotry." Although the merchants of Abbeychurch had promised that no such lectures would ever be permitted again, the vicar, naturally, would never have consented to allow his children to darken the doors of the Institute. And now Elizabeth has done so, and Higgins has gloatingly printed the news in his paper.

One of the worst aspects of Elizabeth's position is that her younger sister, Helen, whom she has been snubbing and contradicting and willfully misunderstanding at every turn, had opposed the excursion to the Institute, and had given as one of her reasons that the place was managed by Dissenters. To the protest that nowadays "Church-people and Dissenters put themselves on a level in almost every public place," Helen replies, "They do not meet in every public place on what they agree to call neutral ground [i.e., the Dissenters have the advantage at the Mechanics' Institute] or profess to lay aside all such distinctions and to banish religion" in order to avoid raising disputes. "You know," Helen continues,

> that no subject can be safely treated of, except with reference to the Christian religion. . . . how many people run wild and adopt foolish and wicked views of politics for want of reading history religiously! and the Astronomers and Geologists with-

> out faith question the possibility of the first chapter of Genesis, and some people fancy that the world was peopled with a great tribe of wild savages instead of believing all about Adam and Eve and the Patriarchs. Now if you turn religion out, you see, you are sure to fall into false notions, and that is what these Mechanics' Institute people do.

At thirteen, Helen has not discovered all this on her own, of course; she has overheard it in a conversation of her elders, but her counsel is the right one.

This linking of religious Dissent, political radicalism ("Chartism and Socialism"), scientific scepticism (geologists, astronomers, Genesis), and religious doubt in a little girl's mind in a novel published as early as 1844 by a twenty-year-old young woman who had never left the English West Country is an extraordinary phenomenon. It is also of great interest to the modern reader to note that the vicar in a town like Abbeychurch still had the influence to put a stop to radical lectures by bringing pressure on the local merchants. We are more apt to agree, perhaps, with Higgins's attack on Mr. Woodbourne for bigotry than with Charlotte Yonge's easy assumption that the vicar had done the proper Christian thing, but the contribution of *Abbeychurch* to social history is undeniable.

When Elizabeth realizes the full horror of what she has done in her impetuosity (she had tried to find her father to ask permission to go to the lecture and, when she was unable to do so, had simply gone, in defiance of the advice of the undervalued younger sister), she abases herself: "I was led away by my foolish eagerness and self-will. I was bent on my own way, and cast aside all warnings, and now I see what mischief I have done." And though her father tries to console her, her last thought is the hope that this will be the end of her "self-will and self-conceit, for indeed there is much that is fearfully wrong in me to be corrected before I can dare to think of the Confirmation." That great step—to be followed, of course, by the first communion—lies ahead of Elizabeth, and she is intent on preparing her unruly spirit for it as the novel ends.

A decade later, when Miss Yonge published *The Castle-Builders; or, The Deferred Confirmation* (1854, no. 24), she had already become a great celebrity as the author of *The Heir of Redclyffe* (1853, no. 30), one of the most famous and successful novels of the nineteenth century, to which we shall return below. Her touch is sure, and the traces of juvenile dependence upon earlier models have disappeared. "Castle-building" refers to castles in the air. But the main theme of the novel is precisely that confirmation and communion to which Elizabeth Woodbourne had been looking forward so anxiously and with such trepidation in view of her grave faults of character, which she was determined to try to conquer before her first partaking of the Sacrament. A mature and finished writer, Miss Yonge in this novel is more directly concerned with doctrine, more theological in her argument, and more overtly propagandistic for Tractarian views than usual: she seems to be ignoring Keble's warning against "too much . . . discussion of . . . doctrines," but he approved the book and obviously found it strong and effective.

Emmeline Berners at seventeen and her younger sister Kate at sixteen, at school in London while their mother and her second husband are in India, are being prepared for confirmation by a callow young curate, too bashful to allay their anxieties about the importance of the event and especially about the first communion that will follow. He has approved them for confirmation, but Kate cannot understand how, "if we were fit for Confirmation, we were fit for the Sacrament." At baptism they "promised all these things by our godfathers and godmothers, and are bound to do them now, so it does not seem so much to promise them for ourselves, but the other [i.e., the Sacrament] is a great deal too awful!" Although a kind friend assures them that the Sacrament "is the means, not the reward of goodness," the girls rather welcome the chance of deferring their confirmation when their mother and stepfather return from India and withdraw them from school to live in the countryside. Their mother is languid, hypochondriacal, and interested in society, their stepfather also worldly and interested in money, though a decent man.

Danger besets the unconfirmed girls almost at once. In the country, they find their own vicar crusty and aloof, and they listen to attacks upon him by his enemies. He will not accept them, for example, as volunteer teachers in his parish schools, which he wants to keep under "the management of himself and his curates"; the girls betake themselves to a neighboring parish. Charlotte Yonge never says so outright, but of course this vicar, Mr. Brent, is a proper High Anglican, and his enemies are Evangelicals and Dissenters. A Victorian reader would recognize the issue at once; a modern reader is likely to have lost the necessary clues. Brent has suppressed certain tracts and prevented their distribution in his parish, including one about a hungry man who prayed for food and instantly found a basketful by the roadside: such a document, indiscriminately handed out, would have been an Evangelical effort. Indeed, Emmeline and Kate are criticized by the very distributor of this tract, Brent's enemy, for sticking too closely to the Catechism in their teaching and they have to abandon it. Their Evangelical sponsors attribute all of Mr. Brent's actions—but none of their own—to the spirit of "party." Next the girls begin on well-meant but ill-directed efforts to make clothes and help the poor, but these also fail, as do their struggles to put themselves through a regular course of heavy intellectual reading. Their abortive projects, and their inability to see why they are unsuccessful in everything, all arise from the fact that they are not confirmed and have never taken the Sacrament.

The girls' stepbrother, Frank Willoughby, their stepfather's son by an earlier marriage, has been brought up by a clergyman uncle and, at seventeen, is determined to take orders and become his uncle's curate in his rural parish. His father, a general, wants the boy to go into the army and presses the case so hard that Frank has sadly knuckled under, when—in one of those seaside catastrophes only slightly less common in Victorian fiction than carriage accidents—Frank is killed while saving both Berners girls from drowning. Before his death, the sisters, who have come to love him dearly, sympathize with him in his conflict with his father: it is such a pity, says Emmeline, "when you have never thought of anything but going into the Church all your life." To which the saintly but thoroughly human Frank replies, "I am in the Church." Frank is shocked to learn that his stepsisters have never been confirmed. The Sacrament, he assures them, is essential to help one get through the trials of life: he could never face his disagreement with his father, had he not had "that," as he calls the Sacrament. "Is it not putting one's trust in forms and ordinances?" asks Emmeline. "Stuff, Emmie," he answers, "no more than it is for the beggar to ring at the gate. . . . It is not all, but . . . it is the means, as the Catechism says, and that's it," and he accuses her of having acquired her attitude from the Low-Church people she has known. Frank's own father is impatient at his continued attendance at daily communion: "Always at it!" he grumbles, and calls it "a perverse clinging" to his "former intentions. . . . Remember you're not a parson now."

Needless to say, the erring father bitterly mourns Frank after it is too late. Uncle Willoughby, the country vicar, arrives to comfort everyone: "an old child," Miss Yonge calls him, hitting off in a phrase that mixture of guilelessness and experience which Keble represented to those who loved him. A saintly Tractarian, Mr. Willoughby of course urges that the girls proceed with their confirmation and first communion. How fortunate they were not to have drowned before it: as the Catechism says, these things are "generally necessary to salvation." Confirmation, he instructs them, "is the solemn vow that brings all our baptismal promises home to us." The giving of the Holy Spirit at baptism is effective for children who have not been confirmed, but this is ineffectual later, "except ye eat the Flesh of the Son of Man." This is "the root of all, the life of all." Love and trust in our savior is the stairway to heaven, and the ordinances of the Church are the individual steps. For the second time the sisters begin to receive instruction looking towards confirmation, this time from Mr. Brent. But they are still timid, and Emmeline uses her continued weakness after the accident as an excuse not to attend; so when Mamma decides to take them off to London to enjoy society and get rid of their morbid thoughts after Frank's death, the confirmation is deferred for a second time.

Now the consequences grow truly alarming. Emmeline—ignorant of the dangers of frivolity—actually dances both waltz and polka and becomes far too much interested in the worldly-minded son of an empty-headed fashionable family. Worse: she agrees to attend a Roman Catholic service with these people, who are not themselves Catholics, but go occasionally to hear the music because it is the thing to do in London. The Catholic church is

> a most beautiful edifice, built according to the rules of perfect architecture, and adorned with exquisite taste, with great richness and splendour, and with attention to the emblematic sig-

> nification of each ornament, one of the places in which Romanism is displayed with the greatest possible attractions to educated and imaginative minds, keeping back as much as possible all that is offensive to a truly Catholic principle [i.e., Anglo-Catholic as well as Roman Catholic] and putting foremost what is really true and beautiful, what it possesses as being a Church, and hiding much of what belongs to Romanism *as such.*

The music is superb, the best in London. The service is beautiful, the preacher is the famous Dr.______ (Newman?) whose "name is in everybody's mouth. . . . There is always such a rush when Dr.______ preaches. . . . You cannot guess what beautiful language it is—so powerful and metaphorical. It is perfect poetry." Never having been confirmed, and so lacking the proper sense of purpose, Emmeline, "with the ordinary ignorance about the Roman Catholic services," knows Latin and understands what she is hearing. She is "taken by surprise at finding so little that was objectionable, and so much that was extremely beautiful." It all enchants her and makes her "feel more devout than she had ever been before."

First the irritations and pitfalls of Evangelical practices have beset the girls, next the deeper and more dangerous snares of Rome itself. Rescue comes only with the return from abroad of a beloved brother-in-law, a proper Tractarian clergyman, with whose family the sisters go to live. More by example than by precept, this good man overcomes Emmeline's and Kate's weakness. He gives up a beautiful rural parish for a living in a busy port with a poor fishing population, and he insists, despite his personal fortune, on living in the old cramped parsonage in a waterfront slum instead of a house in the upper-class part of town. Jaded and thinking she wants to die (like Mariana in the moated grange), Emmeline is convinced by this pious relative that the waltzing and the Catholic service—the only two things she thinks she cares about—were equally bad for her and reprehensible. Under her brother-in-law's tutelage she recognizes her own faults and comes to believe that for "rest . . . comfort of mind . . . true wisdom . . . strength . . . firmness . . . abiding sensation of love and fear of God," confirmation and communion are essential. Properly prepared, the girls finally are confirmed and receive the Sacrament, "that unspeakable Gift . . . that, unless they fall away, will increase daily more and more, till they come to the everlasting kingdom." The reader leaves them at last "admitted to the partaking of that Meat and Drink . . . which can preserve their souls to everlasting life."

The Castle-Builders, didactic though it is—far more explicitly so than most of Charlotte Yonge's novels—is full of entertaining incidents, calculated to keep the attention of teen-age girls and of older readers as well. The confirmation and the communion cure Emmeline's malaise, but their deferment enables Charlotte Yonge to give a vivid sketch of the terrible boredom to which a well-to-do young woman was liable without the solace of the Church—in addition, of course, to the risk of damnation she was running and the traps into which she was likely to fall. Miss Yonge fully understood what later generations would call neurasthenia and depression, and she sketched them quite recognizably. The sisters are well contrasted with one another, despite their great mutual fondness and dependence. And—as with Helen in *Abbeychurch,* only even more dramatically portrayed—there is a neglected and misunderstood younger sister in *The Castle-Builders,* shunted aside by the whole family without love or praise, always regarded as obstinate and naughty and unattractive, when all she requires is a little understanding and sympathy. This she gets only from a much exploited, frightened little governess and, eventually, from her eldest sister, wife of the saintly clergyman. But in the end, *The Castle-Builders* will be remembered (or rediscovered) for its extraordinarily vivid dramatization of Tractarian sacramental views: truly Catholic, but distinctively Anglo-Catholic. It takes a permanent place as an important religious novel.

Conversation—easy and natural and credible—is one of the striking features of Charlotte Yonge's novels. Her people talk as people did and still do talk: about the events of the day, the problems of their families, and the books they have been reading. In these literary discussions, Miss Yonge often revealed her own ideas about other authors' books and their characters, and thus supplied clues to her own intellectual attitudes and development. So, for example, in *Abbeychurch,* the young people are delighted with Scott, using *Ivanhoe* and *Quentin Durward* as works of history; but the shrewd Elizabeth knows that *Ivanhoe* is inaccurate, and prefers her history straight. She enjoys Froissart as a man who knew his own characters; like the youthful Charlotte Yonge, she hates abridgments, and prefers original sources. "I cannot bear dry facts," she says; "who cares who won a battle if one does not know the participants?" In *The Castle-Builders*, the girls try vainly to emulate a learned young woman who is already writing articles for the serious quarterlies on classical and historical subjects. In Miss Yonge's most famous novel, *The Heir of Redclyffe* (1853, no. 30), the books the characters discuss assume a fundamental importance.

The Edmonstone family and their cousin Sir Guy Morville, who at seventeen has just succeeded to the baronetcy and comes to live with them, talk, for example, a great deal about *Sintram* (1814), a romantic tale of the middle ages by the German Friedrich de la Motte Fouqué (1777-1843), which tells of a young Norse warrior's struggle against evil. From early boyhood, Sintram believes himself pursued by "Death and another" and has an attack of overpowering terror every year at the same time. The dreadful visitation was originally brought upon the child by an apparition of death and the devil, who came to assist the boy's father in fulfilling a heathenish vow he had made to commit a sinful murder. Though routed by Sintram's saintly mother, whose prayers prevent the murder, death and the devil revisit Sintram every Christmas. Guilt-stricken, though still a man of violent passions who retains the pagan custom of swearing at Christmas by a gilded boar's head, Sintram's father has allowed Verena, Sintram's mother, to become a nun and pray for her suffering son. As Sintram grows older, death terrifies him, while the devil tempts him to do wicked deeds: last-minute repentance—usually inspired by prayer, by the sign of the Cross, or by a memory of his mother, the nun, whom he has never seen—keeps him pure, and he eventually banishes the devil altogether and obtains a promise from Death that he will not come to him for many years. His father dead, Sintram visits his mother in her convent and is allowed to return each week.

Sintram was inspired by Albrecht Dürer's famous engraving of "The Knight, Death, and Satan" of 1513, sent to la Motte Fouqué by a friend, who asked for a ballad on the subject and elicited instead this strange and beautiful tale, the one of Fouqué's tales of the four seasons which he associated with winter. A copy of the Dürer engraving hung in the Yonges' household and belonged to Charlotte all her life. *Sintram* had a great impact on others also: on Newman, for example, with his convinced belief in the Devil and constant awareness of sin, who burst into tears on reading it. Quite independently of Fouqué, Sir Walter Scott tells us, he had heard a similar Scotch story—of a young man "whose efforts at good and virtuous conduct were to be for ever disappointed by the intervention . . . of some malevolent being," but who triumphed in the end after a fearful struggle. In his introduction to the 1829 edition of *Guy Mannering* (first published in 1815), Scott tells how he had planned to turn the tale into a novel, but—after the first few chapters had been written—altered his intention. Of course, Charlotte Yonge knew both *Sintram* and *Guy Mannering*, as well as the Dürer engraving. Forty-three years after the publication of *The Heir of Redclyffe*, she wrote an admiring introduction to a new English illustrated translation of *Sintram*.

Guy Morville's grandfather is a fierce and savage counterpart of Sintram's father (Guy's own father had died before he was born); Guy has never seen his mother, who died at his birth, just as Sintram's had withdrawn into her convent. Sintram's struggle with temptation—in his case mostly sexual—parallels Guy's struggle with his powerful impulsive temper. Guy's dramatic exploit off the rocky shore of his ancestral estate, when he braves a storm and rescues the victims of a shipwreck, is parallel to Sintram's long residence in the "castle of the moon-rocks." When Guy himself reads *Sintram* for the first time, his expression alters and, like Newman, he finally rushes from the room in tears. He buys a copy for himself, reads and rereads it, and stands looking at the Dürer engraving "as if he was in a dream." His own remote ancestor at the time of Charles II had committed dreadful crimes and finally had gone mad and killed himself. Guy is sure that just "such a curse of sin and death as was on Sintram rests on the descendants of that miserable man," including, of course, himself. In each successive generation, he thinks, the curse has worked its doom. One of his cousins reminds him that "the doom of sin and death is on us all, but you should remember that as you are a Morville, you are also a Christian," to which her sister Amy, who already loves Guy, answers, "He does remember it!"

Amy's words eventually bring home to Guy "the hope and encouragement of that marvellous tale," and Amy's mother, his kind aunt Mrs. Edmonstone, who has taken him in hand, speaks to him "cheerfully of a successful conflict with evil" and makes him realize that "his temptations were but such as are common to man." Yet later, Guy once again complains, in a moment of self-pity, that he is doomed like Sintram, and Amy Edmonstone, whom he marries, reminds him that after all Sintram conquered his doom. Repeatedly—when they are engaged and again on his deathbed—Guy calls Amy "my Verena," heedless of the fact that Verena was Sintram's mother and Amy is Guy's wife. He clearly sees in Amy the saintly traits of the nun in the story and of the mother whom he himself had never known. When his posthumous daughter is born, Amy names her Mary Verena Morville, in memory of what *Sintram* has meant to Guy and herself.

Repentance and humility: they are the key to *Sintram* and to *The Heir of Redclyffe*, and they also serve as important themes in Manzoni's Italian novel *I Promessi Sposi* (*The Betrothed*, 1827), enormously popular in England. Philip Morville, priggish elder cousin of Guy and the Edmonstones, very early in *The Heir* reads aloud a chapter from Manzoni, in which "Fra Cristoforo humbled himself, exchanged forgiveness, and received" the bread of pardon. On hearing it, Guy is greatly moved: "tears hung on his eyelashes." If Philip had profited equally by the lesson of *I Promessi Sposi*, he would have claimed his bride, Amy's sister Laura, in spite of his own lack of means: instead, he sinfully temporizes and evades his duty. So Fouqué and Manzoni receive Miss Yonge's official approval: her most wholehearted disapproval is reserved for Lord Byron.

Philip, who has heard Guy quote a stanza from "The Giaour," warns him that Byron is "bad food for excitable minds." And years later, in Italy, when Philip wants to borrow "Childe Harold" from Guy, Guy—who has now fully mastered himself—is able to retort that he has heeded Philip's advice. Guy "little knew," says Charlotte Yonge, "how much he owed to his having attended that caution; for who could have told where the mastery might have been, in the period of fearful conflict with his passions, if he had been feeding his imagination with the contemplation of revenge, dark hatred, and malice, and identifying himself with Byron's brooding and lowering heroes?"

Even Byron's descriptions of scenery are dangerous, Guy declares, because a man like Byron "is sure to misunderstand the voice of nature . . . to link human passions with the glories of nature, and so distort, defile, profane them." Only "men with minds in the right direction"—religious men—are qualified to write about nature: Shakespeare, Spenser, Wordsworth, Scott, and—surprise from the High-Anglican Miss Yonge and Guy—Milton, "though his religion was not quite the right sort." Indeed—for such a devotee of Charles I as we shall find the typically Tractarian Guy to be—acceptance of the Puritan Milton was extremely broad-minded.

Anti-Byronic though Miss Yonge was when discussing Byron directly, paradoxically she made Guy himself a good deal of a Byronic hero. In his struggle for self-mastery, he displays fierce passions, biting his lip until it bleeds, his face "a burning glowing red, the features almost convulsed, the large veins in the forehead and temples swollen with the blood that rushed through them," and his eyes flashing "with dark lightning." When outraged at an unfair accusation that he has been a gambler, Guy is swept by "a violent storm of indignation and pride":

> On he rushed, reckless whither he went, or what he did, driven forward by the wild impulse of passion, far over moor and hill, up and down, till at last, exhausted by the violent bodily exertion, a stillness—a suspension of thought and sensation ensued; and when this passed, he found himself seated on a rock which crowned the summit of one of the hills, his handkerchief loosened, his waistcoat open, his hat thrown off, his temples burning and throbbing, with a feeling of distraction, and the agitated beatings of his heart almost stifling his panting breath.

So Charlotte Yonge used Byronic action and imagery for her own purpose: to teach the lesson that Byronic instincts and behavior must be rigorously checked. She offered the forbidden fruit with one hand and snatched it away with the other. Almost at once, Guy realizes the "frenzy of his rage and his own murderous impulse . . . appalled at the power of his fury. . . ." And he schools himself in self-discipline.

He can do it, because he is not only Sintram and a Byronic hero but also Sir Galahad. When playing with his cousins a game in which each player lists his favorite characters in history and fiction, Guy's favorite fictional character is Sir Galahad. In 1853, when *The Heir of Redclyffe* appeared, it was still half a dozen years before Tennyson's *Idylls of the King* was published; so it is understandable, if surprising, that all these well-read young people have never heard of Galahad, or the Siege Perilous, or the Saint Greal. Guy must explain: he has learned about Galahad from Malory's *Morte d'Arthur*. Of the others, only the intellectual twenty-five-year-old Philip has ever looked into it, and he declares it "a book that no one could read through." Guy defends it heatedly—"the depth, the mystery, the allegory,—the beautiful character of some of the knights"—but Philip snubs him as usual. However, after Guy has won the victory over himself and is married to Amy, a great artist who meets him begs him to sit for a portrait of Sir Galahad; the sketch for the painting—a splendid likeness—becomes Amy's great comfort after Guy's death.

Even before his regeneration, Guy's saintly qualities are hinted at: he looks like one of the angels in the Sistine Madonna, Mrs. Edmonstone discovers, one of the "winged boys . . . a wonderful pattern of childlike piety. . . . what faces they have. Perfect innocence—one full of reasoning, the other of unreasoning adoration." Guy resembles the larger of the two, but only in his good moods! This is perhaps a bit steep for a modern reader, but Miss Yonge meant her symbolism in all earnestness. As Guy and Amy kneel before the altar on their marriage day, the sun suddenly shines through a stained-glass window, "casting a stream of colour from a martyr's figure in the south window, so as to shed a golden glory on the wave of brown hair over Guy's forehead." It is a "crown of pure angelic light" hardly suitable for a mortal, and it foreshadows Guy's death and salvation.

Guy, then, sprang in part from the inspiration of literary heroes and antiheroes. He also had at least one model in real life: Hurrell Froude, the charming, brilliant, ascetic Tractarian, whose *Remains*

Newman had published, somewhat shockingly revealing to the world Froude's struggles against temptation. Froude fasted and mortified the flesh and repented at length over his arrogance in social behavior, analyzing his faults, subjecting himself to merciless scrutiny, and declaring, "I must fight against myself with all my might, and watch my mind at every turning." He took as his only purpose "resolute and implicit obedience to the lessons and rules of the Church of England." Charlotte Yonge quite consciously used him as one of her models for Guy: even Froude's self-tortures with the lash are once hinted at—she could hardly do more than hint—in a passage where Guy, out for a drive, remarks, "I want something unpleasant to keep me in order. Something famously horrid," and then he repeats it, "smacking the whip with a relish, as if he would have applied that if he could have found nothing else." His aunt can hardly help laughing "at this strange boy," who feels that life in her family "is enough to do me harm; it is so exceedingly pleasant." His is a "serious, ascetic temper, coupled with . . . high animal spirits," in fact exactly like Hurrell Froude's. Charlotte Yonge was much pleased when her own mother spotted the resemblance between Guy and Hurrell and wrote to a friend, "I hope it is a sign I have got the right sow by the ear"—a fine earthy metaphor.

How far and in what respects is *The Heir* a recognizably Tractarian novel? With no new church to consecrate or dissenting radicals to shun (as in *Abbeychurch*), with no specific doctrinal lesson to be taught (like that of confirmation and communion in *The Castle-Builders*), *The Heir of Redclyffe* seems to hide its Tractarianism, as Keble preferred. But when one seeks it, one can find it. There is, for example, Guy's passionate devotion to Charles I. He responds with fury to even a casual teasing sneer about the tragic execution of Lord Strafford in 1640, which Charles did not intervene to prevent. "Ungenerous, unmanly . . . to reproach him with what he so bitterly repented. Could not his penitence, could not his own blood" have availed to save him from taunts now? One may not even joke about Charles I: he "is too near home; he suffered too much from scoffs and railings; his heart too tender, his repentance too deep for his friends to add a word even in jest to the heap of reproach. How one would have loved him . . . for the gentleness so little accordant with the rude times and the part he had to act—served him with a devotion half like a knight's . . . to his lady-love, half like devotion to a saint. . . . And oh! . . . how one would have fought for him!" One of the earliest bonds between Amy and Guy is forged when he learns that she had been found "dissolved in tears" before a Van Dyke portrait of Charles I in a neighboring country house. And when it comes to the game of choosing favorite characters, Guy's favorite in history is Charles I, as his favorite in fiction is Galahad. This devotion to Charles the Martyr—with its implied, and often stated, hostility to the Puritans, to Cromwell, to the regicides, to aggressive Protestantism generally—was a Tractarian shibboleth.

Guy's tribulations when he is wrongly suspected of gambling arise from his wish to make a large contribution of his own money (still in Mr. Edmonstone's control) to a new Anglican sisterhood, which is still a secret, so that he cannot tell what his purpose is. Such sisterhoods were a Tractarian innovation, much criticized even by other Anglicans. The two maiden sisters whom Guy is planning to help are blamed for "taking pauper children into their house, where they educate them in a way to unfit them for their station, and teach them to observe a sort of monastic rule . . . preaching the poor people in the hospital to death, visiting the poor at all sorts of strange hours," even "at twelve o'clock at night, in a miserable lodging-house, filled with the worst description of inmates." A "strong party" has arisen against the two sisters, because, Miss Yonge says in an aside, there is a " 'tyrannous hate' in the world for unusual goodness." This hatred "impedes their usefulness and subjects them to endless petty calumnies." Temporarily prevented from endowing the sisterhood by Mr. Edmonstone's refusal of the money, Guy leaves them a large sum in his will.

When Guy is smitten by fever on his honeymoon in Italy and is on his deathbed, his greatest wish is fulfilled: an English clergyman is found to perform the last rites for the dying. Guy confesses his sins and is absolved. The young priest, himself a sick man, says to Amy afterwards, "One longs to humble oneself to him. How it puts one to shame to hear such repentance with such a confession." This emphasis upon confession and absolution (remember *Ellen Middleton*) is also wholly Anglo-Catholic. And similarly, when poor widowed Amy has been delivered of her little girl and has "brought

Guy's daughter to be baptized," the sacramental aspect of the action is given great emphasis, in the Anglo-Catholic way. Amy feels that her work on earth had been incomplete until that moment and—briefly—wishes that she could follow her beloved husband, but she quickly remembers that Guy had entrusted the upbringing of the child to her: "The sunshine was past, but she had plenty to do, and it was for his sake . . . with the sense of renewed communion with him that she had found in returning again to church."

If one were to have asked the innumerable Victorian readers of Miss Yonge's novel the apparently foolish question, "Who is the heir of Redclyffe?" most of them would almost surely have answered, "Guy, of course." But in fact Guy has inherited Redclyffe before the book opens, and the news comes in its earliest pages. It is *Philip* Morville, his cousin, who is, in fact, the heir throughout the novel, until—with Guy's death—he comes into the inheritance. *The Heir of Redclyffe* is as much the story of Philip Morville's conquest over himself as it is of Guy's. But Philip—overbearing, conceited, self-satisfied, and Guy's personal enemy—is so disagreeable a character that the reader can easily emerge from the book without realizing that Charlotte Yonge intended Philip's development to be as important as Guy's and to teach another variety of the same lesson. Philip is an intellectual—something always a bit suspect to Miss Yonge—who has had to abandon his Oxford career because of his father's early death and accept a commission in the army instead. He is jealous of Guy's wealth and title and knows that, were it not for Guy's existence, he himself would be rich. He constantly rebukes Guy and arrogantly advises him; he starts the (groundless) rumor about Guy's alleged gambling that jeopardizes Guy's engagement to Amy, and he clings to the truth of the charge long after it has been disproved. He refuses to attend the wedding.

Worse: knowing that he cannot afford to marry, he allows himself to propose to Amy's sister, his cousin Laura; and she accepts him, although the engagement cannot be made public. He thus violates the lesson of *I Promessi Sposi.* Still worse: Philip and Laura do not mention their attachment to her parents: this concealment and deception is regarded by Charlotte Yonge as a grievous sin. If this seems far-fetched to us—as it did to some readers even in the decade after *The Heir of Redclyffe* appeared—we can still appreciate it as self-seeking, as unfairness to a woman by a man, and as disloyalty to family obligations: moral issues that are still with us. Philip's insistence, despite Guy's advice, on travelling alone through an area of Italy in which fever is known to be raging brings desperate illness upon him; it is in nursing him that Guy himself is fatally stricken with the same fever.

Philip finally inherits Redclyffe and marries Laura: but he is tortured with feelings of such guilt (he has secretly wished Guy dead, and he is responsible for Guy's death) that he hardly can bear to accept his inheritance, much less enjoy it. His repentance is sudden and complete; from being arrogant, he becomes abject, and grovels in asking forgiveness of all those whom he has injured. Guy on his deathbed had magnanimously forgiven Philip, and this continues to haunt Philip too. The book ends with Philip in a proper state of total Yongeian submissiveness, but the cost has been so great that the modern reader is likely to be repelled. Together Guy's story and Philip's teach lessons not only Christian, but also specifically Anglo-Catholic. Of the two men, Guy is "essentially contrite," despite his fearful natural temper; Philip is "naturally self-satisfied." What Philip gains on earth through his mistreatment of Guy is more than compensated by Guy's early rewards in the life to come.

Dante Gabriel Rossetti and William Morris loved the book: its personification of a true knight in Sir Guy-Galahad-Sintram no doubt struck sympathetic mediaeval chords in their pre-Raphaelite bosoms. An Oxford undergraduate, later a celebrated scholar, longed to die a death like Guy's; and wrote, "how glorious it would be for the survivor to be such as Amy." While Charlotte Yonge was writing the book, Sir John Coleridge—later Lord Chief Justice—who had read it in manuscript, begged her to let Guy's and Amy's baby be a boy, so that Philip would not inherit Redclyffe; but she clung to her purpose: it enabled Amy to continue Guy's noble acts of conciliation and heaped new coals of fire on Philip's head. What a pleasure, Charlotte's brother declared, it would have been to kick Philip all around the courtyard of an Oxford college. Henry James said that Charlotte Yonge was "almost a genius" and had a "first-rate mind . . . which is the master and not the slave of its material." So one cannot dismiss the novel as a mere book for teen-aged girls.

It is an absorbingly well-told story and a major religious document of the Victorian age. Having gone all out on its behalf, however, one takes a certain pleasure in recalling also the lone contemporary critic who cried out that it was a tissue of "Pusey-stricken fancies," and even objected to the name of the hero, Sir Guy Morville, as "invented in a spirit of gentility" only to be compared to that which inspired Dickens when he named "Morleena" Kenwiggs in *Nicholas Nickleby*.

In her *Clever Woman of the Family* (1865, no. 71), Charlotte Yonge introduces us to one of those Victorian females of whose existence we have always been sure, but who are rare in the pages of fiction: a rebel against the enforced idleness of the intelligent, well-to-do, energetic young woman. "Here is the world around me," says Rachel Curtis, aged twenty-five at the outset of the story,

> one mass of misery and evil! Not a paper do I take up but I see something about wretchedness and crime, and here I sit with health, strength, and knowledge, and able to do nothing, *nothing*—at the risk of breaking my mother's heart! I have pottered about cottages and taught at schools in the *dilettante* way of the young lady who thinks it her duty to be charitable; and I am told that it is my duty, and that I may be satisfied. Satisfied, when I see children cramped in soul, destroyed in body, that fine ladies may wear lace trimmings! . . . Satisfied when I know that every alley and lane of town or country reeks with vice and corruption, and that there is one cry for workers with brains and with purses!

Unexceptionable sentiments, one would think. It is only her mother's insistence that Rachel is to marry which holds her back. She "must not be out late, must not put forth my views, must not choose my acquaintance, must be a mere helpless, useless being, growing old in a ridiculous fiction of prolonged childhood, affecting those graces of sweet seventeen that I never had." It is a ringing feminist statement: at first the reader thinks of Miss Yonge, and wonders whether she may not have felt this way herself, so effectively has she put the case. But one reminds oneself that she was a most skillful devil's advocate.

Full of zeal, Rachel plans for the lace-making girls in the village a kind of trade school designed to emancipate them from the cruel conditions under which they work. It is the Female Union for Lacemakers' Employment; but when Rachel realizes that the acronym would be "F.U.L.E." (everybody in the sixties read Artemus Ward's American humor), she hastily changes the name to Female Union for Englishwomen's Employment. A clever swindler in pseudoclerical dress deceives her, misappropriates her money, and starves and mistreats the poor girls, one of whom must die before Rachel begins to think that she may have been wrong in her goals and methods. A self-satisfaction as pronounced though not as nasty as Philip Morville's leads Rachel into trouble, of course. But there is more: Rachel is on the wrong religious path. And although the Tractarian lesson of *The Clever Woman* is more visible than that of *The Heir of Redclyffe*, it is so cunningly embedded in the windings of an elaborate and well-told story that it needs to be separated out.

Rachel dislikes the curate of the village church, Mr. Touchett. He is only "gentlemanlike," not a real gentleman, and therefore cannot—she thinks—be expected to have a true gentleman's feelings. Moreover, he has substituted a choir for the former fiddlers in church, driving the disgruntled musicians into the arms of Dissent, and yet never—because of his own incompetence—managing to produce a choir that can sing very well. He must recruit his singers from amongst the same fisher boys of the village that Rachel teaches; since they are at sea on every weekday but Saturday, he has scheduled his choir practice to conflict with her classes. Her protests have been unavailing; Touchett has boldly defied her, daughter of the important local gentry family though she is. He believes "praise in its highest form the prime object of his ministry," which is to say, he insists on choir music; we may be sure the Tractarian Charlotte Yonge agreed with him. Rachel, however, "found the performance undevotional, and raved that education should be sacrificed to wretched music." There is, then, "party-spirit" in the village, and Rachel is enrolled in the opposition party to Mr. Touchett. He does, however, have a large following among the local ladies and does not need her: "so many volunteers were there for parish work that districts and classes were divided and subdivided, till it sometimes seemed as if the only difficulty was to find poor people enough who would submit to serve as the *corpus vile* for charitable experiment."

Touchett, we see, despite the uncouth noises that his choir still makes, is right, and Rachel wholly wrong. Sneering at the parish ladies who follow his ideas, she writes an article against what she calls "Curatolatry" and has to be reminded that she is combining Latin and Greek roots and that the proper word would be "Curatocult." Rachel goes to church now only on Sundays; she sneers at a devout young governess who goes each morning to early services as behaving like a character in "a little mauve book" of pious fiction for children. For a governess, the old motto *laborare est orare* (to work is to pray) should be enough. What wonder, then, if the impostor who calls himself Mauleverer, and who has a long criminal record, fools Rachel completely? After a few conversations with him, Rachel is defending him as "one of the many who have *thought for themselves* [italics mine] upon the perplexing problems of faith and practice, and one who has been sincere, uncompromising, self-sacrificing, in avowing that his mind is still in that state of solution in which all earnest and original minds must be ere the crystallizing process sets in." Of course, he is *not* in clerical orders, despite his misleading clothes, but Rachel assures him that she "can fully appreciate any reluctance to become stringently bound to dogmatic enunciations before the full powers of the intellect have examined them."

Instantly we see that, plausible though Rachel and Mauleverer sound, they are guilty of precisely that "reprehensible presumption" of attempting to "think for themselves in matters connected with religion" which our old acquaintance, Anne Brontë's Puseyite parson, denounced. Charlotte Yonge, devout Tractarian, agreed with the man Anne Brontë had been satirizing. It was, of course, the authority of the church, rather than any dangerous exercising of one's own intellect, that could instruct the perplexed individual what to believe. What Rachel is doing and saying is anathema to Charlotte Yonge, and so Rachel's schemes inevitably end in the affecting death by diphtheria of a girl who still can say, as she dies, that she knows Christ had been scourged for her. The poor neglected child is at least a devout Christian.

Chastened by the death—as Philip Morville had been by

Guy's—Rachel realizes how deeply she longs, "as for something far away, for the reality of those simple teachings—once realities, now all by rote." Her faith is "all confusion." When she refuses a proposal from Alick Keith, the man she loves, she tells him, "I do believe, I wish to believe; but my grasp seems gone. I cannot rest or trust." Her "old implicit reliance is gone, and all observances seem like hypocrisy and unreality." Alick reassures her that her faith will come back. And since her besetting sin of "self-sufficiency" has now been conquered, she has only to take the next steps before she can recover her spiritual equilibrium. It is fortunate for Rachel that Alick's uncle is the saintly Mr. Clare, a blind, gentle, scholarly clergyman of the good old school (the story is set in the year 1859). Mr. Clare "belonged to that generation which gave its choicest in intellectual, as well as in religious, gifts to the ministry, when a fresh tide of enthusiasm was impelling them forward to build up, instead of breaking down, before disappointment and suspicion had thinned the ranks . . . or doctrinal carpings had taught men to conduct a search into their own tenets." In short, Mr. Clare was a contemporary of Keble himself, and Miss Yonge was surely thinking of Keble when she wrote those words. Because of Mr. Clare, Rachel is able to recapture what she had so nearly lost forever.

The reader sees that Rachel, who had always been viewed with awe by her family as their "clever woman," had never been clever at all. Just as Philip, not Guy, was really the *heir*, so another character in this novel is really the *clever woman*: the staunch, beautiful, crippled, impoverished lady, Ermine Williams, who writes articles under the pseudonym "Invalid" for current critical journals, and manages at the same time to take care of her brother's young daughter. Learned, unassuming, intelligent, and modest, Ermine is all those things that Rachel wishes to be and misguidedly believes she is; Rachel blandly patronizes Ermine until she discovers by accident that the periodicals which are rejecting her own offerings compete to accept Ermine's. The originality of *The Clever Woman* in the Charlotte Yonge canon, however, comes in her introduction for the first time of religious doubt into one of her novels. Here doubt takes the form of Rachel's partly atrophied faith, combined with her intellectual arrogance and her bland assumption that she can, if she likes, find the answers for herself. There is nothing wrong with her impulse to dedicate herself to social service; she goes astray when she allows personal considerations and trivial snobbery to lead her to exercise her private judgment and follow a course independent of that which her clergyman would approve.

Miss Sewell and Miss Skene

Like Miss Yonge a lifelong spinster who lived a secluded life and was a devout High Anglican, Elizabeth Missing Sewell (1815-1906) differed from her in having experienced in childhood and young womanhood the spiritual growing pains which we in the twentieth century regard as the ordinary fate of mortals in adolescence, but which, so far as can be discovered, left Miss Yonge almost unscathed. Again and again, appreciative modern critics look in Charlotte Yonge's fiction for traces of repressed hostilities and frustrated spinsterhood, but they never find anything at all convincing. Either her life was a masterpiece of deceitful concealment of the hatreds that other women in similar positions have generally felt, or Miss Yonge simply conquered hers without resentment. Miss Sewell—who knew Charlotte Yonge when she was twenty-five and Charlotte seventeen—in any case did not, but instead struggled against "secret sins": she vowed in a moment of fury that she would kill her mother, and then debated with herself whether she must carry out the vow. It was only after a stormy period of doubt and resistance in her youth that she achieved religious and personal serenity, and learned to pray briefly and rapidly whenever a twinge of scepticism or rebelliousness swept over her.

Quite possibly the overpowering presence of her brother William, author of *Hawkstone* (1845, no. 2), both made Miss Sewell's task of conquering herself more difficult and underlined the importance of submission. She tells us herself that she loved him far too much and "teased" him by her excess of fondness. He arrogantly assumed that she could not understand difficult books, but indoctrinated her in Tractarian principles. William's name alone appeared as that of "Editor" on the title pages of his sister's earlier novels, the first of which were written primarily for young girls and are not included in our series. Over her fourth, *Margaret Percival* (1847, no. 26), the shadow of William still fell heavily. She wrote it because he urged her to produce a cautionary tale for young people which would convey the lesson that his *Hawkstone* had so vividly rammed down the throats of adults: the dangers of Rome. After she had written it, he "edited" it. We cannot be certain what changes he may have made, even though he declared that he had only recommended "the line of argument to be employed," but he would surely have hardened the anti-Catholic position of the book, if anything. After it appeared, there were protests against its contents, which Sewell characteristically labelled "falsehoods" that had been "invented and circulated" against it. In a special new preface to the second edition, he defended the book.

Young readers would find, he wrote, that in the story they were urged to "abstain from controversy and inquiry." This was because the only "safety is flight," if one is not properly equipped intellectually to argue with Roman Catholics; otherwise the result is "an aggravation of error." "Young persons, especially young females" have not been educated to argue properly. None of this implies any doubt whatever that the Church of England is based on "unimpeachable and triumphant grounds of argument." It is. But young people do not know what they are. Moreover, *Margaret Percival* shows Romanism in a favorable light, not because it has not a darker side (as the man who invented the Jesuits in *Hawkstone* well knew!), but because the purpose of the book was to show how misleadingly attractive Catholicism may be made to seem. Finally, when one encounters individual members (or clerics) of the Church of England who are inadequate for some reason, they alone should be blamed and not the institution.

When the widowed Countess Novera, who had come of an old English Catholic family and married an Italian nobleman, returns to England, she makes a friend of Margaret Percival, a girl in her late teens. The Countess had seen Margaret kneeling in a Catholic church in Rouen, and had leaped to the erroneous conclusion that the girl was a Catholic. Now, in England, she and her private confessor, Father Andrea, go promptly and subtly to work to convert Margaret to Rome. Quickly, Margaret shows how little able she is to defend herself: in her first conversation with Father Andrea, she grants at once the name "Catholic" to the Roman Church, makes no distinction between the "Established Church of England" and the "Established Church of Scotland," and even refers to a Unitarian minister as a "clergyman." She is vulnerable, just as Mr. Sewell warned in his preface, to subtle argument. Soon, having incautiously expressed a dislike for Milton's Puritanism, Margaret is being grilled—and is stumbling—on the reasons why High Anglicans and Puritans are opposed to one another. It is Father Andrea's plan to cause her first to "see that Dissenters have an equal claim" with Anglicans to her respect, and then to bring down the entire edifice of her Anglican faith. "First shake her faith in her Church, and then arouse her feelings, and appeal to her taste, and the work is accomplished."

The local Anglican clergyman has too many poor parishioners to attend to them all; Dissent is making headway. Father Andrea quietly needles Margaret on these points and then talks of Catholic sisterhoods of charity and of the Jesuit missions to Paraguay. Despite her initial bridling at the name Jesuit ("You know," she tells him, "the name in England has passed into a proverb for double dealing"), she listens eagerly to his eloquent account of the order (he assures her he is not a member). The tragic deathbed of a poor Catholic girl, combined with reading in books carefully chosen by Father Andrea, including Saints' Lives and wholly biased accounts of Catholic practices and beliefs (veneration of the Virgin, purgatory and indulgences, infallibility of the Roman Church, the identity of the Roman worship with that of primitive Christianity): all this "had not completed the work of conversion." Margaret is by no means convinced, but she feels such a tumult of doubt that the truths she had accepted all her life "were often shaken to their foundation."

The arrival of Margaret's uncle, Mr. Sutherland, a High Anglican, opens the counterattack. Restless, worn, in deep trouble, Margaret expects that he will produce the stock counterarguments to the stock arguments she has heard; but he knows that this would only lead to a kind of debate with Father Andrea over Margaret's soul. Instead, he says, "As a baptized member of the English Church you are obliged to remain in her communion," making the appeal to authority and not to ratiocination. "Read your Bible" he urges, "and pray with your Prayer-book, and keep a careful watch over a criticising, discontented spirit, and you will never become a Romanist." When doubts arise, Margaret is to pray briefly and earnestly. "Afterwards, repeat verses, walk about, read, sing, do any thing which shall be actual occupation for the moment." The Church of England wins the day in the end. There is much of William Sewell's intransigence in this book; but its whole tone is gentler and more forbearing than anything he could presumably have written.

In writing *The Experience of Life; or, Aunt Sarah* (1853, no. 26), Miss Sewell was wholly independent of her brother William, and her own personality strikes through. Now in her late thirties, she had attained the inner peace that had eluded her in her youth. Sure that she was destined for spinsterhood, glad to embrace her fate, knowing how much comfort and happiness a loving spinster can confer upon other people and especially on other people's children, no longer racked by doubts but content with the simplest and least questioning faith, Miss Sewell wrote a simple, heartfelt, memorable novel, in which the protagonist has good cause for hatred, but learns to arrange her life as Miss Sewell had arranged her own. *The Experience of Life* deserves close comparison with Miss Sewell's own autobiography, published after her death more than half a century later. Psychologists, social historians, and lovers of Victorian fiction will find *The Experience* an unheralded little masterpiece.

Told in the first person by Sarah Mortimer, the ugly duckling of a large family of brothers and sisters, the story gives a vivid picture of more than half a century of quiet English family life—most of it in the days before the railways—its apparently placid surface troubled only by problems of human relations, money, and religion, its joys simple, its sorrows and disappointments keen, its lessons hard to learn. From childhood, Sarah's great-aunt, for whom she has been named, gives her the affection, the moral support, the gnomic wisdom of a dedicated spinster's experience; she crushes in Sarah all tendencies toward self-pity, hypochondria, the expression of often justifiable dislikes and suspicions. So well does Aunt Sarah do her work that long before she dies, Sarah herself has become another such woman, less astringent perhaps, more radiant, but in all important senses a reincarnation of her great-aunt. Aunt Sarah dies at eighty-five; by the time the younger Sarah takes her farewell of the reader she herself is seventy-six. Miss Sewell declared in her *Autobiography*, "I had no Aunt Sarah to comfort me." We infer that both Aunt Sarah and the younger Sarah are versions of Elizabeth Sewell's idea of herself and of her own life, the younger woman admiring what she will become, the older woman recalling what she was to begin with and the stages of her development. Most of the personages and some of the events are fictional (although the Mortimer family's financial troubles were founded on those of the Sewells), but the psychological and spiritual development of the main character is autobiographical. "Sarah's troubled mind was a record of my own personal feelings," Miss Sewell later wrote.

Altogether lacking in *The Experience of Life* is the bitter anti-popery of *Margaret Percival* that smacked so much of William. Catholics are mentioned only once in the entire novel, when Sarah at forty says to her aunt, "I sometimes think that I should like to lead such a life as one hears described by Romanists; not exactly, perhaps, that of a nun, but of a sister of charity." To which Aunt Sarah answers, "It might be a good and holy life for many . . . and it might be better for us Church people if such things were possible; the time may come when it may be." Here Miss Sewell—writing as of a period before the Tractarian leaders had begun to found such sisterhoods; often against public opposition such as we found described in *The Heir of Redclyffe*—expresses her gentle approval of the institution. But immediately Aunt Sarah says that there will be many "who can't live the life, and yet they must be single, and, as most folks think, lonely." This is to be Sarah's fate, of course, as it was Miss Sewell's; but loneliness is kept at bay by work, by self-sacrifice, by charity, by close family ties, and, above all, by the Church itself.

In *The Experience of Life*, Dissent, not Catholicism, is the enemy that troubles the devout Church of England people: most of the novel takes place in the High-and-Dry days, before the Catholic revival inside the Church of England and outside it. Thus, at Lowood, the estate of Sarah's friend and patroness, Lady Emily Rivers, the village rector is elderly, unintelligent, and neglectful of his flock, though well-meaning. The church is crowded with the pews of the well-to-do, intimidating and shutting out the poor; the Dissenters have daily services, not merely weekly, Sunday, services; the Dissenting preachers are "energetic" and "talk to the people in language that can be easily understood. . . . They mix with them daily, and know their needs." All the "religion in England," says a deeply worried Anglican young woman, will "in another fifty years be found amongst the Dissenters." The rector has sent a dying, poor parishioner some broth, but has not called on him for more than a week; the Dissenting minister has been to see him every day even though the sick man is no Dissenter. "Those fellows get about everywhere," says the rector himself; they are "indefatigable," says his critic. The rector blames the situation on Lady Emily and her husband, the squire: they are too tolerant. "He says that if he were the squire he would not have a tenant on his estate a dissenter; he would turn them all out. But Mr. Rivers [a staunch churchman himself] can never come round to this view of treating the evil." If he should, it is indeed predicted, "two new dissenters would spring up for every one that he ejected."

The worst of it is that the Dissenters are not the bad people of the parish but the best, "the neatest, most industrious, most honest." Lady Emily's school for the village children is the one thing that keeps their families in the Church, since the children must all attend, but this too would have been ineffective if the rector's advice had been taken: he had wanted to forbid any child at the school ever to go to a Dissenting meeting. Lady Emily has learned that "by attacking dissent we increase it . . . the lesson of all persecutions." We may contrast Miss Sewell's gentle warning with William's fierce sneers at Dissenters in *Hawkstone* (1845, no. 2).

These passages look ahead longingly to reform in the Church of England such as the Tractarians would sponsor: no more pews, daily service, and, it was hoped, active and personal attendance on the sick and dying poor; but there are no sneers about the Dissenters' lower-class status or their religious customs. The entire experience of Lowood—in Sarah's girlhood—is her first introduction to the possible inadequacy of her own church under certain circumstances. It distresses her deeply. She has seen Dissent "as an active, progressive power, working with some great influence which it seemed that no one could withstand." She is almost reduced to her "former agony of doubt." But Aunt Sarah has taught her the Sewell lesson, to "crush thought with prayer." And, like Margaret Percival, with "terrible struggle" she does it. "Even in early youth, without argument, without sympathy, without external aid, but simply with the force of prayer, and the strong will to crush the very shadow of a rising doubt," peace can be obtained, and one can find one's faith intact and one's conviction restored that it is truly reasonable.

The reader of *The Experience of Life* will find in the foundation of Lady Emily's own private school for girls, and in the various discussions of its principles, a suggestive preview of many a Victorian controversy. The governess in Lady Emily's own household, a Church of England woman but one of the sharpest critics of their do-nothing rector, eventually turns Dissenter herself: "because the dissenting teacher was a more zealous man than the parish priest, she argued, as many have done before, and are likely to do hereafter, that Dissent must be right and the Church wrong." *The Experience of Life*, then, is a Tractarian novel set in the days before Tractarianism, and its Tractarian lessons are conveyed altogether by indirection.

Of these, by far the most important are exemplified in the rigorous schooling that Sarah must go through. Aunt Sarah—often sternly, but always with love—teaches Sarah what she has learned in life, lessons both secular and religious. Sometimes she is unexpectedly witty, as when she says of dinner parties, which Sarah detests, "They may be dull and heavy as the money of the Spartans, but they serve as the medium of exchange; and we grave, stiff English folk are not fit for anything else—if we were we should have found it out before this." Often she is acid, as when accurately telling Sarah—still a young girl of fifteen—exactly what are the defects of each of her many sisters and brothers, and emphasizing her duty to her mother as the one truly responsible and affectionate member of the family. In the money trials, and the personal trials, and the discovery of human nastiness which beset Sarah, Aunt Sarah is always effective.

She makes spinsterhood—with its innumberable opportunities for giving love and helping others—seem positively attractive. She teaches that in families it is well to have everybody's obligations formally agreed upon well in advance. It is always best, Aunt Sarah declares, to have two sets of troubles, unrelated to one another, so that one is prevented from brooding overmuch about either set by regularly transferring one's mind to the other. Aunt Sarah coins the Sewell aphorism, "Don't think but pray," which serves in the end to smother young Sarah's doubts. And it is because of Aunt Sarah that Sarah, an old woman, surrounded by the family of a loving younger sister, still finds that her "real home is the Church." Often she goes there to pray and feels "how little the life of a member of Christ's Church can ever be called lonely. 'One Lord, one Faith, one Baptism, one God and Father of all'—were I without earthly friends, without human relations—could they not all in that life be mine? Not each for himself, and by himself, we travel towards Eternity; but together—one, though many;—united, though separate;—ever living though ever dying;—with interests which began with Creation, and cannot cease with Time." Few works of fiction so convincingly celebrate the joys of faith as this best and most popular novel of Elizabeth Sewell.

In passing, we may note briefly that William Edward Heygate, in his *William Blake; or, the English Farmer* (1848, no. 27), treats some of the same religious subjects as Miss Sewell in *The Experience* and from the same Tractarian point of view. Here again—in a book designed, however, primarily for young people—we have an English rural community. It lacks a generous squire and his wife, which Lowood had, but possesses a High-and-Dry Rector, and Dissent is beginning to lure the few seriously religious farmers. The rest are far gone in dissipation, even profligacy, and the rural laborers are wholly without religious education, and so freely commit theft and other crimes. The advent of a new High-Anglican rector ushers in a new era. Not only—in true Paget-fashion—are the long-overdue repairs made to the church and pews abolished, but William Blake, one of the sons of a prosperous farmer, also seeks out the new rector in a time of personal trial and receives a truly godly education from him. Confirmation and first communion follow—late, but not too late. With every step of Blake's upon the road to godliness, his fiancée, desperately ill, takes a parallel step toward recovery.

This seems to the modern reader quite immoral, as promising similar almost miraculous good fortune to those who heed the example. Moreover, Mr. Lee, the good rector, is not beyond imposing what seems to us a vindictive punishment. An elderly village woman who has told a lie is "struck off the coal club, and clothing club," which will deprive her of her share of the village charity of fuel and warm flannel. The student of the religious novel may make no startling discoveries in *William Blake*, but it includes a most significant list of books prescribed by Mr. Lee for William Blake to read. Divided into three categories—history, devotional books, and general books—the list of forty-one titles would prove extremely informative for the social historian who wanted to know exactly how the Tractarians tried to reach the people in the late forties. One of the books is *Sintram*, so important a key to *The Heir of Redclyffe* five years later: it was obviously not only Charlotte Yonge who found the book a valuable instrument of Tractarian instruction. Another is Henry Manning's sermons. In the early forties Manning had repudiated Tract 90 and had preached a sermon against Romanism (1843); the *Sermons* (1844) reflected this position. But in 1848 he was visiting the Pope, and by 1851 he had gone over to Rome. The presence of the book on Heygate's list is of considerable interest.

Felicia Mary Frances Skene (1821-1899) had enjoyed a far more varied youthful life than Charlotte Yonge or Elizabeth Sewell before she too settled down to many decades of High-Anglican spinsterhood and novel writing. For her the writing of fiction was (as it was for the Catholic Lady Georgiana Fullerton) a means of raising money for her favorite charities. True: Charlotte Yonge devoted all the profits of *The Heir of Redclyffe* to the fitting-out of a missionary ship, and contributed all her large earnings to religious projects, but she herself was a professional novelist and woman of letters. Felicia Skene, by contrast, was first of all an active worker in the slums and prisons of Oxford, and remained an amateur at writing fiction. Miss Skene's father, James Skene, was the close friend of Sir Walter Scott, who paid him affectionate poetic tribute in the introduction to the fourth canto of "Marmion" (1808). Her mother was Elizabeth Forbes, whose brother, Sir William Forbes, had married Scott's first love (Mrs. Skene was the only woman to whom Scott revealed the authorship of the *Waverley Novels*). As a child, Felicia knew the great man well. In her case at least, the charge often levelled at Scott by Evangelicals—that he had imbued a whole generation of readers with "Popish nonsense" and Jacobitism—was true. Felicia had a year of schooling in Paris as a child and at seventeen went out with her family to Athens to live; her brother married a Greek girl. They stayed eight years; she learned to speak Greek fluently, accompanied her father on many long and adventurous excursions on horseback through the wild mountainous countryside, and visited Constantinople and the Danubian Balkan territories.

After the family's return from Greece, Felicia in the late forties came under the influence of Anglo-Catholic clergymen, especially Thomas Chamberlain of St. Thomas-the-Martyr in Oxford. She persuaded her parents to move to Oxford, and lived there half a century. St. Thomas's church had had no resident incumbent since the Reformation; it lay in what was then a filthy slum, extending to the very gate of the richest Oxford college, Christ Church. Chamberlain instituted daily services, choral celebrations, and a society for the practice of Gregorian music. He founded a little series of books called "The Englishman's Library," in which the Tractarian stories of Gresley and Paget were published. Cardinal Wiseman on his return to England would emulate them in "The Catholic Popular Library," in which his *Fabiola* and Newman's *Callista* would make their first appearance. But Chamberlain did not confine his reforms to ritualism and publishing: he embarked on "incessant parochial visiting" (of the kind so neglected by the "High and Dry" clergymen in *Father Oswald* or *The Experience of Life*), and he established a sisterhood of the kind that Sarah Mortimer had so longed for in *The Experience* and that Guy Morville had supported in *The Heir of Redclyffe*. Rigorous in his self-discipline and in the discipline he urged upon his followers, Chamberlain overcame his initial unpopularity by his self-sacrificing zeal in a cholera and smallpox epidemic. When the poor saw him daily risk his life by nursing and comforting the sick, they were ready to acknowledge him as a friend.

Miss Skene had published her first novel, *Use and Abuse* (1849, no. 28), before she moved to Oxford. It is a wild combination of devout Tractarianism with the stage effects of *The Mysteries of Udolpho* school, with a bit of Ottoman reminiscence thrown in for good measure. No matter how she disciplined herself, Miss Skene could never discipline her prose or her imagination, and she never lost her addiction to scenes of horror. After 1850, she threw herself into the work of Chamberlain's sisterhood, but never became a Sister herself, retaining her freedom to act and write under her own direction and even ceasing to go to confession. In *St. Albans; or, The Prisoners of Hope* (1853, NIS) she drew an admiring portrait of Chamberlain; she labored heroically among the poor in a new cholera epidemic; she helped train nurses to go out into the Crimea (but her parents forbade her to go herself, although she was by then in her early thirties). After they had died and she lived alone, she never locked her door at night, so that anyone who wanted her help might walk in and claim it. The young Mary Arnold—later Mrs. Humphry Ward and a famous novelist (see below for discussions of *Robert Elsmere*, 1888, no. 82, and *Helbeck of Bannisdale*, 1898, no. 19)—remembered Miss Skene in the Oxford of her own youth as "a saint of goodness, humility, tenderness," even though they had already begun to differ on religious matters. Mrs. Ward read Miss Skene's novel *Hidden Depths* (1866, no. 28), but as a young woman, she recalled, she "could understand, of course, very little of what such a subject meant." Of course not: the subject was prostitution, and Miss Skene dealt with it frankly, though without prurience. Despite its many faults, it is an extraordinary Victorian novel.

In her work among the Oxford poor, Miss Skene naturally saw many prostitutes; she came to learn how brothels were run, how girls were ruined, what were the possibilities of rescue and rehabilitation in a society that regarded fallen women as irretrievable derelicts, and how to get a girl out of jail (gaol) and into a penitentiary, a very different kind of institution literally intended as a house for repentance, where the rules, however, were usually harsh and the restrictions on liberty almost as great as in a prison. All this she put into *Hidden Depths*, in which Ernestine Courtenay, a brave young woman of good family, undertakes to find and rescue from prostitution the surviving sister of a girl her brother had seduced and driven to suicide. The search takes Ernestine to "Greyburgh," which is Oxford, and to a meeting with the High-Church clergyman, Mr. Thorold, who is another portrait of Chamberlain.

The novel hammers away effectively at the immoral double standard that condemns to perdition the woman who has illicit sexual relations but allows her seducer to escape scot-free, even though he may have added every sort of cruelty to his initial deception. It also reveals all the sordid details of prostitution as a business. There are few more horrifying characters in fiction than the lying bawd who murders the children of the helpless inmates of her brothel, in one case by locking them in a room and burning them alive in a straw mattress. Miss Skene was not imagining this episode: the actual perpetrator of the crime was tried at Oxford for it but was acquitted because she had taken care to provide herself with an alibi.

Miss Skene's Tractarian views are found not only in her depiction of Thorold but also in many other aspects of the novel. Dr. Granby, the Rector of St. Gregory's, of whom Ernestine makes an inquiry while searching for the lost prostitute, Annie Brook, declares that he could not possibly help: he knows only "respectable characters," seeks out the "lost and erring" only "within proper limits . . . where there is not risk of my sacred person—I mean, my sacred office—being treated with irreverence." He literally shrieks with horror at the thought that Annie might be brought into his house to talk with Ernestine, and tells Ernestine that she "should properly be supposed to be ignorant" of the very existence of such a person and "all her class." No doubt prostitutes have souls, but why should Ernestine "interfere with their damnation—I mean with their salvation?" Not wishing to be thought uncharitable, Granby reports that his own daughters do "works of charity, piety, and necessity. My sweet Louisa visits the infant-school once a week, and it is most cheering to see how she has taught the innocent little ones to clap their hands in unison." As she leaves his house, Ernestine scornfully reflects that Granby is the "representative of Him who came to seek and save the lost." Mr. Thorold, who is "always among thieves . . . at it night and day in the most blackguard places in the town . . . never gives any one up, be they ever so bad," is her sort of clergyman.

The friendly gaoler calls Thorold a "trump, none of your stuck-up parsons," and tells Ernestine about the time when Thorold insisted on being locked in the punishment cell ("Black hole") of the prison with a hardened, infuriated assassin, and reduced the ungovernable man to tears of repentance in an hour. By contrast to Thorold, Miss Skene includes not only the pompous, heartless Granby, but the deeply intellectual Vincent, an Oxford don. Vincent has been the teacher of Ernestine's younger brother, Reginald, still an undergraduate, now mortally ill of consumption but unable to die in peace because of deep spiritual malaise. This proves to be Vincent's fault: a year earlier, already knowing he was sure to die soon, Reginald had happily decided to spend his remaining months in studying divinity, full of faith in an everlasting life and in all the principles of the Church of England. But Vincent—in a wish to help Reginald—had "enforced upon me strongly what he considered the duty, as well as the privilege of 'free inquiry' as to matters of faith. He said it was unworthy of the reason with which God had endowed us, that we should rest in . . . the hereditary belief we derived from our parents . . . without testing its truth for ourselves." These and other "casual expressions of Vincent" led Reginald to wonder if his faith were right; so he had put himself under Vincent's tutelage, and within a few months "his work was done; the blackness of darkness had fallen over my soul. . . ." Doubt had triumphed.

Vincent himself, Reginald assures Ernestine, never "in so many words" questions the "great Truths" of Christianity, but he does "cast more than doubt on the means whereby they are revealed to us; and, by denying certain facts," undermines the entire system. Vincent is, then, a Biblical critic, questioning the traditional historical views of revelation. "Traditionary belief," as he calls it, he regards as "the undeveloped conclusions of the world in its infancy." With progress, more and more of it is sloughed off. Where Vincent has been able to stop short of infidelity, Reginald has not. All of Vincent's teaching has seemed to lead towards a denial of the Incarnation ("the one glorious doctrine on which the whole of Christianity hinges") and has deprived him forever of Christ and His love. The death Reginald had been welcoming now has come to seem sheer terror; he cannot face it. In his despair he had embarked upon a life of vice; so that if Christianity were true, he had ("by my wanton defilement") cut himself off from salvation forever.

Not only does Ernestine attack the well-intentioned but destructive Vincent ("You cut away the old foundations from beneath his feet, and opened the way to dangerous speculations") for having damned her brother (though unintentionally); she also instructs him that "the reason the Creator" gave to men is *not* their guide: "Whoso will do the will of my Father which is in heaven, he shall know of the doctrine, whether it be of God." In short, personal holiness alone can teach one the truth. Why do men like Vincent "tamper with the faith of others? . . . Your own life is given you as a prey, but the souls of others are in the hands of God." Ernestine reduces Vincent to abject contrition, comforts Reginald by proclaiming that the evidence of her soul alone has given its foundation to her own faith, *without* intellectual inquiry, and pushes aside science and logic, in the face of the obvious "perfection, the unearthly loveliness" of Christ's life and character. At the end, it is Thorold who performs the last rites for Reginald and gives him absolution.

So Miss Skene shares the anti-intellectual preconceptions common among the Tractarians: just as Miss Yonge always distrusted the merely clever or learned (like Philip or Rachel), and just as Miss Sewell's motto is "pray, don't think," so Miss Skene attacks the arrogance and dangers of exalting free inquiry. Ernestine Courtenay's much-loved fiancé, Hugh Lingard, has also been led into laxity in a similar way: like many thousands of his contemporaries "who are clever without being deep thinkers," he has let "the foundations of the old faith, to which . . . he had given a superficial assent" become obscured. But instead of exercising his free inquiry, like Reginald, he has simply decided that "it was vain to seek the truth amongst so many conflicting theories and contradictory opinions, and that there was nothing to be done but to make the best of life in its visible aspect, and leave the problem of the grave to be solved by that sure death which alone had the key to it." So Lingard is a comfortable sceptic, while Reginald is a tortured sceptic. Deep in his soul, Lingard knows how superficial and unprincipled he is being. It is of course astonishing that the devout Ernestine should be in love with such a man; but Miss Skene does not seem to have worried about the improbability of it. Indeed, it is necessary for her plot: on the deathbed of the poor abandoned prostitute Annie, whom Ernestine has saved, Lingard enters the room, and Annie recognizes him at once as the seducer who had started her—as a child of sixteen—on her downward path. Of course all thought of an engagement between Ernestine and so wicked a man must be abandoned.

Thus the doubters in the novel suffer various degrees of punishment, and yet the hardest punishment is reserved for Ernestine, whom the Lord loveth. Miss Skene's criticism of the social institutions that deal with criminals and prostitutes is unsparing and loaded with ironies. She had herself seen the things she reports; *Hidden Depths* is a documentary novel revealing aspects of Victorian life ordinarily untouched by the novelist. Besides Miss Skene, only James Anthony Froude, of the novelists here selected, touches briefly and knowledgeably on the subject in his short story "The Lieutenant's Daughter" (in his *Shadows of the Clouds*, 1847, no. 68), discussed below. The conditions in a workhouse in which Annie has been found mortally ill are horrible beyond description, and the chaplain has not visited her: "He'll see her in his regular rounds; and her turn ain't likely to come for a week or two yet," by which time she is sure to have died without him. Miss Skene quotes the actual answer recently made by a bishop to a prison chaplain who had asked him to confirm a murderer awaiting immediate execution: "His Lordship would make his biennial confirmation tour in the course of a year and a half, and would be happy then to receive any candidates who might be presented to him." Too little, too late, and too sordid: this is the church's smug response to the grimy Victorian underworld of prostitutes and criminals to which Miss Skene, who knew it at first hand, introduces us.

Mrs. Oliphant: An Outsider's View

Contemporaneously with Miss Skene's *Hidden Depths* in the sixties, there were appearing in rapid order a series of novels called "The Chronicles of Carlingford," by Margaret Oliphant Wilson Oliphant (1828-1897), one of the most prolific of all the prolific nineteenth-century novelists. Almost from girlhood, she led a life punctuated by domestic tragedies, and she never attained financial security or enjoyed a long period of happiness. The pressures upon her would have turned a lesser artist into a hack. But Mrs. Oliphant never became a hack; her novels were always readable, and at intervals she produced fiction worth reviving. The Carlingford series as a whole probably embodies her best and most sustained work. All five novels are here reprinted. Two (*Salem Chapel*, 1863, no. 58, and its sequel, *Phoebe Junior: A Last Chronicle of Carlingford*, 1876, no. 92) deal chiefly with Dissenters and are discussed below.

The series as a whole, as well as the title of its fifth and last member, was obviously inspired by Anthony Trollope's six Barsetshire novels, which appeared between 1854 (*The Warden*, NIS) and 1867 (*The Last Chronicle of Barset*, NIS). Mrs. Oliphant's efforts are Trollopian, to the extent that they also deal in intimate detail with the lives of a large group of people from varying social classes who are connected with one another sometimes only by proximity. But Trollope painted on a wider canvas, his novels presenting an unforgettable picture not only of the clergy of the county, from the bishop in his palace to the most underpaid curate struggling to make ends meet, and from High Church to Low, but also of the county gentry, like the Greshams of Greshamsbury, the Dales of Allingham, and the Courcys of Courcy Castle. In Mrs. Oliphant's novels, this class is hardly represented at all; she did not know or understand them and their interests as Trollope did, and she confined herself largely to the townspeople of Carlingford itself, although an occasional county family on visiting terms in the town makes its appearance. If she does not reach as high as Trollope into the Victorian social hierarchy, she does reach lower, giving her reader a view of the lives of shopkeepers and other members of the lower middle class in a way that Trollope never attempted. In *Phoebe Junior* alone, Mrs. Oliphant directly borrowed Trollopian themes: that of an old established Church of England sinecure like Hiram's Hospital in *The Warden*, and that of a clergyman in deep financial difficulties because of a check, like Mr. Crawley in *The Last Chronicle of Barset*. But her series is, as the name implies, a series of novels of a small town, not of a county.

Forced to write in haste, Mrs. Oliphant was careless at times about chronology and between novels sometimes forgot the exact names of her characters. The Reverend Mr. Wentworth, Perpetual

Curate of St. Roque's, who is the hero of *The Perpetual Curate* (1864, no. 90) is "Frank" in that novel: he had been "Cecil" in *The Rector* (1863, no. 89). But she conveys with skill the sense of the passage of time and of the importance of the religious views of a given incumbent. The first Rector of Carlingford is the Evangelical Mr. Bury, "low—profoundly low—lost in the deepest abyss of Evangelicalism," so successful that he had "half emptied" the Dissenters' meeting house, Salem Chapel. But as he attracted the Dissenters, he drove away his own High-Church communicants, and he had also "half filled" St. Roque's, where Mr. Wentworth, "young, handsome, and fervid," was "at the topmost pinnacle of Anglicanism."

Mr. Bury—whom we come to know well in the fourth novel of the series but the earliest in point of time, *Miss Marjoribanks* (1866, no. 91)—regularly takes tea with the Dissenting minister; his sister feels that there is "something soul-degrading and dishonouring to religion in all the mummeries of Popery." She violently objects when a young barrister, talking about the forthcoming execution of a murderer, declares that there will soon be one party that will try to "prove that a man so kind-hearted never existed outside of paradise, and . . . another that will prove him to be insane," but that most of the spectators will be amused at the hanging. "Sir," said Miss Bury, "when you speak of amusement does it ever occur to you what will become of his miserable soul?" And then the poor overwitty fellow destroys himself by saying, "wretches of that description have no soul." Outraged, Miss Bury declares that she has heard of murderers "coming to a heavenly frame of mind, and giving every evidence of being truly converted," and thus experiencing the decisive moment in the life of an Evangelical Christian, for whom such a "conversion" was necessary for salvation.

But after Mr. Bury, the next Rector, Mr. Proctor, is an Oxford don, who has never held a living. Mr. Proctor is cleverly inscrutable: "What his 'views' were, nobody could divine. . . . He made no innovations . . . but he did not pursue Mr. Bury's Evangelical ways, and never preached a sermon or said a word more than was absolutely necessary." He will not even discuss "the progress of Dissent," on the one hand, or comment on "all that lovely 'Romish' upholstery," with which the Tractarian Mr. Wentworth was decorating St. Roque's, on the other hand. "He was neither High nor Low, enlightened or narrow-minded; he was a Fellow of All Souls." A timid bachelor who loves his mother, the scholarly Mr. Proctor fears that he may be captured and married by one of his parishioners and finds that he cannot "give comfort to the dying poor." He soon resigns and is succeeded by another Fellow of All Souls, who has been waiting for a decade for a living so that he may marry. It is here that Mrs. Oliphant's Tractarian novel, *The Perpetual Curate* (1864, no. 90), third in her series, begins. As for Carlingford itself, it has "no trade, no manufacture, no anything in particular except very pleasant parties and a superior class of people," who have very little to do. The center of life is the clergy, "the administrators of the commonwealth, the only people who have defined and compulsory duties to give a sharp outline to life . . . in a leisurely and unoccupied community."

Mrs. Oliphant—who was herself a Scotch Presbyterian by birth, but worshipped in the Church of England all her mature life—took no sides in the internal Anglican controversies. Indeed, in 1862 she published a two-volume life of Edward Irving (1792-1834), the Presbyterian-born founder of the "Catholic Apostolic Church," which we have seen Newman ridiculing—along with other fringe groups—in *Loss and Gain.* Mrs. Oliphant, though by no means an Irvingite, deeply sympathized with Irving, whose home village presbytery in Annan, Scotland, expelled him from the Presbyterian Church the year before he died. So Mrs. Oliphant took a detached view of the factions in the Church of England and gave them fair play in *The Perpetual Curate.*

Frank Wentworth, young, handsome, well born but with no money of his own, is "as near Rome as a strong and lofty conviction of the really superior catholicity of the Anglican Church would permit him to be." His chapel of St. Roque is a recent building "by Gilbert Scott [1811-1878]," one of the leading architects of the Gothic revival, in contrast to Carlingford church, an eighteenth-century structure "of the churchwarden period of architecture . . . high pews and stifling galleries" and a three-storied pulpit with reading desk and clerk's desk beneath. Wentworth has launched a sisterhood whose members wear gray cloaks, and has taken over as his own the poverty-stricken Wharfside district of

Carlingford, where he has founded a school and consecrated a chapel. He is the only cleric in Carlingford who cares about the poor.

On Easter, at St. Roque's, the "carved oaken cross of the reredos was wreathed tenderly with white fragrant festoons of spring lilies." There are two lines of choristers in white surplices. But Frank's sermon is a mere collection of "choice little sentiments of the beneficence of the Church in appointing such a feast, and of all the beautiful arrangements she had made for the keeping of it." There is nothing about the true significance of the Resurrection. Here Mrs. Oliphant permitted herself a mocking dig at the frequent prissy reluctance of the High Anglican to preach on anything save externals. Yet Frank's sermon in Wharfside that same Easter tells the slum congregation "about the empty grave of Christ, and how He called the weeping woman by her name, and showed her the earnest of the end of all sorrows. There were some people who cried, thinking of the dead who were still waiting for Easter, which was more than anybody did when Mr. Wentworth discoursed upon the beautiful institutions of the Church's year."

Frank Wentworth has three maiden aunts, sisters, who are dedicated Evangelicals and who have at their disposal a family living which they would like to confer on him, if only it were not for his opinions. Led by the formidable Aunt Leonora, they move to Carlingford for a long stay to check up on his activities. They totally disapprove of the candles on the altar and of the sisterhood. Roman Catholicism, says Aunt Leonora, "is a slavish system and a false system, and leads to Antichrist at the end, and nothing less." To her "the church is a missionary institution. Unless you are bringing in the perishing, and saving souls, what is the good?" Yet in Wharfside, Frank *is* "bringing in the perishing" and Aunt Leonora approves, at least until she finds in his chapel a pocket à Kempis, out of which drops "a little German print . . . the meek face of a monkish saint, inscribed with some villainous Latin inscription . . . which began with the terrible words *Ora pro nobis*." If Frank is "preaching the rubric and diffusing Tractarianism" among the poor, he is wicked; only if he is "carrying the real Gospel to the people" is his effort worthy. "Good works," says Aunt Leonora, "may be beautiful sins, if they are not done in a true spirit"—a thoroughly Evangelical opinion, implying, of course, that "justification" is by faith alone.

As if his problems with his Evangelical relatives were not enough, Frank Wentworth must also fight a skirmish at the other end of the ecclesiastical battlefield. His elder half brother Gerald, an Anglican clergyman, married and the father of a good-sized family, is determined to become a Roman Catholic and a priest. Gerald's wife, Louisa, is almost insane with anxiety. Gerald has the Wentworth family living and is well known and liked in his parish. He could have become as High an Anglican as he pleased, moans Louisa: "He might have preached in six surplices if he had liked . . . who would have minded? And, as for confession and all that, I don't believe there is anybody in the world who had done any wrong that could have helped confessing to Gerald; he is so good. . . . And then he goes on talking about subscription and signing articles and nonsense till he makes my head swim. Nobody . . . wants Gerald to subscribe or sign articles. I am sure I would subscribe any amount . . . a thousand pounds if I had it, Frank, only to make him hear reason." But reason is just what Gerald is not prepared to hear. He keeps referring to Louisa "and her children," not noticing that they are his children too.

When Frank urges that Gerald go ahead and be converted to Catholicism, but content himself to remain a layman and not force the issue of the priesthood, Gerald insists, "I am a priest or nothing. I can't relinquish my life." Of course the problem is wholly artificial. Frank all along knows—and Gerald should have known—that the Roman Church will not accept a married man with children as a convert and then allow him to repudiate his wife, without her consent, in order to become a priest. Frank reassures Louisa, "The Church of Rome does not go in the face of nature. She will not take him from you." Squire Wentworth, father of Gerald and Frank, makes a furious speech against Rome, "Instead of an easy-going Bishop and friendly fellows for brother clergymen, and parishioners that think everything that's good of you, how do you suppose you'll feel as an Englishman when you get into a dead Frenchified system, with everything going by rule and measure and bound to believe just as you're told? It'll kill you."

The issues that we have so often seen as tragedy through the eyes of those directly involved in the struggle, Mrs. Oliphant turns into the comedy that they so readily become when coolly observed by an outsider. She wrote above all for money and the critical recognition that would bring it. The fact that she devoted so large a portion of the Carlingford novels to the clergy and their problems in itself provides valuable evidence that the English reading public took an enormous interest in such matters and had an infinite eagerness for variations on familiar themes. The series was by far the most successful of her literary efforts over a lifetime of steady writing. She was paid £1,500 for *The Perpetual Curate*, the highest price she ever received. Her Scotch publisher and friend, John Blackwood, was disquieted by an installment of the novel that seemed to indicate that Gerald Wentworth would actually succeed in jettisoning Louisa and her five children, with another on the way. Not at all, Mrs. Oliphant reassured him: she had been in touch with a Roman Catholic cardinal, and he had told her that the Church would not act without the wife's consent. She does not ignore the human anguish involved in Gerald's eventual abandonment of his Anglican orders to become a mere Catholic layman, but her histrionics can never be taken as seriously as those of writers who were themselves under the tension about which they wrote.

A Prime Minister Speaks Out

In 1870 there appeared, with great publicity and excitement in the world of fashion, the first novel ever written by an ex-Prime Minister of England: Benjamin Disraeli's *Lothair* (no. 32). He had written eight earlier novels, it is true, but none since *Tancred* in 1847. Out of office since December 1868, and with more leisure than at any time in the past twenty-odd years, Disraeli turned to the burning questions of the day: the continental revolution, notably in Italy, now closing in on Rome itself, and its great enemy, the Roman Catholic Church, growing ever more influential in England, notably among the very highest aristocracy. No doubt the recent conversion to Rome of the enormously rich young Marquis of Bute gave Disraeli part of his theme. But as a converted Jew, he had always been deeply interested in the Christian churches, and much drawn to the Roman as the most venerable and gorgeous among them.

As early as *The Young Duke* (1831, NIS), Disraeli had sided with his fictional Duke's Catholic guardian on the question of Catholic Emancipation, and against the firm anti-Catholicism of the Duke's uncle. In *Contarini Fleming* (1832, NIS), whose hero is an admiring self-portrait, the impressionable young Contarini spontaneously falls to his knees and declares himself a Catholic because of the overpowering beauty of the church, the pictures, the music, and the mass. But Contarini is only temporarily experimenting with Catholicism, and immediately thereafter begins to experiment with secret revolutionary societies and other anti-Catholic groups. Disraeli was still only twenty-eight, a new arrival on the social scene in London, a *poseur* and a dandy; the "conversion" of Contarini was only a play to the gallery. *Henrietta Temple* (1836, NIS) includes a member of the old Catholic aristocracy whose tutor had been educated by the Jesuits; the author is friendly to both. In *Venetia* (1837, NIS), Disraeli ridicules a violent anti-Papist squire; in *Coningsby* (1844, NIS), he contrasts the strong social conscience of a Catholic landowner with the hard-hearted Anglicans' willingness to leave the poor to the tender mercies of the Poor Law. In *Sybil* (1845, NIS), a Tractarian clergyman is idealized, while Sybil, the Catholic heroine, has been called "a glowing idealization of the England of Catholic days." In *Tancred* (1847, NIS), Disraeli makes it clearer than heretofore that his pro-Catholic views were only a part of his overriding pro-Jewish views: after all, the Church of Rome "was founded by a Hebrew, and the magnetic influence still lingers."

So in the novels of his earlier years, Disraeli had shown himself friendly towards the Catholics. But the anti-Popery of 1850 made him see that this position, hitherto politically safe—and indeed part of the mythology of "Young England," the group whose ideology Disraeli had strongly favored—was now politically dangerous. He wrote no more novels until *Lothair*. By 1870 he had further cause for showing the Roman Church in an unfavorable light. In 1868 his ministry was shaken by the failure of a plan he was hatching to use government money to endow both the Roman Catholic and the

Presbyterian Churches in Ireland as well as the already established Anglican Church, and to found a Catholic University in Dublin. Disraeli had thought he had the support of Henry Manning, who had succeeded Wiseman as Archbishop of Westminster in 1865. The plan failed because Gladstone torpedoed it by an unexpected speech in the House favoring the disestablishment of the Anglican Church of Ireland. But Manning, Disraeli believed, had misled him with regard to the Irish Catholic hierarchy's willingness to accept the idea of the new university. He did not forgive Manning, and portrayed him vindictively as Cardinal Grandison in *Lothair*. So by 1870 Disraeli—now the completely successful politician and man of the world—no longer believed in the possibility of realizing the idealistic goals that had enchanted him in the 1840's, and was ready to join the many novelists who had satirized the Catholics in fiction.

Everybody in *Lothair* is preposterously rich, and lives and entertains in surroundings of more than Babylonian luxury and splendor. "The Duke," who is so grand that he is not further named, owns so many splendid palaces scattered about England and Scotland in which he is obliged to live for portions of the year that—poor man—he has no real home, which is his only sorrow. Some contemporaries were quick to accuse Disraeli of a "Jewish taste for tawdry decoration." But in fact Disraeli was hardly exaggerating the external pomp and show displayed by the great nobles of his day, whose landed estates—always rich sources of revenue—had during the mid-century years of industrialization sometimes doubled or tripled in value. As a young man, Disraeli had hoped that the nobles of England might galvanize themselves into a new and generous active ruling class in alliance with the workers. These hopes had dissipated, and he now realistically saw the nobility as the often charming, glittering parasites that they had become. In *Lothair* he was satirizing them, but with such affection that they did not notice it. As James Anthony Froude put it in 1890, "Students of English history in the time to come, who would know what the nobles of England were like in the days of Queen Victoria will read *Lothair*." Baron Rothschild named a race horse after the Duke's daughter, Corisande, heroine of the novel, and the filly proceeded to win a major race. A popular song, a new perfume, a street, and a ship were all named for Lothair himself.

In addition to Cardinal Grandison (Manning), a "gliding" master of manipulation, *Lothair* contained some other recognizable portraits. The bishop is the friend of Manning's youth, Samuel Wilberforce, who had become Bishop of Winchester in 1869 after having been Bishop of Oxford for twenty-four years. The Oxford professor—a far less important character ("of advanced opinions on all subjects . . . clever, extremely well-informed, so far as books can make a man knowing, but unable to profit even by his limited experience of life from a restless vanity and overflowing conceit which prevented him from ever observing or thinking of anything but himself . . . a social parasite," who wants to "get rid of religion" at Oxford) was Goldwin Smith, once Regius Professor of History at Oxford, an old political enemy of Disraeli's who had migrated to Cornell, and who exploded in a furious letter to the newspapers when he recognized himself. Disraeli's words about him, said Goldwin Smith, were "the stingless insults of a coward." But this only amused Disraeli and helped the sales of *Lothair*.

In the struggle for Lothair's allegiance, three women take the lead: Lady Corisande, a staunch Anglican, for the Church of England; Miss Arundel, a devout Catholic, for the Church of Rome; and the "divine Theodora," married to an American, who is an ardent sympathizer with Garibaldi. Theodora wins the first round. Like Moreton in Dering's *Sherborne* (1875, no. 12), Lothair goes to Italy to fight, but on the antipapal, not the papal, side. Theodora is killed on the battlefield, and Lothair promises her before she dies that he will never become a Catholic. But he is badly wounded and loses his memory in part, so that when he comes to himself as a convalescent in the great Roman house of Miss Arundel's noble English family, he is in the hands of the *monsignori*. They have cooked up a story—which they do not tell Lothair—that he was actually wounded fighting on the other side, and that his rescue from the battlefield was by a miraculous intervention of the Virgin herself. Obviously he must now be converted. Having discovered the deception, however, Lothair escapes and returns to England, Corisande, and "the Church of his baptism."

There are moments of high comedy when Lothair turns peevish as he cannot understand why everybody in Rome hails him as "one of the most favoured of men" and as living proof that "His Church was never more clearly built upon a rock than at this moment": he has not yet been told about the miracle wrought for him. Before he can hear the news, Cardinal Grandison himself shows Lothair the sights of Rome, introducing him to the Cardinal Prefect of the Propaganda and his worldwide apparatus, explaining away the Inquisition as "wilfully and malignantly misrepresented," and its occasional ruthless conduct as limited only to Spain and the "Moorish and Jewish blood" that had poisoned the Spaniards. The papal hospitals, prisons, schools, are represented as the best in the world. The only reason for the papal troops is the threat from "the Secret Societies of Atheism." A special thanksgiving Mass is to be offered in a Jesuit church by Miss Arundel—at the express command of the Pope himself—for the divine mercy vouchsafed in saving Lothair's life: obviously he must attend it, as Grandison makes clear. And when he agrees—forty-eight hours before the ceremony that he will attend—the *monsignori* are jubilant. "It is done at last," says one, but Lothair must be watched every minute until the Mass takes place.

It is, of course, gorgeous beyond all description (except Disraeli's). When Lothair arrives at the church, "had this been a conclave, and Lothair the future Pope, it would have been impossible to have treated him with more consideration." Lothair finds himself literally pushed into the solemn procession—headed by a special banner of the Virgin. He is preceded by six veiled ladies "who were said to be daughters of the noblest houses of England," at the side of a seventh, Miss Arundel. The new banner of the Virgin, when hung over the altar, shows the Virgin addressing a nurse on a battlefield. And when the long service, "sustained by exquisite music, celestial perfumes, and the graceful movements of priests in resplendent dresses," comes to an end, many people outside the church beg for Lothair's blessing and kiss the hem of his garment. Those in the know predict that the entire English nobility will soon return to the Roman Church. The congratulations multiply. What, the reader—and the puzzled Lothair too—ask themselves, is going on here?

Not until he reads the next morning's newspapers does Lothair understand. With his face changing from pale to scarlet, and his heart palpitating, he is plunged into a cold sweat and is finally unable even to see. It appears that a beautiful woman had spoken to Miss Arundel and told her to seek out Lothair in his hospital: he "will not die if you go to him immediately and say you came in the name of the Virgin." Two priests who saw the woman had seen that she had a halo; she had then given flowers to two children and told them the flowers would never fade: and they had not faded. The Holy Office has scrupulously checked the evidence, and it is all perfectly clear: it was the Virgin herself who had intervened for Lothair, wounded in the papal cause, and that is why he is "the most favoured of living men." Lothair knows he fought for Garibaldi; he sees that he has been duped: "he thought he was leaning on angelic hearts, when he found himself in the embrace of spirits of another sphere." He is desperate, but he consoles himself that the Cardinal, who had not been in Rome during much of Lothair's stay there, cannot be involved in the deception. The Cardinal is "an English gentleman, with an English education, once an Anglican, a man of the world, a man of honour, a good, kind-hearted man."

But when Lothair tells the Cardinal that he feels "indignation . . . alarm . . . disgust" at what he has read in the newspaper, the Cardinal says it is all true, even when Lothair insists he was fighting for the other side. "I know," says Grandison-Manning, "that there are two narratives of your relations with the battle. . . . The one accepted as authentic is that which appears in this journal; the other . . . which can only be traced to yourself, bears no doubt a somewhat different character"; but, he adds, it is improbable and there is no evidence to support it! It is hallucination: Lothair must be weaned from it, abandon "the freaks of your own mind about personal incidents," and accept the opinion of society as to which side he was on. The story of the miracle has already been spread over the world. "You are in the centre of Christendom, where truth, and where alone truth resides. Divine authority has perused this paper and approved it. It is published for the joy and satisfaction of two hundred millions of Christians, and for the salvation of all those who unhappily for themselves are not yet converted to the faith. It records the most memorable event of this century." It is the first appearance of the Virgin at Rome. "Some of the most notorious atheists of Rome have already solicited to be admitted to the offices of the Church; the Secret Societies have received their death-blow; I look to the alienation of England as virtually over." Lothair will be the apostle who takes the lead in the work. And to begin with, the Pope himself will tomorrow receive him as a Catholic.

Froude, an early and most perceptive biographer of Disraeli, and himself a veteran of the religious conflicts of his youth, as we shall see from his novels (no. 68), declared that "nowhere in English fiction is there any passage where the satire is more delicate than the Cardinal's rejoinder." It is a superb piece of casuistry; gently the lie is proclaimed as truth, and the truth as a dream. *Lothair*, wrote Froude, "opens a window into Disraeli's mind, revealing the inner workings of it more completely than anything else which he wrote or said." Lothair feels that the impending crisis is the "darkest hour of his life." He is not a believing Catholic; he knows perfectly well which side he had fought on in the battle; he remembers his promise to Theodora on her deathbed. He will be "a renegade without conviction." He has been a victim of sorcery like a knight in a fairy tale, robbed of his "valour, and will and virtue" by "malignant influence." He sees the spirit of Theodora and faints. The doctor orders him out of Rome. The Catholic plot has failed. The rest of the novel, though always entertaining and often brilliant, is anticlimactic. When Lothair apprehensively returns to London, he finds that he has hardly been missed, and the Cardinal, as outwardly kind as ever, is now full of the Ecumenical Council being planned to declare the infallibility of the Pope in matters of faith and morals.

While Disraeli's biographers have always rated *Lothair* very highly, at the time of its appearance the critics were mostly scornful; Disraeli had dismissed them in advance in the text as "men who have failed in literature and art." "A feeling of stage properties," said Trollope, "a smell of hair-oil, an aspect of buhl, a remembrance of tailors, and that pricking of the conscience which must be the general accompaniment of paste diamonds." Henry James, still only in his mid-twenties, reviewing *Lothair* anonymously in the *Atlantic Monthly*, chided the English reviewers for political bias against the author, and redressed the balance by treating the book without reference to Disraeli's politics. He found it amusing, but could not take it seriously: it was clever, but it lacked all "honest wisdom" and was full of "deplorable levity." Of Lothair himself, James remarked that "one can hardly say that he is weak, for to be weak you must begin by being," a wicked dig but not unjustified: Lothair is a stick. To Henry James, Disraeli's "anti-Romish enthusiasm is thoroughly cold and mechanical. Essentially light and superficial throughout, the author is never more so than when he is serious and profound. . . . His ecclesiastics are lay figures,—his Scarlet woman is dressed out terribly in the table-cloth, and holds in her hands the drawing-room candle-sticks. . . . Lothair. . . . will make no Cardinal's ears tingle." Disraeli's "almost infantine joy in being one of the initiated among the dukes" is only one case of "the frequent betrayal of the . . . innocence of one who has been supposed to be nothing if not knowing."

James's literary judgment is witty and mature. But, one must point out, it *is* only literary. James, I think, was quite wrong, for example, about the tingling of the Cardinal's ears. He hardly appreciated the impact upon the Catholics of such an onslaught as *Lothair* written by such a man as Disraeli, who would, indeed, become Prime Minister for the second time only four years after the book was published. Contrasting strongly as it does with his earlier attitude towards them, it notified them that they had turned a most important friend into a self-proclaimed enemy. It put Disraeli firmly on the side of Charles Kingsley in the bitter controversy with Newman over the attitude of Catholics toward the truth, which had led in 1864 to Newman's *Apologia pro vita sua.* Whatever its shortcomings as fiction (and perhaps they are not as great as James imagined), *Lothair* is a major document in the nineteenth-century religious wars.[2] And if one feels the need to laugh at it, rather than with it, Bret Harte's brilliant brief parody, here reprinted at the end of the third volume, will puncture Disraeli's pomposities more effectively, perhaps, than James's counter-pomposities.

2. We should note that, in his last novel, *Endymion* (1880, NIS), largely written by 1878, Disraeli included another and far gentler portrait of Manning as Nigel Penruddock, Archbishop of Tyre: in the interim, Manning had had a quarrel with Gladstone and had pleased Disraeli by denouncing Gladstone to him.

Enter the Aesthetes: Inglesant and Marius

Early in 1880, a rich Birmingham chemical manufacturer of reclusive habits, Joseph Henry Shorthouse, took to a printer the manuscript of an historical romance which he had completed some four years earlier after a decade of private reading, reflection, and writing. Shorthouse ordered one hundred copies of the long novel, and in July he received them, beautifully printed and bound in heavy white vellum lettered in red. He gave them away to friends, except for twenty-five copies that were sold to the public. After two newspapers had reviewed the book favorably, one or two enthusiastic friends urged Shorthouse to give it to a commercial publisher, who rejected it, not in the least disturbing the author. But a friend who had liked the novel loaned his copy to Mrs. Humphry Ward, who thought it so remarkable that she took it along on a visit to the publisher Alexander Macmillan. And Macmillan, like Shorthouse a great devotee of Plato, was so impressed that he wrote begging to be allowed to publish it. Shorthouse consented, on condition that no changes whatever be made in his text, and about eighteen months after Shorthouse had first decided to take the manuscript out of a desk drawer, *John Inglesant* (1880, no. 33) reached the general public at last.

The firm that had rejected it—Smith and Elder—must have regretted their folly. Mr. Gladstone, then Prime Minister for the second time, praised it and was photographed holding a copy. He invited Shorthouse to visit him in Downing Street. *John Inglesant* was naturally pleasing to High Anglicans. It also deeply impressed Major Maurice, son of the leading "Broad Churchman," Frederick Denison Maurice, whom Shorthouse had long admired. The major was then engaged in writing his *Memoir* of his father, and begged Shorthouse to review it when it appeared. Thomas Henry Huxley, the noted agnostic, spoke enthusiastically of *Inglesant*'s "rare delicacy" and—in a phrase to be savored—remarked that although he could not agree with the deeply pious, mystical Anglicans of Shorthouse's novel, "God knows how I admire and appreciate them." The book was the wonder of the London social season, and so much monopolized conversation that some invitations to dinner went out with the proviso that it must not be discussed. And it made its way year after year with the general public in England and America, deep into the twentieth century. Only Lord Acton complained about its historical inaccuracy; but his criticism—several long pages—was confined to a personal letter and was not published for many years.

Born in 1834 to a Quaker family, Shorthouse was not converted to the Church of England until 1861: he left no account of the intellectual and spiritual processes through which he passed before reaching his decision, but it seems likely that they were as protracted and as exhausting as those of many of the characters in the novels we have been considering. The anxiety weakened his health, always delicate. His baptism into the Anglican Church, we know, made him feel "transformed into a different man." When asked by an admirer how long *John Inglesant* had been in his mind, Shorthouse responded, "I don't think I can remember the time when it was not." Though he wrote several shorter novels after *Inglesant*'s success, none is remotely comparable in interest. *John Inglesant* sums up—in the form of a romance—the growing convictions of a mature and devout life.

Yet these convictions are by no means obvious to readers of the novel. At the time of its appearance, the religious controversy between High and Low was quite undiminished in its intensity; in 1865, the Evangelical "Church Association" appropriated £50,000 at a single meeting to "put down" Ritualism by financing legal action against its practitioners, and so won the name "Persecution Company Ltd." But even with the vocabulary of High and Low opponents thoroughly familiar to the general public, Shorthouse found, to his dismay, that his own position was not often recognized for what it was. "I have been called Romanist, Agnostic—anything you please," he complained, "but few have deduced English Churchmanship from my book." As between High and Low, Shorthouse was a "strong Sacramentalist," as one can see by his comment on his own baptism. Brought up as he was in a loving Quaker household, and remaining a Quaker until the age of twenty-seven, he retained all his life deep traces of his Quaker training and environment: moderation, a distaste for excess, and a sensitive discrimination. Moreover, the Quaker practice of listening for the voice of divine inspiration remained with him: what Shorthouse himself called, after his conversion, "the indwelling of the Divine Word." He broadened his views, however, after conversion, no longer listening to his heart alone, or only to the voice that warned against the vanities of the world, but listening also to the voices of nature, of the arts, of cultivated sensibility, of beauty generally.

In 1871, Shorthouse wrote a remarkable letter to Matthew Arnold: taking Arnold's contrasted pairs—Hellenism versus Hebraism, Literature versus Dogma—he added a third, Revelation and Humor. These he did not oppose to one another, but rather called for a synthesis between them. "The effort of the divine principle to enter human life," Shorthouse wrote, was in effect the entire history of the world; but the contrast between our "sacramental hours" and our daily life had become so "appalling" as to strain the very fabric of love for Christ. Only in *Don Quixote* had Shorthouse found "a representation" of these efforts of the divine principle to reach humanity, couched humorously, but in the "very highest sense" in which the word "humour" could be conceived. But in Cervantes' novel the principle failed. Don Quixote acknowledged his madness; his life had been a mistake. It now remained for Matthew Arnold, Shorthouse urged, to "*point out the possibilities* of . . . a synthesis of Revelation and Humour," so that men's daily lives might be reconciled with faith. He called Arnold "such a disciple of Christ as I fancy Plato would have been could he have known Him." And indeed, together with Quakerism, Plato—whom Shorthouse read again and again, and about whom he wrote several essays—constantly informed Shorthouse's thinking and writing. Plato's influence too will be found in *John Inglesant.*

Almost as hostile to Romanism as the Evangelicals, as little interested in dogma as the Broad Churchmen (in one of his essays he urged complete tolerance and an affectionate welcome for any agnostic who came to church only for the beauty of the services), Shorthouse was a most peculiar specimen of High Anglican. His sacramentalism, his "Churchmanship," his emphasis on individual holiness and on the Inner Voice rather than on good works or social activity among the poor, his Quaker mysticism, his Platonic identification of the Divine Intellect with the God in whose image mankind was made, blended together in his life and in his major novel to make an amalgam not exactly paralleled elsewhere. On the one hand, Shorthouse's charming villa at Edgbaston near Birmingham lay only a few yards from the Oratory where Newman was living all during the years when the novel was written; there was much in Shorthouse's mysticism that is reminiscent of Newman. On the other, Shorthouse both shows and openly argues in *John Inglesant* that the submission of private judgment to authority required by the Catholic Church is unacceptable. Anglican "freedom and reason" must in the end be preferred to Catholic "obedience and faith." And Catholic sacerdotalism and the interposition of the confessional and penance between the worshipper and the supernatural must be repudiated.

Freighted with these convictions, Shorthouse steeped himself in the writings of the seventeenth century, deliberately choosing as his setting the period he felt to be most like the nineteenth in the intensity of its religious struggles and the complexity of its political life. Into his text he wove long passages, sometimes using them word for word, from seventeenth-century diaries, histories, travel books, philosophical treatises, and other literary sources. Burton's *Anatomy of Melancholy*, Evelyn's *Diaries*, Hobbes's *Leviathan*, Aubrey's *Brief Lives*, are only a few of the best-known works of the period that Shorthouse deliberately pillaged. Yet such was the skill with which he used the passages and so authentically seventeenth-century in style did he learn to make his own felicitous prose, that for forty-five years after *John Inglesant* was published, nobody called attention to this wholesale plagiarism. And when, in 1925, the first real study of Shorthouse's sources did appear and the extent of his dependence on other men's writings was for the first time revealed, even the author of the study obviously felt that Shorthouse's practice had not in any important way damaged his novel. He was not producing a Ph.D. thesis or a work that masqueraded as scholarship—although it was scholarly enough in all conscience—but a novel in which he was striving for verisimilitude, and this he certainly attained by his skillful mingling of seventeenth-century original writing with his own. If the style was altogether genuine, the history was not. For his own purpose, Shorthouse telescoped and recombined historical events, especially on the Continent, a thing which made Lord Acton grumpy but does not in the least affect the merits of the novel.

Everything about *John Inglesant* is subtle, beginning with the hero's name and the title of the book. "Inglesant" sounds like "English saint," and Shorthouse certainly intended his protagonist to resemble an English saint. When the aged Duke of Urbino, one of Inglesant's powerful friends on the Continent, is dying, he bestows on Inglesant a "suit of superb armour which had been made expressly" for his own son, who had died. When Inglesant puts it on, the duke declares that he "well represented the patron saint of his nation, St. George of England" and calls him "il Cavaliere di San Giorgio." The duke has already given him some landed property (a "fief") named after Saint George; so Inglesant is a knight of St. George in the literal sense of the term. Moreover, when he wears the armor ("the superb but useless and fantastic armour of the seventeenth century, with cuirass, greaves, and cuisses of polished and jewelled metal, worn over the ordinary dress, and combined with the lace and velvet which ornamented the whole"), he does "certainly resemble somewhat closely a splendid Renaissance St. George." The duke insists that Inglesant is to wear the armor when he "goes to meet his bride."

On his way to his marriage, Inglesant encounters in an Italian mountain pass his most desperate enemy, Malvolti, the murderer of his twin brother, who had made an earlier effort to assassinate Inglesant himself. With a strong escort, Inglesant has Malvolti completely at his mercy, and the man richly deserves to be killed outright, as all Inglesant's servants expect and recommend, and as any contemporary gentleman would have felt free to do. But Malvolti prays for mercy in the name of Christ and the Virgin, and Inglesant does not kill him, but instead takes him as a captive to a nearby mountain village church, where, after mass at which he partakes of the Sacrament, he turns him over to the priest: "I give him over to the Lord. I give up my sword into the Lord's hands, that He may work my vengeance upon him as it seems to Him good. Henceforth he is safe from earthly retribution, but the divine Powers are just."

Instructed by Inglesant, the simple country priest takes the sword and puts it on the altar. To the "child-like" priest to whom the saints and angels are as real as his peasant flock, it does not seem "strange that the blessed St. George himself, in jewelled armour, should stand before the altar in the mystic morning light, his shining sword in his hand." To Inglesant he says, "It is well done," and he begs Inglesant to intercede for him "when thou returnest to thy place and seest again the Lord Jesus." Inglesant does not realize that the priest thinks he is truly St. George; to us Shorthouse's meaning is clear enough. At this moment when he has so nobly foregone vengeance, his hero is truly saintly. Whereas Guy Morville could be no more than an image of Sir Galahad, Inglesant becomes the English saint *par excellence*, as his name had predicted.

Trapped in the nineteenth century, Guy Morville can only proclaim how loyally he would have fought for Charles I, if he had only had the chance. John Inglesant, however, actually does save the king, under circumstances that Guy Morville could hardly have understood and with results that would have made Guy very angry. From his earliest youth, Inglesant has been educated by a kind and learned Jesuit, who intends to use him as a special agent serving as intermediary between the Churches of Rome and England. Since any such plan would have been instantly aborted had Inglesant become a Catholic, Father Holt makes sure that he does not have a wholly Catholic education, but is steeped in Plato; and later—so that Inglesant's mind may be infused "with a large measure of rational inquiry"—he is introduced to Hobbes himself. Quoting his *Leviathan* (although it had not then yet been written!), Hobbes denounces the Roman Church, with the effect on Inglesant that the Jesuit had intended. Loyally carrying out Father Holt's instructions, Inglesant often feels that he is "the agent of a mighty will of a system which commands unhesitating obedience . . . which is part of my very being." He is drawn towards Rome at times.

Just before the outbreak of the Civil Wars, Inglesant, always in obedience to Father Holt's schemes, becomes an "Esquire of the Body" to Charles I. Among his many adventures, Inglesant is the only one aside from the king to see the dreadful apparition of Lord Strafford's ghost which comes to reproach Charles two nights after the execution. Where Guy Morville, with the Tractarian romanticism of 1853, could not bear to have Charles blamed for the execution because the king had repented it, Inglesant sees the ignominy of the entire episode. He also attends Laud on the scaffold. Sent by Charles on a secret mission to Ireland to negotiate with papal agents, Inglesant is arrested, and bravely lies about the royal origin of the mission. Imprisoned, interrogated by the parliamentary authorities, and condemned to death (John Milton alone quickly appreciates his double role), Inglesant is saved from execution only a few days after Charles himself has been beheaded. Although Charles is represented as remorseful for a new betrayal of a loyal agent (after Strafford and Laud), he does little about it: as a cynical Royalist puts it, "When did the King help any of his friends?" Shorthouse's Charles I is the genuine historical weakling; Charlotte Yonge's, the sentimentalized demi-saint of the Puseyite Victorians. Perhaps this was one of the reasons why many readers did not see at once how high an Anglican Shorthouse himself really was.

Some modern readers will find John Inglesant's personal elegance—always scrupulously dressed, always courteous, ever the British gentleman—hard to credit. Others will find his subservience to the Jesuit, whose faith he can never fully share, more and more unnatural. On the whole, Inglesant is passive, despite the tumultuous happenings through which he bravely moves and in which he plays a part. He is another Lothair, to whom every possible experience is happening, and one may echo Henry James's complaint about Lothair: "to be weak you must begin by being." But this is not an ordinary novel, to be judged by ordinary standards. Inglesant is a mystic, who has second sight, and experiences hallucinations and states of mind where things are unclear and disturbing: quite probably derived from Shorthouse's experiences as an epileptic. His own unbalance reflects the lack of balance in the seventeenth-century world, in which scenes of violence and bloodshed are punctuated with moments of heavenly peacefulness, as among the Anglicans of Little Gidding. Only after the Restoration of Charles II—when the convulsions of the previous years have ceased and quiet has settled over England—can the book end, with Inglesant devout, resigned, even cheerful, reported in a final episode by a new matter-of-fact narrator in a document to emphasize the change of pace.

Calvinism, Quietism, Astrology, Magic, all are given a sympathetic hearing. The more Protestant the outlook, the less can survive of the blessings of culture, all the beauty in the world that alone makes life worth living. The more Catholic the outlook, the more one has to abandon one's individual freedom. Only the Church of England has the *via media*, the happy medium. If Shorthouse reveals the influences upon him of Hawthorne and Thackeray, he yet wrote a novel very different from any of theirs. Paul Elmer More, the American High-Church Episcopalian, admired it extravagantly as "the nearest approach in English to a religious novel of universal significance" and "the one great religious novel of the English language." Margaret Maison—the Catholic—echoes the Catholic Lord Acton, finding the hero "drab . . . feeble, almost 'phoney,' " though his adventures are a "superb historical mosaic." One thing is clear: anyone interested in the Victorian novel of religion will want to read *John Inglesant.*

If Lothair and Inglesant seem to us inactive despite the battles and intrigues in which they engage, both are Lancelots or Rolands by the side of the endlessly introspective noble Roman youth who is the protagonist of *Marius the Epicurean* (1885, no. 34), by the celebrated critic and humanist, Walter Pater (1839-1894). Lothair marries Lady Corisande (or at least, having received the gift of a rose at her hands, he is expected to do so), and Inglesant twice falls deeply, if not altogether convincingly, in love, losing the first girl to an early death and marrying the second. But Marius only once even thinks—fleetingly—of marriage: to Cecilia, the Christian matron and widow. Discovering her household and its faith only after a long spiritual pilgrimage, the pagan Marius visits it again and again because of "the charm of its poetry, a poetry of the affections, wonderfully fresh in the midst of a threadbare world"; he finds a "range of intellectual pleasures, altogether new to him, in the sympathy of that pure and elevated soul" and, above all, the "sentiment of maternity." But if—Pater hastens on—"Marius thought at times that some long-cherished desires were now about to blossom for him, in the sort of home he had sometimes pictured to himself . . . that in this woman, to whom children naturally clung, he might find such a sister, at least, as he had always longed for," he instantly "reminded himself" that Christians might not marry a second time. He has also heard a rumor that even among married Christians there is no sexual intercourse ("They which have wives be as they which have none"). Where, one asks, did Marius think that all those many Christian children came from?

So Marius is rather like Newman's Agellius in *Callista,* who at least nerved himself up to a proposal, even though he was relieved when it was rejected and he could remind himself how overpowering are the responsibilities of marriage. But Marius is far more squeamish than Agellius: he knows he wants a mother or even a sister ("at least"), but he obviously does not want a wife, although he does not say so. Within a few pages of these reflections, we find Marius believing that Cecilia will marry his friend Cornelius; so the whole suggestion that Christians may not marry for a second time had been only a pretext for *not* proposing. Seeing Cecilia occupied with the funeral services for the child of one of her household, Marius reminds himself that whenever he has seen dead children or children's graves in his earlier life, it has marked "the failure of some lately-born hope or purpose of his own." Cecilia's expression makes Marius feel "that he too had had to-day his funeral of a little child," that is, the death of his hope of marriage.

But the sudden death—for these obscure reasons—of this alleged hope does not much affect Marius: he always has taken "flight from any too disturbing passion, from any sort of affection likely to quicken his pulses beyond the point at which the quiet work of life was practicable." There is "a certain disappointment at his heart, greater than he could have anticipated," and—it is autumn—"the mental atmosphere within himself" is "perceptibly colder." Like Newman's Charles Reding in *Loss and Gain,* who knew from his boyhood that he was marked out for celibacy, but with less apparent knowledge of himself, Marius is not a lover of women. Instead he has two absorbing friendships, each with a young man whose physical beauty is emphasized: Flavian, the somewhat older pleasure-loving pagan poet of Marius's student days at Pisa, who dies of the plague; and Cornelius, the Roman knight, who is a Christian—although Marius does not know this for a long time—and whose life Marius saves at the sacrifice of his own. Like Pater himself, Marius is "simply uninterested in the heterosexual experience," as a recent critic remarks. Marius is also obsessed by corpses and burials and death.

In discussing *Loss and Gain,* we had occasion to note the suggestion put forward by some that Newman was homosexual. In the context of Newman's life and achievement, it seemed to us, the truth of the suggestions made very little difference. Pater's case is different, however, because his attitude to religion, which particularly concerns us here, is bound up in a bundle of other attitudes all of which can easily be associated with his sexual preferences. Not until *The Way of All Flesh* (1903, no. 87), which Samuel Butler kept in his desk for a quarter of a century and which was not published until after he died, will we encounter a fully recognizable, aggressively homosexual ritualist parson, who tries vainly to seduce the protagonist, Ernest Pontifex. But we cannot doubt that the ritualists' emphasis on elegant vestments and splendid church fitments, on gold and silver and jewels and incense, together with their emphasis on celibacy, had a greater natural attraction for homosexuals than, let us say, strict Evangelical or Calvinist forms of worship. Pater, at any rate, was a man of homosexual leanings and, paradoxically, while he was not a fully believing Christian, by the time he wrote *Marius* he was once more a ritualist, as he had been in his boyhood.

In recent years, there has been a flood of Pater scholarship, some of it enormously helpful. As Pater's major piece of fiction, *Marius* has naturally undergone careful scholarly re-examination. Newman's direct influence on Pater, for example, not previously realized, has now been fully demonstrated.[3] Four times in *Marius*, Pater significantly uses the words "loss and gain" in such a way as to echo Newman. Like Charles Reding, Marius is exposed to a bewildering variety of opportunities for religious choice. After the briefest attraction to Evangelical views (parallel to a much longer Evangelical period in Newman's own youth), Charles remains a High Anglican moving towards Rome, until he actually takes the great leap. Living in the second century after Christ and reaching maturity in the reign of the cultivated Stoic emperor Marcus Aurelius (116-180), Marius has a more elaborate evolution.

He begins with Roman paganism, "the religion of Numa," the ancestral provincial faith of his fathers, still piously practiced on his remote family estate during his childhood, which is parallel to

3. David J. DeLaura, *Hebrew and Hellene in Victorian England. Newman, Arnold, and Pater* (Austin and London: University of Texas Press, 1969).

Pater's early Anglican faith. At the University—Pisa—Marius adopts a form of Epicureanism (called "new Cyrenaicism" after its founder, Aristippus of Cyrene), a religion of sensation and delightful experience like Pater's own youthful philosophy. At Rome, Marius shifts to the Stoic philosophy to which Marcus Aurelius himself was so devoted. Finally Marius encounters and admires Christianity. But *did* Marius in the end actually become a Christian? Ever since the novel first appeared, critics have debated this point, and the argument still goes merrily on in the 1970's. So if Marius is like Charles Reding in *Loss and Gain*, Pater's novel—like *Callista*, which he greatly admired—is an effort to treat nineteenth-century religious problems in the guise of historical fiction about the ancient Roman world. More important even than *Callista* for Pater was Newman's *Grammar of Assent* (1870).

Each reader will have to decide for himself, of course, the question of Marius's conversion to Christianity. But since it is *the* fundamental question for us, we must examine the evidence. Towards the end of the book, Marcus Aurelius sanctions a new persecution of the Christians, the first in many decades. By then, Marius has become deeply interested in the beauty and dignity of the Christian ritual as practiced on Cecilia's estate. At Easter, during "the sweet singing of the Eucharist, . . . as the pathetic words of the psalter relieved the tension of their hearts, the people . . . wore upon their faces their habitual gleam of joy, of placid satisfaction." But after the ceremonies, there is read an "Epistle from the churches of Lyons and Vienne," towns in Gaul where the persecution has begun, telling of the dreadful fate of the martyrs. Marius resolves to go to the emperor "with an appeal for common-sense, for reason and justice." But he is deterred from making the "chivalrous effort at enlightenment" because the emperor is busy with other matters: the reader may feel that if Marius had wanted to do so, he might have persisted.

Then, after a sudden earthquake near Marius's own ancestral home, peasants attack a little group of Christians; Marius and his friend Cornelius are arrested as being Christian, which Marius of course is not. But Marius, who thinks that Cornelius is to marry Cecilia, bribes a guard to set Cornelius free. He performs a truly heroic act. He has "delivered his brother," yet he "is no hero, no heroic martyr"; he has "indeed no right to be," that is, he is not formally a Christian: he does not believe that his expected execution will be more than an execution. He falls ill, is delirious and near dying, is abandoned by the soldiers, and is cared for by a group of Christians. For Marius "revelation, vision, the discovery of a vision, the *seeing* of a perfect humanity in a perfect world" has always been more important than *having* or *doing* anything. And in his recollection of his many visions of beauty, the "touching image of Jesus, apprehended dimly" assumes the climactic place. Marius is grateful; but he feels the sense of self-pity, of "wasted power." Yet each of his successive visions, "throughout that elaborate and lifelong education of his receptive powers," has prepared him for "possible further revelation some day." And now he is ready for it, his "unclouded receptivity of soul . . . at its height." The tablet of his mind is blank "for whatsoever divine fingers might choose to write there."

As the weariness of oncoming death surrounds him in his weakness, and he wakes from a last earthly sleep, the people about his bed are "praying fervently—*Abi! abi! Anima Christiana!* [Depart! depart! O Christian Soul!] In the moments of his extreme helplessness their mystic bread had been placed, had descended like a snowflake from the sky, between his lips." And once he has died, the Christians take up his corpse and bury it secretly "with their accustomed prayers, but with joy also, holding his death, according to their generous view in this matter, to have been of the nature of a martyrdom; and martyrdom, as the church had always said, a kind of sacrament with plenary grace [full forgiveness of sin]." The final chapter, of which these are the final words, is entitled *Anima Naturaliter Christiana*, "A Soul that is by nature Christian."

In the last prayers of those Christians around Marius's bed, the very Latin words "abi" and "anima" have a special importance. The pagan Roman Emperor Hadrian (117-138) wrote a celebrated poem addressing his own "little soul," beginning "Animula, vagula, blandula/ Hospes comesque corporis,/ Quae nunc abibis in loca?/ Pallidula, rigida, nudula," or "O little soul, little wandering one, little caressing one,/ the guest and companion of my body,/ to what places will you now depart?/ little pale one, stiff one, little naked one." These celebrated lines of Hadrian's Pater used as an epigraph for an earlier chapter of *Marius* immediately after the funeral of Marius's hedonist pagan friend, the imaginary poet Flavian, who at the very moment of his death from the plague is writing a brilliant poem in honor of love.[4] Flavian's death seems to Marius a proof of "the soul's extinction. Flavian had gone out as utterly as the fire among those still beloved ashes."

In contrast to the "little fluttering creature," the pagan soul (*animula*)—departing for unknown places, if any, and more probably as extinct as the ashes of its erstwhile host and companion, the body—we have at Marius's death the "naturally Christian soul," no longer a diminutive *animula* but a full-fledged *anima.* When it is urged to depart (*abi*), there is no Hadrianic query (*quae nunc abibis in loca?*) about the places it will depart to; its heavenly destination is certain. Though Marius has perhaps never consciously made the final decision—the leap to Christianity paralleling Charles Reding's leap to Catholicism—yet his heroic act of substituting himself for Cornelius is as surely an act of Christian sacrifice as that of a martyr. Marius feels only "satisfaction at his courage, at the discovery of his possession of 'nerve.' " But the Christian God will know how to interpret the act and will generously regard him as a martyr. The people's belief and the churches' belief are in agreement, and plenary grace—full absolution—will be vouchsafed to Marius. Without a full-fledged, deliberate, conscious conversion, Marius—it seems clear enough—has indeed become a Christian.

Now, we must add, this is a highly controversial opinion. Pater is ambiguous, and his ambiguity is heightened by the involutions of his prose. Professor DeLaura says that Marius "ends in the life of the Christian community"—perhaps, rather, in the true *death* as believed in by the Christian community. Professor Knoepflmacher regards the death only as Marius's climactic "passive absorption" of a "final 'atmosphere.' " And in the end, his Christianity is still "a possibility but a possibility only."[5] A hoax, says another scholar of

4. The *Pervigilium Veneris* (Virgil of Venus), a famous anonymous poem with the haunting refrain "cras amet qui numquam amavit, quique amavit cras amet"—Tomorrow may he love who has never loved before, and whoever has already loved, may he love tomorrow—for which Pater invented Flavian as author.

5. U. Knoepflmacher, *Religious Humanism and the Victorian Novel: George Eliot, Walter Pater, and Samuel Butler* (Princeton: Princeton University Press, 1965), pp. 218-219.

Marius's martyrdom, but apparently without much thought as to Pater's propensity or lack of propensity for hoaxing. Not a "true" conversion, or "not quite" a conversion, say others: perhaps, but enough of a conversion to be a conversion, at least so Pater clearly says. Professor Dahl, believing flatly (as I do) that "Marius dies a Christian," points to the other characters in the nineteenth-century novels of ancient Rome, including Wiseman's heroine Fabiola, who are truer Christians than many Christians and yet never formally become members of the Church.[6]

Long ago T.S. Eliot, perhaps understandably, grew impatient, declaring that Marius "simply *drifts* towards the Christian Church if he can be said to have any motion at all." He proclaimed the book "incoherent" and a "hodge-podge." Reviewing it favorably when it first appeared, Mrs. Humphry Ward—a personal friend of Pater's in Oxford and soon to publish *Robert Elsmere* (1888, no. 82), still the most celebrated single novel of Victorian religious doubt—remarked that the ambiguity of Marius's death "in which, while not a Christian, he suffers with the Christians, fitly corresponds with the ambiguity of the life which had gone before it." It is, she declared, only a "half-Christian death," although she quotes in full the final passage from which we have given key sentences above. To my knowledge, however, nobody has previously noted the echoing Latin words pagan *Animula*—Christian *Anima*, pagan *Quae nunc abibis*—Christian *Abi*, which seem to underline Pater's real intention.

Mrs. Ward—and here virtually all critics since 1885 have agreed—saw in *Marius* "a wonderfully delicate and faithful reflection of a real mind . . . of the nineteenth century, and not of the second." She emphasized its autobiographical character, disguised in the reticent English manner as fiction: the English prefer novels to "the avowed specimens of self-revelation." *Marius* is one of those books which "the future student of the nineteenth century" will have to read to understand the age. As Mrs. Ward said, Marius begins life in accordance with the teachings of Pater's *Studies in the History of the Renaissance* (1873), which, in its original conclusion, seemed to urge young men to seek all possible pleasure through

6. C. Dahl, "Pater's *Marius* and Historical Novels on Early Christian Times," *Nineteenth-Century Fiction* 28, 1 (June 1973): 15.

their senses. ("What we have to do is to be for ever curiously testing new opinions and courting new impressions. . . . High passions give one this quickened sense of life, ecstasy and sorrow of life, political or religious enthusiasm, or the 'enthusiasm of humanity.' Only be sure it is passion. . . .") But then, Mrs. Ward continued, as Marius grows older the continual pursuit of sensation is incompatible with the "ethical tradition. . . . the broad main stream of human history," and he soon becomes aware of the danger of isolation from human experience generally. In Marius's case, his soul can no longer "live solitary in the midst of a dainty world of its own choice . . . because . . . such a worship of beauty defeats its own ends." By joining the human race (to put it crassly) Marius's soul actually "increases its own chances of beautiful impressions, of 'exquisite moments.' " "What makes the great psychological interest of the book," wrote Mrs. Ward, "while it constitutes what seems to us its principal intellectual weakness, is the further application of this Epicurean principle of an aesthetic loss and gain [note these words] not only to morals but to religion."

For Marius, "acquiescence in the religious order" of the surrounding world, just like his acquiescence in the moral order, is also essentially rewarding because of the fresh "exquisite moments" it offers him. Christianity is "bright, blithe, sweet"; it makes death more tolerable than any of the other systems (and Marius, like Pater, is deeply preoccupied with death). The message is: "submit to the religious order about you, accept the common beliefs, or at least behave as if you accepted them, and live habitually in the atmosphere of feeling and sensation which they have engendered and still engender; surrender your feeling while maintaining the intellectual citadel intact; pray, weep, dream with the majority, while you think with the elect; only so will you obtain from life all it has to give, its most delicate flavour, its subtlest aroma." Mrs. Humphry Ward, with gentle indignation, found this an unworthy betrayal of the Christian religion. Better not to adhere to it merely for the sake of the "beauty, charm, consolations to be got out of the intricate practical system," while remaining sceptical about it; better instead, like Arthur Hugh Clough, the poet and doubter, to "put no fairy tales knowingly into the place which belongs to realities," and to suffer the harsh consequences. But Mrs. Ward made her protest gently and almost parenthetically.

Into her review Mrs. Ward put, of course, her own growing preoccupation with religious doubt and the courage required to face up to it—the theme she was just embarking upon as she began to write *Robert Elsmere.* Knowing Pater so well personally and liking him, she understood much about him: his ingrown isolation from so many of his Oxford colleagues and his unhappiness with the university generally she would portray in Langham, one of the most interesting figures in her own novel. In other respects, however, she drew Langham from the Swiss sceptic, Amiel, whose journal she had recently translated. (Reviewing it, Pater had criticized Amiel adversely for letting doubts trouble him.) But there was also much about Pater that Mrs. Ward missed, or at least chose not to say in print. Pater's "Conclusion" to the *Studies in the History of the Renaissance* indeed lent itself to misunderstanding as a plea for unbridled hedonism: Oscar Wilde, who read it in 1874, later said that it had exercised a "strange influence over his life"; and there were other young men, Wildeian aesthetes in embryo, around Oxford who found Pater's ideas fascinating in a way he had perhaps not fully intended.

Worse still: W. H. Mallock—a brilliant young Oxford undergraduate, who found Pater's aestheticism laughable, as indeed he did all the other fashionable ideas of the mid-seventies—published in 1877 *The New Republic* (NIS, but see below), introducing a quite obvious portrait of Pater as "Mr. Rose" and cleverly satirizing Pater's views as he apprehended them. As an Oxonian, Mallock had the advantage of knowing Pater by sight and reputation, and could lampoon the "lukewarm" vitality, apt to retreat into "affectation," which others saw in him. After Pater died in 1894, Henry James wrote of him as "faint, pale, embarrassed, exquisite Pater." Mallock's "Mr. Rose" exaggerates, as is the way of successful satire, the mannerisms and writings of the original.

Says Mr. Rose, "I rather look upon life as a chamber, which we decorate as we would decorate the chamber of the woman or the youth [NB] that we love, tinting the walls of it with symphonies of subdued colours, and filling it with works of fair form, and with flowers, and with strange scents, and with instruments of music." He has "learned the weariness of creeds." Successful life consists "simply . . . in the consciousness of exquisite living—in the making our own each highest thrill of joy that the moment offers us. . . ." He welcomes social dissolution as "the true condition of the most perfect life," setting free the individual. The man of culture is like "an Aeolian harp, which the winds at will play through—a beautiful face, a rainbow, a ruined temple, a death-bed, or a line of poetry. . . ."

Mr. Rose walks at night in London hoping for the thrill of seeing a prostitute fling herself from Waterloo Bridge into the Thames. He gladly assists a servant—"a pretty boy with light curling hair"—to arrange some tumblers on the grass. He is loud in praise of Achilles and Patroclus, of David and Jonathan, of "our English Edward [King Edward II, notoriously a homosexual] and the fair Piers Gaveston." He has an intense interest in bric-a-brac, such as Chelsea shepherdesses, and he tries to buy a pornographic book surreptitiously.

He reads aloud a sonnet "by a boy of eighteen—a youth of exquisite promise—, I think, whose education I may myself claim to have had some share in directing," a sonnet which tells of three visions—of Narcissus, of Venus, and of Thomas Aquinas in his cell: the first two flee the author, and then only does he yearn for religion as exemplified in the third. This, says Mr. Rose, is "a true and tender expression of the really Catholic spirit of modern aestheticism, which holds nothing common or unclean." And he finds ("when . . . in the weary mood for it") some of the Ritualist services in the Church of England "managed with surprising skill. The dim religious twilight, fragrant with the smoke of incense; the tangled roofs that the music seems to cling to; the tapers, the high altar, and the strange intonation of the priests, all produce a curious old-world effect, and seem to unite one with things that have long been dead," indeed far more so than Catholic services themselves. Mr. Rose, then, is effeminate, affected, perverse, a very early aesthete indeed, in the days just before Oscar Wilde and his fellows (about 1880) burst upon a startled London, and Gilbert and Sullivan promptly satirized them in *Patience* (1881).

Obviously disturbed by Mallock's onslaught, which had a

measure of misunderstanding in it, Pater first suppressed the conclusion to the *Renaissance* when the book went into a second printing, then later revised it substantially for subsequent editions. But he also wrote *Marius* in part, at least, as a reply to Mallock. Marius's life and philosophic history were intended to refute the charges of irresponsibility or immorality implicit in the portrait of Mr. Rose. Like Newman and Wiseman, and many other writers of novels of antiquity, Pater intended to comment on nineteenth-century England. He constantly intrudes modern references into his delicately woven prose pictures of persons and emotions and institutions of the ancient world, damaging the illusion, one imagines, for many a modern reader. References to Goethe, Dante, Shakespeare, Calvin, Jonathan Edwards, Swedenborg, St. Louis (Louis IX, King of France 1226-1270), Giotto, Raphael, Francis of Assisi, Théophile Gautier, throng the pages of the novel. At one moment Pater says, "that age and our own have much in common—many difficulties and hopes. Let the reader pardon me if here and there I seem to be passing from Marius to his modern representatives—from Rome, to Paris, or London." And, one should add, to Oxford.

Marius's "modern representative" is above all Pater himself, saying to Mallock, saying to the world, "You have misunderstood me. I do *not* think that religion is a mere spectacle, or to be embraced when one is weary, if only it is well enough 'managed.' I believe that religion is necessary. But our times, like those of Marius, offer a bewildering variety of choices, and furious disputes among pious men." Behind Pater stands Matthew Arnold as well as Newman. Marius's first step from the faith of Numa to New Cyrenaicism parallels Pater's move from traditional Christianity to Arnoldian "culture," from Arnold's "Hebraism" to his "Hellenism." The second step—from New Cyrenaicism to Stoicism—is a step from happy youthful experiment to mature pessimism of the sort radiated by the emperor himself. The third step, towards Christianity, is precipitated by Marius's delight in Christian joyousness, and his ever-deepening sense of the brutality of his own society and the wretchedness of the human suffering that it, often deliberately, causes. Before he makes the move, before he has even consciously encountered his first Christian or had his experience of Christian life and behavior, he has—in a chapter called "The Will as

Vision"—a revelation of his own, significantly enough in an olive garden.

There Marius sees "himself moving, as if in another life and like another person through all his fortunes and misfortunes." In addition to his beloved friends, the dead Flavian and the still living Cornelius, he feels that he has always had another dear companion, "a self not himself" at his side, of the sort he had read of in Plato and in the writings of Marcus Aurelius. This friend at his side—for the Greeks the "eternal reason," and "ideal of the spirit within him"—Marius now formulates as "that reasonable Ideal to which the Old Testament gives the name of *Creator* . . . and . . . the New Testament the *Father of Men.*" (Neither portion of the Bible was then or ever available to Marius.) With his entire physical self engaged in "passive surrender" to the sense of "a thousand combining currents from earth and sky," Marius feels that his thoughts also are the "remote and therefore imperfect pulsations" of an external "intellectual or spiritual system."

Wholly Platonic is the concept of physical objects, including human bodies and intellectual and spiritual "pulsations" of the human mind and soul, as reflections, as the creations of that "one indefectible mind" outside, thus accounting for the continuing apperceptions of the same reality from generation to generation of men. At the moment of this vision, the material world itself seems to dissolve for Marius, who joyfully welcomes the revelation: his "divine companion" is no longer merely "an occasional wayfarer beside him," but the "unfailing 'assistant,' without whose inspiration and concurrence" he cannot breathe, see, or think. "The sense of a friendly hand laid upon him amid the shadows of the world" leaves this unique moment of revelation as a landmark in Marius's life: he knows now that he must seek for the earthly equivalent of this "*Great Ideal.*" He is ready for his first exposure to Christian practices and attitudes.

But the Christianity that Marius (and Pater) are prepared to embrace is only one sort of Christianity. Marius is lucky, Pater makes clear, in that he is alive at the right time in history, "a period when . . . the church was true for a moment, truer perhaps than she would ever be again, to that element of profound serenity in the soul of her Founder, which reflected the eternal good will of God to man." Before the Antonine era in which Marius lives, and again afterwards, the church—says Pater—passed through periods of austere asceticism. Especially after Christianity became the state religion (during the fourth century), Pater finds the church steeped in the "exclusiveness . . . puritanism . . . ascetic gloom" which had set in with Marcus Aurelius's persecutions, and which "characterised a church under misunderstanding or oppression, driven back, in a world of tasteless controversy, inward upon herself." "A world of tasteless controversy": here is a reference to Pater's own day, as well as to the "dark ages" of European history.

That sort of Christianity, Pater clearly implies, would never have suited Marius, who lives instead in the last days of a happy church, which owed its chance to breathe to Marcus Aurelius's father, the "pagan saint," Antoninus Pius, who never shed Christian blood. "Amiable in its own nature, and full of a reasonable gaiety," Christianity responded to similar traits in the emperor and could "expand and thrive for a season." It was "a charmed period," and it would not recur until the Renaissance, when St. Francis, Giotto, Dante, could reassert once again the earlier lost values.

"In the history of the church," then, Pater writes, "there are two ideals. . . . The ideal of asceticism represents moral effort as essentially a sacrifice . . . of one part of human nature to another . . . while the ideal of culture represents it as a harmonious development of all the parts of human nature, in just proportion to each other." The contrast between an ascetic Christianity, which is repulsive to Pater and would have been so to Marius had he chanced to live when it was dominant, and a Christianity of culture, which attracts Marius and Pater, reflects Matthew Arnold's contrast between Hebraism, with its emphasis on morality, and Hellenism, with its emphasis on intelligence. But Pater, as DeLaura has well said, has created a kind of "factitious" Christianity of his own. This acceptable Paterian Christianity is described by a series of favorite words recurring with a special insistence in this portion of the novel: "serene, blithe, debonair, sweetness, humanism, appreciation of beauty, freshness, grave and wholesome beauty, gracious spirit, amiable, reasonable gaiety, the grace of graciousness, tact, good sense, urbanity and moderation, cheerful liberty of heart, aesthetic charm, comely order. . . ."[7] In fact, this Paterian Christianity is astonishingly like Paterian paganism. He was still the Pater of *The Studies in the History of the Renaissance.* He might try to throw Mr. Rose out with a pitchfork, but bits at least of Mr. Rose would keep on coming back.

This Christian church of Pater (and of Marius) manifests itself in a "wonderful liturgical spirit . . . unparalleled genius for worship." It puts "beautiful furniture" into the old pagan temples and converts them to its use. It develops a "wonderful new music and poesy." With "a generous eclecticism" it manages, from Gnostic, Jewish, and pagan sources, to "adorn and beautify the greatest act of worship the world has seen." Latin lines from the Catholic liturgy of the Eucharist (*Tantum ergo*) close the chapter. Like so many of his Latin and Greek quotations that stud the pages of *Marius,* Pater does not translate them. In the words of the standard translation we are exhorted: "Let us then before him bending/ This great sacrament revere./ Types and shadows have their ending/ For the newer rite is here."

There follows an entire chapter on "Divine Service," as Marius first encounters it in Cecilia's villa, a "wonderful spectacle . . . of those who believe," old and young, who seem to have received a message of hope from outside the "flaming rampart of the world" (Pater translating Lucretius here). Finally Marius apprehends a little of the meaning of all this beauty, and learns for the first time of the Atonement: "We adore thee, O Christ, because by thy cross thou hast redeemed the world," sing the (beautiful) young men in surplices, suggesting the human nature of the divinity they are invoking: "the image of a young man giving up voluntarily, one by one, for the greatest of ends, the greatest gifts; actually parting with himself." To the worshippers it seems a recent event. To Marius it seems "as if the very dead were aware"—their tombs are near at hand on Cecilia's estate—and were associating themselves with "this exalted worship of Jesus." The partaking of the eucharist, an act literally of "thanksgiving," leaves Marius "with a kind of thirst, for all this, over again." Matthew Arnold's ideas underlay Pater's

7. DeLaura, *op. cit.*, p. 282.

here too, as in Marius's subsequent realization of the need to thrust aside any indifference to the sufferings of others and to love one's fellow man. But Pater's hero remains a visionary and expectant, whereas Arnold was ready to embrace "an agnostic Christian moralism."

For Pater, as he said elsewhere, the Church offered an "atmosphere based on the positive imageries of a faith so richly beset with persons, things, historical incidents," and Christ's "infinite nature had led to such diversities in preaching as St. Francis, and Taylor, and Wesley," that a man of truly philosophical temper could find himself at home in it, without worrying about doctrinal details. In the end, then, Pater emerges as a strange amalgam. He is a ritualist primarily on aesthetic grounds, which links him (as does his Platonism and Marius's vision of his friend Cornelius as a knight in shining armor) to Charlotte Yonge and Shorthouse, Guy Morville-Galahad and John Inglesant-St. George. On the other hand, he is wholly untheological and undoctrinal. While admiring Mrs. Ward's *Robert Elsmere*, which he reviewed in 1888, three years after she had reviewed *Marius*, he protested that if Elsmere had only possessed the "perfectly philosophical or scientific temper," he would not have felt the need to leave the Church of England. Now *if* Elsmere had indeed stayed in Anglican orders (always imagining him as a real person instead of the hero of a novel), he would have been behaving as many Broad Churchmen were behaving in the seventies and eighties: pushing his doubts aside, ignoring his worries about the Thirty-nine Articles, working for liberalization from within the Church, and doing good. In 1888, Mrs. Ward disapproved of such men, although much later she would adopt their views as her own.

So if Pater is a ritualist and if *Marius* earns its place in this chapter as a "Tractarian" novel, it is as a most peculiar kind of Tractarian novel indeed, with a strong overlay of disbelief, or lack of interest in the content of the religion, even of doubt, and, above all, of ambiguity. "He never returned to Christianity in the orthodox or intellectual sense," said Mrs. Ward herself, writing of Pater, "but his heart returned to it." The compound of ritualism and scepticism, as prescribed for those already satiated with experience and world-weary, an impressionistic religion of beauty without theological content, is a long way from anything we have come to think of as Anglican Christianity.

Like Charles Reding, then, Marius takes an intolerable time making up his mind; but unlike Charles Reding, he never in fact makes it up: it is made up for him by his self-sacrifice and by the communion given him in error on his deathbed. Marius does not make Charles's or Newman's act of faith; he disregards the warning that Lucian of Samosata, a Greek pagan writer introduced into the story by Pater, gives him to get on with it lest he die of hunger while still preparing the banquet. The Greek epigraph on the title page of *Marius* (left untranslated) calls the book "A winter's dream, when the nights are longest." It is as indecisive as a dream, and sometimes as baffling; and the night is a long one indeed.

Some Anti-Tractarian Fiction

Many novels carrying an anti-Tractarian message were primarily designed as arguments in favor of some other religious point of view. Even the Catholic *Loss and Gain*—with its portraits of Bateman, interested only in externals, and of White, speedily ready to marry and abandon his vaunted Catholic preferences by settling into a comfortable Church of England living—has its anti-Tractarian aspects; but one could hardly classify it as *primarily* an anti-Tractarian novel. So, too, under the headings of Evangelical, Broad Church, Dissenting, and doubting fiction of all shades, the reader will naturally find a rich treasury of anti-Tractarian sentiment, expressed with varying degrees of seriousness ranging from the mildly satirical to the venomous. But in addition to these novels, which are discussed, with comment on their anti-Tractarianism, in other portions of this book, there is a large class of novels whose chief, if not sole, purpose it is to denounce "Puseyism" root and branch.

These primarily anti-Tractarian novels, though well worth reading, and indeed often highly entertaining, do not call for much detailed comment. Writers who were anti-Catholic often feared Tractarianism as much or more, regarding it as the first step towards Rome, a corrupting influence within the Church of England. Beginning in the 1840's, soon after the general public had become aware of the "Romanizing" current flowing so strongly at Oxford, anti-Tractarian fiction grew increasingly strident and violent with the passing decades. In Anne Howard's *Mary Spencer. A Tale for the Times* (1844, no. 41), the Puseyite enemy is still given credit for good intentions: "a set of foolish young men, just come from college, (where some, who ought to be wiser, have turned their heads)." In this vein, but far more wittily, the irrepressible Charles Maurice Davies, a Broad-Church parson, in his first novel, published as *Philip Paternoster. A Tractarian Love-Story* (1858, no. 31) under the pseudonym "An Ex-Puseyite," ridiculed the flummery of Puseyism, which he himself had only recently abandoned. It will never appeal to ordinary men, says one young Oxonian drinking wine with another, who is already a convinced Tractarian: "Mr. Hodge [the typical English peasant], who must be a decent citizen" will never understand it:

> "You would haul him to church . . . and Gregorianise him and incense him (perhaps in more meanings than one of the word) and then you would show him your coronae and all the other pretty things—which he could not in the least understand or appreciate—and your relics—a fragment of the toe of St. Seraphina, with a portrait of the venerable damsel. . . . You would tell him how she lived in holy virginity—a statement, which from your portrait aforesaid he would have no sort of difficulty in believing—and existed upon bread and butter and mushroom ketchup, . . . teach him to sing ancient hymns in a voice harmonious as a bear's, absolve his past peccadilloes, and turn him out of your oratory, or wherever you had converted him, to go—whither think you?"
>
> "Well, whither?"
>
> "Back to the beer-shop, as sure as you are a sucking parson. Pass the bottle."

In a more serious vein, many well-known authors took great alarm at Tractarian practices. Clerical celibacy, for example, inflamed the pugnacious Charles Kingsley (1819-1875) into many a violent attack on the enemy, Catholic or Tractarian, and many an impassioned defense of earthly marriage in all its carnal joys. His

Hypatia (1853, no. 47) (reserved for fuller discussion as an exposition of his Broad-Church views), we have already seen as the stimulus to Wiseman's *Fabiola* and Newman's *Callista*. His first novel, *Yeast* (1848 in *Fraser's Magazine*, 1851 in book form, NIS), while not primarily religious in theme, nonetheless sounds this favorite note. Much of the social evil of England derives, in *Yeast*, from "Romanist" sexual abstinence: even the unsanitary drainage conditions in the village in the novel (another obsession of Kingsley's) are attributed to the curse of a sixteenth-century nun. Lancelot, the hero of *Yeast*, tells Luke, his Tractarian cousin, to "take your saints and virgins, relics, and miracles," and "give me the political economist, the sanitary reformer, the engineer."

But Luke turns Catholic, and his spiritual adviser, a recent convert, is presented as dainty and effeminate, and is surely intended as a portrait of Newman. He listens to Lancelot "with the most winning courtesy and sweetness." "With so sweet and arch a smile that it was impossible to be angry," he refuses to reveal Luke's whereabouts, but does admit that Luke is entering an order devoted to the worship of the Blessed Virgin and is following "the star of Mary." Lancelot explodes, "I want not a mother to pet me but a man to rule me." To contemporaries, Kingsley's defense of sexuality in marriage seemed rather overheated (Lancelot makes a drawing of his fiancée—*not* from the life—showing her in the nude[8]); Tractarian reviewers were quick to denounce the book as licentious. But Kingsley was not a defender of profligacy: *Yeast* condemns extramarital liaisons as vigorously as it does celibacy.

The pitch to which anti-Tractarian sentiment could mount, even in the minds of respectable and much-read novelists, is illustrated by Mrs. Lynn Linton's *Under Which Lord* (1879, no. 35) and Robert Buchanan's *Foxglove Manor* (1884, no. 36). The peculiar personality of Eliza Lynn Linton (1822-1898) and the development of her agnostic religious views we consider below as a case history in doubt, as described in her fictionalized autobiography. Her only true love among men is identified by her nephew and biographer, G. S. Layard, as a Catholic, a mysterious "Brother Edward," who

8. In this he was only imitating Kingsley himself.

would not abandon his views any more than she would her own. Marriage was impossible for them, but they corresponded for forty years. Mrs. Lynn Linton's dislike for Catholicism was virulent: "How any one who can read can be a Roman Catholic, is more than I am able to understand," she wrote in a personal letter, and in *Under Which Lord* she says of certain persons, "They were Catholics, not men." But she hated Tractarians even more: at least the Catholic clergy were personally disinterested members of a powerful hierarchy, whereas the Tractarian clergy were free to build up their enormous personal influence without restraint. "You boggle at discipline outside yourself," says a Catholic character in *Under Which Lord* to a Tractarian, "and want to be at the head of all organization and authority."

Despite his personal effeminacy, Lascelles, Mrs. Linton's repulsive High-Church parson, is enormously attractive to women, and makes his female parishioners fall in love with him. Confession is the handiest device for obtaining the devotion of the women. Through confession, Lascelles deliberately destroys the happy marriage and family life of his leading parishioner by securing a hold over the wife, who is the legal owner of the estate. A deeply religious agnostic, her husband, Fullerton, is driven from his household into poverty. Just as wicked is Lascelles's sister, whose ritualistic devotion spreads Romanism, misery, and death among the young women of the parish.

It seems astonishing that so crude a novel—reminiscent of the great anti-Jesuit scare and the fiction of the fifties—could have appeared as late as 1879. But public receptivity to these old-fashioned bogeymen had been newly reawakened by the private publication in 1877 of *The Priest in Absolution*, a High-Anglican handbook for confessors. The uproar created by this document takes us back to the days of *Ellen Middleton* (or even to *Poverty and the Baronet's Family*). Disraeli's Tory Home Secretary declared that *The Priest in Absolution* ought to be prosecuted as obscene literature, and one Evangelical clergyman demanded capital punishment for any Anglican clergyman who heard confessions. In this anti-ritualist atmosphere, *Under Which Lord* sold well, despite the reviewers' generally contemptuous attitude towards it—the *Saturday Review*, for instance, declined "to characterise the ravings which pass for interviews between an English clergyman and his female parishioners."

Even more lurid was *Foxglove Manor*. Robert Buchanan (1841-1901), a poet of some reputation, and a novelist who had protested in 1872 against what he felt to be the sensuality of the pre-Raphaelites in a celebrated article called "The Fleshly School of Poetry," now committed offenses infinitely greater than those with which he had charged Rossetti (who had promptly replied in a counterblast called "The Stealthy School of Criticism"). Despite its crudities, *Foxglove Manor* showed that Buchanan realized, as perhaps Mrs. Lynn Linton did not, the extent to which the Ritualists depended upon sensuous impressions: color, form, fragrance, music. By using "colour and form," Santley, Buchanan's Tractarian clergyman, seduces a beautiful young woman and then repudiates her. But Santley reaches new heights of improbable indecency when he begins to find himself "gazing on the Madonnas in his own study, with a satyr's delight in their plumpness, their naked arms, their swelling breasts." It may be true, as Buchanan's adopted daughter and biographer (she was also his sister-in-law) declares, that his novels of the eighties were written merely as potboilers. But even that hardly excuses the vulgarity of *Foxglove Manor*.

Perhaps sensuality was the favorite sin attributed to Tractarians by their novel-writing opponents. But it was far from the only one. Sir Walter Besant's *In Deacon's Orders* (1895, no. 88), a novelette by a famous and popular novelist who had the respect of his brother writers and, as in questions of copyright law, for example, was often selected to serve as their spokesman, told the story of a young aspirant for the Anglican priesthood, whose ordination is sensationally prevented by the objections of a woman at the ceremony itself in a great cathedral. The youth, already a deacon, is a cheat, a thief, a forger, and a seducer. Yet as a boy he "had a lovely face and a lovely voice; they took him into the choir, and he used to sing solos with so much fervour—such spiritual rapture—in his angelic countenance, that all the ladies fell in love with him." He has "the typical clerical face." And in the end, after a notable career of crime followed by exposure, he dies an edifying religious death, showing "humility . . . at the last consolations of the Church" and turning "his dying eyes to heaven" in "rapture." In a preface, Besant explains that his target is not religion but "religiosity," which is at war with true religious feelings. But the reader of his story will find him protesting too much.

In a far more deeply felt novel, *Red Pottage* (1899, no. 88), Mary Cholmondely (1859-1925) portrayed a clergyman whose chief sin is self-satisfaction leading to an obtuseness so powerful that his own bishop is in despair. A man of dim perceptions and coarse fibre, Mr. Gresley victimizes his sensitive, highly intelligent, and creative sister, who has written a novel which he surreptitiously reads and disapproves. The reader of *Red Pottage* will have to find out for himself what Mr. Gresley does then. But the book is not only a vigorous attack on the smugness of the Anglican clergy; it is also a notable document in the history of feminist literature, and deserves rediscovery for this among many other reasons. Mr. Gresley is not even particularly High-Church: for example, he espouses temperance—one of the Evangelical causes—with all possible vigor.

In a far more agreeable vein, though sharply satirical, Thomas de Longueville's anonymous (or pseudonymous!) brief and witty *The Life of a Prig*, by One (1885, no. 14), teases the Tractarians unmercifully from the Catholic point of view. Writing in the hope that his work may make "even one prig more priggish," the prig solemnly advances his credentials: "My father was a fellow of his college; my grandfather wrote a commentary of thirteen volumes on the Ephesians; my uncle on my mother's side was the writer of the well-known and popular children's tales, called *Gilded Pills*, and my maternal grandfather was a famous preacher. My one married aunt wedded a dean, and five of my unmarried aunts never miss the two daily services at Boredom Cathedral." No doubt there were many Anglican families who fitted this description, but perhaps knowledgeable readers were intended to think of the Wilberforces. Headed for Oxford as a matter of course, the promising prig at sixteen writes in his diary:

> Resolved to lose no opportunity of improving myself. While washing my teeth this morning, reflected upon the solemnity of life. In my bath, thought of our first parents in the garden

> of Eden. While buttoning my braces, asked myself this question, "What do I live for?" Much moved at family prayers with feelings of thanksgiving . . . that I am of a clergyman's family; that I am a member of the Church of England; that I live within reach of a cathedral town; that I am going to Oxford; that I have never been exposed to the temptations of school; that I have the inestimable blessing of a mother who can read Greek. Resolution at breakfast not to talk much in society or make myself too agreeable. A profitable morning. Herodotus. Trigonometry. For mortification at dinner, put sugar into beer and mustard into pudding, but secretly, lest, being observed, pride might supervene. . . . Algebra, Hecuba, Greek verses and Hume till tea. Feeling of oppression after tea. Thoughts of death. What are those strange sensations from which I sometimes suffer? Have I some mysterious disease? How many have died young! Why should not I? Entertained myself by reading *Anatomy of Melancholy* until supper time. Earnest conversation with Uncle George about the future of the Chinese missions. Felt much fervour at family prayers. In my own room, self-examination. Oh, how I have wasted today! Opportunities neglected! Eaten too much at tea. Oh, why do we gorge ourselves with the luxuries of this life? Resolution. Will endeavour, as much as possible, to check the flippancy of those around me.

This is wicked, and was doubtless intended to suggest Hurrell Froude's *Remains*.

Discovering at Oxford that, although he is a High Churchman, there are others still higher, the Prig determines "not to be beaten" on this point. His progress higher and higher is set forth in hilarious detail. Private services, the usual Puseyite "crucifixes, monstrances, and ciboriums" for the private oratory, going to confession, confessing and receiving absolution by mail, "reserving" the sacrament in his own room, flagellation: he goes in for it all; yet there are still persons "higher" than he: monks. He is prepared for ordination by the "fathers of the order of Friars Green," which is three months old (echoes of Newman at Littlemore?), undergoes further mortification of the flesh, is saved from death by a miracle, and tours the Continent attending Catholic churches, creeping nearer and nearer to Roman observance with every day, but never with any real sincerity. Was he not a heretic, people would ask, in the eyes of true Catholics? "To such silly remarks . . . no scholar could condescend to reply." His activities grow more and more farcical. Each of his gingerly approaches to Catholicism itself meets with the rebuff it deserves. His attempts to fly even higher than Rome, while bypassing Rome, lead him to turn to Zoroastrianism, Hinduism, Buddhism, Confucianism, and Islam. The exercise leaves him still unable to speak a word of comfort to a dying man. Agnosticism then claims him; but he runs into difficulties with an agnostic boy—cleverer than he is—to whom he has been appointed tutor. And so it goes. Longueville, as a Catholic secure in his faith, needing only the authority of the Roman Church to define his beliefs, found the Prig's intellectual presumption and total lack of humility not only ridiculous but also damnable. With restraint and good humor, he said so indirectly and in short compass.

A Summing Up

The Tractarians originally mobilized against the danger that the Church of England would be secularized in the wave of reform of the 1830's. However real the danger may have been, it soon evaporated, in part, no doubt, as a result of their militant efforts. Their insistence on Apostolic succession and on the individual's submission to the authority of the Church, their revival of practices which they attributed to the "primitive" Church of the early Christian centuries, their "sacramentalism," their "Churchmanship," aroused waves of sympathy amongst those alarmed at the do-nothing complacency of the High-and-Dry school, and corresponding waves of antipathy among those devoted to "Protestantism" and alarmed at any Romanizing trend. From the earliest novelists—Gresley and Paget—whose fiction amounted to little more than sugar-coated tracts, one moves to the novels—genuine novels—of Charlotte Yonge. Her propaganda is usually so subordinated to art, in keeping with Keble's advice, that the Tractarian message is often effectively concealed from any but the most alert modern reader.

The massive *oeuvre* of Miss Yonge, extending as it does from the early forties to the turn of the twentieth century, provides us with a veritable fictional library of Tractarian views, social as well as ecclesiastical. Changing only very little with the passing decades, her novels—of which we have provided no more than a small sampling—give the modern reader, once he knows how to read them, the most valuable possible clues to the Tractarian outlook, not only on doctrine and practice in the Church, but also on family relationships and the mutual obligations of the social classes. Miss Sewell, more outspoken and propagandistic, especially in her early novels, and Miss Skene, more activist in her message of the need for charity among the poor and the criminal, together with Mrs. Oliphant, a cool and observant reporter within the setting of a small town, help complete our mid-Victorian picture of the High-Church people.

With Disraeli's ascent into the rarefied atmosphere of the terribly noble and frightfully rich, we encounter, in *Lothair*, the first early whiff of fin de siècle worldly cynicism. The Catholic Church—at least its administration and machinery—is so riddled with outright fraud that the "Church of one's ancestors" provides the only possible refuge for a gentleman of the upper classes. Doctrinal and liturgical questions never appear in the pages of a novel which does, however, earnestly warn against the threat of revolution and anarchy, if the forms of religious observance are not properly observed. With Shorthouse's *John Inglesant*, the underlying quietism of the author's Quaker youth combines with his ritualist predilections of the years after his conversion, his Platonism, and his learning in the religious conflicts of the seventeenth century, to produce a uniquely clever historical rationalization and defence in fiction of nineteenth-century High-Church positions. And with *Marius*, aestheticism and deliberate ambiguity, reflecting the spiritual preferences and ultimate bewilderment of Pater himself, cannot conceal—even behind the veils interposed by the Antonine setting of the romance and by Pater's opaque prose—the author's Ritualist preferences, however hesitant and diluted by disbelief.

At their most strident, the novel-writing enemies of the High Church—whether Broad, Low, or infidel themselves—are hardly to be distinguished from the Jesuit-haters. Both schools of alarmists worry equally about what went on in the confessional, and show an equal distaste for the same features of the ritual. To balance this attack from the left comes the mockery from the right: from those like Newman who have made the whole journey and can now safely ridicule the Batemans and Whites, and from those like Longueville, birthright Catholics, to whom the entire Tractarian movement seems like so much imitative flummery. Still largely ahead of us lies the Evangelicals' fiction, making their own positive case somewhat uneasily in a form which they always mistrust as such (novels are almost as wicked as stage plays), but which they recognize they must adopt if they are to hold their own in the propaganda wars of religion that have replaced the battlefields of the seventeenth century.

As the nineteenth century draws to a close, the charge levelled against the Tractarians since their earliest days—that they emphasize the externals of the church service at the expense of their social duties to the poor and unfortunate—grows shriller. Of course, many High Churchmen had from the beginning devoted themselves to unceasing labors of charity, and we have encountered them in Charlotte Yonge's *Castle-Builders* and in Miss Skene's *Hidden Depths.* But as a minority for decades denied preferment by the crown itself, the Tractarian leaders remained on the defensive, and were often removed from the life of the church. Not until the seventies and eighties did Tractarians—largely through Gladstone's influence over the Queen—obtain bishoprics and other preferment to influential positions. The nineties saw the foundation of High-Anglican religious orders devoted to charitable purposes, among them that of the Society of the Divine Compassion launched in 1894 by the Honorable and Reverend J. G. Adderley.

The year before, Adderley's *Stephen Remarx* (1893, no. 38) told the story of a socialist High-Church priest, whose activities literally bring about his martyrdom. The "Marx" in the hero's preposterous name is no accident: himself a convinced socialist, Adderley puts into the mouth of Remarx his own view that the callousness of businessmen and manufacturers is wholly inconsistent with Christianity. And of course, as in Miss Skene's *Hidden Depths,* the Church itself is full of un-Christian clergymen. We may view Adderley's little novel as he himself viewed it: "This is a Tract, not a Novel," he wrote in a preface to a later work of fiction, anticipating the reviewers who would otherwise say, as they had said before, "This is a bad novel." At the end of the Victorian age, then, we are, so far as the Tractarian novel is concerned, back where we started, with Gresley and Paget. Although their themes are now different, the Tractarians are once again writing tracts.

CHAPTER 3.

THE LOW CHURCHMEN [EVANGELICALS] AND THEIR ENEMIES

The "Great Change" and Other Evangelical Tenets

In many of the novels we have been considering—beginning with the very first, Grace Kennedy's *Father Clement*—we have encountered Evangelicals, bitter opponents of Rome and Romanism, and by that token often even more bitter opponents of the Tractarians. The second great party within the Church of England, the Evangelicals of one shade or another commanded the loyalty of most of the Church's communicants. By the early fifties, High Churchmen were strong in the southwest, in the dioceses of Exeter and of Bath and Wells, and at Oxford. Elsewhere (except for a small pocket in the Episcopalian Church of Scotland) the Evangelicals held sway, more particularly in the populous towns. But it was the Catholics, the converts to Catholicism, and the Tractarians who chiefly caught the public eye, beginning with Catholic Emancipation in 1829, and continuing with the spread of the Oxford movement in the thirties, with the conversion of Newman in 1845, with the Maynooth controversy, and with the re-establishment of the Catholic hierarchy in England in 1850. These trends captured the headlines and inspired the novelists—friendly and unfriendly—the apologists, and the enemies.

Although we have given attention in passing to the Evangelicals and their views of their opponents, it has hitherto not been possible to emphasize properly how greatly their beliefs differed from those of the High-Church party. High and Low extremists seem to the modern student to have been virtually members of two different faiths. They were not, of course; all were still recognizably Christian, and those matters which they believed in common were more important than those on which they differed. But the beliefs they held in common needed and received little discussion, while the doctrines about which they differed became the cornerstones of their new fortresses. It is these that made such apparently irreconcilable enemies out of High and Low—these, and the social tastes and distastes to which they gave rise.

Of these doctrines none was more important for the Evangelical than his insistence upon the necessity of a specific "conversion" to Christianity by every individual, and upon the primacy of "justification by faith" as against good works. Both doctrines had their roots in Puritanism, inside and outside the Church of England; the Methodist revival of the eighteenth century—first inside the church and then outside it—laid equal stress upon them. Of the Evangelicals within the church, William Wilberforce (1759-1833), for example—zealous pioneer (who, with his fellow Evangelicals in Parliament and out, led the way in so many major philanthropic reforms)—had four sons, three of whom became clergymen. To his little son Samuel (later the celebrated Bishop, first of Oxford and then of Winchester) the senior Wilberforce wrote in 1814, when the boy was nine years old:

> You must take pains to prove to me that you are nine not in years only but in head and heart and mind. Above all, my dear Samuel, I am anxious to see decisive marks of your having begun to undergo the *great change.* I come again and again to look to see if it really be begun, just as a gardener walks up again and again to examine his fruit trees and see if his peaches are set; if they are swelling and becoming larger, finally if they are becoming ripe and rosy. I would willingly walk barefoot from this place to Sandgate to see a clear proof of the great change begun in my dear Samuel at the end of my journey.

This "great change" is the conversion for which Evangelical parents anxiously looked in their children. Its signs were the manifestation of outward piety, of religious earnestness, of "seriousness," not necessarily gloomy or austere, indeed often accompanied by "joyousness," provided it was "Christian joyousness." More specifically, conversion meant the acceptance of the Christian religion and the Evangelical doctrines.

Despite their key importance to the Evangelicals, actual "conversions" are relatively infrequent in fiction. They are seldom fully described, and may be precipitated in many different ways. Perhaps naturally, they are most often to be met with in Evangelical stories for children, designed to edify and presumably to speed the conversion of the young reader. Thus in Catherine Sinclair's *Holiday House* (1839, NIS), young Harry and Laura Graham, around whom the story revolves, have a fifteen-year-old elder brother, Frank, who—it is clear—has already experienced his conversion. He reads his Bible assiduously. It is "evident that by the blessing of God, he had been early turned away from the broad path that leadeth to destruction, in which every living person would naturally walk, and led into the narrow path that leadeth to eternal life." Even in the navy, Frank continues to read the Bible, and takes such delight in it that he becomes a favorite in the officers' mess. It is important to note in passing the key place taken in Evangelical thinking by "the Bible and the Bible alone," and to remind ourselves, for example, of the way in which the Catholics in *Father Clement* vainly try to keep it out of the hands of their young charges, and how, when they have failed, conversions to Protestantism follow rapidly. Frank Graham's death converts the naughty (but not wicked) Harry and Laura. "All was changed within and around them—sorrow had filled their hearts." They had "witnessed the realities" of the world; "they had experienced the importance of religion—they had learned the frailty of earthly joy"; and "they had received, amidst tears and sorrows, the last injunction of a dying brother to 'call upon the Lord when He is near, and to seek Him while He may yet be found.' "

In the case of Harry and Laura, then, it is the particular experience of Frank's death that leads to the "great change." We shall find conversions occurring under other circumstances to other persons in fiction. For moderate Evangelicals, the necessity of conversion meant only that human beings are by nature selfish and need to have their higher instincts awakened by growing religious awareness before they can practice Christian behavior: in this form, the doctrine is hard to reject. But many if not most Evangelicals, at least those who wrote novels and who appeared in novels, took and advocated a far more extreme position: that "every individual must experience," at some given day or hour, "certain prescribed sensations in a particular order." Harry and Laura Graham did so, and we shall be able to refine our ideas of the Evangelical conversions by looking at other case histories in other novels. Such individual "conversions" of persons—notably children—already nominally Christian did not enter the purview of a High Churchman, for whom the sacrament of infant baptism—providing regeneration—served until confirmation and the first communion to cleanse the Christian child of sin. The Low Churchman put far less emphasis on the sacraments than the High, denying the regenerative power of infant baptism.

"Justification by faith" means that forgiveness of sins ("justification") and therefore salvation derive only from faith, not from any mere "routine of outward observances," but from a consciousness of union with the Savior. As an Evangelical hymn put it, "When upward I fly—Quite justified I," a verse particularly scorned by the Broad-Church Master of Balliol, Benjamin Jowett: "How cocky they are!" he would say, contemptuously, "who can repeat a thing like that?" Pushed to extremes, the doctrine implies that moral behavior in one's lifetime counts for nothing in attaining salvation: "good works" here on earth are of no use. Such a view reduces faith itself to little more than a faith in one's own salvation.

This brings one into line with the Calvinist belief in predestination and in the inability of any man to change God's unalterable decision, made before the world began, about the future of his soul. For the Calvinist, earthly comfort can derive only from seeking for external signs that one *is* in fact among the elect; to this extent, a man who does good deeds may be more likely to have been from the beginning one of God's chosen than a man who does evil deeds. Yet conduct is essentially irrelevant and immaterial: good deeds cannot save and bad deeds cannot damn. The sins of the believer, the man with faith, were forgiven before they were committed: he is "justified" by faith. And the good deeds of an unbeliever count for nothing: they are only "splendid sins"; he has no faith and cannot be justified—acquitted.

Like most theological tenets, this one is seldom argued as such in the pages of novels, except in those which are merely theological debate disguised as fiction. But the principle—assumed by both its proponents and its opponents to be thoroughly understood by all readers—underlies many episodes in Evangelical and anti-Evangelical fiction; so a modern reader must apprehend it as keenly as did a Victorian reader. In another children's story, for example—this time an anti-Evangelical one by Newman's Tractarian sister, Harriett Mozley, *The Lost Brooch* (1841, NIS)—a devoutly Evangelical girl of sixteen, Constance Duff, argues fiercely against her High-Church cousins that faith in Christ alone—not the sacraments of baptism or the Lord's Supper, and certainly not penance—brings regeneration. Only the "inner Witness" can assure a believer that he does in fact believe. To this Constance adds the (originally Lutheran) doctrine of "imputed righteousness": only because Christ had an inexpressibly large oversupply of righteousness, which he was ready to "impute" or share out with those who were justified by their faith in him, is salvation attainable at all. "My sins," says Constance Duff, "are washed away by His blood, and my heart renewed by His spirit; I renounce my own righteousness and His righteousness is imputed to me."

It is little wonder that Constance finds the chapels of Dissenting sects more agreeable to her than any service, no matter how "Low," of the Church of England. In fact, after a tour among the Dissenters, Constance prefers the Quakers to all other sects and tries to persuade members of the Church of England to attend Quaker meetings with her. She attacks their argument that "if you profess to be of the church, you must submit to her teaching," which her own brother advances against her. We shall often find in novels this close relationship between extreme Evangelicals, nominally members of the Church of England, and Dissenters (Nonconformists) who are outside the Church: these two groups are far closer to one another than many Low Churchmen are to the members of any other party within their own church.

In Constance's brother's argument, one sees also the High-Church teaching that one must "submit" to the authority of the Church. Not at all, said the Evangelicals. One must exercise one's right of "private judgment." This great argument between Low and High we have often encountered: in *Loss and Gain*, for example, we remember Newman's assertion that Charles Reding had the duty to exercise his private judgment until the moment when it took him into the Church of Rome, and that thereafter he must abandon it and submit to authority. Charlotte Yonge's clever woman courted ruin by exercising private judgment. But in *Father Clement* and other novels, we have heard Protestants arguing that one must search scripture to help guide one's private judgment—a precept which, the Catholics gleefully retorted, led to every man's interpreting the Bible in his own way, and so to a multiplication of warring Christian sects, each one of which deplored the existence of all the others.

For one who regards "the Bible and the Bible alone" as the "religion of Protestants," every word in the Bible is just as inspired as every other word; the entire book is a single work dictated by God himself. It cannot err. If it seems to err, or if there seem to be internal contradictions, these must be reconciled by casuistry. Since all books of the Bible are equally valuable, and the Old Testament is four times as long as the New, the mere equal division of one's time uniformly over the whole text leads to the spending of four times as much on the Old as on the New. This in turn leads to various forms of "Judaizing."

Mrs. Tonna, a leading Evangelical novelist (see no. 40), whose pen name was "Charlotte Elizabeth," wrote (and published) a letter to the newly appointed Anglican Bishop of Jerusalem, urging him to have his sons circumcized. In Harriett Mozley's *Fairy Bower* (1841, NIS), the Duff children's Evangelical governess is so strict a Sabbatarian that like the Jews, she will never perform any activity after six o'clock on the day preceding the Sabbath. This attitude was responsible for the dreariness of the Evangelical's or Nonconformist's Sunday. "Haste put your playthings all away,/ To-morrow is the Sabbath day," said one Evangelical Saturday-night hymn for children, while in the Evangelical Infant Schools the hapless youngsters were taught to sing, "We must not laugh on Sunday;/ But we may laugh on Monday./ On Tuesday and on Wednesday,/ On Thursday, Friday, Saturday,/ Till Sunday comes again." It was obvious "to any animal with a head of a higher order than a Chimpanzee," declared the extreme Evangelical newspaper, the *Record*, that the Crystal Palace and other places of public worldly entertainment should be closed on Sunday.

The Victorian Evangelicals were of course the immediate spiritual and cultural heirs of the great founders of the movement itself, which had accomplished such prodigies not only of social reform but also of transformation in popular behavior. During the last decades of the eighteenth century and the first of the nineteenth, under the influence of Evangelical tracts and propaganda of all kinds, the free and easy indecency of the eighteenth century virtually disappeared. Dramatic literature languished, as the theatre suffered first censorship and then loss of public interest. Hannah More (1745-1833), enormously influential arbiter of cultural matters who condemned all theatrical performances out of hand, shared with her fellow Evangelicals an almost equally powerful suspicion and dislike of novels. "One of the most universal as well as the most pernicious sources of corruption," she wrote, but she did not altogether forbid them to her readers; and for this she was criticized in firm but friendly fashion by a clergyman who thought that she should have denounced "the whole race" of novels without exception.

The powerful *Evangelical Magazine* in the early 1790's published a "spiritual barometer" assigning different levels of wickedness to various pastimes. Novel reading it regarded as worse than adultery and equally vile with scepticism: novels were "instruments of abomination and ruin." This attitude towards fiction, except for tracts, had of course greatly diminished by the opening of the Victorian age, when the novel had become so popular a form of art. But a residue of dislike for it, a lingering suspicion that the novel in truth was dangerous and wrong, remained in the Evangelical consciousness. Evangelical novelists found it necessary to apologize to themselves and to their readers for writing novels at all, and to find good excuses for doing so. This tended to make them, in early Victorian times at least, highly self-conscious and often awkward about what they were doing. It is no accident, then, that we begin our discussion of the Victorian Evangelical novel with an attack on the Evangelicals by a moderate churchwoman or that we shall find our best and most sympathetic picture of Evangelical influence and way of life in a novel by one of their own renegades.

Cartwright, Ashton: The Cons and the Pros

Well before the Tractarian movement had made much of an impact on the public, Mrs. Trollope—still at an early stage in her career, with only *The Domestic Manners of the Americans* (1832, NIS) and a couple of novels behind her—trained her sights on the Evangelicals with the same energetic malice she later directed against the Catholics in *Father Eustace* (1845, no. 4: see above). In *The Vicar of Wrexhill* (1837, no. 39) she voiced her contemptuous distaste for an immoral Evangelical clergyman and for certain Evangelical practices that she found as objectionable even at that early date as did many later generations of High-Church writers. The fact that she took her own vicar at Harrow-on-the-Hill, the Reverend John Cunningham, as her model for her fictional Mr. Cartwright sharpened her barbs and made her venom deadlier. But she was too good an artist to limit herself to personalities: Cartwright is indeed lascivious, hypocritical, and brutally cruel to anyone in his power, but each aspect of his unsavory character is linked to some Evangelical doctrine or practice.

Cartwright's appointment is political: the living is in the hands of a Whig cabinet minister who follows the wishes of the Prime Minister, "my Lord M_____" (Melbourne, of course, who held office from 1835 to 1841). "Though a bit of a saint," Cartwright is "a *capital clerical* Whig," and so the request of the late Tory vicar's Tory High-and-Dry son to be appointed to the living must be turned down. Cartwright is a graduate of Cambridge, where many think him "quite an apostle." At Oxford, however, his views on "elective grace [pure Calvinism] are famously quizzed [we would say 'kidded.']." Cartwright is the forerunner of all the hypocritical and untrustworthy Low-Church clergymen of Victorian fiction, notably including Mrs. Trollope's son Anthony's Obadiah Slope in *Barchester Towers* (1853, NIS): they usually have Old Testament first names (Cartwright's is Jacob); they are not gentlemen socially; they are often repulsive physically. But women—foolish creatures—fall in love with their amiable and oily manners. A widower, Cartwright blesses people, notably young ladies, with extreme volubility and fervor when they meet or part, which Mrs. Trollope assures us is normal for Evangelicals.

To the rich widow Mrs. Mowbray, whose daughter Fanny is greatly attracted to him, Cartwright issues the warning that "it is just such sweet and gifted creatures as your Fanny that the Evil One seeks for his own," but he assures the mother that if she watches and prays, it will be her destiny to save her daughter. When Mrs. Mowbray asks him for advice, because her fellow executor of her husband's will has quarreled with her over its provisions, Cartwright declaims, "Vengeance is mine, saith the Lord": were it not for that salutary caution, he would himself grapple personally with her antagonist. His advice to Mrs. Mowbray is entirely motivated by self-interest, and he eventually gains complete ascendancy over her, marries her, and obtains control of her fortune.

Cartwright is given to extempore praying, especially in private and with pretty girls. For the anti-Evangelical writer, this practice was the equivalent of the confessional for the anti-Tractarian or anti-Catholic writer: it was by private interviews and heated praying, accompanied by caresses, that the Evangelical villains won their influence over unsuspecting women. Cartwright closes the door of the library, pulls down the shades, smoothes Miss Fanny's curls gently, and kneels down beside her. He is violating the very Scripture, Mrs. Trollope angrily declares, to which the Evangelicals were always proclaiming their attachment, which instructs that prayer should be private. He implores "especial grace for the not yet awakened soul" of the pretty young girl, who—we quickly see—has not yet had the "conversion" that Evangelicals required. "Turgid rantings, and familiar appeals to the most High God, in volumes of rapid, careless wordiness," Mrs. Trollope calls Cartwright's performance, and adds that it is "perhaps the most offensive outrage" for "Christians not converted," or rather "perverted from the solemn reverence our church enjoins in the utterance of every word by which we venture to approach the Deity." Cartwright implores the Lord not to let the Prince of Darkness turn Fanny's talent for poetry into a snare. Fanny is soon weeping passionately, and only a timely interruption forestalls Cartwright's advances.

It is both profane and indecent, Mrs. Trollope assures her

readers, to carry on in this way. Cartwright's own daughter detests her father and warns the sensible heroine, Rosalind Torrington, against him. Rosalind has been brought up by her own father, "a clergyman of the established church," and therefore cannot "continue to make her residence in a house where irregular and extempore prayer meetings are held"; she threatens to leave unless it stops. Banned from the house, Cartwright continues the even more inflammatory sessions in the shrubbery. All he intends by it is seduction: his real object is to marry Fanny's mother, but he is simultaneously toying with the affections of several susceptible young girls.

When asked "at what age . . . one should begin to instil the doctrine of regeneration into a little girl," Cartwright replies, "Not later than ten. . . . A very quick and forward child might perhaps be led to comprehend it earlier. Eight and three quarters I have known in a state of most perfect awakening; but this I hold to be rare." This case has been published, and "nothing can be more edifying than the outbreakings of the Spirit through the organs of that chosen little vessel." Cartwright quickly sets the village ladies to selling copies of the tract about the wonderful child (now "alive . . . in heaven") to their friends for a shilling apiece. He has a little volume of "sacred words" set to the music of popular tunes, which he likes to have sung instead of secular music at social gatherings. When rebuked by the brave Rosalind, Cartwright accepts the reprimand as "persecution for righteousness' sake." Before long, he is reading the Bible with Fanny privately in her bedroom: he has made her plaster her ringlets flat to her head; she now has "an inward conviction of the sin and folly of dressing our mortal clay to attract the eyes and admiration of the worldly." Teased by her brother, she is delighted: Cartwright has told her that "persecutions would begin as soon as my election was made sure!" Fanny has had her "conversion." And her brother deplores "the grievously schismatic inroad into our national church which these self-chosen apostles have made."

Here, from the pen of a middle-of-the-road Anglican who detested Romanism as much as Calvinism, is a very early fictional attack upon "schism" as produced by the extreme Evangelicals. A "shining light" to some, Cartwright is a "ranting, canting fanatic" to Mrs. Trollope and all right-minded characters in the novel. That Mr. Cunningham furnished her with a complete model for Cartwright seems improbable. Cunningham's own "novel," *The Velvet Cushion* (1814, NIS), is a rather mild "autobiography" of a velvet cushion which has been used in the Church of England ever since the reign of Mary Tudor. The device gave Cunningham the opportunity to sketch English history since the sixteenth century; he is anti-Catholic, but also anti-Roundhead, and generally far milder and less offensive than Cartwright. But Cunningham's behavior among the ladies of Harrow did allegedly elicit from Mrs. Trollope an acid warning to one of them that "the kiss of peace changes its quality if repeated!" And there can be little doubt that Mrs. Trollope obtained her fluent Evangelical vocabulary from the sermons and extemporaneous prayers of Mr. Cunningham. The reader of *The Vicar of Wrexhill* can become a connoisseur of this peculiar language by careful study.

Cartwright causes general havoc in Wrexhill. He persuades a nine-year-old girl not to eat her pudding because it is "a sin to care for your vile bodies, and we ought to love nothing but the Lord"; three local girls are "bitten by this black tarantula" and tell their sorrowful mother that "she is doomed [by a divine decree decided on thousands of years before her birth]" to everlasting perdition, and that their only chance of escape is never more "to obey her or listen to her." Mrs. Mowbray feels the "overwhelming influence of Calvinist terror on one side, and Calvinist pride at presumed election on the other." The village shopkeepers boycott Cartwright's opponents: "Mrs. Richards had been refused bread by a converted baker; beer by an elected brewer, and soap and candles" by an equally pious tallow chandler.

Fanny is in terror when her brother tries to reason with her, convinced that she is listening to an agent of the devil, who is speaking to her "of works" when works are useless in obtaining salvation. Mrs. Mowbray's house is turned into "a perfect conventicle," in which Cartwright every night delivers long extempore sermons, and where missionary boxes are hung up behind every door and carried about by the butler whenever anyone calls. Books vanish from the household, which is now filled with "Evangelical Magazines, Christian Observers, Missionary Reports, and Religious

Tracts of all imaginable sorts and sizes." Though the family schism has its humorous side, it is also deeply pathetic; Mrs. Mowbray tells her only son that she has come to believe that her entire past life was a sin, that "living in peace and happiness with your unregenerate father was an abomination in the sight of the Lord," and that her only hope for salvation lies in hating everything that she once loved. By the time Cartwright actually proposes, the canting mixture of heavenly and carnal language is almost too much for the reader's stomach, as Mrs. Trollope intended.

The withholding of money from the poor until they have convinced Cartwright's agents that they are of the elect; the writing of tracts, sold for a penny apiece, by all the young ladies of Mr. Cartwright's coterie; the effort to ruin the village schoolmaster because he opposes Cartwright's evening lectures and "expoundings," a favorite Evangelical practice; the wooing of Cartwright's disillusioned daughter by the Evangelical curate, to whom she confesses first that she is not Evangelical, and finally that she is an atheist—neither of the announcements noticeably affecting his fervor: all these scenes are managed with much vigor. Cartwright greatly inceases the expenses of Mrs. Mowbray's menage after they are married: his advertisement, "Wanted to live in the country, A SERIOUS FOOTMAN," elicits many responses; it is exactly the sort of advertisement that filled the columns of the *Record*, organ of the extreme Evangelical sect. Despite the occasional tediousness of the efforts that Mrs. Trollope had to make before she could bring her novel to a relatively happy conclusion, it remains a memorably hostile documentary portrait of the Evangelical as he seemed to his enemies.

The few modern readers who have ever had the courage to tackle Lady Catherine Long's *Sir Roland Ashton. A Tale of the Times* (1844, no. 41) have been antagonized by the priggish hero, the intolerable sentimentality of the love story, and the long pages of preaching that clog its pages. Yet the brave student of the religious novel as a social document and a reflection of Victorian thinking can positively enjoy it as a mirror image of Mrs. Trollope's *Vicar of Wrexhill.* Everything that Mrs. Trollope hated and satirized, Lady Catherine admired and advocated. Moreover, where Mrs. Trollope scorned Evangelical theology too much to study it or discuss it,

Lady Catherine had done her homework earnestly—*how* earnestly!—and intended to edify her readers and speed them toward their own conversions if possible. "I know," she wrote in her preface of dedication to the Countess of Carnarvon, "that there are many excellent people who do not approve of religious sentiments being brought forward through the medium of fiction." But, she went on, she had learned that novels "have often been instrumental in awakening and exalting spiritual feelings . . . [and] conveying vital truths to the soul." Daughter of the Earl of Orford (collateral descendant of Sir Robert Walpole) and wife of a wealthy country gentleman, Lady Catherine was that relatively rare specimen, an Evangelical noblewoman, lending the prestige of her name to a piece of intense Low-Church pleading. It is true, of course, as critics duly note, that *Sir Roland Ashton* is anti-Tractarian, but its chief emphasis is on the positive propagation of Evangelical views rather than on the effort to destroy those of the opposition.

Conversions stud the pages of the novel: when we meet the angelic hero, we learn that "the light of holy truth had early shone upon him . . . his soul was stayed upon his heavenly father," and his greatest fear is "a coolness of heart toward God," typical Evangelical phraseology for the deeply personal individual intimacy with God that Evangelicals felt and preached. Indeed, Roland's childhood was always godly, brought up as he was by right-thinking Evangelical parents, "nursed . . . with love and kindness." It was not until he reached the age of seventeen or eighteen, however, that the "great change" was wrought. Lying on a hillside and listening to the tolling of a church bell, Sir Roland had been suddenly convinced that he had not loved God enough and could not answer to him for a thousandth part of his sins. In his anguish he had thought of the scriptural passage, "Thou hast destroyed thyself, but in Me is thy help." Then the Holy Spirit "opened my soul to the joyful reception of the free unpurchaseable salvation of Christ." As for Sir Roland's close friend Scott (later Lord Wentworth), he has been brought up "in the world" and has led a life of dissipation. It is Scott's elder cousin Singleton, an Evangelical clergyman, who brings about his conversion, causing him "to see things as the Almighty saw them" and producing "a great and happy change," which is not further described, but whose nature we now understand.

Much of the first volume of the novel is taken up with Roland's active effort to convert a sad infidel, Mr. Anstruther, an English diplomat on the staff of Sir Roland's uncle, Lord N____, ambassador to "a northern court" in Europe in "a dissipated capital." Here Sir Roland, at twenty-five, is shocked at the seamy side of diplomacy, and protests to his uncle about the lying that seems to be required as part of the day's work. The admiring but worldly uncle decries Sir Roland's "unnecessary scrupulosity," but Sir Roland stoutly maintains that "if God means nations to have diplomatic relations, such intercourse must be carried on according to His laws." This particular reform project apparently proving too difficult, Ashton contents himself with lecturing to Anstruther, a task facilitated by the fact that Anstruther is on his deathbed in any case.

In contrast to Sir Roland, Anstruther has had a most unhappy childhood, his devout and loving mother having knowingly married an infidel. When she had tried to convert her husband, he had quoted Scripture at her, "Be ye not unequally yoked together with unbelievers": she had always known that he had no faith; so she should not now "intrude" her "cursed cant" upon him. At the moment when she lay dying, the senior Anstruther had literally torn their young son from her arms. What wonder if Anstruther has grown up a cynic? Lady Catherine—whatever her literary shortcomings—has at least perceived the importance of early childhood surroundings in determining later attitudes toward religion, and both Sir Roland's piety and Anstruther's impiety are psychologically credible.

Unable to believe that after a life of sinfulness it is not too late for divine forgiveness, Anstruther—having for the first time in twenty years read the Bible (loaned him by Sir Roland)—can now be reminded that "the blood of Christ cleanseth from all sin." Does not this mean, however—as the Evangelicals' opponents always asserted—that a mere last-minute repentance can save a hardened sinner? No, says Sir Roland: although "by Christ's merits *alone* can we be saved," yet "without holiness no man shall see Christ." Our sins were cancelled out in advance at the moment of Christ's crucifixion; but personal holiness, a true faith in Christ, a longing after righteousness, are all indispensable. Did not Christ say to the thief on the Cross, "Verily today shalt thou be with Me in Paradise?" So

Lady Catherine stresses the need for good works as well as faith, taking a position far less extreme than that of many Low Churchmen and so putting herself in a position to argue the matter with the opposition.

In due course, Anstruther is convinced and converted, and on his deathbed he receives the sacrament from Singleton, the Low-Church clergyman whom he prefers to the frivolous chaplain of the embassy. Singleton consents, but only upon ascertaining that Anstruther's conversion is genuine: "I really could not have done it . . . if he had been one of those, who, having neglected religion all their lives, take this rite, at the last gasp, as a sort of moral or spiritual panacea; and place as much dependence on it as the deluded Papist does on the 'Viaticum' of his church." Yet the receiving of "the Lord in his heart," which really saves Anstruther, remains a vague process. By way of vivid contrast to his son's edifying end, Anstruther's incorrigible father appears at the funeral service and commits suicide on his son's grave.

Although Anstruther is eager for the sacrament and Singleton administers it, the episode in itself has none of the awe-inspiring quality of Guy Morville's deathbed or Marius's deathbed, or of the moment of partaking as described in *Loss and Gain* by Charles Reding's Catholic friend, Willis, "It is wonderful . . . quite wonderful!" For Lady Catherine Long, as for the Evangelicals generally, such sentiment would be the characteristic of "a religion of sacraments," not of "the religion of Christ." Not only does Singleton, Lady Catherine's spokesman, deny the "real presence" of Christ in the bread and wine of communion; he regards the elements only as "a continual remembrance of the sacrifice of the death of Christ." The Lord said, "This do in remembrance of me," and that is all there is to it: there is nothing miraculous about the Lord's Supper; one must not take the words "body" and "blood" literally; it confers no benefit in itself: after all, Judas partook of it, and it surely did him no good! What an astonishing contrast to, say, the young girls of *The Castle-Builders*, for whom the confirmation and the first communion represented a critically important moment of moral and spiritual reawakening.

Similarly with the other sacrament of the Anglican Church, baptism: this is a mere baptism by water, an "outward act . . . admission into the visible Church of Christ." The true baptism is by the Holy Spirit, and this cannot take place until the conversion (the taking the Lord for one's God) which for the Evangelicals is the necessary prerequisite for the remission of sins. Baptism is not necessary for salvation; the blood of Christ saved *all* infants, not merely Christian infants, and baptism confers no regeneration. Until children are old enough willfully to "sin against God," they are safe anyhow; thereafter, they are subject to the full rigor of the law and "can be saved only by an individual appropriation of the merits of Christ to their own souls [imputed righteousness], claiming the benefits of His atonement for themselves, and laying all their sins upon Him."

Finally, as against those Anglicans who emphasized the power of the priest to confer absolution, opening the way to confession, even to penance, virtually a third sacrament, Singleton declares flatly that the Church cannot remit sins, that no clerical mediator is needed between God and man, that the apostles did not have bestowed upon them the power of remitting sins and were themselves not absolved of their own sins. Lady Catherine does not enter into the kind of theological argument against confession that we found in favor of it in *Ellen Middleton*, for example, nor does she indulge in such denunciation of it as we found, for example, in Mrs. Lynn Linton or Robert Buchanan. She simply lays down the Evangelical law: hers is not a religion of sacraments.

Yet she wears her Evangelicalism with a difference. Sir Roland quotes Keble's *Christian Year*: it is "a lovely book of poetry, and was my delight long before I thought any thing about Puseyism, and, indeed, before that fearful evil had shown itself openly to any extent. . . . in Keble's poems there breathes a spirituality of mind. I despise no good thing let it come from what quarter it may." Sir Roland has been rebuked for quoting Keble, but he rejoins, most significantly, that "we [Evangelicals] are too often apt to forget that though salvation is a free . . . gift, yet . . . labour and love are the appointed paths to heaven. Too many of us are satisfied with being safe, without striving sufficiently to be holy." And Keble's poems "bring our duties as well as our consolations continually before us." Here, as in the dialogue over Anstruther's deathbed, Lady Catherine reveals her preoccupation with a very weak point in the Evangelical armor: the disregard by so many of the need for good works as well as faith, for being "holy" as well as "safe," for "labour and love." She never uses the words "good works," but she obviously is referring to them, declaring that for her, faith is really *not* enough, and that too many Evangelicals acted as if it were.

Not only does her paragon, Ashton, quote Keble, but he likes the restoration of old church architecture, the beautifying of churches where this is not "overdone," more frequent services, greater discipline within the church, improvements in music, and an emphasis on education: all, as we know, important parts of the Tractarian program. But for the most part, it is true, Puseyism remains a "great evil." Even in *The Christian Year*, Sir Roland can trace "portions of the leaven which has worked so fearfully in the author's mind." Keble is an "archangel ruined," his mind corroded by a malign poison. How can a man permitted to remain in the Church of England say that "the Atonement is to be preached with reserve"? The Puseyites do not separate themselves from the vanities and follies of the world: "in the morning at church—at the midnight hour with the God-forgetting world in the dissipations and vanities of the ball-room." Sir Roland has never been to a ball, and he staunchly refuses to give one even when it is considered his social duty. It is a "sickening mixture" when the Puseyites fast one day and plunge into "all the abominations of the theatre" the next. Sir Roland, then, is Puritan in his attitude toward worldly amusement.

Puseyism is a sign that the end of the world is near ("the end of this dispensation" as the Calvinistic Evangelicals called it), since it is clear that Satan is now hastening: witness the "rapid strides of this fearful apostacy," Tractarianism. Singleton argues learnedly and with references to Scripture against the High-Church view of apostolic succession: one of the original seven deacons consecrated by the apostles was the author of the Nicolaitan heresy, which twice in Revelation (ii.6 and ii.15) God himself declared that he hated; obviously the laying on of hands does not insure orthodoxy. Not only are all the High-Church views of the sacraments combatted, but the "proud, pragmatical, Papistic Puseyites" are said to seek only one object: "to exalt themselves and their order [i.e., the Anglican priesthood] and to ride on the necks of the people." Even the Evangelicals, who once were "ever wakeful to the necessities of souls, ever desirous to promote God's kingdom on earth," are now intent only on exalting the merits and power of the apostolic succession: the Tractarian movement has had a pernicious impact even on the Low Church.

Ashton, of course, bows his "whole soul to the Bible, but I am afraid that Dr. Pusey would think me a terrible and audacious heretic were I to say that I adhere to the Church of England, not as taking her for my guide, but as a mere matter of preference." He is "not a churchman, but a man who goes to church." On the day—so greatly anticipated by the High-Church faction—when the Church of England is reunited with the Church of Rome, Ashton will leave her—or rather, she will have left him. Here is private judgment not merely defended but exemplified in all its independence.

No two novel-writing ladies of noble birth were further apart in their views on religion than our Evangelical Lady Catherine Long and the High Anglican, and soon Catholic, Lady Georgiana Fullerton. Yet once one has accepted them as spokeswomen for opposite sides in the struggle, one is struck by the comical resemblance in the behavior of their male characters when personal emotions rather than religious opinions are at issue. Like the Byronic, proto-Brontë-esque Henry Lovell of Lady Georgiana's *Ellen Middleton*, published in the very same year (1844), the priggish Evangelical Sir Roland Ashton and his equally devout Evangelical brother Henry in Lady Catherine Long's novel burst into wild Byronic ranting when crossed in love. Without knowing of his elder brother's engagement, Henry Ashton falls in love with Roland's fiancée. When he learns of the engagement, he recoils in horror, shrieks, walks up and down "in a state of distraction; his wild actions and frantic exclamations spoke the intensity of his anguish. . . . His whole soul melted with agonizing remorse," and the knowledge that the lady loves him better than Roland, though "delightful," brings "with it pangs unspeakable. . . . Raising his arms a moment as if in supplication to heaven, he dashed himself to the ground."

And this is only the beginning of his performance, which is unexcelled until Sir Roland—some hundreds of pages later—learns that he is supplanted in the lady's affections, and puts on an even more melodramatic show of his own. Sir Roland rushes out of doors and towards the shore:

> Regardless of the chill and biting wind, and of the cold, sleety rain which fell on his uncovered head, he went on—on. . . . The remembrance of . . . his hopes and fears—now all turned to despair . . . overcame him, and he fell almost lifeless to the turf. No burst of anguish came to relieve him—no tear flowed to ease his burning brain; and, excited almost to madness, it seemed as if all the demons from the depths of hell had risen with fury to take possession of the soul from which they had so long been exiled. . . . Jealousy, hatred, revenge—all in turn weakened him; till, writhing under their deadly influence, in the frenzy of despair he exclaimed, "My God! my God! why hast Thou forsaken me?"

After this, sleeplessness sets in, and then, of course, brain fever. From which one may conclude that in 1844 Anglo-Catholic young men and Evangelical young men were both duty bound to indulge themselves in Byronic behavior under these circumstances. Not even all of Sir Roland's piety avails him in this crisis.

Long afterwards, however, Sir Roland, reflecting on the lessons of his disappointment, declares that "the simple bereavements of earth" are nothing when compared to "the deliverance of my soul from the power of Satan." God humbled his pious but "wavering" heart: but afflictions of this sort "are not punishments—witness Job." Ashton has come to believe that "no suffering . . . comes from the hand of God Himself, for 'from him cometh every good gift,' not evil ones." His friend Scott protests that "we are told that 'sanctified afflictions are amongst the chief mercies,' " but Roland answers that "the sanctification is the mercy, not the afflictions." All trouble comes direct from Satan and is "permitted by God, not commanded." Pressed by Scott for scriptural evidence supporting this novel belief, Sir Roland produces some, and with cheerful gloom continues to support his private judgment on the matter. Here we may leave him, commending him once again to the reader as the perfect specimen of Evangelical hero, whose views, though thoroughly Low-Church, have yet some individual distinction of their own, and whose behavior and conversation provide an excellent handbook to Evangelical patterns of thought and action.

Eric and Janet: Two Studies in Repentance

Of all the novels selected for this series, F.W. Farrar's *Eric; or, Little by Little* (1858, no. 42) may have been the most widely read. Written for schoolboys, and enormously popular in its own day (some fifty-odd editions were called for), it was from the first the subject of controversy. One schoolboy wrote the author that "it was through reading Eric that I first learnt to hate sin, and ever since that time, about four years ago, I have tried to live a pure, brave and true life in school." Charlotte Yonge, Tractarian that she was, in 1869 criticized *Eric* as a "morbid dismal tale, which we hope no mother or boy reads." All it could do, she added, was to "make them unhappy or suspicious," and in addition, it demonstrates "by numerous telling examples, that the sure reward of virtue is a fatal accident." Kipling's schoolboys in *Stalky and Company* (1899, NIS), forty years after *Eric* was published, loathed it, and they turned its hero's name into a pejorative verb, displaying their contempt for "beastly Ericking." A modern scholar dismisses Farrar's schoolboy world as "the nightmare emanation of some morbid, introverted brain."

In later years the novel slumbered virtually unread, and was mentioned only to elicit a knowing sneer. It is now experiencing a modest revival: at least three scholarly articles have appeared on it since 1967. The first praises it as a thriller, admiring its verisimilitude and hailing it as "a remarkably penetrating novel of adolescence, and . . . an invaluable document in nineteenth-century education." The second dislikes the "pious prose," but insists on the importance of the novel as a social document; the third demonstrates in fascinating detail the exact resemblances between school life as it was portrayed in *Eric* and as it is recorded in many nonfictional sources of the period. Many of the incidents dismissed as the most "improbable" or "contrived" actually happened.[1]

But none of the recent rediscoverers of *Eric* has examined its religious message. Farrar was the product of the Evangelical King William's School on the Isle of Man, the original of Roslyn School in *Eric*. He then went on to the University of London and to Cambridge, where the strong Evangelical influences were continued. And although he later fell under the influence of the liberal-minded Broad Churchman F.D. Maurice, he never abandoned his Evangelical fervor. He took orders, taught at Harrow and the Marlborough School, became Headmaster of Marlborough, and eventually Dean of Canterbury. He wrote three other novels of school and college (*Julian Home*, 1858; *St. Winifred's; or, The World of School*, 1862; and *The Three Homes*, 1872) and two novels of the ancient world, in addition to many articles. In one he praised John Wesley's "noble, evangelistical, apostolical, and self-denying labours." He also wrote a famous *Life of Christ* (1874), which had an enormous sale. At an Oxford dinner party, Farrar unwisely complained aloud that all he himself had ever made from it was three hundred pounds. To which—it being Oxford—came the answer, "You forget that in the good old days the same job was done for thirty pieces of silver."

Like Lady Catherine Long, who acknowledged that novels about religion were widely disapproved among Evangelicals, Farrar retained the residual Evangelical suspicion of the novel as such. Long after they had begun to read and write fiction, Evangelicals somehow felt that they must always "impressively remind the reader of futurity." They felt that they must not allow themselves to be caught up in their narratives as mere story tellers. They insisted repeatedly that they were *not* writing fiction but were dealing with "facts." And they constantly stood aside and preached, underlining all their points heavily. For Eric's parents in India religion is "not a system but a habit—not a theory but a continued act of life." And

1. See Mary Hobbs, "Fair Play for Eric," *Times Literary Supplement* (November 30, 1967): 1150; A. Jamieson, "F. W. Farrar and Novels of the Public Schools," *British Journal of Educational Studies* 16 (1968): 271-278; P. G. Scott, "The School Novels of Dean Farrar," *ibid.* 19, no. 2 (1971): 163-182.

throughout the story religious observances play a negligible part. Just as Sir Roland Ashton is wholly unsacramental, and belongs to the Church of England as a matter of convenience only, so the emphasis in *Eric* is on private prayer and on the constant necessity to fight original sin in one's own nature. Eric has much good in his character but, like many schoolboys, is too weak to resist the attractions of easy popularity and to hold out against temptation, as some of his schoolfellows are able to do.

So "little by little" he succumbs to the pressure to commit the schoolboy sins: he tolerates and then uses bad language; he smokes, drinks, keeps evil company, and neglects his prayers. He never tells a lie or steals, which are the two worst sins for Evangelicals, but he cannot exculpate himself from a charge of theft, and so runs away from school. Not even the deaths of a virtuous friend and an equally virtuous little brother can redeem him, although he grieves over both. As these episodes take place, Farrar steps from his role as narrator and preaches, sometimes to his readers ("O young boys . . . pause and beware. The Knowledge of evil is ruin, and the continuance in it, hell. . . . That beginning of evil . . . will be like the snowflake . . . from the mountaintop, which, as it rushes down, gains size, and strength, and impetus, till it has swollen to the mighty and irresistible avalanche."), sometimes directly to poor Eric ("Now, Eric, now or never! Life and death, ruin and salvation, corruption and purity, are perhaps in the balance together, and the scale of your destiny may hang on a single word of yours. Speak out boy! Tell these fellows that unseemly words wound your conscience; tell them that they are ruinous, sinful, damnable: speak out, and save yourself and the rest."). *Eric*, indeed, belongs to a whole genre of Evangelical fiction for the young—*Death of an Infant Scholar, You Are Not Too Young to Die*, and the like—in which the Evangelicals concentrated on frightening children into believing that every breath might be their last, and that they had better speed up their individual conversions. These fictionalized tracts have wholly vanished from our view. But *Eric* survives because of Farrar's genuine literary skills, now once again being appreciated, and because of the extraordinary success which those skills won for the book.

The modern reader will be unprepared for the vicious beatings at school, on which Farrar seems to dwell with such loving attention to the gruesome details. No doubt, these were "facts" of life for the schoolboys at King William's School where he had gone himself and whose customs he was so faithfully reproducing in his pages. But they were also the facts of life as he thought they ought to be, and as he made them for his pupils at Harrow or Marlborough. Even if a boy has not committed the fault for which he is being unjustly punished, Farrar, like many schoolmasters of his day and of later days as well, sees something redeeming about the beating itself. Mr. Rose, the teacher whom Farrar most admires, beats and humiliates the pupils as a matter of course, and his "noble moral influence gained tenfold strength from the respect and wholesome fear that he then inspired." Schoolmasters were surrogate fathers, and fathers were reflections on earth of the Evangelical God: one did not spare the rod without spoiling the child; one chastened those one loved. There were many texts to justify a program which seems to most of us scarcely diluted sadism. "Sin and punishment are twins," as Mr. Rose says.

Aboard the ship on which he has been shanghaied after running away from school, Eric receives the ghastliest beating of them all: it almost kills him. For Eric this is a necessity: he has allowed his mind to become corrupted, so that he no longer even "knows his own infirmity." The snowflake has turned into the avalanche, and gentle correction is no longer possible: "He had long flung away the shield of prayer and the helmet of holiness, and the sword of the Spirit, which is the word of God [i.e., the Bible] and now, unarmed, and helpless, Eric stood alone, a mark for the fiery arrows of his enemies, while, through the weakened inlet of every corrupted sense, temptation rushed in upon him perpetually and unawares." So he needs the murderous shipboard lashing, and—sure enough—his conversion follows promptly:

> In the valley of the shadow of death a voice had come to him—a still small voice—at whose holy utterance Eric had bowed his head, and had listened to the message of God, and learned His will; and now, in humble resignation, in touching penitence, with solemn self-devotion, he had cast himself at the feet of Jesus, and prayed to be helped, and guided, and

> forgiven. . . . Yea, for Jesus' sake he was washed, he was cleansed, he was sanctified, he was justified; he would fear no evil, for God was with him.

Eric is now justified by faith; he has undergone the "great change," but he has been literally battered into it. It is surely one of the cruellest conversions in all Evangelical literature: even the hardened reprobate, Anstruther, in *Sir Roland Ashton*, experiences no comparable suffering, while Sir Roland himself goes through only a moment or two of doubt and fear, as the church bell tolls, before he is converted. True: Ashton's mind and heart were prepared, and he had committed no sins. But even some Evangelical readers of *Eric* found his treatment by Farrar extreme (after such a conversion, there is nothing left for Eric but an edifying death), while High-Church readers, like Charlotte Yonge, turned away from the book as repellent.

Yet behind the stern Evangelicalism that eventually brings Eric to his reward through such suffering, Farrar was espousing the intellectual and social ideals of a far gentler man, Thomas Arnold, the great headmaster of Rugby (1795-1842), whose régime was unforgettably pictured in *Tom Brown's Schooldays* (1857, NIS) by Thomas Hughes (1822-1896), a Victorian school story equally famous with *Eric.* Attention to learning, industriousness, enjoyment of the outdoors and exercise, moral purity and earnest piety: these were the ideals of the Broad Churchman, Thomas Arnold. And they were also Farrar's, but with the addition of the fierce Evangelical religious message that Arnold would wholly have repudiated. As Hugh Kingsmill once wittily remarked, *Eric* was "the kind of book Dr. Arnold might have written had he taken to drink" and become intoxicated with romanticism.

In October 1856, Marian Evans, then thirty-seven and an experienced critic of literature and student of religion, who had translated Strauss's famous *Life of Jesus* and Feuerbach's *Essence of Christianity* into English, contributed an article to the *Westminster Review* entitled "Silly Novels by Lady Novelists." She wittily and effectively demolished some of the popular fiction writers of the day, reserving a climactic place for what she christened "the *white neck-cloth* species, which represent the tone of thought and feeling in the

Evangelical party," and amount to little more than "a kind of genteel tract on a large scale, intended as a sort of medicinal sweetmeat for Low Church young ladies." She singled out *The Old Grey Church* (1856, NIS), whose author she did not name, presumably because the book was published anonymously, but who was actually Caroline Lucy, Lady Scott (1784-1857). "Utterly tame and feeble," said Marian Evans, typical of its genre: it had as its hero an Evangelical curate of high social background ("for Evangelical silliness is as snobbish as any other kind of silliness"), and the author, as usual, had no real knowledge of the social circles she was trying to depict; so she was both ignorant and vulgar in her efforts to depict them. "It is less excusable in an Evangelical novelist than in any other," said Marian Evans, "gratuitously to seek her subjects among titles and carriages. The real drama of Evangelicalism—and it has abundance of drama for any one who has genius enough to discern and reproduce it—lies among the middle and lower classes." Why cannot Evangelical novelists show us "religious life among the industrial classes in England," where people do not keep carriages, or eat with silver forks, or even speak correct English?

Having asked the question, Miss Evans—or Mrs. Lewes as she now called herself, although of course she was not and could not be married to her lover, George Lewes, the novelist, critic, and student of science—proceeded instantly to answer it. She remembered the curate of Chilvers Coton in her girlhood, John Gwyther, an Evangelical clergyman who had served there between 1831 and 1841, and she wrote a short novel or long short story about him, calling it "Amos Barton." Early in November 1856, Lewes submitted it to the editor of *Blackwood's Magazine*, writing him that it would be the first of a series of "tales and sketches illustrative of the actual life of our country clergy about a quarter of a century ago; but solely in its *human*, and *not at all* in its *theological* aspect." Since Goldsmith's *Vicar of Wakefield* and the novels of Jane Austen, Lewes added, "we have had abundant stories polemical and doctrinal," but none "representing the clergy like any other class, with the humours [i.e., personal characteristics], sorrows, and troubles of other men." The story appeared anonymously in *Blackwood's Magazine* in January and February 1857, and thereafter Marian Evans assumed the name of George Eliot, under which *Blackwood's* presented two additional stories, first serially and then in book form as *Scenes of Clerical Life* (1858, no. 43).

Amos Barton, like John Gwyther, is a most ordinary man, middle class, middle-aged, "not *very* ungrammatical . . . superlatively middling, the quintessential extract of mediocrity." A Cambridge man, Gwyther had been ousted from his curacy after ten years by the vicar, who wanted the post, with its wholly inadequate stipend, for his own brother. This episode was fact, as were some details of Barton's appearance, manner, and behavior in the pulpit and out; but the troubles that Barton gets into at "Shepperton" were George Eliot's own invention. One can date the time when it is supposed to be taking place as late in 1837 or early in 1838: *Pickwick Papers* has recently been completed and published in book form. As Lewes wrote Blackwood, the theological aspects of Amos Barton's views concerned George Eliot far less than his "humours, sorrows, and troubles." But even these are wholly dependent upon his being Evangelical. His church itself still has the coat of stucco over the original stones, its old gallery, its "huge roomy pews," its music produced by a "bassoon, two key-bugles, a carpenter understood to have an amazing power of singing 'counter,' and two lesser musical stars." He himself alienates parishioners because of his Evangelical emphasis on sin. Prosperous old Mrs. Patten complains that "when Mr. Barton comes to see me, he talks about nothing but my sins and my need o' marcy," and insists that she has never been a sinner: "If I'm not to be saved, I know a many as are in a bad way." Despite Barton's foundation of a Tract Society, the congregation has fallen off; the poor among the churchgoers are mostly heavy drinkers, and only the Dissenters in the village are sober men. Barton, however, believes he is making great headway against Dissent: "He preached Low Church doctrine" entirely similar to what the Dissenters heard in their own chapel. But he "made a High Church assertion of ecclesiastical powers and functions. Clearly, then, the Dissenters would feel that 'the parson' was too many for them."

So theology is important after all. Mr. Barton indeed is a curious hybrid. Himself the son of a Dissenting (Congregationalist) deacon, and trained at Cambridge under Mr. Simeon, he would have subscribed to the extreme Evangelical *Record* if he could have afforded it. Yet in the late thirties, the impact of the "tractarian agitation" and "satire" on the Low-Church party has become marked. Mr. Barton has come to believe that "an Episcopalian Establishment" is praiseworthy; "and on many other points he began to feel that he held opinions a little too far-sighted and profound to be communicated to ordinary minds. He was like an onion that has been rubbed with spices; the strong original odour was blended with something new and foreign. The Low Church onion still offended refined High Church nostrils, and the new spice was unwelcome to the palate of the genuine onion-eater."

The impact of Low-Church doctrine, expressed as the heavy-handed Barton expresses it, is just as unfortunate among the paupers in the workhouse, where he preaches regularly, as in Mrs. Patten's comfortable cottage. He simply cannot get a message across to the ignorant and suffering, because he has not the imagination to see things with their total absence of information or interest. When he preaches, he talks "of Israel and its sins, of chosen vessels, of the Paschal lamb, of blood as the medium of reconciliation," all wholly beyond them. When he talks of unleavened bread, his hungry hearers cannot get their minds out of the dough-trough. Not only has he a "natural incapacity for teaching," but he is tactless as well, when it comes to appealing to the individual pauper. To old Bessy, who depends on snuff for her sole remaining pleasure in life, and whose snuff-box is empty, all Barton can say is, "So your snuff is all gone, eh?," and while she is hopefully awaiting a new supply, he crushes her with, "Ah well! you'll soon be going where there is no more snuff. You'll be in need of mercy then. You must remember that you may have to seek for mercy, and not find it, just as you're seeking for snuff." But as soon as he begins, "the lid of her snuff-box went 'click!' and her heart was shut up at the same moment." Similarly, to a pauper boy aged seven, who has been beaten by the master of the workhouse, Barton says, "If you were not naughty, you would not be beaten. But if you are naughty, God will be angry . . . and God can burn you for ever. That will be worse than being beaten." Now, as we know, there were plenty of clergymen of other persuasions who neglected the poor or were tactless with them when they tried to help them. But this particular form of tactlessness is wholly Evangelical. For his own congregation—all of whom devoutly believe in the Incarnation, but none of whom has the remotest idea who the Unitarians (Socinians) are—Barton preaches a powerful sermon attacking the Socinians on the question of the Incarnation, which is doubly useless.

In "Mr. Gilfil's Love-Story," the second of the *Scenes*, George Eliot moved backward in time, Mr. Gilfil himself being drawn from Bernard Gilpin Ebdell, vicar of Chilvers Coton until his death in 1828, three years before John Gwyther had become the curate. But the main action of the story takes place in the 1780's, half a century before that of "Amos Barton." It provides the reader with a series of echoes, as it were, of "Amos Barton": the beautiful Italian Tina, Mr. Gilfil's love and eventually his wife, dies in the same room of the same vicarage as the saintly Milly Barton. A key to the story's mournful beauty is provided by a melody from Gluck's *Orfeo* that Tina sings which symbolizes her ability to abandon her romantic dream of marriage to the dissolute heir of the manor and all its glories, and to welcome happiness with the staunch Gilfil, who has loved her from the first.

There is less theology in "Mr. Gilfil" than in "Amos Barton." Gilfil, of course, is *not*, as some readers have believed, an Evangelical clergyman, but rather the best sort of "High and Dry" parson characteristic of the late eighteenth century. We meet him first as an elderly, childless widower, long since bereft of his beloved Tina. When he chats amiably with the disreputable Dame Fripp, a beggar despite her possession of a fine fat pig, whom she prefers to keep as a friend, he says good-bye to her "without asking her why she had not been to church, or making the slightest effort for her spiritual edification"; but he sends her a large piece of his own bacon so that she may taste the meat again and keep her pet pig too: a most un-Evangelical course of conduct. Mr. Gilfil does not "shine in the more spiritual functions of his office," but performs them "with undeviating attention to brevity and despatch." From his "large heap of short sermons, rather yellow and worn at the edges," he selects two each Sunday, impartially, "without reference to topics," and preaches one at Shepperton in the morning and the other at Knebley—to which he rides over—in the afternoon. Here he absentmindedly sometimes forgets to take off his spurs before putting on his surplice and realizes what he has done "only . . . by feeling something mysteriously tugging at the skirts of that garment as he stepped into the reading desk." In his youth Mr. Gilfil had "had many a good day's hunting" with the squire, although they later quarrel over the squire's hard-fistedness.

Gilfil's affection for the little village boy who commands him not to step on his spinning top, his deep knowledge of breeding cows and horses, his maintenance of his own stock farm, his habit of talking in the rural dialect with the farmers without ever losing social caste by it, his parishioners' insistence that Mr. Gilfil in person marry them and baptize their children ("the benefits of baptism were supposed to be somehow bound up with Mr. Gilfil's personality"), and their love for his oft-repeated sermons ("not doctrinal, still less . . . polemical . . . amounting . . . to little more than an expansion of the concise thesis, that those who do wrong will find it the worse for them, and those who do right will find it the better"): all this is a gentle, affectionate, shorthand caricature of the High-and-Dry riding and hunting parson of the days before "that dangerous fruit of the tree of knowledge: innovation." No wonder that a "flippant town youth" wins his bet that he can write a sermon as good as Mr. Gilfil's, or that the Dissenting minister inveighs against Mr. Gilfil's "darkness," or that, as he grows older, Mr. Gilfil gives up dining out at the "best houses in that part of the county" and by preference stays at home with his pipe and his gin and water.

In the third of the *Scenes*, "Janet's Repentance," however, we are back in the late 1820's (slightly earlier than the date of "Amos Barton") and dealing once again directly with the Evangelicals. But we have moved from little Shepperton (Chilvers Coton) to the large nearby town of Milby (Nuneaton). The newly arrived Evangelical Perpetual Curate of the Chapel of Ease at Paddiford is an idealized portrait of the Reverend John Edmund Jones, who arrived in 1828 in the same role at Stockingford Chapel, Nuneaton, thanks to the influence of the new Evangelical Bishop of Lichfield and Coventry. Jones's success in the pulpit of his chapel led the bishop to license him to give a series of evening lectures in Nuneaton parish church, then in the ineffectual hands of the High-and-Dry Harold Hughes, whose sermons were inaudible to a rapidly dwindling congregation. "Janet's Repentance" reproduces the situation faithfully: the Reverend Mr. Crewe, on whose behalf such a hue and cry is raised against the project of the evening lectures, is Hughes, and the Reverend Mr. Tryan, the energetic (but physically delicate) curate, is Jones.

Jones had soon filled the Nuneaton church, not merely with Church of England listeners, but with Dissenters as well; a religious revival was under way, and the opponents of change were furious, threatening Jones with violence, and maintaining their hostility until his death in 1831. The opposition was led by a Nuneaton lawyer, J.W. Buchanan, who is the "Dempster" of the novel; his wife, who, in opposition to her husband, became a sympathizer of the Evangelical Mr. Jones, is the "Janet" of the story. Only, as George Eliot wrote to Blackwood, the "real town was more vicious than my Milby; the real Dempster was far more disgusting than mine; the real Janet, alas! had a far sadder end than mine." So "Janet's Repentance" is perhaps closer to an actual episode than the other two *Scenes*, but as with them history has been greatly transmuted by art.

When Mr. Jones died, Marian Evans was only twelve years old, but she had heard him preach, and—more important—Maria Lewis (principal governess at the Nuneaton grammar school, but "more like a friend than a governess," says Professor Haight, George Eliot's biographer) became a devoted follower of Jones's. So the influence of "Mr. Tryan," directly or indirectly, played a part in fixing Marian Evans's girlhood sympathies for Evangelicalism. Her father, too, had been drawn away by Jones's "innovation" from his own former High-and-Dry loyalties, and greatly admired the new clergyman. As a girl in her teens, Marian Evans adopted the Evangelical view that novels were spiritually harmful except for "standard works"; but soon she was reading Scott (whom she had excepted from her ban) and finding that he did not uniformly associate types of character with types of religious outlook. Even Bulwer's *Devereux*, which she had read at thirteen, left in her mind a sympathetic portrait of an atheist. Gradually, by stages well sketched out by her biographer, she came to rebel against Evangelical principles as ardently as she had at first embraced them. This shift in outlook took place in the years 1840-1841, sixteen years before she sat down to write the *Scenes*, and became George Eliot.

By 1856-1857, she was able to take a balanced view of what had always been admirable in the Evangelical views that she had first adopted and then rejected: and this the more easily since she had consistently believed that moral excellence should be made the standard by which all ideas and creeds should be judged. In 1855 she denounced a popular Evangelical preacher (Dr. Cumming) for failing to see that those who differed with him were not necessarily on a lower moral level than he, but that they might indeed, on careful examination, have found his doctrines to be "subversive of true moral development." There was nothing inconsistent in her remembering the true moral excellence embodied in the teaching and behavior of some of the Evangelical clergymen of her girlhood, and in her treating Mr. Tryan with admiring justice. With the balance of a mature woman, though some of the faults, no doubt, of a novelist as yet inexperienced in her art, she wrote a story still capable of moving readers deeply a century and more after its first appearance.

"The collision in the drama is not at all between 'bigotted [sic] churchmanship' and evangelicalism," George Eliot wrote to Blackwood, who had criticized the opening installment of "Janet's Repentance" without realizing what was to come, "but between irreligion and religion. Religion in this case happens to be represented by evangelicalism, and the story . . . is a real bit in the religious history of England." It is a conflict "between immorality and morality. . . . Mr. Tryan will carry the reader's sympathy. It is through him that Janet is brought to repentance. Dempster's vices have their natural evolution in deeper and deeper moral deterioration. . . . My irony . . . is not directed against opinions—against any class or religious views—but against the vices and weaknesses that belong to human nature in every sort of clothing." With this authoritative guide from the author herself, "Janet's Repentance" can hardly be misinterpreted. But though Dempster is wicked, he *is* also a foe of Evangelicalism, and though Tryan is noble, he *is* an Evangelical, and the episode *did* take place. George Eliot would not have been attracted to it, perhaps, had it not been for its moral conflict, but for us it comes through as a beautifully rendered "bit in the religious history of England."

Dempster, brutal drunkard and sharp lawyer, poses as the voice of Anglican orthodoxy: he "will take every legal means to resist the introduction of demoralizing methodistical doctrine into this parish," and fight the "insult to our venerable pastor." His fellow committeemen, who hope to dissuade the bishop from licensing Tryan's lectures, are the ignorant rich miller, Tomlinson, who opposes the lectures because they may educate the ignorant poor (he hates "schooling and newfangled plans"), and the choleric womanizer, Budd. Dempster too is ignorant: he attributes the founding of the Presbyterians to a certain John Presbyter, "a miserable fanatic"; but he is also furiously prejudiced against the "lower classes": "the brood of dissenting vermin that crawl about in dirty alleys, and circumvent the lord of the manor in order to get a few yards of ground for their pigeon-house conventicles." When he is corrected about the origin of the Presbyterians, he denounces the man who has set him right as a person who is "ignored by the very fleas that infest the miserable alley where you were bred."

Although this speaker, Byles, has been correct in his history and unobjectionable in his sentiments ("these Evangelicals are not Churchmen at all," says Byles; "they're no better than Presbyterians"), Dempster calls him "a meddlesome, upstart, Jacobinical fellow . . . an insolvent atheist . . . a deistical prater, fit to sit in the chimney-corner of a pot-house, and make blasphemous comments on the one greasy newspaper fingered by beer-swilling tinkers." The invective itself indicates how deeply colored with the fear of the French Revolution ("Jacobinical," "atheist," "deistical") such unreasoning social prejudice remained early in the 1830's. Dempster's invective is meaningless, except to him and his fellows. His later address to his fellow townsmen reaches a still higher pitch of shrillness and inner contradiction, as Tryan is called "a fanatical, sectarian, double-faced, Jesuitical interloper!"—a preposterous series of epithets for an Evangelical merely trying to launch a series of evening lectures.

When defeated by the bishop's decision to authorize the lectures, Dempster brazens it out: "I knew we had nothing else to expect in these days, when the Church is infested by a set of men who are only fit to give out hymns from an empty cask, to tunes set by a journeyman cobbler"; he denounces the bishop (not the episcopacy, of course, just *this* bishop) for giving in. And then Dempster plans mob violence. The playbill that he concocts against Tryan—with the help of Janet, who is still hostile to any apparent insult to old

Mr. Crewe, the High-and-Dry incumbent—is a masterpiece of anti-Evangelical obscurantism. It is full of puns on the names of Tryan and his local followers, and of attacks on Evangelical doctrine: the Misses Linnet, referred to as "a pair of regenerated Linnets!" are only two in the "large collection of *reclaimed and converted Animals*!" who are scheduled to perform. The playbill reaches its climax with a "*Screaming Farce*," called "THE PULPIT SNATCHER!" in which all the parts ("Mr. Saintly Smoothface, Mr. Worming Sneaker, Mr. All-grace No-works, Mr. Elect-and-Chosen Apewell," and the rest) are to be played by "Mr. Try-it-on." But Tryan's loyal friends help him survive the near riot that Dempster precipitates.

Tryan himself—who preaches extempore, expounds the Scriptures in cottages, and attracts the Dissenters—is the first Evangelical "who had risen above the Milby horizon," a tardy arrival in "one of the last spots to be reached by the wave" of the new movement. He is "treated as a joke" as long as he is only heard in Paddiford Common, an industrial suburb. But when he begins to attract persons of substance in Milby proper, and Evangelicalism is seen to be "invading the very drawing-rooms . . . threatening . . . to stifle Milby ingenuousness," and the lecture project is broached, alarm becomes general among the conservatives. Tryan is thirty-three and personally attractive; his followers soon include several formidable maiden ladies, including the blue-stocking Miss Pratt, who has already published *Letters to a Young Man on his Entrance into Life* and *De Courcy, or the Rash Promise, a Tale for Youth*, and now produces her "Six Stanzas" addressed to Tryan, beginning, "Forward, young wrestler for the truth!" Miss Pratt deeply approves of Tryan's new list of works suitable for popular reading, including notably our old friend Grace Kennedy's *Father Clement* (1823, no. 1), "a library in itself on the errors of Romanism." Tryan has shown Miss Pratt that the worst error of the Catholics is the denial of the doctrine of justification by faith. Personally ascetic, Tryan lives in discomfort in a poor neighborhood, despite his own gentle birth. Indeed, the mere fact that he does belong to the upper classes, unlike the other evangelical parsons whom Milby has heard of, hardens the hearts of his enemies still further.

Tryan appeals to the Dissenters in Milby, where the Baptists and the Methodists are struggling in obscurity, and only the Independents (Congregationalists) have prosperous members like the excellent Mr. Jerome. Milby's Salem Chapel—like the one in Carlingford that Mrs. Oliphant would describe in her novel *Salem Chapel* (1863, no. 58), which we shall be discussing—is "unfortunate in the choice of its ministers." The mutual disenchantment between the Milby congregation and its successive pastors resembles that in Carlingford, although—again as in Carlingford—some members of the Church of England attend the services. But Mr. Tryan's advent provides a great attraction for the Dissenters. Mr. Jerome supports him, and Mrs. Jerome, who had left the Church of England for the Congregational Chapel on her marriage, is quite ready to move back again "without performing any spiritual quarantine": she sees little difference.

Jerome, innocent of later Dissenting arguments about the wickedness of a state-established church, is "simple and non-polemical," and likes Tryan's personal goodness and powerful preaching: "Before you came to it, sir," says Mr. Jerome to Tryan, "Milby was a dead an' dark place; you are the fust man i' the Church to my knowledge as has brought the word o' God home to the people. . . . I've been a Dissenter ever sin' I was fifteen 'ear old; but show me good i' the Church an' I'm a Churchman too." So he marches with Tryan in the face of the threat from Dempster's bully-boys, exemplifying in his own person the strong natural bond between Dissenters of this type and Evangelical members of the Church of England. Those Anglicans who are discontented or bored with Mr. Crewe's High-and-Dry Anglicanism join many Dissenters in the new Evangelical revival which Tryan is leading.

Of course, says George Eliot, speaking in her own person as narrator, the revival has a mixed effect. A few listeners develop only a more inflated verbiage without necessarily undergoing a compensating spiritual growth ("Some . . . had gained a religious vocabulary rather than religious experience."), and simply grow "silly and sanctimonious." Children in the Sunday school "had their memories crammed with phrases about the blood cleansing, imputed righteousness, and justification by faith alone, which an experience lying principally in chuck-farthing, hop-scotch, parental slappings, and longings after unattainable lollypop served rather to darken than to illustrate." But the shallow aspects of the Evangelical impact are outweighed by the tremendous good which, George Eliot declares, the revival had brought to pass: Milby society was for the first time sensitive to "that idea of duty, that recognition of something to be lived for beyond the mere satisfaction of self, which is to the moral life what the addition of a great central ganglion is to animal life." The great central ganglion, the very backbone of spiritual existence, was for George Eliot the development of a moral sense; and this she now attributed to the very Evangelicalism which she had embraced as a child and repudiated as a young woman. Even the frivolous learn that there is "a divine work to be done in life," and although "the notion of a heaven in reserve for themselves was a little too prominent," yet they sense that the way to get there is through "purity of heart . . . Christ-like compassion . . . the subduing of selfish desires." Color-blindness, says George Eliot, is better than total blindness. "They might give the name of piety to much that was only puritanic egotism; they might call many things sin that were not sin; but they had at least the feeling that sin was to be resisted."

And though the social critic may call Mr. Tryan "not a remarkable specimen," and add, "the anatomy and habits of his species have been determined long ago," yet such subtle "analysis of schools and sects" misses the point. One must, says George Eliot, salute the labors of so splendid an individual human being as Tryan. And for us—almost a century and a half after Tryan worked, and only a quarter of a century less since George Eliot immortalized him—for us, who cannot any longer count on subtle contemporary analysis for recognition of Tryan's type, *Scenes of Clerical Life* is the most powerful existing tribute to the good that Evangelicalism once wrought.

Of course, Janet's redemption is Tryan's most dramatic single achievement. He frankly tells her the story of his own youthful sin and the conversion that it had brought about in him. When he gives her the courage to abandon the drink to which she has turned in her wretched marriage, and to nerve herself to undertake the work of self-rehabilitation, he does the Lord's work in its purest form. He speaks "words of consolation and encouragement" when she needs them most, and when she is in most danger of yielding to temptation once again: "She had been unable to pray alone; but now his prayer bore her own soul along with it, as the broad tongue of flame carries upward in its vigorous leap the little flickering fire that could hardly keep alight by itself." And her quiet walk homeward alone in the starlight across the fields wet with dew is the climax of her spiritual life:

> The Divine Presence did not now seem far off, where she had not wings to reach it; prayer itself seemed superfluous in those moments of calm trust. . . . Had not rescue come in the extremity of danger? Yes; Infinite Love was caring for her. She felt like a little child whose hand is firmly grasped by its father, as its frail limbs make their way over the rough ground; if it should stumble, the father will not let it go. That walk . . . remained for ever in Janet's memory as one of those baptismal epochs, when the soul, dipped in the sacred waters of joy and peace, rises from them with new energies, with more unalterable longings.

Thenceforth, Janet is "a changed woman—changed as the dusty, bruised, and sun-withered plant is changed when the soft rains of heaven have fallen on it."

In short, Janet—like Eric, Sir Roland Ashton, Scott, and Anstruther—has undergone a "conversion." She has experienced the "great change" for which William Wilberforce was watching in his nine-year-old son, Samuel, which the children in *Holiday House* undergo at a slightly later age, and which Mrs. Trollope mocks in *The Vicar of Wrexhill* as Cartwright hypocritically discourses on the extraordinary case of the eight-year-old child's conversion. There may be little theology in "Janet's Repentance," as Lewes warned Blackwood, but there is much more than at first meets the eye.

Janet's conversion is not discussed in theological terms: but the deliberate double use of the word "changed" and the supernatural quality of the experience itself, when Janet feels buoyed up and released by a new-found faith, unmistakably identify what has happened to her with the Evangelical concept of the major indispensable human experience. That George Eliot, herself technically an unbeliever who had repudiated Evangelicalism a decade and a half earlier and had within two years excoriated the Evangelical Dr. Cumming, should in her first, deeply felt and intimately remembered fiction adopt not only the Evangelical doctrine of conversion but also the Evangelical terminology of "change," argues eloquently for her heartfelt conviction that—at least in Milby, and at least in the early 1830's, and at least in the person of a man like Tryan—Evangelicalism had been a mighty force for good. The ultimate irony is that the Evangelical cause should owe to a sceptic by far the most moving and convincing existing account in fiction of its own accomplishments. Janet, like Eric, had suffered, in part through her own fault; but it is probably safe to say that no mature reader then, and no modern reader now, can be genuinely moved by Eric's conversion or feel that it is emotionally "true." Janet's is. Critics object that the nascent love springing up between the dying Tryan and Janet mars the story with its sentimentality, and it is hard to argue this point with them. But though "Janet's Repentance" may have its soft spots, it is hard and clean as a diamond on doctrine and the soul of man.[2]

Throughout, George Eliot's plea is for humanity, for individual judgments, against the easy generalization. Let us not dismiss a man and sneer at his mistakes by giving him a label. Is he a Low Churchman? Let us not call him "Evangelical and narrow" and leave it at that. Is he a High Churchman? Let us not call him "Anglican and supercilious" and leave it at that. Is he a Broad Churchman? Let us not call him "Latitudinarian and Pantheistic" and leave it at that. Let us instead realize that whichever he is, he is human, and very likely in torment because of the hard things he has to say and do in his daily work. It is a plea worth heeding as we make our way through the religious novels of the age.

2. It is true, of course (see T. W. Noble, *George Eliot's Scenes of Clerical Life* [New Haven and London: Yale University Press, 1965], chapter 30), that George Eliot had hammered out her own "doctrine of sympathy," according to which ethical and generous behavior towards other human beings is the essence of religion, and true as well that only Tryan's kindness towards Janet enables her to triumph over her misery. But it is equally clear that in "Janet's Repentance," the exercise of sympathy takes the form of Evangelical behavior at its best, Evangelical doctrine, Evangelical theology.

Three Forms of Popular Evangelicalism: Emma Worboise, "Hesba Stretton," Elizabeth Charles

Far more typical of the novels the Evangelicals wrote about themselves were those produced in large numbers by Emma Jane Worboise (1825-1887), afterwards Mrs. Guyton, three of whose more than fifty works of fiction are here included. Appearing in the same year as *Scenes of Clerical Life*, the first of the three, *The Wife's Trials; or, Lilian Grey* (1858, no. 44), deals with the grim experiences and final triumph over adversity of Lilian, a young girl of few social pretensions from a small country town, who marries Basil Hope, the spoiled heir of a rich family. In Kirby Brough, where Lilian has spent her childhood, "the inhabitants thought they were good, consistent Church-people, because they congregated once or twice every Sunday in the grand, old church," and took communion four times a year. "No sectarian or party spirit" had penetrated to the town: "High Church and Low Church were terms but imperfectly understood, and never discussed. Tractarianism and the Evangelical Alliance were alike unknown." So Lilian is naturally "altogether wanting" with regard to religion, and has never seen "the light of truth which every day grew clearer and stronger."

Her marital trials are, then, inevitable, even though her friend, the saintly invalid Alice Rayner, gives her a Bible as a wedding present. Basil's mother and sisters prove intolerant of Lilian's inadequate education. When she thinks of Christ, her emotions are "no deeper" than if she were reading a novel about the crusades. She has a "vague idea" that she is a sinner and that Christ had died for the fallen; but "she did not love Him . . . ; she never felt the need of Him." When asked if she is Evangelical, she answers yes "for want of a better answer"; it is fortunate that she does, since the Hopes are "strictly Evangelical" but "eschew anything like *Low Church*!" This distinction naturally baffles poor Lilian: she trips when she is told that a new local rector is "very low" and replies that she wonders that "they allow *low* men in the Church . . . a clergyman should always be a gentleman!" Lilian believes that "Roman Catholics were very wicked, and Dissenters very vulgar, and the State Church about right, though there was no knowing what the Establishment might come to if *low men* were permitted to receive ordination." Determined Emma Worboise got the largest possible mileage from each such effort at humor by repeating it until the reader was sure to have got the point.

Basil's increasing neglect and his tastes for gambling and drink, Lilian's own feverish addiction to fashionable London parties, virtually destroy her and directly lead to the death of her infant son. Only then does she turn to that Bible which she has so long needed. Then, as if by magic, the combination of her sorrows and a single reading of John xiv brings about a conversion: Lilian's soul cries out to God for peace, and—in a lush passage full of scriptural prose that strikes the modern reader as almost indecent—the light of illumination comes to her. Lilian's is the least convincing of all the conversions we have been considering. It is deepened by a visit to Alice on her deathbed, during which Lilian solemnly renounces "the vain shadows which all my wasted life I have unceasingly pursued. I trust in the mercy of Jesus Christ, my Lord and Saviour, for the remission of my sins. . . ." Basil's conversion takes longer, requiring a nearly fatal illness to get him into the right mood to listen to Lilian recite, "There is a fountain filled with blood,/ Drawn from Emmanuel's veins." Again, instantly, he realizes that like the most hardened sinner, he too may be washed clean, and "all silently the cry of the perishing soul went up to Heaven—'Lord, I believe, help Thou my unbelief! Lord save me; I perish!' " John xiv completes the work for Basil as it had for Lilian.

Mrs. Worboise's characters are as unconvincing to the modern reader in their repentances and speedy conversions as in their conventional sins. The Victorian reader obviously found her satisfying. Without the polemic capacity of Lady Catherine Long, or the vivid story-telling ability of Dean Farrar, and light-years distant from the talents of George Eliot, she is a good average specimen of Evangelical novelist. Her hero, Basil, is from the first reassuringly anti-Tractarian despite his own vicious shortcomings and unregenerate condition. Possibly the best passage in *The Wife's Trials* is Basil's denunciation of his High-Anglican brother-in-law, who has rebuked him for his wastrel's life. Basil calls him a "hypocritical, canting,

Puseyite," and so turns the tables by attributing to him the very vices for which the High-Church writers most commonly denounced the Evangelicals. Basil continues:

> A Puseyite indeed! daring to lecture *me*! a poor, puling, whining, lackadaisical Puseyite, that is neither flesh, fish, nor fowl. Such a hybrid of Romanism, and Anglicanism, and schism, and heresy, and dissent without the name, to talk about his priestly authority! But . . . I told him there were three things I detested and despised—Birmingham jewelry, gooseberry champagne, and Puseyism. The mean, pitiful, black-coated fellow!

Quite different in tone and subject matter, though just as devoutly Evangelical, are the tales of Sarah Smith (1832-1911), who wrote under the pseudonym "Hesba Stretton," the forename made up of the initials of her brothers and sisters, and the surname taken from the Shropshire village of All Stretton. Daughter of a local bookseller, she began her writing career with several full-length conventional novels for adults, but in 1867 struck her best vein with *Jessica's First Prayer* (1867, no. 45), a short story primarily for children, and published, like her later successes, by the Religious Tract Society. Hesba Stretton was skillfully combining two popular genres of fiction. In part she was inspired by the "sensation novel" of mystery and crime for adults, which underwent a great revival in the 1860's, beginning with Wilkie Collins's *Woman in White* (1860), Mrs. Henry Wood's *East Lynne* (1861), and Mary Elizabeth Braddon's *Lady Audley's Secret* (1862). In part, she was following the decades-old tradition of "Tract books," short Evangelical moral stories, often distributed free and aimed at "cottage families," the rural poor, to whose children—destined to go into domestic service—the tales gave good advice on being content with their lot. However poor the readers might be, the little tracts proclaimed, there were others still poorer. Moreover, pure and devout children often had special missions in life: to rescue their drunken fathers from grog shops, to bring the truths of religion home to even unregenerate adults. A corresponding body of stories was designed to teach richer children their duties to the poor: Maria Louisa Charlesworth's *Ministering Children* (1854, NIS) was perhaps the most celebrated: the benevolent rich "ministering" children experience a thrill of self-approval every time they give a poor family coal, warm clothes, or blankets.

But the "tract books," whether written for poor or rich children, usually dealt with the countryside, leaving untouched the problems of the poor of the great industrial cities. Hesba Stretton was breaking new ground when she turned to "ragged London depravity" for her themes, and she was adopting a new mode of writing religious stories for children when she dealt with her material somewhat in the fashion of the "sensation novel," then widely disapproved in just those Evangelical circles in which she would have her greatest success. *Jessica's First Prayer* first appeared in a magazine called *Sunday at Home* late in 1866, and in the new year it was published as a small book. It sold more than 1,500,000 copies and was translated into all the languages of Europe, and into many Asian and African languages as well.

Jessica, the street waif, neglected by her drunken mother, is befriended by Daniel, the proprietor of a street coffee stall, who is also caretaker of a large church. Seeking for Daniel there, the child is told that the church is "for ladies and gentlemen," and that she must go away. She learns that the rich pray there and is told that prayer means asking God for what you want. But why should the rich want anything, and what is God? This pathetic question—often asked by children being interviewed by investigators for parliamentary committees—revealed a horrifying ignorance. No matter how indifferent to the material suffering of the poor, religious Englishmen or Englishwomen were aroused when they learned of the existence of children so deprived that they had never even heard of God. Novelists—such as Mrs. Trollope in her *Michael Armstrong, Factory Boy* (1840, NIS)—exploited this pathos in their novels. But Hesba Stretton was for the first time bringing the harsh facts home to those children of the well-to-do who were previously acquainted only with the pious, subservient, rural poor of *Ministering Children.*

When Jessica hides in the church to hear the service, and is discovered by the clergyman's children, they want to invite her into their pew, but realize that she is too ragged and dirty. Yet they know that the Bible commands that "a poor man in vile raiment" be treated the same as one "in goodly apparel." The Church itself, therefore, is flouting Scripture. Even the kind clergyman can only allow her to sit at the steps of the pulpit. He does assure her that God will let her speak to him as readily as he would a well-dressed child. And so Jessica offers up her first prayer: "O God! I want to know more about you. And please pay Mr. Daniel for all the warm coffee he's given me." By nature, one sees, Jessica is an Evangelical: she calls at once with confidence upon a personal God, whom she summons as a father, and who answers her prayer. And, as happened so often in the "Tract books," the child becomes the instrument for the conversion of the man. Daniel, who has attended church every Sunday without his heart being truly touched, becomes a "saved man" only after listening to Jessica's searching questions.

It is, in fact, the church that is inadequate, in Hesba Stretton's little story. In order to live in the clergyman's house, Jessica would have to be "washed and clothed in new clothing to be fit for it." The words have a double meaning: of course, the ignorant and neglected child must be taught, and so put on new spiritual garments. But it is literally true also that the ragged dirty waif cannot be taken as she is into the proper middle-class household of God's clergyman. Every day those who are most committed to following the precepts of Scripture violate those precepts. Society equates poverty with sinfulness; the church and its leaders and its membership are purse-proud and self-conscious: they have departed from Christian ideals. Herself secure in the Evangelical middle class, but a notable practicing philanthropist in London, where she helped to found the Society for the Prevention of Cruelty to children, Hesba Stretton was sounding a new note in Evangelical fiction.

It is not surprising that Charles Dickens was a great admirer of *Jessica's First Prayer* and that he published other stories by Hesba Stretton in his own periodical. But it is noteworthy that Charlotte Yonge, who regarded the Evangelicals with such distaste and who scornfully coined the term "Street Arab Tales" for the whole genre that Hesba Stretton founded, should nonetheless have selected *Little Meg's Children* (1868, no. 45) as one of the two best. Somewhat more substantial than *Jessica's First Prayer*, this second of Hesba Stretton's Religious Tract Society's publications deals even more directly with the horrors of the London streets. Where Jessica's mother had been an alcoholic actress, Kitty, who kindly takes care of Meg's little brothers and sisters, is obviously a prostitute. When drunk, Kitty allows one of her men companions to quiet Meg's baby sister by giving the child so much gin that it dies. Under the bed in ten-year-old Meg's wretched top-floor room is a bag of gold pieces that she believes must be guarded intact for one of her absent father's shipmates. But when her father comes home—having been converted at sea—the gold proves to be his own, and he is prepared to reward his surviving children by giving them a happy and prosperous new life.

Unlike Jessica, Meg knows all about God. Everything is in his hands. "If people do grow up bad," she says, "God can make 'em good again, if they'd only ask him," a belief that eventually brings about the repentance of Kitty. Under Meg's direction, Kitty asks God to have mercy on her and make her a good girl again. Immediately Kitty's estranged mother takes her back. While lying ill overseas, Meg's sailor father—who had formerly been a brutal drunkard—had reflected that Christ had died to save him. "I'd nobody to fly to but Jesus if I wanted to be aught else but a poor, wicked lost rascal. . . . And now, please God, I'm a bit more like a Christian than I was." In this shamelessly sentimental yet oddly moving story, even the deaths of Meg's mother and of the baby poisoned by gin are God's doing and are signs of his kindness.

Hesba Stretton's *Alone in London* (1869, no. 45) and *Pilgrim Street* (1872, no. 45) ring the changes on her themes. The virtuous street urchin who has never heard of Christ is by now a familiar character; but the determined hard work by which he raises himself from the depths of penury to the proprietorship of a muddy street-crossing as a sweeper, and eventually to a pleasant outdoor job in the country is a satisfying story for an Evangelical audience. Because every bed in the Children's Hospital is full, little Dolly must die, and in the Evangelical fashion Hesba Stretton extracts the maximum of pathos from her death, simultaneously reassuring the weeping reader that there is nothing tragic about it: Dolly has only "gone home to the father's house," and is waiting there for her parents, who in any case soon have another child. The fully developed picture of Manchester poverty—a grade or two worse than that in London—presented by *Pilgrim Street* makes it perhaps Hesba Stretton's best book, as it is the most elaborately plotted of those reproduced here. But her own protest against the church's defects as a social institution comes through most clearly in *Jessica's First Prayer.*

The last of our Evangelical novelists differs so widely from all the others in tone as virtually to raise the question whether indeed she can properly be called Evangelical at all. As a child in Devonshire, Elizabeth Rundle Charles (1828-1896) had strong literary leanings. James Anthony Froude, later the celebrated historian, only a decade older than she and soon to be the author of two novels of religious doubt (no. 68: see discussion below), read her juvenile fiction and found "traces of genius" in it, while Tennyson praised her verses. On a trip to France in her teens, Elizabeth Rundle, influenced as well by the Tractarians, contemplated joining the Catholic Church; but the intervention of a Swiss Protestant pastor saved her for the Evangelical wing of the Church of England. Married at twenty to the owner of a soap and candle factory in Wapping, a Thames-side slum of London, Mrs. Charles did what we would call social work among the families of her husband's employees and the other poor of the district. She also wrote busily, both Evangelical fiction and nonfictional religious works.

Her earlier books were all modestly successful, but the novel that made her world-famous was *The History of the Schönberg Cotta Family* (1862, NIS), set in early sixteenth-century Germany with Martin Luther as its main character. Promptly translated not only into German and French but also into Arabic and several Indian dialects, it enjoyed decades of popularity in America as well as England. Many of Mrs. Charles's later novels were also historical, some with Catholic heroes and heroines, but a few were set in her own day, including several about a family named Bertram, of which the last is here republished: *The Bertram Family* (1876, no. 46). Widowed in 1868, Mrs. Charles was able to live on the royalties from her fiction, and remained an active philanthropist, devoting herself to the Hospital for Consumption (of which her husband had died), to the Home for the Dying, and to the National Association for Befriending Young Servants. It is noteworthy that her friends included persons of widely varying views on religion, from Pusey himself at the Tractarian extreme to Dean A. P. Stanley of

Westminster and Benjamin Jowett, Master of Balliol, both Broad Churchmen.

The breadth of her close acquaintance and perhaps her youthful interest in Catholicism, as well as her careful research for her historical fiction, made her by far the most tolerant and cultivated Evangelical novelist of whom we know. *The Bertram Family* is written wholly without bitterness or even polemic. Compared with Mrs. Worboise, Mrs. Charles is a latitudinarian; compared with Lady Catherine Long, she seems almost a heretic. Urbanity marks her characters' attitudes and conversations as no doubt it did her own. Her family of Leighs (their mother was a Bertram) are descended from the leading characters in her other novels, the Schönberg-Cottas of the German Reformation, the Draytons of the English Civil Wars, and the rest: their ancestors perhaps witnessed so much bloodshed and turmoil in the name of religion that in their own generation the Leighs have come to behave gently and courteously. The numerous grown Leigh children differ widely from one another and discuss every issue: one son—who attends a middle-class grammar school—is "fastidiously reactionary," while his brother, at an ancient public school, is "liberal to the most advanced stage"—anti-aristocratic, anti-bourgeois and anti-plutocratic—and advocates the confiscation of private property. Obviously, Mrs. Charles had a certain quiet humor based on keen insights into human nature.

The father of the family, Maurice Leigh, saintly but not stuffy, is the active rector of a riverside slum parish, perhaps suggested by the Wapping in which Mr. Charles's factory stood. His wife and children admire him deeply and try to follow his example. For Mr. Leigh the fight against evil is never won; each victory only requires mobilization for the next, and he is ready with learned historical parallels to show what he means: "The most elaborate refutation of the Monophysite heresy," he says, truly, "or the most elaborate proofs of the doctrine of Athanasius in his own words, would not . . . have edified the brewers and bakers and tanners of my congregation, although it did intensely interest the tanners and bakers of Constantinople." And, he goes on, "the most elaborate refutation of justification by works, or of the efficacy of indulgences, would not touch anybody today." What the Church does need, however, is the "truth for which Athanasius fought, the Unity of the Godhead, as the Father and the Son and the Spirit, to love and save us, instead of its division into a stern Judge to condemn and a Saviour to rescue." This sounds thoroughly critical of much evangelicalism; it sounds like Broad-Church doctrine. But it is Luther and Wesley whom Mr. Leigh quotes as believers in a forgiving, not a condemning, God.

When Mr. Leigh dies in a cholera epidemic, the local Belgian Catholic priest and the intransigent minister of the local Baptist chapel mourn him equally. To the poverty-stricken priest Leigh had given French Catholic books as a present: they included the book on Christ, *Le Rédempteur* by Pressensé, which had been hailed by one of the archbishops murdered by the Paris Communards in 1871 as an answer to Renan's heretical *Vie de Jésus.* The Baptist, too intolerant to attend Leigh's funeral, nonetheless declares that he had been the holiest man of his acquaintance and that he is certain that he has gone to heaven. The bereaved wife and children carry on bravely, determined to surmount all their difficulties, including religious doubts.

In deep trouble, Mrs. Leigh's son Eustace confesses to his mother that it is no longer "a question of the double authorship of Isaiah, or the growth of myths, or of what our ancestors might have been millenniums since." So he has passed beyond the usual troubles of the era created by Biblical scholarship, by the arguments that Christianity is only another legend, and by evolutionary theory ("what our ancestors might have been"). He is troubled "about what we may be tomorrow, and . . . what my father is to-day," and has come to question the whole doctrine of the atonement and of eternal life. He is, therefore, not merely one of "the young men who glorify the nineteenth century and modern thought, and have too much culture to receive the Old Testament"—whatever the level of their knowledge of science or of "oriental criticism." What saves him is "a real, earnest, painstaking study of the Bible itself, as of any other literature." It leads him not only back to his religious faith, but also to the determination to become a clergyman like his father. In this episode, Mrs. Charles is causing Eustace to follow the advice of her friend Jowett, who—in *Essays and Reviews* (1860), a sensationally disturbing volume—argued that the Bible should be studied like any other book. But she accepted Jowett's challenge, and instead of allowing the recommended study of the Bible to lead Eustace to Broad-Church latitudinarianism or—worse—to doubt, she has it bring him back to faith and Evangelicalism.

To Austin, another son, who has always been deeply devout, but is now unable to believe, his mother quotes Tennyson's lines from "The Passing of Arthur" in which all is "Confusion. . . . For friend and foe were shadows in the mist." Not only Arthur—in Tennyson's *Idylls* a great Victorian hero—but also even she herself at times has "seen only mist" when looking upward for heaven. The death of Mr. Leigh has created a new chasm in her life, and a deepening of faith is needed to fill it. And one's entire faith goes at once, if it has been based—as the Leighs' has been—on Christ and Christian life. Mrs. Leigh has overcome her uncertainties, and she can pray for her son to overcome his. There is much that is reminiscent of Newman in the passages in which Mrs. Charles emphasizes the slowness with which such difficulties in faith must pass. Progress toward faith is maddeningly slow and often seems like retrogression.

In *The Bertram Family* there are no dramatic conversions, although one somewhat cynical cousin is launched by his love for one of the Leigh daughters on a process that in the end brings him to full belief. Handling the problems of a large affectionate family with all the skills of Charlotte Yonge, Mrs. Charles is almost as muted in asserting her Evangelicalism as Miss Yonge is in asserting her Tractarianism. But where Charlotte Yonge's hero is Charles I, Mrs. Charles's heroes are Cromwell and Latimer and the martyrs to the persecution of Mary Tudor. As unobtrusively as Miss Yonge introduces pleas for apostolic succession and ecclesiastical authority, Mrs. Charles defends the Bible stoutly against "vague crumbling criticism," against the feeling that "between the divine words and our feeble minds we need some softening or interpretative medium," and against exaggeration of either its human fallibility or its mysterious divinity. Do not, she pleads, declare (like Catholics and Tractarians) that the Church alone can interpret the Bible, or declare (like Latitudinarians) that the Book is "dry and ancient" and insist on "the living spirit." No: the Bible itself "has the answer to both these depreciations."

Yet Mrs. Charles—eloquent though she is in defense of the Scriptures—is no "Bible and Bible alone" Protestant. She is strongly sacramental, paying devout tribute to the eucharist, and insisting on a "real presence." Yet her Christianity is "supremely rational," and doubts when they arise are "not to be quelled by authority." The skillfully-managed love stories of the young Leighs, the long—some will think interminably long—discussions of religious problems, the occasionally saccharine quality of the emotional scenes, all these are common to both Miss Yonge and Mrs. Charles. But the doctrines towards which they wish to move their readers are opposite doctrines. Mrs. Charles is as surely Evangelical as Miss Yonge is Tractarian. But Mrs. Charles, paradoxically for an Evangelical, often so intransigent, is far gentler: she concedes to the opposition goodwill, even a glimpse of the truth, and she does not—as Miss Yonge does—condemn those of her characters who do not follow her straight and narrow path to severe chastisement.

A Summing Up

While the latest of our Catholic and Tractarian novels belong to the 1890's, our Evangelical novels stop with the mid-seventies. Evangelical fiction continued to be written in the later Victorian decades, but the message remained essentially unchanged. Catholics and High Churchmen moved with the new currents—sometimes, like Father Barry, attacking them, sometimes, like Mrs. Craigie, allowing themselves to be greatly influenced by them. But the Low-Church clergyman Edward Jonathan in Barry's *Two Standards* would have been perfectly at home in the pages of Lady Catherine Long more than half a century earlier. She would have admired him as much as Father Barry detested him, but she would have recognized him at once. In a period when the question is more and more not "what shall I believe?" but "can I believe at all?" the Evangelicals cling to their original positions and restate their case without inspiration.

Yet although there seems to be no further development after the mid-seventies, Evangelical fiction, within the briefer forty-year span of the early and mid-Victorian eras, exhibits a surprising degree of variety. We began with the fierce little tracts of Mrs. Tonna—even less fully developed as fiction than the Tractarian novels of Gresley or Paget—in which children and their parents discuss for pages on end textual *cruces* in the Old Testament, and both together frustrate the wicked efforts of Papists to encroach on the Protestant shores of England. (" 'My little Protestant,' murmured the Mother; and her tears fell upon the bright face that nestled in her bosom," as little Jane—in *Falsehood and Truth* [1844, no. 40]—announces that she intends to "poke down" the Pope with her Bible.) But almost at once, in the relatively sophisticated Lady Catherine Long, we found an unexceptionable Evangelical mingling her exposition of Protestant doctrine with a warning against the prevalent Evangelical underemphasis on the necessity of "holiness"—i.e., good works—as well as faith for salvation.

It is true that Dean Farrar put Eric through the harshest possible conversion, but Farrar himself was a disciple of Maurice so far as eternal punishment was concerned, and embraced instead the Broad-Church doctrine of eternal hope. Hesba Stretton emphasizes the importance of philanthropy as heavily as Lady Georgiana Fullerton, the convert to Catholicism, or Felicia Skene, the Tractarian activist. Emma Worboise cares as deeply as Elizabeth Sewell for the reconciliation between the demands of faith and of life in the world upon her female characters. And George Eliot, who knew Evangelicalism at first hand from the inside, and who had revolted against it, gives a more appreciative picture than any other novelist of its enormous contribution to English life.

No "summing up" of Evangelical fiction, however, can be complete at this stage. Artificially separated by the barriers of the Church of England from tens of thousands of nonconforming fellow Protestants outside the Church, the Evangelical novelists give, for example, only a faint picture of the total impact of Calvinist doctrine upon individual lives. Until we have examined the novels of Dissent we shall have only a partial appreciation of this major theme. And—partly in revulsion against extreme Evangelicalism—there had already formed the third and most elusive of the major parties within the Church of England: the Broad-Church party, of which we caught echoes in Mrs. Charles's *Bertram Family* and elsewhere. " 'What is a latitudinarian, Mamma?' " asks little Sarah, in Mrs. Tonna's *Falsehood and Truth*, and the answer is " 'A person . . . who pretends to be very liberal in his opinions, regarding with equal favour all religions or none.' " This is a dreadful thing, as the children realize; but there is more to it than Mrs. Tonna was conceding. Before leaving the Church of England and crossing to the Dissenters, we turn first to the Broad-Church thinkers and to their sparse but critically important crop of novels.

CHAPTER 4.

BROAD CHURCH

The "Cambridge Network"

The terms "High Church" and "Low Church," even if not precise, do at least suggest large and reasonably well-defined areas of doctrinal difference and of political conflict within the Church. "Broad Church" is a far more difficult concept to understand, far less easily described in terms of theological doctrines or liturgical practices held in common, and not, to the same degree as High or Low, descriptive of a well-defined party within the Church. The term itself, heard occasionally in the mid-forties, was used by Arthur Penrhyn Stanley—later Dean of Westminster—in the summer of 1847. But it passed into general use only in 1853, when it was publicized in a widely-read article on "Church Parties" by the Reverend W. J. Conybeare (1815-1857) in the *Edinburgh Review*. So "Broad Church" positions did not even acquire that name until the early 1850's, although they were articulated well before then, and it is typical of the incoherence of the movement that Frederick Denison Maurice (1805-1872), who is usually singled out as its most important intellectual leader, always denied being a part of it and in various ways kept his distance from it.

The Broad-Church current of thought goes back to the great Romantic poet Samuel Taylor Coleridge (1772-1834), who—with William Wordsworth, his coauthor in 1798 of *Lyrical Ballads*—at first welcomed the French Revolution, but later drew back in horror from its excesses. Having lost his religious faith in his youth, Coleridge recovered it. But for him the recovery was not an intellectual but an emotional experience, a visceral, instinctive feeling of the need for religion. "Make a man feel the *want* of it," Coleridge wrote in *Aids to Reflection* (1825), "rouse him, if you can, to the self-knowledge of the *need* of it," and he will work out his own intellectual rationale. Away with proofs and counterproofs: arguments were of no avail. Rather like Newman (and Newman's Charles Reding) a couple of decades later, Coleridge made the leap: he acted as if he believed, and he did believe. But he was repelled by shallow eighteenth-century rationalism, by rigid High-and-Dry orthodoxy, and by Evangelical or Methodist emotionalism and rant.

Rejecting the "outline of any single dogmatic system," Coleridge was in part inspired by the anti-intellectual mystical German shoemaker and philosopher Jacob Boehme (or Behmen, 1575-1624), by George Fox (1624-1691), founder of the Quakers, and by William Law (1686-1761), an English disciple of Boehme: "all the products of the mere *reflective* faculty," Coleridge wrote, "partook of DEATH." Coleridge was never a systematic thinker: much of his most brilliant perception flowed out in conversation, and his writings on religion are fragmentary and were mostly published posthumously. In Coleridge, as later in Maurice, one finds everywhere the influence of Plato: inquiring into the meaning of everyday facts and thoughts of men, seeking explanations outside the rational sphere. Plato's divine being was one that would "satisfy the wants of man," as contrasted with Aristotle, collector and classifier of all available facts, for whom divinity was "the first Cause of Things." Coleridge and his followers, then, are distinguished by a Platonic *cast of mind*, by an emphasis on what Coleridge called the "reason," which discerns spiritual reality—real knowledge—as against the "understanding," which deals with material reality—merely abstract, quantitative, superficial knowledge.

When applied to the Bible, Coleridgean thinking takes on particular importance for us. Coleridge deplored the standard view that the entire Bible had been dictated by the Supreme Being, and therefore that each and every portion of it was equally and infallibly true. This "petrifies" the Bible, Coleridge wrote, depriving it of its flesh and blood, and turning a "breathing organism" into a mere lifeless conduit for a voice. To him it was a "sure and constant tradition, that all the several books . . . were composed in different and widely distant ages under the greatest diversity of circumstances and degrees of light and information."[1] The Bible, to Coleridge, was God's word "because it is true and holy"; it is not "true and holy because it is somehow known" later as God's word.[2] All one needs to do is to *read* the Bible: conviction of its nature follows. "In the Bible there is more that *finds* me than I have experienced in all other books put together. . . . and whatever finds me brings with it an irresistible evidence of its having proceeded from the Holy Spirit."

This does away at once with the textual arguments that lay at the root of so many individual crises of religious doubt. For anyone feeling as Coleridge felt, it no longer matters *what* scholars say about the time of composition of any portion of Scripture. One *feels* that the Bible is inspired, and that feeling withstands any new textual discovery or interpretation. What a relief to the troubled! Let us welcome all the information scholars bring us about the text of the Book, and let us not waste our time and ingenuity in trying to explain away "difficulties." There are none. We are still some distance away from the "Broad-Church" Professor Jowett's incendiary statement in *Essays and Reviews* (1860) that the Bible should be studied like any other text; in fact, Jowett was emphasizing the need to open one's mind to the results of precisely the sort of textual scholarship whose insignificance—when confronted by faith—Coleridge was proclaiming. Yet one can see in Coleridge the germ of the future Broad-Church position on Scripture.

Breadth, as contrasted with any narrow sectarian view of the Church, is to be found also in Coleridge's views on society and on the proper role of the Church in society. For him society was an organic whole, in which the naturally static influence of landowning and rural pursuits was leavened by the naturally dynamic influence of industry and commerce, while both were elevated and civilized by the "clerisy," Coleridge's word for the sages or intellectuals in general, including the clergy. Scholars in every field, lawyers, mathematicians, musicians, together with the churchmen constituted the "National Church." And the Christian National Church of England,

1. *Confessions of an Inquiring Spirit* (1840).

2. Alec Vidler, *F. D. Maurice and Company. Nineteenth Century Studies* (London: SCM Press, 1968), p. 211.

with the monarch as its constituted head, was part of the Catholic Church, which had no head but Christ. Coleridge gave to the Tractarians with one hand (by identifying the Church of England as part of a universal Catholic Church), but he took away with the other (by emphasizing the national character of the Church of England within the larger Church). Newman regarded Coleridge as "an original thinker, who . . . instilled a higher philosophy into inquiring minds, than they had hitherto been accustomed to accept"; yet in the same breath he declared that Coleridge "indulged in a liberty of speculation which no Christian can tolerate." Carlyle, who once said that if there had been no Coleridge, there would have been no Puseyism, wildly overstated his case. But it is not an exaggeration to say that if there had been no Coleridge, the development of Broad-Church views would be hard to imagine.

With regard to the key doctrine of justification by faith—so greatly at issue between High and Low Church—Coleridge put himself in direct opposition to the Tractarians, and sought to reaffirm what he called "pure Lutheranism," as embodied in the controversial Articles XI ("We are accounted righteous before God, only for the merit of our Lord and Saviour Jesus Christ by Faith, and not for our own works and deservings. . . ."), XII ("Albeit that Good Works, which are the fruits of Faith, and follow after Justification, cannot put away our sins . . . yet are they pleasing and acceptable to God in Christ, and do spring out necessarily of a true and lively faith. . . ."), XIII ("Works done before the grace of Christ and the Inspiration of the Spirit are not pleasant to God, forasmuch as they spring not of faith in Jesus Christ, neither do they make men meet to receive grace . . . yea rather . . . we doubt not but they have the nature of sin."), and XIV ("Voluntary Works besides, over and above God's commandments, which they call Works of Supererogation, cannot be taught without arrogancy and impiety. . . .").[3] As they exist, the Articles represent an effort to strike a balance between what the divines of the sixteenth century felt to be the Roman Catholic overemphasis on the importance of

3. Note that "imputed righteousness"—Luther's "legal fiction" that Christ's righteousness is "imputed" to sinners and their sins "imputed" to him, so that sinners draw, as it were, upon the treasury of Christ's righteousness—is *not* included in the Thirty-nine Articles.

good works, which suggested that one could earn merit and forgiveness (justification) by them, and the Lutheran underemphasis on works, which suggested that faith alone could save, and even—as we have seen—that the believing Christian could safely behave as he pleased, free from the moral law (antinomianism).

The Church of England after 1688 followed the Dutch moderate Arminius (James Hermann, 1560-1609) in admitting the importance of good works in salvation; the Methodists, in opposition to Arminianism, reverted, at the end of the eighteenth century, to staunch advocacy of justification by faith alone. The Evangelicals, responding to the Methodist challenge, adopted the same emphasis within the Church of England. Although the early nineteenth-century dispute centered on the efficacy of infant baptism for salvation, the underlying issue was justification by faith. Repudiating alike the Calvinist insistence that men could not earn or merit justifying faith and were therefore predestined either to salvation or to damnation, and the Arminian emphasis on man's free will, the efficacy of works, the importance of penance, and the possibility of universal salvation, Coleridge took a middle, or "pure Lutheran," view.

The "faith" that justifies is for Coleridge, as we have seen, the outcome not of an intellectual process but of an emotional process, forcing the will to comply in a moral assent. But Coleridge perceived the danger of overenthusiasm inherent in emotional processes, and he had before him the example of Edward Irving, that founder of the so-called Catholic Apostolic Church, whose followers Newman lampooned in *Loss and Gain.* Irving, Coleridge declared, went too far, as did the Methodists, in their "reliance upon excitement."

Moderation in emotionalism: this was Coleridge's keynote; yet without the initial emotional commitment and the priority of the emotions, the will and the understanding could not, he argued, play their necessary role in a man's commitment to the faith that justifies. In his own *Lectures on Justification* (1838), thirteen years after Coleridge's *Aids to Reflection,* Newman, still an Anglican, repudiated Article XI and Coleridge's "pure Lutheranism," and declared that not faith but the sacraments, notably the baptism of infants, were the "immediate . . . instrument of justification," while faith was "secondary, subordinate." While Newman openly discarded the

Thirty-nine Articles on justification, Coleridge upheld not only their emphasis but also their formulation. And in doing so, he rejected rationalism and embraced mystery:

> Without faith, there is no power of repentance: without a commencing repentance no power to faith: . . . that is a power of the will either to repent or to have faith in the Gospel sense of the words, is itself a consequence of the redemption of mankind, a free gift of the Redeemer; the guilt of its rejection, the refusing to avail ourselves of its power, being all that we can consider as exclusively attributable to our own act.[4]

So if Coleridge's position was nearer to the Tractarians on the Catholicism of the Church of England, it was nearer to the Evangelicals on justification by faith.

Very close to Coleridge, and in some ways an inspiration to him, was the thinking of Thomas Erskine of Linlathen (1788-1870), a Scotch lawyer and layman, who became a retired country gentleman and quietly exercised an enormous—and perhaps not yet fully appreciated—influence on several generations of religious thinkers. Erskine's writings (notably *An Essay on Faith*, 1822, and *The Brazen Serpent*, 1831) belonged to his youth. Sympathetic with the zeal of Scotch Evangelicalism, Erskine repudiated its extreme Calvinist insistence that God had died only for the elect, which we shall find vividly pictured in the novels of George MacDonald, who, like Erskine, and in considerable part under his influence, detested it. How could one reconcile an all-loving God with a God who—so the Scotch Presbyterians insisted—would laugh with pleasure at the spectacle of the damned roasting eternally in hellfire? ("There ye wull lie," a proper dominie declaims from the pulpit in a well-known anecdote, "broilin' i' the flames, wi' yer banes roastin' an' the marrow i' them boilin' and the odor gaein' up into the nostrils o' the Laird. An' ye'll cry oot in yer agony, 'Laird, Laird, we didna ken, we didna ken.' And the Laird, *in his infinite maircy*, wull luik doon upo' ye, an' wull say, 'Aweel, ye ken noo!' ") Erskine believed in a loving, fatherly God: God would indeed punish sinners, but he

4. *Aids to Reflection* (1825), as quoted by James G. Boulger, *Coleridge as Religious Thinker* (New Haven: Yale University Press, 1961), p. 63.

would not relish his power for its own sake, using it instead to teach his children. Christ's atonement was for all mankind, not only for the elect, and as a consequence the doctrine of eternal punishment must be rejected. As a layman, Erskine could promulgate these ideas unscathed; his friend John M'Leod Campbell (1800-1872), a minister who shared his views, was deposed from his ministry in 1831. In his emphasis and elaboration upon the emotional prerequisite for faith, Erskine went further than Coleridge, who tried to curb enthusiasm.

Second only in importance to Coleridge as a "founding father" of Broad Churchmanship was Thomas Arnold (1795-1842), headmaster of Rugby School and celebrated for his educational reforms there. By no means an uncritical follower of Coleridge, Arnold classed himself as an Aristotelian, not a Platonist, and was disturbed by Coleridge's lack of a profession and by his spending all his time on contemplation. Yet he regarded Coleridge as the greatest man of his time. Friend of Keble as an Oxford undergraduate and Fellow of Oriel in the years 1814-1818, just before Newman's arrival, Arnold was one of the Oriel "noetics": liberal opponents of party spirit in the Church, differing with one another, but all formidably intelligent and full of verbal agility, distrusters of dogma. Like Coleridge, Arnold regarded the Bible as "human writing" containing a "human history" rather than a perfect revelation. By no means so subtle or so persistent a philosopher and theologian, Arnold lived a far more active life.

In brief intervals of leisure from his duties as a headmaster, he spoke out vigorously for the "revival of the church of Christ in its full perfection." The Church of England, he believed, was only in his day emerging from long stagnation; like other institutions, the church changed with the passing generations. Arnold vigorously attacked the Catholic and Tractarian principle of church authority ("as rotten a staff as ever was Pharaoh's"), and sometimes despaired of the Church of England. His *Principles of Church Reform* (1833) was radical indeed: he wanted to admit Dissenters into the Church of England, thus making it broad enough to accommodate most Englishmen. Within such a church, allowance would have to be made for the widest differences of opinion: its articles would need to be few and as little dogmatic as possible—belief in God, Christ the Saviour, the Bible as revelation, and Christian morality. Having celebrated the Anglican liturgy on Sunday mornings, parish churches should open their pulpits in the afternoon to former dissenting ministers. Arnold declared that only Catholics, Unitarians, and Quakers would refuse to join such a church. Utopian and impractical, his proposals met with little but scorn: even a friend inquired "why Christian unity would be better promoted by assembling in the same buildings at different hours than by assembling in different buildings at the same hour."[5]

Opposed to "priestcraft," strongly emphasizing that the church included the laity as well as the clergy, critical of the aristocratic and royal connections of the Church of England, which tended to make it condescending to the people and unpopular with them, urging the greater participation of the laity in church government, belittling the importance of apostolic succession, Arnold was a natural enemy of the Tractarians. "Dr. Arnold," Newman once asked, "*is* he a Christian?"—a remark that was quickly relayed to Arnold and increased his intense dislike for Newman and what he stood for. When Dr. Hampden (whom we encountered in *Loss and Gain* caricatured as "Dr. Brownside") was nominated by the king as Regius Professor of Divinity in 1836, and the Tractarians wrote violent pamphlets of protest and tried to reverse the nomination, Arnold wrote for the *Edinburgh Review* a vitriolic account of the pamphlet literature on the subject. The editors gave his article the title "The Oxford Malignants and Dr. Hampden," and although Arnold had himself not sanctioned this wording, which has become famous, the tone of the article justified it.

"Monstrous," "almost incredible," Arnold began, as he examined the opposition to Hampden. When fully warmed to his subject, he denounced the "fanaticism of the English High Churchmen" as

> the fanaticism of foolery. A dress, a ritual, a name, a ceremony;—a technical phraseology;—the superstition of a priesthood without its power;—the form of Episcopal government without its substance; a system imperfect and paralysed,

5. Quoted in Chadwick, *Victorian Church*, I, p. 46.

> not independent, not sovereign, afraid to cast off the subjection against which it is perpetually murmuring.

If the Tractarians got what they wanted, it "would lead to no good, intellectual, moral, or spiritual—to no effect, social or religious, except to the changing of sense into silliness, and holiness of heart into formality and hypocrisy."[6] Dr. Hampden's detractors were guilty of "moral wickedness." Arnold preferred, he wrote later, a Roman Catholic ("an enemy in uniform") to a Tractarian ("an enemy disguised as a spy").

But Arnold was almost equally harsh against the Evangelicals: they were good Christians, he admitted, but "with a low understanding, a bad education, and ignorance of the world." His God was not the Calvinist God of power, but a God of truth and goodness. The Bible was not to be accepted as absolute authority ("a command given to one man, or to one generation of men, is, and can be, binding upon other men, and other generations, only so far forth as the circumstances in which both are placed are similar"). And "the revelations of God to man were gradual, and adapted to his state at the several periods when they were successively made." Arnold disliked the Thirty-nine Articles as too dogmatic, too theological. He put his emphasis not upon truth but upon goodness: the moral improvement of mankind. And his emphasis on good had political implications: the national Church should "expose the wickedness of spirit which maintains the game laws [a great source of grievance with the rural poor, violently attacked by Arnold's Broad-Church ally, Charles Kingsley, in his novel *Yeast* (1848 serially, 1851 in book form, NIS)] and in agriculture and trade seems to think that there is no such sin as covetousness. . . ."

In one of his denunciations of the Oxford movement, Arnold declared that the "Cambridge movement," which he associated with Coleridge's influence, was far superior, because it "enforced great points of moral and spiritual perfection which other Christians had neglected" and "preached Christ." Coleridge indeed had been at Cambridge, and his teachings found an echo and a further development among many Cambridge men. A careful recent student of the subject prefers the term "Cambridge network," because the

6. *Edinburgh Review* 63 (April 1836): 235.

Cambridge Broad-Church thinkers were not as closely knit as the Oxford Tractarians.[7] The "network" included a group of young mathematicians, who played an important role in the advancement of science in the university and in the nation at large. Connected with them, and more directly connected with developments in the Church, were a group of humanists, of whom Julius Charles Hare (1795-1855) was perhaps the most notable.

Taken by his parents to Weimar as a child to learn German and to meet the great Goethe, Hare became a devotee of German scholarship and owned a large library of German books: "the man best acquainted," said A. P. Stanley, the Broad-Church Dean of Westminster, "with all modern forms of thought here or on the Continent." Rector of Herstmonceux (Sussex) from 1832 until his death, Hare was a great admirer of Coleridge ("the profoundest thinker whom England has produced for centuries"). To Coleridge, Hare dedicated his *Mission of the Comforter* (1846). In the 1820's while still a Fellow of Trinity College, Cambridge, he was tutor in classics to both John Sterling (1806-1844) and Frederick Denison Maurice (1805-1872), two key members of the "network" only a decade or so younger than Hare.

Like Arnold, Hare favored a large increase in the number of bishops (perhaps tripling the number of twenty-six in 1843) in order to enable them to know their clergy more intimately. He also advocated lay participation in a National Synod (council) of the Church and, like both Coleridge and Arnold, he opposed parties in the church. He wrote "vindications" for a good many people, living and dead, of various shades of opinion, who, he considered, had been unfairly attacked: Luther, Hampden (whose nomination in 1847 to be Bishop of Hereford created a new outburst like that precipitated in 1836 by his appointment as Regius Professor), and the Tractarian Priscilla Sellon, foundress of a sisterhood. The Catholic Sir Thomas More (now a saint) also won Hare's wholehearted admiration. With Connop Thirlwall (1797-1875), Bishop of St. David's, Hare translated (1828) the first volume of the *History of Rome* by the German historian, B. G. Niebuhr, attacked as heretical by the conservatives for having questioned the possibility that the

7. W. F. Cannon, "Scientists and Broad Churchmen," *Journal of British Studies* 4, no. 1 (November 1964): 66.

entire human race could be descended from a single couple, Adam and Eve, and for viewing the Mosaic genealogies with scepticism.

In 1848, Hare wrote a biographical memoir of John Sterling, four years dead, whose tutor he had been at Cambridge and who had briefly served as his curate at Herstmonceux. Still another disciple of Coleridge ("To Coleridge, I owe *education.* He taught me to believe that . . . Faith is the highest Reason. . . ."), of whom he saw more personally than any other members of the "network," Sterling shared Coleridge's attitude toward the Bible. In 1831, Sterling, who had radical democratic leanings, organized a small raiding party of fifty-five Spanish refugees to land on the coast of Spain; he had intended to accompany them, but stayed behind to marry; and when the revolutionaries were captured and executed, Sterling never forgave himself. He resigned his curacy at Herstmonceux because he lost his faith, partly as a result of reading Strauss's famous *Life of Jesus.* When Sterling died, he left his papers to Hare and Thomas Carlyle; Hare undertook to write the memoir because he realized that otherwise Carlyle would write it and would use Sterling's life for his own purposes.

Hare did his best for Sterling—one of those men who possessed while living a charm for his friends that is not communicated after his death by his writings—and warned against the insidiousness of Strauss. William Palmer (1811-1879), a learned scholar and extreme High Churchman, attacked Hare's biography in an anonymous review, in which he blasted Hare, Coleridge, and Arnold, along with Ralph Waldo Emerson, Connop Thirlwall, Newman's younger brother Francis (who passed through many religious phases before ending as a Unitarian), and a good many other "liberals" whose views Palmer disliked. Hare was accused of introducing to England the poison of German theology and of spreading infidelity. Hare responded in a long pamphlet, "*Thou shalt not bear false witness against thy neighbour.*" He had viewed Sterling's doubts with deep pain, he said, but nonetheless continued to admire the nobility of his nature. As for German theology, of course it did include some dangerous writings; all the more reason for helping English students distinguish between the good and the bad. Palmer remained unrepentant.

Hare's memoir of Sterling did not prevent Carlyle from writing his own in 1851. In it Sterling almost disappears, while Carlyle denigrates Coleridge and exaggerates his own influence over his protagonist. It had been foolish for Sterling to take orders in the first place, said Carlyle (combatting Hare). Sterling won proper emancipation from all such superstition only when he listened to Carlyle, abandoned the Church, and devoted himself altogether to literature. In the midst of the Sterling controversy, the Evangelical *Record* discovered that there existed a "Sterling Club," whose members had included Sterling during his lifetime, and who dined together regularly (at the Freemasons' Tavern!): Carlyle himself, the Broad-Church Hare, Maurice, Thirlwall, and Stanley, Henry Manning, the High-Church Archdeacon of Chichester (later to be converted to Rome), and Samuel Wilberforce, Bishop of Oxford! A shocking thing, shouted the *Record*: why not call it the Strauss Club and be done with it? Although the members explained away all the charges of infidelity against them, they soon afterwards changed the name of the club.

It is high time to introduce Frederick Denison Maurice in person. Hare had married his sister; his own second wife was Hare's half-sister. Maurice's father was a Unitarian minister, a radical of the eighteenth-century stamp, who had himself been converted to Unitarianism from Presbyterianism. As a youth, Maurice lived in a household constantly engaged in religious debate so heated that the various members at times communicated with one another only by letter although living in the same house. Maurice was an only son, with three older and five younger sisters. One older sister became a Moravian (in communion with the Church of England); two others and their mother abandoned Unitarianism for a severer Calvinistic faith. For Maurice himself these were "years of moral confusion and contradiction." His mother could never convince herself that she was of the elect. She was neurotic, ill, hypochondriacal, anxious. Maurice could never finish his various later efforts to describe his childhood in writing. The Calvinism to which the women of the family were attracted, and the absence of a personal deliverer in the Unitarianism which they were rejecting, were an essential part of his psychological development and perhaps underlay his later wish to reconcile opposites and to seek for unity. At Cambridge between 1823 and 1826, he had radical political views—strongly opposed, however, to the utilitarianism of Bentham and Mill—but was kept from losing his religious faith, he felt, largely because of his devotion to Coleridge, whom he repeatedly saluted in his later writings. For some years, his religious views were vague, romantic, idealistic.

In the late twenties, Maurice became editor of the *Athenaeum*, then a new critical journal, well described by a contemporary admirer as "Platonic-Wordsworthian-Coleridgean-anti-Utilitarian." But even then Maurice was opposed to party conflict as such: he cared, as he said appreciatively of Julius Hare, more for "the deepest principles of the human mind" than for "the question of infant baptism or episcopacy." As early as these *Athenaeum* days, Maurice—in explaining Shelley's atheism—attributed it to "the tyranny and self-sufficiency of those who . . . proclaim that the God, who became man from love of man, is a cruel and revengeful being, and will punish even errors of the intellect by an eternity of suffering, without the slightest design of reforming the sinner." "An eternity of suffering": this Calvinist view, so widespread among the Evangelicals, was, we see, repellent to Maurice as early as 1828, before his own conversion to the Anglican faith. It was, he said, "a degrading and polluted idea of God." This unalterable conviction, as he proclaimed it more and more insistently with the advancing decades, gives us one major key to Broad-Church ideas and influence: the Maurician concept (like Thomas Erskine's) of a loving God who would be a loving, if stern, father, and who would forgive rather than condemn, brought spiritual relief to untold thousands who feared eternal damnation, and had learned to think of God as vengeful.

In 1829, Maurice became a member of the Church of England, after a long inner spiritual struggle, weary, as he later said, of his "sham creed and pretentious toleration." He had begun to write a novel, and he read its chapters, as he completed them, to his favorite sister, Emma, who was dying, and whom he was nursing. Not published for four years after he finished it, Maurice's *Eustace Conway; or, The Brother and Sister* (1834, NIS) should perhaps have been included in this series: it is surely in large part autobiographical. Some have seen in the hero a portrait of John Sterling rather than of Maurice himself, and the melodramatic involvement of the hero in Spanish revolutionary affairs was surely inspired by Sterling.

Eustace Conway, moreover, passes through utilitarianism, "Low Radicalism [also Benthamite]," spiritualism, and pantheism, which Maurice of course did not, on the way to conversion to Christianity. The novel is so incoherent and confused, and Maurice had so little ability to make his characters credible human beings, that few modern students find it readable. The final conversion of the hero—stimulated by his devout sister on her deathbed—surely reflects Maurice's own experience. Like Maurice, Eustace Conway is contemptuous not so much of the rival creeds, which he finally repudiates, as of himself for not having embraced them with true dedication. In Maurice's view it was almost better to be wrong and committed than right and superficial.

But the fictional Honoria Conway is only a shadow of the overpoweringly pious Emma Maurice, dying at twenty-three and yearning (pathologically, it seems to us) to be "purged" of all her sins, "even if the furnace be kindled seven times hot," so that her soul may be "left in the immediate presence of God, enjoying the vision of his face." Like his sister, and inspired by her influence and by his own grief at losing her, Maurice too experienced the mighty emotional experience of conversion. He was rebaptized in the Church of England in 1831 and ordained in 1834. Thereafter the direct influence of Coleridge upon his development lessened. Recent biographers emphasize Maurice's "compulsive need to care for unquestionably neurotic sick women": two sisters and his second wife (who survived him) kept him in attendance for long periods of years.

The complexities, incoherencies, and apparent contradictions of Maurice's religious thought are legendary. His friend Sterling wrote of him in 1839 that his "incapacity of conceiving a fact except as an illustration of his own theories is something quite singular." Maurice never abandoned his repudiation of the Calvinist "God of Damnation." Yet he insisted, with the Calvinists, that "God be first in our thoughts" and that no theory of "human free will" be substituted for the equally mistaken theory of "Divine predestination." In part these views were influenced by Edward Irving, whose beliefs in glossolalia and healing Maurice repudiated, but whose theocratic Calvinism he admired. Maurice was also deeply influenced by Thomas Erskine of Linlathen's *Brazen Serpent*, whose subtitle was

Life Coming Through Death; and by its theme that "Our true deliverance is on the other side of death, and we must pass through death to get it." Since Christ was "a crucified and risen man. . . . those who abide in Him are those who are dying daily in the flesh and present things, in the hope of the future glory." It was a romantic concept, which transformed morbidity into Christian hopefulness, and no doubt helped Maurice achieve consolation for the death of Emma. Rejecting the Calvinists' belief that Christ had died for the elect alone, Erskine also argued that their doctrines of justification by faith and predestination had turned faith itself into a kind of good work. Instead of focussing their attention on God, men concentrated on themselves and on how they might assure themselves that they were elect. God's will, said Erskine, was a will to deliver all men from evil. Maurice agreed, and he acknowledged that Erskine had first brought home the conviction to his mind.

Too little noticed has been the influence on Maurice of the Rector of Lympsham, Somerset, Joseph Stephenson, for whom he served as curate in 1833. Stephenson was a "Millenarian," who believed that the Kingdom of Christ was already in existence on earth: it did not need to be established. Maurice followed Stephenson's method in searching the Book of Revelation for historical allusions, and he used it as his chief scriptural support in asserting that after the Romans destroyed Jerusalem in 70 A.D., the throne of Christ was established immediately; that present society and humanity were *already* divine realities; that "the ransomed children of God" would enjoy felicity on this earth, "redeemed, purified, and regenerated." From Stephenson, Maurice—as he acknowledged—took the mystic concept of Christ as king and Christ's church as an established kingdom. The Millenarians, Maurice always felt, had "done an infinite service to the Church" by preaching that men should not focus their attentions upon Heaven, "which makes us indifferent to the future condition of the earth."

A man, then, who strove to "know" God "as a friend," Maurice easily found in the Bible evidence that its authors had the same desires, and so also did "every patriarch, prophet, and priest from Adam downward." He had rejected his father's Unitarianism as unsatisfactory: Christ's atonement and resurrection as the center of a Trinitarian faith lay at the core of true Christianity. Christ must be fully man, as well as fully God, exposed to all human temptations. And Christ, the God-man, is in every human being. Theologians, instead of erecting systems, should seek for and proclaim God's presence and glory. Man's relationship to evil, to his own yearnings for improvement, and to God must be dealt with in an immediately practical way. So—always as a theologian—Maurice was active in politics, as one of the chief leaders of the Christian Socialists of the late 1840's and as a social and educational reformer, in working-men's schools, lecture foundations, and the like.

While openly acknowledging that his discovery of Christ in every man was a Quaker doctrine and therefore heterodox, Maurice nonetheless achieved the gymnastic feat of interpreting the Thirty-nine Articles to his own satisfaction as supporting his views. He found in them, as in himself, support for the Puritan reformers: Cromwell was his hero, Charles I and Archbishop Laud his enemies. Paradoxically, then, while engaged in radical activities and believing in a radical creed, he conformed wholly not only to the Articles and to the Church of England, but also to the structure of society as it was. A monumental waste of intellectual power, said John Stuart Mill: all of Maurice's ingenuity and perceptiveness "served him not for putting something better into the place of the worthless heap of received opinions on the great subjects of thought, but for proving to his own mind that the Church of England had known everything from the first," and that the Thirty-nine Articles contained the essence of truth.

Maurice had the same kind of timidity, Mill believed, that drove other men to the Church of Rome in search of firm authority. Whether "timidity" is the right word for it hardly matters: at the root of Maurice's tortuous thought there certainly lay some deep personal problem. For example, although baptized as an infant in the name of the Father, Son, and Holy Ghost by his Unitarian father, Maurice nonetheless made the solemn but quite unnecessary decision to be rebaptized when he entered the Church of England. Perhaps he was striving to throw off a great weight of paternal influence. Yet all his life he loved his father, and he always maintained that from his father's love of him he had first learned to think of the loving paternal aspects of God.

Converted at the moment of crisis over the Reform Bill and the uncertainties that faced the Church of England, when Arnold was demanding the inclusion of the Dissenters in the Church, and Keble was preaching on "National Apostasy" and sounding the tocsin for the Oxford reformers, Maurice soon found himself deep in controversy. Though he joined the Tractarians in defending the requirement that university men subscribe to the Articles, he broke with them over Pusey's massive Tracts 67, 68, and 69, written against the Evangelicals and affirming the efficacy of infant baptism to convey regeneration. During 1837, Maurice wrote belligerently trying to reconcile High-Church baptismal regeneration with Evangelical insistence on justification by faith. He succeeded in mystifying and alienating both parties: the Tractarians, whom he denounced for maintaining that baptism changed the nature of the recipient, and the Evangelicals, whom he denounced for failing to accept its necessity as a "covenant," if not a sacrament. Pusey found Maurice so irritatingly ignorant and shallow that he declared he preferred the Low-Church *Record* as an opponent.

Maurice's massive *Kingdom of Christ* (1838) reflected both his appreciation and his ultimate rejection of Quakerism, Calvinism, and Tractarianism. He believed—and many of his admirers strengthened his conviction—that the time had come for a "New Reformation," sweeping away party conflict and unifying the warring sects. For Maurice's New Reformation, the old Reformation was crucial. In the very same years when Newman declared that the "spirit of Luther is dead," Maurice found in Luther a "strong, steady current of thought and meaning flowing through all his perplexities and contradictions." And the personal psychological conflicts within Maurice's own spirit echoed Luther's own.

Happily married to John Sterling's sister-in-law (1837) and appointed (1840) to a professorship at King's College, London (a Church of England institution founded as a counterweight to the wholly secular nonsectarian University College), Maurice was not a successful lecturer. ("The fourteenth century," began a student parody of his lectures, "was preceded by the thirteenth, and followed by the fifteenth. This is a *deep fact* . . . profoundly instructive, and gives food for inexhaustible reflection.") Supporting the Tractarians against their opponents' efforts to silence them, supporting the Evangelicals on the burning issue (1842) of their plan—violently opposed by the Tractarians—to erect a Church of England bishopric in Jerusalem, attacking both as parties, yet refusing to join a "No Party" alliance because it savored too much of party, furiously defending orthodoxy against Carlyle's praise of Emerson, unhappy at Carlyle's increasing influence over John Sterling, Maurice was consistently inconsistent and irritating to everyone. At a moment when increased education was advocated by most students of social ills, Maurice actively attacked state education and defended education by the clergy of the Church of England, ignoring the Dissenters' natural antipathy to such a solution. Conservative in his devotion to the institutions of the family, the monarchy, and the Church—national in form but universal in its embrace—Maurice was a radical in his personal faith and in his gadfly attacks on orthodoxy.

The death of his wife from tuberculosis (1845), after she had nursed John Sterling on his deathbed from the same disease, plunged Maurice once more into sadness. Now began his friendship with Charles Kingsley, fourteen years younger and then only twenty-five years old, who had been more influenced, he said later, by Maurice's *Kingdom of Christ* than by any other book he ever read. The intensity of Maurice's faith, "which," Kingsley wrote, "explains all heaven and earth to a man," was "infinitely above the half-faith of our present systems." With Kingsley and John Malcolm Ludlow, Maurice formed a triumvirate at war with the growing social misery of the late forties, anxious to Christianize the socialism then beginning to spread among hungry and discontented English laborers, and launching their own series of "Tracts for the Times," published as *Politics for the People*, and advocating cooperative associations, notably in the tailoring trade. Kingsley's novel, *Alton Locke* (1850, NIS), is in part the record of these efforts, and we shall later meet him in the pages of Mark Rutherford's *Clara Hopgood* (1896, no. 65).

But as soon as the others tried to form a "Health League" to improve the dreadful conditions of sewage and water supply and to combat the raging cholera, Maurice's ingrained suspicion of any such grouping led him to oppose it, as he did a central board to organize the Working-men's Associations. His own chief interest in the tailors' associations was as an audience for his *Tracts on Christian So-*

cialism. On the platform, Maurice's natural tendency to grant that his opponents had much right on their side stood him in good stead when angry workmen spoke their minds and attacked the clergy as part of the social conspiracy against them: he often turned enemies into well-wishers. His manifest honesty and obvious effort to throw off his class consciousness and mingle with the poor made the movement many friends. But Maurice's Christian emphasis was wholly at variance with Ludlow's socialist emphasis, and it led to increasingly heated personal conflict between them.

In 1851, Maurice had Ludlow removed from the editorship of the paper, the *Christian Socialist,* in which he had been advocating a church altogether free from state control and militantly socialist: Thomas Hughes (1822-1896), who had attended Rugby under Thomas Arnold and who would soon write the famous *Tom Brown's School Days* (1857, NIS), replaced Ludlow. As President of the Christian Socialist Society, Maurice grew personally authoritarian. He disliked the "un-English" character of socialist theory, and stoutly called (1852) for "Monarchy, Aristocracy, and Socialism, or rather Humanity, recognized as necessary elements and conditions of an organic Christian Society," all of which Ludlow impatiently thought of as outworn. In any case, Maurice's own interests came to be concentrated upon the new Working Men's College (founded 1854), and the Christian Socialist movement petered out.

Much affected by Sterling's loss of faith, largely as the result of Carlyle's influence, and determined to reach other doubters, Maurice, a most effective preacher as chaplain of Lincoln's Inn, and as leader of Bible classes in his own house, felt obliged to challenge "the religion we make for ourselves"—virtually any contemporary formulation except his own—and so incurred much antagonism. The autobiographical novel by Kingsley's brother-in-law and Hurrell Froude's younger brother, James Anthony Froude, *The Nemesis of Faith* (1849, no. 68), discussed at length below, impressed him deeply. Had Froude's hero, Markham Sutherland (who is Froude himself), only possessed his own trust in God, he would never, Maurice wrote, have allowed his doubts over the Old Testament God to shake his faith. But Sutherland had given in first to "Newmanic" influences and then to those of Carlyle. The Tractarians taught a "religion *about* God," Carlyle a "religion of man," a "religion against God." What Sutherland needed was a Maurician "belief *in* God." It was as simple as that. In all his manifold works, Maurice felt, he was in effect only writing a continuous review of Froude's novel. Such views and such frequent iteration of them led to more controversy.

William Palmer's attack (1848) on the *Life of Sterling* by Julius Hare, now Maurice's brother-in-law, which damned Maurice with the others, elicited an answer from Maurice as well as from Hare. Accused of a scepticism derived from the German philosophers, Maurice warned against the complacency of English High Churchmen, like Palmer, in the face of increasing sectarianism and doubt. No existing system could withstand this. The ultra-Evangelical *Record* soon was attacking this last point: "with the Bible in hand," said the *Record*, they needed no further system. And then came the furor about the "Sterling Club." Soon this was compounded by Maurice's *Theological Essays* (1853) addressed to the Unitarians, reaffirming and many times restating his belief in the continual struggle between the "All-Good" and the "All-Evil." The Evil Spirit "directly and absolutely opposed to the Father of Lights . . . the God of absolute goodness and love"—Maurice declared (in a notable use of the words "Father of Lights" which we shall later find in his disciple George MacDonald)—could be found in the New Testament. It was the assaults of this evil spirit that made men evil: wickedness was *not* their original nature, a "horrible notion which has haunted moralists, divines, and practical men." Maurice did not actually proclaim a belief in the Devil, but the effect of his writing was the same as if he had. Because he was addressing Unitarians—less likely than any other sect to accept the idea of a personalized evil spirit—Maurice made this emphasis especially heavy and tried to prove that the New Testament was a literal historical record of events.

In his essay on "Eternal Life and Eternal Death," Maurice reasserted his ancient conviction that the "everlasting fire" of Matthew xxv.41 and the "everlasting punishment" of Matthew xxv.46 are not to be understood literally. The tortuousness of the argument by which "everlasting" or "eternal" was made to mean not an endless time, but a quality of life, "not time extended but time abolished," and in which "everlasting punishment" meant being at war with God's love, as a "death which men choose for themselves," baffled even expert theologians. Was Maurice really denying the doctrine of eternal punishment, as his Evangelical enemies loudly declared? Dr. Jelf, principal of King's College, thought so, but couldn't be sure; the theologians he consulted mostly said that Maurice seemed confused. The Thirty-nine Articles, by which Maurice always stood, did not include an article on eternal punishment: there had been such an article in the Forty-two Articles of 1553, but it was dropped from the Thirty-nine permanently adopted in 1573.

Questioned by Jelf about his belief, Maurice stood on the Articles: he would not be judged by "religious coteries or newspapers." Indeed, the *Record*, in full cry, was calling Maurice's doctrine "a strange compound," in which they saw Unitarianism, Carlyle, Coleridge, Edward Irving, and even Pusey and Keble intermingled and "glossed over with an Evangelical phraseology." It was a more confident analysis of the elements in Maurice than modern students would dare to make. But that he was obscure none would deny. Julius Hare defended him; Samuel Wilberforce, who did not like the *Essays*, nonetheless said that Maurice was orthodox. But led by the Bishop of London, Blomfield, the forces in opposition got Maurice dismissed from his professorship (1853). The public, apprehending little more than that he was being punished for denying the necessity of eternal hellfire for sinners (which many of them did not believe in), on the whole took his side. He became Principal of the Working Men's College, where his staff of lecturers included not only Thomas Hughes but also Dante Gabriel Rossetti and John Ruskin.

Almost immediately, Maurice became embroiled in another controversy, this time with a learned Oxford theologian, Henry Longueville Mansel (1820-1871), later Dean of St. Paul's, who had published a pamphlet against Maurice's *Theological Essays.* On the question of eternal punishment (Mansel called it "Mr. Maurice's theory of a fixed state out of time"), Maurice, said Mansel, had made the mistake of attributing to God the nature and character of Christ; of course, in such a context, eternal punishment was not conceivable. But with our "limited capacity" we do not know and cannot know what God is, but only how God wants us to think of

Him. So we cannot simply deny the possibility of eternal punishment, which may well be possible. To which Maurice replied that God made man in His image; so man *could* know what God is, indeed, could not be a man without knowing it. Mansel's teaching, said Maurice, now swinging wildly, was typical of the English attitude toward Revelation: that it told men things which were not true, but which they "ought to believe and act upon as if they were true." Infallible Bible (said the Evangelicals); infallible church (said the Tractarians): both of them were "unconscious plagiarists from the canons" of Mansel and his school, which saved men "from what the world calls mysticism," from Maurice's own concept of a Revelation that actually did reveal.

To this Mansel simply answered privately that he and Maurice were unlikely ever to reach a mutual understanding, and Maurice was angry at what seemed like a condescending effort to break off the discussion. For Maurice, God's nature—in the sense of the sort of Being that God was—could indeed be discerned in the person of Jesus; and in Christ's death and resurrection God and man were reconciled. One did not have to cling to what Maurice felt to be the abstruseness of Mansel's insistence that to know God one had philosophically to know (obviously impossible) God completely in His essence. And in his Bampton Lectures of 1858 Mansel—as difficult to understand as Maurice himself, but far more rigorously logical—reaffirmed the unknowability of God, and therefore the futility of erecting a philosophy of God. Revelation represented "the infinite God under finite Symbols, in condescension to the finite capacity of man." Human reason and conscience help us in determining whether an act of God is revealed or not. Man must receive the Bible in its entirety as inspired by God. Other philosophers besides Maurice challenged Mansel; indeed almost everybody got in on the act. But Maurice, for whom the immediate personal experience of divinity was an essential "given," was the most vociferous of all, in his *What is Revelation?* (1859). Has "the Infinite and Eternal God" revealed himself to man or has he not? That was the question, Maurice insisted: and he insisted that Mansel denied it and he affirmed it.

When *Essays and Reviews* appeared the next year, Maurice, though disliking the book intensely, characteristically defended its authors' right to be heard and attacked their attackers: it was the same spirit in which more than thirty years earlier he had defended the proposal for a monument to Byron in Westminster Abbey. Only in his last decade of life did Maurice begin to receive recognition, ending his days as a professor at Cambridge and receiving much support and admiration. But his ideas did not develop, had never greatly developed, since his conversion of 1831. His social and political conservatism, his radical, combative, and mystic faith, his personal relationship with the Divinity, his challenge to all other views, his hatred of party, his refusal to acknowledge that he had himself become a party leader, and the extreme difficulty of understanding what he was saying: these qualities combined to make him a unique figure on the Victorian religious scene, the most important member of the Cambridge Network, whose very existence he would have disputed, and the chief single inspiration of Broad-Church thinking, deny it though he would.

Broad Churchmanship, Alexandrian Style: Hypatia *(1853)*

Though Maurice's disciple and fellow Christian Socialist, Charles Kingsley (1819-1875), put many of his master's and his own principles into his first two novels, *Yeast* (1848 serially, 1851 as a book, NIS) and *Alton Locke, Tailor and Poet* (1850, NIS), they were not primarily religious novels. His third novel, however, *Hypatia; or, New Foes with an Old Face* (1853, no. 47), was a religious novel of the ancient world, which, as we have seen, elicited both Wiseman's *Fabiola* (1854, no. 9) and Newman's *Callista* (1856, no. 6). Set in Alexandria, with scenes in Cyrene (in present-day Libya) in the early fifth century, it introduces some historical characters: Hypatia, the learned and beautiful Neoplatonist lecturer on pagan philosophy; Cyril, the Patriarch of Alexandria; Synesius, Bishop of Cyrene; and St. Augustine, Bishop of Hippo (Bône in modern Algeria). The era of persecutions, which both Wiseman and Newman were to choose, was over: Christianity became the state religion of the Roman Empire in 381. But the Christians themselves had now produced persecutors of their own, of whom certain Egyptian monks were the most fanatical. And there were still many pagans, by no means all of them intellectuals like Hypatia and her father. As in classical times, the Jews of Alexandria continued to live on hostile terms with the Greeks and Egyptians.

Kingsley had studied the historical sources for his period, and commanded a vivid and engaging prose style. Colorful and tumultuous, pervaded by mob violence, steeped in cruelty, his fifth-century Alexandria is surprisingly authentic. But of course, he was commenting obliquely on his own age. The "new foes" of his subtitle are the foes of the good in nineteenth-century England. At the very end of the novel, Kingsley says to his readers, "I have shown you New Foes under an Old Face—your own likenesses in toga and tunic, instead of coat and bonnet. . . . The same Devil who tempted these old Egyptians tempts you. The same God who would have saved these old Egyptians if they had willed, will save you, if you will. Their sins are yours, their errors yours, their doom yours, their deliverance yours." But of course this is both too general and too vague to enable modern readers of *Hypatia* to decipher Kingsley's intentions, which were far more specific and more polemical.

To Maurice, Kingsley wrote, while still planning *Hypatia* in 1851, that he wished "to set forth Christianity as the only really democratic creed, and philosophy, above all, spiritualism, as the most exclusively aristocratic creed." By "spiritualism" Kingsley meant, as he told his publisher, "the Emersonian pseudo-spiritualism of the present day," which, he argued, "has less hold on the human sympathies than even the lowest forms of orthodox Christianity." He intended, he said, not to argue this thesis but to show it "in action." So the aristocratic Hypatia is intended to personify transcendentalism—"Emersonian Anythingarianism," Kingsley called it—and to illustrate the dangers of the intellectual arrogance which falsely persuaded individual human beings that they could seek and find their own deity, ignoring the Church and religious tradition. Not so, Kingsley had stoutly declared in *Alton Locke*, where an American ex-minister preaches "An Emersonian Sermon," and Kingsley's own Scotch spokesman points out that "God cam' down to look for puir bodies, instead o' leavin' puir bodies to gang look-

1. John Henry Newman, 1844, from a drawing by George Richmond.

2. Oriel College, Oxford, showing Newman's rooms (the three second-floor windows in the wing on the right).

3. Frances Milton Trollope, 1839.

4. Charlotte Mary Yonge, about 1858.

5. Joseph Henry Shorthouse, 1887.

6. Walter Pater.

7. George Eliot, 1860, from a drawing by Samuel Lawrence.

8. Frederick Denison Maurice, 1846, from a drawing by Samuel Lawrence.

9. Charles Kingsley.

10. George MacDonald, 1892.

11. Margaret Oliphant Wilson Oliphant, 1895, from a drawing by Janet Mary Oliphant.

12. William Hale White (Mark Rutherford), 1887, from a drawing by Arthur Hughes.

13. The Old Meeting, Bedford.

14. Eliza Lynn Linton.

15. James Anthony Froude.

16. Mrs. Humphry Ward, 1876, from a water-color painting by Mrs. A. H. Johnson.

ing for Him." Emersonianism meant that the few who think themselves geniuses monopolize philosophy and come up with "bottled moonshine [a phrase coined by Carlyle]," while the ordinary man is left "in his superstition and ignorance to fulfill the lusts of the flesh."

And, indeed, *Hypatia* does set forth these views in action. Hypatia regards herself as a new Julian the Apostate (Emperor 361-363), determined to revive paganism in its Neoplatonic form. She is so sophisticated that she sees the pagan gods only as symbols of the life-giving forces in nature. To her, Christianity exalts "all that is human and low-born, illiterate and levelling." It is "an anthropomorphic adumbration of divine things fitted for the base and toiling herd." And that, of course, is just the point. What she scorns is actually the only road to salvation for humanity. Hypatia is most attractively drawn—Kingsley himself admires her—but her self-confidence is eventually shaken. As she comes to realize the corruption of the ancient faith, she is conscious that she has lent herself to a deception, and she finds it difficult to write an Ode to Aphrodite for the show in the amphitheatre that is to celebrate the successful conspiracy of the Prefect Orestes to make himself Emperor and Hypatia his consort. The conspiracy is a failure, of course, and Hypatia, at a moment when she is on the verge of seeing the Christian truth, is murdered by the mob, stripped naked on the high altar itself below the crucifix.

It is not only transcendentalism, however, that Kingsley is attacking in *Hypatia.* Her anxiety over the truth of her outworn beliefs reflects the fact that "she did not know yet that those who have no other means for regenerating a corrupted time than dogmatic pedantries concerning the dead and unreturning past, must end, in practice, by borrowing insincerely, and using clumsily, the very weapons of that novel age which they deprecate, and 'sewing new cloth into old garments' till the rent become patent and incurable." Here the target is the Tractarians and the Catholic converts, the Newmans, whom Kingsley believed to be groping in the dead past for outworn dogmas and practices. In general, Kingsley distrusted the intellect and—like Coleridge and the Broad Churchmen—felt that emotional commitment was the only way to faith.

When Hypatia herself lectures on Homer, she asks what

difference it makes whether Hector, Priam, Helen, and Achilles ever lived or spoke or thought as Homer says they did. What does it matter whether Homer himself ever lived?

> The book is here,—the word which men call his. . . . Let the thoughts thereof have been at first whose they may, now they are mine. . . . parts of my own soul. . . . part of the universal soul. What matters, then, what myths grew up around those mighty thoughts of ancient sects? Let others try to reconcile the Cyclic fragments, or vindicate the Catalogue of ships. What has the philosopher lost, though the former were proved to be contradictory, and the latter interpolated? The thoughts are there and ours. Let us open our hearts lovingly to receive them.

For Homer substitute the Bible, and for the scholarly questions at issue in the *Iliad* all the literature of nineteenth-century biblical criticism. Kingsley was impatiently pushing it aside and making Hypatia, the intellectual, his spokesman. The saintly Abbot Pambo declares that he has seen "many a man wearying himself with study and tormenting his soul as to whether he believes rightly this doctrine and that," not knowing "with Solomon that in much learning is much sorrow. . . . " As a man becomes "a more and more learned theologian, and more and more zealous for the letter of orthodoxy," he grows "less and less loving and merciful, less and less full of trust in God." "While he was puzzling at the letter of God's message, the spirit of it was going faster and faster out of him." So Kingsley ranges himself clearly with the anti-intellectuals, themselves often highly trained scholars, in the Broad-Church movement.

Kingsley's hatred of celibacy, and especially of clerical celibacy, pervades *Hypatia* as one would expect. Philammon, the young Greek monk from the monastery on the upper Nile, who is warned most particularly against women when he comes to Alexandria, makes "a whole regiment of women acquaintances" within four days of his arrival. But, says Kingsley, "Providence having sent into the world about as many women as men, it may be difficult to keep out of their way altogether. Perhaps, too, Providence may have intended them to be of some use to that other sex, with whom it had so mixed them up." Kingsley is not always sardonically semi-humorous on this favorite subject. Raphael Aben-Ezra, the rich, cynical, sensual young Jew, sceptical of all religions but courageous and adventurous, is drawn to Christianity by his love for a young Christian woman, Victoria, and also by the arguments in the Epistle to the Hebrews and by the kindliness of Christians towards the poor and distressed. But he is utterly horrified to hear that Victoria's father wants her to become a nun. Bitterly, he remarks that he had "nearly deluded" himself "into the fancy that the Deity of the Galilaeans [pagan term for Christians] might be, after all, the God of our old Hebrew forefathers . . . who believed that children and the fruit of the womb were an heritage and gift which cometh of the Lord. . . . " But Raphael has now discovered instead that the Christian God enjoys "seeing his creatures stultify the primary laws of their being."

It is only when Raphael visits his old friend Bishop Synesius of Cyrene that he can be set straight upon the point. Synesius is usually

> up at four in the morning, always in the most disgustingly good health and spirits, farming, coursing, shooting, riding over hedge and ditch after rascally black robbers; preaching, intriguing, borrowing money; baptizing and excommunicating; . . . comforting old women, and giving pretty girls dowries; scribbling one half-hour on philosophy and the next on farriery; sitting up all night writing hymns and drinking strong liquors; off again on horseback at four the next morning; and talking all the while about philosophic abstraction from the mundane tempest.

Not only has Kingsley made out of Synesius a Victorian sporting parson, full of good works and his own muscular Christianity (there is a splendid ostrich hunt on horseback, with all the excitement of a fox hunt), but—of course—Synesius is married. In fact, Synesius had refused to be made a bishop unless he were allowed to keep his wife. As a vicious celibate puts it, Synesius "despised the gift of the Holy Ghost in comparison of the carnal joys of wedlock, not knowing the Scriptures, which saith that those who are in the flesh cannot please God!" To Synesius, Raphael unfolds at length a new interpretation of the Song of Songs, not as an allegory of the "marriage between the soul and its Creator" and an argument for celibacy in the standard Christian way, but as an allegory of the glory of monogamy: Solomon leaves his whole harem for the "undefiled who is but one," and "feels that he is in harmony for the first time in his life with the universe of God, and with the mystery of the seasons. . . ." Now a widower, but still a believer in Christian marriage, Synesius encourages Raphael, and a fortunate encounter with St. Augustine completes the conversion.

Even after Raphael has almost come to believe—after hearing Augustine preach and arguing philosophy with him—that "the Jehovah of the old Scriptures" is not only the God of the Jews, and the "Divine Wisdom" of the Jewish thinker Philo of Alexandria, but "the Lord of the whole earth and the nations thereof," and that the "strange story" of the crucifixion and the resurrection may be true, he still balks at Christianity: "celibacy and asceticism, nonhuman as they were, what had they to do with the theory of a human God?" Raphael—who has been a Platonist, a Stoic, an Epicurean, a Cynic, and a Sceptic (and who has even become sceptical about scepticism)—can become a Christian only after Augustine, who has already praised virginity, proceeds to deliver a eulogy on marriage. Raphael remarks that it is a pity that Augustine himself had never married, but he regrets his impertinence: he sees an expression on Augustine's face that tells of deep sorrow: a clear reference to the concubine that Augustine had put away from him after his conversion, and to their son. This episode was unknown to Raphael, who had of course not read the *Confessions*, but well known to Kingsley, who had. Hypatia too, though a pagan, is vowed to chastity and has never known sexual fulfillment before she is horribly murdered by the Christian mob. In the personages of his fifth-century story, Kingsley carried forward his own nineteenth-century battle for monogamous sexual love against the celibacy of the Catholic clergy and of many Tractarians. He drew the character of Raphael from Alfred Hyman Louis, an English Jew whom he himself had baptized, but he probably also had Disraeli in mind.

If Synesius and Augustine represent Christian virtue, the leading Christians of Alexandria embody a variety of nineteenth-century Christian vices. True, they do engage in social work: the *parabolani* of Cyril labor in the "squalid misery, filth, profligacy, ignorance, ferocity, discontent" of the slums, among people "neglected in body, house, and soul, by the civil authorities," starving and rotting, "heap on heap." Only two or three years away from his most vigorous endeavors in the London slums with Maurice and Ludlow, Kingsley was here surely not thinking primarily of the ancient world. The *parabolani* are "district visitors," who bring food and clothing, nurse the sick, and bury the dead. But their charity towards the poor does not preclude sectarianism, petty maneuvering for position, and backbiting.

Patriarch Cyril, for example, has a feud with the learned Isidore of Pelusium (whose more than two thousand letters full of valuable sidelights on the society of the period still in 1976 await their first complete scholarly edition). Flatterers and tale-bearers in Cyril's entourage are constantly intriguing: "The sleekest and the oiliest, and the noisiest; the man who can bring in most money to the charities, never mind whence or how; the man who will take most of the bishop's work off his hands, and agree with him in everything . . . and save him, by spying and eavesdropping, the trouble of using his own eyes; that is the man to succeed in Alexandria, or Constantinople or Rome itself." Or, one might add, in Canterbury, London, or York. Had it not been for the protests of Isidore of Pelusium, gossip has it, Cyril himself would have sold a bishopric to the highest bidder. Christian brotherhood has disappeared, say the complainers, ever since the persecutions stopped. Priests are jealous of deacons, bishops of metropolitan archbishops, the Church of Egypt of the Church of Africa (which has a schism of its own), and the Pope and the Patriarch of Constantinople of the Patriarch of Alexandria. Church councils, which are supposed to settle such matters, actually evoke "every evil passion in men's hearts."

And if the high politics of the Christian Church are in disarray, the results can be seen everywhere in society. A fashionable lady arriving at church in her luxurious sedan chair wears a dress richly embroidered with the stories of Dives and Lazarus and of Job. Moreover—and here Kingsley did not even need to substitute a toga for Victorian costume—"her gown was stuffed out behind in a fashion which provoked from the dirty boys who lay about the steps . . . the same comments with which St. Clement had upbraided from the pulpit the Alexandrian ladies of his day." It is a fifth-century crinoline! With a jewelled manuscript of the Gospels around her neck, and crosses on her diadem, her dress, and her slippers, this veteran of a pilgrimage to Arabia, "to kiss the very dunghill" where Job had sat, is on her way to confess her sins and buy absolution with rich presents. Moreover, she "has such a delicate sense for orthodoxy" that she can scent a heretical comment in a sermon, and with her fellow rich and pious women she settles matters of church preferment: she even has the ear of the Empress Pulcheria, far off at Constantinople, in whose hands (in the year 413) effective government of the Empire rested. At the level of the *parabolani* with whom Philammon is laboring, there is scandalous gossip too, about "who had stayed for the Eucharist the Sunday before, and who had gone out after the sermon; and how the majority who did not stay could possibly dare to go, and how the minority who did not go could possibly dare to stay. . . . Endless suspicions, sneers, complaints . . . what did they care for the eternal glories and the beatific vision?"

As for Patriarch Cyril, he follows the "alluring path of evil-doing that good might come." In the years after the action of *Hypatia* itself, as Kingsley explicitly says, this led Cyril into committing "many a fearful sin, and left his name disgraced forever." But, says Kingsley in extenuation, posterity has forgotten both the "pandemonium" against which Cyril fought and his intense faith: perhaps he was "no worse, even if no better, than themselves." In a more final judgment, however, Kingsley excoriates the "ferocity" of the Egyptian Church. Eventually it tore itself to pieces, he says, and "ended as a mere chaos of idolatrous sects, persecuting each other for metaphysical propositions, which, true or false, were equally heretical in their mouths, because they used them only as watch-words of division. Orthodox or unorthodox, they knew not God, for they knew neither righteousness, nor love, nor peace." And eventually came the Muslims and seized Alexandria. Impressionistic as is this view of the fifth, sixth, and seventh Christian centuries, it is quite defensible historically; and it clearly warns the contentious sects in Kingsley's own England that they too are set upon the path of unrighteousness.

On the chief question at issue in the Christian controversies of Cyril's age—the relationship between the human and divine natures in Christ—Kingsley remarks that "the notion of that God-man was receding fast to more and more awful and abysmal heights, in the minds of a generation who were forgetting His love in His power, and practically losing sight of His humanity in their eager doctrinal assertion of His Divinity." The comment is prompted by Philammon, who had been temporarily drawn away from the fanatical monks by the power of Hypatia's learning and beauty, and who, returning to his Christian faith, finds himself unable to pray directly to Christ for his erring sister, Pelagia. It is too presumptuous to address Christ directly: all Philammon can do is pray to the Magdalene to intercede with Christ. Kingsley's appreciation of the important implications of the fifth-century controversy over Monophysitism is keen and accurate: inherent in the Monophysite emphasis on Christ's divine nature, prevalent in Egypt, lay precisely the danger that Christ's human nature would be forgotten and the atonement therefore neglected: how could a divine being suffer the pains of crucifixion? In the nineteenth century, as in the fifth, such a diminution or even disappearance of the human nature of Christ for men like Maurice or Kingsley threatened the very basis of the faith. So here too—perhaps obscurely to readers in his own day, and surely to readers in ours—Kingsley was fighting the "new foes with an old face."

It would be unfair not to emphasize how readable, how exciting, *Hypatia* is. The Jewish sorceress, Miriam, is as arresting as Newman's dreadful witch, Gurta, in *Callista.* Kingsley's passionate belief that the English race is essentially Teutonic, and that German blood and German vigor lie at the root of its historic glories, can be seen embodied in the characters and the conversations of his Goths, living in Alexandria and contemptuous of the effeminate Mediterranean inhabitants. Kingsley's admiration for these crudely virile muscular Christians (though Arian!) is as interesting for a student of Kingsley as his onslaught on celibacy and unsanitary conditions. The ghastly massacre of the captive black women and children in the amphitheatre, the final murder of Hypatia by the mob (in which the mere appearance of the word "naked" brought down a storm upon Kingsley's head), the portrait of Synesius: all these remind one that Kingsley was a professional novelist of a high order, as well as a Broad-Church polemicist.

To Kingsley's first book, *The Saint's Tragedy* (1848, NIS), a blank verse drama about the conflict over celibacy in the mind of St. Elizabeth of Hungary, Maurice had contributed a preface, which some critics had declared unnecessary or pompous, and others (as usual) had found obscure. So this time, Maurice—by 1853 under fire at King's College—declined to allow Kingsley to dedicate *Hypatia* to him, and urged him instead to dedicate it to his parents: it did, after all, celebrate the importance of monogamous marriage and family life. Kingsley assented, but he did not, of course, fail to support Maurice enthusiastically in his troubles; he needed to be curbed rather than urged on. Nor did the absence of Maurice's name make *Hypatia*'s reception notably easier: Queen Victoria loved it; so did Tennyson, but he objected to Hypatia's being stripped in the final scene. Kingsley was apparently not much disturbed by the criticisms: he was already moving on to write *Westward Ho!* (1855, NIS), a novel ostensibly about Elizabethan seafaring, but in fact a thinly disguised recruiting tract for the Crimean War of 1854-1856, which exhibited the celibate Jesuits in a most unlovely light. But in the early sixties, when he had been recommended by the Prince of Wales himself for an honorary degree at Oxford, the offer was withdrawn because of *Hypatia*'s alleged indecency. This greatly disappointed Kingsley, who later refused to lecture at the university which had acted so meanly. The "new foes" were still active, still effective, still petty, still backbiting, a decade after his finest novel had shown them their old faces.

"Broad Church" or "Hard Church"?: Perversion *(1856)*

William John Conybeare (1815-1857), in whose brilliantly incisive essay on "Church Parties" the term "Broad Church"—as we have noted—first gained currency, came of a long line of unusually gifted West Country clergymen. His great-grandfather was Bishop of Bristol in the mid-eighteenth century; his uncle and his father were scientists and clerics. The uncle—theologian, scholar and translator of Anglo-Saxon poetry, geologist and chemist—published important studies of the geology of Devon and Cornwall in the 1820's; the father—Vicar of Axminster in Devon and even more eminent as a scientist—cooperated with Cuvier, wrote pioneering works on the Hydrographical Basin of the Thames and on the Ichthyosaurus, christened the genus Pleisiosaurus, and studied volcanic phenomena on Madeira. He is still remembered for his fundamental paper on the "Progress, Actual State, and Ulterior Prospects of Geological Science" (1842). William John, educated at Westminster and Trinity College, Cambridge, was brought up, then, in a family atmosphere in which the contemporary conflicts between science and religion had been resolved. Appointed at twenty-seven to be the first principal of the new Liverpool Collegiate Institute, he was obliged to resign the post because of ill health, and in 1848 succeeded his father as Vicar of Axminster. Joint author of a successful work on *The Life and Epistles of St. Paul* and author of a series of essays for the *Edinburgh Review*, including the celebrated one on Church Parties, frequently reprinted, Conybeare died young of tuberculosis, and his father, overcome by grief, had a stroke and died immediately afterwards.

Conybeare's only novel, *Perversion; or, The Causes and Consequences of Infidelity* (1856, no. 48), is an extraordinary production. The word "perversion" meant in the 1850's "conversion" from the Church of England: apostasy. Conybeare had a clear, fast-moving, facile style, and a sometimes sardonic, sometimes farcical, sense of humor. *Perversion* has much of the vigor of the picaresque novels of the eighteenth century, with which it shares a surprising lack of prudery. But Conybeare had only rudimentary skill in creating credible characters. Like other novelists of the period, Bulwer-Lytton among them, he "typified" instead, and his personages emerge as bundles of abstract qualities rather than as convincing human beings. Moreover, Conybeare lacked a sense of structure, and allowed himself to ramble freely from each episode to the next. Lively and thoroughly readable, however, *Perversion* is a long and convincing argument by case history, rather than by sermonizing, for the liberal theological and practical views of Coleridge and Thomas

Arnold. It also exhibits certain disquieting features not uncharacteristic of the Broad-Church novel.

From his earliest days at school, Charles Bampton, the hero, is dogged by the persecutions of George Armstrong, a vicious but intelligent bully, which almost prove fatal. Conybeare takes a cool, unemotional attitude toward the horrors of school life: after only two months at school, Charles "learned to swear with tolerable ease, and could listen to indecent conversation without the sense of horror and the painful blushes which it caused him during the first month of initiation." Instead of injecting an emotional appeal like those of Farrar to Eric two years later, "Now Eric, now, or never," Conybeare seems to accept brutality at school as inevitable in "a primitive state of society, under the law of the strongest." Besides, Lyngford Grammar School has a stupid and callous Evangelical headmaster ("What, sir! not happy in my school? Not happy at Lyngford Grammar School, sir? see the corruption of your nature, sir."), who imprisons Charles in the "black-hole" and flogs him savagely in public.

Charles finally manages to escape, and his stupid but affectionate widowed mother allows him to stay at home under the care of a tutor, a German revolutionary exile named Gottlieb Schrecklich(!). A sound scholar (the Germans are sounder scholars than the English because "they never go out to tea . . . never go out to ride, and . . . save much time daily by letting their beards grow long and cutting their ablutions short"), Schrecklich is a good tutor, but a Hegelian Pantheist. He does not attempt to indoctrinate the twelve-year-old Charles, but it is obvious that "the light of revelation was not the guiding star of his . . . moral being," and his vague answers to "religious questionings" leave the boy "in a state of mystification and incipient scepticism." Given Mrs. Bampton's utter incompetence to supply religious guidance, one must regard Schrecklich's tutorship, when added to Armstrong's bullying, as one of those "causes of infidelity" in Charles of which Conybeare's subtitle speaks.

Expelled from school, Charles's enemy, Armstrong, joins the army. A passive unbeliever since boyhood, because he dislikes the supernatural, has a hypocritically pious father, and prefers a life free of the moral restraints imposed by religion, Armstrong—stationed near Manchester—becomes acquainted with the family of a rich Unitarian fellow officer, a " 'liberal' *par excellence*." The Unitarians have "renounced everything of Christianity except the name, and many of them repudiated the name also" because they think it creates "an invidious distinction" between them and the Jews. Their conversation and books solidify Armstrong's "floating doubts into a systematic structure of infidelity." He accepts their negative views but not their positive deism: to him the spirituality of the deists seems pure sentimentality, and its morality is unacceptable. In this respect Armstrong is a Benthamite, denying the existence of a moral sense. Steeping himself in Comte, he rejects all belief in a Creator and a creation and accepts the view that "the very notion of *sin* as applied to human conduct is absurd." Human actions are only links in a chain of necessary events.

Armstrong, says Conybeare, has come to agree with Henry Atkinson and Harriet Martineau. These two had recently published *Letters on the Laws of Man's Nature and Development* (1851), a strange and shocking book. Atkinson was handsome, plausible, (probably homosexual), a dilettante and phrenologist, intellectually third-rate, now joined in a curious collaboration with Miss Martineau, who was considerably older, a neurotic, blue-stocking essayist and famous popular writer on political economy. He had assisted in her mesmeric cure from a severe illness and had accompanied her on a trip to the Near East in 1846-1847. Born a Unitarian, Miss Martineau herself had now lost her faith in a personal God and immortality. In the *Letters*, she "gushed and Atkinson ranted."[8] Denying free will and individual moral responsibility, attacking the vested interests of the clergy and Christian dogma, the book made quite a sensation: "There is no God," said Douglas Jerrold, "and Harriet is his prophet." George Eliot, while appreciating the courage and apparent disinterestedness of the book, disliked its advocacy of mesmerism and found its language "studiously offensive." Miss Martineau's brother and girlhood idol, James, a Unitarian divine, himself wrote a devastating review. Miss Martineau was soon to become a Comtist, like Armstrong.

The "consequences of infidelity" in Armstrong's case follow

8. R. K. Webb, *Harriet Martineau* (London: Heinemann, 1960), p. 294.

immediately. He lures his colonel's mistress, Julia, into what he plans as a false marriage; but his trick misfires: the marriage is in fact a genuine one. When Armstrong takes Julia to America, they fall in with a party of Mormons, and he becomes a Mormon and the editor of their newspaper in New Orleans. So the next stop on Conybeare's *tour d'horizon* of the mid-nineteenth-century religious scene is Mormonism, on which he had made himself a hostile expert, having studied it and written a thorough paper on it for the *Edinburgh Review*. The Mormon section of *Perversion* is one of the most unexpected and most rollicking of all. Armstrong writes up accounts of Mormon miracles, propagandizes for the faith, collects the tithes from all Louisiana (as President of the New Orleans "High Priests' Quorum"), and attends a national Mormon convention, all in a thoroughly businesslike and unreligious spirit.

In Washington he meets Lyman, one of the "twelve apostles," an ex-Unitarian minister, who openly tells Armstrong that he has no belief in the "miraculous legend of Joseph Smith." Is there nothing in it? asks Armstrong. "On the contrary," answers Lyman, "there is everything in it . . . . the colonisation of Utah . . . the presidency, and the high priesthood, and all the dozen ranks of the hierarchy . . . the tithing of a hundred thousand converts . . . my income of 5,000 dollars per annum . . . your editorship and future prospects. . . ." For such results, one needs "some tangible myth." Lyman adds that, like Comte, all the leading Mormons are really atheists, and supports his argument with many (authentic) quotations from the contemporary Mormon press. Like Carlyle, the Mormons have learned how to prepare the public for pantheism or worse by using Christian phraseology. Armstrong is easily able to persuade his Mormon friend to take Julia off his hands. Free of this incubus, he goes back to England as a Mormon agent, inherits a small estate, and changes his name to Archer. Still under twenty-one, he is off to Oxford, where Charles Bampton is also an undergraduate. Armstrong's appearance has greatly changed as the result of a face wound in a duel, and Charles does not recognize the former school bully under his new name.

Charles's mother now falls under the influence of Mr. Moony, an Evangelical clergyman, who closely resembles Mrs. Trollope's Cartwright, the Vicar of Wrexhill. Moony has provided Mrs.

Bampton with a new prayer book of his own authorship, "Protestant Devotions." Handsome and with a fine voice, Moony displays "a mixture of fawning and familiarity which absolutely sickens one, especially when it is joined with the most irreverent introductions of sacred words and sentiments." He preaches windy and incomprehensible sermons extempore. A widower, like Cartwright, he would like to marry Mrs. Bampton. Moony introduces into the Bampton household Mr. Murphy, a representative of the Millenarian Society. Unlike Maurice, who deeply respected the Millenarian Stephenson, Conybeare mocks them: Murphy is a greedy blusterer and cheat. He identifies the French Revolution of 1848 with the battle of Armageddon, predicting that it will lead in 1852 to the restoration of the Jews to Palestine, and in 1853 to the end of the world. He cannot explain why his calculations are any more trustworthy than those of others who fix the Millennium for different times. Moony treats the poor of his parish with neglect: he is typical of the "popular religionists of the day," as exemplified in their organ, "The Rouser" (obviously the *Record*), to which Mrs. Bampton now subscribes.

But before leaving the "worldly-minded and self-indulgent" Evangelicals, with their religion learned by rote, their toadying to the rich, their love of Jews, hatred of Papists, and general humbug, Conybeare cautions the reader that there are in fact many "worthy" Evangelical clergymen. In the same town other Evangelicals, who make much less noise than Mr. Moony, are working among the poor. They hold livings bought up by Mr. Simeon of Cambridge for bestowal upon Evangelicals, and are devoted "Simeonites." Even their lack of charity towards those who differ with them comes from an earnest desire to save souls. It is "intellectual comprehensiveness, not catholic love" that is lacking. Thus Conybeare pays tribute to the truly "apostolic" men among the Evangelicals: it would have been fortunate for Charles and his twin sister, Clara, he says, had they fallen under such benign religious influences, but Mr. Moony's Evangelicalism is as unacceptable to them as to Conybeare himself. So much "folly, guile, and malice" do they see Moony perpetrating daily that not even an angel in the guise of an Evangelical clergyman would have won a hearing from them.

Naturally, Charles's next religious exposure is to the Tractarians. Not yet "earnestly seeking for a principle of action which might guide his life and control his will," and disgusted with Evangelicalism, Charles is still a nominal Christian. The charms of architecture, music, and the " 'dim religious light' " of the High-Church party, with its "air of poetic mysticism and reverential reserve," appeal to him. So a young Tractarian Aristotelian Oxford teacher, Lapwing, newly ordained, who constructs arguments from Aristotle's *Ethics* in favor of the Tractarian theory, and uses Aristotle's metaphysics to "illustrate the doctrine of the Real Presence," is the next specimen in Conybeare's ecclesiastical zoo. Lapwing is "addicted to the extemporaneous formation of the most singularly sentimental and schoolgirlish attachments," always to members of his own sex, writing verse in English and Latin in praise of their beauty, sending them passionate love letters, but breaking off each affair suddenly to embark upon a new one. Conybeare describes this obvious case of Tractarian homosexuality with less ambiguity than many Victorian novelists, and treats it as essentially ridiculous. The fickle Lapwing soon transfers his affections to a young lordling, who also cuts Charles out with a pretty girl: Charles is "twice jilted in a single term."

Conybeare mocks the Tractarians by a solemnly hilarious description of the Ecclesiological Society's meeting and a learned paper on an early English village church, in which all the pseudo-mediaeval longings of the members are given full play. But the gentle foolery becomes far sharper when he introduces the Reverend Henry Morgan, a High-Church clergyman, who succeeds the Low-Church Moony in Mrs. Bampton's affections and who—despite an initial preference for celibacy—eventually marries her when he discovers how rich she is. Morgan's father, the archdeacon, engages in "pantomimic attitudinizing" during a confirmation service, gesticulating in accordance with the words of his son's sermon, listening to the Gospel as if he has never heard it before, and, when it comes to the miracle of the raising of the widow's son, assuming "a look of devout amazement." Ill-tempered, "full of Mammon-worship and worldly cunning," the archdeacon is a mere playactor. His son preaches in his surplice, its train borne by six Sunday-school children all in surplices too. He is just as eager to propagate the Gospel among the colonies as is Mr. Moony to push the cause of the Millenarians. For Morgan, the Evangelicals are schismatics, while converts to Rome are "unfilial hearts." Yet he recommends a manual for recently confirmed young people written by a convert, though allegedly published before conversion.

Conybeare also introduces Morgan's curate and his wife, who are, interestingly enough, High-Church people from the lower middle class, ignorant and full of malapropisms and mispronunciations. It is now 1850, the moment of the Low-Church "Protestant agitation" against Catholics after Wiseman's return, and the Tractarians are mounting a counterattack against the Evangelical Prime Minister, Lord John Russell. Conybeare pours ridicule upon a pair of Tractarian agitators, one Anglo-Catholic, the other Roman. The Anglican has been baptized by the Russian, Armenian, and Abyssinian churches, as well as the Church of England, just in case the rite has been defective in England ("lest any real or alleged schism in one or other of the churches in which I sought the sacrament might vitiate it, I thought it best to have it performed by bishops of three distinct churches which mutually anathematize each other"). The Roman Catholic is an ex-Anglican clergyman, a "pervert," who had joined the Roman Church in order to ingratiate himself with a rich Catholic nobleman. His patron has obtained for him a commission in the Austrian army, and he now sports a uniform. His assumed military bearing, his false moustache, his insistence on ordering masses said for his infuriated Church of England relatives, all render him ridiculous.

Disillusioned with both Low and High, Charles Bampton is now fair prey for Archer's systematic attempts to undermine what little faith he has. Archer begins with ridicule, and progresses to higher criticism, easily showing that the Bible cannot be regarded as a single text, and that modern geologists and Genesis are in conflict. Charles fails to remember that the apostles themselves had not pretended to be superhuman. He

> did not perceive that a revealer of religious truth is not required to be infallible except in the subject matter of his revelation. He did not consider that the historical and scientific infallibility which he sought in the sacred writing would (had it existed) have superseded the researches of history, and

> anticipated the discoveries of science, and would thus have been incompatible with the designs of Providence. . . . He had been taught to substitute an infallibility of the letter for the infallibility of the Spirit, and his idol being overthrown, his worship perished with it.

In short, Charles, not having been exposed to Broad-Church ideas, is trapped into infidelity. Archer clinches his victory by prescribing books arguing that revelation from without is an impossibility, and that miracles must be "rejected as simply impossible."

Soon he introduces Charles to a club of freethinkers ("the friends of light" or " 'Licht-freunden,' for they greatly affected German phrases"), glib pretenders to knowledge, scientific and otherwise, on all subjects, parlor revolutionaries urging the assassination of kings, displayers of indecent pictures and statuary (nudes by Raphael, Correggio, Titian, which "if published in a cheaper form would have exposed the publisher to a prosecution by the 'Society for the Suppression of Vice' "). They listen to an essay in favor of licentious behavior (Christian asceticism is bad for youthful morals), written by a young man who has paid a pilgrimage to the shrine of George Sand herself and returned with a button of her "masculine integuments" as a souvenir, or rather a relic. Why not? Conybeare argues, half indignant, half flippant: had not Lord Herbert of Cherbury said that "yielding to our physical passions is no more to be blamed than drinking when we are thirsty," and Emerson that "purity of heart is identical with the law of gravitation"? Thus, there can be "no impurity in obeying the force which draws our hearts to pleasure." The freethinkers are sensualists, and Conybeare waxes indignant against Goethe and Etty as advocates of the nude. But this episode too ends in slapstick when an innocently pious freshman comes into the freethinkers' room in search of a group practicing Gregorian chants, and is persuaded to accept a High-Church interpretation of the "indecent" paintings.

At Cottonham, where Charles's elder sister has married a rich manufacturer, social pretentiousness and industrial misery are the order of the day. Both derive from a lack of Christian faith and an unbridled lust for wealth. Only a few manufacturers are exceptions to the general rule of "sordid selfishness." Charles encounters an experienced and devout doctor, who faces these facts manfully but is not without hope for improvement. Believing the Bible, he looks "for a certain and eternal triumph of good at last." Charles sees that "religion, whether true itself or not, was a useful and almost indispensable antidote to the corruptions of the world." Yet the local Cottonham clergyman is "a divine of the good old orthodox school," elderly, fat, red-faced, nephew of an eighteenth-century bishop, holding an enormously rich living, and denouncing church reformers as "atheistical dogs." Hating both "popular preachers" (Evangelicals) and "the frivolous ceremonies of tractarianism," he has had no time to read the *Tracts for the Times* because he is too busy fishing and farming the glebe. He barely interrupts himself in a fishing story long enough to say grace at dinner, opposes national education, and has only reluctantly founded a parish school, in which the children are taught nothing. So Conybeare includes a specimen of the "High-and-Dry" in his gallery of clerical portraits.

The vicious but brilliant unbeliever, Archer—who exercises "moral mesmerism" on his victims—not only deprives Charles of his faith, but also succeeds in making Charles's beloved twin sister, Clara, fall in love with him and marry him. Not a speculative person, never enjoying a firmly rooted faith, like Charles disgusted with extreme Low- and High-Church clerics, Clara succumbs easily to Archer. He works as a radical journalist, promoting the extirpation of Christianity, which he hates with the "acrimonious hatred of a soul devoted to the cause of evil." Through Archer Clara meets a variety of atheists and agitators. But Archer is, of course, still legally married to Julia, who has entered upon Mormon matrimony without realizing that her new husband already has several wives. She escapes from Utah (her life among the Mormons is described entertainingly and at length) and returns to England to sue Archer for bigamy. Ultimately he is convicted and sentenced to six years' hard labor. Released for good behavior, he goes to New York and plans a political career in the "ultra-democratic party" in America. In taking leave of him, Conybeare looks forward to his reappearance as American Ambassador to the Court of St. James's: a heavy-handed satirical hit, revealing the anxiety about revolutionary tendencies that haunted those Englishmen of the early 1850's who were politically conservative even if liberal in their views of the Church.

Shattered by the ruin of her marriage, Clara commits suicide. As for Charles, he must undergo severe tuberculosis, a shipwreck, a long convalescence in Madeira under the care of a devoted clergyman's wife, and a final conversion. While he is still an invalid, the good Samaritan Mrs. Williamson daily reads to him stories by Miss Sewell or Miss Yonge, oddly Tractarian fiction for a reprobate and anti-Tractarian sinner. But it is the opportunity to do works of Christian charity that eventually redeems him: he undertakes the rescue of a poverty-stricken family of Madeiran grape growers. By imitating the example of Christ, who healed the sick and did good to the poor, Charles begins to have a glimmer of the truth. Mr. Williamson, admirable though he is in character, is an Anglo-Catholic after the pattern of George Herbert, a devoted parish priest. Here at last is the example of a good High Churchman so long wanting in this novel to balance the bad. But Williamson is "not familiar with the doubts and perplexities of the present day, nor capable of meeting the cavils of modern unbelief." So Charles's conversion must wait.

The rescue of a prostitute to whose delinquency he had himself contributed as an undergraduate is the next practical step towards christianizing Charles. The process is speeded when he learns that his own death cannot be long postponed. This produces "a deeper earnestness"—at last a sign of the key Arnoldian virtue—and a "thirst for truth." Charles's encounters with Hawkins, chaplain of the hospital for fallen women to which he has consigned his former victim, play a vital part: like Charles, Hawkins had once been a freethinker at Oxford; misfortune had taught him the key lesson, "It is more blessed to give than to receive." So Charles turns to him, in distress over his guilt and his irrevocable sin (in ruining the young girl), and asks for a redeemer or sanctifier.

While Charles cannot believe in a personal God, he now shrinks from the pantheist conclusion that "self-conscious humanity is the highest God." He cannot reconcile God's omnipotence and benevolence with the existence of evil, an ancient problem, of course, on which he has read widely, but finds all answers unsatisfactory. Moreover, Charles still cannot convince himself of the genuineness of the Christian miracles. As a result of his reading in science and the higher criticism, he doubts the inspiration of Scripture. And finally, how can mankind live up to Christian ideals? Are they not too lofty and impractical?

Hawkins replies, as Conybeare, Coleridge, Thomas Arnold, or Maurice would have replied: intellect alone does not suffice to convince us that God exists; it is only the heart that can do this. All attempts to explain the existence of evil *are* futile: we must cling to the Gospel assurance that a time will come when "the divided empire of good and ill shall cease, when pain and sin shall be no more, when God shall be all in all." Nor can sufficient evidence be summoned to demonstrate the truth of miracle, although the probabilities favor it. But the "perfect adaptation" of Christianity to the "spiritual needs of mankind" converts men's hearts. Mankind has an "internal affinity for the Gospel" and bad men are changed to good men when they receive it.[9] Heart, conscience, and will must answer the question before the "sceptical understanding" can follow along. Charles's act of seeking for communion with God's spirit will surely be answered. As for the Bible, the apostles need not be infallible, and their mistakes "cannot affect their credibility as ambassadors of Christ." And if ordinary men strive towards the Christian life as expounded in certain New Testament texts, they will at least have goals worth attaining, as contrasted with Goethe's outworn epicurean precepts of "know thyself," "follow thy bent," "push nothing too far." Prayer is the answer, and the ability to pray comes with praying.

The practical social work of the parish where Hawkins is one of the curates drives home the lesson to Charles. Infidelity amongst the lower classes is the direct result of ignorance, and with education and assistance in their problems, they become naturally drawn to religion. A manufacturer who gives his workmen opportunities for playing healthy games, who participates with them in their sport as in their prayers, who teaches them and has established a library

9. This quotation Conybeare attributes to "Tholuck," who is Friedrich August Gottreu Tholuck (1799-1877), Professor of Theology at Halle, antirationalist, author of commentaries on Romans, John, and Hebrews, and of *The Authenticity of Gospel History* (1837).

for them, and who even encourages them to invest in the factory, has been brought to all these acts of decent Christianity by reading the life of Dr. Arnold. Charles becomes convinced that "Christianity is a living and working power, not only confessed in the pulpit and the Sunday school, but leavening the most secular transactions, penetrating the details of commerce, and influencing the relation between capital and labour." Here is the practical sort of endeavor to which Arnold devoted himself at Rugby, and Maurice, a generation later, among the London workingmen. And, Conybeare stresses, such genuine living Christianity can be sought by men of any theological beliefs. The rector of the parish, for whom Hawkins is a curate, is a strong Evangelical, but will not let party spirit affect his social work.

Visits to the deathbeds of the suffering poor open Charles's mind for Thomas Arnold's sermon on the moral certainty of the Christian's resurrection. Hawkins quotes the key passage:

> Once think of any one as devoted to God—as living principally in relation to him—and it becomes as difficult to conceive of such a one that he is perished, as to conceive of any other that he will not perish. For here we have a man possessed with faculties and with affections that nothing on earth has satisfied or can ever satisfy; his life is imperfect; he seems to have been cut off most untimely, if that God, whom here on earth the very best man can only see, as it were, through a glass darkly, shall never be known to him more fully. And when we see such a man going on quietly, attracting no great notice or glory on earth, yet ripening continually in all goodness; suffering with cheerfulness; labouring with unwearied zeal; making the best possible use of earthly things, yet ever looking beyond them;—it is manifest that his conversation is not here, and that if the grave close on him for ever, he who has lived better than any other class of men, will alone of all men never have reached the haven which he desired, nor attained the end of his being. It is like those foreign plants whose flowers and fruit will not come to perfection in our climate: but whose natural strength and beauty make us feel only the more sure

> that they must have elsewhere a better and more genial climate of their own.

The very deathbed of such a man is evidence of a certain future life. "If there were many such, faith would scarcely be faith, but would be almost changed into sight."

Precisely such an opportunity comes to Charles that day, as Hawkins is suddenly struck low by cholera. During his intense prayers that Hawkins's life be saved, Charles comes to know "within himself that his prayer was not unheard, that he had a Father in heaven, and a Saviour who could be touched by his infirmities. . . . Henceforward Charles Bampton was a Christian; not, as he had once been, by name and profession only, but by the conviction of the conscience, and the consent of the enlightened reason and of the converted will." Charles dies helping the sick and wounded in the hospital at Scutari during the Crimean War.

Perversion provides an overview of mid-Victorian religious attitudes more extensive than any other to be found in fiction. Sharply satirical of High-Church and Low-Church foibles, Conybeare nonetheless concedes that excellent individual clergymen are to be found even amongst the extreme partisans of both contesting parties. Though he condemns the Mormons and the various schools of free thought, he says nothing about Methodists or indeed about any Dissenters except the Unitarians. His hero's spiritual pilgrimage brings him at last to peace within the framework of Broad-Church Christianity. A modern reader wonders how much Charles Bampton's own knowledge that he has only a brief time to live has to do with his readiness to accept Hawkins's example and his precepts. Would Bampton have remained an unbeliever if he had kept his health? The more readily one accepts Charles Bampton's ordeal as credible, the less one can believe in Armstrong-Archer's continued baleful influence. The inherent improbability that Charles would never have recognized in his evil spirit—and brother-in-law—the bullying schoolboy who had wrecked his childhood looms larger and larger.

But even if one dismisses from one's mind all uncertainties about the plot, one retains a nagging sense of dissatisfaction with

Conybeare's novel. Clara's tragic marriage and suicide, Charles's repeated hemorrhages and eventual death, must be taken seriously if they are to be effective. Yet the prevailing tone of the book is highly satirical, with strong overtones of slapstick farce: one half of a moustache falls into the soup; one luxuriant whisker is shaved off an undergraduate as a practical joke; there is a library of indecent books (George Sand, Paul de Kock, Rabelais), all of them mere dummies with leather backs, palmed off as suitable library furniture on the gullible Mrs. Bampton, just as there is a collection of indecent Old Masters in the freethinkers' rooms. It is easy to accept either the ridicule or the tragedy, but difficult to accept both. Other Broad-Church novelists also often seem unable to control an irrepressible frivolity. The overall effect is an unfortunate one of jaunty flippancy, surely unintended, which dilutes the religious message.

A vitriolic review of *Perversion*, objecting to it on somewhat different grounds, appeared in the *National Review* immediately after the novel's publication in 1856. Anonymous, but by Richard Holt Hutton (1826-1897), coeditor of the periodical with Walter Bagehot, the article later appeared much revised in Hutton's *Essays, Theological and Literary.*[10] Hutton christened *Perversion* a "Hard Church Novel," "uniting the tone of a schoolmaster to a spirit of intellectual scorn," a degradation of what he called the "Church of Common Sense." The Church of Common Sense—of Paley, Whately, and others—is "Broad in inclusion . . . because it demands but *few* articles of belief . . . the resort of the strong-minded theologians." It "forms a Court standing midway between the narrow crypts of Low Evangelical doctrine beneath, and the venerable decay of the High Church towers above." But the Hard Church is the "morally ossifying type" of this Broad Church, says Hutton, imitating Conybeare's own typologizing of Church parties in his *Edinburgh Review* essay. Unlike Maurice and Julius Hare, Conybeare browbeats his adversaries instead of granting them leeway (and Conybeare surely made few concessions, while Maurice made

10. Second edition, 2 vols. (London: Macmillan, 1880), I, pp. 303-333; first in *National Review* 3 (1856): 127-146, from which all quotations in the text are taken. This is important because so much of the first version was later altered, and almost all the commentary on Conybeare cut out.

many); and Conybeare sees in theology not a "deep philosophy like Coleridge . . . nor a Divine reconciliation of the many contradictory yearnings of human nature, like Maurice," but "a decisive chain of circumstantial evidence." Hard-Church thinkers dismiss "as immaterial or practically misleading, all those fluctuating elements of human life which do not seem to be deeply imbedded in the average notions of average men."

Disliking "that hybrid species of composition of which religious novels almost always consist," Hutton yet believes that "there is no better sign for the theology of the present day than its disposition to try itself by literary tests. Theology and Literature . . . need to go hand in hand, and are only just beginning to know it." So far, however, the only successful writers of religious novels have been "one or two ladies with characters yielding enough to bend wholly to the high Anglican theory, and with intellects sufficiently delicate" to portray the disagreeable consequences of their form of faith: probably he meant Miss Sewell, possibly Charlotte Yonge. If, says Hutton, the High-Church "sacerdotal conceptions of the legitimate anxiety of conscience, and the duty of *detecting* a captivity for the will where it does not offer itself, were engrafted on the genial trustfulness of Protestant faith," we would all be breathing a "consumptive air," full of "feverish debility." As for Evangelical or Low-Church novels, they are "mere forms; you see every where that the life consciously or unconsciously believed in, and the life inculcated, are totally distinct." Hutton praises the Broad-Church Kingsley for his efforts to indicate "the type of manly religious life in which faith and nature may be fused into a living whole." Kingsley aims at "something far nobler and healthier than the Anglican school," but has not been so successful. But "the points at which real religion strives, whether successfully or vainly, to enter the hearts of ordinary men" are not yet revealed in fiction. The Church of Common Sense, even if uncomprehending of the emotional needs of less rational beings, is at least tolerant of them.

But the Hard Churchmen "go about like theological detectives, without any care or compassion for the sins . . . of the defaulters they arrest." Coarsely triumphing over "supposed error or real evil," their lack of sympathy is the sort that makes men "hurl back the charges at their accuser." Conybeare, says Hutton, is obviously reporting from life all the "miserable shams which pass in such quick succession before us." His weapons are ridicule, censure, and disgust. And he does not limit himself to caricaturing religious deviants. Hutton expresses particular outrage at Conybeare's satire on the manufacturing classes and on the Unitarians of Manchester, and calls Conybeare's denunciations of them only "mild specimens of the *throng* of dark and yet hard triumphant representations of vulgarity and wickedness . . . High Church, Low Church, heterodox, and sceptical" that fill *Perversion.*

One of the ablest essayists and critics of the entire Victorian age, the son and grandson of Unitarian ministers, Hutton had himself been trained in Manchester for the Unitarian ministry; so he was naturally cut to the quick by Conybeare's stinging attacks on the Unitarians of Manchester and on the manufacturing classes generally. Much influenced by James Martineau, whom Conybeare also satirizes, Hutton was also offended by the sneers at the "shallow deism" of Francis Newman and by the denunciation of the American Unitarian Theodore Parker's "absolute religion" as "substituting a mutilated Christianity for the preaching of the Faith." Three years before he wrote his review of *Perversion,* Hutton had met Maurice and become a great admirer of his. He was on his way into the Church of England. But naturally he retained an affectionate understanding for the Unitarianism of his ancestors and of his own youth, and a tender sympathy for all doubters. Himself a Broad Churchman of a wholly different stamp from Conybeare, Hutton was bitterly offended by what he felt to be the slashing intolerance of *Perversion.* It did not seem funny to him. But the anger of his review, though understandable, should not blind a modern reader to the effectiveness of the novel. "Hard Church" it may be, but it has far more in it of Coleridge and Maurice than Hutton admitted. And it stems immediately from Thomas Arnold, whom Hutton does not mention. Conybeare and Hutton, then, illustrate the great variations in religious emphasis to be found within the Broad-Church party.

Portrait of a Seer: F. D. Maurice in George MacDonald's David Elginbrod

The Scotsman George MacDonald (1825-1905), remembered today chiefly for his popular and disturbing children's books—*At the Back of the North Wind* (1871), *The Princess and the Goblin* (1872), and *The Princess and Curdie* (1883)—or for his tales of dream fantasy for adults—*Phantastes* (1858) and *Lilith* (1895)—was a Congregationalist rebel against Scotch Calvinism when Maurice and Maurice's disciple A. J. Scott brought him, like Hutton, into the Church of England in the early 1850's. He wrote twenty-five novels for adults, in which he preached a generally Broad-Church message. In several of his novels reprinted here, he painted a vivid picture of Scotch Calvinism; occasionally, as we shall see, he portrayed most unsympathetically the narrowness of the English Congregational chapel folk like those among whom he had held his first and only ministry. In his first full-length novel for adults, *David Elginbrod* (1863, no. 53), whose chief character is a heroic liberal anti-Calvinist Scottish patriarch, MacDonald, whose own spiritual ancestry derived from Boehme, Swedenborg, Blake, Novalis, Hoffmann, Wordsworth, Coleridge, and Erskine of Linlathen, included a portrait of Maurice himself.

Maurice appears climactically, after the young Scotch hero, Hugh, has come to England, and has attended various church services there. First he hears a High-and-Dry country clergyman comically and confusingly described by a loyal parishioner to his guest, Mrs. Elton, a baffled Evengelical lady, as "quite a respectable preacher, as well as a clergyman. . . . an honour to his cloth. . . . no Puseyite either, although he does preach once a month in his surplice"; he is not original, for "how is a man to be original on a subject that is all laid down in cold print . . . and has been commented upon for eighteen hundred years and more?" Relieved at this, Mrs. Elton says, "We don't want originality. . . . It is only the gospel we want. Does he preach the gospel?" She is sardonically reassured, "How can he preach anything else? His text is always from the Bible." "Chaotically bewildered," she replies, "I am glad you hold by the inspiration of the Scripture," to which the answer is "Good heavens, Madam. . . . Could you for a moment suppose me to be an atheist? Surely you have not become a student of German neology."

The village church (like the Church of England itself, says MacDonald ironically) is old and would have been beautiful had it not been plastered over; its stained-glass windows are (significantly) "half concealed by modern appliances for the partial exclusion of the light." It had suffered the same fate as "Chaucer at the hands of Dryden." So had the truth, "flickering through the sermon," bought ready-printed for eighteenpence, which proves that "God is no respecter of persons." Since the gentry, their servants, and the "common parishioners" occupy three distinct levels in this very church, the message is singularly malapropos. Death, says the clergyman, will lower the rich to the level of the poor, and the future life will raise the poor to the level of the rich. Fortunately, Hugh thinks, the Bible and the liturgy are beyond the "reach of such degenerating influences." The complacent host is quite satisfied: no Puseyism, no Radicalism: the uneducated have been shown how "to do their duty in the station of life to which God had called them." But the Evangelical Mrs. Elton feels the lack of the Gospel. Later that Sunday, she urges that justification by faith and a peculiarly muddled idea of the atonement (all her own invention, it is clear) should henceforth be preached.

In London, Hugh meets a fellow Scot, Robert Falconer—about whom MacDonald five years later published an entire novel (1868, no. 60)—a strong anti-Calvinist mystic, who enunciates his own philosophy of death: whenever it arrives, it "comes as the best and only good" possible for the dying man. We think of death too much "as the culmination of disease, which, regarded only in itself, is an evil, and a terrible evil. But I think rather of death as the first pulse of the new strength, shaking itself free from the old mouldy remnants of earth-garments, that it may begin in freedom the new life that grows out of the old. The caterpillar dies into the butterfly." The good, welcome death that is the beginning of true life was, we know, an idea promulgated by Erskine of Linlathen and accepted by Maurice. It pervades MacDonald's fiction, and is perhaps his most important moral lesson, one that brought comfort to his many thousands of readers.

The fierce Evangelical faith of Mrs. Elton so disturbs her little son Harry that he dreams of heaven's being a great church exactly like the one his mother goes to. God, in the pulpit converted into a throne, terrifies him until Jesus, at the reading desk below, hides him from the baleful glare. "Dead wooden shapes," says MacDonald of Evangelical religion, "substituted for the forms of human love and hope and aspiration." Harry's dream is "no more incongruous than the instruction that prompted it." Like MacDonald himself as a little boy, Harry—pondering the doctrine of election—declares that he does not want God to love him if He does not love everybody. He expects God to forgive him for his sins and to say, "Come along, never mind. *I'll* make you good. I can't wait till you *are* good, I love you so much." The little child has an instinctive Maurician appreciation of eternal forgiveness. Mrs. Elton's clergyman, however, preaches a fatuous sermon to the effect that even the great Queen Victoria worships the Christ, who "dwells with his own elect, the chosen ones, whom he has led back to the fold of his grace." Hugh says to Falconer that the clergyman seems "quite proud of the honour done his Master by the Queen," to which Falconer returns, "I do not think that his master will think so much of it, for he once had his feet washed by a woman that was a sinner."

Impatience with the Calvinism that permeated the Low Church, combined with a romantic eagerness for death and not a little social radicalism, makes Hugh and Falconer breathless listeners at the church of still another clergyman of the Church of England. After the morning service and the litany have been read, "in an ordinary manner though somewhat more devoutly,"

> from the communion-table rose a voice vibrating with solemn emotion, like the voice of Abraham pleading for Sodom. The sermon which followed affected [Hugh] no less, although, when he came out, he confessed to Falconer that he had only caught flying glimpses of its meaning, scope, and drift.
>
> "I seldom go to church," said Falconer, "but when I do, I come here; and always feel that I am in the presence of one of the holy servants of God's great temple not made with hands. I heartily trust that man. He is what he seems to be."
>
> "They say he is awfully heterodox."

"They do."

"How, then, can he remain in the church, if he is as honest as you say?"

"In this way. . . . He looks upon the formulae of the church as utterances of *living* truth—vital embodiments,—to be regarded as one ought to regard human faces. In . . . human faces others may see this or that inferior expression, may find out the mean and the small and the incomplete; he looks for and finds the ideal; the grand, the sacred, the God-meant meaning; and by that he holds as *the* meaning of the human countenances, for it is the meaning of Him who made them. So with the confession of the Church of England; he believes that not man only, but God also, and God first and chief, had to do with the making of it; and therefore he looks in it for the Eternal and the Divine, and he finds what he seeks. And as no words can avoid bearing in them the possibility of a variety of interpretations, he would exclude whatever the words might mean, or, regarded merely as words, do mean, in a narrow exposition; he thinks it would be dishonest to take the low meaning as *the* meaning. To return to the faces: he passes by moods and tempers, and beholds the main character,—that on whose surface the temporal and transient floats. Both in faces and in formulae he loves the divine substance, with his true, manly, brave heart; and as for the faults in both,—for man, too had his share in both—I believe he is ready to die by them, if only in so doing he might die for them. I had a vision of him this morning, as I sat and listened to his voice, which always seems to me to come directly from his heart, as if his heart spoke with lips of its own. Shall I tell you my vision?

"I saw a crowd—priests and laymen—speeding, hurrying, darting away, up a steep, crumbling height. Mitres, hoods, and hats rolled behind them to the bottom. Every one for himself, with hands and feet they scramble and flee, to save their souls from the fires of hell which come rolling in along the hollow below with the forward 'pointing spires' of billowy flame. But beneath, right in the course of the fire, stands one man, upon a little rock which goes down to the centre of the great world, and faces the approaching flames. He stands bareheaded, his eyes bright with faith in God, and the mighty mouth that utters his truth fixed in holy defiance. His denial comes from no fear, or weak dislike to that which is painful. On neither side will he tell lies for peace. He is ready to be lost for his fellow-men. In the name of God he rebukes the flames of hell. The fugitives pause on the top, look back, call him *lying prophet*, and shout evil, opprobrious names at the man who counts not his own life dear to him, who has forgotten his own soul in his sacred devotion to men, who fills up what is left behind of the sufferings of Christ, for his body's sake,—for the human race, of which he is the head. Be sure that, come what may of the rest, let the flames of hell ebb or flow, that man is safe, for he is delivered already from the only devil that can make hell itself a torture, the devil of selfishness—the only one that can possess a man and make himself his own living hell. He is out of all that region of things, and already dwelling in the secret place of the Almighty. . . .

"He trusts in God so absolutely that he leaves his salvation to him—utterly, fearlessly, and, forgetting it, as being no concern of his, sets himself to do the work that God has given him to do, even as his Lord did before him, counting that alone worthy of his care. Let God's will be done, and all is well. If God's will be done, he cannot fare ill. To him, God is all in all. If it be possible to separate such things, it is the glory of God, even more than the salvation of men, that he seeks. He will not have it that his Father in heaven is not perfect. He believes entirely that God loves, yea, *is* love, and therefore that hell itself must be subservient to that love, and but an embodiment of it; that the grand work of Justice is to make way for a Love which will give to every man that which is right, and ten times more, even if it should be by means of awful suffering,—a suffering which the Love of the Father will not shun, either for himself or his children, but will eagerly meet for their sakes, that he may give them all that is in his heart."

Freely granting that these are his own views of the preacher, who is, of course, Maurice, and is not "accountable" for any of them, Falconer declares that "this is how I seem to myself to succeed in understanding him." Falconer was MacDonald's own spokesman. Acknowledging that Maurice is hard to understand, and not certain that he has understood him thoroughly, he nonetheless ventures this somewhat turgid, lengthy, exultant exposition both of the key aspects of Maurice's theology—the dismissal of predestination, election, and eternal damnation—and of the key aspects of his character—bravery, boldness, and utter devotion. How is it, then, Hugh wants to know, that "so many people call him heterodox"?

Falconer, speaking once again for MacDonald, answers that he does not mind that:

> I am annoyed only when good-hearted people, with small natures and cultivated intellects, patronize him, and talk forgivingly of his warm heart and unsound judgment. To these, theology must be like a map,—with plenty of lines on it. They cannot trust their house on the high table-land of his theology, because they cannot see the outlines bounding the said table-land. It is not small enough for them. They cannot take it in. Such can hardly be satisfied with the creation, one would think, seeing there is no line of division anywhere in it. They would take care that there should be no mistake.

Such intellectuals would make their lines into "Chinese walls of separation." But the kind of lines that God draws are "pure lines without breadth, and consequently invisible to mortal eyes." These theories in religion that "are so hard to see" are puzzling only to intellectuals. But if they are good-hearted they will "get to heaven, which is all they want," and thereafter they will understand Maurice, "which is more than they pray for." Till they have done being anxious about their own salvation, we must forgive them their ability to contemplate "with calmness the damnation of a universe, and believe that God is yet more indifferent than they." Of course such men—Evangelicals and Calvinists generally—say that Maurice and his followers do not understand them either; but until "the Spirit of God" decides the matter, "the Right must be content to be called the Wrong, and—which is far harder—to see the Wrong."

A mystic who cared little for the intellectuals' "lines on a map," MacDonald with considerable ability expounded here in the pages of a novel those portions of Maurice's doctrines that most appealed to him as a refugee first from Scotch Calvinism and then from Congregational Dissent. And more important than any doctrine is the whole-hearted, whole-souled admiration for the quality, the integrity, the courage of Maurice himself. The only attempt to portray Maurice in a novel, to my knowledge, this passage in *David Elginbrod* reflects both MacDonald's bewilderment (like Hugh's) at his first listening to one of Maurice's sermons, and his later interpretation (put into the mouth of Falconer) of its essential meaning. Richard Holt Hutton, on whom Maurice had had an equally great influence—and who had an intellect so much more precise than MacDonald's that one might have supposed that he would either understand Maurice thoroughly or repudiate him for not putting enough lines on his map—in fact responded the same way.

When Bagehot first took his friend Hutton to hear Maurice preach, he told him that "he would not exactly answer for my being impressed with the sermon, but that at all events he thought I should feel that something different went on there from that which goes on in an ordinary church or chapel service, that there was a sense of 'something religious' . . . in the air which was not to be found elsewhere." And Hutton wrote forty years later that "the voice and manner of the preacher . . . in the reading desk as much as the pulpit—have lived in my memory ever since, as no other voice and manner ever lived in it."

> The half-stern, half-pathetic emphasis with which he gave the words of the Confession, "And there is *no* health in *us*," throwing the weight of the meaning on to the last word, and the rising of his voice into a higher plane of hope as he passed away from the confession of weakness to the invocation of God's help, struck the one note of his life—the passionate trust in eternal help—as it had never been struck in my hearing before. There was intensity—almost too thrilling—and something too of sad exultation in every tone, as if the reader were rehearsing a story in which he had no part except his personal certainty of its truth, his gratitude that it should be true, and his humiliation that it had fallen to such lips as his to declare it. This was what made his character present itself so

> strongly to the mind as almost embodied in *a voice*. He seemed to be the channel for a communication, not the source of it. There was a gentle hurry, and yet a peremptoriness, in those at once sad and sonorous tones, which spoke of haste to tell their tale, and of actual fear of not telling it with sufficient emphasis and force. . . . They seemed put into his mouth, while he, with his whole soul bent on their wonderful drift, uttered them as an awestruck but thankful envoy tells the tale of danger and deliverance. . . . His countenance expressed nervous, high-strung tension, as though all the various play of feelings in ordinary human nature converged, in him, towards a single focus—the declaration of the divine purpose. . . . The more Maurice believed in Christ, the less he confounded himself with the object of his belief, and the more pathetic was his distrust of his own power to see aright, or say aright what he saw.

So Hutton's and MacDonald's impressions of the great preacher were almost identical.

Hutton's account, which has been much abridged here, goes on to emphasize Maurice's humility ("the sins of others produce such sin in me," he wrote, "and stir up my unsanctified nature so terribly")—a statement both revealing his "profound sense of unworthiness" and explaining the heat he poured into his polemic. Others, of course, took a harsher view of Maurice. Augustus Hare, nephew of Maurice's second wife and as a child a great sufferer at her hands, commented that Maurice

> maundered over his own humility in a way which—even to a child—did not seem humble, and he was constantly lost mentally in the labyrinth of religious mysticisms which he was ever creating for himself. In all he said and wrote, there was a nebulous vagueness. . . . When he preached before the University of Cambridge to a church crowded with undergraduates, they asked one another as they came out, "What was it all about?"

Nor is this inconsistent with MacDonald's experience: he too did not catch more than "flying glimpses" of Maurice's "meaning, scope, and drift." But MacDonald did not mind bewilderment: other men did. John Ruskin found Maurice "puzzle-headed"; Matthew Arnold spoke of him as "always beating the bush with profound emotion but never starting the hare." "Like eating pea soup with a fork," said Aubrey de Vere, and Mountstuart Elphinstone Grant-Duff, after hearing Maurice thirty or forty times, "never carried away one clear idea, or even the impression that he had more than the faintest conception of what he meant himself."[11] "Not a clear idea in his head," said J. B. Mozley, "and his reputation will collapse as soon as it is touched." "Misty and confused," said Jowett, but "a great man and a disinterested nature, and he always stood by anybody who appeared to be oppressed." "Of all the muddle-headed, intricate, futile persons . . . about the most utterly bewildering," said Leslie Stephen. And yet James Martineau declared that "for consistency and completeness of thought and precision in the use of language, it would be difficult to find Maurice's superior among living theologians," and in 1902 W. E. Collins pronounced him "the greatest seer of the [nineteenth] century."[12] Just because opinions of Maurice in his own day were so deeply contradictory, one welcomes still more heartily the long glimpse that *David Elginbrod* gives us of the inspiration he conveyed to MacDonald, who was a serious religious thinker and a popular, prolific, and influential novelist.

Two Popularizers: Robinson and Davies

F. W. Robinson (born 1830), one of those Victorian professional novelists whose books are counted by the dozen, published his first novel in 1854. *The House of Elmore* (NIS) and its immediate successors are utterly forgotten now, and perhaps deserve obli-

11. Hutton in "Frederick Denison Maurice," *Essays on Some of the Modern Guides to English Thought in Matters of Faith* (London: Macmillan, 1891), pp. 316 ff.; Hare in *The Story of My Life* (London, 1895), I, p. 72; Ruskin in *Praeterita* (London: Rupert Hart-Davis, 1949), pp. 451-452; the others in Amy Cruse, *The Victorians and Their Books* (London: George Allen and Unwin, 1935), p. 111.

12. These opinions reported in A. Vidler.

vion; but in 1860 appeared the first of Robinson's four novels written in rapid succession about contemporary religious issues. A glance at the opening words of *High Church* (1860, no. 49)—"It was a large town. It was a quiet old town. It was a steady, matter-of-fact, business-like town, that throve well and turned a fair face to society"—is enough to tell the reader that he is dealing with a devoted disciple of Dickens. Robinson's constant aping of the master, in fact, grows both comic and tiresome: "Murder!" begins the account of a trial, "The trees beyond the open window might have been rustling the name, and the bee that had strayed in and was 'worriting' the nose of a reporter might be humming it to itself."

But *High Church* merits resurrection as an account, however prejudiced and improbable, of the impact produced in the 1840's on a country town by the arrival of a pair of Tractarian clergymen, father and son, John Stone and Geoffrey Stone, who serves as his father's curate. Familiar though we are by now with the Tractarian innovations in the service and with the objections of their opponents, we have never encountered anything like the vehemence of the opposition in Tenchester as portrayed by Robinson, who ranges himself firmly on that side. His spokesman, the hero, Martin Chester, a local businessman, loves "a plain, simple service," like his parents before him, and, though personally tolerant, feels a twinge at the introduction of new practices. In church, the prayer books are now "embellished with brass crosses, and the communion-table . . . covered with black velvet, on which a huge cross stood forth in bold relief"; but this, the intoning, the choir, and "some incomprehensible bowing" during the service are not as objectionable as the flowers at Easter. Then the Stones put on an "ecclesiastical flower show." Flowered wreaths, crosses, and letters hang on each pillar. Camellias, lilies, and *immortelles* on the altar are set off by veils of embroidered lace. An embroidered green velvet cloth is spread on the altar, and above it a "superaltar" gives "elevation to a large cross and two massive candle-sticks." Most people, says Robinson, could have prayed better without all this; it can only

> startle and pain those brought up in a simpler fashion, and inclined to worship God with their hearts, instead of hanging up

> flowers, and lace, and velvets, and calling *that* religion. They had called *that* religion in the darker times, before Martin Luther burned the papal bull—they had called it so in Bloody Mary's time—they had called it so when Protestant Laud was Archbishop of Canterbury, and a nation with one voice had thundered "NO" to it.

The Tractarians, says Robinson, are the "mountebank sons" of the church. They will "drop off in their time," and "this sect-oppressed world" will see them form a new church of their own. Meanwhile, the ordinary people of Tenchester grow more and more incensed with the innovations, and are whipped into fury by demagogues. A Low-Church churchwarden becomes embroiled in a lawsuit with the Stones; the "No Church" rabble make menacing noises. Despite his anti-Tractarianism, Robinson himself is not a fanatic. He uses the word "nuisance" for the local tailor who denounces the Stones as papists leading Tenchester to the feet of the scarlet woman. As discontent grows in the town, disharmony grows in the marriage of Martin Chester, who dislikes the innovations, and his wife, Ada, who likes them. The marriage collapses when Ada confesses to Geoffrey Stone, and Martin—quite unfairly, it seems—insists on a separation. "The canons of our Church," Geoffrey Stone has said to Ada, "authorize, in peculiar cases, the confessions of the afflicted, give us power to console them in their trouble, and solace them with godly counsel. We do not seek the outpourings of the heart, but we are not bound to reject them. . . . Ours is not the Romish confession. . . . It is not in my power to absolve you from sin. . . ." This way of putting it suggests that Robinson did not fully understand the Tractarian theological views on the question: they unquestionably *did* claim the power of absolution. Moreover, Stone has concealed even from himself that he has been falling in love with Ada Chester: so Martin's suspicions of hanky-panky in the confessional are after all to some degree justified. We are here back in the world of Mrs. Lynn Linton's *Under Which Lord* and Robert Buchanan's *Foxglove Manor*.

Both the public crisis in Tenchester and the private crisis in the lives of the Martin Chesters reach melodramatic climaxes. The church is burned down, not by the mob, which has confined itself to riotous and blasphemous behavior, but by a local tramp with a grudge against Geoffrey Stone, who is eventually murdered. And the rehabilitation of the marriage is prevented by Mrs. Chester's edifying death. All the tragedy is laid—unfairly even within the limits of the plot—at the door of Tractarianism. Robinson closes by quoting indignantly from an unnamed "clerical wiseacre" who has claimed that never has a member of the Church of England previously "known to be well informed in what are termed Church or Catholic principles . . . conformed to the Romish Communion." This seems preposterous, of course, when one remembers Newman and all the other devout Anglicans who actually did become Catholic. To the end, Robinson sees implicit in Tractarian practices the lure of Rome. The "flock," he says, is in danger from "choral effects and floral embellishments, and ceremonies of all kinds." It is a simplistic, even a primitive, view, that gives no consideration to theology or to church politics. But such views were frequent among Englishmen who were themselves not necessarily Low Church. Robinson is thus a better guide to popular opinion than many a more sophisticated novelist.

In Tenchester, Robinson christens the party of the poor workingmen, many of them hard-drinking reprobates, the "No Church" party. And he used the term as the title for his next novel. *No Church* (1861, no. 50) is the natural party for Richard Calverton, the vicious proprietor of a public house in the London slums and the father of two daughters: Lotty, the elder, a youthful prostitute, whom he himself has brought up, and the younger, Bessy, brought up by Matthew Davies, a pious Methodist uncle in Wales, her mother having died in prison. Narrow-minded and miserly, but not unkind, Uncle Matthew and his daughter Mary give Bessy eight peaceful years, although he never unbends enough to show her any real affection for fear of spoiling her. "We shall see her a blessing to us some day, perhaps; though we mustn't take credit for good works," is Uncle Matthew's view. The unexpected arrival of Stephen Speckland, a young London carpenter on holiday in the Welsh hills, changes their lives. Unaware that he is a stage carpenter and therefore "on the way to perdition," Uncle Matthew lets Stephen do some necessary household repairs. On leaving, Stephen gives Bessy a book of fairy tales. Bessy knows that her uncle will object to such a book, because "it is not all truth," but she is enchanted with it. Uncle Matthew's attitude towards literature, as we know, was not untypical among Evangelical writers, who often apologized for writing novels at all. When Uncle Matthew discovers the book of fairy tales, he confiscates it ("a book of lies, without an object or a purpose even in its lying") and burns it in Bessy's presence. Soon her real father claims her, and she must go off to London with him. But she takes with her a Bible as a present from her cousin Mary: "a substitute for the fairies."

The sordid life of the El Dorado, her father's pub, the presence of her Dickensian stepmother ("Humble as the earth, and trodden under foot as much, ever since the awful time when my character was lost and everything went wrong, and I went from prison to the streets, and from the streets to prison, what's the use of keeping back from you what everybody knows, and taunts me with? Crushed from fifteen years of age—crushed now!"), her father's insistence that she too sing for the customers in the bar: all this threatens Bessy. But rescue comes in the form of Mr. Parsloe, a Church of England clergyman with messages from Uncle Matthew and Mary in Wales. He begs Bessy not to forget the lessons she had learned as a child, and never to forget God. As he leaves the El Dorado, the stepmother warns him to stay away—"We're of No Church here, and allus shall be"—and almost before the words are out of her mouth a group of brawlers erupts from the doors of the pub, and Parsloe is robbed in the mélée. Bessy manages to recover his money and returns it; her erring but affectionate older sister Lotty contrives her escape from the El Dorado, rather than let her start on the downward path by singing indecent songs. Bessy leaves Lotty Mary's Bible.

Parsloe obtains work for Bessy, and before long she has once again met Stephen Speckland, the donor of the book of fairy tales, and his family: his elder brother, Hugh, is a talented wood engraver, on his way to becoming a successful artist. Self-respecting artisans though they are, the Specklands are equally "No Church" with the denizens of the El Dorado. Mr. Parsloe is constantly fighting for the Specklands' souls, though they are not his parishioners. Hugh Speckland has seen converts to religion: "the man that lived next door took the pledge last year, and is now a drunkard and a beast; the churchman swears to thirty-nine articles and then goes over to Rome." Under Parsloe's influence, Hugh himself had gone to church and been faced by "flowers, lace, velvets, and other trumpery," intoning, bowing to the east, and a "half-minister, half-priest" purveying a mere "sponge-cake religion." Nor did the Dissenters please Hugh any more. Bessy has more success with Stephen, who does accompany her to church, more out of love for her than out of interest in religion. But the true conversion is that of Lotty: it is due to the Bible alone, which brings about her repentance, though she cannot yet believe that she may be forgiven.

Reunited in London with Mary Davies, Bessy finds her now taking "broader, larger views of religion and its duties" than the narrow Methodism of her father. His last illness and death had taught Mary that "much of her best feelings, most of her sympathies, had been kept down." Having inherited his money, she now had "some of the old Catholic spirit of expiation," in her determination to do with it the kind of good that he had been too miserly to do. Although Mary is a Methodist ("a worthy sect, take them all together—a little narrow in their views"), Mr. Parsloe says she belongs to the Church, the same Church that he belongs to: "better than High Church or Low Church, chapel-going or open-air preaching . . . the one and the true, and that's Broad Church." Parsloe's declaration of faith is Robinson's own, and the first that enables a reader to be sure that the author is not after all a mild Evangelical. "It is a wide creed, has love and sympathy for all classes, and shuts the door in no one's face—be he Jew or Gentile," Parsloe continues. "It don't seek to reach heaven by singing, intoning, or high mass—and its worshippers are from all churches and all degrees of life." It is to be noted, however, that even in the proclamation of liberal toleration for all, Parsloe, like Robinson, gets in an additional dig at the High Church. The followers of Broad Church are still few in number, says Parsloe, but they will grow, "and all the pomps and vanities and prejudices that pollute the sanctuary will be as far removed from actual, working, religious life, as the racks and thumbscrews that tried to force a creed in [Bloody] Mary's time."

Hugh Speckland, in love with Bessy like his invalid brother, Stephen, is for a time a churchgoer on these terms, but when misunderstanding clouds their engagement, Hugh becomes "No Church" once again. Bessy herself works assiduously with Parsloe and Mary Davies in doing good in the slums. And when Parsloe is offered a living in the country, he marries Mary, who formally abandons Methodism for the Broad Church. "Religious opinion is one thing, and true religion another," she says; does it matter what sect we are if we love God and keep his commandments? And in the end, Hugh embraces Bessy and Broad Church simultaneously. Robinson seems far more at home with the lower-middle-class and lower-class, even criminal, characters of *No Church* than he was among the upper-middle-class town gentry of *High Church*. While the earlier novel was largely a display of negative prejudice, *No Church* fervently (and very simply) argues a positive case.

In *Church and Chapel* (1863, no. 50), Robinson expands the thesis voiced by the liberal Mr. Parsloe. In the town of Chipnam, the Dissenting minister, James Bayford, is a decent man but vigorous in his preaching against the vanities of the Church of England. Of the two Church of England clergymen, the more popular, Frederick Alland, is a learned and energetic preacher, High Church in his leanings, but not given to the "furbelows" which Robinson so greatly detests. He is, however, over-intellectual, and likes to preach about recent scholarship and the proper interpretation of texts. Bayford and Alland are at daggers drawn. Striving to mediate between them is the incumbent of the second church, William Chark, an older man whose health is feeble and ambition limited, and whose main goal is to improve relations between church and chapel-goers. His proposal of a series of public lectures, in which all three clerics are to participate along with laymen, arouses the doubts of Bayford and Alland, but they agree to cooperate. The lectures fail, and it is only after a melodramatic and tragic series of events that Chark's efforts lead to what we would call a happy ecumenical relationship between churchmen and Dissenters in the town.

As usual, Robinson is vague about theology: it is not even clear to what sect of Dissenters Bayford and his congregation belong, probably (from one reference to an "elder") the Presbyterian. Although Alland is compared to a Jesuit ("disciple of Loyola"), his sermon simply

> touched on the miracles, analyzed and expounded, sifted, weighed, and suggested fifty methods of accounting for them, any but the plain, simple way which the Bible intended—nothing of doubt expressed, only implied by a mass of erudition and hard gleaning from a hundred books; no scepticism intended to be conveyed to the minds of his listeners, only a desire to evince his own knowledge, and show how much light he could throw on any Bible mystery.

The phraseology here demonstrates Robinson's inveterate distrust of scholarship (one did not *need* to be a scholar to be anti-intellectual among Broad Churchmen), and incidentally suggests that Robinson himself knew what "the Bible intended." Alland's sermon, then, is "hardly the sermon to strike home to sinners, and make them better and more humble Christians." So Robinson's own Evangelical leanings can clearly be seen beneath the Broad-Church veneer. So "Low" are they indeed that he makes no effort to conceal his preference for the Dissenters over the High Anglicans. He does lampoon excessive zeal in Dissenters too: for example, his "red hot dissenter," the irascible Josiah Glade, objects violently to the project of the lectures as "too much gabble about amusing the masses," time-wasting with magic lanterns, and "egotistical narrations of . . . idleness in foreign parts. . . . sliding in . . . their own pernicious doctrines under cover of amusement." But Robinson regards Glade with amused tolerance, rather than with the bitter dislike he reserves for the Tractarians.

Drawn as an appealing peacemaker between Church and Chapel, Mr. Chark regards both Bayford and Alland as bitter and outrageous in their mutual enunciations. His doctrine, he says, "advocates peace on earth, and good-will amongst all men." He does not want "the walls which divide one sect from another . . . run up so high that we cannot shake hands over the top." He differs with Alland on points of biblical criticism, but he argues mildly and is "soon lost in the fogs of discussion." As Chark develops his antisectarian program, the reader assumes that, like Parsloe in *No Church*, he advocates "the Church that's better than High Church or Low Church . . . Broad Church." But the only time that Robinson identifies Chark's own theological position he calls him "Low": Bayford's brother, Robert, engaged to Chark's ward, Miss Saville, who is a communicant at Alland's church, much prefers Chark, and decides that after he is married, "High Church must be exchanged for Low—Mr. Alland for Mr. Chark." This is perhaps a verbal slip—Robinson is often careless—but it underlines the real essence of his alleged "Broad Church" position. Robinson is not "Low-gone-Broad," but "Low masquerading as Broad and pretending to be Low-gone-Broad." Yet no proper Evangelical would be content for a moment with Robinson's opposition to sectarianism, however much he might appreciate his anti-Tractarianism.

Robinson's picture of Chipnam contains much that is arresting: apropos of the first lecture, he notes that the "*canaille*" do not attend, but remain hanging about the doors outside, setting dogs on to one another "after the usual fashion." Those who come are "the poorer class of church folk . . . in fair force, a few of the tradespeople, and just a sprinkling of the dissenters—not the high dissent but the broad. For there are High, Low, and Broad Dissent, as there are High, Low, and Broad Church." He leaves it at that, but the idea is original, and one wishes it had been illustrated further. As in *High Church*, Alland, the Tractarian clergyman, "discovers" that he is in love with another man's fiancée only *after* he has contributed to the breaking of the engagement: Robinson inherently distrusts relationships between Tractarians and women. True: Alland does "not even consider himself a Tractarian," and is "man of sense enough to abjure the candle-lighting, the shuffling, and bowing and 'flip-flapping,' common to very High Church establishments." But he is "fond of music, and long anthems, and critical sermons that did no one any good." Even this small measure of High-Church practice receives the brickbats of the Dissenting minister, Bayford, who has "no longer any respect for persons when he saw the Protestant religion verging on Romanism. The Church of England was formal enough; but this High Church was an abomination." Yet Alland is *not* really High Church.

Over Chark's long-protracted deathbed Bayford and Alland are turned into allies instead of enemies. To Alland Chark says, "You and I are members of the same church, have signed the same articles of religion, have been supposed to make the same exact study, and form the same interpretations of the Holy Scripture." But Alland's mind, "in its eagerness to grasp at every small truth, occasionally lets slip the grand and simple ones." Alland goes in too much for fine points of translation and interpretation, and Chark tells him to turn his energy "to the one great effort to save sinners . . . the form and manner of saving does not matter." Better not to add any "trappings" than to send one parishioner away in anger at innovation. It is noteworthy that Chark's parallel admonition to Bayford is omitted; Robinson says only that he does not wish to be accused of sermonizing on his own. Chark tells Bayford to be more considerate in his attacks on the church and "not . . . to despise the set prayers and set forms of the church from which he held himself aloof; to remember that the churchman gave the same glad tidings to his listeners, taught the same holy precepts, fought side by side with him the same battle against evil."

As Chark lies dying, Alland and Bayford promise to think less of "*sects*" and to work together. They shake hands after Chark has preached them a deathbed sermon on cooperation. Within two years you can "see a dissenting family taking tea with a churchman's"; Bayford and Alland walk up the High Street arm in arm; neither man gives up his characteristic way of preaching, but both acknowledge from the pulpit that there are "various ways of doing good." Church of England churchwarden and Dissenting elder go fishing together; both ministers visit the poor and sick irrespective of allegiance; even the lecture series is revived and is successful. Chipnam becomes "a model town." Together, says Robinson, "we are at the head of an army whose power and strength there is no calculating. SECT IS NOTHING!" In heaven, "there is no sect . . . it is broad and open to us all, as our creed should be, whatever it is, and to whomsoever we preach." God loves his erring children and will be merciful towards them. "There are different ways of telling these truths, of seeking that mercy not denied to Jew or Gentile, but the best way is that which thinks most of the mercy, and very little of the *form* by which the mercy is sought." The final note, then, is liberal and Broad Church. The intellectual content of the doctrine in Robinson's version is very small; its emotional message, however, is of major importance in the England of the sixties.

Charles Maurice Davies (1828-1920) we have already encountered as the author of the humorously anti-Tractarian *Philip Pater-*

noster (1848, no. 31) which he wrote as an "ex-Puseyite." Of Welsh origin, and educated at Durham University—newly founded in 1832 from part of the enormous wealth of the Chapter and Bishop of Durham, richest of the English dioceses—Davies went over to the Broad-Church wing of the church after his brief period as a Tractarian. Though ordained as a priest, Davies by the mid-fifties took only an occasional preaching assignment; he spent most of his life as schoolmaster, novelist, and journalist. An able reporter, he visited and wrote articles on literally hundreds of the places of worship in London. The articles were collected and published as four major books: *Unorthodox London* (1871) and *Heterodox London* (1872) reported on Dissenters and Freethinkers in all their rich variety including the most peculiar; *Orthodox London* (1873) reported on the Church of England "as by law established," and on the spokesmen for its various branches; and *Mystic London* (1878) reported on "Phases of Occult Life."

About this last, Davies told much less than he knew: since the mid-fifties, he himself had been a convinced spiritualist, dabbling in mesmerism, hypnotism, astrology, and white and black magic. His book *The Great Secret* (1896), recounting his personal experiences of these matters over forty years, was published anonymously. His occultist leanings were, however, well known, and in 1869 he was made a member of the commission appointed by the "London Dialectical Society" to investigate and report on the alleged phenomena of spiritualism. His fellow members included Thomas Henry Huxley, the great scientist; George Henry Lewes, George Eliot's consort; and Charles Bradlaugh, the famous atheist. These associations aroused much criticism against him as a priest of the Church of England. Davies himself never saw anything inconsistent or improper about his remaining an active clergyman while exploring what others regarded as the lunatic fringes of belief, and participating in séances and the like. But to Davies, as he himself remarked in his preface to *Unorthodox London*, all the types of worship he was describing—even the most eccentric—were "gradual approximations to truth." In 1882, he resigned his orders. A competent classicist, he spent his later years on commission from Cecil Rhodes supervising the preparation of a series of translations of Gibbon's sources for the *Decline and Fall of the Roman Empire*, which were not published but remain in Rhodes's library in South Africa. As a Broad Churchman, Davies was about as "latitudinarian" as possible.

In his busy life, Davies probably regarded his novels as little more than potboilers. In *Broad Church* (1875, no. 55), he continued to satirize the Tractarians, although this was no longer his principal theme. The Reverend Cyprian Gules is the High-Church curate of the High-and-Dry Mr. Denton, Rector of Sturminster village, and the Reverend Claude Vallance is his Broad-Church curate. Gules is made ridiculous by an exaggerated espousal of all the familiar Tractarian foibles: he perverts the language of the Catechism, which says that only two sacraments—baptism and holy communion—are "generally necessary to salvation," to mean that the other five are "specially necessary"; and he has many other "little heresies." Vallance, whom one expects to be Davies's true hero, is "awfully broad." He has a "decided penchant for an ornate ritual." His favorite topics in the pulpit are "the probabilities of future sympathetic existence, and the reflex action of such a faith on present life and duty." "This," he argues, is the "ground for belief and motive-power of action which lay at the bottom of the creeds, not only of Christendom but of the world, which gave them the good which all in various degrees possessed, and which was compatible with any and every form of expression, however divergent in faith and practice." In Vallance one sees the same latitudinarian eagerness to find in all faiths what Davies, in *Unorthodox London*, had called an "approximation to truth."

Vallance's morning sermon on the text, "Prove all things. Hold fast to that which is good," celebrates the Church of England as "the Church of Private Judgment, and so of Individual Responsibility." He offends both the High-and-Dry and High-Church partisans in the stagnant conservative village, where Dissent is unknown. He preaches that everyone must think things out for himself. Each human being has something within him "greater than Church or Bible . . . your own Conscience, which is the voice of God. . . . Follow that. Treat a religious question exactly as you treat other questions in life. . . . God has given you free-will, and by your exercise of that great privilege you will be judged at last." That same evening, he preaches that "the strongest sanction of all for Christian duties" is "love for the . . . dead, and hopes of reunion with them."

In a single day's sermons, as a sharp-tongued spinster remarks, he has both "demolished the Universal Church, and done away with the Day of Judgment." One suspects that Vallance's sermons are Davies's own.

When some of his new acquaintances think it extraordinary that he should ever have taken orders, Vallance explains his attitude towards other professions: literature is all very well "as an addition to other pursuits," but should not be a man's sole occupation. For himself, he believes "that the principles of the English Church, apart from extremes in their interpretation, are the very truest embodiments of Christ's own teachings. If I felt strongly on the Sacraments, I would go to Rome. The mere disciplinary arrangement of the Pope's supremacy would be as nothing compared with the recognition of the Real Presence. If Bishops were an unmitigated stumbling-block, I would join the Free Churches. But I think no more of Bishops than of the Pope." For Vallance, Ritualism is "out of date and out of place in the Church of England. We cannot ignore the Protestant Reformation." Vallance feels he has nothing in common with the Tractarians. He knows he could make more money with his pen, but "some fascination, which is nothing at all like *esprit de corps*" keeps him in the church. But "a very little persuasion would make me lapse into a layman." Of course such a man soon has his enemies, objecting to his "newfangled nonsense," as they object to Gules's "mummery." But the rector finds Vallance and Gules "a capital set-off" against one another. However, the bishop responds affirmatively to complaints and revokes Vallance's licence to preach.

Vallance's private life, however, raises even a modern reader's eyebrows: he swears eternal fidelity to Ada Parkinson, a fine young woman whom he cannot afford to marry, and actually marries himself to her in a private Church of England ceremony before the altar, without witnesses and conducted after the canonical hour of noon. So it is not a valid marriage. But, one would think, it ought at least to be morally binding on the clerical bridegroom. Yet Vallance, who bows cheerfully to the bishop's edict (and is replaced by a young Evangelical), is equally pliable when separated from Ada, and is eventually swept up into marriage with another woman. He leads the fast life of a London playwright and editor of a new

Sturminster newspaper in the radical interest. Regularly now, in the columns of his newspaper, Vallance's latitudinarian opinions receive far more publicity than they ever could have, had he remained in the pulpit. The bishop is horrified, and more so when the local radical duke makes Vallance his private chaplain, preaching radical sermons (in his surplice!) in the duke's chapel as a "Free Christian" church. Vallance has, he says in a sermon, "a special work to do in the way of combining the sacred and secular influences of society, and broadening somewhat the often narrow views of religion which pass current." Vallance will lecture on "secular" subjects, but he wants his congregation to think of everything as sacred and of nothing as secular. Again, one can imagine Davies himself addressing a congregation in this way.

Why, then, has he made his own spokesman such a contemptible man? Can he actually admire the immoral Vallance? One is slowly forced to believe that he does. Despite the feeble plot machinery designed to convince the reader that Vallance believes Ada to have given him up, he actually never makes any effort to find her and marry her properly. And, says Davies, Vallance's "doubt resolved itself into a pleasant principle that he should eat, drink, be merry, make money, and love." Before long, however, Vallance and his new wife's "hours of passion" are outgrown. "With that satiety" comes the "old ambition to act the priest . . . to infuse into the apparently effete system of the Church of England some at least of that enthusiasm of humanity which belonged to it when men were chosen for the priesthood because they were born for it. . . . " The Vallances now often attend "the little Positivist School in Chapel Street," where the Comtists teach that the theological age of the human race had corresponded to infancy in the individual, a period now all in the past. Unbridled sensuality becomes their religion. And yet Vallance still preaches in London as well as in Sturminster, creating a "school of the Sceptics," or, as Vallance's Bohemian clubmates call it, "a pious music-hall."

A reunion and a series of clandestine meetings ("Platonic Love") with Ada hardly improve Vallance's moral position. He now develops "a simple service which should reproduce . . . the genius of Primitive Christianity," which "centres around the Eucharist as a Feast of Love," and he and Ada celebrate "their first Agape" together. Calling his entirely irregular establishment "the Oratory of the Holy Spirit," Vallance invents his own Communion service (perhaps no great step for a man who had once performed his own marriage service and then ignored the fact). The "system" at the new Oratory is "a sort of recoil from Positivism." Vallance has "great personal power in private as well as in the pulpit." He would, Davies declares, have made "a capital father-confessor as well as a successful preacher, if he could have narrowed his range of vision so far as to fall in with the position of the Ritualistic cultus." His simple communion service gives great comfort to the many busy doubters, men and women, who come to it.

If Davies had set out to convince his readers that the latitudinarian wing of the Broad Church was as dangerous as most of them feared, he could hardly have been more persuasive than he was in his description of the secular and religious behavior of Claude Vallance. Not only is Vallance a bigamist in everything but the legal sense, but also he and Ada live quite comfortably, if "Platonically," with their unconventional situation. And the peculiar religious experiments—drawn with authentic touches from all Davies's own wide experience among the odd sects of London—complete a picture which must have proved most offensive to his readers. His "solution" of Vallance's difficulty is even more outrageous than the difficulty itself. Separated from his wife, living intimately with Ada, a churchman by courtesy only, Vallance is nonetheless invited by the new bishop to resume preaching, and he does so. Eventually he is rewarded for his sins by the living of Sturminster itself.

The title page of the novel bears an epigraph from the 1874 presidential address by the antireligious scientist John Tyndall to the British Association at Belfast—"To yield reasonable satisfaction to the religious sentiment in the emotional nature of man is the problem of problems of the present hour"—but the novel hardly addresses itself to that problem in any serious or convincing way. Tyndall was horrifying enough to the ordinary Christian, who feared that such laxity as his would lead to the breakdown of morals. Davies's novel seemed to prove that all these fears were justified. "Vulgarity and slovenliness," said the *Athenaeum*; "the characters whom we are meant to admire are despicable," the hero a "thorough scoundrel and a consummate snob." "Clever and readable," said the *Spectator*, "but often distinctly offensive to good taste." It was an "unworthy" book, and yet Davies did not seem to realize it. A century later, one cannot fail to share these views. *Broad Church* is a most irreligious religious novel.

Its successor, *'Verts; or, The Three Creeds* (1876, no. 56), deals equally frivolously with conversion to and from Catholicism, with the falsification of wills and misappropriation of estates, and with murder, ending cozily with Broad-Church messages once again. Its lack of all restraint suggests either that Davies had no control over his material and did not realize what he was doing, or that his cynicism was matched by his determination to outrage his readers, and to show up the entire religious world of the mid-seventies as a joke and a sham. A reading of Samuel Butler's *The Fair Haven* (1873, no. 54)—discussed below in the chapter on doubt, in connection with his own religious development and its climax in *The Way of All Flesh* (1903, no. 87)—is likely, however, to redress the balance and to remind one that the Broad-Church movement did indeed have an underlying theological (or at least philosophical) rationale, and that its adherents usually accepted men's lives and religious troubles as important.

A Summing Up

Although the Broad-Church party was so much less coherent and unified than either the High-Church or the Low-Church parties that it hardly deserves to be thought of as a party at all, a small group of novels does clearly reflect its position: in the court, as Hutton puts it, that stands between the "narrow crypts of low Evangelical doctrine and the venerable decay of the High Church towers above." Maurice's own inspiration is seen directly in Kingsley's *Hypatia*, combined with Kingsley's own idiosyncratic preferences; Maurice himself, reverently portrayed, if still puzzling, makes his appearance in MacDonald's *David Elginbrod.* More Arnoldian, perhaps, than Maurician, but harking back also to Coleridge, is the positive message of Conybeare's *Perversion*, whose comprehensive demolition of Evangelical and Tractarian extremists and of the various forms of unbelief seemed to Hutton so harshly intolerant that he failed to appreciate how much of Maurice's doctrine Conybeare had in fact imbibed.

It is worth emphasizing that Charles Bampton's eventual salvation in *Perversion* is directly attained by his commitment to helping the poor and the wronged, whether the prostitute he has himself helped to ruin or the wounded in the Crimean War. Like Charles Bampton, Kingsley's otherwise fanatical Alexandrian Christians labor vigorously in the slums, and MacDonald's Robert Falconer devotes his life to the cause of London unfortunates. Maurice, Kingsley, and MacDonald had all worked among the poor themselves, and Conybeare recognizes the effectiveness in this field of those "good" and "apostolic" men among the Evangelicals, whom he otherwise despises. So the Broad-Church novel also voices the social theme which we have already heard from Catholics, Tractarians, and Evangelicals.

In F. W. Robinson, Broad-Church doctrine is reduced to a mere repudiation of Tractarianism, combined with simplicity and human decency, not very far removed from mild Evangelicalism, and quite stripped of philosophical depth. In C. M. Davies, on the other hand, the reader encounters a determined effort to capitalize on the author's explorations of the furthermost reaches of mid-Victorian eccentric sects. The Unitarians, so often dismissed as not Christians at all, seem positively ritualistic when compared with the Comtists and other fringe groups from whom Claude Vallance pilfers ideas for his synthetic sermons in *Broad Church.* To the question of little Sarah in Mrs. Tonna's novel, "What is a Latitudinarian, Mamma?" we now have a satisfactory answer in fiction in the person of Vallance, for whom anything that goes on in the name of religion is an "approximation of truth." But the determined light-heartedness of the author suggests, as with Conybeare, that there may have been something incorrigibly frivolous that prevented Broad-Church novelists from taking their subject matter seriously.

The novels discussed in this section fail to convey the enormous importance of Maurice's repudiation of eternal punishment. The transformation of a vengeful Calvinist God into a loving Broad-Church God, still stern, still paternal, but not condemning any of his children to perpetual hellfire, saved literally tens of thousands of mid- and late-Victorians from depressions that often bordered upon psychopathic despair. The Broad-Church novels fail to do more than hint at this startling change made possible by Broad Churchmen. The failure may perhaps be ascribed to the fact that the pure Calvinist doctrine of election and eternal damnation was held within the Church of England only by extreme Evangelicals. It was among the Calvinist Dissenters—Presbyterians, Congregationalists, and others—that the doctrines were universally preached. It is to the novels of Dissent, therefore, that we next turn.

PART III.

THE DISSENTING CHURCHES

CHAPTER 5.

DISSENT

Outsiders and Renegades: Mrs. Oliphant, George MacDonald, William Hale White, Edmund Gosse, and Others

The religious census of 1851 listing the number of worshippers at every service on Sunday, 30 March, recorded more than 4,500,000 persons attending Dissenting houses of worship, only about 750,000 fewer than those attending Church of England services. Unreliable as they are, the statistics are all we have. They omit Unitarians, Quakers, and other smaller sects, and reflect only Methodists (perhaps half the total number of Dissenters), Independents (Congregationalists, rather more than half the remainder), and Baptists (rather less than half the remainder). Despite their numerical importance in Victorian England, however, the Dissenters themselves produced few novelists. Like Uncle Matthew, the Methodist in F. W. Robinson's *No Church*, they usually detested or at best mistrusted fiction as displaying what was not strictly true. Moreover, many of them came from the less well-educated lower middle classes who read little fiction and wrote less.

Our fictional portraits of individual Dissenters and glimpses of life among the Dissenters, therefore, often emanate from hostile observers, sometimes former Dissenters. William Sewell's savagely anti-Catholic *Hawkstone* (1845, no. 2), for example, directs its sarcasm also against all religious beliefs other than Sewell's own rigorous High Anglicanism. When the Hawkstone Temperance Society holds a festive anniversary tea-drinking in the ruins of an old priory, throngs of happy men, women, and children ("so decent and quiet, so very respectable") arrange their trestle-tables in the former sacred precincts, and light the fires for their tea-kettles on the former altar itself. The Presbyterian minister, the Baptist, the Independent (Congregationalist), the Quaker, the Unitarian, are all present, and so also, to Sewell's disgust, is the Church of England curate of the parish, Mr. Bentley, an Evangelical: otherwise he would never have been there. He says a special grace omitting the Prayer Book ending, because he does not wish to hurt the feelings of the Unitarian minister "by introducing any allusion to particular doctrines." When Bentley joins hands with the Dissenting ministers, he notes that the mediaeval sculptured face of a bishop frowns at him reproachfully. Despite his own opposition to the state religion, the Unitarian proposes Bentley's health—the laws, he says, should be obeyed as long as they are in force—and he praises Mr. Bentley's Christian liberality—if all churchmen were like him, there would be no sectarian strife. Bentley's honest reply is stumbling and ineffectual: he feels embarrassed. Indeed—Sewell maintains—"in delivering a message from his Maker," a clergyman need only "deliver it plainly, intelligibly, effectively." Therefore "popular preaching, and popular speaking, and appeals to the passions, and all the trickery of platform discussions and proprietary chapels, are out of place in members of a Church, and only do harm."

The Presbyterian minister calls the tea-drinking "a truly Protestant assembly." In an impassioned plea for total abstinence, he vows that if the Pope were present, he would have challenged him to defend "his bloody and atrocious system." He contrasts the vile deeds (fasting, idle mummery of dress, absurd processions and pilgrimages) with which the priory ruins had once been filled to the present happy group there assembled. The festivities close with a rousing speech from a Whiggish reforming candidate for Parliament. Sewell's scornful distaste for the profanation of the priory is satirically expressed in the speech: "dens of superstition . . . abodes of bigotry. . . . bloody altars" have all been crushed, says the politician, by which he means, Sewell explains, that "Henry VIII had driven out a number of poor old religious men to starve in the roads, had pulled down their houses, turned their chapel into a cow-house, and put their money into his own pocket."

So too, at a session of the Hawkstone ladies' Dorcas Society, the Dissenting ladies join with the Evangelical Church-of-England ladies, and the Church shows to its disadvantage at every turn. Its members have abandoned the "good old way of no mixing with Dissenters." The Presbyterian lady even tells the Anglican lady that "in Scotland we are the Church and you are the Dissenters." So bitingly does Sewell cut at the Dissenters and their half-reluctant, wholly incompetent ally the Evangelical curate, that one might be misled into thinking him pro-Catholic were it not for the savagery of his attack on the Roman Church that follows in the later portions of the novel. To Sewell it seemed weak folly for Low Churchmen to collaborate with Dissenters, who were no better than heretics.

In the years after Sewell wrote, other novelists from time to time gave occasional fleeting treatment to the Nonconformists who made up so large a portion of the English population. Elizabeth Cleghorn Gaskell (1810-1865), for example, included a most appealing Dissenting minister in her *Ruth* (1853, no. 57). He and his sister give shelter to the pathetic, betrayed heroine. They tell the curious townsmen that she is a young widow, making it possible for her to gain acceptance and to bring up her illegitimate son free of the taint of bastardy: until the deception is discovered. The story of Ruth's seduction shocked contemporaries, who were even more horrified at the minister's connivance in a lie, a sin for which he also blames himself severely. His sect is not specified, but he is not a Methodist or a Unitarian, like Mrs. Gaskell's guardian, who served as her inspiration, or like her own husband, who was minister to one of those cultivated well-to-do Manchester Unitarian congregations so sneered at by Conybeare in *Perversion.* Except for some charming descriptions of the chapel, and a fine portrait of the self-righteous merchant who is a leading member of the congregation, however, *Ruth* tells us little about the Dissenters as such. As for the sinning heroine, even the Church of England rector of the town comes to admire her greatly because of her services as a nurse during an epidemic. In her superb novel *Adam Bede* (1859, NIS), George Eliot included an authentic saintly Methodist heroine, Dinah, an idealized portrait of George Eliot's own aunt, once a Methodist preacher. George Eliot knew, for example, the ways in which Methodist faith and religious fervor loaned a special exaltation to the language of village courtship, raising the ordinarily warm emotions of young love to a feverish heat in which human and divine aspiration were bewilderingly mingled. But melodrama rather than Methodism lies at the center of *Adam Bede.*

The Dissenting way of life received perhaps its first major treatment by a novelist in Mrs. Oliphant's *Salem Chapel* (1863, no. 58). Critics at the time recognized the originality of the book with horrified admiration: among contemporary novels, said one writer, it stood out "like a piece of newly-coined gold in a handful of commonplace shillings." The public had long since had plenty of novels dealing with "pastoral life and clerical experience," but "the relative position of pastor and flock in a Nonconforming 'Connection' were but guessed at by the world outside, and terrible is the revelation." Here for the first time the "sacred things of the conventicle" were spread before the fascinated reader, almost as if he were reading a report on a newly discovered African tribe.

Son of a Dissenting minister and educated for his duties in a Congregational College, the young bachelor Arthur Vincent is full of zeal when he receives his first call: to Carlingford to succeed the elderly Mr. Tufton as pastor of Salem Chapel. Convinced that the Church of England, despite its apparent prosperity, is "profoundly rotten," he sees himself as an eloquent spokesman for the truth who will soon conquer all of Carlingford. But he is wholly unprepared for the character of his congregation, whose elite is made up of "greengrocers, dealers in cheese and bacon, milkmen, with some dressmakers . . . and teachers of day schools. . . ." Their houses are "clean, respectable, meagre." They like things as they are; they never have anybody in the "Connection" who has not been in trade: "Bein' all in the way of business, except just the poor folks, as is all very well in their place, and never interferes with nothing, and don't count, there's nothing but brotherly love here, which is a great deal more than most ministers can say for their flocks." Yet these "cheerful folks, and no display" make constant social demands on Vincent. He is expected regularly to come to tea with his deacons and visit their families. Phoebe Tozer, daughter of the dealer in butter and bacon, archly and coyly determines to marry poor Vincent, who is not at all attracted by her (she is "pink all over—dress, shoulders, elbows, cheeks, and all,") and finds himself utterly uninterested in the trivial subjects of his flock's conversation and in the vicious backbiting gossip and mutual jealousies so quickly revealed to him.

The managers of the congregation have a keen eye for finances: their chief goal is to rent all the pews in the Chapel, and they pay their minister according to his success in attracting new subscribers. For the purpose they are convinced that inspirational—not intellectual—preaching is the best, and Tozer urges Vincent to "give it to the Church folks a little more plain," emphasizing the anomalies of the Anglican system: "the bishops in their palaces and the fishermen as was the start of it all"—that's the sort of thing that "always tells . . . lay it on pretty strong." Nothing loath, Vincent gives a series of special lectures on Church and State, for which his deacons hire the town Music Hall. He thunders against the Church of England, expatiating upon "the Kingdom that was not of this world. If these words were true, what had the Church to do with worldly possessions, rank, dignity, power? Was His Grace of Lambeth [the Archbishop of Canterbury] more like Paul the Tentmaker than his Holiness of Rome?" The series is a great success, and all of Carlingford comes.

But the flock arrogates to itself the right to control their pastor's social life. Too fastidious for the sturdy company of the lower middle classes, and with strong social aspirations of his own, Vincent meets and falls hopelessly in love with Lady Western, a beautiful young widow living in one of the town's largest houses, a Churchwoman, of course, whose kindness encourages him in the false hope that she may return his love. It is this looking outside the flock for society that eventually proves ruinous to Vincent's pastorate: to the flock, Lady Western is "one of those painted ladies . . . with low dresses and flowers in their hair," not "fit company for a good pastor." After all, the flock is paying him:

> If a minister ain't a servant, we pays him his salary at least, and expects him to please us. . . . If it weren't for that, I don't give a sixpence for the Dissenting connection. Them as likes to please themselves would be far better in a State Church, where it wouldn't disappoint nobody. . . . if the Chapel folk's a bit particular, it's no more than a pastor's duty to bear with them, and return a soft answer. . . . A man as goes dining with Lady

> Western and thinks as she's going to make a friend of him, ain't the man for Salem.

Which is too bad, as there are now only three pews still unrented.

As Vincent becomes ever more deeply involved in an effort to thwart the machinations of a desperate villain who has tried to kidnap and seduce his sister (a melodramatic and not very credible but typical "sensation"-novel theme of the 1860's), his congregation more and more resents his having to take time off for his own affairs: "Business of his own! a minister ain't got no right to have business of his own, leastways on Sundays. Preaching's his business. He's in our employ, and we pay him well. . . . if he don't mind us as pays him, another will." His substitute is welcomed for preaching "a *sweet* sermon. That's refreshing, that is. . . . good gospel preaching and rousing up." And even Vincent's advocate among the deacons, Tozer the butterman, warns him that there will be trouble unless he apologizes for neglecting his social duties: "them ain't the sentiments for a pastor in our connection. That's a style of thing as may do among fine folks, or in the church, where there's no freedom; but them as chooses their own pastor, and pays their own pastor, and don't spare no pains to make him comfortable, has a right to expect different."

At a meeting of the congregation called by the opposition, disgruntled because Vincent is "too high" (not at all in the sense of "High Church" or with respect to doctrine of any sort, but simply in his social aspirations), the loyal Tozer carries the day for Vincent against the opposition in a tremendous speech, which emphasizes Vincent's success in filling the church, and ends with a peroration rebuking the jealous members of the flock for their censoriousness:

> to go for to judge the pastor of a flock not by the dooty he does to his flock, but by the times he calls at one house or another, and the way he makes himself agreeable at one place or another, ain't a thing to be done by them as prides themselves on being Christians and Dissenters. It's not like Christians, and it *is* like Dissenters, the more's the pity.

But it is too late: Vincent resigns his ministry; he "throws it all up," and—dreaming of "an ideal corporation," a future great and simple church—he becomes a writer on philosophical subjects and the founder of a new periodical.

Salem Chapel hardly touches upon doctrine. Except for their hostility to the Church of England, and their delight in good "rousing-up" preaching of the gospel, Carlingford's Congregationalists have few apparent tenets. Even Vincent himself, with all his education, is surprised when a sophisticated woman of the upper classes, a Churchwoman born and bred, deserted by an unworthy husband and miserably unhappy, regularly attends his services. When he hopes that his sermons may give her comfort, she answers scornfully, "*Comfort!* . . . all the old churches in all the old ages have offered comfort. I thought you new people had something better to give us: enlightenment . . . religous freedom, private judgment. . . . Comfort! One has that in Rome!" But she alone seems to recognize the advantages that a sensitive Christian might derive from his emancipation from the authority of the Church and from a new ability to think for himself. Vincent is either too young or too insensitive to have made this discovery on his own, nor does he take advantage of it when it is presented to him. *Salem Chapel* may have owed the inspiration for its plot machinery to Wilkie Collins and Mary Elizabeth Braddon—both of whom were far more skillful at manipulating the elements of "sensation" than Mrs. Oliphant—but it deserves to be revived for its pioneering sociological explorations into the world of the small-town, lower-middle-class Dissenting congregation so little-known to the class-conscious Anglican novel-reading public.

How accurate was the picture she drew? It received extraordinary confirmation in the very next year, in Florence Williamson's forgotten novel, *Frederick Rivers, Independent Parson* (London: Williams and Norgate, 1864, NIS), written from the inside of the Congregational "connection" by an author with a more extensive personal knowledge than Mrs. Oliphant could have possessed. Mrs. Williamson's hero is the son of a Dissenter, whose "temperament rendered him wholly indifferent to the ceremonialism of the older communions, . . . his slightly radical political creed had no place for bishops or for ecclesiastical state patronage." So, while "Fritz" would have enjoyed the status of a clergyman of the Church of England, he cheerfully accepts the only views he knows, and studies for the Independent (Congregational) ministry. He finds his college "a quiet retreat for pious mediocrity," fostering priggish behavior; his fellow students are "charming characters . . . redolent of sanctity, but . . . unquestionable humbugs." Inadequate Greek, Latin, and theology are offered; what Mrs. Oliphant only suggests about Vincent's poor preparation at his Congregational college, Mrs. Williamson spells out: few of her readers would know or care, she supposes, about such a matter, yet, since "a good many hundreds of thousands of the people of England are Dissenters," it is, she insists, important that "their theology and social habits, and even morality are influenced" greatly by the wretched college training of their ministers.

When seeking for a new minister and listening to the sermons of candidates, the deacons speak a language like that of their counterparts at Carlingford. When they like a sermon, it is "the very marrow and fatness of the blessed Gospel—wine on the lees. None of your new-fashioned notions that one never heard of before." To one of them, interviewing Fritz, Christian doctrine was really "all in a nutshell."

> There's the Blessed Trinity . . . a great matter but beyond us. And then there's the Atoning Blood . . . what should we be without the Atoning Blood? And then there's the Holy Ghost, and the blessed influences of the Spirit poured out on the blind eyes of the carnal mind. And then . . . there's Election, up to glorified, 'them he also glorified.' And then . . . there's 'the Holy Bible, book divine, precious treasure, thou art mine,' on which it all rests.

Had Mr. Tozer and his fellow deacons of Carlingford been a shade more intellectual, this doctrinal summary is one they would have approved. About any complexities beyond this crude and oversimplified statement they do not wish to hear.

In a suburban London parish, Fritz succeeds so extremely Puritanical a minister that "it was a mystery half the congregation had not turned Papists for a change from the dull monotony." Disliking the "tyranny" which the Puritans had introduced, which seemed to him to empty life of "symbol and beauty" and to "cut religion off completely from the ordinary duties and enjoyments of mankind," Rivers preaches in his gown and drives out one of his intransigent congregation. Like Vincent, he gradually builds up the congregation in numbers, and like Vincent, he runs into trouble: he is known to possess the books of F. D. Maurice, which is tantamount to heresy; malicious gossip flourishes among his parishioners, as it does at Salem Chapel; Mr. Lush's view of the matter is like Mr. Tozer's—"He was inclined to think a . . . chapel might be a capital business investment if properly managed. 'Pay well,' he used to say, 'get your talent, have a large place, and the thing's done.' "

It is Lush and one of his colleagues who soon warn Fritz Rivers that "there's a something," that the people are not being "fed with the marrow and fatness of the Gospel," and that there has been talk about his possession of Maurice's writings. Rivers has not denounced the recent "heretical" *Essays and Reviews* or preached a fire-breathing sermon on "Infidelity in Lawn Sleeves" (i.e., attacking as heretics High Anglicans who preached in surplices). At a meeting like the one at which Vincent was barely saved from dismissal, Rivers is protected from cross-examination on his doctrines only by his friends' assistance and his own defiance. Unlike Vincent, he clings to his pulpit, though his opponents secede from the congregation. He makes up some of his lost income by writing. But the crisis convulses the poor minister's personal life. So *Frederick Rivers* offers welcome testimony to the accuracy of Mrs. Oliphant's observations of an Independent Congregation in the period of the late fifties and early sixties.

Mrs. Oliphant also faithfully and wittily recorded the changes that took place in the course of the next two decades. In her *Phoebe, Junior. A Last Chronicle of Carlingford* (1876, no. 92), the charming and self-possessed daughter of the all pink Phoebe Tozer, who had failed to catch Mr. Vincent, takes the center of the stage. Phoebe, senior has married Vincent's successor at Salem Chapel, Beecham, who has gone on to a brilliant career, at first in the North of England, where the Dissenters are "very superior . . . a different class of society. . . . In the great towns of the North, Dissent attains its highest elevation, and Chapel people are no longer to be distinguished from Church people except by the fact that they go to Chapel instead of Church." Eventually Mr. Beecham comes to London as pastor of "the most comfortable chapel in the whole connection," in which everybody is very rich and "would have been disconcerted if the poor had come in to take shelter." In contrast to the gulf that had yawned between young Arthur Vincent and Church of England clergymen, Beecham now has "many friends in the Low and some even in the Broad Church." He appears on platforms to promote various public movements along with clergymen of the Church. He speaks of "our brethren within the pale of the Establishment, always with respect, sometimes even with enthusiasm. . . . What should we do in the country parishes where the people are not awakened? They do the dirty work for us, dear brethren, the dirty work." Here a Congregational minister in a novel is found acknowledging one of the key facts about religion in Victorian society: by and large the Church was strong in rural parishes, while the Dissenters found themselves at home chiefly in the towns.

Carlingford itself—where Phoebe junior must go to take care of her ailing grandmother, Mrs. Tozer—also reflects social change. Old Tozer, the butter and cheese merchant, so long ago the friend and sponsor of Mr. Vincent, has now retired and taken his wife to live in that very house in Grange Lane which Lady Western had formerly owned. Personally unchanged, the Tozers themselves still feel themselves inferior. But the rigid dividing lines of the fifties have by the seventies begun to break down even in Carlingford. Young Phoebe, with her good education, her virtuoso piano-playing, her cultivated good manners and natural ease in society, is worlds away from the narrowness and vulgarity of her own mother in her youth. Though her mother is aware that she will be shocked at the "lowly place held by the connection in an old-fashioned, self-conceited Tory town like Carlingford," Phoebe is more disturbed to find that her own grandfather is "an old shopkeeper, very decent and respectable, but a little shabby and greasy," and that in her grandparents' fine house in Grange Lane there are no books except for "a few volumes of sermons and a few back numbers of the Congregational Magazine," and nothing but her grandmother's gossip to pass the weary hours away. Her aunt is worse, a vulgar, pushing virago; but Phoebe says to herself, "if this is what we have really sprung from, this is my own class, and I ought to like it; if I don't like it, it must be my fault. I have no right to feel myself better than they are. It is not position that makes any difference, but individual character." She knows that Dissenters are looked down upon, but "when people have any sense, as soon as they know us, they do us justice."

Phoebe's great admirer is Clarence Copperhead, son of an arrogant, purse-proud millionaire, the pillar of her father's London congregation, a bully who never fails to boast of his wealth, and who takes the practical view that a place like Carlingford, with no factories, should be destroyed. He is lavishly generous to his son, however, and at a ball at the Copperheads', Phoebe meets Ursula May, a young Carlingford girl, daughter of the Perpetual Curate of St. Roque's, an impoverished Anglican clergyman. Soon Phoebe is a regular visitor to the Mays' house, and acquires a second earnest suitor in the person of Ursula's brother. Class and sectarian lines are blurring, even though Phoebe in the end prefers young Copperhead.

And as if to emphasize the geographical differences among Dissenters as well as the newly possible intimacies across religious barriers, Mrs. Oliphant introduces one of those gentleman-Dissenters from the North, Horace Northcote, well-off and well-educated, temporarily acting as pastor of Salem Chapel, and finding his parishioners "poulterers and grocers" as limited in their outlook as Arthur Vincent had found them twenty years earlier. Northcote is "a youthful fanatic on the subject of separation of church and state, more successful on the platform than in the pulpit, believing that the Church is the drawback to all progress in England, an incubus of which the nation would gladly be rid." He is scrupulously careful to distinguish his own dress from theirs: "he would not plagiarize the Anglican livery, and walk about in a modified soutane and round hat." The Church of England clergy whom Mr. Beecham calls "our brethren" Northcote regards as enemies; he takes pains that his black frock coat be short, his white tie as stiff as possible, his hat uncompromisingly tall: he is "clerical but not of the clergy, a teacher of men, yet not a priest of the Anglican inspiration." One of his fellow-speakers at a great meeting of the Disestablishment Society declares that "there are good men among the clergy of the Church of England, but they are nothing but slaves, dragged at the chariot-wheels of the State, ruled by a class of hard-headed lawyers, binding themselves in the rotten robes of tradition." Northcote himself violently attacks a Carlingford sinecure, the well-paid chaplaincy of an almshouse with only six aged inmates and few prescribed duties, which Phoebe's admirer, the son of the Perpetual Curate, has just assumed. A state church, declaims Northcote, "so cows the spirit and weakens the hearts of its young men" that able-bodied young clerics, "educated and trained and cultured," stoop to accept its emoluments instead of seeking honest work.

Of course, this produces much ill-feeling between the two young men. Gradually Northcote learns to appreciate the enormous amount of voluntary work among the poor done by the man he has so scorned, and he grows ashamed of his own earlier violence. Slowly becoming an intimate of his former opponent's family, Northcote falls in love with and eventually marries Ursula, the daughter of the house, Phoebe's friend. In this union between the erstwhile violent enemy of the Church of England with the daughter and sister of its priests, the sectarian barriers disappear altogether. Northcote is better off than his brother-in-law, and as well-educated; he has come to appreciate the beauties of tradition: the fifteenth-century chapel of the almshouse, the feeling that its chaplain is "heir to the centuries," touch his heart. Mrs. Oliphant supplies unspoken ironical comment on the match, which would have been a disgrace only twenty years before: Northcote's bride's father, the Perpetual Curate, has in his poverty actually committed forgery; he dies before he can be prosecuted, but it is Northcote who pays his father-in-law's debt. Irony upon irony—it is Tozer's name that the Perpetual Curate has forged. Yet old Tozer feels always that his relationship to the young Anglican chaplain is "semi-servile," while his relationship to Northcote—who after all is acting as pastor of Salem Chapel—is "condescending and superior." So the humble dissenting victim—implacable against the man who has injured him—is in the end repaid by the proud dissenting minister, who has married the Anglican criminal's daughter.

Sometimes dotting her i's and crossing her t's, but more often leaving her social commentary to be found by the appreciative reader, Mrs. Oliphant in *Phoebe, Junior* dealt subtly with complex aspects of English social and religious life left virtually untouched by her fellow novelists. Even the loyal Phoebe Junior thinks that England would *not* be "much nicer if we were all Dissenters" and declares that (as Vincent, and Frederick Rivers, and Northcote himself would agree) "Congregations are not pleasant masters." "Dissenters," remarked Newman in *Loss and Gain*, "put themselves above their system, not below it; and though they may in bodily position 'sit under' their preacher, yet in the position of their souls and spirits, minds and judgments, they are exalted high above him."

In 1848—just about the same time as the fictional Arthur Vincent or Frederick Rivers—a young Scot named George MacDonald (1825-1905) began his training at Highbury, one of the Congregational colleges. After periods of service like theirs as "supply" minister to various congregations, MacDonald was called in 1850 to be pastor at Arundel, Sussex, at a salary of 150 pounds a year, barely enough to support himself and his wife and young daughter. A rebel against Scotch Calvinism, tubercular, and strongly under the influence of Wordsworth and the German romantic Novalis, MacDonald was as little charmed by the pettiness, gossip, and possessiveness of the Arundel "connection" as was Vincent at Carlingford or Rivers in his London suburb. Soon his deacons suspected that he was tainted with "German" theological ideas: a charge easily levelled in those days against anybody whose orthodoxy did not agree in every detail with the simple views of the Nonconformist establishment.

Arising initially from the malaise created by German efforts to study the Bible critically or to treat Jesus as an historical personage (as, for example, David Friedrick Strauss had undertaken to do in his famous *Life of Jesus* [1835] which George Eliot at twenty-seven translated into English in 1846), the term "German" in the England of the 1850's meant little more than a minister's disquieting display of interest in anything previously unknown to his congregation. So when MacDonald affirmed that the heathen would eventually be saved, and preached a sermon suggesting that man's beloved pets would also go to heaven (as a Romantic, he already liked animals at least as well as people), the deacons were quick to take offense and cut his annual salary to 115 pounds. "Annoyances" and "spiritual weakness in high places" followed, and led to his resignation in 1853. Though he never revealed in detail what had happened, those who have followed the experiences of Vincent or Rivers in the pages of novels will easily guess what happened to MacDonald in real life: the Arundel counterparts of the Tozers and Lushes made life unbearable for him.

He never had another pulpit, but over the years he became a famous novelist and writer of successful fairy romances for children and adults. Yet he always thought of himself as a preacher. Brought into the Church of England by Maurice—whom, as we have seen, he portrayed in *David Elginbrod* (1863, no. 53)—he developed a liberal theology of his own, influenced by Maurice and by Maurice's disciple, the former Presbyterian minister A. J. Scott, and proclaiming the eventual salvation of all mankind. In his twenty-five novels for adults, MacDonald seldom reverted to his unhappy experiences at Arundel. But in *David Elginbrod* the hero for a time acts as tutor in the family of a Nonconformist grocer "whose religion consisted chiefly in negations, and whose main duty seemed to be to make money in small sums, and spend it in smaller." Like one of the children of the Arundel "connection," a son of the grocer boasts that he has five bags of gold in the Bank of England.

The clearest echo of MacDonald's Arundel experiences, however, are to be found in *Paul Faber, Surgeon* (1879, no. 62), in which there reappear—although incidentally to the story—the petty-minded, sanctimonious lower-middle-class tradesmen, many of whom cheat despite their piety. In their sermons they want polemics; mere "edification in holiness" is not enough for them. They care not "to grow in grace, but in social influence." And their minister's college training has put all its emphasis on "pulpit-success, the lowest of all successes and the most worldly." Here the experienced and sadly mistreated MacDonald is commenting on his own youthful rejection. Yet the minister in *Paul Faber* at times gives vent to mystical speculation in the pulpit, and the quotations that MacDonald supplies from his sermons almost surely reproduce what he himself had said to outrage the Arundel congregation more than a quarter-century earlier. And as with himself, so with his fictional minister: the congregation accuses him of Germanism.

Born and brought up in the Aberdeenshire village of Huntly, and surrounded in his youth by uncompromising Calvinists who believed wholly in the doctrine of election and in eternal damnation for those who were not saved, as a child George MacDonald declared roundly that he did not want God to love him unless He loved everybody. Fearing hellfire for himself and shrinking even at a tender age from the horrible thought of human beings roasting for eternity, he later put into his best novels both the maturer theological conclusions he had reached after abandoning Calvinist views for those of the Broad Churchmen and a series of striking and sympathetic portraits of a variety of Scots who had clung to their ancestral doctrines. *David Elginbrod* (1863, no. 53) drew its initial inspiration from a seventeenth-century Scotch epitaph which put into lapidary form some of MacDonald's own ideas on the nature of the deity: "Here lie I, Martin Elginbrod,/ Hae mercy o' my soul, Lord God;/ As I wad do, were I Lord God,/ An' ye were Martin Elginbrod." MacDonald made the protagonist of his novel a descendant of the dead Martin Elginbrod, who shares the views expressed in the epitaph: it is a "daring, maybe a childlike way" of judging the Lord himself, saying that if he, Martin Elginbrod, would have mercy, then surely the Lord was not less merciful than he. He felt that the mercy in himself was one of his best qualities, and he could not think that there would be less of it in the "father of lights," from whom cometh every good and perfect gift.

A noble sage, gentle, childlike, and reverent, David Elginbrod has been educated on the driest and most uncompromising books embodying the grimmest Calvinist doctrine: books to which MacDonald's own grandmother had introduced him in his own childhood. She belonged to a splinter sect, known as the "Missionars" from their emphasis on overseas missions to the heathen, who had found even the tenets of ordinary Scotch Presbyterianism too mild for their liking. The books dwelt on the torment of hellfire, making religion a dull and negative and frightening thing: human nature is naturally depraved; nothing a man does may be considered a good work if Christ has not already chosen and accepted him. Along with these terrifying books on David Elginbrod's shelf, however, MacDonald has put as a symbol another book, from the library of the dead Elginbrod of the epitaph, a copy of the first—1612—edition of Jacob Boehme's *Aurora* (*Morgenland in Aufgang*), a mystical tract which had influenced many generations of mystics and poets—Swedenborg, Blake, Novalis—and profoundly inspired Maurice and

MacDonald himself. David cannot read Boehme's German, but he treasures the book: independently he has reached the same conclusion as Boehme about the all-loving God, who treats all his children like a father.

Speaking in his own person, MacDonald attacks the Scottish divines for emphasizing Calvin's harshest doctrines to the exclusion of "what he loved most," and so depriving God of all lovable attributes. And David Elginbrod, who has declined "with a queer smile" the invitation to be an elder of the kirk, attacks the doctrines of justification by faith and imputed righteousness as presented from the pulpit: justification can only be obtained, says David, by a man who puts himself trustingly and unreservedly—sins and all—into the hands of the Father, "and that," he says—and I paraphrase his Scotch—"will not be done by putting a robe of righteousness upon him before he's got a clean skin beneath it. As if a father could not bear to see the poor encrusted skin of his own poor sinful child, but had to have it all cleaned up before he could let the child come near him!" Such an idea of justification, such a reliance upon the imputation of Christ's righteousness, has in it a germ of hiding from God himself. Perhaps there is truth in all these doctrines, but the result of them is that they put a distance between man and God, shrouding God in such a thick mist that His poor children cannot see Him holding out His arms in mercy to receive the sinner—and the more grievous the sinner the warmer the welcome—to His own heart. "If," says David, "preachers gave up all this doctrinal talk and simply persuaded their flocks to talk directly to God alone, the loss would be very small and the gain very great." But of course God must punish sin: it would be no kindness to neglect punishment.

In *Alec Forbes of Howglen* (1865, no. 59) MacDonald modifies his direct attacks on the Presbyterian Church of Scotland by making its minister, Mr. Cowie, a kind and gentle man, ready to supply comfort to an alarmed orphan girl, who has listened too intently to the sermon of his "Missionar" colleague, and is sure that she is damned eternally. Mr. Cowie tries to reassure her: from time to time, he says, there comes a day when she does not think about her own dead father, and she knows that he would readily forgive her: well, would not her heavenly Father do the same? After all, He sent His only Son to die for us. "Ay, for the eleck, sir," replies Annie, to which Mr. Cowie can only supply a lame reassurance: "Go home, Annie my child, and don't trouble your head about election and all that. It's not a teaching we can understand. No mortal man could ever get to the bottom of it. I think it has not much to do with us. Go home, my daughter, and say your prayers to be preserved from the wiles of Satan," and he gives her a shilling.

Had she gone to the Missionar preacher, he would have been kind too, but would have gloated over her wretchedness "as a sign of grace bestowed and an awakening conscience." Thomas Crann, the village stonemason, tells Annie how he could never rest until he learned that he was one of the elect: he had "plagued the Lord night and day" until he got the answer. All night long lying in a peat bog he prayed to the Lord for grace, and after three days in bed on nothing but a little milk and water, he had his revelation: "I went to my work with my head swimming and my heart almost breaking for joy. I *was* one of the chosen." But when Annie asks him how he *knew*, all he can say is, "Get a glimpse of the face of God. It's all in the spirit. When you see it you'll know."

In both *David Elginbrod* and *Alec Forbes*, the young hero experiences a revelation of the true MacDonald religion through Wordsworth and the beauties of nature. The novels are memorable for their refutations of Calvinism accompanied by sympathetic and wholly convincing portrayals of individual Calvinists. In *Robert Falconer* (1868, no. 60), MacDonald develops his theology at the expense of the narrative but to the benefit of the student of Scotch Calvinism. Here the staunch Missionar grandmother of the hero is drawn from MacDonald's own grandmother, praying to God to save her reprobate son, Robert's father, from eternal flame: "If you were a mother yourself, Lord, you would not let him burn in Hell." The story tells at length of Robert's devotion to social work among the London poor, and of his discovery and rehabilitation of his drunken derelict of a father.

But the reader will remember longest the formidable old woman and the indelible impact she makes upon the grandson she loves, although her religion prevents her expressing her affection. The boy,

> tormented by the fear of Hell . . . made many frantic efforts to

> believe that he believed; took to keeping the Sabbath very carefully . . . by going to church three times, and to Sunday school as well; by never walking a step save to or from church; by never saying a word on any subject unconnected with religion . . .; by never reading any but religious books; by never whistling . . . all the time feeling that God was waiting to pounce upon him if he failed once.

He was denying God "as the maker of the world," and worshipping him "as a capricious demon." Robert reads in Klopstock's *Messiah* of the rebellious angel, Abaddon, who repented, and conceives of a "plan for almost emptying hell." On his own first night in heaven, he explains to his grandmother, he intends to rise at table and say that his heart is breaking to think of the souls in hell. He will call upon all those present who have friends and neighbors in the pit to abstain from food and to pray the Lord directly to remit the sins of the damned and summon them to join the saved. The idea is a practical extension of MacDonald's childhood cry that he did not wish God to love him if He did not love everybody.

Mrs. Falconer will have none of such heterodoxy, of course. She even finds and burns her grandson's violin, his secret comfort and inspiration, and so cuts him off from the one resource that has kept "the finer faculties of his mind awake." As a youth, Robert has to suffer in silence, but when he is a young man, he becomes an ever more vocal defender of the MacDonald doctrine of a loving God, and even argues his case with his grandmother. Reluctantly, once again, I translate from their broad Scotch. Robert says, "You speak about God as if he were a person like a policeman, full of his own importance, and always ready to arrest anybody that did not show constant respect to his office, always concentrating on his own glory; whereas he is really a quiet, mighty, grand, self-forgetting, all-creating, all-upholding, eternal being, who took the form of man in Christ Jesus in order that he might have it in his power to bear suffering and be humbled for our sakes. Whatever is not like Christ is not like God." "But laddie," remonstrates his grandmother, "he came to satisfy God's justice by suffering the punishment due to our sins; to turn aside his wrath and curse, to reconcile him to us. So he could not be *altogether* like God." But Robert stoutly denies it, striking at the root of Calvinism. "He did nothing of the kind, grannie. That's all a lie. He came to satisfy God's justice by giving him back his children, by allowing them to see that God was just; by sending them weeping home to fall at his feet and grip his knees, and say 'Father, you are in the right of it.' He took our sins upon him not by any sleight of hand, not by any lawyers' quibbles about imputing his righteousness to us, and the like . . . but he took them and he took them away." Like Thomas Crann, the stonemason in *Alec Forbes*, old Mrs. Falconer arouses the reader's sympathy for the torments that true believers must suffer, while she inflicts further torments on those in her power.

In MacDonald's own day, there were many who were outraged at his brisk refutation of Calvinism: it was no light thing in 1868 to write that the teaching of imputed righteousness was "all a lie." His revulsion against Calvinism, they felt, had broken all bounds. His idea that it was possible to repent in hell, and so to qualify for redemption, created—the critics declared—a sort of "Protestant purgatory," and could even be used to justify a massacre, since the victims might begin their repentance in hell and so speed their own salvation. Sentimental overemphasis on love alone led to the neglect of the meaning and implications of sin. MacDonald's "benign determinism," his overoptimism, his use of "domestic emotions"—the love of sons for fathers—as the scale by which to measure God and the principles of God's rule, was to derive theological conclusions from "facile surface emotion for the offspring," and to reduce ethical mysteries to "a sweet and effeminate type of domestic love." Mrs. Falconer's views were, the critics maintained, *not* "all a lie." In the MacDonald theology, they scornfully declared, "we are each of us blessed with a nature good enough from the beginning, and, once we cleanse away a trifle of rubbish that overlays or obscures it, we 'find ourselves,' and very soon find our God." Such reasoning was "sentimental vaporing." These strictures serve to show the continued power of Calvinism down to the turn of the twentieth century. The vehemence of both MacDonald's supporters and his opponents reflects his key importance as a sympathetic portrayer of individual Scotch Calvinists (both Church-of-Scotland and "Missionar") and as a powerful critic of their doctrines. When one remembers in addition his own career in the Congregational ministry in England

and his first-hand knowledge of the small-town English nonconformist congregation, one unhesitatingly puts him into the front rank of the novelists of Dissent.

Coming from an English rather than a Scotch background, William Hale White (1831-1913) nonetheless had much in common with George MacDonald. Born and brought up in Bedford, Hale White came from a middle class family who were loyal members of "Bunyan Meeting," a stronghold of highly Calvinistic Dissenters, founded in the seventeenth century by John Bunyan himself, the great Puritan author of *Pilgrim's Progress*, so inspiring to MacDonald and Hale White and uncounted thousands of other readers and writers. It was to the Puritanism of Cromwell, Milton, or Bunyan that Hale White's father—and Hale White himself in his youth—felt the closest affinity. Yet Bunyan Meeting at Bedford, like many Dissenting congregations, had been so swept up by the Evangelical revival that the pure Calvinist doctrines of election and of limited atonement had become blurred in the enthusiasm for the Evangelical teaching that all men could repent and be saved (justified) by faith in Christ. As Dissenters became wealthier and joined the middle classes, they were often attracted by the Church of England and its higher social position. Many Dissenting ministers therefore ceased to emphasize the doctrine of election—uncomfortable even for so blameless a child as Annie Anderson—and began to "moderate" their Calvinism. Neither Hale White's affectionate father nor Hale White himself was comfortable with the change: if "moderate Calvinism" had any meaning at all, Hale White himself wrote long afterwards, "it was that predestination, election, and reprobation were unquestionably true, but they were dogmas about which it was prudent not to say much."

In his *Autobiography of Mark Rutherford* and *Mark Rutherford's Deliverance* (1881, 1885, no. 63), Hale White wrote an extraordinarily powerful and moving mixture of autobiography and fiction. Mark Rutherford suffers from extreme poverty. This Hale White himself never experienced, being unemployed for only a few months in 1852, when he was only twenty-one, and later holding a reasonably lucrative (if often uncongenial) job as a civil servant in the Admiralty, rewarded by promotions, pleasant holidays, loving children, and close friendships, and always enjoying good physical health. It was in his profound spiritual suffering and unsatisfactory marriage that he most resembled Mark Rutherford. Hale White, like George MacDonald, studied for the Congregational ministry, but did not progress as far along the path to a ministerial career. In 1851, the same year that MacDonald's congregation at Arundel forced his resignation on the charge of "Germanism," Hale White and two classmates at the Congregational New College were expelled for heresy. Undergoing examination on a lecture by their Principal on "The Inspiration of the Bible," they raised questions about "the propriety of treating the Bible" as a single book, and questioned the claim that all its authors had been "miraculously impelled" to write all of the Bible as it now existed. All three were shocked by a sudden and final act of expulsion which declared them unfit not only for the ministry but also for continuing their studies.

Fully supported by his father—whose own rigid ideas had been undergoing gradual modification, and who even wrote a pamphlet entitled *To Think or Not to Think*, in his son's defense—Hale White suffered a deep blow. His biographers have found also in his wife's tragic illness that lasted over many years, and in his feelings of guilt, because he and she were not fully congenial and he could not quench his own feelings of self-pity and hostility, the mainsprings of his own continued emotional malaise. He did not publish his first novel until he was fifty, and he cloaked it and its successors under double anonymity. Although the two continuous *Mark Rutherford* volumes, then, are by no means wholly autobiographical, their view of the Dissenters and of the protagonist's agonizing spiritual pilgrimage were Hale White's own.

In Mark Rutherford's country town, he tells us, everybody was "formed upon recognized patterns, and those who possessed any one mark of the pattern had all." There was the wine merchant, a perfect representative of his class: Tory, Church-going, shunning the company of lesser tradespeople, "knowing no 'experience,' " and never having felt "the outpouring of the Spirit." Then there were the Dissenters, such as the ironmonger, a "deacon, presiding at prayer-meetings, strict Sabbatarian, and believer in eternal punishment." The deacon would not have argued, however, that the wine merchant ought to be converted, and the Dissenters as a congregation would not have thought any better of the wine merchant had he left the church to join them. A third class was represented by " 'Guffy' . . . real name unknown, who got drunk, unloaded barges, assisted at the municipal elections, and was never once seen within a place of worship." The pattern was "of immemorial antiquity," and any change, such as the "conversion" of the Anglican wine merchant, "would have broken up our foundations and party-walls, and would have been considered as ominous and anything but a subject for thankfulness."

Within this pattern, Rutherford's shopkeeping family belongs to the "rigid Calvinistic Independents [i.e., Congregationalists]." His boyhood is characterized by the familiar bleak Sabbath with its Hebrew features of no work whatever on that day, all preparations being made the day before and most of the food served cold. Sunday school is followed by three chapel services, with long "maundering" extemporaneous prayers addressed to God: "our minister seemed to consider that the Almighty, who had the universe to govern, had more leisure at His command than the idlest lounger at a club." The sermons are even worse. Yet Rutherford's religious training gives him a permanent regard for truthfulness and for personal chastity, which he regards as major assets.

His "conversion" takes place when he is fourteen, when he is told that the time has come for it. "Conversion," he writes, "among the Independents and other Puritan sects, is supposed to be a kind of miracle wrought in the heart by the influence of the Holy Spirit, by which the man becomes something altogether different to what he was previously. It affects, or should affect, his character; that is . . . he ought to . . . be better in every way than he was before: but this is not considered as the main consequence. In its essence it is a change in the emotions and increased vividness of belief." During his childhood, he says, conversions were sometimes genuine, but usually not, and not in his own case. He himself becomes "perhaps a little more hypocritical." His church-going becomes even more intense, and he thinks he is interested in it, "but what I really liked was clanship and the satisfaction of belonging to a society marked off from the great world." All the Evangelical conversions we have encountered in fiction were genuine. This is the first false one.

The College at which Rutherford is prepared for the ministry resembles in every detail those which Frederick Rivers and George

MacDonald attended. It is startling to find once again the wretched quality of the instruction in classics and theology, and the suspicion of the very word "German": a "term of reproach signifying something very awful, although nobody knew exactly what it was." When Rutherford is nineteen, he begins an apprenticeship as "supply minister" in various congregations. Not long after comes a first chance encounter with Wordsworth's poems. This produces Rutherford's genuine conversion. Wordsworth's "real God is not the God of the Church, but the God of the hills, the abstraction Nature, and to this my reverence was transferred." A "new and living spirit" now replaces "the old deity, once alive, but gradually hardened into an idol." At this juncture, Hale White himself was expelled, but Rutherford continues. As with MacDonald or Vincent or Rivers, his sermons are too intellectual, too little dogmatic; although he increases church attendance, he has enemies among the deacons, of whom the reader obtains a fine series of portraits.

The famous Mr. Snale, Rutherford's chief opponent—like some of MacDonald's nastiest English Congregationalist characters, a draper by trade—is perhaps the most revolting specimen of a Dissenting hypocrite in fiction. Rutherford's confrontation and denunciation of Snale are highly dramatic and bring the reader some of the same satisfaction that he feels at the similar discomfiture of Uriah Heep (thoroughly Snalelike) in *David Copperfield*. But the conflict means that Rutherford, like George MacDonald, must resign his ministry. "Congregations," as Phoebe, Junior remarked, "are not pleasant masters." Disappointment leads to what we would call a severe depression, not unlike the terrible spiritual trials that beset William James (and his father, the elder Henry James), which William called a "vastation," and from which Rutherford never fully recovers.

Though never able to become a Congregationalist Minister, Hale White in 1856 did serve briefly in a Unitarian pulpit. And now, needing employment, Rutherford too takes the ministry in a Unitarian village church, one of those which had originally been Presbyterian, but over the decades had abandoned the Trinitarian creed. Its meager congregation "still testify against three Gods in one and the deity of Jesus Christ." Like the Congregationalists, they are mostly small tradesmen. But unlike the hospitable Tozer and his fellow deacons of Carlingford, they are stingy and inhospitable. On Rutherford's first visit to the chapel, there is no fire on a cold day and nothing to drink except stagnant water in a bottle; midday dinner at a parishioner's house is unaccompanied by any conversation, and the parsimony of the entertainment is positively comic: Rutherford is asked whether he will have potatoes *or* cabbage, and two shillings are deducted for the meal from his fee of a guinea. The congregation consists of five families. Despite the Unitarian "freethought lineage," it is a "petrified sect."

> They were perfectly orthodox except that they denied a few orthodox doctrines. Their method was as strict as that of the most rigid Calvinist. They plumed themselves, however, greatly on their intellectual superiority over the Wesleyans and Baptists around them; and so far as I could make out, the only topics they delighted in were demonstrations of the unity of God from texts in the Bible, and polemics against tri-theism. Sympathy with the great problems then beginning to agitate men they had none. Socially they were cold. . . . They had no enthusiasm for their chapel, and came or stayed away on the Sunday just as it suited them, and without caring to assign any reason.

The student of English social and religious life will be hard put to it to find elsewhere in fiction a comparable account of the Unitarians.

Starved for human warmth and companionship, and for sympathy and love, Rutherford holds out as their minister for about a year. Despite a series of ever more distressing personal and emotional trials, he does not "go off into absolute denial" or form a penchant for any "sect, party, or special mode." Rather than struggle with speculation about the fundamental religious problems, he reaches "a peace not formally concluded, and with no specific stipulations, but nevertheless definite. He was content to rest and wait." Imagining himself suddenly elevated to the pulpit in St. Paul's Cathedral, with the opportunity to deliver a sermon to thousands, he realizes that all he could say would be, "Dear friends, I know no more than you know; we had better go home." Yet Rutherford now practices rather than preaches Christ's teachings. With his friend, M'Kay, who shares his horror at the grimness and hopelessness of life in the London slums, he rents a room in the heart of one of the worst areas, Drury Lane, to which anybody may come to rest and perhaps be taught ways of facing wretchedness. Without theology, the two friends hope to create a Christian spirit.

Rutherford recalls several of the human beings in direst anguish whom he and M'Kay succeed in helping: the porter who carries the coals for the fires in a government office building—lowest man on the totem pole—the victim of bullying by the messengers, who are bullied by the clerks, who are bullied by the officials; the waiter in a Strand chophouse worrying about his drunken wife and his abused child; the ex-commercial traveller with the bitterly uncongenial jealous wife; and the unhappy clerk who must spend all of each day in addressing newspapers to be sent out of London, while listening to the foul language of his fellow workers. The sympathy, the absence of patronizing feeling, the anxiety for the decent dregs of society that characterize Rutherford's accounts of these four, and his modest descriptions of the simple and effective ways in which he and M'Kay—themselves virtually penniless—contrive to alleviate their troubles constitute a picture of Christianity in action as moving as anything in nineteenth-century literature. The pastors and ministers of Salem Chapel were made uncomfortable by the small-town poor; it was the Anglican clergy who ministered to them in Carlingford and in the English villages; but Rutherford, who has left formal faith behind and who has no comfortable rectory or vicarage to return to, is a ministering angel among human creatures only a little worse off than he.

Neither church nor chapel, Rutherford declares, would have done these people much good. Had they gone to either, they would only have heard discourses on problems that did not concern them: "Their trouble was not the forgiveness of sins, the fallacies of Arianism, the personality of the Holy Ghost, or the doctrine of the Eucharist. They all *wanted* something distinctly." Only practical remedies could be of use to them. Beyond these, the room offers a quiet shelter and a place for reflection. Rutherford and M'Kay give such practical help when they can, and strive "to create in our hearers contentment with their lot, and even some joy in it." Never emphasizing sin as the cause for God's estrangement from men, Rutherford and M'Kay in their "Drury Lane Theology" still seek to create a reconciliation, to mitigate the inescapable agonies of pain and death. All great religions have done the same; all deserve to be preserved for this quality; pre-eminent among those that have done it successfully, Rutherford declares, is the Roman Catholic faith.

Despite all of his own tribulations—material as well as spiritual—Rutherford is convinced that the world is steadily improving, not only "in the gross" but also for each individual human being. Nor does he—authority on troubled faith that he is—admit the general contention that "it is pure doubt which disturbs or depresses us"; it is instead "dogmatism in the cloak of doubt," i.e., the acceptance of doubt as a matter of faith: it is just as dogmatic to say of a dead man, he is gone forever, as to say, he is gone to heaven. "The proper attitude . . . enjoined by the severest exercise of the reason is, *I do not know.*"

With the insight born of experience, Rutherford remarks that the dissenting Calvinism of his own background is "entirely metaphysical" as a religion, and

> encourages, unhappily, in everybody a taste for tremendous problems. So long as Calvinism is unshaken, the mischief is often not obvious, because a ready solution taken on trust is provided; but when doubts arise, the evil results become apparent, and the poor helpless victim, totally at a loss, is torn first in this direction and then in the other, and cannot let these questions alone. He has been taught to believe they are connected with salvation, and he is compelled still to busy himself with them, rather than with simple external piety.

These sentences from *The Deliverance* might be taken as a text for the earlier portions of Hale White's next and perhaps most famous novel, *The Revolution in Tanner's Lane* (1887, no. 64), a two-part historical story set in the years after 1814, at a moment when Bunyan's pure faith, deeply felt by the protagonist, Zachariah Coleman, was only beginning to be shaken. Confronted by his friends and fellow radicals from France, who are children of the enlightenment, Zachariah finds that it is "a century and a half too late" to persuade them of the Calvinist truths. Himself a sinner, he has somehow been forced to apply these truths himself. The system is "still the same, but the application had become difficult." Forty years before Mark Rutherford, Zachariah finds that "doubts arise" and "evil results become apparent."

And in the second portion of the novel, when the scene shifts to the Bedford of Hale White's youth, Calvinism has degenerated from the "old time religion" that always kept its hold on Zachariah into the "moderate" form that both Whites, father and son, deplored. As the gluttonous new minister remarks, "Let us follow our Lord and Master and warn our hearers against sin, and leave the application to the Holy Spirit." All "disputed topics . . . all particular offences" are to be avoided in the pulpit. Only the great London minister, Bradshaw—probably modelled by Hale White on Caleb Morris (1800-1865), an inspired Welsh Congregational preacher—can bring the doubting George Allen, protagonist of the second part of *Tanner's Lane*, to even a temporary sense of true religion. But George is of a new generation: Bradshaw and his childhood beliefs can stand firm for Zachariah despite their testing. George's faith cannot stand the tests to which it is put. When the "Revolution"—only the last of the many revolutions in the novel—comes to Tanner's Lane, it is through the appointment to the ministry there of a third minister, who actually echoes some of Hale White's own ideas, and so represents a third generation of increasingly unstable Calvinism.

In the three earlier novels of William Hale White, then, the reader finds a vivid picture of small town Dissent, authentic, moving, and, by now, celebrated among an ever widening circle of Hale White's admirers. But he also finds, crisply expressed in the sentences we have just been considering, and implied by the whole course of Mark Rutherford's life, as by the generational difference between Zachariah Coleman and George Allen, one major key to the diagnosis of the most complicated problem we have yet to face: the origin and the nature of the multiform doubt that flourished so widely alongside the proliferations of varied Victorian piety. We shall find Hale White's later fiction opening our investigations into the varieties of doubt, as we have found his earlier fiction closing our investigations into the varieties of faith.

Before abandoning the Dissenters for the Doubters, however, we must pay tribute to one of the most revealing autobiographies in English, *Father and Son* (1907, NIS) by Edmund Gosse (1849-

1928). Not a novel, of course, it tells us more about Dissent in Victorian England than any novel. Moreover, it incidentally provides us with an authentic view of the Plymouth Brethren, most Puritanical of all the sects, known to one another as "the Saints," whom we have so far encountered only incidentally. A prolific literary critic, who was one of the first to plead the cause of Ibsen in England, and a friend of the leading poets and novelists of the late Victorian and Edwardian periods,[1] Gosse published his autobiography anonymously. With an easy prose style, a wry humor, and much pathos, he recorded the story of his own childhood.

His parents were devout Plymouth Brethren, his father, Philip Gosse, a former Methodist and a well-known and prolific marine zoologist, his mother a former Anglican and a poet. As epigraph for *Father and Son*, Edmund Gosse used (in German) a line of Schopenhauer, "Faith is like love; it cannot be compelled." Dedicated to the Lord by his strong-willed parents when he was less than two months old, and intended for the ministry, Gosse more than half a century later produced what he called "a *document*" of "educational and religious conditions, which, having passed away, will never return . . . the diagnosis of a dying Puritanism." All our reading about Evangelicals and Dissenters fails to prepare us for the degree of religiosity that dominated the Gosses' lives. "My parents," Gosse wrote, "founded every action, every attitude, upon their interpretation of the Scriptures, and upon the guidance of the Divine Will as revealed to them by direct answer to prayer. . . . So confident were they of the reality of their intercourse with God, that they asked for no other guide. They recognized no spiritual authority among men, they subjected themselves to no priest or minister, they troubled their consciences about no current manifestation of 'religious opinion.' "

Mrs. Gosse believed that "to tell a story, that is, to compose a fictitious narrative of any kind, was a sin." All novels, all narrative verse, were therefore outlawed. Keble's *Christian Year*—which even

1. Gosse also wrote a short novel, anonymously published, which deals vividly and charmingly with a romance between an upper middle-class High Anglican youth and the delightful daughter of a Baptist minister in London. The girl has depth and character, the man none. Entitled *The Unequal Yoke*, the story appeared serially in *The English Illustrated Magazine* No. 31 (April, 1886), pp. 500-512; No. 32 (May, 1886), pp. 562-576; and No. 33 (June, 1886), pp. 604-615. It was never published in book form.

the Evangelical Sir Roland Ashton read with relish, if with some misgivings—was forbidden, like all other High-Church poetry and hymns. There was little company, there were no other children to play with; it was life in London "in a Calvinist cloister." Mrs. Gosse wrote tracts, "testimonies to the blood of Christ" as their admirers called them. Mr. Gosse pursued his researches. Both believed in the absolute truth of every statement in the Bible. Like the Millenarians and Maurice, they enjoyed interpreting the Book of Revelation as prophetic of things to come in their own lifetime. So anti-Catholic were they that Mrs. Gosse's dying hours in 1857 (when Edmund was still only seven) were cheered by the thought that the Papacy was in danger from the Italian rebels. "My Father celebrated the announcement in the newspapers of a considerable emigration from the Papal Dominions by rejoicing at 'this outcrowding of many throughout the Harlot's domain, from her sins and her plagues.' "

When Gosse and his widowed father moved to Devonshire, the father strove—in his *Omphalos* (1857)—to combat the scientific theories of Sir Charles Lyell, the geologist, by demonstrating that "when . . . creation took place, the world presented, instantly, the structural appearance of a planet on which life had long existed." Edmund Gosse recalls the publication of his father's "curious, obstinate, fanatical" book, which seemed to critics to be saying that "God hid the fossils in the rocks in order to tempt the geologists into infidelity." Philip Gosse's fellow scientists rejected the book, and his friend Charles Kingsley wrote him that he could not "give up the painful and slow conclusions of five and twenty years' study of geology, and believe that God has written on the rocks one enormous and superfluous lie." Edmund's life grew even gloomier in the face of his father's depression and conviction that the repudiation of his book was the punishment for sin. Believing that Christmas was a Popish feast, and sinful to celebrate, he threw away a plum pudding made surreptitiously by the servants.

The Devon village Plymouth Brethren worshipped in a room over a smelly stable. They were, Gosse wrote, a "quaint collection of humble, conscientious, ignorant and gentle persons. In chronicle or fiction, I have never been fortunate to meet with anything which resembled them." Baptism consisted of total immersion, before the whole congregation. Only the baptized were admitted to communion, "the Breaking of Bread." Gosse gives an unforgettable portrayal of individual "saints" and recalls with horror the dreadful smell of their undrained cottages when he visited them as a child doing "pastoral work in the Lord's service." His only pleasures came from sharing in his father's search for specimens of marine life in the still unplundered tidal rockpools that educated so many nineteenth-century amateur naturalists, including Kingsley, whose *Glaucus; or the Wonders of the Shore* (1855) and *Water-Babies* (1863) were popular and famous. But the grim Calvinism of Philip Gosse closed in like a prison. If Edmund burned his finger, his father "would solemnly ejaculate: 'O may these afflictions be much sanctified to him!' " before offering any remedy for the pain. In spite of snubs ("Tell Mr. Kingsley that I am engaged in examining Scripture with certain of the Lord's children") Charles Kingsley would wait, "nervously careering around the garden," until Philip Gosse would see him.

> As we would expect of so deep-dyed a Calvinist, in dealing with the peasants around him . . . my Father always insisted on the necessity of conversion. There must be a new birth and being, a fresh creation in God. This crisis he was accustomed to regard as manifesting itself in a sudden and definite upheaval. There might have been prolonged practical piety, deep and true contrition for sin, but, these, though the natural and suitable prologue to conversion, were not conversion itself. People hung on at the confines of regeneration, often for a very long time; my Father dealt earnestly with them. . . . Such persons were in a gracious state, but they were not in a state of grace. . . . But on some day, at some hour and minute . . . the way of salvation would be revealed to these persons in such an aspect that they would be enabled instantaneously to accept it. They would take it consciously, as one taking a gift from the hand that offers it. This act of taking was the process of conversion, and the person who so accepted was a child of God now, although a single minute ago he had been a child of wrath. The very root of human nature had to be changed, and *in the majority of cases*, this change was sudden, patent, palpable.

The italics are mine. "In the majority of cases" means that Philip Gosse did not wholly exclude the possibility that the child of godly parents might at an early age have had his conversion "unperceived and therefore unrecorded." Since conversion could not happen twice, it was important to recognize in these rare cases that it *had* happened once, and to accept the person into communion. Philip Gosse believed that little Edmund, now nine, had experienced this sort of rare conversion and should be admitted to the communion of saints.

Two of the elders examined Edmund: Fawkes, the builder, "was so long in coming to the point," Edmund writes, "that I was obliged to lead him to it myself, and I . . . testified my faith in the atonement with a fluency that surprised myself. Before I had done, Fawkes, a middle-aged man, with the reputation of being a very stiff employer of labour, was weeping like a child." The examination went swimmingly:

> My answers had been so full and clear, my humility (save the mark!) had been so sweet, my acquaintance with Scripture so amazing, my testimony to all the leading principles so distinct and exhaustive, that they could only say that they had felt confounded, and yet deeply cheered and led far along their own heavenly path, by hearing such accents fall from the lips of a babe and a suckling. I did not like being described as a suckling, but every lot has its crumpled rose leaf. . . .

So Edmund's public baptism—"the central event of my whole childhood"—followed, after which he felt so "puffed out with a sense" of his own holiness that he stuck out his tongue at other little boys "to remind them that I now broke bread as one of the Saints, and that they did not."

But the comedy Gosse did not perceive until many years later. The remainder of *Father and Son* describes in moving detail the sense of intolerable pressure he felt at the thought of becoming a minister, "imprisoned forever in the religious system which had caught me." But fortunately, mitigating circumstances made the rest of his childhood far more bearable, despite the horrors of Lord's Day observances, with early domestic prayers followed by morning, afternoon, evening, and late night services and prayer meetings.

Deep into Edmund's young manhood, however, after he had left home and gone up to London, his father inexorably pursued him with letters, putting the "ceaseless inquiry" to him: "Let me know more of your inner light. Does the candle of the Lord shine on your soul? . . . Do you find the ministry of the Word pleasant, and, above all, profitable? Does it bring your soul into exercise before God? The Coming of Christ draweth nigh. Watch, therefore, and pray always, that you may be counted worthy to stand before the Son of Man."

In reflecting upon his father's spiritual attitude, Edmund Gosse remarks that "his aspirations were individual and metaphysical." And this, he declares, was characteristic of the form of Puritanism, of which Philip Gosse was the "latest surviving type," still finding the "great panacea now, as always, in the study of the Bible." But nowadays, Edmund points out, "all classes of religious persons combine in placing philanthropic activity . . . in the foreground." The old subjectivity had been replaced by a new objectivity. "Nowadays a religion which does not combine with its subjective faith a strenuous labour for the good of others is hardly held to possess any principle worth holding." Gosse's childhood and his loving and horrified study of his father enabled him to see this fundamental transformation of Victorian religion at first hand. We have seen it in the novels of all shades of English religious opinion. By the end of the nineteenth century, Catholics, High-, Low-, and Broad-Churchmen, and Dissenters alike are to be found putting their emphasis upon beneficence, "constant attention to the moral and physical improvement of persons who have been neglected." And although, as Gosse points out, this idea "seems to have formed some part of the Saviour's original design," it did not triumph wholly until the late Victorian age. So strongly indeed does it come to pervade men's consciousness now that—as we shall see—even doubters share it with believers.

Gosse's final judgment is that

> evangelical religion . . . divides heart from heart. It sets up a vain, chimerical ideal, in the barren pursuit of which all the tender, indulgent affections, all the genial play of life, all the

exquisite pleasures and soft resignations of the body, all that enlarges and calms the soul, are exchanged for what is harsh and void and negative. It encourages a stern and ignorant spirit of condemnation; it throws altogether out of gear the healthy movement of the conscience; it invents virtues which are sterile and cruel; it invents sins which are no sins at all. . . . There is something horrible . . . in the fanaticism that can do nothing with this pathetic and fugitive existence of ours but treat it as if it were the uncomfortable antechamber to a palace which no one has explored and of the plan of which we know absolutely nothing.

PART IV.

"NO CHURCH"
VARIETIES OF DOUBT

CHAPTER 6.

"ONLY INFINITE JUMBLE AND MESS AND DISLOCATION"

Preliminary

We have already encountered many doubters in the novels about faith, such as the Oxford freethinkers in Conybeare's *Perversion.* Conybeare's Armstrong-Archer—in his passage from indifference via Unitarianism all the way to atheism without even a stop-off at a Pantheist way-station—is perhaps the fullest case history yet; and the tools he employs to undermine poor Charles Bampton's vestigial faith—books of higher criticism casting doubts on the authenticity of the Bible—were indeed effective in weakening the religious beliefs of many Victorians. But Armstrong-Archer and Bampton inhabit a novel primarily devoted to purveying the Broad-Church message. Similarly, in Felicia Skene's *Hidden Depths,* the heroine's brother loses his faith at Oxford because an overzealous tutor has caused him to read widely and exercise his private judgment. But the chief emphasis of the novel is not on doubt but on Tractarian values. Novels dealing primarily with doubt do, however, abound. They vividly illustrate the almost infinite shadings of disbelief that characterized the period, shadings more diverse, perhaps, than even the varieties of Christian faith with which we are by now familiar.

Many a man who spent his mature life in the service of the Church of England had passed through a doubting phase in his youth. Newman's opponent, Charles Kingsley, to mention only one, in rebellion against his clergyman father's Evangelicalism and repelled by the celibacy of the Tractarians and the Catholics, as we know, nonetheless felt while at Cambridge that he must be either a Catholic or a mere deist, but could not—despite self-flagellation severer than Hurrell Froude's and a momentary attraction to the life of a monk—embrace the Church of Rome. His re-entry into the Church of England (called a "conversion" by his latest biographer, Lady Chitty,[1] but hardly that in the sense in which we have been using the term) was intimately connected with the stormy course of his courtship. Once he was sure that Fanny Grenfell truly loved him, he listened to the "still small voice" that told him that only in the Church of England could he find rest for his "troubled spirit." He made his own "atonement" for his past offenses by taking a solemn vow to become a clergyman.

Thomas Arnold himself warned his Rugby boys in a sermon (published in 1834) that their hearts would be "hardened by the coming years. . . . It may be that our faith may fail . . . our hearts will ever be whispering, what if it be all but a cunningly devised fable? What if there be no resurrection, no Christ, no God?" And one of Arnold's most devoted pupils, Arthur Hugh Clough (1819-1861), at eighteen wrote verses proclaiming that fear, and possibly despair, always accompany a boy's passage from youth to manhood. Faith was needed, but would it be possible? At Balliol, Clough's tutor, the Tractarian W. G. Ward, who later followed Newman into the Roman Church, introduced Clough to the writings of John Stuart Mill, in the hope that once his orthodox belief had been sapped, he would be the readier to accept Tractarianism: it would be all or nothing. Only the first part of the operation was successful. Clough's tendencies toward scepticism—usually too little recognized by those who attribute the entire outcome to Ward—were strengthened, and he found, as he wrote in his *Bothie of Toper-na-Vuosich* (1848), that he saw "Only infinite jumble and mess and dislocation" in the contemporary religious scene.

Judgment suspended, Clough did not deny Christianity outright, but adopted for himself a "religion of silence." He did not feel the power of the Christian faith working upon him and was not sure that he could believe in it. "What is the meaning," he wrote, "of 'Atonement by a crucified Saviour'? . . . the Evangelicals gabble it, as the Papists do their Ave Mary's—and yet say they know; while Newman falls down and worships *because* he does not know

1. Susan Chitty, *The Beast and the Monk. A Life of Charles Kingsley* (New York: Mason/Charter, 1975), pp. 59-60.

and knows he does not know." So Clough became an agnostic. Partly under the impact of a meeting with Ralph Waldo Emerson, he resigned his fellowship at Oriel because he did not wish others to think that he still accepted the Thirty-nine Articles: he was sorry he had ever subscribed to them. Other deeply personal factors—a feeling of friendlessness, political radicalism, a "loosening of social pressures"—all contributed to his convictions and his behavior. Though Clough was a rarity in the 1840's, his views as set forth in his poetry had by the sixties won him many admirers in the universities and out. James Russell Lowell wrote that Clough would a century later "be thought . . . the truest expression in verse of the moral and intellectual tendencies, the doubts and struggles towards settled convictions, of the period in which he lived."[2]

Other sensitive intellectuals found Christian doctrines ethically repugnant. "A great many intelligent and moral people think Xty [Christianity] a bad religion," Clough wrote to his friend James Anthony Froude; "I don't;—but I'm not sure, as at present preached, it is quite true." Froude himself, as we shall see, had gone through a tremendous period of emotional struggle and eventually rejected Christianity out of hand as a doomed religion, ethically unacceptable: why *should* Christ's crucifixion atone for *our* sins? Moreover, was not an emphasis upon the next world wholly inappropriate for dwellers in a real world in which there was so much to be done to improve man's lot? John Henry Newman's brother, Francis (1805-1897), found not only the atonement but also the Calvinist ideas of election (to which he had been far more exposed in his Evangelical youth than Froude), and even the idea of baptismal regeneration, wholly unacceptable on ethical grounds. His *Phases of Faith* (1850), his spiritual autobiography, details his long and varied religious pilgrimage from Evangelical Anglicanism to the Plymouth Brethren to the Baptists, and eventually to free thought. Like Froude, he felt Christianity an inappropriate religion for the nineteenth century. Only late in life did he become a Unitarian. And George Eliot, as we know, firmly abandoned the faith of her youth.[3]

2. I am much indebted here to P. G. Scott, "A. H. Clough: A Case Study in Victorian Doubt," *Schism, Heresy and Religious Protest*, ed. Derek Baker (Cambridge: Cambridge University Press, 1972), pp. 383-389.

3. Howard R. Murphy, "The Ethical Revolt Against Christian Orthodoxy in Early

Sometimes repugnance toward Christian doctrine did not make a doubter. Benjamin Jowett wrote in 1855 that "the doctrine of the Atonement has often been explained in a way at which our moral feelings revolt. God is represented as angry with us for what we never did; He is ready to inflict a disproportionate punishment on us for what we are; He is satisfied by the punishment of His Son in our stead. The sin of Adam is first imputed to us; then the righteousness of Christ. The imperfection of human law is transferred to the Divine. . . ."[4] But Jowett, of course, did not abandon his faith: he became a leading spokesman for the Broad-Church party and argued that the primitive ideas of original sin, the atonement, eternal punishment—which reflected man's own crudeness—should be purified and refined until, so his opponents would argue, there was nothing left of them or of Christianity.

The very same doubts that made freethinkers out of Froude or George Eliot made Jowett a certain kind of believer. Doubt, then, is a most complex phenomenon, varying with each individual, differing in its origins, its intensity, the conclusions to which it leads. Far more than the believers, each such intellectual doubter necessarily had his case history. To believe was normal and accepted; to doubt required a positive revolt against family training, social pressures, and accepted behavior. While the rebellious and tormented intellectuals were more articulate than any other class of doubter, and far more likely to tell their stories in novels, they were by no means the only sort of doubter in Victorian England. We shall perforce meet more of them than of the less articulate and more numerous nonintellectuals in the following chapters, but we must recognize from the beginning their relative statistical insignificance.

Indeed, according to even the most optimistic contemporary interpretations of the official statistics gathered on the attendance at religious services in England on Sunday, 30 March, 1851, it appeared that more than five and a quarter million persons (of a popu-

---

Victorian England," *American Historical Review* LX, 4 (July 1955): 800-817, deals with these three doubters.

4. Quoted from Jowett's *The Epistles of St. Paul to the Thessalonians, Galatians, Romans* (1855) in the fine article of D. W. Dockrill, "The Origin and Development of Nineteenth Century English Agnosticism," *Historical Journal* (University of Newcastle, New South Wales) I, 4 (February 1971): 16.

lation of about eighteen million) who should have been present were not. This estimate was based on a series of more or less plausible conjectures, but it was impossible to estimate how many of the absentees on 30 March were habitual absentees. It was promptly assumed that most of those who stayed away belonged to the laboring classes: resentful of the social distinction that confined them to "free seats," while reserving pews for the well-to-do, suspicious of religion as a possession of the middle and upper classes, or living in such squalor that things of the spirit had no meaning for them. In cities, where such poverty was the greatest, it was clear that there was not enough space in houses of worship to accommodate all those who stayed away, and enthusiasts proclaimed that many more (two thousand was the number selected) churches and chapels were needed. At one level, perhaps the simplest, the working-class absentee from religious services embodied religious doubt, although few of them, perhaps, would have put it this way: religion simply did not enter their consciousnesses.

Such unfortunates appear from time to time in the pages of novels, usually in pathetic scenes where respectable church-going persons are horrified to discover poor people—often children—who have never even heard of God or of Christ. At the beginning of *Jessica's First Prayer* (1867, no. 45), Jessica is of course in such a predicament, as are others of Hesba Stretton's "street Arabs." So is Mark Rutherford's bargee "Guffy," whom he takes as a prototype of the anonymous laboring classes of his native town, "never once seen within a place of worship." At Carlingford, too, there is the bargees' district, Wharfside (a reminder that much of England's commercial traffic moved by canal), abandoned to misery and paganism by the Dissenters and by a succession of rectors, where young Frank Wentworth, the High-Church Perpetual Curate of St. Roque's, consecrates a schoolroom for church services, visits the poor, and, on one memorable Easter morning, baptizes six children of the same family, thus incurring the wrath of his nominal superior, the Rector of Carlingford.

William Hale White's Freethinkers

But beyond these multitudes of anonymous laborers (symbolically Guffy's "real name is unknown") .to whom religion was a matter of indifference or of ignorance, were other freethinking members of the working classes who had made the conscious decision to reject it. On their depressing Sunday walks in London, Mark Rutherford and M'Kay, for example, several times visit a "freethinking hall," where they hear the audience roar with laughter at comic accounts of Noah and Jonah, and listen to "demonstrations of the immorality of the patriarchs and Jewish heroes, and arguments to prove that the personal existence of the devil was a myth." On one occasion they witness a debate between a dissenting minister (who has volunteered) and the freethinkers' spokesman. The audience gives the minister a respectful hearing; they even applaud when he prays for them as "poor wandering souls who have said in their hearts that there is no God"; they regard his long prayer "as an elocutionary show-piece." His address is a sermon; it dwells on the fact that great men—Locke and Newton—had accepted the Old Testament, and that the Old Testament constantly prefigures the New. Warning his hearers of their doom if they reject Christ, and holding forth to them the prospect of eternal bliss if they accept Him, he is again loudly applauded even by his opponent in the debate.

This "little man with small eyes," however, a practiced orator, soon has it all his own way. Who wants to go to heavenly bliss in the company of the Old Testament worthies? When you got there would you want to leave your wife alone with David? Or do you want to spend eternity with the bishops of the Church of England, who, "on their departure from this vale of tears tempered by ten thousand a year, are duly supplied with wings?" It is, he shows cleverly, impossible for the Old Testament to include those references to Christ which his opponent had stressed. Nor is there any use in trying to reconcile the Bible with science. What the minister had said might do for the young women of his congregation, but it is far too elementary for his present audience. So William Hale White gives us a picture of an active working-class freethinking organization, virtually—one might say—an "anticongregation," since the freethinkers are just as religious in denying the truth of Scripture as the Christians are in affirming it. With his usual melancholy, Rutherford declares that—in view of all the work to be done in the world—it is surely just as "imbecile" for them to waste a Sunday morning in ridiculing such stories as that of Jonah as to waste it in proving the stories literally true.

After leaving the last of his ministerial posts with the Unitarians, Mark Rutherford works for a time in the employ of Mr. Wollaston, a publisher of sceptical books, a portrait of John Chapman, editor of the *Westminster Review*. Before Wollaston will employ Rutherford, he inquires into his views of the miracles in the Bible: Wollaston's antagonism to the prevailing religious orthodoxy is such that "belief or disbelief in it was the standard by which he judged men." Rutherford explains that he does not suppose that the miracles really happened, but regards each miracle as "a statement of divine truth . . . felt with a more than common intensity." This is acceptable, and Rutherford is soon an inmate of Wollaston's household. Wollaston does not much care for individuals, but is generally philanthropic: a not unfamiliar type. And he has notably "liberal" (the quotation marks are Hale White's) ideas about relations between the sexes, believing in a form of free love without being a libertine, and speaking freely before his unmarried niece, Theresa, on all subjects: "he had a theory that she ought to receive precisely the same social training as men, and should know just what men know." Although much given to scientific verbiage and to discussing "psychology," Wollaston is not profound or well-read. As for Theresa herself, whom Rutherford comes to love, she is at least a partial portrait of Marian Evans, not yet George Eliot, who was also a lodger in Chapman's house and a member of his peculiarly complicated household. William Hale White apparently worshipped her from afar.

Far more acute than Wollaston is Rutherford's atheist friend, Mardon, a printer like so many other nineteenth-century atheists and radicals. Mardon not only believes that the Gospels cannot be reconciled with one another but also rejects Rutherford's counter-suggestion that it does not much matter whether Christ existed historically or not, since the Christ-idea is "eternally true." Not at all, says Mardon, it is of supreme importance "whether we are dealing with a dream or with reality," since only if Christ's crucifixion is a reality can a man nerve himself up to a comparable sacrifice. Besides, "the commonplaces which even the most freethinking of Unitarians seem to consider as axiomatic" are to Mardon unbelievable. The concept of omnipotence requires some resistance to become credible; but in the case of God's hypothetical omnipotence, there is no such resistance postulated. God is made up, says Mardon, of such "abstract, illimitable, self-annihilative attributes," which are all nonsense. It is Mardon who urges Rutherford to abandon the ministry and "prefer the meanest craft," and who tries to demonstrate that Rutherford's alleged belief in God is no different from his own belief in the "laws which govern the universe and man," and that it makes no difference whether or not one thinks of an "intellect" behind creation, since in any case one can affirm nothing more about that intellect. It is Mardon, on his own deathbed, who challenges the generally accepted views of personal immortality. In short, Mardon is a real philosopher, of a rather homespun kind, who has not elevated his atheism to the level of a new religion.

The freethinking orator, Wollaston, and Mardon are all antireligious men whose thoughts have been profoundly if not always directly affected by the new science and Biblical scholarship of the forties and fifties: even the freethinking spokesman produces "a clever exposition" of scriptural inconsistency and "a really earnest protest against the quibbling by which those who believed in the Bible as a revelation sought to reconcile it with science." These are manifestly men whom Hale White knew in his maturity: he was only twenty-eight when *The Origin of Species* was published in 1859. Hale White's last three novels, *Miriam's Schooling* (1890, no. 64)—hardly more than a long short story or *nouvelle*—*Catherine Furze* (1893, no. 65), and *Clara Hopgood* (1896, no. 65) are set in the 1840's, the time of Hale White's own boyhood: in all three, theology as such moves far into the background. Yet all are religious novels centering upon a woman's emotional and spiritual development and achievement of the "deliverance" that Mark Rutherford had so hardly won.

Self-willed, untamed, almost pagan in her lack of discipline, Miriam Tacchi "had no religion, although she listened to a sermon once each Sunday." So strong is her impulse to help the downtrodden, however, that she is willing to lie in order to give an alibi to a man she believes to be falsely accused of setting a fire. After experiencing poverty in London and falling in love with a man unworthy of her, she is in the midst of a deep suicidal depression when she is caught in a thunderstorm ("the flashes were incessant and flamed round the golden cross of St. Paul's nearly opposite her"); she recovers from her subsequent fever determined to "do something for her fellow-creatures." It is a "conversion." Like those men who feel that life has nothing to offer them, and who therefore follow "the best recommendations of the Catholic Church," she goes to work in a hospital, where she is put to scrubbing the floors. Yet she is ineffectual, "self-sacrificing but not soldierly," and she loses her job.

Her real chance for self-mastery and a form of happiness comes after her marriage. A naturally literary but untutored woman, she discovers Shakespeare. Though at first she finds her plodding husband wholly unsympathetic with her tastes, she slowly comes to appreciate his extraordinary skills: he builds an orrery, for example, with which he can demonstrate and explain the movements of the solar system. Miriam learns the lesson of humility. Though "churches and philosophers had striven and demonstrated for thousands of years; yet she was no better protected than if Socrates, Epictetus, and all ecclesiastical institutions from the time of Moses had never existed." She is thrown back upon herself. Reconciliation replaces rebellion: she will find salvation that way.

In *Catherine Furze*, a longer and more complex but not more perfect story, the sacrifice that brings redemption comes from renunciation. Deeply kind-hearted and possessed of a powerful independent will, Catherine can dominate her doting father and combat her socially ambitious mother on better than even terms. Mrs. Furze forcibly moves the family from Dissent into the Church of England purely out of social ambition, while Furze himself, a small-town ironmonger, is like Mrs. Oliphant's Tozer, who can never feel socially at ease with persons he thinks of as his superiors. Catherine falls in love with a clergyman, Mr. Cardew, married to a wife who as little understands his literary bent as Miriam Tacchi's husband understood hers. Mrs. Cardew "had been brought up as an Evangelical, but she had passed through no religious experience whatever, and religion . . . was quite unintelligible to her. Had she been born a few years later, she would have taken to science and done well at it, but at that time there was no outlet for any womanly faculty . . . which has an appetite for exact facts." Yet she loves her husband profoundly, and is deeply troubled by his growing indifference.

Cardew, himself an "ultra-evangelical" theologian in his youth, has a creed that is dangerous for him. "Always prone to self-absorption," he finds this tendency accentuated by his religion. Love for Catherine sweeps this introspective man off his feet. In her he finds a woman who understands not only St. Paul and Milton but an extraordinary short story which he himself has written—and which "Mark Rutherford" reproduces—about a Greek named Charmides living in Rome about 300 A.D. who is converted to Christianity. Charmides cannot, however, accept miracle. The Christians' "fantastic delusions, their expectations that any day the sky might open and their Saviour appear in the body, were impossible to him; nor could he share their confidence that once and for all their religion alone was capable of regenerating the world." Charmides is nonetheless convinced that there is more certainty in Christianity "than was to be found in anything at that time current in the world. Here, in what Paul called faith, was a new spring of action. . . ." Yet "even in those moments when he was nearest to a confession of discipleship he was restrained by faintness and doubt." His decision to become a Christian is precipitated by his love for a beautiful Christian girl, and by his determination to die with her. They are executed together, but "Charmides was never considered a martyr by the Church. The circumstances were doubtful, and it was not altogether clear that he deserved the celestial crown."

The nineteenth-century parable hidden in the little historical tale is clear enough. Was Charmides "justified" by faith of this sort even if he died for it? As with Marius, the circumstances are indeed doubtful, and so are those of the love for Catherine that "literally possessed" Cardew. At a riverside meeting between the two, things hang in the balance: "it was a perilous moment; one touch, a hair's breadth of oscillation, and the two would have been one." But—at the sound of a note of thunder, as decisive as the thunder and lightning in *Miriam's Schooling*—Catherine breaks off the interview with a word of fervent praise for Mrs. Cardew and her "brains for scientific subjects." No word of love is ever spoken.

Catherine Furze is by nature a true Puritan born out of her time: "Had Catherine been born two hundred years earlier, life would have been easy. All that was in her would have found expression in the faith of her ancestors, large enough for any heart or any intellect at that time. She would have been happy in the possession of a key which unlocks the mystery of things, and there would have been ample room for emotion." But Bunyan's days are over: nowadays "each man is left to shift for himself, to work out the answers to his own problems," and "the result is isolation." As a woman of the early nineteenth century (the story is set in the 1840's), Catherine is isolated. With much irony, Rutherford admits that she would have been more fortunate had she been born later: there was as yet no "new education . . . no elaborate system of needle-points, Roman and Greek history, plane and spherical geometry, political economy, ethics, literature, chemistry, conic sections, music, English history, and mental philosophy to draw off the electricity within her. . . ." But caught where she is, her isolation leads her eventually to death. And on her deathbed, Cardew says to her, "*You have saved me*," to which she can only reply, "*You* have saved *me*." As with Miriam, Puritanism has failed Catherine.

Catherine Furze's sacrifice is repeated even more dramatically if possible in Hale White's last and finest novel, *Clara Hopgood* (1896, no. 65), so casual and seemingly offhand in the telling that it has sometimes misled the critics. Doubt in the formal sense—rather than the mere loss by Puritanism of its power to give security, which brought so much misery upon Miriam Tacchi and Catherine Furze—now takes center stage once more. Once again deliberately set in 1844 and the years immediately afterwards, when freethought was a far greater rarity than in the time when Mark Rutherford and M'Kay walked the London streets some years later, *Clara Hopgood* introduces a most extraordinary family. Mr. Hopgood, bank manager in Fenmarket, an East Anglican town, has "never been particularly in earnest about religion," a simple indifference about which we hear no more. His wife is a believer, but neither High nor Low Church, rather "inclined towards a kind of quietism not uncommon in the Church of England, even during its bad time [presumably the eighteenth century], a reaction against the formalism which generally prevailed." She seldom goes to church, although she grows more devout personally with advancing years: she explains this by saying that she is too restless, not admitting that the church is "horribly dead." She is disinclined to criticize her husband's freedom, while he has a high regard for her faith.

They educate their daughters, Clara and Madge, in an equally distinctive way: both girls go to Germany, to Weimar, where they move in pleasant society, hear good music, study literature, talk about Strauss's *Life of Jesus*, and learn to think for themselves. Before going abroad, Madge does spend one year at an Evangelical girls' boarding school in England, where her anomalous religious position causes consternation. When Selina, her Evangelical roommate, daughter of a City merchant who lives in Clapham, learns that Madge has never been christened, she half believes that "something dreadful might happen if she should by any chance touch unbaptized naked flesh." Is Madge perhaps a Dissenter? Dissenters are of course "to be pitied and perhaps even to be condemned," but some of them may be "among the redeemed," and some are among Selina's parents' friends. But no: Madge has not been "immersed" any more than she has been sprinkled. Is she then perhaps a Jew or a heathen, in which case Selina might convert her? Especially had Madge been a Catholic, Selina would have begun by pointing out how absurd was her idolatrous behavior. But no: Madge's father is "nothing." True: Madge does say the Lord's Prayer on rising and at bedtime, but she adds to it "no petitions of her own"; such people were "formalists, and it was always suspected that they had not received the true enlightenment from above." In the end, Madge has to leave the school, but enjoys her expulsion as a joke. Indeed, Hale White has made rare comedy of it.

The Hopgoods go on being not quite like anyone else in fiction. Having engaged herself to marry a suitable young man, who is deeply in love with her, and whom she thinks she loves, Madge breaks the engagement *after* she knows herself to be pregnant by him—she gives herself to him during one of Hale White's crucial thunderstorms. But she is sure she does not really love him: he does not appreciate her sensitivity in poetry; and her mother and sister

(Mr. Hopgood has died) accept the disgrace and the forced departure from Fenmarket for London. For Madge, there is none of the comfort that she would have derived from religion had she been a Christian:

> Had she believed in the common creed, her attention would have been concentrated on the salvation of her own soul; she would have found her Redeemer and would have been comparatively at peace. She would have acknowledged herself convicted of infinite sin, and hell would have opened before her, but above the sin and the hell she would have seen the distinct image of the Mediator abolishing both. Popular theology makes personal salvation of such immense importance that, in comparison therewith, we lose sight of the consequences to others of our misdeeds. The sense of cruel injustice to those who loved her remained with Madge perpetually.

Madge, then, the unbeliever, emerges as a braver and more tender woman perforce than a Christian woman in the same situation: she lacks the consolation of faith, and so she feels even more keenly the trouble she has brought on others: on her mother and sister above all, but on her jilted suitor as well.

In their new circumstances in London (their mother shortly dies and leaves them alone), Clara and Madge encounter several workingmen who are active Chartists, and who discuss radicalism and religion with them. Some of the people who address their Chartist meetings are clearly identifiable as real persons behind the fictional names that Hale White has given them. His "Frederick Dennis," the wood engraver, is W. J. Linton, the radical artist, who was briefly and unhappily Eliza Lynn's husband, while "Henry Vincent," who winds up his speeches to the Chartists with scraps of poetry, is Charles Kingsley, who on a famous occasion had declared himself to be a "Clergyman of the Church of England . . . and a Socialist." "I know what Vincent's little game is," says one of the Hopgoods' friends, "and it is the same game with all the rest. They want to keep Chartism religious, but we shall see. Let us once get the six points [of the Charter] and the Established Church will go, and we shall have secular education, and in a generation there will be not one superstition left."

But Clara, a hard-headed girl, thinks Utopia is not just around the corner: "I do lose a little patience," she says, "when I hear it preached to every poor conceited creature who goes to your Sunday evening atheist lecture that he is to believe nothing on one particular subject which his precious intellect cannot verify, and the next morning he finds it to be his duty to swallow wholesale anything you please to put into his mouth." Soon, she predicts, "the tyranny of the majority may be more dangerous than any ecclesiastical establishment that ever existed." Although written half a century after the events it is supposed to be describing, *Clara Hopgood* rings true to life as the expression of the views of two remarkable young women of the forties brought up without religion. Like the freethinkers of Mark Rutherford, the atheists at large among the Chartists only want to prove to the poor that "there was never no Abraham and no Isaac, and that Jonah was never in a whale's belly," and this is as little satisfactory as Christian doctrine itself.

A. J. Scott, Maurice's disciple and George MacDonald's honored elder friend, appears briefly in the pages of *Clara Hopgood* under his own name: he has been a friend of the girls' father and is a friend of Baruch Cohen, the skilled workman and half-Jewish bibliophile who is at first Clara's suitor, but whom she refuses in the quiet act of self-sacrifice that forms the mainspring of the novel's plot, and on which the critics have naturally focussed their attention. Clara and Madge sometimes hear Scott lecture, but Hale White says nothing about what they hear him say or about its impact upon them: it is rather as if Scott's name were being dropped as an act of piety toward one of the most inspirational and courageous radical Broad-Church thinkers of the Victorian age. Madge and one of her friends occasionally go to the Catholic chapel to hear a Mozart mass. Like so many others in real life as in fiction (for example, Emmy Berners at sixteen and her fashionable friends in Charlotte Yonge's *Castle-Builders* [1854, no. 24]), it is primarily the Catholics' music, so much finer than anything the Church of England—let alone the Dissenters—could offer, that attracts Madge. But Clara also suspects that possibly Madge is somewhat drawn toward the Catholic faith itself. As for Clara herself, rationalist and clear thinker that she is, she is

> not disposed to be a convert. Once for all, Catholicism is incredible, and that is sufficient, but there is much in its ritual which suits me. There is no such intrusion of the person of the minister as there is in the Church of England, and still worse among the dissenters. In the Catholic service, the priest is nothing; it is his office which is everything; he is a mere means of communication. The mass, in so far as it proclaims that miracle is not dead, is also very impressive to me.

With all her training and her powerful intellect, Clara has obviously reached a position similar to that bluntly stated by a poorly educated Chartist friend of hers, "if you must chuck your reason overboard, you may just as well be Catholic as Protestant." And it is arresting to hear Clara—wholly without religion as she is—echoing the powerfully argued views of the starchiest and most vociferous of Anglicans, William Sewell (in *Hawkstone* [1845, no. 2]), that the less a clergyman intrudes his personality into his service, the better: he is a messenger with a message to deliver and should simply deliver it clearly. As Clara puts it, "the priest is a mere means of communication." Here the views of two authors—Hale White and Sewell—worlds apart in social and religious outlook, converge in an interesting and revealing way. For a sensitive, refined, reflective, and intellectual nature schooled in disbelief, the paradox is that the form of religion most likely to be effective or appealing is the Catholic, which dispenses with argument, in which the divine speaks with authority through an intermediary messenger, which proclaims—without discussion—in the ceremony of the Mass that miracle is not dead.

On the Victorian scene the Hopgood sisters are exceptional because they are eighteenth-century people deliberately recreated in the nineteenth by the mode of education chosen for them. Weimar, still redolent of Goethe, was indeed by the English standards of the 1840's subversive. Dimly perceived by Mrs. Tubbs, the Fenmarket brewer's wife, as "injudicious and morally wrong," the Hopgoods' decision to send their daughters there makes the young women forever out of place in England. They are at once behind their times by virtue of their continental culture and eighteenth-century rationalist viewpoint, and ahead of their times by virtue of their early exposure not only to their father's religious indifference (rather than active scepticism) but also to Strauss in his German home, just after he had published the *Life of Jesus* and long before it became generally known in England. The girls have had nothing in their upbringing to revolt against: all society is out of step except for them. Hale White, who did not invent characters, must have known the Hopgoods, and he surely rendered them immortal.

Mrs. Lynn Linton and Christ as a Communist

Perhaps the Hopgood sisters' nearest analogue in real life was the novelist Eliza Lynn Linton (1822-1898). Far less reticent, far more militant, and brought up altogether differently, she nonetheless arrived at a very similar religious position. At the age of sixty-three, she wrote her autobiography in the form of a novel. She switched the sex of the protagonist, however, and told her story as *The Autobiography of Christopher Kirkland* (1885, no. 80). The transformation of Eliza into Christopher sometimes creates a problem for the reader: were the various women, for example, whom Christopher Kirkland is represented as loving, actually men whom Eliza Lynn had loved? Or—since she had a masculine character and Lesbian tendencies—were they really women all along, whose original sex could be preserved in the novel since it was appropriate to have them loved by a man? It is not always possible to answer, and in some instances it may not be very important: Mrs. Dalrymple, the mystical inspiration of Kirkland's late adolescence, or Althea Cartwright, the heartless vamp of his youth, or even Cordelia Gilchrist, the woman whom he cannot marry despite their love because she is a Catholic, may perhaps in real life have been either women or men, although one is inclined to think that they were women all along.

But "Esther Lambert," the woman Christopher marries, is just as surely a portrait of Eliza Lynn's husband, W. J. Linton (the Frederick Dennis of Hale White's *Clara Hopgood*) with his sex changed to female, as Christopher Kirkland is Eliza Lynn herself with her sex changed to male. The account of the beautiful and neglected "Lambert" children whom "Christopher" loves, and of their dying "father" bequeathing them to "Christopher," who then marries their hopelessly impractical radical feminist lecturing "mother," is historically true if one changes the sex of all three adults concerned. W. J. Linton's wife did bequeath her children to Eliza Lynn, who married Linton "with more sense of duty than of attraction." "Our roles," writes Christopher Kirkland, "were inverted from the beginning and I had to be man and woman both." This was indeed true of Eliza Lynn, but in her novel she inverted the inversion. Besides this detailed account of a celebrated marriage and separation, *Christopher Kirkland* contains an extraordinary gallery of Victorian portraits: Landor, the Brownings, George Eliot, Lewes, Thornton Hunt, John Chapman, and dozens more, sometimes introduced by name, sometimes anonymously or under pseudonyms. The book gives an unparalleled view of radical social, political, and intellectual circles in the forties and fifties. Less a novel than a reservoir of gossip—agreeable and disagreeable—often thrown together hastily, it is an interesting (and neglected) book. It is upon the protagonist's religious development that we concentrate here, usually calling her Eliza Lynn rather than Christopher Kirkland.

Born and brought up in a remote Lake Country parsonage, in a region where eighteenth-century attitudes and conditions still prevailed, Eliza is the youngest of a large family born to the parson, who is soon widowed. Himself the son of an autocratic and lordly bishop, her father is indolent, learned, and fierce tempered, agonizingly aware of his own sins, and praying and weeping aloud late at night to ask for their forgiveness. Towards his children he displays a strange mixture of affection and brutality, neglecting their education, refusing to discuss their problems with them rationally, and taking an especial dislike—so she says—to Eliza (Christopher). The elder children tyrannize over the younger, and Eliza suffers the most as a result: "teased and bullied until I became as furious as a small wild beast," and then flogged for being furious. Not even the small scope of the family library and the indifference of the rector, however, can blunt Eliza's zeal for knowledge; she teaches herself French, Italian, German, Spanish, Latin, and some Greek, but naturally neglects grammar and focusses on learning how to read.

She bitterly resents her father's failure to provide instructors for her or send her to school (her brothers suffer equally), but at seventeen she is nonetheless still a devout Christian, indeed an ascetic, who, if she had been a Catholic, would have entered "some severe disciplinary order. My whole inner life was one of intense religious realization. God was far off, the paternal King and inexorable Judge of all, and His 'unlidded eye' ever watched me with awful attention." Such a state of mind is of course far more natural for the daughter of an authoritarian, religious, neglectful father than for a son. What is hard to believe of Christopher is easy enough to believe of Eliza. Her "effort after godliness," with all the "spiritual endeavour and frustration" it involves, only irritates her father, who testily urges her to leave superior piety alone and content herself with conformity. An Evangelical curate—in charge of one of "Mr. Kirkland's" parishes in his absence—causes him much difficulty; yet he dislikes the Tractarians also. He is "High and Dry." And, while he is a High Tory in politics, his daughter—full of *Sturm und Drang*—is already a Republican and a Chartist (one day she even fraternizes with some local Chartists who come to attack the Rectory in her father's absence), sympathizing with O'Connell and the cause of Irish freedom, hailing the French Revolution and all the European national struggles for freedom from the Turks or the Russians.

The arrival in a neighboring parish of a new rector, F. W. Myers (called Henry Grahame in the novel), an admirer of Coleridge and a pupil of Maurice, gives Eliza her first opportunity to read Coleridge, Wordsworth, and Carlyle. But Myers feels utterly convinced of the eternal truth of all the teachings he has accepted, and he treats with scorn any doubting questions put to him. He regards Mr. Kirkland as "arid, unenlightened, fossilized," while Mr. Kirkland regards him as "unsound, fanciful, unreal." Passing through a "mysterious" and "weird" period of deep interest in alchemy, astrology, Rosicrucianism, mesmerism, ghosts, and the like, and reading and rereading classical mythology, Eliza suddenly finds herself asking the question: what difference is there between classical stories of virgin births and the Bible, "between the women made mothers by mysterious influences and those made mothers by divine favour?"—again a far more natural preoccupation for the genuine female Eliza than for the hypothetical male Christopher.

The idea itself strikes her almost like a lightning bolt. And the mystery of the incarnation now seems "a matter of perplexity and doubt . . . no longer exceptional and divine, it had become historic and human." It all boils down to the question: was the Virgin Mary's word as to what had happened any more reliable than that "of the Greek girl who told how she had met the god in the reeds by the river side?" And while puzzling over the question of whether God had indeed ever become man, Eliza has a night vision, a revelation:

> Then, as vividly as if I had seen Him in the body and spoken with Him face to face, I saw Christ as a peasant translated to our own time. I realized the minutest circumstances of His humanity; when a loud voice, like the rushing wind, seemed to echo from earth to sky—to fill all space and to command all time, till I was conscious of nothing but these words: "Man—not God; man—not God."

For an adolescent girl in the rebellious state of mind of Eliza Lynn, this is in its way a conversion fully as decisive as any of those experienced by Evangelical or Dissenting youths. Discovering her in a "state of spiritual anguish and confusion," her father seals the experience by harshness and by a refusal to kiss her.

Thereafter, the questions and doubts only multiply: what really *was* the relationship between God and Christ? why was Christ not born earlier? All that Myers can say is that the question is beyond reason, beyond comprehension, and that it is wrong to compare the Christian story to "the absurd legends of a rude people in a rude age." Eliza (Christopher Kirkland) is now set firmly on the path towards freethinking. The details of her self-questioning are all in the novel, interspersed with her other experiences of life. Myers's eclecticism, Maurice's books, which he loans to Eliza, cannot remove her doubts. Nor does it help—when she wonders why Christ did not impart the truths of science to his contemporaries—for Myers to reiterate simply that "His kingdom is not of this world."

She is now a monotheist, a Unitarian believing in the "divine life in man," but not as "incorporate Godhead," simply as "inspiration." Hell and the devil now are subject to doubt, like the Incarnation and the Atonement.

A hopeless adolescent love affair is followed by Eliza's departure for London, and by life in the big city as a journalist and novelist. But before she goes, a new book, *Vestiges of the Natural History of Creation* (1844, anonymous, but by the Scotch journalist and publisher, Robert Chambers)—a misguided and ignorant effort to interpret scientific advance, embarrassing the scientists, but enormously popular and highly misleading—has reached the parsonage and become "a priceless treasure" to her, and "a deadly and diabolical sin" to her father. Thereafter, her London friends include atheists; socialists; believers that living beings are but "a fortuitous concourse of atoms"; enemies of capital punishment favoring the rehabilitation of criminals; pacifists interested in the "foundation of a quasi-masonic community—a kind of cryptic church of free-thought"; intimates of European revolutionaries (Mazzini, Louis Blanc, Kossuth); dabblers in phrenology, mesmerism, clairvoyance, herbalism, and Daniel Dunglas Hume's spiritualist seances; Voltaireans; Swedenborgians; and believers in metempsychosis.

She also encounters many feminists, including "the most pronounced of the man-haters and woman-defenders of her time," for whom "sex determined everything. To be a man was to be a monster, to be a woman was to be probably a saint and certainly a victim." Again, how much better one understands the novel, and all of "Christopher's" subsequent associations with the feminists, if one realizes that "Christopher" is really Eliza! Rather shamefacedly, she admits that she can never agree wholeheartedly with the militant feminists, since so many of them are physically unattractive. Experience of life in Paris teaches her much about marriage: in France, "adultery is condoned because divorce is impossible." In England, she has learned, for many reasons "post-nuptial dissatisfaction is fatally common," and divorce by mutual consent, she argues, ought to be easy.

One woman friend advocates suicide as a natural step, with moral and social value, and later commits it herself; many engage in free love, some with discipline, others without. Eliza's moral absolutes dissolve as her theology had done: "the sanctity of marriage was effaced in favour of the imperialism of love"; hedonism takes over, as duty becomes "a superstition, and pleasure the final cause and great end of existence." Her new acquaintances "made morality discretionary and not compulsory; and changed the granite stability of right and wrong into a nebulous kind of individualism where all was convertible according to convenience." She is in the heart of London intellectual radicalism and freethought. Even Wordsworthian Pantheism, once so daring, now is laughed to scorn: "I cannot for the life of me find God in a stagnant horse-pond," says one intimate of Eliza's (Christopher's), who also finds it positively blasphemous to "believe that this world, with all its pain and misery . . . is the deliberate work of an Omnipotent and Omniscient Deity." It is all as if Eliza were a mediaeval student dabbling in the Black Arts, "peeping into forbidden places and listening to forbidden sounds."

Despite the rejection of formal religion, contemporary religious controversy continues to play a part in Eliza's life. For example, in 1847-1848 when the interminable "Gorham case" began—in which the dictatorial Tractarian Bishop of Exeter pitted himself against an Evangelical clergyman in his diocese (who had advertised for a curate "free of Tractarian error," and whose views on baptismal regeneration were suspect)—all the London freethinkers, Eliza's friends ("who cared nothing about the intrinsic merits of the question"), sided with Gorham. "It was easy," writes Eliza, "to foresee the tyranny of the High Church should it ever have supreme power." Although "men suffer individually from the moral grip of the Low Church ministers," this is "more congregational than organic," and can be shaken off. Yet Eliza's real view is that both factions are loathsome: the "profoundly abhorrent" Evangelicals have such "constricted human sympathies," hate science so bitterly, and so superstitiously adhere to every word of the Bible that they are condemned as sanctimonious and repulsive. Her anecdotes of her experience with Low Churchmen amply explain her views of them.

Despite the bewildering impact of her freethinking friends' views, Eliza clings to a belief in divine providence, in man's soul, in goodness, in the perfectibility of man and the rapid advance of society towards that perfection, in the sweeping away of hell, and in a God "neither Christian, nor Jewish, neither Mohammedan nor Brahmin, but everywhere, in all beliefs, in all heroic deeds, in all faithful effort. . . ." She is a "fervent Deist and by no means an ethical latitudinarian; though . . . so far a hedonist . . . that I thought happiness a human good, and pain and misery evils." A love affair with a Catholic girl cannot make "Christopher" accept the Divine Incarnation or become a Christian of any denomination, which would enable the two to be married. He cannot believe and he cannot lie. And "Christopher" admits that he has "a strange feeling of tenderness for the Roman Catholic ritual," for incense, for the mass, for the cross. "Hating the system with the whole force of my intellect, I love the worship with . . . idealization of sentiment." So—like her fellow freethinkers the Hopgood sisters—Eliza Lynn admits a paradoxical, lingering admiration for the form of creed ostensibly most remote from her own doubting position.

After the break-up of the marriage to Linton ("Esther"), when Eliza ("Christopher") joins a Unitarian congregation, as "the nearest approach to Truth," she finds "a limitation of inquiry and a dogmatism of unproved assertion." Sir Charles Lyell, the great geologist, is a regular member of the congregation, but—though his presence is reassuring—it is not enough. Depressed, without even a vestige of faith left, Eliza is contemplating suicide, when science enters her life. She discusses in some detail its impact on her self-tutored and not very discriminating mind. She finds it exciting to be alive at a moment when the human intellect is being "emancipated from superstition" and the scientific method substituted for the theological. "Everywhere was a shaking of the dry bones and the clothing of flesh and sinew on what had been dead and useless fragments buried in the earth." The 1860's were to Eliza Lynn Linton as a rejuvenating breath. Eventually, she "confesses only the truths of science."

Repetitious, often verbose, sometimes apparently inconsistent, hastily thrown together, *The Autobiography of Christopher Kirkland* is nonetheless an unmistakably authentic account of one Victorian woman's spiritual travails. Long before she wrote it, as was natural, she put her views into her many other novels. Thus, in *Under Which Lord?* (1879, no. 35), we remember, she drew the portrait of a sinister Tractarian parish priest. It was, however, in the short, eloquent, and still astonishing novel *The True History of Joshua Davidson* (1872, no. 72) that Eliza Lynn Linton concentrated and transmuted into fiction, even allegory, the full force of the religious convictions whose gradual development she describes in *Christopher Kirkland.*

Joshua Davidson is Jesus (the same name as Joshua), son or descendant of David. So we are dealing with the life of a contemporary Christ. In its first edition, the book's full title was *The True History of Joshua Davidson, Communist.* The publishers then bethought themselves, so they said, of the mistaken impression that the title might have created: it was, they decided, "in a measure unfair to the book" because it was not until "well advanced in his career that [Joshua] became convinced that in following the teachings and example of Christ, he was a practical Communist, and then avowed himself as such." So for the second edition they made "a slight alteration in the title page," and now called the book *The Life of Joshua Davidson; or the Modern Imitation of Christ: a Theoretical Novel,* substituting the reassuring reference to Thomas à Kempis, abandoning the incendiary and alarming word "Communist," and soothing the potential reader by the assurance that the novel was actually theoretical anyhow. One doubts if the fiery Eliza Lynn Linton would have approved of such pussyfooting. Her views were radical, and her novel had been intended as propaganda.

A Cornish carpenter boy, Joshua early crosses swords with the overbearing vicar, who, as a rich man, believes that the poor should know their place and the ignorant should not ask questions. Joshua tries to follow exactly the Christian life as set forth in the Gospels: yet his faith cannot move mountains, and when he takes up a serpent it stings him. The laws of Nature being supreme, then, Christ's words must be in large part a parable, and we should "carry on the work in His spirit but in our own way." After a vision in which he sees Church and Society persecuting Truth, Science, Freedom, and Humanity, Joshua goes to London. He finds most of his fellow workmen infidels, although some are Unitarians ("which gave them the most religion with the least dogma of all the sects"). Usually, however, "religion . . . had followed the class antagonism of the artisan." Joshua works with a devoted "Ritualist City priest" called "the Superior," but cannot accept "the largeness of their assertions, the smallness of their proofs. . . . their devotion to the Church rather than to Christianity at large," and their emphasis on the divinity rather than the humanity of Christ. Still less can Joshua abide the Evangelicals, among whom "each man is an independent pope and quite as bigoted as the real one." Already Joshua feels that if he is to accept the authority of any church, it must be the Catholic. "If the keys of life and death are held by a governing body, they are surely held within the Vatican," says Joshua, asking by what authority the Church of England can claim the right to shut off private inquiry.

For Joshua no sect will do: only "the wide creed of Universalism." He studies science. He soon announces that "the sole meaning of Christ . . . is Humanity." The man Jesus "left the social question where he found it . . . His mind not being ripe to accept the idea of a radical revolution, and His hands not strong enough to accomplish it." Joshua must carry on the work of Christianity in the form of a revolution which will destroy caste, poverty, and ignorance: "society is elastic . . . no social arrangements are final . . . morals are only experimental . . . no laws are divine." Christianity is no longer a creed but an organization: "It is Communism." He begins to have meetings for the poor, where he discusses science with them and "a few homely truths in the way of cleanliness, health, good cooking," winding up with a few simple prayers and an attempt to make his hearers "feel the Presence and the Power of God." So far, he is like Mark Rutherford and M'Kay in their Drury Lane headquarters.

Living in the most wretched of slums, Joshua and his friend and biographer—John, the Beloved Disciple—take in a prostitute (the Magdalen), who nurses Joshua when he is ill, and a hardened criminal, a burglar. Joshua and John lose their jobs for consorting with bad company. His followers, a few "enthusiasts set out to realise Christ," rally round to support them. But even the charitable regard Joshua as hopelessly impractical. He becomes an early member of the International Working Men's Association, but without any "dream of barricades and high places taken by assault," opposing any form of social warfare, and favoring "class advancement by peaceable and noble efforts, not . . . universal destruction by violent or ignoble ones." A staunch Republican, Joshua is a gradualist here also. Soon his fellow members of "a little inner and anonymous society which some few of us had formed" suspect him of treachery. But Joshua is saved by Félix Pyat, the French radical then in exile in England, who speaks out for him. Working-class solidarity, "the lawfulness and desirability of trades' unions and strikes": these are the things that Joshua favors in his "religion of politics," a relatively mild program even for the early 1870's.

But when Joshua insists on going to Paris to participate in the Commune, Mrs. Lynn Linton's enthusiasm sweeps her away. Probably she still was not aware of the Communards' excesses (the novel appeared within a year of their suppression). To call the Communards "Christ-men" who swept Paris wholly clear of crime, to say that the "artisan government of '71" had a "brief but noble record," is to display an indiscriminate enthusiasm which renders *Joshua Davidson* far less effective than it might have been if the protagonist had never gone to the Continent. In England, after his escape from Paris, he meets the martyrdom that had always awaited him. In her girlhood, Eliza Lynn had had the great moment of conversion, when she had a vision of Christ as Man alone, not as God. Later she put that vision into the form of this novel: if Christ the man—Jesus the descendant of David—were to return to the England of the mid-Victorians, he would, she argued, become a Communist and would be killed for his efforts on behalf of humanity.

The Hopgood sisters, then, were a pure case. Never having had a faith, they had no need to undergo a disillusionment. Eliza Lynn (Christopher Kirkland) and Joshua Davidson, by contrast, experienced a revelation and had a conversion that was really a deconversion. It took them from Anglicanism into disbelief (in the Incarnation, the Atonement, Hell and the Devil), but not all the way to unbelief. While the Hopgoods never needed God at all, Eliza Lynn passed from Anglicanism through doubt to Deism, Unitarianism, Pantheism and "Communism," yet never reached the stage of being "nothing" where the Hopgoods began and ended. Moreover, because they lost their money and because of Madge's illegitimate child, the Hopgoods were declassed and found themselves living among, fraternizing with—and even marrying—members of the working class, among whom freethought and revolutionary ideas were a commonplace. Eliza Lynn never left the middle classes; no matter how freethinking or radical her London friends, they were always members of the middle classes who wanted in varying degrees to do the working classes good, never actual workers.

Recent scholarship has taught us much about G. J. Holyoake, Charles Bradlaugh, and other militant leaders of the Atheist movement, who tried after the failures of Chartism to capitalize upon the social and economic unrest of the working classes and lead them into political and secularist collaboration with the middle-class radicals of the salons frequented by "Christopher Kirkland." Not yet revolutionary socialists—or at least revolutionary only to the degree that Joshua Davidson was revolutionary—the leadership never fully succeeded in closing the gap between the classes. The working-class atheists continued to prefer the street-corner freethinking orators of the sort Mark Rutherford heard, with their denunciations of the Bible—or their quotations from Tom Paine—to middle-class high-mindedness and intellectuality. Eliza Lynn Linton had to imagine working-class life in order to create Joshua Davidson and his associates. And this—quite apart from the fact that she was a far lesser artist than William Hale White—renders her latter-day Christ, though earnestly imagined, a far less convincing figure than White's Marshall the Chartist or Baruch Cohen in *Clara Hopgood.*

CHAPTER 7.

"SPIRITUAL AGONIZING BELLYACHES"

J. A. Froude and Geraldine Jewsbury

In 1847, when agitation for the Charter was reaching its peak, when the Hopgood sisters were living alone in London, and when Eliza Lynn had plunged into the kaleidoscopic world of metropolitan radicalism and free thought, there appeared a little volume called *Shadows of the Clouds* (no. 68), under the pseudonym of "Zeta." It consisted of two short pieces of fiction. The first, "The Lieutenant's Daughter," told in a series of visions seen in a fit of delirious fever, recounts the seduction and descent into prostitution of the orphan daughter of a naval officer. Extraordinary for its description of a brothel and of the mechanisms whereby innocent women were entrapped ("Lord William offers two hundred pounds . . . if it's quite fresh"), "The Lieutenant's Daughter" does not deal directly with religious problems. The longer story, "The Spirit's Trials," however, does. Overwritten and full of exaggerated sentimental apostrophes, it is nevertheless deeply interesting to the modern reader. "Zeta" was James Anthony Froude (1818-1894), a deacon of the Church of England, Fellow of Exeter College, Oxford, youngest brother of Newman's close friend and colleague, R. Hurrell Froude (1803-1834), and like Hurrell, of course, the son of the Archdeacon of Totnes. Later in life he was to be the brother-in-law of Charles Kingsley, the intimate and biographer of Thomas Carlyle, and a notable historian.

"The Spirit's Trials" tells the lugubrious story of Edward Fowler, youngest of a family of eight, now motherless, pushed ahead as an academic prodigy by his father, Canon Fowler, and sent too young to Westminster School, where he is brutally bullied (the older boys hold lighted cigars to his face when he is in bed at night), and so driven into a malignant case of schoolboy misery, exacerbated by his father's indifference and partiality for whipping his son. It is not an unfamiliar nineteenth-century English story, but the details are more horrifying and presented in a more dramatic way than usual. Fowler wholly lacks physical courage, which only leads the bullies at school and home to further excess. Yet he eventually emerges into a successful Oxford career: popularity with his peers replaces inferiority towards his elders. While an undergraduate, he becomes engaged to Emma Hardinge, daughter of a clergyman who has brought up his own large family on precisely the opposite principles from those of Canon Fowler. The Hardinges are allowed "to do almost anything they pleased that was not wrong," free from restraints "imposed for their own sake as a discipline of obedience." Canon Fowler reluctantly consents to the engagement, but it is broken off suddenly when Edward is discovered to have run up debts at the University.

Both the young people are miserable. As for Edward, "Why should he care any more for good? What had good cared for him? What was his life but wretchedness?" He thinks of suicide, tries dissipation, is redeemed by the disgrace of being "sent down," and resumes his studies. Beset by two suitors, one of whom, her father's friend, is a sexless clergyman, splendid in the pulpit but awkward with women ("Theology makes bad lovers"), Emma eventually marries the other. Some years later, Fowler, smitten by consumption, depressed at the conviction that he must die without leaving any positive accomplishment behind him, his projects unfinished or failures, has come to believe that the delinquencies of his earlier years are forgiveable as a mere bungling start in life, and that "human nature can never take pleasure in evil. Its worst alternatives are bewildered seekings after what is considered good." His melancholy is somewhat dissipated when he saves the child of his beloved Emma from drowning, and he is enabled to die a lingering death amidst the adoration—somewhat too passionate—of his former sweetheart, the gratitude of her husband, and the affection of her son, with whom he engages in much conversation about the life after death.

The entire last quarter of the narrative consists of Fowler's reflections as he contemplates his imminent death. Detached from his past human affections, he believes that God "has all goodness and all power"; he is reconciled to his fate, acknowledges his past delinquencies, and is prepared to suffer for them hereafter if necessary: the very infliction of God's punishment will be good for him. *He cannot, however, believe in the eternity of punishment*, since this would bring no lesson with it and, in fact, not even the worst sinner really deserves it. His "composure was unnatural" and his state of mind quite different from the usual Christian's fear of death. In all this there seems to be nothing that would have disturbed a Broad Churchman. Yet the narrator of the story and Emma's husband, both clergymen, are full of misgivings about their dying friend's state of mind, and from their point of view they are right. Fowler writes an impassioned defense of Newman and attacks Newman's enemies.

Newman, it appears, had personally given Fowler comfort in his darkest hour: "he told me my sins, and wept for me. . . . he was the truest and best friend the Church of England had . . . and she has spurned him from her, and set the seal on her own hollowness. . . . To be sure, she is lenient enough on the other side. All her members have to guard against is, believing too much. They may believe as little as they please." For Fowler, belief in God and belief in duty are now the only needful beliefs for a Christian: "I cannot find that the number of articles you introduce . . . produce any corresponding effect upon character, or that the Socinian [Unitarian] leads a less virtuous life than the Anglo-Catholic." It is unnecessary even to believe in the inspiration of the Bible. Fowler loves, honors, and learns from both Newman *and* Carlyle. When people who fear a revival of Catholic tyranny denounce Newman publicly, they only help bring about the troubles that they fear. A system which ostracizes Newman or Thomas Arnold, at the opposite pole within the Church, should be abandoned.

Luther's effort to influence by popular clamor "what should have been left to the thinkers" was a terrible mistake. This "wretched enemy of all that is bright, and noble, and chivalrous; this water bucket, this miserable negative Anglo-Protestantism is playing the same foolish part over again with none of old Martin's heroic daring. . . . But it is weighed in the balance and found wanting. Its kingdom is divided, and thank God its days are numbered."

Here are doubts indeed. They are perhaps somewhat diluted by the avidity with which Fowler receives the sacrament on his deathbed—even Guy Morville was not more eager for it. In a dying act, he joins Emma's hand with that of her husband once more in a kind of symbolic remarriage. The final long-delayed departure takes place on Easter morning as Fowler's friend reads aloud at his request a turgid passage from Jean Paul Richter (1763-1825) on peace in death. External nature cooperates, as the sun, the sea, the bells of Easter, all repeat the stage effects of Jean Paul's prose. The essays that Fowler leaves behind confirm the fact that he had indeed had a faith, but not "the faith popular at the present day." Beyond God and God's providence everything was "shifting cloud." All the world's religions alike seemed to him partly true and partly untrue. And the narrator ends with excerpts from two of Fowler's letters, of which more in a moment.

The entire story is autobiographical. Fowler is Froude, Canon Fowler the archdeacon. The horrors of school and home life are recollected exactly as they had been. The archdeacon, whom the eldest son, the charming self-confident Hurrell, so deeply revered, was a proper object of loathing to the youngest, the diffident, timorous James Anthony. The pious Hurrell as a young man had amused himself by holding his little brother upside down by his heels with his head under a flowing stream, or by looking on approvingly as the archdeacon flogged the child. The fantasy of "The Spirit's Trials" was a natural result: how sorry my father will be when I'm dead! "Fowler's" unhappy love affair was genuine; but his tuberculosis, his rescue of the child, and all the rest of the narrative Froude invented for the purpose of imagining his own death, which gave him such an unparalleled opportunity for getting back at his father. How outraged the rigorous Anglican archdeacon would be to read his son's denunciation of "this miserable negative Anglo-Protestantism" and the prediction that its days were numbered, together with the account of James Anthony's own substitute faith, so latitudinarian that it indiscriminately embraced, and repudiated, Newman and Carlyle, Arnold, Jean Paul, and, indeed, all the formal religions of the world, clinging to God alone.

The two letters with which "Fowler's" story were ended are actual letters that Froude had written himself; so that it became even easier to penetrate the disguise of "Zeta"—thin enough in any case—and to identify the author of "The Spirit's Trials." In the first letter, written in 1843 to a friend who had reproached him in surprise for having contributed to Newman's *Lives of the Saints* (Froude had written the *Life* of St. Neot), Froude expressly disowns both Catholicism and Protestantism. He himself had been surprised that Newman, who well knew that he disbelieved in miracle, should have asked him to write a Saint's life. There *was*, he admitted, an element of hypocrisy about his accepting, yet most young clergymen were worse: "few things sicken me more than to hear fellows spiritualizing away in the pulpit, and prating of heaven and hell and every holy mystery, whose single preparation has been a course of Port wine and fornication." The second letter recounts a daytime vision or nightmare that Froude had experienced in the Magdalen College Chapel, where he felt himself a mere spectator of a beautiful scene in which he wished for no greater share. His eternal lot, he writes, with an undergraduate's humorless pomposity, was to be an outcast ("God have mercy on such as we"—as the Yale Whiffenpoof song says). Everywhere around him in the chapel Froude is conscious of sin and of profligacy, and at the end of the service he overhears "one surpliced figure" whispering to a girl "under a deep overhanging bonnet." It is an assignation.

No wonder the archdeacon tried to suppress *Shadows of the Clouds*. Full of self-pity, much of it justified, constantly aware of and troubled by sex—as "The Lieutenant's Daughter" also vividly makes clear—Froude, in "The Spirit's Trials," produced a psychological document of major interest despite its literary awkwardness. His ambivalence toward his faith lay deeply rooted in his childhood and boyhood history; and though he expressed his love for Newman, by whom he was clearly fascinated, in fact they did not know one another very well. There must have risen between them the memory of the ascetic Hurrell, the four volumes of whose *Remains* Newman had somewhat imprudently published in 1838 and 1839, almost a decade before James Anthony became "Zeta." High Anglicans (notably Professor Chadwick in his *Victorian Church*) still write harshly of Froude, but whatever Froude's faults as a human being or a would-be novelist, "The Spirit's Trials" remains a vitally important book, usually overlooked even by those who have studied its pendant, Froude's second novel, *The Nemesis of Faith* (1849, no. 68), written during the summer of 1848, a year after *The Shadows of the Clouds* was published.

Markham Sutherland, protagonist of *The Nemesis of Faith*, is just as much Froude as Edward Fowler. But Froude had now put behind him his need for revenge on his father, his schooldays, his self-hatred. Sutherland has a loving family, a kind father ("a more upright, excellent man never breathed," "not very clever," but with "a breadth of solid understanding"). His childhood—we learn far along in the novel—is a kind of idyll, with religion, until his tenth year, a matter of tender feeling; thereafter, improbably enough, he undergoes successively, and without explanation, first a period of firm Protestant indoctrination from ten to sixteen, and then one of Catholicizing. Presumably, this was intended to account for his latent suspicions of both tendencies. Moreover, his classical education proves, as he suggests it always must, a bad preparation for devout Christianity. How can one believe that the cultivated pagan ancients are somehow damned, while the cruder Christian writers are to be preferred? If one wishes to educate a Christian, one should "close up the literature of the world" and confine one's pupil to the reading of the Bible alone. At twenty-four, Sutherland is deeply hesitant to go into the Church, as his father would like him to do.

Not surprisingly, his doubt rests upon a foundation similar to that of Edward Fowler in "The Spirit's Trials." He cannot believe the Old Testament and accept its God as all-just, all-merciful, all-good. We really do not know who wrote the Old Testament or at what date. So the Bible as such is unacceptable. Moreover, he cannot accept the New Testament doctrine of eternal punishment: it too is inconsistent with an omniscient, omnipotent, all-loving God. He accepts "not *the Christian religion*, but *the religion of Christ*—the poor man's gospel; the message of forgiveness, of reconciliation, of love. . . ." Hindus, Muslims, have their holy books, which do "not differ from the Bible in kind," although it is "immeasurably the highest . . . not because it is the most divine but because it is the most human." Like other historic creeds, even paganism, Christianity seems to alter with history, and it is or will be subject to decline and decay as they have been. Moreover, Sutherland does not like the clergy: they are "fatally uninteresting," and all they care about is worldly advancement, despite their loud preaching to the contrary. Only one in fifty has any social conscience or cares for the poor enough "to make a home in those rivers of wretchedness that run below the surface of this modern society, asking nothing but to shed their lives, to pour one drop of sweetness into that bitter stream of injustice. . . ."

Yet when he is offered a living, Sutherland overcomes his reluctance, and pleases his father, and the family friend, the bishop, by taking it. He will follow an active life, having abandoned his speculations as fruitless: "regular activity alone," his uncle the dean advises him, can keep "soul or body from disease." On being ordained, Sutherland is admonished to avoid Puseyism at one extreme and German rationalism at the other: "Walk steadily in the position which our own admirable Church has so wisely chosen, equidistant between these two." Sutherland feels sick at the very thought of becoming an Anglican religious leader. So it is little wonder that within a year he finds himself in disgrace with his prosperous suburban parishioners for having imprudently denounced the Bible Society at a tea party:

> Considering all the heresies, the enormous crime, the astounding follies which the Bible has been made to justify, and which its indiscriminate reading has suggested; considering that it has been, indeed, the sword which our Lord said that he was sending; that not the Devil himself could have invented an implement more potent to fill the hated world with lies, and blood, and fury, I think, certainly, that to send hawkers over the world loaded with copies of this book, scattering it in all places among all persons—not teaching them to understand it; not standing, like Moses, between that heavenly light and them; but cramming it into their own hands as God's book, which He wrote and they are to read, each for himself, and learn what they can for themselves—is the most culpable folly of which it is possible for man to be guilty.

This resounding denunciation, echoing and expanding what "The Spirit's Trials" had only hinted were Froude's unorthodox views of the Bible, leads to Sutherland's having to resign his living, after a moving explanation to the bishop. The rash speech is only part of the problem: Sutherland in an entire year has not preached "a single sermon which might not have been Socinian [Unitarian]," not that he has overtly taught Socinian doctrine, but that he has "not said a word to prove that I had opinions which Socinians did not hold" with respect to the incarnation or the atonement. To this Sutherland replies, "If the Catholic doctrine be true . . . it is so overwhelming a mystery that I cannot think of it without its crushing me. I cannot bring myself to speak in public of it, before such a mixed assembly. . . ."—a typically extravagant Froudeian statement revealing his unfitness to be an Anglican clergyman. To the bishop, his kind old friend, Sutherland summarizes his position, as Fowler on his deathbed had summarized his: God is just and merciful; eternal punishment would not be justice; while he does not disbelieve that "in some mysterious transcendental sense . . . the Catholic doctrine of the atonement may be true," he does not find it a teaching that enables him to appreciate God more highly or love Him more.

Sutherland leaves the Church, goes off to Italy, and falls in love with a young married Englishwoman living on the shores of Lake Como with her young daughter while her neglectful husband leaves her alone for long periods. His love is returned; the child is drowned; the love has been unconsummated, but the sin is great. Yet the wife persists in regarding her loveless marriage, and not her illicit love for Sutherland, as the sin. In the aftermath of the child's death, Sutherland renounces her, and both eventually bury themselves in Catholic monastic institutions, she to die and he to survive in misery.

But before this last Italian portion of the novel even begins, the reader must traverse a summary of Sutherland's philosophical and theological musings, occupying almost half the length of the novel. Called "Confessions of a Sceptic," this clarifies further the nature of Froude's doubts and of the agony that caused him to write *The Nemesis of Faith* with his own heart's blood, as he put it. He seems to doubt the incarnation: Christ was so good a man that his followers made a god of him and told tales of his miracles, declaring it impossible for him to have been born in the ordinary human way, or to have dissolved "in the vulgar corruption of the grave." The result has been that "instead of a man to love and follow we have a man-god to worship. From being the example of devotion, he is its object; the religion of Christ ended with his life, and left us instead but the Christian religion." Here indeed is Froude's "Socinianism." Whereas in "The Spirit's Trials" Fowler had said only that he could not see "that a Socinian led a less virtuous life than an Anglo-Catholic," in *The Nemesis of Faith*, Sutherland has preached nothing contrary to Socinian views in his sermons, and comes out positively in favor of them in his writings. He has pondered the Jewish, the Indian, the Persian, and the Greek philosophical and religious interplay, which, he is convinced, gave rise historically to Christianity.

In a discussion of "private judgment," Sutherland criticizes *both* the Catholic view that a man should "submit his judgment to the judgment of the church" (on the ground that, once a church has lost the physical instruments of compulsion or the sanction of punishment for nonconformity, the church is just a "bereaved lady" unable to compel submission), *and* the Protestant view that a man must exercise his own judgment (on the ground that weak minds cannot do so and will be naturally drawn to the most magnetic nearby influence). Indeed, he says, in recent times the church "had lost its power, perhaps its life, and was decomposing." So there arose a movement insisting that men submit their judgment to hers, a movement whose "leader [Newman] took us all his own way; all that is who were not Arnoldized [the reference is to Thomas Arnold]. And even some of these. . . ." All the time, the Tractarian movement—despite its apparently innocent beginnings and the fact that it "represented pretty exactly Anglican Oxford. . . . where theology is itself the profession"—was leading towards conflict with the establishment. "It became necessary to surrender tutorships, fellowships and the hopes of them: to find difficulties in getting ordained; to lose slowly the prospects of pleasant curacies, and livings, and parsonage houses, and the sweet little visions of home paradises," and then the young high churchmen, frightened, ceased to follow Newman. Self-sacrifice, a kind of martyrdom, was too difficult, especially for the "half-worshippers of truth," for whom it is impossible to give up everything for a mere *idea.*

So on the one side stood Newman: "genius with its pale face and worn dress and torn friendships and bleeding heart. . . . strong only in struggling, counting all loss but truth and the love of God; rewarded, as men court reward, perhaps by an after apotheosis, yet never seeking this reward or that reward, save only its own good conscience steady to its aim: promising nothing; least of all peace—only struggles which are to end but with the grave." And on the other side stood "respectability, with its sweet smiling home, and loving friends, and happy family, a fair green spring, a golden summer, an autumn sinking fruit-loaded to the earth—the final winter rest following on the full finished course of duty done, and for the future prospects, easy and secure." This was the choice. Only a few select spirits could take the harder course; these were the sons of genius, the "church militant, the army of the human race." Perhaps there are three or four such geniuses alive on earth, and one "was at that time rising up in Oxford, and drawing all men towards him": Newman, of course—so far identified by Sutherland only as "N"—with his extraordinary powers of insight into the "hidden life," the "Sanctuary of the mysteries" of the individual man ("I believe no young man ever heard him preach without fancying that some one had been betraying his own history, and the sermon was aimed directly at him").

Despite all this, "it is a problem heavier than has been yet laid on theologians to make what the world has now grown into square with the theory of catholicism"; and this N's disciples, as they "began to leave the nest, and though under his eye, fly out and look about for ourselves," have begun to discover. If the Catholic theory were true, it would be necessary to hate the Reformation, yet at the time of the Reformation the Catholic Church badly needed reform and was "shamed" into it by the Protestants. Moreover, ever since, Catholic countries have been "comparatively" weak; the Catholic church has produced no great intellectual or artist; the "personal character of people in all Roman Catholic countries is poor and mean . . . they are untrue in their words, unsteady in their actions, disrespecting themselves in the entire tenor of their life and temper"; and all this is due to their being priest-ridden. These things are troublesome but not conclusive. At a different level, how could it be true that, mankind having fallen and needing to be redeemed, "from the beginning of time a peculiar body of people, *not specially distinguished for individual excellencies* [the Jews], had been made the channels of grace and their priests divinely guided"? Did not Protestant Christianity as well as Catholic lose credibility from this argument? And had not Protestant Christianity in Europe "uniformly developed into Socinianism, and thence into Pantheism," and from a fact was it not becoming an idea merely? Could one indeed apply reason to Christianity? Or should one not concede that it was a mystery, a matter for the heart alone? Unbelief, as the Bible warned, "was a sin and not a mistake, and deserved not argument but punishment."

All these last considerations return Sutherland to the position where he can grant that the Protestants, by "falling back on individual experience," had "cut away the only support on which Revelation could . . . sustain itself." One must return to the "continued authority of the church's witness" to have anything left at all. And so Sutherland returned to Newmanism and for a time "dreamed" that Newman's views were his own. What, then, about the Church of England? The English were Protestant in temper: all the poets from Chaucer to Milton favored Reform; Oliver Cromwell was the incarnation of the typical Englishman. Yet the Church of England "retained the Succession. . . . the Sacraments . . . Liturgical forms which committed it to the just Catholic understanding of them." For the Tractarians, the question was whether they could "unprotestantize its working character, and reinspire it with so much of the old life as should enable it to do the same work in England which the Roman Church produced abroad." This would make England cease to produce great men and would "substitute devotion, endurance, humility, self-denial, sanctity, and faith" for "poetry, courage, daring, enterprise, resolution, and broad honest understanding." One might think this satire, or conclude that the mere listing of these qualities which the Tractarian program would jettison and those which it would foster revealed Sutherland's—and of course Froude's—bias against it.

But no: he continues:

> What a sight must this age of ours have been to an earnest believing man like Newman. . . ? A foolish Church, chattering, parrot-like, old notes, of which it had forgot the meaning; a clergy who not only thought not at all but whose heavy

> ignorance, from long unreality, clung about them like a garment; selfishness. . . . faith in God, in man, in virtue, exchanged for faith in the belly, in fortunes, carriages, lazy sofas, and cushioned pews; Bentham politics and Paley religion,

the only thought German or the philosophy of Hume and Gibbon, all the spiritual feeling the "light froth" of the Wesleyans and Evangelicals. A "proud, rugged, intellectual republicanism" threatened to do away with "Erastianism, pluralities, prebendal stalls, and pony-gigging parsons," while philosophy, "with Niebuhr criticism for a reaping sickle, mowed down their darling story-books." The first step was to win the clergy, "to wean the bishops from their palaces and lazy carriages and fashionable families, the clergy from their snug firesides and marrying and giving in marriage [note the reference to Tractarian celibacy here], and substitute holy life, prayer, fasting, the confessional." But instead of listening to Newman's message, the worldly Church of England drove him out. So Sutherland tells at length the story of Newman's endeavors that Fowler had summarized in a sentence, the view of the early days of Tractarianism as Froude saw it.

Yet Froude—Sutherland—had left Newman before that, because of another equally great prophet—Carlyle, product of the Scotch Highlands and Goethe's poetry rather than of Oxford, lectures, college chapels, and school divinity. Carlyle's *French Revolution* showed Sutherland how widely two great men may differ and led him to re-examine Newman's dictum that reason must be swept away. One sentence in a sermon preached by Newman—"Scripture says the earth is stationary and the sun moves, science that the sun is stationary and that the earth moves"—was enough to destroy Sutherland's faith in Newman, already shaken by Tract 90. The suggestion that Scripture "instead of a revelation" might become a jumble, a "huge mysterious combination of one knows not what," convinced Sutherland that Scripture must be abandoned. Newman had to go on to Rome; Sutherland got off the moving vehicle of Newman's "advance into the real feeling of Christianity." Convinced of the reality, and the terror, of sin, Newman—like any man in the same position—chose that religion "where the sacraments are most numerous and most constant, and absolution is more than a name." For Sutherland sin had not yet become so real.

Yet in the end—and it is here that we part from Froude's own personal history and find Sutherland once more to be a fictional character—it is Sutherland's great sin of illicit love for a married woman that brings him another step along the path laid out by Newman. For—in an episode utterly preposterous as art—a figure exactly like Newman himself, an English Roman Catholic priest named (for the novel's purposes) Mornington—appears, just as his old friend Sutherland is on the point of taking poison at the foot of a wayside crucifix on the shore of Lake Como, and prevails on him by his "gentleness and fascination" to submit utterly to the Church, to confess, to receive Catholic baptism, and to enter a monastery. But "his new faith fabric had been reared upon the clouds of sudden and violent feeling," and his end is one of miserable solitude, still steeped in doubt.

It is only when one reads Froude's two autobiographical fictions together that one can fathom the religious experiences of his young manhood. The boyhood of Edward Fowler was Froude's own; yet the religious views to which it led and the processes by which they were reached can be fully appreciated only in *The Nemesis of Faith.* But the background of Markham Sutherland was not Froude's own, and the arguments and conclusions of *The Nemesis of Faith* remain oddly impersonal and unconvincing until they are brought together with the true story of Froude's childhood as he perceived it and set it forth in "The Spirit's Trials." Led by Newman up to the threshold of conversion to Catholicism, Froude had drawn back in sudden and not fully rational revulsion and had become—at least in the pages of the novel—an infidel. Like Clara Hopgood, Markham Sutherland had to choose between Rome or nothing, and despite his entry into a Catholic monastery it was nothing that he had in the end.

Of course, *The Nemesis of Faith* produced a sensation. It appeared under Froude's own name. The Catholics wanted Newman to write an answer to it. The Tractarians were outraged. William Sewell, author of *Hawkstone* (1845, no. 2), was vice-rector of Froude's Oxford College (Exeter). Characteristically, he snatched a copy of *The Nemesis* from the hands of an undergraduate who was reading the book and threw it into the fire. This, as the Broad Churchman Charles Maurice Davies (see no. 31, no. 55, no. 56) later remarked, served as an excellent advertisement: headlines in the religious papers screamed out about the "Public Burning of a Blasphemous Book"; so every Oxford undergraduate instantly bought a copy. Broad Churchmen and Unitarians disliked the novel. Carlyle himself, the second prophet of its text and the one who had prevailed, called it "a wretched mortal's vomiting up all his interior crudities, dubitations, and spiritual agonising bellyaches into the view of the public, and howling tragically, 'See!' " The press vilified all those who had helped Froude achieve advancement. He resigned his fellowship, soon married Kingsley's sister-in-law, recovered from his melancholia, and settled down into his long career as historian.

Verbose, lachrymose, sentimental, ejaculatory in keeping with the forms of expression common at the time, *The Nemesis of Faith* is notable not for being a good novel but for preserving—more particularly in the interpolated "Confessions of a Sceptic"—the record of a fine mind and a troubled spirit wrestling with psychological and spiritual problems that proved intractable and left formal faith in ruins. One of Froude's reviewers was a Manchester spinster of thirty-seven, writing anonymously in January 1850 for the *Westminster Review*, which George Henry Lewes had persuaded to take the article, although they would not pay for it. Froude, who, after the scandal, was acting as tutor in a Manchester Unitarian family, could not have known that his reviewer and he had recently met, or that she had found him "a very nice natural young man, though rather like a lost sheep at present," and, as an Oxford man, quite unused to "sectarians and unbelievers" of the kind of which Manchester had so many. The lady saw Carlyle's influence in *The Nemesis of Faith,* and recognized it as "a very powerful picture of the struggles of a religiously disposed sceptic." She found the book oppressive and painful because it made no effort to *explain*—so she thought—Froude's reasons for scepticism. The regretful, complaining tone she disliked; and though these were symptoms of the age, it was unfortunate to publicize them: modesty and reserve would have been better.

The writer of the review was Geraldine Jewsbury (1812-1880), intimate friend of Jane Carlyle, pioneer smoker of "cigarettos," and herself given to such ungovernable passionate, spontaneous expressions of love for men and women indiscriminately that her anonymous recommendation of restraint to Froude is delightfully funny. Four years before *The Nemesis of Faith* and two years before "The Spirit's Trials," Miss Jewsbury had published her own novel of doubt, *Zoe: the History of Two Lives* (1845, no. 67), perhaps the first serious effort to deal with the subject in fiction. "Modesty and reserve" are wholly absent from *Zoe*, set in the eighteenth century and dealing with a handsome married woman, a friend of Dr. Johnson and his circle (all of whom appear), who falls in love with a Catholic priest, Everhard Burrows. But Everhard is not just an ordinary Catholic priest: he is a friend of the eighteenth-century sceptics in both France and England, has taken priestly orders with no profound conviction, and thereafter grows steadily more convinced that the *evidence* for the truth of Christianity is unsatisfactory. Questioning the truth of revelation, he finds himself "in utter ignorance, without a hope or a belief to guide him."

What was Miss Jewsbury to do with him then? She wrote to Jane Carlyle that she could not provide Everhard with "new doctrines to begin to lead the remainder of his lifetime. . . . What can any of us do? What do any of us know?" Having resigned from the priesthood, Everhard first goes in for social work among the Welsh coalminers, but is forced to leave by Wesleyan revivalists who are more popular than he. He writes a book about religion which precipitates a scandal, retreats to Germany, and in that more congenial atmosphere writes a learned philosophical history that makes him famous.

But before Everhard had abandoned the priesthood, he had fallen in love with Zoe. He has never told her so until the night he rescues her from a fire. "A warm palpitating weight," she lies on his bosom (she is in her nightclothes at the time), and soon he "who had never touched a woman" experiences a "whole life of passion" in a single moment. "He crushed her into his arms with ferocious love,—he pressed burning kisses upon her face, her lips, and her bosom; but kisses were too weak to express the passion that was in him. It was madness like hatred,—beads of sweat stood thick on his forehead, and his breath came in gasps." At once, Zoe's own "burning arms were round his neck, and her long hair fell like a veil over him." After a few moments of "delirium," Zoe recovers first, and she begs Everhard to tell her that he has not "lost the esteem" he had had for her. It is this torrid episode that leads directly to his resignation of the priesthood, and so it should. Later on in the novel, Zoe has another love affair with Mirabeau himself, and Everhard dies in poverty.

The love affair between Zoe and Everhard harks back to such famous "Gothic" novels as M. G. Lewis's *The Monk* (1796), in which Catholic monks or priests press unwelcome sexual attentions on fair young women, usually in a vaulted chapel. The only difference is that Zoe welcomes Everhard's embraces (which also take place in a chapel, immediately before the altar). In all other respects *Zoe* is a truly pioneering effort. It is the first novel to sound the notes which novelists were so often to repeat. Scepticism of Christian evidences, sublimation of doubt in sex, social service among the poor as a substitute for faith, the importance of German biblical criticism in undermining belief: all these—entirely new in 1845—we shall encounter again and again in the more famous novels of doubt that we shall be examining. Mrs. Humphry Ward, whose *Robert Elsmere* (1888, no. 82) became the classic of the subject more than forty years after *Zoe*, includes all of these elements except for the sexual: and that, together with all the rest, is a marked feature of the five extraordinary novels of W. H. Mallock (nos. 76, 81, 85, 86, 84), the last of which, published in 1899, brought the century to an end.

Little wonder that, despite its glaring faults, *Zoe* struck Jane Carlyle with a "feeling little short of terror! So much power of genius rushing so recklessly into unknown space!" She added that the "old and young roués of the Reform Club almost go off into hysterics over its indecency." Though *Zoe* did not even have "a fig-leaf of conformity," though its publisher was deeply worried about its outspokenness, and though its reviewers protested against its "fling at the reasonableness as well as the purifying influence of the Christian faith" or found it—quite rightly—"feverish" or "most dangerous," it made a great noise. Had Everhard been an Anglican priest instead of a Roman Catholic (who were, as we know, rather expected to be seducers), the scandal would have been far worse. And, one must emphasize, the doubts that Everhard felt about Christian evidences were Geraldine Jewsbury's own, even as early as

1845. Her cry of "What can any of us do? What do any of us know?" justifies us in regarding *Zoe* too as a kind of autobiography.

Earnestness in the Second Generation: William Delafield Arnold

All those who were not "Arnoldized," Froude had said, and even some of those who were, had been drawn to the leadership of Newman and the Tractarians. Surely, no Oxford undergraduate could ever have been more deeply "Arnoldized" than William Delafield Arnold (1828-1859), who was not only the fleshly son of Thomas Arnold but very much his spiritual son as well. Matthew Arnold (1822-1888) and Thomas Arnold the younger (1823-1900), father of Mrs. Humphry Ward, were his elder brothers. Destined for Holy Orders, William decided as an undergraduate at Christ Church that he could not subscribe to the Thirty-nine Articles. He became an Ensign in the Indian Army, went out to India in 1848, and there won a coveted appointment as Assistant Commissioner in the Punjab. He was home on sick leave in 1853 when he published his novel *Oakfield* under the pseudonym of "Punjabee," with a dedicatory preface disavowing the resemblance of its least attractive characters to any real persons. But harsh criticism of the author for hiding behind a pseudonym led him to acknowledge the second edition, published under his own name (1854, no. 70), and to deny again that he had intended to disparage the "distinguished service," to which he had the honor to belong. Having returned to India as first Director of Public Instruction for the Punjab, Arnold labored mightily in setting up an entire new department. His young wife died in India, leaving four children. Invalided home, Arnold never reached England, but died on the way, at Gibraltar, still only thirty. A month later, walking in Brittany and thinking of his dead younger brother, Matthew Arnold, in "Stanzas from Carnac," lamented

O, could he once have reached the air
Freshened by plunging tides, by showers!
Have felt this breath he loved, of fair
Cool northern fields, and grain, and flowers.

He longed for it—pressed on!—in vain!
At the Straits failed that spirit brave,
The south was parent of his pain,
The south is mistress of his grave.

And later, with almost Wordsworthian pantheism, in "A Southern Night" Matthew Arnold reflected upon his sister-in-law, buried in the Himalayas at Simla and on his brother buried at Gibraltar,

Mild o'er her grave, ye mountains, shine!
Gently by his, ye waters, glide!
To that in you which is divine
They were allied.

To become acquainted with this lost Arnold, we must read *Oakfield*, in which Edward Oakfield's fictional experience and opinions reproduce Arnold's own (although they are deliberately put several years earlier), except that the hero of the novel successfully completes the long voyage home to his family in England and dies there of the disease that Arnold must have known had already doomed himself. So, although *Oakfield* is a far better work than "The Spirit's Trials" or *The Nemesis of Faith*, Arnold, like Froude, allowed himself to fantasize about his own death. Otherwise the active, vigorous, dedicated young soldier and Indian civil servant, with a sense of mission and a personal religious devotion, differed widely in temperament and outlook from the despairing infidel such as Edward Fowler or Markham Sutherland. For one thing, all is harmony and affection in the Oakfield family, happily living—though still mourning their father, early dead like Thomas Arnold—in the Arnolds' own beautiful lake country. Then too, Oakfield's time at Oxford is "a continual flow of unchecked happiness," a "rare and awful happiness." Yet there is a "benumbing influence" at work, which he feels he must shake off. He has a vague feeling he is "going to the devil" in Oxford; and without joy, but with an anxious determination to experiment, he decides to go to India to make his career. Though *Oakfield* is of major importance as an account of the English in India just before the Mutiny of 1857 and a long generation before Kipling, it concerns us chiefly as the self-portrait of a youth beset by religious anxieties.

At Oxford Oakfield for some time "inclined to the Tractarian influence then so prevalent, and thought for a while he had found the help he needed; when lo! again, in an hour of startling conviction, he found that the forms with which he had been so busily lulling his conscience had as little of the divine in them as the forms of common worldly society. The reaction followed, and he hated the Church which he thought had deceived him; the idea of taking orders became intolerable. . . ." His mother is disappointed: she is "fondly attached" to the Church, of which her husband had been "during thirty years, a faithful minister," and had hoped her son would follow in his footsteps. So, despite the fact that Oxford tutorships and livings were sure to come his way, he finds "the Thirty-nine Articles an insuperable barrier." More than a decade before William Arnold went out to India, his father Thomas Arnold had himself written in a letter to a pupil (December 20, 1839) that he had long been satisfied in his own mind that "Ordination was never meant to be closed" to those who could not accept the words of "every part of the Articles and Liturgy as true," but who intended to be earnest ministers of the Church. Now his son—and his son's fictional counterpart—were finding the same block in the way of a clerical career.[1]

If the "Church of England and its ministry" were "always and everywhere" what it had been "here with our dear father in these happy valleys," Oakfield tells his sister, things would have been

1. Dean Stanley of Westminster—an Arnoldian Broad Churchman—argued strongly in favor of relaxing the terms of subscription, which required the clergyman to say "I do willingly and from my heart subscribe to" the articles and to acknowledge "all and every" one "to be agreeable to the word of God." If this were pressed rigidly and literally, said Stanley, not a single cleric in England could remain in his post. In 1865, ten years after William Delafield Arnold died, the new Clerical Subscription Act softened the terms to "I assent to the thirty-nine articles of religion, and to the Book of Common Prayer. I believe the doctrine . . . as therein set forth to be agreeable to the Word of God." Moreover, subscription was interpreted very loosely, and after 1865 clergymen were seldom prosecuted for preaching or writing contrary to the Articles.

different. But even had it not been for the Thirty-nine Articles, he had grown disillusioned with the Church. "In some things I still love the Church of England;—the gentlemanly element in it, as it has been called, and by which I understand the seemliness of its ordinances and its ritual,—so satisfying to one's mere taste—is, and always will be, a great attraction to me," he says; but "its wretched sectarian spirit" and the contrasts between its professions and its practices would in any case have made a clerical career impossible. Oakfield cannot reconcile his "belief in the Bible with ordinary life and its ordinary fashions and practices"; he yearns to combine "the utmost freedom of thought and a firm belief in the New Testament," whereas most religious men are taught to separate these. But essentially he is a religious-minded young man, who finds ordinary society irksome, since he always wants to lecture his friends about religious matters.

He cannot sympathize with the Tractarians:

> I don't the least mean to say that many of those men, with their surplice and white-tie fiddle-faddle, were not excellent men, better men, how often have I felt, than I; the forms which they extol and love may be a help to them, but they were not and never could be, to me; and it would be utterly impossible, when struggling for life and death with such fearful realities as sin and ignorance, to have any true sympathy with those who are for ever thrusting to you, as the one panacea, the shape of a building or the cut of a waistcoat.

And he dislikes their Evangelical enemies even more: while he reveres "the excellence of many individuals calling themselves Evangelicals," he thinks that "their party bitterness, and ignorant, self-satisfied narrow-mindedness, has done more harm to the cause of good than the great Popery lie itself." They belabor Popery too much and damage the truth as badly with their "unlearned semi-magical prophecy disquisitions" as their opponents do with their "surplice follies."

Many a reader of *Oakfield* would have seen a reference to Thomas Arnold himself in his son's description of religious men who are *not* partisans in the strife:

> either they keep their holy secret in their own hearts, and bow in sadness to a state of things which they are not strong enough to alter, or when they are to be seen at all, they are alone, isolated, misunderstood, shedding truth indeed in all directions, which does or will bear fruit somewhen or somewhere, but which has not yet penetrated into society, so as to remodel even a small portion of it.

Such admirable individual men exist, but "societies—or sections of a society of such men—not." Oakfield, then, is not in revolt against his father, as was Edward Fowler; whereas Froude loathed the archdeacon and fostered or at least used his own doubts to strike a vengeful blow at him, William Arnold loved the memory of the Master of Rugby, and the doubts he nurtured were doubts his father would have understood and even honored, while regretting that they were keeping his son from the pulpit.

It is no accident that William Arnold gave *Oakfield* an epigraph from Longfellow: "Life is real! Life is earnest!/ And the grave is not its goal;/ Dust thou art, to dust returnest,/ Was not spoken of the soul." In India, Oakfield is nothing if not earnest. He soon finds he cannot bear the profanity and loose language of the mess, and more and more he withdraws into the company of three or four close friends, from whom he is often separated by circumstance. Though younger than they, he leads them, through "the force of earnestness."

> He had been from his childhood—rare blessing!—accustomed to find those around him in earnest; and this influence had made itself felt; and now . . . in the ripening of his young manhood, he found himself closely questioning life, asking eternal reasons for what he should do. . . . He was an earnest man,—and he was a Christian man. Alas that the two should be so often severed! Alas that the long folly of those "who profess and call themselves Christians" should have done its best to divorce Christianity from wisdom! that so many true and eager hearts, seeing, as they thought, Christianity intimately leagued with sectarianism and narrow-minded dogmatism, should have thought it needful to renounce it as the

> first step toward freedom and truth! Alas that we should now find, to our cost, that Christianity, the new religion . . . should be in danger of confounding itself with things old and ready to vanish away, when it should be . . . lending sanctification and divine light to whatsoever things are noble, whatsoever things are true.

Despite the rhetoric, one can hardly miss the sincerity—the earnestness!—of this dislike for "party" in the Church and its ill effects. Froude's heroes and alter egos, Markham Sutherland and Edward Fowler, are brought by doubt among those "true and eager hearts" who—Oakfield deplored it—have felt it necessary to renounce Christianity. But Oakfield's earnestness, like William Arnold's, has kept him a Christian.

In India, the clerics Oakfield meets are wholly unsatisfactory. The regimental chaplain is "respectable, commonplace . . . worldly," so much so indeed that when one of Oakfield's friends is on his deathbed, they do not send for the chaplain, but by themselves eat and drink "together the bread and wine in remembrance of the death of their Lord and Master." Such a sacramental act can be only symbolic without a clergyman to administer the Communion: it would never have done for Guy Morville or even Sir Roland Ashton. Another Anglican cleric—High Church this time—is instantly gullible when a bibulous wandering Irishman says a few words about the mutual dependence of Church and aristocracy on which the fabric of society rests ("a few sentences of . . . sectarian slang"). The Tractarian maintains that India will be saved by "the one true Church of England, as legally appointed in this country, with its . . . Bishops, Priests and Deacons." But there are only thirty of them in all Bengal: these and these alone he equates with Christianity. He is deeply offended at the suggestion that the Indians must be helped toward physical and intellectual improvement before they will be Christianized.

Once Oakfield has become familiar with the predominantly self-seeking, profane, and cynical (as it seems to him) attitudes and behavior of the English military and civilians, he decides that "a man's duty" is "to help in the work, or to try to set it going" of raising the level of the *English*, "first from the depths of immorality, gradually to a state of comparative Christian earnestness." Only then can the larger task of combatting the "perfectly awful" inertia of native Indian society be undertaken. As long as the English society is "gross" in its lower phases and "false and Mammonish" in its highest, its government will be nothing but a police force, and all the missionary work among the Indians useless. What is needed is "Christ and his Gospel," not "self-worship or sect-worship," and "least of all that most portentous of all lies, Sunday-church-preaching, week-day-Mammon-practising Christianity." Yet the practical pursuit in daily life of goals as lofty as these is discouragingly difficult. Oakfield's wisest friend counsels him to believe in them always, but to pursue them through the more prosaic activity of doing his daily work as well as he possibly can. "The excitement of work" is, indeed, one of the ways to overcome the "hot dull vacancy of Indian life." So to his military duties—slight in peacetime and easily accomplished—Oakfield adds the self-imposed task of learning the native languages and passing the government examinations set in them.

But beyond the work, he seeks for an opportunity to put himself "in opposition to some cherished lie," to expose "the falseness which lies wrapped in some commonplace respectable formula." He finds the opportunity when he is deliberately put into a position where he ought—according to the "code of honor" prevalent in the army—to challenge a foul-mouthed bullying fellow officer to a duel, and refuses, allowing himself to be thought a coward ("coming the religious dodge"), when in fact he is displaying great moral courage. He is obeying "God's and nature's code of honor," although this does not mean abstention in all cases from the "weapons of the flesh." The regimental code of honor, on the other hand, is unlawful authority: "public Opinion,—which is the World—which is enmity with the one center of all authority,—God." Indeed, the articles of war seem *literally* in opposition to the New Testament. Oakfield, then, is "most singularly and genuinely ambitious to serve God; . . . not the last infirmity but the noblest craving, of noble minds."[2]

2. In 1852, while Arnold was writing *Oakfield*, there took place in India an episode that quickly became notorious, and must have come to his attention. A medical officer named Umphelby in Bengal allowed himself to be kicked by a clerk in a government

On active campaign for the first time, Oakfield is struck by the superiority of an army in the field to the same army in its peacetime encampment: it is "at work . . . work involved seriousness . . . seriousness . . . induced reflection," and reflection brings out the best in the individual and enables him to slough off to some degree the bonds of "wretched public opinion." In the absence of "moral earnestness," at least "physical earnestness" is better than nothing. Work, then, is a thing that a man must do as well as he can, into which he must put all his energies; yet "to 'devote himself' to it is a sin," because of his higher duty to God: Oakfield's friends tease him as a clergyman *manqué*, who is always preaching to them, and he acknowledges the charge and admits that he must to some degree conform to the ways of society. When he declares that he has done with all forms, that he

> will never go to a church where God is not worshipped, never mix in a society where only animal life is acknowledged, never even speak with respect of what does not approve itself to me as good, be it priest, altar, or sacrament. . . . I will worship God under the stars, and call good good, and evil evil, and liberal liberal, and the churl churl, the wise man wise, and the fool foolish,

one of his friends answers, "The fit will pass," and of course it does.

Oakfield is young; he is physically brave (the quality that Froude so notably lacked); he behaves heroically in combat. He proves "to his own satisfaction that a man was none the worse soldier for being a Christian." He is professedly "a contemplative admirer of Carlyle" and so finds war attractive despite its horrors. For one of his chapters he uses as epigraph a passage from Carlyle declaring that "difficulty, abnegation, martyrdom, death, are the *allurements* that act on the heart of man." Though strongly liberal in

office, and did not challenge the clerk to a duel. Umphelby was court-martialled for conduct disgraceful to the character of an officer and gentleman for not having issued the challenge. He was acquitted, not because duelling was regarded by the court as wrong, but because, by refusing to issue a challenge, Umphelby had demonstrated that a medical officer was of a social class superior to a clerk, and therefore could not fight him. (Put in Prussian terms, the clerk was not *satisfaktionsfähig*.) Clearly the Umphelby case and the court's primitive and un-Christian attitude toward it were in Arnold's mind when he constructed the plot of *Oakfield*.

politics—as a vivid passage on the year 1848 demonstrates—Oakfield goes out of his way to praise that archconservative, the Duke of Wellington. He is a bit of a prig, or at least terribly thin-skinned and uncompromising, but he learns some tolerance and comes to respect the qualities of some men whom at first he had thought good for nothing. His self-doubts, however, persist until the moment of his death: although sure that God has not forsaken him, Oakfield cannot be certain that his own work in India has actually been a service to God. Worldly activity and godliness seem more and more incompatible, and it remains a puzzle how to lead a godly life. After Oakfield has died, his close friend Stanton says the last word: Oakfield's nature was "anxious and too speculative." He would in time have outgrown the "doubts and suspicions of himself," and "active employment" would have satisfied him. As an authentic portrait (and self-portrait) of the late 1840's and early 1850's, *Oakfield* has no equal.

Voices from South Africa and Australia

A generation later and half a world away from England (or even the India of Oakfield), and springing from a spiritual environment utterly remote from that of any of our English doubters, there emerged in the early 1880's the manuscript of the novel that eventually saw publication under the pseudonym "Ralph Iron" as *The Story of an African Farm* (1883, no. 78). Its author was Olive Schreiner (1855-1920), born in the year of William Delafield Arnold's death, ninth child of a German-born Moravian missionary and his English wife, of Evangelical background, laboring in remote mission stations in South Africa. When Olive Schreiner was still a child, she was fired with enthusiasm by the Sermon on the Mount, and was shocked when her mother told her that people could not these days live according to its precepts: apparently her doubts began then. At the age of twelve, no longer living with her parents but with a succession of relatives, she was already so opposed to the fanatically narrow religion of the family that a brother declined to pray for her recovery when she was ill. She was seduced when she was about seventeen by a man who promised to marry her, and then abandoned her.

She became a governess in a succession of families in South African small towns. She responded with passionate effusions of affection to the friendliness shown her by older women. Her great favorite, obviously a substitute for the mother who had never loved her properly, turned her away: "I have *loved* you, at times with an almost idolatrous love . . . Olive Schreiner," she wrote, but "God in His goodness and wisdom used you as a means to show me what an awful soul-destroying thing free-thinking is." She could not love God and Olive Schreiner at the same time. And Olive Schreiner replied, "I do not at all blame you for not loving me any more." It was no wonder that Olive Schreiner suffered all her life from asthma. Another woman friend, however, a free-thinking liberal, wife of a doctor, encouraged her to write, and by 1880, the manuscript of *The Story of an African Farm* was completed. By the time it was published, Olive Schreiner had been living for more than two years in England.

Two of the three children on the fictional African farm represent different aspects of Olive Schreiner herself: the beautiful young orphan English girl Lyndall (the name was the family name of Olive's mother)—fiercely independent and almost unmanageable—and the boy Waldo, son of the gentle, pious German farm-manager. For Waldo the Bible is everything:

> The leaves of that book had dripped blood for him once; they had taken the brightness out of his childhood; from between them had sprung the visions that had clung about him and made night horrible. Adder-like thoughts had lifted their heads, had shot out forked tongues at him, asking mockingly strange, trivial questions that he could not answer, miserable child:—*Why did the women in Mark see only* one *angel and the women in Luke* two*? Could a story be told in opposite ways and both ways be true? Could it? Could it?* How was it that the Spirit of the Lord chanted paeans over Jael, when she had lied and killed a trusting man in his sleep? *Could the friend of God marry his own sister, and be beloved, and the man who does it today goes to hell, to hell? Was there nothing always right, always wrong?*

Waldo is still able to answer the questions by saying to himself: we cannot understand, but God knows, and God loves men. He yearns to see God soon. But the incredibly sadistic Bonaparte Blenkins, a sinister tramp, is already on his way to high influence at the farm. His devilish cruelty—perhaps the most extreme shown to a child in all fiction—leads Waldo to disbelieve: "There is no God," he tells Lyndall. Waldo's later sufferings and a mysterious encounter with a parable-recounting stranger help turn the wretched little boy into a dim and saintly young man, his talents stunted and thwarted, who eventually dies a mystic Wordsworthian death.

As for Lyndall, she loses her faith as Olive Schreiner lost hers: through a realization that the Christian precepts in the Bible are not taken seriously as rules of conduct even by those who profess to be the most pious Christians, while injustice flourishes everywhere. Her religion—we gather, though the prose is opaque indeed—is replaced by a form of romantic nature-worship and a feeling of unity with all creation not dissimilar to Waldo's ultimate faith. For long periods Lyndall vanishes from the novel; she becomes a militant feminist, cursing the lot of women as mere childbearers, determined to bring about a better future. Proud, sometimes strident, Lyndall meets only with suffering, frustration, and death.

The Story of an African Farm caused a sensation on its publication, partly because of Lyndall's illegitimate child by a mysterious man whom she (like Madge Hopgood) refuses to marry, partly because of the exotic and little-known South African environment. "The ablest book ever written by a woman," said Sir Charles Dilke—absurdly, when we think of the Brontës and George Eliot. Gladstone admired the *African Farm.* Feminists seized upon it eagerly, and they later ranked Lyndall and Nora in Ibsen's *Doll's House* as their two chief literary heroines. Notable English writers and social thinkers—Havelock Ellis, Bernard Shaw—sought out Olive Schreiner. She had, however, put everything she had into this novel, and she never managed to write anything else worth remembering. Each generation produces its passionate defenders of the *African Farm,* most recently Isak Dinesen and Doris Lessing, who compares it in detail to *Wuthering Heights,* with Waldo as Heathcliff and Lyndall as Cathy (although Waldo and Lyndall are really the same person and there is no passionate love between them). Others find the book disappointingly turgid and portentous, immature and vague, promising more than it ever delivers. For us its interest lies in its peculiar exploration of childhood loss of faith in a strangely harsh and beautiful natural environment, which itself comes to be substituted by Waldo and Lyndall for the consolations of religion.

Somehow, despite its faults, the *African Farm* is still remembered. *Sheba* (1889, no. 83), however, by Mrs. Desmond Humphreys ("Rita"), is utterly forgotten, although as the *Farm*'s Australian counterpart it will seem rewarding to many modern readers. "The way Sheba was brought up," says a friend, "was enough to ruin any girl's disposition." Sheba's mother does not truly love her, and the girl revolts against her family's strict evangelical religious principles: she is forced to write each Sunday's sermon down from memory after listening to it in church, which she feels as a "peculiar infliction." Like Waldo and Lyndall, she questions the Bible from early childhood. She is not sure that "God didn't intend Eve to disobey Him from the very first"; otherwise why make such a big world for nobody to live in. What chance did Pharaoh have against God, who first hardened his heart so he had to retain the Jews in Egypt, and then punished him with plagues for doing it? One Sunday, instead of the sermon actually given in church, she writes down one very largely of her own invention: God is remote from man; life is only suffering. "Better the darkness and the void . . . than the . . . misery that never ends." All this is quite worthy of Waldo or Lyndall; but—presumably because "Rita" was already a well-known, rather run-of-the-mill lady novelist—nobody noticed that in this book she was trying something new and different, remembering her own Australian childhood. The *farouche* and feverish Olive Schreiner attracted widespread attention and applause for doing no more.

Sheba's mother is as unsatisfactory as Olive Schreiner's (or Froude's father), and as a young woman she finds that "the vital principle of religion was as a dead letter to her soul." As with Olive Schreiner, the moral is not that she should have persisted in her formal religion, but rather that young women need parental affection. She wants to be independent, rebels against her rich and uncongenial stepfather, encounters a German freethinker and anticlerical who greatly influences her, deeply admires George Eliot, thinks her fortunate for living "apart from society" with a man not her husband, thwarts her mother's plans for her marriage to a detestable man, embarks on a love affair, and finds herself in Lyndall's predicament. But Sheba's suicide attempt fails, and she survives to an uncertain future.

CHAPTER 8.

THE IMPACT OF SCIENCE

The Telescope atop the Tracts

Though Froude ("Fowler," "Sutherland") and Arnold ("Oakfield") underwent their spiritual struggles comparatively untouched by the scientists, since, like Clara and Madge Hopgood, they lived too early to have experienced their full impact, Eliza Lynn ("Christopher Kirkland") was, we know, an early addict of Chamber's *Vestiges of Creation* (1844). But she had already lost her girlhood faith when that half-baked "popular science" volume came her way: it only confirmed her in her Humanist views. Later she came to recognize that Chambers "was in a certain sense pre-scientific" (for one thing, he accepted spiritualism as true), and she paid her major tribute to Darwin ("the true epoch-maker and torch-bearer of this century"). When *Christopher Kirkland* appeared in 1885, Darwin was completely accepted, but a quarter of a century earlier he had been disputed by the learned, derided by the unlearned, and denounced by "the theological remnant . . . as a lying teacher of iniquity." Eliza Lynn claims also to have been enormously influenced by Sir Charles Lyell's *Principles of Geology* (3 volumes, 1830-1833), and later she took comfort in finding Lyell, now an old man, repeatedly attending the same Unitarian services as herself. She also adduces Hugh Miller's *Testimony of the Rocks* (1857) by an extraordinary Scotch workman turned geologist. But Mrs. Lynn Linton was an undiscriminating enthusiast and name-dropper (she also mentions Frederic Harrison, W. K. Clifford, Huxley, Tyndall, and other "unbelievers" without saying much about them), and one suspects that she probably read little and understood less of the original works of the leading scientists, welcoming their impact on society chiefly because it re-enforced her own already heterodox religious opinions.

Although it has become a truism that science—along with the "higher criticism" of the Bible—made doubters out of believers, this may be true in a more limited way than has hitherto been asserted. Study of about 350 accounts by members of the Secular Movement explaining what had caused them to lose their faith has indicated that Thomas Paine's *Age of Reason* and the Bible itself were the two books most responsible. Only two persons in the sample chosen had read Darwin or Huxley and only one Strauss's *Life of Jesus.* And more important than any book was the conviction that the Church was indifferent to the sufferings of the poor, and a force against social advance.

Yet the sample is in some sense unrepresentative for us: it runs from 1850 to 1950, and many of its members fall into the twentieth century and are not Victorians. Nor do they say what *caused* them to read the Bible critically. May it not often have been the case that some inkling of scientific conflict with the Bible—an inkling obtained not necessarily from books by scientists, often hard to read, but from conversation or street-corner oratory—sent the listener back to the Bible to read it again with an eye opened by the second- or tenth-hand reports of scientific advance? Of course, militant atheists circulated Tom Paine, rather than Darwin or Huxley, amongst their audience. Moreover, novel-readers and novel-writers are our subject, and that fact distorts *our* sample in precisely the opposite direction: away from the laboring class and towards readers, intellectuals, would-be intellectuals, and half-baked intellectuals. Among such persons, the evidence is clear: the scientists had an impact, and Malthus and Lyell roused religious doubts long before Darwin and Huxley wrote.

It is not to the novelists indeed that one would look for lucid expositions of scientific discovery even in popularized form. All that one may reasonably expect in fiction is a reflection of the impact of scientific advance on individual beliefs, and even here the results are not conclusive. For example, in *Olive* (1850, no. 69)—an early novel by the popular writer Dinah Maria Mulock, later Mrs. Craik (1826-1887), now remembered chiefly for her *John Halifax, Gentleman* (1856) and for one or two children's stories—

science is important, but it is not easy to specify how. *Olive* is enthusiastically packed full of every catastrophe standard in the Victorian novel, among them deformity, sudden loss of wealth, blindness, illegitimacy, a conflagration, and a severe hemorrhage of the lungs. Its shopworn and bombastic language matches the plot. Yet it provides perhaps the earliest example of a loss of faith, in part due to science, rapidly if not convincingly overcome by argument and love.

Harold Gwynne, an Anglican clergyman, is a clerical Heathcliff (*Wuthering Heights* in 1850 was only three years old) who barely manages to go through the motions of his office. In the pulpit he displays "iron coldness," repeating the liturgy "with the tone of a judge delivering sentence" and substituting a "plain, moral discourse" for the sermon. He cannot properly fold his hands in prayer; he cannot comfort a family whose son has died: "He looked on the dead boy . . . and muttered 'What should *I* do here?' " A widower, he will not allow his little daughter to be taught religion ("I deem it inexpedient that the feeble mind of a child should be led to dwell on subjects which are beyond the grasp of the profoundest philosopher"). As a result, the little girl has never heard of God: she is one of those pathetic children found in the pages of the Victorian novelists, but perhaps the only one to be the daughter of a practicing Anglican clergyman! Under the circumstances, one wonders how Harold has ever managed to escape inquiry and condemnation from his bishop or at least complaints from his parishioners.

Harold had taken orders in his youth, despite unspecified doubts ("doubts came upon my mind as they will upon most young minds whose strivings after truth are hedged in by a thorny rampart of old worn-out forms") only because he was the sole support of his widowed mother, and had to choose between taking a living or letting her starve. Having made the choice, Harold suffers for it ("Though little more than a boy in years, struggling in a chaos of mingled doubt and faith, I bound myself to believe whatever the Church taught. . . . These . . . bonds, this vow, made me, in after years, an infidel"). His cynicism is re-enforced by his marriage to a frivolous young woman whose love for him is half feigned, and who had loved another man first without telling Harold about it.

It is the heroine, Olive Rothesay, preternaturally good despite her congenital slight deformity (she is not quite a hunchback) and despite much harsh treatment by both her parents in her childhood, who leads Harold out of his agonies. She is so devout that she trembles "at the impiety" for even asking the question "Oh, God, why hast thou made me thus?" and has an instant revulsion ("God's immeasurable infinite rose before her in glorious serenity. What was her one brief lifetime in ages of eternity? She felt it . . . in her weakness, her untaught childhood, her helplessness—felt that her . . . body enshrined a living soul"). Olive gets Harold to admit that he believes "in one God, the Creator and Ruler of this world," and he also believes that Olive herself is good. The rest is easy: she asks him "can you believe in human goodness, yet doubt Him who alone can be its origin? Can you think that He would give the yearning for the hereafter, and yet deny its fulfillment? That he would implant in us love, when there was nothing to love; and faith when there was nothing to believe?" This banality appeals to the learned Harold: "You speak plain, reasonable words, not like the vain babbles of contradictory creeds." After a renewed stringent course of Bible-reading, Harold emerges believing that "he who loves God is one with God. There may be a hundred varying forms of doctrine, but this one truth is above all and the root of all." An "almost angelic beauty" comes over his face as he feels his spirit changing within him.

Of course, this will not do for an Anglican priest, and Harold resigns the orders he should never have taken. Through the clouds of verbiage one sees that Miss Mulock has an Evangelical streak: it is the Bible that finally completes the good work that Olive had begun. But essentially the theology—if it can be identified at all—is latitudinarian: Olive herself is a member of the Church of England only because she thinks its forms of worship are pure; she does not "set up the Church between myself and God." Many good words are spoken in the novel both for the Presbyterian Church of Scotland, where much of the action takes place, and for the Catholics: Chrystal, the passionate quadroon, illegitimate half-sister of Olive, passes as a Protestant, but has always been a Catholic and ultimately finds shelter in a convent.

Only if one reads *Olive* carefully can one see "science" looming vaguely in the background. In Harold's parsonage study "dust lay upon John Newton's sermons, while close by rested in honored, well-thumbed tatters, his great namesake, who read God's scriptures in the stars." Of course, Isaac Newton was no infidel—and he seems to be the most modern scientist whose name Miss Mulock knows—but she obviously meant it to be suggestive that Harold has read the scientist to tatters and left the theologian untouched. Then too, even more symbolically, Harold has a telescope in his study, which *rests upon a basket of tracts as a base.* So he is by temperament a scholar and a scientist, rather than a cleric; and after he resigns his pulpit he returns with glee to his "heavy" scientific books. Though wealthy now as the result of a fortunate legacy, Harold, as Olive's husband, "could not relinquish his scientific pursuits, but was every day adding to his acquirements and to his fame." What it is he does Miss Mulock does not tell us; probably her large audience would not have understood or cared; perhaps she did not know or understand or care herself. It was enough in 1850 to be saying that a man tortured by doubt in the pulpit could recover his faith through the love of a good woman and the Bible, and could find happiness in "science," which had always been his vocation and which somehow was not in conflict with the vague devotion to God that Miss Mulock demanded of all men.

An OUTCAST, Alone and Desolate

With Winwood Reade's *The Outcast* (1875, no. 73), however, we come to a novel whose author was a knowledgeable popularizer of science. Written during his final illness (born in 1838, he was only thirty-five at the time), it was his fourth novel and only successful one: he was the nephew of the successful and important novelist, Charles Reade (1814-1884), and it was probably his uncle's fame that prompted him to try his hand at novel-writing. In the early sixties he travelled in Africa as an explorer, anthropologist, and war correspondent, later publishing his journals of life in the bush and an account of the Ashanti war. By far his most celebrated work was *The Martyrdom of Man* (1872), a hard-boiled account of human suffering on earth, which Gladstone bracketed with Herbert Spencer's *First Principles* (1862) as two particular examples of the "noxious crop" of books by unbelievers. Returning to the novel form in *The Outcast*, Reade reconsidered the relationship of men to the cruel godless universe of *The Martyrdom of Man* and, virtually on his own deathbed, emerged with a solution that held out a measure of hope. In the whole range of Victorian fiction, there is nothing quite like *The Outcast*.

Essentially it consists of a memoir of his life by Edward Mordaunt, written in the form of a series of letters to his daughter Ellen, now married and a young mother. Mordaunt has been moved to write his story only because Ellen has read—despite his precautions—a manuscript left behind by another man, Arthur Elliott, who has recently committed suicide at an early age in a fit of madness. So the reader begins with Elliott, a classicist, philosopher, and devout believer. Yet—even when impulsively praying, stimulated by the beauties of nature or the reading of Plato—Elliott's gestures often "grew wild and almost furious, his utterance was choked, and a strange bubbling sound came from his mouth." One of his ancestors had been insane. And soon Elliott has read both Malthus's *Essay on Population* (first published in 1798), which makes him doubt the goodness of God, and Darwin's *Origin of Species* (1859), "which proves that the Law of Population is the chief agent by which Evolution has been produced." Malthus, of course, had long been the property of the novelists, as of everyone else; Harriet Martineau's fictional *Illustrations of Political Economy* (1832-1834, NIS), for example, includes several stories—notably, perhaps, "A Manchester Strike"—in which Malthusian principles (emigration, birth control by the postponement of marriage, and the like) are advanced, in accordance with the views of the *laissez-faire* school, as the only solution for industrial unemployment and workingmen's misery. In *Joshua Davidson* Mrs. Lynn Linton included a Malthusian businessman, and a charitable one at that. But Darwin has "just appeared" when Elliott reads him, and it is the combination of Malthus and Darwin that unseats his reason.

He goes into mourning for mankind and keeps on his study table the two scientific works, bound in dark colors, Malthus entitled "The Book of Doubt," and Darwin "The Book of Despair."

Racked by doubt, Elliott, like other "men of powerful intellect, especially those of the poetic constitution," cannot "shake off the faith" he had learned in childhood. He can neither close his eyes to nature's barbarism nor doubt the dogma of a personal creator. And so he is menaced with insanity until he falls in love and recovers his health. But the sudden death of his fiancée precipitates a recurrence of madness and suicide.

Before he dies, Elliott writes an account of a series of dreams, which he calls "A New Thing Under the Moon." Looking at the solar system from outside (he has grown to be a huge being and sits in a theatre with others equally huge), Elliott observes the horrible tragedies on earth. He is in fact a demigod, and everything that goes on in the world is part of a play designed to amuse the demigods. He leaves the theatre before the performance is over, unable to stand the tragedy. It is not even a very good play, as a review in a demigod periodical wittily demonstrates. The review summarizes the show: the whole history of the earth. But in the end (which Elliott missed) freedom triumphs over tyranny, social equality over personal ambition; war ceases, nature is conquered, vice and disease are eliminated, and the world becomes "a pleasure garden," as men learn to "bear without repining a painless death in extreme old age."

The demigod reviewer thinks of the play as a satire on theology: it was comic to see "these ephemeral creatures . . . building little houses in honour of the First Cause [churches, of course] and glibly explaining mysteries" which not even demigods understand. But why do these creatures who look like us demigods retain so many animal characteristics? Their Creator should have modified his law of evolution: "it might have been less philosophical, but it would have been more decent." Then too, more of these beings were born than could survive, and so a struggle for existence took place: ingenious, but wasteful and cruel. All along, each advance was won by violence: an unforgivable mixture of evil and good. There was too much death, disease, insanity. In short, man had been martyred, and the playwright Creator is blameworthy. Many of the audience left before the play was over, but the performance was in any case cruel and immoral. Next time this "young beginner" produces a world, "we hope it will be one we can take our wives and daughters to see, and one which will give us a more favorable impression of his own character." Here, in Elliott's ostensibly insane visions, Reade incisively summed up in a few pages his own view of the martyrdom of man.

Little wonder that Mordaunt's daughter Ellen is shocked when she reads Elliott's manuscript or that it shakes the faith which Mordaunt has carefully provided for her in her childhood: teaching her to revere "a God compared with whom the God of the Bible is a very indifferent character," but a made-up God just the same. Now she must learn about her father's own religion, the fruit of a long lifetime of suffering, which he summarizes for her in the bulk of *The Outcast.* Five times as long as Elliott's ghastly story, Mordaunt's autobiography is a more conventional novel. Son of a rich, self-denying, scholarly, and brutally severe Evangelical clergyman ("his religion was of the lowest Calvinist type") in a remote parish, Mordaunt as a boy is mistreated much as Edward Fowler had been, comforted only by a loving mother. The parish doctor is a rich man, a scientist with his laboratories, working on "the physiology and chemistry of the vegetable kingdom."

Edward takes orders, and in his first parish meets Fitzclarence, an aristocratic radical, who "sat at the feet of James Mill, dined *tête-à-tête* with the famous Jeremy [Bentham], and wrote for the *Westminster Review*," an agitator for reform, "a violent hater of the Bible and the Church, a second Tom Paine." The conversation turns to "recent discoveries in geology which revealed the world's antiquity and the creation of fish, reptiles, and quadrupeds in epochs separated by vast intervals of time." In his youthful naïvety Mordaunt affirms that the world *was* made in six days, not even aware that some clergymen were already affirming that each of the six days was a geological period. Yet *if* it could be proved that creation took many thousands of years—impossible, of course, says Edward—he agrees that it would also be proved that the Bible was not inspired. This dreadful thing Fitzclarence asserts has actually been done. And before long, Fitzclarence has sent Edward a copy of Lyell's *Principles of Geology.*

Unlike Elliott long afterwards, Mordaunt has never read Malthus, and Darwin is as yet unpublished. But Lyell is enough. Mordaunt is "captivated by the beauty of the style, the modesty of the author, and the wondrous world he opened to my view." The answers to Lyell even by fair-minded theologians seem simply pieces of special pleading. Since there is obviously one mistake in the Bible, perhaps there are others. And with a careful rereading "the scales fell from my eyes." The Bible is a beautiful literary production, but clearly "written by men and by men immersed in superstition." Mordaunt wonders how he can have gone on so long without realizing this earlier. The Incarnation is no longer tenable: "It seemed to me an awful blasphemy to assert that the great God of heaven clothed himself in the body of a man, and I prayed him to forgive me for having believed it." He still believes even more profoundly in the Creator, but of course he realizes he must leave the Church.

A kindly nearby rector emphasizes the disastrous financial consequences of such a move—Mordaunt would have to give up his fiancée—and advises him not to resign: it would be the lesser of two evils in this case to be a hypocrite. "Consider," he says, "how much harm you will do to others if you proclaim yourself an infidel; consider how much good you may do if you remain in the Church. You need never preach a doctrinal sermon; in the New Testament you will find maxims of the purest morality and precepts of the tenderest love. Let these be your texts." Mordaunt could still "convert men and women from a life of brutality and vice." Obviously the counsellor has himself followed this course. Mordaunt accepts the advice, but feels "the most horrible torments of conscience," and has nightmarish visions in the pulpit. Like Harold Gwynne, he is unable to perform the priestly function properly. Suddenly, without warning, upon being offered a far better living, he has his revulsion, and without warning he declares to Margaret, his true love, that he is an infidel, though he still acknowledges a "Divine Ruler," an "eternal spirit of Truth."

Mordaunt's father refuses to receive him, and he feels himself "an OUTCAST; alone and desolate." Chalmers, the scientific-minded doctor of his father's parish, takes him in, and Mordaunt himself now becomes a deep student of science, since Chalmers has three resident scientists in his house: an anatomist, a geologist, and an astronomer, each engaged in research for a learned book of his own, but all prepared to instruct and talk with Mordaunt. Mordaunt's father finds a means to make him leave Chalmers. Work for a publisher, marriage to Margaret on a pittance, financial ruin caused by her spendthrift brother, blindness and total destitution relieved only by the kindness of thieves and prostitutes: all this Mordaunt and his wife and baby daughter must now suffer. Margaret's death in poverty causes Mordaunt to cry out that God has murdered her. He will not pray again to "that monster, that demon, that fiend." In the lowest depths, Mordaunt is rescued by a chance meeting with the bishop, who intervenes for him with his former employers and gets him work to do once more.

Reflecting again upon God, Mordaunt concludes that none of the arguments about His benevolence or power holds water; perhaps all our ideas about God need revision. Francis Bacon's statement that "God worketh nothing in nature except by second causes" next leads him to hypothesize, Epicurean-fashion, that "God has no personal relations with the earth," is incomprehensible, and is only to be apprehended, if at all, through a study of Nature. Yet Nature's laws treat plant, animal, and human life alike, and therefore men "in common with the atoms of water and air . . . are part of the material with which the Creator," through imperfect "secondary" laws, "carries out his scheme, whatever it may be." A sad thought, disposing forever of the hope for a future life beyond the grave: "if man is only raw material," how can he expect to be rewarded later for suffering here? But—and here Mordaunt is obviously still hoping against hope—"the spirit of science" suggests that at least after death "the mind is decomposed (nothing is ever destroyed), and that its elements are recombined into other forms of mental life, so that though the individual intellect perishes nothing is lost to humanity."

The sight of the stars in the night sky suggests the vastness of the universe and the possibility of superior beings in planets of other solar systems "who would look upon us as we look upon the ants and the bees." But then Mordaunt's first sight of a steamboat suggests that, however small man may be with relation to the Universe, he is "great in relation to the Earth." Man's very efforts to make the earth progress "from a lair of wild beasts and savages to a paradise of happiness and virtue" show that he "has been selected to represent the good, to extinguish the evil." Man's realization that his mission is to "battle with the evil in Nature" would lead to a new religion whose adherents would cheerfully labor for the future of the race. Joy fills Mordaunt's heart again, and he determines to proclaim mankind's mission and preach the new religion. But he soon realizes that his role will not be that of the prophet of the new faith, and he adopts instead a life of quiet scholarship.

Realizing that his father's apparent cruelty to him has arisen directly from "his barbarous Calvinistic creed," and that this conviction had given his father great sadness, he reflects that the most important possible mission would be the "Diffusion of Doubt." Doubt "dissipates superstition and softens the rancour of religious life. Without doubt, there can be no tolerance. . . . The scepticism spread by Voltaire humanised the dogmas of the Roman Church; and we ourselves are passing through a silent, gradual, but momentous doubting revolution," which is softening the views of the clergy. Mordaunt has lately "heard a clergyman of the Church of England say things in the pulpit which in my younger days very few laymen would have dared to say at a dinner-party," though of course "much religious persecution goes on and bigotry abounds."

Mordaunt believes in "God the Incomprehensible": to try to comprehend Him is a mere waste of time. He believes in learning, in being kind. He sometimes wishes for his old belief "when . . . God was semi-human and man was semi-divine; and after death life began," yet more often he has no wish for immortality and feels it "just and natural that I should go back to the Earth whence I came." He thinks his "religion of unselfishness . . . is far more ennobling than any religion which holds out the hope of celestial rewards."

Of course, says Mordaunt at the close of *The Outcast*, he may be wrong, and there may possibly be a future life. And if there should be, a doubter like himself who had practiced the religion of unselfishness would be perfectly prepared for it: "We disbelieve in future rewards, and so eradicate all selfish longings from our hearts; but if, contrary to our expectations, there should be a future life with rewards, none will be able to rank with ourselves. For what life is so highly deserving of reward as that which is spent in doing good without the hope or desire of reward?" So Winwood Reade turned "Pascal's Wager" upside down and still came out the winner of his bet.

The Outcast is no mere fictional autobiography like *The Nemesis of Faith* or *Oakfield* or *The Autobiography of Christopher Kirkland.* It is an effort to teach the Victorian novel-reading public the lessons of *The Martyrdom of Man,* and to leave them at the end with some crumb of comfort in the form of a substitute faith which that treatise had virtually denied them. Had Lyell, or Darwin, or Huxley, or Herbert Spencer, or W. K. Clifford written a novel about his beliefs, it might have been a better novel than *The Outcast.* But since they did not, *The Outcast* must stand alone as the effort of a man who had actually studied some science to come to grips in fiction with the impact of his study upon Christian Orthodoxy.

Laxity Combatted

Few novelists can have been further from Winwood Reade's new religion of doubt than Charlotte Yonge. From her point of view nothing could have been more deplorable than the growing laxity of the seventies, which, she saw, was intimately connected with scientific advance: a subject that she can hardly have known much about, but one whose implications clearly troubled her. In *Magnum Bonum* (1879, no. 74), one of her longest, most complex, and best novels, she handled this theme with dignity and subtlety. A typically crowded, complicated Yonge romance about two large linked families of cousins, *Magnum Bonum* is made even more complicated than usual by the fact that the boys in both families have the same first and last names. The reader nonetheless comes to know each person intimately and to follow his fortunes with a real interest in his eventual fate. Adult contemporaries of Miss Yonge would probably not have missed her main point, but a twentieth-century explorer of nineteenth-century fiction may well do so.

Magnum Bonum is the name given in the Brownlow family to an important medical discovery—exactly what it is Miss Yonge perhaps wisely did not specify—some sort of miracle drug or treatment for disease, the research for which is left incomplete by Dr. Brownlow when he dies. To his wife ("Mother Carey") he solemnly bequeaths as a sacred trust his notebook of materials on his experiments, with the injunction that she keep the *Magnum Bonum* a secret until the boys are grown up (if put into the wrong hands the results would be dangerous) and then only "confide it to the one that seems fittest, when he has taken his degree, and is a good, religious, wise, able man, with brains and balance, fit to be trusted to work out and apply such an invention, and not to make it serve his own advancement, but be a real good and blessing to all."

"Mother Carey"—charming, talented, artistic, an affectionate mother, utterly devoted to her husband's memory—of course accepts the charge. But despite all her good qualities she is heading for difficulties: she reads Scott aloud to her children on Sunday and, when reproved, defends herself by saying she does not like "dull and goody" Sunday reading. She "has not got the recipe" for improving her children: "when we've done our church, I see no good in decorous boredom." Here, as often, Miss Yonge has put the case against herself so well that one may be misled. Carey's Bohemian London friends visit her in the country and sing songs boisterously (but innocently) late at night. She is a woman of love and ability; but she lacks "wisdom and judgment." Moreover, the local vicar is "a dull weak man, of a worn-out type," and his sermons are so bad that the only reason for keeping awake is to wait for his hilarious mixed metaphors, such as "Let us not, beloved brethren, as gaudy insects, flutter out life's little day, bound to the chariot wheels of vanity, whirling in the vortex of dissipation, until at length we lie moaning over the bitter dregs of the intoxicating draught." So there is little help in the local church for Carey, little "to lead her higher."

Indeed, the *Magnum Bonum* "had become very nearly a religion to her"—a bad thing obviously—and her boys "must be brought up worthy of the quest, high-minded, disinterested, and devoted, as well as intellectual and religious." As Yongeians, we know that this is *not* religion, not enough. At one moment, in her bereavement, Carey cries out for just one moment with her dead husband to learn from him "how to keep the charge . . . your Magnum Bonum." Then her eye is caught by an engraving of Christ, "the Great Physician, consoling and healing . . . the sick, the captive, the self-tormenting genius, the fatherless, the widow." At that moment

> Something darted through her mind like a pang, followed by a strange throb—"Give yourself to Him. Seek the true good first. The other may lie on its way." But it was only a pang. The too-natural recoil came the next minute. Was she not as religious as there was any need to be, or at least as she could be without alienating her children or affecting more than she felt? Give herself to Him? How? Did that mean a great deal of church-going, sermon-reading, cottage visiting, prayers, meditations, and avoidance of pleasure? That would never do.

Buried unobtrusively in the midst of a very long novel, this little episode is actually the key to Charlotte Yonge's intentions. *Our* twentieth-century sympathies are fully with Carey. Not so Miss Yonge's. It takes an accident on a Swiss glacier threatening two of her sons with death to give Carey "the one thing that was wanting to her sweetness and charm." Her anxiety and the example of a friend make "conscientiousness, or . . . religion, appear winning to her, neither stiff, nor censorious, nor goody."

This is still not enough. At first it seems that none of the Brownlow boys will have the right combination of scientific bent and deep faith necessary to take over the work of the *Magnum Bonum*. Carey's intellectual, ambitious, and self-willed daughter Janet begs her mother to give her the opportunity, after she has passed her examinations, to "claim that best inheritance my father left, which his sons do not heed." But Carey replies that the remaining work involves "a succession of experiments" that would have been very hard even for Dr. Brownlow and would be impossible for any woman. It was "the exceeding difficulty and danger of the proof" that had made him reserve it for a son who should be "good as well as clever, clever as well as good." The rebellious Janet eventually steals the notebook containing the work on the *Magnum Bonum*, and—finding the experiments indeed too hard for her to perform (impossible for a woman: we cannot tell why)—she marries without her mother's knowledge or consent a shady doctor, a Greek (although he has a German name) who thinks the *Magnum Bonum* is some sort of patent medicine that will make him rich, and tries to buy the formula from the outraged Mother Carey. Janet's presumption is of course a capital crime, and it is eventually punished by death.

One of the Brownlow sons, however, does eventually go into medicine, and to him Carey gives the recovered notebook. When he and his namesake, cousin, and fellow scientist examine the document, they realize that much of the discovery has already been worked out and published by another active doctor; they consult with him, and while he does get some valuable ideas from Dr. Brownlow's work, essentially the problem had been solved independently. Thus the *Magnum Bonum*, so carefully held as in a shrine all the intervening years, has proven—whatever its value to mankind—to have been misnamed.

The true *great good*—Charlotte Yonge is saying, although she never underlines her point or states it in so many words—can never be a matter of mere human ingenuity and scientific cleverness: it is the Christian faith. It does not seem to have occurred to her that the sainted Dr. Brownlow's original disposition of his notebook had anything immoral about it: that to keep mankind waiting for so great an alleged benefit until one of his own sons was ready to complete the work had something in it of selfishness and self-aggrandizement; or, if it did occur to her, she glossed it over by emphasizing the dangerous nature of the experiments still left unperformed and the necessity of protecting mankind from the menace of an incomplete piece of scientific work. Yet it is obvious that to Miss Yonge all scientific work—like all other human activity—if uninformed by faith was a mere vanity.

The Brownlow cousins are uncomfortably conscious of the snobbish attitude that contemporary high society takes towards doctors, viewing the profession as somehow not on a level with the army, the navy, the church, or even the law. One of their sons, having overcome this prejudice in himself and having decided that he wants to become a doctor and a scientist, is deeply worried nonetheless by the possibility that his faith may suffer if he follows his intentions. He consults an older doctor, who, for the only time in the novel, deals head on with the problem and tells young Brownlow, "If faith is unsettled by looking deeper into the mysteries of God's work, it cannot have been substantial faith, but merely outward, thoughtless, reception." No doubt "speculations and difficulties" may arise, but there will be "none which real active religion and love cannot regard as the mere effects of half-knowledge—the distortions of a partial view."

This, of course, was what Miss Yonge herself believed, largely untroubled as she was by any substantial acquaintance with scientific advance. The "speculations and difficulties" she calmly foresees are a far cry from the agonies of Edward Mordaunt in *The Outcast.* The contradictions between the Bible and the teachings of the churches on the one hand and the findings of the scientists and higher critics on the other might indeed be made to yield to faith, but only if the churches prepared themselves to answer the questions, to modify their earlier positions, to abandon their bland reassurance. It is not surprising that Charlotte Yonge did not see these things; it is surprising, rather, that she reassured her readers—mostly well-bred, protected, naturally timorous, and conventional young High Anglicans—that careers in science and medicine need not necessarily lead them into infidelity.

To Atheism and Back

In *Magnum Bonum,* there is no real doubt: only Mother Carey's mistaken overemphasis on the value of a scientific experiment when she "made a religion" out of her husband's legacy and ever so slightly neglected what should have been her true religion. But in *Donovan* (1882, no. 77), a runaway best-seller written at the age of twenty-seven by Ada Ellen Bayly (1857-1903), who wrote under the pseudonym "Edna Lyall," doubt takes the center of the stage. At eighteen, Donovan Farrant has every reason to declare that "the people who brag most about the universal brotherhood are the very first to throw stones at their neighbours." He is about to be expelled from school for having introduced card playing among the boys, and he has to run the gauntlet: "The Christian brotherhood are nearly ready for me," he says.

Sent home to England at the age of three while his parents were in India, Donovan had been confided to the care of a small-minded and unkind woman not unlike the one who, at about the same time, was tormenting the young Rudyard Kipling, and who was later immortalized in his "Baa, Baa, Black Sheep." Brought up without any real religion yet in terror of a fierce punishing God, and frustrated in his efforts to read and learn, sure that he is wicked, he is rejected at eight by his selfish mother when she does come home. He is repelled by her "conventional religion" and hypocritical church going, and by the time he has his first tutor, he has decided that "They are all shams, these Christian people."

Donovan's determination to profess no faith receives "amused encouragement" from his tutor, a "clever, but shallow," man who

> had dabbled in science, and rather prided himself on being able to appreciate the difficulties which great minds found in reconciling the new discoveries of science and the old faiths. He quoted Tyndall and Huxley with great aptness, and, though on occasion he was quite capable of appearing to be exceedingly orthodox, yet he was rather fond of styling himself an Agnostic when quite sure of his audience. He . . . liked talking of his "intellectual difficulties," and regarded scepticism as "no bad form nowadays."

He allows Donovan to discard the classics and "devote most of his time to scientific subjects." The damage is advanced by the sudden death of Donovan's sympathetic father, who has been kind to him in his disgrace at school. It is completed by Donovan's attendance at an atheist lecture, "The Existence of a God—Science *versus* Superstition," delivered by a handsome, eloquent speaker, whose profession is to overthrow courteously but effectively "the mischievous delusion of popular Christianity," and who crushes those in the audience who try to argue with him. Luke Raeburn, the atheist, upholds "self-restraint, self-sacrifice, temperance, truth at whatever cost," precepts that Winwood Reade's Mordaunt would also have promulgated as his own. The combination of Raeburn's skill and his opponents' ineptitude sends Donovan home "a confirmed atheist, a bitter-hearted despiser of Christianity." Known to be reading Mill and "books on positivism," and to have attended the lecture, Donovan is shunned by the careful neighboring gentry, and their snubs add to his bitterness.

Donovan is unquestionably a tear-jerker: at the deathbed of his beloved little crippled sister, the only person who loves him and whom he loves, he prays aloud that God *may* exist, so that He may stop the invalid's pain; he repeats, without any sense of the "hideous mockery," her favorite hymn, Newman's "Lead Kindly Light," but he cannot bring himself to kneel at her funeral. "The consistency of an atheist rarely received anything but hard words, and all the spectators were inexpressibly shocked." He is thought to be "hard and unfeeling" and is subjected to "looks of shrinking aversion or righteous indignation." Turned out of his father's house by his wicked and dishonest stepfather, Donovan slips into a life of cardsharping. Recovering from a severe illness, he reads by chance the Gospel of St. Matthew and is struck for the first time by the life of Christ; he progresses to Renan's *Life* of Jesus. Without in the least acquiring faith, he now *behaves* like a true Christian, restoring a fortune he has won at baccarat to a French gambler whom he has inadvertently ruined, abandoning card playing, and sinking into the direst poverty.

A kindly Cornish doctor, whom Donovan has known in the past, rescues him—still only twenty-two—and plays the Good Samaritan. Knowing all the worst about Donovan, the doctor's wife and children take him in and make him feel, for the first time in his life, a member of a family. No sheep is lost forever, says the doctor; and "lost" means only "not found yet." In the last third of the novel, Donovan is gradually "found" again: partly through the kindness of others towards him; partly through his own self-sacrifice—the "road of the cross"—his increasingly Christ-like behavior towards others, climaxed when he nurses through the smallpox his stepfather, the man he has best reason to hate; partly through the influence of Osmond, an Anglican clergyman with a London slum parish. Osmond's Christianity is exactly that of George MacDonald: the fatherly behavior of earthly fathers is only the barest reflection of the fatherly love of God for His children. This God—like MacDonald's called the "Father of lights"—of course makes the most appeal to those whose fathers—like Donovan's or George MacDonald's own—have been kind to their sons: such an appeal could never have been made, for example, to Edward Fowler—Froude's projection of himself—or to Edward

Mordaunt in *The Outcast*, since their earthly fathers had been cruel and tyrannical.

During these years of his movement away from atheism, Donovan is a medical student, and so constantly learning more about the science which had so largely contributed to his original doubt. His hard and fast atheism is early replaced by agnosticism, but this proves far more painful: it had not been difficult to be stoical when denying the existence of God, but "to waver in doubt, to know nothing, to feel that in knowledge only could there be rest, and yet to despair of ever gaining that knowledge . . . was . . . a misery. . . ." Science, as his friend the doctor tells him, "great and noble and mighty as she is, cannot satisfy all a man's needs." But Donovan wants *proof*: "in science all is proved with exquisite clearness; in religion there is absolutely no proof." And here, of course, as Coleridge argued, is where Donovan goes wrong: one must have faith *before* one can believe. The whole matter is not really an intellectual one; what is needed is rather "the awakening of a spirit which slept." As a scientist, Donovan cannot account in any way for the "existence of that immaterial thing, the will," yet he *feels* that it exists: similarly the doctor "knows and feels" the existence of God. "One of the greatest men of science of the present day is obliged to own that *consciousness* is not mentally presentable, although it exists."

Doubts are natural; while one is doubting one needs only to go on living—and doing the right thing. On Donovan's shelves, a cause of alarm to the aggressively pious, are "Maurice, Renan, Haeckel, Kingsley, Strauss, Erskine [presumably Thomas Erskine of Linlathen] and at the top an open volume, Draper's 'Conflict between Religion and Science' [1875: by an American scientist]." Among his fellow medical students there are "plenty of Freethinkers," who discuss "the points of discord between religion and science." Their conversations often seem irritatingly puerile to Donovan: one says triumphantly that he has never found a soul in the dissecting room; so immortality must be impossible; but the reply, "No one but a fool would look for one there," elicits Donovan's applause.

Donovan's friend Osmond, the clergyman, astonishes him by declaring that he himself regards the theory of evolution as "in absolute harmony with all that I know or can conceive of God. . . . an imperfect glimpse of the beauty of His plan, the best and clearest that science can give us." And if spontaneous generation of cells—as yet unproven—should be demonstrated, this would "merely carry us one step further back in our appreciation of the original will-power. We shall still recognise the one Mind impressing one final and all-embracing law upon what we call matter and force, and then leaving force and matter to elaborate the performance of that law." Even Donovan himself is not prepared to argue very hard for the standard contemporary unbeliever's hypothetical concept of a "fortuitous concourse of atoms" as against Osmond's primordial Law. As for *Genesis*, "it expresses in a simple, clear way, such as a wise teacher might use with young children, the very truths that recent researches have wonderfully enlarged upon." Again like George MacDonald—and some of the German theologians—Osmond is cheerfully ready to concede the likelihood of an eternal life for animals: St. Paul "asserts the deliverance of the *whole creation*"; Osmond admits that he is, with Tennyson, a believer in the "Higher Pantheism."

In Osmond, Donovan has been made to encounter a clergyman of advanced liberal views—views which would still have horrified many in 1882—but the only sort of clergyman likely to be able to move Donovan further along the road away from agnosticism. While we may feel it improbable that Donovan himself should not only give his stepfather medical assistance but also tender him spiritual consolation and preach to him the doctrine of eternal fatherhood, we do not feel it at all impossible. And this is because "Edna Lyall," within her limited role as a novelist not writing for intellectuals but seeking to entertain as well as to enlighten, has dealt honestly with her readers: science plays a part—together with human cruelty—in making Donovan an atheist, and—together with human kindness—science cannot be left unreconciled with religion as he is triumphantly returned to a highly liberal form of early 1880's Christianity.

In short, Osmond is a Maurician clergyman, who has made it part of his belief that atheists and agnostics are children of God like the rest of us. They must be listened to even when they say that there is no God, because one may learn what side of the truth they have been able to apprehend. Such a clergyman was Arthur Penrhyn Stanley, Dean of Westminster, who maintained friendships and engaged in discussions with many scientists and was the personal pastor of the strongly anti-Christian scientist John Tyndall. When we come to consider the works of W. H. Mallock, we shall find this sort of latitudinarianism vigorously satirized.

Science, Religion, and Samuel Butler

Of all the novels under discussion in this book it seems probable that Samuel Butler's *Way of All Flesh* (1903, no. 87) is today the most widely read. Yet, paradoxically, few of its many admiring readers are likely to have appreciated the multiple intentions of its author, a fact which would have given him intense pleasure. Musician and composer who disliked all music after Handel, painter who adored the works of Giovanni Bellini, excellent scholar of Greek and Latin, pragmatic philosopher of science without being a scientist, lifelong bachelor who in his maturity visited the same prostitute every Wednesday afternoon for years, notable eccentric (some would have said a crank), tireless controversialist against real and imagined opponents, Samuel Butler (1835-1902) deeply enjoyed mystification. He always saw the other side of any question, even after he himself had taken a position on it, and would frequently argue anonymously or pseudonymously against himself in the columns of newspapers or periodicals to be sure that the subject got a thorough hearing and that it would be he who put the case for both sides and for some sort of compromise between them.

Unsure of what it was he wanted from public opinion—except the appreciation which he almost never received in his lifetime—he was an individualist of individualists, far ahead of his contemporaries, a pioneer in the understanding of the human unconscious, in the awareness of the threat to mankind from machines, in the critique alike of evolutionary theory and of Christian dogma, witty and rewarding. *The Way of All Flesh*, it is obvious, belongs with *The*

Nemesis of Faith and *Oakfield* as another largely autobiographical document describing the passage of a Victorian young man from faith to doubt. Not so obviously, but just as truly, the novel also embodies the essence of Butler's advanced anti-Darwinist theories of evolution. It belongs, then, properly to the novels of doubt in which the new science plays a major part; but here Darwinism does not lead to the loss of faith: it is the author's counteroffensive against Darwinism that leads to a form of new faith. A unique specimen, the novel provides a suitable climax for this chapter.

In the year 1873, aged thirty-eight, Butler read George Eliot's *Middlemarch* at the suggestion of his friend Miss Eliza Savage, a former governess. She was lame and not particularly attractive, but so clever and so good a judge of his personality that she was often able to persuade him to do what she wanted him to do, which was invariably the best possible thing he could have done. Miss Savage's purpose was to stimulate Butler into writing a novel of his own: he was "an admirable novel-making machine," she said, and should be "set going." As she had anticipated, Butler was convinced that he could write a better novel than *Middlemarch*, and he began *The Way of All Flesh*. For the next twelve years he worked at it on and off, sending Miss Savage installments, always obtaining encouragement and sometimes helpful criticism (in 1883 she wrote him, "the grand catastrophe wants vraisemblance [i.e., Ernest's arrest seems improbable]," and though Butler revised it, modern readers will mostly agree with her). But in 1885 she died, and in 1887 Butler did the last of his work on the manuscript, which remained—still not quite finished—in his desk drawer, to be published only the year after his death. It was hailed then by Bernard Shaw, as it has been hailed by thousands of delighted readers ever since, as the quintessential commentary on a Victorian upbringing and career.

Like Froude and W. D. Arnold, Butler came from a clerical family: his grandfather, for whom he was named, was a reforming headmaster at Shrewsbury School, like Thomas Arnold at Rugby, and later became Bishop of Lichfield. It is only one of the bewildering paradoxes in Butler's life that in his later years he should have devoted much time and energy to writing a formal Victorian *Life and Letters* of this clerical grandfather, and to violently attacking those who he fancied were hostile to his memory. Yet like some of the other paradoxes, this one becomes easier to understand when one begins to appreciate the full complexity of Butler's intellectual and spiritual development. His father, Thomas Butler, who had wanted to go into the Navy, was forced by his father to take clerical orders instead. He was Rector of Langar, near Nottingham, and later Canon of Lincoln; his wife, originally a Unitarian, became a devout Churchwoman. These are the two who sat for the portraits of Theobald and Christina, the awful, yet often hilariously funny, parents in *The Way of All Flesh.* Samuel Butler's parents may have seemed kindly or humorous to other members of their family; what is important for us is the way they seemed to Samuel Butler, and this he set down imperishably.

Even after his Langar childhood, Butler himself was planning to enter the Church. At Cambridge between 1854 and 1858 he had "never met anyone who entertained a doubt" of the miracles in the New Testament. He did detest the "Simeonites," the extreme evangelical undergraduates, in part for social reasons, as is shown by the caricatures he drew of them in *The Way of All Flesh*; but he also mistrusted all excessive zeal. In an attack he wrote on the Simeonites (which was probably stuffed into their Cambridge mailboxes), he commented that "Men are disgusted with religion if it is placed before them at unseasonable times, in unseasonable places, and clothed in a most unseemly dress." The "Sims," he suggested, were humbugs. But there is no indication that Butler had yet heard of the new science or that any misgivings about taking orders were based upon doubt. He went to London to work among the poor and to prepare himself for ordination. There he discovered that some of the poor boys in his evening classes had been baptized and others had not; yet baptism had made no difference in their character or their behavior. This, he said, destroyed his faith in dogma, and he declined to go into the Church. He really wanted to be a painter; so there was an element of rationalization in this explanation. After a disagreement with his father in 1859, Butler went out on his own to New Zealand to try his hand at sheep farming. The night before he left he did not say his prayers, and he never said them again.

On the way to New Zealand he read Gibbon's *Decline and Fall,* with its anti-Christian eighteenth-century rationalist bias; once in

New Zealand, he read Darwin for the first time. He was a success in the frontier environment, and he managed to get a piano conveyed to his sheep ranch, which he played each night after the long day's hard work. He also wrote, in a New Zealand newspaper in 1862, a dialogue between a pro-Darwinian and an anti-Darwinian, in which the pro-Darwinian—acknowledging that there is a conflict between Darwin and Christianity—argues that this must be honestly confronted in order that it may be reconciled. Both the friend of evolution and its enemy actually represented Butler. And in the dialogue he emphasized two ideas that even then preoccupied him: an offspring resembles its parent, but any variation which makes it better adapted will improve the line; and a change in climate or environment can well produce such a variation (this latter a point made by Lamarck, but accepted by Darwin). These two aspects of evolutionary theory were to prove of major importance in Butler's later writing: by changing the Christian climate of his upbringing, the hero of *The Way of All Flesh* will improve on his heredity. In another article in 1863, "Darwin among the Machines," Butler pointed out, perhaps half in fun, the danger menacing man from his own offspring, the machine, already itself evolving from generation to generation and growing more complex. The answer? Kill the machines! As he often did, Butler answered his own article with a counterblast extolling machines, and with a third paper reconciling the earlier two: if machines evolve, man will evolve with them and maintain his ability to control them.

Home in London after five years, and busy learning to be a painter, Butler continued to face the problem that Darwin had caused for him: what to substitute for the Christian Deity. A deity must be personal, he thought, and *The Origin of Species* put nothing in God's place. Moreover, Butler's close examination of the Gospel evidence for the Resurrection led him to write a pamphlet rejecting that miracle on historic grounds. In Butler's *Erewhon* ("Nowhere" spelt backwards [1871, NIS]), a Utopian fantasy, the hero must leave behind him at the entrance-pass into the mysterious new country ten statues through which the wind blows with a hollow ghostly sound: in fact, the Ten Commandments, which we must reject if we are ever to embark upon a vision of a new world. Most of the names in *Erewhon* are reversed, and many Victorian absurdities are ridiculed, but the Erewhonians have their own, which are not very different. Here crime is an illness, treated by a "straightener" much like a psychiatrist: Senoj Nosnibor (Jones Robinson), the rich banker, who has embezzled money from a helpless widow, is not in jail but is being straightened out in regular sessions. On the other hand, illness is a crime, and sufferers from severe disease are sentenced to life imprisonment and harshly denounced by judges.

The people worship at Musical Banks (the Church of England), depositing there a special form of valueless currency: the ceremonies are absurd, but dignified, and hallowed by tradition. Profits are divided every thirty thousand years, and it has been only two thousand years since the last distribution (the birth of Christ). The people get on very nicely without a personal God. Their real object of worship is the goddess Ydgrun (Mrs. Grundy). The "High" Ydgrunites are handsome, athletic gentlemen, admirable in every way, who have faith only in her, like Victorians generally, while the "Low" Ydgrunites are often hypocrites. There is no afterlife, but there is a forelife, and every child signs a formula declaring his parents innocent of any responsibility for his existence: he asks forgiveness for having maliciously troubled their peace. The Erewhonian Church's claim to possessing absolute truth, its incompetent ministers, and its stifling of new ideas; the Erewhonian birth-formula which ridicules baptism; these are uncomfortably like their counterparts in the world the hero has left behind. There is one sect preaching a faith in which those who "had been born strong and healthy and handsome would be rewarded for ever and ever"; in other words, immortality is a reward for eugenics.

In *Erewhon*, the anti-Darwinist of Butler's early dialogue has won some new victories: acquired characteristics are important in heredity, and unconscious memory is emphasized. Butler was moving towards the crystallization of an evolutionary but anti-Darwinian faith. In *The Fair Haven* (1873, no. 54), he produced an extraordinarily guarded novel, in the guise of a "defence of the miraculous element in our Lord's ministry on earth," preceded by a memoir of the alleged author, John Pickard Owen (who had ostensibly died), by his alleged brother, William Bickersteth Owen. The device of putting himself at two removes from his material enabled

Butler to construct a most elaborate literary shell game, ambiguous throughout, and baffling when a reader tried to discover what the author was really getting at. In the memoir of Owen, we begin to get Butler's own reminiscences, but they are sometimes turned upside down. The father of the Owen brothers, for example, who dies early, is "a singularly gentle and humorous playmate," the exact reverse, of course, of Canon Butler or Theobald Pontifex of *The Way of All Flesh.* And, says Owen, "children's earliest ideas of God are modelled upon the character of their father. . . . Should the father be kind, considerate, full of the warmest love, fond of showing it, and reserved only about his displeasure, the child, having learned to look upon God as his Heavenly Father through the Lord's Prayer and our Church Services, will feel towards God as he does towards his own father." Of course, the reverse is also true: "if a man has found his earthly father harsh and uncongenial, his conception of his Heavenly Parent will be painful." He will shrink from God as from "an exaggerated likeness of his father."

Butler is saying explicitly what Froude said implicitly in "The Spirit's Trials," when he so vividly contrasted Edward Fowler's harsh and unloving father (who was his own father, the archdeacon, as Froude perceived him), with the tender, loving father of the Harding family, with whose daughter Fowler falls in love. The identification of a kind earthly father with a kind heavenly father (which, Butler says, "will stick to a man for years and years after he has attained manhood—probably it will never leave him") is nowhere better exemplified than in the life and writing of George MacDonald, as we have seen. Yet the possession of a kind father on earth, against whom a son must mask his natural rebelliousness, created psychological problems for MacDonald (as for other men with loving fathers), of which Butler—who in most moods so strongly hated his own father—could have no inkling.

But the Owen boys are left to their mother to bring up, and she has been "trained in the lowest school of Evangelical literalism." Later on in life, says the memoirist, both brothers agree that this school was "the main obstacle to the complete overthrow of unbelief." Penetrating the triple negative, one sees that the Owens felt that religious faith would have triumphed all along the line, had it *not* been for Evangelical literalism, the great nurse of doubt. Like

Butler himself, John Pickard Owen makes the discovery that baptism has not made the baptized youths in his Sunday class any better than the unbaptized. This leads him to become a Baptist: if infant baptism does not work, then adult baptism must be the answer. But the Baptist view of predestination is unacceptable, and Owen becomes a Catholic. The Catholic insistence upon accepting the authority of the church and the stifling of free inquiry force him to move on again. From Deism, he takes the usual path toward doubt, and eventually swings back—for all the world like Donovan—to a latitudinarian Broad-Church position. But he has had enough now; melancholia sweeps him into inertia and death. For Owen, as for Butler, it had been a terrible fight: others, properly brought up, were given as their birthright the freedom he had to struggle so desperately to acquire.

This early portion of *The Fair Haven* is only the preface to the expanded republication—as by Owen, this time—of Butler's earlier essay "The Evidence for the Resurrection of Jesus Christ as Given by the Four Evangelists, Critically Examined" (1865). Of course, the Gospel accounts won't stand up as history, and the miracle of the Resurrection cannot be proven. But—by a Butlerian paradox—the very inconsistency of the accounts should serve to strengthen faith, not to weaken it: if there were not some distortion in the accounts, it would be too perfect a version for humanity to have written or to accept. Here, Butler was satirizing the reconcilers of the higher criticism; he was satirizing their opponents; he was satirizing Owen, and by that token he was even satirizing himself. Like Gosse's father Philip—whose *Omphalos* (1875) proclaimed that God had put fossils on earth to test man's faith in the perfect truth of the chronology of Genesis, and that Adam, though not born of woman, was given a navel by God just the same—Owen (Butler) finds satisfaction and reassurance in the very discrepancies that so worried others.

In a concluding passage, Butler with savage irony pretends to prefer the mediaeval ascetic ideal of Christian sanctity ("wasted limbs. . . . clothed in the garb of poverty— . . . upturned eyes piercing the very heavens in the ecstasy of a divine despair") to the classical ideal of physical beauty and the pleasures of the flesh. His readers were duly edified. Indeed, *The Fair Haven* puzzled and deceived many of the keenest Victorian polemicists against doubt, who welcomed it as a serious defense of orthodoxy. Even Darwin wrote to Butler saying that if he had not known who wrote it, he would never have suspected that the author was not orthodox. "What has struck me . . . is your dramatic power . . . the way you earnestly and thoroughly assume the character and think the thoughts of the man you pretend to be." *The Fair Haven* is no hors d'oeuvre to be recommended to one just beginning to feast upon Victorian religious fiction; but there are few better savories for the blasé banqueter who has sampled all the other dishes.

While working at intervals on *The Way of All Flesh*, Butler completed his own theory of evolution. While actually writing *Life and Habit* (1877), he suddenly hit on the compromise between evolution and Christianity for which he had been seeking ever since his first dialogue published in New Zealand. Darwinian natural selection, with its survival of the fittest, seemed to him less and less satisfactory as a theory. He put his emphasis upon Lamarck's idea of the unconscious memory, and explored and developed it with a persistence that was ridiculed by scientists at the time, but with a rigor and an effectiveness that some twentieth-century critics have begun to appreciate. How is it that we know best those things of which we are actually least conscious? How is it that a pianist can play a difficult piece while simultaneously carrying on a conversation? How is it that we follow in the paths of our ancestors without conscious purpose?

The more conscious our knowledge of a subject, the less we really know about it. Far from being the coming religion, science is only a new superstition, and the scientist must "be well-watched by those who value freedom," lest a fearful new tyranny be established. At the same time, "we are still drawn" to the "unspoken teaching" of the Church "with a force that no falsehood could command." True: these days churchmen are too introspective, too talkative, too conscious of themselves, and the more conscious they are of knowing, the less they know. But the Church's ideal "is in grace." As with knowledge, so with will: the less conscious we are of wanting something, the more we actually want it. We have to learn how to eat, but we know how to swallow. We have to learn to walk, to talk, to read: all these are peculiarly human characteristics; but we digest without consciousness: digestion "we have in common even with our invertebrate ancestry." The unborn chick grows a bill to peck a hole in its egg shell because of "infinite practice on the part of the chicken's ancestors." Individual human beings are the sum total of all the influences upon them: " 'we,' 'our souls,' our 'selves' or 'personalities' . . . are but the *consensus* and full flowing stream of countless sensations and impulses on the part of our tributory 'souls' or 'selves.' "

Butler developed the implications of his theory with incisiveness and wit: "What is the discovery of the laws of gravitation as compared with the knowledge that sleeps in every hen's egg upon a kitchen shelf?" When a hen eats a grain of corn, that grain has nothing in its ancestral memory to prepare itself for being inside a hen's stomach, and so it adopts the hen's memories: "There is no such persecutor of grain as another grain when it has . . . identified itself with the hen." Man is the dominant animal on earth because he can more often put other organisms into a position with which their forefathers have been unfamiliar than the other way around. And why are hybrids infertile? Obviously because their memories are incompatible. Darwin's five hundred crossbred eggs that never matured were "distracted by the internal tumult of conflicting memories" and were therefore "puzzled to death."

In a hilarious passage (of the sort that convinced his scientific opponents he was not a serious debater, but that strikes us quite differently) Butler uses the Church of England to combat Darwin's assertion that the Lamarckian concept of inherited habit is disproved by neuter insects: in the Church

> The bishops are the spiritual queens, the clergy are the neuter workers. They differ widely in their structure (for dress must be considered as a part of structure), in the delicacy of the food they eat, and in the kind of house they inhabit, and also in many of their instincts, from the bishops, who are their spiritual parents. Not only this, but there are two distinct kinds of neuter workers—priests and deacons; and of the former there are deans, archdeacons, prebends, canons, rural deans, vicars, rectors, curates, yet all spiritually sterile. In spite of this sterility, however, is there anyone who will maintain

> that the widely differing structures and instincts of these castes are not due to inherited spiritual habits? Still less will he be inclined to do so when he reflects that by such slight modification of treatment as consecration and endowment any one of them can be rendered spiritually fertile.

Opposing natural selection and its apparent corollary that blind chance determined variation and therefore survival, Butler did not rely upon such humorous analogies as this. But humor accompanied him even in his most serious biological arguments. With regard to the leaf-moth, which can look like foliage at all the stages of the leaf, he declared that these could no more be "the accumulation of minute, perfectly blind and unintelligent variations" than the artificial flowers in a woman's hat or the plain clothes put on by a detective to conceal the fact that he is a policeman. Men don't make mouse traps or steam engines because they don't want them. In his *Evolution Old and New* (1879), Butler made much of Darwin's predecessors, including Darwin's grandfather, Erasmus Darwin, and fiercely attacked Darwin himself as not fully understanding his own theories. Into the complex polemic that followed (Butler wrote two more books on evolution) we need not go, but with some justice Butler felt himself slighted and neglected by Darwin's apparent refusal to take him seriously, combined with what seemed like covert attacks.

By 1887, then—though his ideas were to undergo further development in later years—Butler had reached the conclusions with respect to human life and religious faith that are embodied in *The Way of All Flesh*, which he put aside in that year and left virtually untouched thereafter. In the "continued personality" passing not only from parent to child but also from each entire generation of mankind to the next, he found the substitute for the personal Deity of which Darwinism had originally robbed him. Since men live in their descendants, they obtain a form of immortality. The mere wish to live, to know, to do, is in itself an act of faith: suicide is the ultimate demonstration of lack of faith. This is "the vital principle." And the presence of unconscious memory is the prerequisite for life. The healthy ancestral memory provides the best possible life, and the inverse is equally true.

Now that we know what kind of man wrote *The Way of All Flesh*, we can fully appreciate the meaning of all the attention he devoted to Ernest Pontifex's ancestry. Great-grandfather John, the hard-working carpenter and organ builder, untroubled by intellectual matters, at home in his skin, so to speak, who says farewell to the sun the night before he dies, has made the single invaluable contribution to what we would call the genes of his great-grandson. John has died in a state of grace and like Abraham (Genesis xvi.12-16) he has been vouchsafed the revelation that in the fourth generation his seed will be fruitful. At ancient Rome a "pontifex" was a priestly patriarch and magistrate: John Pontifex, it is subtly implied, is *Pontifex Maximus*, the highest priest of all; *maximus* also signifies the earliest of those who have been our *maiores*, our ancestors, or greater ones.

Note John's epitaph: he was "unostentatious but exemplary in the discharge" of his "religious, moral, and social duties": a true statement, although the stone was erected by his unworthy son George, a sanctimonious religious publisher of evangelical books, a mean man, who unfortunately takes most of his characteristics from his narrow-minded, disagreeable mother. Grandfather George uses his money to keep his hold over his children, forces *his* son, Theobald, to become a clergyman against his will, and lies about having broken the bottle of water from the Jordan used in baptising his grandson Ernest. George too has an appropriate epitaph (was it by Theobald?): "HE NOW LIES AWAITING A JOYFUL RESURRECTION AT THE LAST DAY. WHAT MANNER OF MAN HE WAS THAT DAY WILL DISCOVER."

So Theobald's outrageous behavior is foreordained: he has inherited George's acquired characteristics. He is also a dull man, his "Harmony" of the Old and New Testaments a futile scissors-and-paste job. Moreover, he does not like children: why could they not be born grown up? "If Christina could have given birth to a few full-grown clergymen in priest's orders—of moderate views, but inclining rather to Evangelicalism, with comfortable livings and in all respects facsimiles of Theobald himself—why there might have been more sense in it." Naturally he is therefore the kind of father who (as we know from *The Fair Haven*) will eventually cause his son to look unfavorably upon God. And so Ernest is beaten as a baby for mispronouncing words, and suffers intellectual forced feeding, domestic religiosity, and paternal self-righteousness. Though she is in so many ways a figure of fun (her reflections provide some of the funniest writing of the nineteenth century), Christina's betrayals of Ernest to his father are deadly serious. (As a spinster she won Theobald in a card game with her married sisters: natural selection at work.)

There is intent in Ernest's first name as well as his last; it was his grandfather George who insisted upon it: "The word 'earnest' was just beginning to come into fashion, and he thought the possession of such a name might, like his having been baptized in water from the Jordan, have a permanent effect upon the boy's character." Arnoldian earnestness, then, is with us once again; Butler's novel, like Wilde's comedy, could have been given the punning title *The Importance of Being Ernest.* And of course, when Ernest goes off to "Roughborough" (Shrewsbury) to school, the headmaster, like Arnold and Butler's grandfather, is "irreproachable"; his foremost quality is "what biographers have called 'the simple-minded and childlike earnestness of his character,' . . . which might be perceived by the solemnity with which he spoke even about trifles."

Ernest's misery at school is alleviated only because of his Aunt Alethea (the name means "Truth" in Greek), drawn in part from Miss Savage, "in religion . . . as nearly a freethinker as anyone could be whose mind seldom turned upon the subject. She went to church, but disliked equally those who aired either religion or unreligion." Though she is George's daughter and Theobald's sister, Alethea has obviously inherited grandfather John's good genes. She moves to Roughborough to be near Ernest, and gives him also his first chance to realize and utilize this inheritance from his great-grandfather. She tells Ernest about John Pontifex, and the boy goes in for carpentry and builds an organ. It is the first thing he has ever really enjoyed doing. John Pontifex speaks out in Ernest too, when the boy, in a railway compartment, absentmindedly—like John—begins to talk to the sun, until a fellow traveller remonstrates. But it requires a long time and much suffering before Ernest can surmount the troubles that his own parents' influence and his own weakness are still to bring down upon him. Would it not be better after all if the generations did not overlap? "Why cannot we be buried as eggs in neat little cells with ten or twenty thousand pounds each wrapped round us in Bank of England notes, and wake up, as the sphex wasp does, to find that its papa and mama have not only left ample provisions at its elbow, but have been eaten by sparrows some weeks before it began to live consciously on its own account?" The name "Pontifex" literally also means a "bridge builder," and the "earnest bridge builder" still has a long way to go before he can cross the chasm into his own proper way of life.

Butler reminds us that between *Vestiges of Creation* in 1844 and *Essays and Reviews* in 1860 (Butler wrongly dates it 1859) "there was not a single book published in England that caused serious commotion within the bosom of the Church." This is to overlook Darwin, of course; but the very statement is interesting as reflecting the closed little world of Evangelical Christianity. At Cambridge in his day, *Vestiges* had been forgotten; "Tractarianism had subsided into a tenth day's wonder . . . at work . . . but not noisy; the Catholic aggression scare had lost its terrors. Ritualism was still unknown to the general provincial public. . . . Dissent was not spreading. . . . there was no enemy to the faith which could arouse even a languid interest." Yet older men knew that the "wave of skepticism which had already broken over Germany" was on its way.

Ernest's adventures with the "Simeonites" reflect Butler's own. An Evangelical sermon points him in that direction, and it is high comedy when the naturally Evangelical Theobald finds to his horror that his son now shares his sentiments. Ernest views "the doctrines of baptismal regeneration and priestly absolution" with contempt and wants to reconcile Methodism and the Church. What business has *he* to think about such subjects, his father feels? Theobald "hated the Church of Rome, but he hated dissenters too." But gradually the neighboring clergy has been becoming more and more High Church, and Theobald has been reluctantly moving along with the current, tolerating "many practices which in his youth he would have considered Popish." Ernest is beginning to swim against a tide, and Theobald has the pleasure of telling him he is a fool. Still later, Theobald preaches in a surplice, chanting is introduced in his church, the congregation and he turn eastward, the "Belief" becomes the "Creed"; but he always refuses to say "Alleluia" instead of "Hallelujah."

Unlike Butler himself, Ernest is ordained. Once in London, he falls under the influence of the High Churchman Pryer, who argues, among other things, that "no practice is entirely vicious which has not been extinguished among the comeliest, most vigorous, and most cultivated races of mankind in spite of centuries of endeavor to extirpate it. If a vice . . . can still hold its own . . . it must be founded on some immutable truth or fact in human nature. . . ." The clergy must have absolute freedom to experiment, and marriage is absolutely taboo ("I can hardly express the horror with which I am filled by seeing English priests living in what I can only designate as 'open matrimony.' "). Pryer is "restless, as though wanting to approach a subject which he did not quite venture to touch upon, and kept harping on . . . the way in which the vices wanted regulating rather than prohibiting." Ernest clearly is too innocent to understand Pryer's homosexual advances; but he has an "embryo mind," and so it is no wonder that he is influenced by Pryer's doctrines, even though he had been an Evangelical only a few days earlier. "It is no more to be wondered at that one who is going to turn out a Roman Catholic, should have passed through the stages of being first a Methodist and then a free thinker, than that a man should at some former time have been a mere cell, and later on an invertebrate animal."

On his missionary efforts in his London rooming house, Ernest encounters a learned freethinking tinker, Mr. Shaw, who easily routs him in an argument about the Resurrection. Forced to examine—as "John Pickard Owen" and Butler had been forced—the conflicting Gospel accounts, Ernest is shocked and bewildered. He reads the *Vestiges of Creation*—now more than fifteen years old and, interestingly enough, not sneered at by Butler for its naïveté—and the shock increases. But it is not until after his arrest (the novel's climax which, Miss Savage felt, lacked verisimilitude) that Ernest, now in prison, loses his faith. Perhaps his surroundings have something to do with the change, "just as the cocoons of silkworms, when sent in baskets by rail, hatch before their time through the novelty of heat and jolting." Now, Ernest's "belief in the stories concerning the Death, Resurrection, and Ascension of Jesus Christ, and hence his faith in all the other Christian miracles, had dropped off him once and forever": like a cocoon, in fact. "He would probably have seen it years ago if he had not been hoodwinked by people who were paid for hoodwinking him." His new rationalism, he realizes, may not be permanent, any more than his earlier phases have been; but he is convinced that no shock less severe than that of his arrest and imprisonment would have produced the same effect.

Nor indeed is it the final phase. Down and out, having lost everything, Ernest realizes that reason must be abandoned and that "instinct is the ultimate court of appeal . . . a mode of faith in the evidence of things not actually seen." He feels "the power that was in him": he has Butler's vital principle now in the forefront of his consciousness. He feels "that Christianity and the denial of Christianity after all met as much as any other extremes do; it was a fight about names—not about things; practically, the Church of Rome, the Church of England, and the freethinker have the same ideal standard and meet in the gentleman." What is needed is "charitable inconsistency," what must be abandoned is dogma. And "of course he read Mr. Darwin's books as fast as they came out and adopted evolution as an article of faith."

But the Butlerian (not Darwinian) theory is exemplified in Ernest's life to the very end: he has his son and daughter—illegitimate, as it turns out—brought up in the countryside in a bargeman's family, where they are blissfully happy in the outdoor life, wholly untroubled by intellectual or religious problems, and content, the girl to marry a bargeman, and the boy to go to sea. In the fifth generation, the good genes of John Pontifex have been encouraged to manifest themselves. And since Ernest concerns himself very little about the children personally, except that he visits them occasionally and gives them some of Aunt Alethea's money that he has inherited, he is coming as close as possible to imitating the sphex wasp. Although not eaten by a sparrow before his children come into the world, he leaves them alone as much as any father could. "A man," says Ernest, "first quarrels with his father about three quarters of a year before he is born. It is then he insists on setting up a separate establishment; when this has been once agreed to, the more complete the separation forever after the better for both."

In order to present the largely autobiographical *Way of All Flesh* with proper sardonic detachment, Butler tells the story through Ernest's godfather, Overton, who, as a relatively detached observer, can give a Butlerian view of Butler's own experiences. It was the same trick he had played in *The Fair Haven*, and it enabled him to take both roles, the observed and the observer. Overton, rich bachelor writer of burlesques for the London stage, is as much Butler in maturity as Ernest is Butler as a child and a young man. And once Ernest is free of wife, children, and financial worries, he becomes a second Overton, a rich bachelor writer, living a quiet life and occasionally travelling. His book of six or seven essays, "semi-theological, semi-social," purporting to be by six or seven different authors, is a kind of answer to *Essays and Reviews* and a thoroughly Butlerian project.

All of the essays support the Church of England (one is on the Resurrection, like the essay that lay at the core of *The Fair Haven*). Why should not the Church follow the practice, familiar in the law, of allowing the meaning of the ancient words of the prayer book and articles to change with time, "a righteous and convenient" thing to do? The Church rests on faith, not on reason, and "it was not a little true and not a little false" depending upon the amount of beauty or ugliness it had fostered. What is important is that nobody feel too strongly on any issue: "We should be churchmen, but lukewarm churchmen." In fact, "the book rang with the courage alike of conviction and lack of conviction." At the center of all was good breeding: "That a man should have been bred well and breed others well; that his figure, head, hands, feet, voice, manner and clothes should carry conviction upon this point. . . .": that is what is needed. The highest good is to increase the number and happiness of such people. Ernest himself—having too much of a Christian in him—can never be one of these new "elect," like the "High" Ydgrunites of *Erewhon*, but he has built the bridge into posterity, and, it is hinted, his descendants are likely to achieve this ideal status.

After all the storms through which he has passed, Ernest Pontifex, it is clear, has emerged just as outrageous and impossible and amusing as his creator. And if the paradoxes strike a familiar note, and the reader of *The Way of All Flesh* is reminded of Bernard Shaw, it will not be accident.

CHAPTER 9.

EARNESTNESS IN THE THIRD GENERATION: MRS. HUMPHRY WARD

Robert Elsmere*: "The typical process of the present day"*

"Mamma and I," wrote Gladstone—then Prime Minister—to his daughter, "are . . . engaged in a death grapple with *Robert Elsmere*" (1888, no. 82), and to Lord Acton he said "one could no more stop in it than in reading Thucydides." The devout Tractarian Gladstone disapproved of the great classic novel of Victorian doubt, and wrote a long, signed, unfavorable review of it in the *Nineteenth Century*, which did not in the least prevent him from having friendly and lengthy conversations with its author. But he did concede that *Robert Elsmere* was "eminently an offspring of its time." He predicted that it would make a deep impression, not only "among mere novel readers, but among those who share, in whatever sense, the deeper thoughts of the period." He added that Mrs. Humphry Ward, the author, had a "generous appreciation of what is morally good, impartially exhibited in all directions," a strong "sense of mission," and above all "earnestness and persistency of purpose." Indeed she had: it was, once more, true Arnoldian earnestness; for Mrs. Humphry Ward (1851-1920) was the granddaughter of Thomas Arnold of Rugby, and the niece of William Delafield Arnold (see above: *Oakfield*, 1854, no. 70) and of Matthew Arnold.

Her own father, Thomas Arnold the younger (1823-1900), intelligent and personally most attractive, was a Rugbeian as a matter of course, went out to Tasmania as Inspector of Schools, there married Julia Sorell, a beautiful woman of devout French Protestant (Huguenot) background and upbringing, and in 1856—when their daughter Mary was five—was converted to Catholicism. He promptly lost his job, and had to move to Dublin to teach for Newman himself, the most "malignant" of his father's "Oxford malignants," while his daughter Mary went to live with her Arnold grandmother in the beautiful Westmoreland Lake country that "Oakfield" had so yearned for while in India. The conversion was a terrible blow to the family, of course: Julia Arnold was intensely Protestant and—as was traditional—was allowed to bring up her daughters as Protestants, but had to surrender her sons to the Catholic enemy. Nine years later, Thomas Arnold returned to the Church of England. Mary—then thirteen—intensely shared her mother's joy; the family was reunited in Oxford, where Thomas Arnold took pupils and obtained a lectureship in history.

In the Oxford of the late sixties and early seventies, the influence of Newman was reviving, but the old moulds had been broken: in 1871 Dissenters were admitted to all degrees except those in divinity. Powerful voices were raised in favor of applying historical scholarship to the Bible: in the famous *Essays and Reviews* (1860) Benjamin Jowett, Master of Balliol, urged that Scripture be interpreted "like any other book," beginning with the ascertainment of its meaning, "in the same impartial way that we ascertain the meaning of Sophocles or Plato." Mark Pattison, Rector of Lincoln, once a Newmanite, now a sceptic, fought to make university appointments depend upon a candidate's scholarly achievements rather than upon his religious beliefs. Thomas Hill Green, a Balliol philosopher and Hegelian, accepted the dubious historical arguments of the German scholar Ferdinand Christian Baur that the miracles of the New Testament were not attested to by the kind of historical "testimony" that would satisfy the standards of modern scholars, and that therefore belief in these miracles could no longer be required of Christians. In practice, this meant the jettisoning of the entire historical basis of Christianity. Brought up in a devout Evangelical tradition, Green put his emphasis upon Christian morality, Christian ethics, Christian love: good works, self-sacrifice, social service among the sick and the poor, the seeking for God within oneself. He regarded himself as a devout Christian, and preached occasional "Lay Sermons" to his followers, expounding his philosophy. Though not fond of one another, Jowett, Pattison, and Green all became young Mary Arnold's personal friends, and exercised much influence upon her.

Unable as a woman to attend the university, she was nonetheless told by Mark Pattison to "get to the bottom of something . . . choose a subject and know *everything* about it!" and made herself a learned authority on the early mediaeval Spanish church, working in the original sources: the records of Church Councils, Visigothic Law Codes, chronicles, saints' lives. Married at twenty to T. Humphry Ward, a young don, and before long the mother of three children, she was planning a book on early Spanish history. As a preliminary step she undertook to prepare the biographies of early Spanish churchmen for Wace's *Dictionary of Christian Biography*. Her study of the early mediaeval sources re-enforced her interest in Green's ideas about Biblical testimony; like the Gospels, her saints' lives included many miraculous episodes told as facts, which, however, could not be accepted as facts by a nineteenth-century intellectual: they were rather examples of the attitude of mind of the mediaeval writer, other instances of historical "testimony."

By the time she was twenty-five Mary Arnold Ward was a staunch partisan of wholly free Biblical criticism; she denied the historicity of miracles; she disbelieved in the Incarnation and the Atonement; Christ was only a great teacher. All this, a friend wrote, "was a striving after righteousness, sincerity, truth," a search for Arnoldian earnestness. In that same year, 1876, her father, who was the leading candidate now for the vacant Chair in Early English at Oxford, suddenly announced that he had been reconverted to Catholicism. He lost the election and his position in Oxford, and had to return, after twelve years, to Dublin once more. In tears, his daughter ran through the streets of Oxford to the house of the Greens, who comforted her in this new family crisis.

In 1881, she heard the Reverend John Wordsworth—great-nephew of the poet, later Bishop of Salisbury—lecture on "The Present Unsettlement in Religion" and stoutly maintain that all who failed to hold orthodox opinions were guilty of sin. Aroused to anger, she wrote a pamphlet, "Unbelief and Sin," attacking these views and espousing those of Green. She and her husband embarked on literary careers in London, and after a children's story and a first novel, she translated into English the *Journal Intime* of Henry Frédéric Amiel, a Swiss philosopher and professor at the University of Geneva, a mystic who believed that organized religion was decadent. Mrs. Ward herself rejected Amiel's views and clung tenaciously to her liberalized Christian belief: Christ's life and teaching lay at the center, and she longed, with "immense tenderness," for a sweeping away of the complex theological formulas that—she thought—put Christianity beyond the reach of the masses, and for a "simplification of the creeds" which would make Christ's message directly available to all mankind.

Into *Robert Elsmere*, the massive and moving novel that she published early in 1888, she put the crystallization of all her past experience and thinking: the tensions and conflict created in a family when a husband and wife who truly love one another disagree about religious belief; Mark Pattison's attitude toward scholarship and religion; T. H. Green's ethical and moral philosophy; the paralysis of the will characteristic of many intellectuals, notably Amiel; her own passionate interest in Christian social work among the poor; and of course her highly intelligent observation of contemporary men and manners, as well as her professional scholarly attainments. Gladstone's prediction that the book would make a deep impression on "those who share the deeper thought of the period" was, sometimes ludicrously, overfulfilled.

Its sales got off to a moderate start, but after the Prime Minister had reviewed it and made it a byword in everybody's mouth (Mrs. Ward was congratulated by his political enemies for taking Gladstone's mind off the Irish question), *Robert Elsmere* simply took off, selling 70,000 copies within the first three years in England alone. In the United States, it was, said Dr. Oliver Wendell Holmes, "the most effective popular novel we have had since *Uncle Tom's Cabin*." The absence of an international copyright law left it wide open to American publishing pirates; cheap editions proliferated; perhaps half a million copies were sold in the first eighteen months after publication; there was a price war, as Jordan Marsh's department store in Boston offered copies for four cents apiece, and the line of waiting buyers stretched around a large city block, while the Maine Balsam Fir Soap Company countered by giving a copy away free with every cake of soap they sold. An alleged sequel, *Robert Elsmere's Daughter*—with which Mrs. Ward had nothing to do—was produced by an enterprising American publisher under her name: indeed, the American publishing atrocities committed against her in the case of *Robert Elsmere* contributed notably to the eventual adoption of the first International Copyright Act that prohibited such actions in the future.

It was not only Gladstone who reviewed it, but also almost everybody else in the intellectual world. Walter Pater called it "a *chef d'oeuvre* of that kind of quiet evolution of character through circumstance, introduced into English literature by Miss Austen, and carried to perfection in France by George Sand [who is more to the point, because, like Mrs. Ward, she was not afraid to challenge novel readers to an interest in religious questions], it abounds in sympathy with people as we find them, in aspiration towards something better. . . ." Pater—perhaps remembering Mrs. Ward's sympathetic review of *Marius*—praised her style, both its individual sentences and its larger structure, illuminated by "a rare instinct for probability and nature." *Robert Elsmere* is a profound novel, true to life, and, for the most part, extraordinarily well written: a point well worth making, since one of the ablest of our own contemporary scholarly critics emphasizes what he calls its "artistic demerits" (meaning presumably "shortcomings") and still makes the old assertion that the book's "historic significance exceeded by far its intrinsic merits." We have often been willing here to ignore the literary distinction of our novels, emphasizing instead precisely their historic significance; but we are all the more eager, when the novel which we are discussing has high literary merit as well, to proclaim that fact. In the end, literary merit is and will remain a matter of taste; and in the case of *Robert Elsmere,* I prefer Walter Pater's view to that of Professor Ulrich Knoepflmacher, who, as a learned student of Pater himself, will perhaps not blame me too severely.

Robert Elsmere is the climactic Victorian novel of religious doubt. It appeared at a moment when all the chief Victorian arguments against the Christian faith had already been thrashed out by the intellectuals, and their discussions in a simplified form had filtered down to the general public. Mrs. Ward dedicated it to two deceased friends, one of whom, T. H. Green, had died in 1882. In Mr. Grey, the Oxford don who exercises so strong an influence upon her hero, Robert Elsmere, she deliberately drew a loving portrait of Green, quoting verbatim from time to time from his "Lay Sermons" as published under the title *The Witness of God.* Langham, Elsmere's languid and sceptical tutor, has much of Amiel about him, but—perhaps in the combination of fascination and fear he feels for women—has also much of a certain familiar type of English academic of whom Walter Pater was one. The girl that Elsmere marries, Catherine Leyburn, conscientiously dedicated to the family tasks her beloved Evangelical father had bequeathed to her, unquestioningly and rigidly devout, yet full of sexual passion for her husband, is in part at least Mrs. Ward's mother, the long-suffering Huguenot woman who twice saw her beloved husband turn Catholic. And the squire, Roger Wendover (why did Mrs. Ward name him after a mediaeval English chronicler?) resembles Mark Pattison in his enormous erudition, his Tractarian youth, his liberal reaction, and his ultimate scepticism, although as Mrs. Ward later insisted, Pattison—unlike the squire—would have been kind to his tenants had he been a landowner. Newman himself appears in a minor role as a Ritualist priest—not a Catholic but an Anglican—called "Newcome" by Mrs. Ward, "a saint clearly, though perhaps . . . an irritable one."

But the interest of the novel only begins with these full or partial portraits of real persons. Elsmere goes to Oxford, takes orders, obtains a country living, marries Catherine—whom he finds in her ancestral Westmoreland, headquarters of the Arnold family—and leads a joyous life of service as a country parson. His scholarly researches—and the goading of the atheistical learned squire Wendover—precipitate a personal crisis of doubt originating with the question of testimony. Elsmere feels it his duty to give up his living and—having rendered himself and his loving wife wretchedly unhappy and imposed a severe strain upon their marriage—moves to London, embarks upon social work, founds a "new church," and dies of overwork. It is the richly developed nuances of character, the superb conversations and debates, the leisurely and interesting portrayal of persons in the round, and the argument of all sides of vexed issues that make this simple and familiar story as arresting today as it was in 1888.

Science—one should note immediately—is not an important issue in Elsmere's life. He did not read *The Origin of Species* at Oxford, and later comments that "we used to take the thing half for granted" (how different his generation is from its predecessor—as Eliza Lynn Linton pointed out), but in his Surrey parsonage he has now read it: "To drive the mind through all the details of the evidence, to force one's self to understand the whole hypothesis and the grounds for it, is a very different matter. It is a revelation." To which his friend Langham answers, "Yes, . . . but it is a revelation . . . that has not always been held to square with other revelations." True: not always, but apparently it now causes Elsmere no more trouble than other churchmen experienced. Indeed, the 1884 Oxford Bampton lectures of Frederick Temple, Bishop of Exeter and future Archbishop of Canterbury, "assumed Evolution as an axiom."

Mrs. Ward has made Elsmere handsome, charming, vigorous, athletic, tactful, proud but self-controlled, generous, and self-denying: Henry James rather wickedly wrote her that he feared her hero might "suffer a sunstroke from the high oblique light of your admiration for him." Yet for once, perhaps Henry James was too quick to judge: Robert Elsmere takes only second-class honors. With all his enormous attractions and his considerable intellect, his is not wholly a first-class mind: probably Mrs. Ward could not have made him wholly first-rate and still have had her story. Had he been first-rate, he would have become a full-fledged disciple of Green ("Grey") while an undergraduate, and would not have taken orders and have had to go through the conflict of resigning them. When Langham first sends Elsmere to hear one of Grey's lay sermons, he is sure that Grey will influence him, and thinks sarcastically, "Well, no one can say I have not given him his opportunity to be 'earnest.' " And Mrs. Ward adds that the sarcasm would in an earlier generation have been applied to the " 'earnestness' of an Arnoldian Rugby." It would have been well, surely the granddaughter of Arnold of Rugby would have thought, for Grey's influence to have been paramount with Elsmere from the first. But—while admiring Grey on sight (he never lost "the memory of the outward scene" and was "filled with a fervour and an admiration which he was too young and immature to analyse")—Elsmere finds the sermon largely "beyond him." Had he been able to understand then, however, what Grey was saying (and Mrs. Ward quotes it in part) about "testimony" and the miracle of the resurrection, he would have been spared his later ordeal.

So while admiring Grey, Elsmere goes along instead with the

others at Oxford who were reacting "against an overdriven rationalism," who were joyously discovering that "after all Mill and Herbert Spencer had not said the last word." He joins in the new wave of High-Church romanticism (still influenced by Newman from without) and falls in love with "the stateliness and comely beauty of the Church order as it was revealed to him at Oxford." In a revealing little scene when Grey seems to take it for granted that Elsmere will get only a second class, Elsmere tells him he plans to enter the Church. Grey asks, "You feel no difficulties in the way?" and Elsmere answers that he never has felt any, perhaps "because I've never gone deep enough." To which Grey answers, "You will probably be very happy in the life. . . . The Church wants men of your sort." Langham too, Elsmere's tutor, openly declares that to him Christianity is a "respectable mythology." Elsmere will have none of this, insists that Christian theology is a system of ideas "made manifest in facts," and defends the factualness of these "facts" in such a way that Langham decides that "the intellect had precious little to do with Elsmere's Christianity." Is it not clear that Mrs. Ward intended Elsmere as a fine "second-class" undeveloped young mind, too immature to experience early the doubts that would torment him later?

Ultimately the Evangelical traditions of his family and Grey's influence steer Elsmere away from the High-Church party, and—now wholly without partisan bitterness—he eagerly accepts the family living. Once there, he is in part a "muscular Christian," playing cricket with the village lads ("his batting was of a fine, slashing superior sort") and spending a good deal of time in fishing, talking of it "with constant quotations from Kingsley." But his major interest is social work: his Institute, where he reads stories aloud to the village youths; his Naturalists' Club, which develops their interest in birds, insects, and flowers; and above all, the village poor, some of them housed in squalor through the neglect of Squire Wendover and the corrupt stewardship of his estate manager, against whom Elsmere declares war. Wendover's social views are retrograde: not only does he disregard the conditions under which laborers on his estates must live, but he also openly challenges Elsmere, by attacking "all the fools with a mission who have teased our generation—all your Kingsleys, and Maurices, and Ruskins . . . bent on making any sort of aimless commotion which may serve them both as an investment for the next world and an advertisement in this." It takes seven deaths in a diphtheria epidemic in the unsanitary cottages to change the squire's mind on this point.

Yet Elsmere's "enthusiasm" on social questions is as yet secondary to the question of his faith. Like Winwood Reade's Mordaunt and many others, even the secure Elsmere sometimes thinks of all the generations of men who died before the birth of Christ and had to bear their anguish without Christian comfort. And, stimulated surely by the new scholarship in comparative religion—whose traces we have already found in those doubters who think of Brahmins or Buddhists or ancient Egyptians or others as possessing a faith comparable to Christianity (and, who knows, perhaps influencing it through the Jews?)—Elsmere, too, "thought of Buddhist patience and Buddhist charity; of the long centuries during which Chaldaean or Persian or Egyptian lived, suffered, and died, trusting the gods they knew." Moreover, he contemplates all the sufferings for which Christianity had been directly responsible.

But Elsmere is happy in his work because—so Langham thinks—of his "passionate acceptance of an exquisite fairy tale, which at the first honest challenge of the critical sense withers in our grasp." The "fairy tale," the "mythology of Christianity," are terms used by his old friend Grey; but the challenge to Elsmere's faith comes from his own scholarly work (on early Frankish history, instead of Mary Ward's early Spanish subject) and from his deepening acquaintance with Squire Wendover. Personal friend of Schelling, Humboldt, Niebuhr, Strauss, Baur, and the other Germans, and author of *The Idols of the Market-Place* (an attack on English beliefs) and *Essays on English Culture* (an attack on English education), Wendover is formidable indeed.

In *The Idols*, the squire has his jaundiced say about "The Pentateuch, the Prophets, the Gospels, St. Paul, Tradition, the Fathers, Protestantism and Justification by Faith, the Eighteenth Century, the Broad Church Movement, Anglican Theology. . . ." The "coolness and frankness" of his method shocks the religious, but "the subtle and caustic style" forces everybody to read the book just the same. It becomes a major center of controversy, and many intelligent people believe that its publication marks an epoch. Probably no single actual book corresponds to Wendover's *Idols. Essays and Reviews* created an uproar in the years after 1860, but that was a collective work by seven authors, only one of whom was a layman, and its tone—despite the protest—was generally reverent. Perhaps the anonymous *Supernatural Religion* of 1874-1876 (actually by a certain W. R. Cassels) most closely fits the case, but unlike Wendover's imaginary book, it confined its attack to the authenticity of the New Testament tradition; and its ostensible scholarship was soon refuted by professional experts; while, apparently, Wendover's *Idols of the Market-Place* was sound.

In any case, when Elsmere reads Wendover's analysis of the evidence for the Resurrection ("testimony" once more) and the squire's dismissal of the story as "legend," he feels "as though a cruel torturing hand were laid upon his inmost being." To the squire's book are added elements from his own historical research, and "from the secret half-conscious recesses" of his mind. It is the beginning of his loss of faith, although he determines not to debate such matters with the squire until he feels more confidence that his own learning can compete on more even terms. His gentle defiance of Wendover ("I believe in an Incarnation, a Resurrection, a Revelation. If there are . . . difficulties, I want to smooth them away, you . . . to make much of them. . . .") is only erecting a child's "sand-barrier against the tide." Naturally, Elsmere shrinks from telling his wife, Catherine, anything about his travail. In view of her character and beliefs the shock to her is certain to be a dreadful one when it comes.

Catherine, in her earliest acquaintance with Elsmere, "shrinks" upon hearing him give high praise to the unorthodox Grey: Mr. Leyburn, her father, was "a fanatic—as mild as you please—but immovable. . . . Evangelical, with a dash of Quakerism," who had much in common with the Wesleyans, but was a loyal churchman, a visionary, who had passed through Oxford at the time of the Oxford movement, and had, "so to speak, . . . known nothing about it, while living all the time for religion. . . . He would have had the Church make peace with the Dissenters. . . . But he drew the most rigid line between belief and unbelief. He would not have dined at the same table with a Unitarian if he could have helped it." He had written an article against admitting Unitarians to the universities or allowing them to sit in Parliament. "England is a Christian state . . . they are not Christians; they have no right in her except on sufferance." And these views his loving eldest daughter, Catherine, only sixteen when her father died, has taken over undiluted from him; she has made them the center of her entire life.

She even feels about her gifted younger sister Rose's violin a little bit the way Robert Falconer's infinitely fiercer Calvinist grandmother had felt about his violin, and a Wesleyan aunt has "special leadings of the spirit" against the instrument. Catherine reads St. Augustine, à Kempis, Keble, Wordsworth, Dante, and Milton, but is baffled when during their courtship Elsmere talks of contemporary books and men or "speaks the natural Christian language of this generation," tolerant and flexible, in contrast with the intense devotion of her father and herself. Elsmere argues in favor of Rose's violin-playing "as Kingsley would have argued"; he adduces its beauty, its employment of a God-given talent, and its humanizing impact upon the poor. Catherine knows nothing of passion and its claims, and agonizes before she feels she can marry Elsmere. She is a Puritan. After marriage, she cannot bring herself to like Langham or Grey. And Langham, when he comes to know her, thinks, "she is the Thirty-nine Articles in the flesh! . . . For her there must neither be too much nor too little."

Living at Wendover's gates, and growing more and more deeply engaged in his own researches, Elsmere cannot stop his progress towards loss of faith. The squire is engaged in writing just that massive *History of Testimony* which T. H. Green and Mrs. Ward had both thought so necessary: he has learned several oriental languages, including Sanskrit, and for thirty years has been "sifting and comparing the whole mass of existing records": a massive undertaking indeed, of which the first portion, from the beginnings to the sixth century A.D., is now completed. Wendover is not only far more erudite than Elsmere: he is also strongly anticlerical, and deliberately *wants* to demolish Elsmere's faith. So their discussion of the book on testimony becomes "the turning-point" of Elsmere's life. He skillfully defends "all that was most sacred to himself and to Catherine," but this conversation with Wendover—and Mrs. Ward actually gives her readers much of it verbatim—ends Elsmere's "happy unclouded youth."

As with so many clerics in real life, so with Robert Elsmere: the Book of Daniel is a crux. The late date attributed to it by scholars had driven Renan out of the Catholic Church: if the Church had been wrong on that, how could one be sure that she had been right on everything else? Divine inspiration disappeared. A Protestant might argue that Christ quoted Daniel, and therefore it cannot be late and apocryphal, and a liberal Anglican might say that Christ quoted it, but only as literature; but this cannot satisfy Elsmere: he has already reached the shocking conclusion that Christ was "purely human." It comes to him not as the same revelation ("Not God, but man") had come to Mrs. Lynn Linton ("Christopher Kirkland"), but as intellectual conviction.

And the first consequence is that Elsmere now preaches sermons which constantly and imaginatively dwell on "the earthly life of Jesus." Just as Markham Sutherland in Froude's *Nemesis of Faith* more than a full generation earlier had preached nothing that "Socinians" might not have preached, so Elsmere is now permanently shaken in his Anglicanism. He still believes in God: Theism, he notes, can never be disproved; unlike Christianity, it is philosophical, not historical or literary. He believes in Christ the teacher and martyr, but not in the "man-God, the Word from Eternity," not in the Incarnation, the Resurrection, the Atonement, not in miracles: they "*do not happen!*" Neither Catherine's pleading nor "Newcome's [Newman's]" call to submit and be a slave to Christ can now prevail over "Grey's" message that God is not unintelligible but "forever reason." In Catherine, the "Puritan independent fibre" is only strengthened by her husband's disaster. If the Gospel is not "true as history," it has no value for her.

The resignation of Elsmere's living does not follow immediately. As Wendover cynically puts it, he would not "be the first parson in the Church of England who looks after the poor and holds his tongue." The financial need for his living is not an issue, as it had been with Edward Mordaunt in *The Outcast*, who nonetheless found it impossible to "be a hypocrite" as his friend the neighboring rector advised; with Elsmere it is purely a matter of conscience: his *feeling* for his priestly role has vanished; all is dreary and shallow and worthless. He confers with Grey and tells him the whole story. It has been, Grey declares in Elsmere's case, "the typical process of the present day." Abstract thought has had little to do with it; it has "all been a question of literary and historical evidence. . . . all experimental, inductive." Like Wendover or Mordaunt's adviser, Green reminds Elsmere that both of them know many men with similar opinions who are still "doing admirable work" inside the Church. Yet Elsmere cannot adopt that solution, cannot imagine "standing up Sunday after Sunday to say the things you do *not* believe." He cannot now possibly preach another Easter sermon.

Grey recognizes what a terrible wrench it is—"the rending asunder of bone and marrow"—to part with "the Christian mythology." But God, he declares, is everywhere, in reason as well as faith, and the die is cast. Readers of the novel may possibly overlook the central importance of Elsmere's decision to leave the pulpit after the loss of his belief in miracle; but there can be no question but that Mrs. Ward so viewed it. Many men were compromising, staying in the Church to do good, and keeping quiet about their convictions. She thought it wrong, and through her hero movingly and powerfully argued her convictions. By 1899—eleven years later—she had changed her mind, and believed that men in Elsmere's position should stay inside the Church and reform it from within. This idea she later embodied in her novel *The Case of Richard Meynell* (1911, NIS), which falls outside our period.

Elsmere's first work in London is under the aegis of a Broad-Church vicar, whose views do not differ from his, but who believes that one must "keep things going" inside the Church. "Prudent silence and gradual expansion from within" is a policy that seems to Elsmere to vitiate this man's whole life. They cannot work together long. A far more promising opportunity arises with a Unitarian minister in a slum parish (Rotherhithe?) where his rivals are a group of Puseyite Ritualists: for some time there has been a "private war" between "hectic clergy heading exasperated processions or intoning defiant Litanies on the one side" and "mobs, rotten eggs, dead cats, and blatant Protestant orators on the other." (Perhaps Mrs. Ward was thinking of the notorious case of St. George's-in-the-East in 1859-1860.) Elsmere's new Unitarian friend—by appealing to the "aristocracy of artisans" opposed to Puseyism but not violent men—establishes a successful mission. Despite Catherine's ancestral distrust of Unitarians, amounting to hatred, Elsmere finds his real work among them. He does write two articles on "disputed points of Biblical criticism" in the *Nineteenth Century*, but his place now is in the slums with his "high Utopian vision" driving him on.

And what does Elsmere do amongst the urban poor? He gives a series of story-telling evenings, like those "which had been so great a success" in his rural parish. He founds a "Scientific Sunday School," like the Naturalists' Club he had founded in the country. In short, after all the torments and soul searchings, Elsmere finds himself doing exactly the same things among the "upper classes" of the urban poor that he had done among the rural poor. Critics of the novel have been too overwhelmed by its authority, its omniscience, its extraordinary vividness, to ask themselves whether all the agonizing and torment was really worth it. It is a small result indeed that Elsmere has achieved, and Mrs. Ward seems not to have noticed this, possibly the chief failure of her imagination in the entire novel. True: aroused by obscenities in a poster of the Crucifixion put up by the powerful local Freethinking organization to advertise their paper, Elsmere delivers an Easter Eve lecture on "The Claim of Jesus upon Modern Life." Catherine refuses to come to hear him: "Your historical Christ," she says, "will never win souls. If he was God, every word you speak will insult him. If he was man, he was not a good man."

It is a meeting like the one Mark Rutherford and M'Kay had attended a quarter of a century earlier, and Elsmere gets "fair play," just as the anti-Freethinking Dissenting minister had on that occasion. But of course Elsmere's address is far more effective. He tells the audience about himself: he is neither a Unitarian nor an Anglican, but a historian and a believer in God, in Conscience, and in Experience, "in an Eternal Goodness—and an Eternal Mind—of which Nature and Man are the continuous and the only revelation." It is in *Experience*, "that unvarying and rational order of the world which has been the appointed instrument" of human education since the beginning, in the history of the world and of man, that the revelation of God lies. Miracles do not happen, and the rational view gives no place for a Resurrection or an Ascension, but that does not mean that it is decent to make obscene mock of Christ. Just because Jesus' life has been shrouded in legend is no reason to discard his teachings. His life is part of us. "We are what we are tonight . . . largely because a Galilaean peasant was born, and grew to manhood, and preached, and died."

In answer, one of the Freethinkers says exactly what modern social historians have discovered that he would have said: "old Tom Paine was as good a scholar as any of 'em, and most of 'em in the hall knew what *he* thought about it. Tom Paine hadn't anything to say against Jesus Christ. . . . He was a workman and a fine sort of man, and if he had been alive now he'd have been [like Joshua Davidson] a Socialist." But other people "got up the Church": Tom Paine called them "Mythologists," and now they had been found out, and "serve 'em right." The answer is a distinct intellectual advance upon the counterthrusts of Rutherford's Freethinker, with his satirical comments on David's morality or Jonah and the Whale. And it is followed by other and more radical speakers: Mr. Elsmere's New Church—with its aim of bringing the life of Jesus "into real and cogent relation" with our modern lives—would "only be a fresh instrument in the hands of the *bourgeoisie.*"

But despite the atheist and Marxist objections, Elsmere has made an impression. A group of workmen asks for a course of lectures on the New Testament. Elsmere effectively seeks for help and understanding in the fashionable drawing rooms of London, a city "honeycombed with vice and misery," but also "with the labour of an ever-expanding charity." Only Catherine grows "more wintry and more rigid." No wonder; Elsmere, somehow without the imagination to realize how she will react, invites to dinner a Comtist colleague and his wife, who have recently had one of their children baptized "with full Comtist rites." Elsmere is at times a fool; but the charge that Mrs. Ward has no sense of comedy should be reconsidered after an examination of this scene. Despite a variety of absorbing subplots the whole last portion of *Robert Elsmere* drags, once Elsmere has discovered his new faith. Well before Elsmere's death, Catherine becomes aware of her cruelty to him and is reconciled to his new life.

The last of the seven "books" into which the novel is subdivided Mrs. Ward entitled "Gain and Loss," reversing the title of Newman's famous novel. In it Elsmere proceeds with the organization of his "new church," a "lasting and organic" institution based upon faith, in which the workmen are to take their full share of government, a "sect," a "conventicle," a "new Company of Jesus." The workers assent, but at first largely because of Elsmere's own personal magnetism. By the time the new church is launched, Catherine has "undergone that dissociation of the moral judgment from a special series of religious formulae, which is the crucial, the epoch-making fact of our day." She is now aware that (as Mrs. Ward had argued against John Wordsworth) unbelief is *not* sin, and that "the rebel of yesterday" is "the rightful heir of tomorrow." So she participates in the meetings in which the details of "The New Brotherhood of Christ" are hammered out. To a sympathetic observer it seems like a rekindling of the spirit of devotion that inspired St. Benedict or St. Francis, Luther, Calvin or George Fox. Mrs. Ward imagines it all: the room, the services, the adherents. And though at the end—after Elsmere has died in Algiers—she assures us that "The New Brotherhood still exists and grows," and that the struggle was not only Elsmere's, we cannot help doubts of our own from creeping in at this stage. Yet to have imagined the spiritual developments and the vicissitudes that lead to the founding of a new religious movement is in itself an enormous achievement.

As early as 1869, T. H. Green had written that "*mere* religious agency does but touch the surface of modern rottenness: . . . the people who cry 'Lord, Lord' do no wonderful works and never get nearer to any organisation of life: . . . the only hope lies in such 'secular' agency and 'human' philosophy as requires a religious zeal, not less self-denying and much more laboriously thoughtful than that of the monk, to bring into action." Here was the call to action that Elsmere heard. In the years immediately following *Robert Elsmere*'s publication, Mrs. Ward herself played a major part in the foundation of a settlement house, Passmore Edwards Hall, similar to Elsmere's "Elgood Street Settlement," and emphasizing both social work among the laboring classes and a Unitarian religion of ethical endeavor much like his. The library was named for Green, and one of his former students was the first director. It accomplished much in social service, but as a "New Church" it failed utterly, and by 1898 its missionary activities came to an end. Passmore Edwards Hall, now named for Mrs. Ward herself, still stands on its original site, not in a slum region south of the Thames like R———, where Elgood Street lay, but in proper middle-class Bloomsbury, where the Wards themselves lived. Whatever was preached there, the "upper working classes" obviously did not get the message or feel that it was addressed to them. The workers' rallying to Elsmere's New Church strains credulity in the pages of the novel, and in real life we know that it did not happen.

"The Grand Intellectual Novel": Helbeck of Bannisdale

Mrs. Ward's *Helbeck of Bannisdale* (1898, no. 19), a decade later than *Robert Elsmere,* is a superb complement to it. By 1898, the three-volume novel had vanished—only three or four of them had been published in 1897 as a final death gasp—and the now mandatory one-volume form encouraged brevity. Still massive but far less discursive and far faster moving than *Robert Elsmere, Helbeck* has the sweep and inevitable dénouement of a Greek tragedy. Once again, Mrs. Ward came to grips—this time more directly—with the tragic tensions and conflicts of her own family background. Once again, the central drama of her story lies in the torments suffered by a man and woman who love one another but cannot agree on religion.

This time, however, the conflict arises not between two members of the Church of England, one of whom is eternally rooted in Evangelical piety—almost a Puritan—while the other experiences the "typical process of the present day" and moves from orthodox Anglicanism to ethical Theism, but between an unshakably convinced Roman Catholic and a born unbeliever. In *Elsmere,* it is the woman, Catherine, who is staunch in belief, and it is the man who shocks her orthodoxy; in *Helbeck,* it is the man, Alan Helbeck himself, who is the devout Catholic, and the woman, Laura Fountain, sixteen years younger and only twenty, whose father had brought her up—but failed to educate her—who is the thorough-going enemy of religion. In *Elsmere,* the two protagonists are husband and wife, while in *Helbeck* they desperately wish to marry, but in the end cannot. How closely the conflict in *Helbeck* reflects that between Mary Arnold Ward's parents, or—perhaps more likely since both her father and mother were religious—that between the twice-converted Catholic Thomas Arnold the younger and Mary Ward herself, his highly "Liberal" daughter, is a matter for speculation and is in any case not very important. He was still alive and active when she wrote the novel; she consulted him about it, and he liked it. Her love for him and her association with him during all the years of his religious vagaries taught Mrs. Ward much about Catholicism that most non-Catholics could never have learned. And those things she put into *Helbeck*.

Helbeck is a somewhat impoverished Westmoreland country gentleman of ancient family—twenty generations of loyal Catholics—inhabiting a lonely Elizabethan manor house, now partly stripped of its ancient and valuable contents, sold to raise money for the owner's many religious charities. The story is a contemporary one; but because Westmoreland is so remote and Helbeck himself is utterly devoted to his religion to the exclusion of all pleasures except for fishing, the atmosphere resembles that of rural England a century earlier. The country folk—except for the rare Catholic among them—detest and fear and suspect Helbeck in the ancient fashion of the Protestant peasantry, egged on by a fiercely Evangelical curate. To the great house on all sorts of business come not only the family priests but also a Jesuit friend (a convert) and the Mother Superior and nuns of a nearby order, for whom Helbeck is building an orphanage. In the private chapel at Bannisdale, by special favor, the Sacrament is "reserved," that is to say, allowed to remain constantly on the altar rather than imported for each communion service.

Helbeck himself, educated by Jesuits, is a Franciscan tertiary, a subsidiary of the brotherhood reserved for pious laymen. "What *time* this religion took! Apart from the daily Mass, which drew him always to Whinthorpe before breakfast, there were the morning and evening prayers, the visits to the Sacrament, the two Masses on Sunday morning, Rosary and Benediction in the evening, and the many occasional services for the marking of Saints'-days and other festivals." Lent at Bannisdale is like Lent in a monastery. Were it not for Helbeck's responsibilities as a landowner, he would himself have become a Jesuit. He reads only Catholic devotional works, including saints' lives. Many years before—he tells Laura at a moment of crisis in their relationship—he was on the verge of an illicit love affair, but the woman in question "saved" him by immuring herself in a convent. Since then, he has remained unmarried "for the church's sake," living the life of an ascetic.

Helbeck is more exclusively and rigidly Catholic even than his Jesuit adviser and than the local Catholic bishop, clinging to the motto "No Salvation outside the Church" (*Extra ecclesiam nulla salus*), a motto which the Jesuit himself repudiates: it has done the Catholics "deadly harm in England. . . . We forget that England is a baptised nation, and is therefore in the supernatural state." But when Helbeck hears that part of his land is being purchased in order that a new Anglican church may be built upon it, he cancels the sale, declaring that he will "give no help, direct or indirect, to a schismatical and rebellious church. . . . They have filched enough from us Catholics in the past." He laughs with cruel pleasure at stories of discomfiture suffered by Anglican missionaries in Africa.

Laura is the stepdaughter of Helbeck's recently widowed elder sister, whom she accompanies to Bannisdale after her father's death. Her father, a Cambridge scientist, the son of a local Westmoreland peasant family, had been a confirmed atheist, sure that his religious views had hindered his career. So Laura feels a deep repulsion, at times sexual, for the persons and ceremonies and atmosphere at Bannisdale. She seeks out her nearby farming cousins, one of whom—in most respects a hopeless yokel but a talented musician—calls Helbeck "a *snake*," who "sticks in folk's gizzards aboot here," and makes Laura aware of the causes of the local hostility. "For . . . all of us," says a Jesuit to Laura, "doubt is misery." She answers, "Papa taught me—it was life—and I believe him."

The love between Helbeck and Laura is genuine and passionate on both sides. Helbeck's friends—all Catholics—are shocked and disturbed. But Laura has been baptized: her mother had insisted on that, and so there is no impediment to their marriage. Helbeck's hopes are concentrated upon her eventual conversion, but he sternly resists the temptation to spend time with her that would otherwise have gone to his religious duties: "Devotion to the crucified

Lord and His Mother, obedience to His Church, imitation of His saints, charity to His poor—these are the means by which the Catholic draws down the grace . . . he seeks. . . . the more he loved her, the more rigid became all the habits and purposes of religion. . . . inflamed by that profound idea of a substituted life and a vicarious obedience which has been among the root forces of Christianity." Laura, on the other hand, "represented forces of intelligence, of analysis, of criticism, of which in themselves she knew little or nothing, except so far as they affected all her modes of feeling. She felt as she had been born to feel, as she had been trained to feel."

But she has no arguments at the ready to meet the Catholic arguments. To her the nuns display "unintelligible virtues and . . . very obvious bigotries and absurdities"; the priests seem sly or absurd or superstitious, "doing perpetually the most futile and foolish things." She wavers between efforts to compromise and certainty that she cannot. Horrified by what seems to her an inhuman episode in a saint's life she has been reading, she says to Helbeck that her father belonged to "an Ethical Society at Cambridge," which discussed such problems. He answers gently but contemptuously, "Mercifully, darling, the ideals of the Catholic Church do not depend upon the votes of Ethical Societies." When she loves him most, she decides that it would be "a crime—a crime" to marry him, and she runs away. But not even a brilliant (and it is brilliant), long, and analytical conversation among some of her father's rational former Cambridge colleagues about the Catholic Church and its place in history can keep her away. She returns to Bannisdale, to reconciliation, to a renewed engagement, and to a second revulsion culminating in suicide.

Helbeck of Bannisdale might easily be considered a novel of Catholicism (and in this series we have indeed so listed it) because of the detail, the insight, the unshrinking analysis Mrs. Ward gives to some of the major aspects of the faith in nineteenth-century England. Yet it is more appropriate to bracket it with *Robert Elsmere*, as a sophisticated and informed study of the conflict—so sharp this time as to be fatal—between faith and doubt. More than that: it is a fine novel, whose wealth of incident and breadth of interest and excitement have hardly been indicated here in this brief analysis of

Mrs. Ward's treatment and resolution of its central problem. Of all the novels in this collection, none will better repay the rediscoverer. As Paul Bourget wrote to Mrs. Ward, "It is easy to write novels of passion, harder to write novels of manners, and harder still novels of conscience. But the grand intellectual novel, one in which ideas are shown *alive* in their active and intimate relationship with sensibility and will, that, I maintain, is the rarest and loftiest form of our art. In that you have once again succeeded, and your subject is of so great an importance that in my opinion this is your most important work."

CHAPTER 10.

"SOULS BEREAVED" THE NOVELS OF W. H. MALLOCK

"A Systematic Stock-taking of the English Mind"

In March 1877, there appeared anonymously an astonishingly witty book called *The New Republic; or, Culture, Faith, and Philosophy in an English Country House* (NIS). Essentially it was a series of conversations among a large group of worldly men and women at a house party, whose host set them the task of determining the principles upon which an ideal nineteenth-century state—like Plato's *Republic*, only "New"—should properly be based. Knowledgeable readers soon discovered that at least seven of the most important characters were recognizable portraits of seven of the most towering intellectual figures of contemporary English life, whose views—as each spoke them—were satirized, sometimes mercilessly but always cleverly, and always in such a way as to make them more readable and more easily understandable than the originals. Thus "Dr. Jenkinson" was Dr. Jowett, the latitudinarian Master of Balliol (friend of Mrs. Humphry Ward, as we know), philosopher and professional, though indifferent, Greek scholar. "Mr. Rose"—labelled a "Pre-Raphaelite"—was Walter Pater, as we have seen. "Mr. Luke" was Matthew Arnold; "Mr. Storks" Thomas Henry Huxley; "Mr. Stockton" John Tyndall; "Mr. Saunders" Professor W. K. Clifford, the brilliant mathematician, who had moved from advanced Anglo-Catholicism to atheism; and "Mr. Herbert" John Ruskin, the great art critic and social theorist. All except Ruskin were skillfully ridiculed by utterances only mildly exaggerating their own.

Hailed at once by Disraeli and Oscar Wilde, *The New Republic* was soon known to be by William Hurrell Mallock (1849-1923), then twenty-seven, member of a Devonshire gentry family, nephew of the late Hurrell Froude and of James Anthony Froude, great-nephew of the archdeacon, Balliol graduate, amateur of the classics, and man about London, sophisticated and conservative. Working in the vein of Thomas Love Peacock's satirical novels of the early nineteenth century, Mallock also freely adapted the famous episode of Trimalchio's Feast in the *Satyricon* of Petronius Arbiter. Although the house party is ostensibly held in "an English country house," the house itself is a most un-English modern villa built by the sea in late Roman style by the late uncle of the host, "a lettered voluptuary," enormously rich and altogether cynical. So luxurious are the house and gardens and so elaborate the furnishings and decorations that Mallock pretended that he could not even describe them himself, but supplied instead a long footnote of lush prose which he attributed to the daughter of a former housekeeper in the villa, now transformed into a lady novelist: it is a cruel and telling parody of the popular novelist "Ouida" (Louise de la Ramée). And of course, in addition to Peacock and Petronius, Plato, author of the original *Republic*, provided the essential inspiration of the dialogue form in which Mallock cast his book.

The New Republic is not truly a novel, and religion is only one of its concerns, but it contains many clues to the ideas of Mallock's later novels, which primarily concern us. The host of the house party—Laurence—in thinking of a topic for his guests to discuss "that anyone can talk easily about, whether he knows anything of it or not," is at first considering religion. No, says his friend Leslie, this might scare off the ladies; how about simply asking "the question 'Are you High-church or Low-church?' There is something in that which at once disarms reverence, and may also just titillate the interests, the temper, or the sense of humour." But in the end, this too is dropped, and religion as such does not form one of the set topics. Yet it naturally pervades the discussion: and while Pater's aesthetic paganism, Arnold's cultural relativism, Clifford's strident atheism and scientism, and Huxley's scientific agnosticism are all impartially lampooned, it is Jowett's Broad-Church vagueness and personal style that Mallock most sharply attacks. He had disliked Jowett personally at Balliol, regarded him as muddle-headed (and as a social climber), and loathed his religious views.

Jowett ("Jenkinson") appears as "the great Broad-Church divine who thinks that Christianity is not dead, but changed by himself and his followers in the twinkling of an eye." He agrees that society is in a bad way: "Many thoughtful people think that there is more that is bad in the present than there has ever been in the past. Many thoughtful people in all days have thought the same." Yet these times are really better than the past after all: "We have got rid of a vast amount of superstition and ignorance and are learning what Christianity really is. We are learning true reverence—that is, not to dogmatise about subjects of which we cannot possibly know anything." Even when others assure him that "if you take four out of five of the more thoughtful and instructed men of the day, you will find that not only have they no faith in a personal God or a personal immortality, but the very notions of such things seem to them absurdities," and tell him that in the past thirty years atheism has supplanted Christianity, "Jenkinson" is cheerful: "There's plenty of religion now. The real power of Christianity is growing every day. . . ."

Jowett is made to preach a long sermon, wickedly set on the stage of the private theatre of the estate (there is no chapel). The decor is provided by "scantily draped" and nude pagan goddesses and muses, fauns, and women in a Bacchanalian procession, and on the curtain is Faust, "not a man to be abashed by incongruities," with a naked witch. Jowett opens the service with a passage from the Koran, follows it with a selection from the English morning service, omitting the creed, and concludes with a prayer by St. Francis Xavier, the sixteenth-century Jesuit. His sermon on the text "The fear of the Lord is the beginning of wisdom" is a masterpiece of obfuscation and bewilderment, beginning with Plato and Aristotle, discussing science and religion, and wholly lacking sharpness of definition or even of diction. He quotes from himself the same passage from *Essays and Reviews* that we quoted above about the need to study the Bible as one studies all other books, and going on to "clear our eyes of any false theological glamour." When we see Christianity as wholly a subject for study, we shall realize that there has always been difference of opinion about the dogmas of religion, and that—like Judaism and primitive Christianity—the Church of England too is composed of "a variety of systems, all honestly and boldly thought out, differing widely from each other, and called by the honourable appellation of heresies."

Everything is confused and doubtful, even "the details of the divine life of our Lord," but we should not be disturbed, because "we can be quite sure that He lived, and . . . went about doing good." So we must embrace science and modern Biblical criticism: "we should surely learn henceforth not to identify Christianity with anything that science can assail, or even question. Let us say rather that nothing is or can be essential to the religion of Christ which, when once stated, can be denied without absurdity." Even when warring theologians and rival sects have been most at odds, they have really been in agreement without realizing it.

"All the most enlightened men" of the present day are gradually coming to these conclusions, and we must not rebuke "our weaker brethren" who may cling to past "evils" like the doctrines "of eternal punishment, or of sacerdotal absolution, or . . . the mystical paradoxes of the Athanasian Creed," all of which have been useful in their day. "And even if we do occasionally come across some incident in the history of our religion—some doctrine or body of doctrines, which seems, humanly speaking, to subserve no good end at all—such as our own Thirty-nine Articles—let us not suffer such to try our faith, but let us trust in God, believing that in His secret councils He has found some fitting use even for these. . . ." Properly considered, evil is only undeveloped good; so we may cease our "fretful wailings" over the badness of our own times, the "unbelief of our neighbours, the corruption of society, the misery of the poor, the luxury of the rich, or the decline of commercial morality." The times we live in are the best for us, and "we could not, as a whole, alter anything in them for the better." Each of us should do his duty.

No summary can do full justice to Mallock's marvellous deadpan satire on the complacent vagueness of Jowett's form of Broad-Church Christianity. It reminds one of Jowett's own remark after hearing one of Maurice's sermons: he gathered, he said, that "today was yesterday and this world the same as the next." Mallock's "Jenkinson" is also shown busily toadying the rich and powerful: attending a dinner in honor of Baron Isaacs (Lord Rothschild?) in honor of his horse's having won the Derby; leaving the party when it is over in the carriage of the social-climbing Lady Ambrose, whose husband is a man of great wealth and dubious social origins; and commenting, as the last word in the novel, that after all, the Utopia the house guests have been constructing is only present-day society "with its homelier details left out." The present, the Doctor comfortably assures us, is the "highest state of things conceivable." "Dr. Jenkinson's Christianity," as one of the guests remarks, "is really a new firm trading under an old name, and trying to purchase the goodwill of the former establishment." No wonder that Jowett was piqued by *The New Republic*: he is supposed to have said that "Ninety-nine young men of talent could have written it, but the hundredth would have been too much of a gentleman to have it printed."

The New Republic introduces the reader to many aspects of Mallock's personal interests besides his contempt—amounting to hatred—for Jowett's latitudinarian opinions. The Vicar of the Parish—modelled on Dr. Pusey—makes a brief appearance. He seems unaware of religious infidelity amongst the upper classes, believes that irreligion is now "confined . . . to the half-educated artisans in our large towns," on whom the Church has lamentably relaxed her hold, and is more interested in the possible reunion of the Anglican and Greek Orthodox Churches and the detailed theological considerations involved therein than in any practical ethical problem of the present day. The Puseyites are hopelessly impractical and out of date.

The host at the house party, Laurence, not fully developed as a fictional character, is an embryonic early sketch of the heroes of Mallock's later novels. He is "one of those of whom it is said till they are thirty, that they will do something; till they are thirty-five, that they might do something if they chose; and after that, that they might have done anything if they had chosen." At thirty-two, Laurence is three years "gone into the second stage" and is listless, sybaritic, and unhappy. He is looking for a cause, but cannot find it: "Politics have turned into a petty, weary game; religion is dead; our new prophets only offer us Humanity, in place of the God of which they have deprived us. And Humanity makes a very poor Deity, since it is every day disgracing itself and is never of the same mind from one week's end to another. And so here I am utterly alone,—

friendless, with nothing to help me. . . ." At the very end of *The New Republic*, Laurence has almost made up his mind to go to Italy with "Mr. Herbert" (Ruskin), who is congenial: "We both want to pray, and we neither of us can."

To the beautiful Miss Merton, a Roman Catholic, Laurence says, "I cannot pray, because I do not believe in God. Will you pray for me?" and when she confesses that she has already done so, he is about to propose marriage to her. But they are interrupted and the proposal is postponed. The young infidel who hates his own infidelity and yet cannot change, but who yearns for the stability of Catholic faith, is a stock Mallock character, reflecting his own doubts and desires. Typical also is the interrupted proposal: marriages are infrequent in his novels, though love affairs are numerous. Mallock inserted in *The New Republic* an admirable verse parody of Matthew Arnold's "Dover Beach," and a single quatrain which he attributes to Clough, but which of course he wrote himself: "Ah, well-a-day, for we are souls bereaved!/ Of all the creatures under heaven's wide cope,/ We are most hopeless who had once most hope,/ And most beliefless who had once believed." It is from these verses that I have chosen the words which serve as title to this chapter. They nicely epitomize Mallock's attitude and views.

The year after *The New Republic*, there appeared Mallock's *The New Paul and Virginia; or Positivism on an Island* (1878, NIS), which he called "a short satirical story in the style of Voltaire's *Candide*," and in which he returned to the battle against his enemies, the "liberal" philosophers. This time, instead of inventing exaggerations of their own opinions to put into the mouths of his characters based on them, Mallock used their actual words, but made them ridiculous by the circumstances in which they were spoken. Was the decline in religious belief affecting morality, and how severely? This question was being seriously discussed on all sides, and was debated in the *Nineteenth Century* by members of the Metaphysical Society, including Huxley, Tyndall, W. K. Clifford, Frederic Harrison—an out-and-out Comtist Positivist—and others. In the pages of the periodical, Mallock answered them in articles later published (1879) in a volume dedicated to Ruskin and entitled *Is Life Worth Living?* But meanwhile, he gave his views bite and wider circulation in *The New Paul and Virginia.* Jowett had been so thoroughly refuted in *The New Republic* that his ideas do not reappear, but those of Huxley, Tyndall, and Clifford do. All those, indeed, who repudiated orthodox religion and sought to substitute for it an "enthusiasm for humanity" or "a passion for the welfare of posterity" or "a godless deification of domestic puritanism for its own sake" now became Mallock's butts.

A recent English reissue of Bernardin de Saint-Pierre's famous sentimental idealistic novel *Paul et Virginie* (first published in 1788) no doubt prompted Mallock to choose a title redolent of qualities he also intended to satirize. The new "Paul" is both Darwinist and positivist, married to an Evangelical woman who hopes to restore his belief in hell. The new "Virginia" is the young ex-mistress of "the heads of many distinguished families," who as a result is a rich woman at thirty, converted to Ritualism, and married to the Bishop of the "Chasuble Islands," who "besought her to share with him his humble mitre, and make him the happiest prelate in the whole Catholic Church." When the ship they are traveling aboard goes down, Paul and Virginia lose their spouses, but are themselves saved, and land on an uninhabited island with all the comforts of home already installed. This put Mallock in a splendid position to assault those who elevated the idea of personal human happiness to the level of a religious tenet.

Paul and Virginia are joined by a curate also rescued from the ship and already well advanced towards Paul's religious conviction that there is no law except the law of matter. As they drink champagne together, Paul remarks that what he is enjoying is the champagne that the curate is drinking, while what the curate is enjoying is the champagne that Paul is drinking. "This is altruism, this is true benevolence," says Paul, the Huxleyite. But the curate is transformed by the wine into a Cliffordite who believes in instantly pursuing pleasure; so he kisses Virginia and wants to go on doing so. Since Paul is stronger, the laws of matter prevail, and the curate, unable to continue, slides under the table.

So much for the laws of matter, altruism, and some aspects of the "enthusiasm of Humanity." The idea that it is posterity which benefits by the good we do on earth or suffers from the evil—and indeed that "we live in others after death," a favorite Comtist doctrine expounded by Frederic Harrison—receives its *reductio ad absurdum* when Virginia finds a box of chocolates saved from the ship and, as she eats them, is told by Paul that their dead owner "is immortal" because she is eating his erstwhile chocolates. When the now hopelessly alcoholic curate falls over a cliff, Paul hails his death as "unspeakably holy . . . it is for the greatest happiness of the greatest number. . . . Let us prepare ourselves," he says to Virginia, "for realising to the full the essential dignity of Humanity . . . which has come, in the course of progress, to consist of you and me." Virginia's illicit love for Paul, which seems to contradict his theories, he wards off by quoting Tyndall and Huxley at her. But she seizes upon Huxley's remark that some men may possibly worship sensual enjoyment and says *that* is her religion. Together they try to express "cosmic emotion" by howling at the moon ("more rational than the Lord's Prayer" because easily understood), and, just as Paul is about to kiss Virginia ("rational religion" is showing itself to him "under a new light"), their spouses suddenly reappear. Struck by the contrast between Virginia and his newly recovered, ugly wife, Paul suddenly believes in hell, while the advent of the Bishop only restores Virginia's lost belief in heaven.

Amusing for those who had been reading the solemn debate in the pages of the *Nineteenth Century* and who could recognize the ludicrous twist that Mallock had given to the words of the debaters when put into his new context, *The New Paul and Virginia* is a sophisticated piece of polemic, but it is less of a novel even than *The New Republic.* Together they form "a systematic stock-taking of the English-speaking mind," as H. G. Wells said in 1917, when he lamented that there had been nothing like them for forty years. And while they are not novels, and are therefore not included in this series, they provide the best possible background for the five consecutive novels by Mallock that are here reproduced: only Mrs. Oliphant and William Hale White have as many.

The few critics who have bothered to read the later novels are disappointed and disapproving: while *The New Republic*, one of them wrote in 1895, "burst like a bomb over modern Oxford," and men expected great things of its author, he gave his readers "his best wine first" and became a "half-failure," who lacks the power to "integrate and achieve." Mallock's characters speak and behave and feel convincingly, he admitted, but somehow they "lack human vibration." As recently as 1960, a sympathetic scholar faulted Mallock for his inability to construct a plot, and attributed this defect to his participation in the "spiritual distress of the later nineteenth century," deriving from the inability to reconcile science and religion. Because Mallock was unable to find and propose solutions, the action of his novels remains "irrelevant." I would argue in response that the novels have never been properly appreciated. Yet even if I am wrong, they are absorbingly interesting as illustrating the ways in which fiction can be made to reflect the varieties of doubt.

Sex, Melancholia, and Religion

The first, *A Romance of the Nineteenth Century* (1881, no. 76), is sensational indeed. Ralph Vernon, its hero—like Laurence in *The New Republic*—is rich, well born, charming, and disillusioned. "There was many a mother in London of the best and purest type who thought his character so cold, so unprincipled, and so repulsive, that he could atone for it only by becoming her daughter's husband." He has broken his engagement because his fiancée's family have been unwilling to accept his requirement—unexpected and inexplicable in a man without faith—that all his children shall be brought up as Catholics. He has lost a close Parliamentary election. And now he is on the French Riviera, in a villa as lush as Laurence's (Mallock himself now takes over the role he had assigned to Ouida in *The New Republic* and describes it in detail), living idly and luxuriously and making love to all available attractive women, including *demi-mondaines* and other men's wives.

The exquisitely beautiful young Cynthia Walters, however, is neither. As they grow ever more attracted to one another and Vernon finds himself falling seriously in love, Cynthia hints ever more broadly at something dreadful in her past. While repeatedly insisting that they be nothing but friends, she also keeps throwing herself in Vernon's path (she is most inadequately chaperoned) and giving him kiss after kiss in more and more heated embraces. She too has lost faith and needs reassurance. More like a schoolboy than the hardened man of the world he believes himself to be, Vernon keeps telling her how noble and pure she is. The modern reader feels that it would have been a better idea to make her his mistress instead. But in the intervals between their meetings Vernon cannot keep himself from dalliance with other women, for whom he does not care, nor can he summon up the necessary fervor to sweep Cynthia off her feet.

Eventually Vernon learns what he has been trying not to believe (and what the reader who picks up Mallock's clues has long suspected): Stapleton, the middle-aged sportsman and sensualist, who holds so inexplicably privileged a position as an old friend of Cynthia's family, had seduced her in her girlhood and has kept her as his occasional mistress since. Unable to tell Vernon this in so many words, the girl shows him a recent present from her lover: an album of photographs "such as in England the police would seize upon." Since Stapleton had earlier tried to show the pornographic pictures to Vernon, he knows at once what they are and who sent them. As Cynthia herself says, "The very fact that such a thing should be sent me will throw some light for you on the character of the sender, and the sort of character which I have let him impute to me." Though inexpressibly shocked, Vernon does not give her up. He listens to her detailed story of her seduction, and even absorbs the fact that she has had other lovers: "Do you think," she asks, "that such affection as Colonel Stapleton gives a woman is of a kind likely to keep her faithful during his absence?" But though he still loves her and would be ready to marry her, he is somehow unable to take the necessary steps. Colonel Stapleton gets her back, and the novel ends in tragedy.

A Romance of the Nineteenth Century may well be the most outspoken English novel of that century. It is inexplicable that Chatto & Windus, Mallock's publishers, should not have objected, and even more surprising that no outcry arose from the circulating libraries, which exercised so stringent a censorship over the novels they would accept, and whose refusal of any novel meant its inevitable failure. George Moore, whose *Mummer's Wife* (1884) was far less explicit but was nonetheless banned, was understandably bitter about the acceptance of Mallock's novel. And Hardy abandoned novel writing forever, because of the critics' objections to "offenses" in *Tess* (1891) and more particularly in *Jude the Obscure* (1896) far more pardonable than Mallock's. Mallock got away with putting "Blessed are the pure in heart" on Cynthia Walters's tombstone a decade before Hardy was attacked for calling Tess "a pure woman," yet by any standards Tess was far purer than Cynthia. Criticism of Mallock's Zolaesque candor eventually did lead him to alter some of the details of *A Romance of the Nineteenth Century*, but not until eleven years after its first appearance. Some of its torrid embraces seem prurient to a reader even now.

For us its main interest lies in the strongly religious theme that mingles so persistently with its sexual themes. Frederic Stanley, Cynthia's cousin and a close friend of Vernon's, is a Catholic priest. Once "the cleverest of our Oxford idlers" and thereafter a guardsman, he serves in a limited degree as the confidant of both protagonists. He has observed Vernon performing an act of Christian charity for the lame child of a nearby French peasant family. He remembers that at Oxford Vernon used to talk continually of theology, "never with any reverence, though sometimes with thought and knowledge." For Vernon religion is an intellectual question only, his friends think, "a tiresome riddle that piques him because he can't answer it." His casual behavior in his relations with women, which "deadens human love, deadens divine love also," says a close friend. But Vernon replies by reminding him that he had broken his engagement because of the Catholic question, and asserts that it is wanton self-indulgence and cruelty to give children no faith to guide them. Vernon reads Augustine's *Confessions* and weeps, but is instantly full of contempt for his own tears. He writes a lengthy confession of his own, bemoaning his wretchedness, declaring his yearning to speak to God, "to lay bare my soul . . . and to cry to Thee to have pity," calling on God to teach him to know himself: that is, if there is a God at all, and God is not "only a dream—an idea—a passing phenomenon in man's mental history."

Remembering his childhood, Vernon writes how he had loved God then: "Hardly an hour passed in which, without kneeling, I did not say some word to Thee." Increasingly a sense of the world's sinfulness and of "how Thou wast being grieved and blasphemed everywhere" came over him, and often when he had seen "some young soul corrupting itself" he had thought, "I would die if he might be saved from sinning." Vernon recalls the deep emotion of his first communion, when he "received Thy Son's self into me with fear and trembling." For five years, even when enjoying gaiety and subject to temptations, he remembered Christ. And then, very gradually, God was slowly withdrawn from him, *not through his forgetting God but through his thinking about Him always*: "I studied much and many things; and whatever I studied, I applied it to Thy Church and Thee. And new lights broke on me, and new roads of knowledge; and my soul suffered violence, and the sight of its eyes was changed." So "all that I had once been taught about Thee, the Sacraments also, through which I once thought I approached Thee, became to me like outworn symbols." None of his efforts to revive his faith have been successful. It is, then, not his sins that have cost Vernon his God, but "the very things by which I resisted sin; it is my reason, my intellect, and my longing for what is true." It is the new learning—whether science or Biblical criticism, or both, Vernon does not say—that has effectively destroyed his faith.

He has been told that he may gain faith in God through love of other human beings—but to him this is putting things the wrong way around: it is through love of God that one should come to the love of other human beings. The woman he had hoped to marry "would have made me into *her* God instead of guiding me to *mine*." Continuing to call upon a God of whose very existence he cannot be sure, Vernon is in a pitiable state, and his long Augustinian confession is a painful cry of the heart. Reminded of Herbert Spencer by the sight of one of his books, Vernon concludes his writing by commenting that "to the prophets of humanity an unskilled bricklayer is a more tragic object than a ruined soul!"

Cynthia—who reads Strauss and Renan herself—is told by Stanley, the priest, that "The wrong or right of a book depends on what the reader gets out of it, and out of modern science one may get good or evil, according to the condition that one approaches it in." She is not a Catholic, although the best people she has known have been Catholics. She had once thought of joining the church, but it would have been mental suicide. "With their eyes open, they swallow so much non-sense": how could an absolution provided by Stanley after confession, for example, relieve her of her sins? Why, adds Vernon, should God forgive sins at all, much less through Stanley's agency? Perhaps, she suggests, "what we do to ourselves" is not important, and the real question will be "what work have your hands done? not whether we have kept them quite clean in doing it." Both duties, Vernon thinks, to ourselves and to humanity, are equally important: at least that is what the Church teaches. And when she asks him if he is a Catholic, he says he does not know what he is. About to commit himself more deeply in his relationship with her, he reluctantly misses an appointment with her in order to take the lame child to the doctor. Vernon, says Stanley, is "like a peach-tree: always blossoming and being always nipped with frost." When he does a kind thing he does it "as though he were anxious to disarm affection." There is in him "a remnant of what might once have made him a saint."

Yet Vernon continues to wallow in self-pity and self-hatred, continuing his written confession at length, and moving without pause from self-accusation to paeans of praise for Cynthia. He seeks to persuade her—and himself at the same time—that everyone has a soul to be saved, although of course it cannot be proved. His own soul has "become demagnetized"; it no longer points toward God, but he knows God is still somewhere. He thinks that the way to find God again is through devoting himself to others by a return to public life. Yet although he still has "the wish to act," he has "lost the will." Paralysis of the will—as we would put it—is indeed what affects Vernon. Besides that—as Cynthia tells him herself when he cannot understand her repeated hints about her past (she has told him she is worse than any Magdalene)—he is a "very innocent-minded person." He keeps on telling her that she is "akin to all that is best and holiest," and she keeps on telling him that she is depraved.

After he knows the truth about Cynthia, he has a final conversation with Stanley, who is writing a small book on St. Thomas Aquinas. And Stanley makes Vernon see that—religion apart—happiness must depend on an occupation that will keep his active mind busily employed. It is "one of the worst spiritual signs we can detect in ourselves" if we are "touched with the pathos of our own condition." And when Stanley urges him to do things for others as a pathway to finding contentment, Vernon reveals that he already gives away two-thirds of his income, yet gets no pleasure out of it. Vernon feels that before loving a woman, he must be certain that they both have souls, and that the only way "in which human love can be allied with divine love and blessed by the Christian church . . . is by treating it as a mutual exhortation . . . to the service and love of God." Not so, says the priest: God made everything, including man's affections, and St. Thomas Aquinas's "interior instinct" was given to every human being. "Souls may be moved to God" through the affections, before they know of God's existence. Human affections, rightly exercised, are holy in themselves and may prepare the way for the love of God. Stimulated by this conversation, Vernon wants again to die for Cynthia, to bear her sins, and to leave her "once more spotless."

Just before the final catastrophe, a new political opportunity opens up for Vernon, and he is galvanized into making a decision. And with it he determines to revive an earlier abandoned project for a "kind of workhouse arranged on a new principle" for the East End of London, where he has some property. It will be more generous than the usual charitable relief establishment. So—as with Rutherford and M'Kay, with Joshua Davidson, with Robert Elsmere—it is the philanthropic urge that helps to bring comfort and in this case enables Vernon to overcome paralysis of the will. Stanley quotes W. K. Clifford ("one of the bitterest of the younger generation of English freethinkers") to Vernon, drawing the distinction between the kind of inference one makes in physics and the kind one makes when one realizes that another person is thinking thoughts similar to one's own. Even the antireligious Clifford, says Stanley, implies the reality, the creativity, the necessity, of love. Nobody who loves truly can logically be a sceptic. Buoyed up by this inspiration, Vernon encounters the sudden final ruin of his hope and his life.

To some degree, of course, Vernon—like Laurence of *The New Republic*—is a self-portrait of Mallock, who was not as rich as they, but who shared their doubts and anxieties. Into *A Romance of the Nineteenth Century* he put a lovingly drawn portrait of the first Lord Lytton—Edward Bulwer-Lytton, the novelist, playwright, and poet, who had died in 1873—a dandy of the early century, and a finished mournful man of the world. "Lord Surbiton" Mallock called him:

he had been Vernon's friend and had given him early encouragement when Vernon as an Eton schoolboy had brought him his first poems; he can even still recite them with appreciation: "Oh Goddess, I am sick at heart, o'er worn/ With weariness,/ For the weight of life is bitter to be borne/ Companionless." So it is clear that Vernon's melancholia went back deep into his early manhood, as did Mallock's own. And a shrewd woman remarks of Vernon that he will never marry—as Mallock did not—because he's "exactly like a younger edition of Lord Surbiton." I think one must conclude that—even had Cynthia Walters been of the most unquestioned purity (which would of course have deprived the novel of its irony and its bite), even had Vernon married her and been elected to Parliament and engaged in philanthropy, even had he been converted in the end to the Catholicism he regarded as essential for his children—he would never have conquered his malaise and gained emotional and spiritual equilibrium as a human being. The novel therefore is a deeper and more compelling one than even Mallock's kindest critics have ever before suggested.

The Social Question and Religion

In his next novel, *The Old Order Changes* (1886, no. 81), Mallock's themes underwent important variations and expansions. His hero, Carew, is not listless, like Vernon, but at thirty-five he is without a career. He knows that to launch himself satisfactorily he will need the companionship of a congenial wife who shares his goals and purposes. The heir to ancient encumbered family estates in Devonshire and—from another source—to the fortune that will enable him to clear them of debt and assume his proper position, he is a passionate believer in the perpetuation and strengthening of the aristocracy as a class. In addition to theology and philosophy, he has made an intensive study of the "social question" and has come to hold views much like those of Disraeli and his friends in the "Young England" group of the 1840's: the interests of the aristocracy and of the working classes are identical; the enemy of both is the manufacturing middle class. Perhaps not since Disraeli's own famous *Sybil; or, The Two Nations* (1845, NIS), in which the "two nations" were the rich and the poor, had this particular social theory been given so thorough an airing in a novel.

Mallock brought matters up to date by putting much of the vituperation against the middle-class Whig radicals, who pretend to be friends of the working man but are not, into the mouth of a Marxist revolutionary. In Carew's French cousin's castle in the hills north of Nice, he assembles a house party among whose members is the Socialist "Foreman," a hardly veiled portrait of H. M. Hyndman, the English socialist leader and atheist, who had repudiated his own middle-class origins. "Foreman" outdoes even the most reactionary of Carew's Tory friends in his vituperative attacks on "Japhet Snapper," the Liberal Radical leader, a vitriolic caricature of Joseph Chamberlain, portrayed as taking cruel advantage of the "Birchester" (Birmingham) workers whose interests he pretends to uphold, and as lying in wait to buy Carew's ancestral property, so that he may become a member of the very landed gentry he professes to hate but actually envies. The year 1886, when *The Old Order Changes* was published, saw the Trafalgar Square riots led by Hyndman; Mallock gives a vivid picture of these, as viewed from Carew's club in St. James's Street. Mallock comments on the international socialist and anarchist network that extended to America, where the Chicago Haymarket riots took place in the same year. In its subject matter and timeliness, then, the novel somewhat resembles Henry James's *Princess Casamassima*, also published in 1886, but Mallock's views of socialism, though hostile, were well informed, not merely intuitive like James's.

Carew's (and Mallock's) interest in the working classes is of a somewhat limited kind: in an unguarded moment Carew refers to them as "dirt," and the stream of rioters in the West End reminds him of a flow of sewage. He wants to do them good from above, in some part, one sees, as a protective measure to ensure the future of his own upper class. Mallock's hatred of the social climbers of the middle class is embodied in the ridiculous (but trouble making) character of Mr. Inigo, the name-dropping snob, who turns out to be "Foreman's" own half brother, and who has made a large annual contribution to the Socialists as blackmail to keep the fact of the relationship dark. "Lord Aiden"—poet, diplomat, and sophisticated man of the world—is an affectionate portrait of Robert, second Lord Lytton, the poet "Owen Meredith," Ambassador to France, later Viceroy of India and first Earl of Lytton, son of the novelist Edward Bulwer-Lytton, whom we met as "Lord Surbiton" in *A Romance of the Nineteenth Century*. Some of Mallock's best epigrams are put into his mouth: "The relation that prevails, and indeed always has prevailed, in England, between birth and riches, between rank, power, and talent, may not, perhaps, be the most important problem in the world; but, excepting for Chinese grammar, I doubt if anything is more complicated; and a judgment of it that even approaches truth is as nice a thing as the most delicate chemical compound."

The sexual passions of *A Romance of the Nineteenth Century* are muted and far less explicit here, but love plays a central part in the novel. Not an emotional basket-case like Vernon, Carew nonetheless shares with him the ability to amuse himself cheerfully with almost any attractive woman in the absence of the woman he thinks he loves the best. Falsely suspected of an involvement with a noblewoman of ill repute, he is coldly treated by the sisters and guardians of his true love, Consuelo Burton, beautiful, devoutly Catholic, and possessed of a strong social conscience. During an enforced separation from Consuelo—to whom he has never fully committed himself—Carew makes love, desultory at first, to a charming American girl, Violet Capel, who responds eagerly and piquantly to his advances. Before long she warns him that she is "bespoke": engaged to be married soon to a rich nobleman, "one of the most dissolute men in Europe, and . . . one of the silliest." Carew and she continue their flirtation just the same, and—though, like most Mallock heroes, he does *not* commit himself—Violet lets him know that she really loves him. She could never be his partner in his planned career, however, and if he married her, he would also be disinherited. Especially after the misunderstanding with Consuelo's family is cleared away, and it is obvious that she will marry him if he asks her, Carew is faced with a delicate dilemma: how far is he bound to try to rescue Violet from her imminent marriage and—if he succeeds—to make a shipwreck of his own hopes?

But it is religion that provides the unifying theme of *The Old Order Changes*. Carew, like Vernon, is sympathetic to the Roman

Church, and has been expected to become a Catholic, but has not taken the plunge. His royalist French cousins, in whose chateau (where one feels that "one is actually living before the French Revolution") the earlier portions of the novel are laid, are of course Catholics. So are his Italian cousins, in whose equally sumptuous lakeside villa on Lago Maggiore the later episodes unfold. Frederic Stanley, the Catholic priest of *A Romance of the Nineteenth Century*, reappears as a major character. His monograph on Thomas Aquinas is completed, and he has just prepared the first translation into English of Marx's *Das Kapital*, "the profoundest piece of imperfect reasoning I ever met with in my life." Thoroughly steeped in socialist literature, and delighted to meet and debate with "Foreman," Stanley is determined to reach out for a synthesis between the Positivist-humanists, the socialists, and the Catholics, and to make it serve the necessary practical purposes in the economic and social crisis of the period. In this, he has the assistance of Consuelo Burton and other influential Catholic friends of Carew, who obtain papal approval for their scheme, which is, of course, Mallock's own. In a climactic scene, Stanley preaches an extraordinary sermon in the chapel of the villa to an audience including a positivist professor and "Humbert Spender," the scientist—Herbert Spencer, of course—whom Mallock hardly bothered to disguise.

Carew's friends associate themselves together in a "small informal society" of well-born people all of whom are convinced that they have a duty to humanity. All are also Christians or "at least regard Christianity with minds open to conviction." Their two protracted meetings, one in France and the other in Italy, have something in common with *The New Republic*; indeed the parallel is drawn almost explicitly: "no doubt for us it is a very delightful thing to look across lakes and gardens at purple mountains and sunsets, and talk about the sorrows of men who live in back-yards and alleys. It is delightful to dream of the new duty which we owe them, and new ways of discharging it. It's a delightful intellectual exercise, just as Plato's 'Republic' was." But the difference is that this time the symposiasts are actively seeking new solutions to real problems in the world. Had "Humbert Spender" made his appearance in *The New Republic* (or in *The New Paul and Virginia*), he would have presented at length a credible yet burlesque summary of his chief ideas and would then have been refuted by one of the other characters. In *The Old Order Changes* he appears but says nothing in particular. This novel comes to grips with more concrete questions in a far less comic vein.

Consuelo's brother, brought up in "one of the last of the really great households in England," had three Italian priests as tutors; the place swarmed with retainers, "endless horses in the stables, . . . constant coming and going, . . . meets, . . . scarlet coats, . . . the foreign ecclesiastics . . . gliding [!] quietly up and down the huge passages"—all of which has rendered him and his elder sisters wholly unequipped to deal with the modern world. To Consuelo, her sisters' constant efforts for the poor seem "like weeding a flower-garden instead of ploughing a field." They are more pleased to see two hundred people in church than they are pained to see twenty families in one house. "When I watch her trotting off to Mass in the morning, looking as though she were doing the whole duty of women," says Consuelo of one sister, "I feel as if . . . I should never be religious again." She thinks that "men like Mr. Foreman are the only men who are right when they tell us we must begin by attacking the circumstances" under which the poor must live. She is disturbed because "the world is changing, and the Church stands apart from the change." Yet she can as little understand why Carew is not a Catholic as he can understand why she is dissatisfied with Catholicism. Often when she has heard the organ, she has thought, "Hang the organ! Let me listen to the crying of the children!"

Convinced that he and his class "are made of different clay from the others," and that he must stop sneering at the claims of the poor as if they "were nothing but the cant of a sect or of some scheming radical faction," Carew believes that only with Consuelo can he do his bit to see that "Civilization must cease to rest on squalor and misery." He wants to cut through "the sense of doubt and bewilderment," so widespread amongst all social classes and especially in the upper class, "as to what we should do with ourselves, not only as moral beings, but also as people inheriting a special place in society." For him the aristocracy is a foundering vessel, and religion already derelict. Some of the members of the informal society that discusses the question, then, are Catholics; others, like Carew and

Aiden, "incline to Catholicism. It was not true, but no other view was tolerable." Only one or two feel annoyed when "a respectable but an indifferent superstition" is called "The Faith." The influential Lady Chislehurst, who has the Pope's own ear, "had sought, and . . . had made, the acquaintance of nearly everyone, to whom she saw any chance of being either a friend or a benefactress, and she thus has a wide experience of all ranks except the middle."

Confronted by a Catholic priest who knows as much Marx as he, "Foreman" is left without an answer when Stanley puts it to him that a socialist state would be possible only if "we were all equally clever and all equally industrious" or if mankind as a whole could "rise to heights of zeal and self-sacrifice to which saints and heroes at present find it very hard to attain." Stanley declares that the most rigorous asceticism of the Catholic Church—regarded by the Church as suitable for only a small fraction of mankind (and of course detested by "Foreman")—"does far less violence to our average human nature" than the changes in it that Socialism would require. "It would be easier . . . to make men Trappists than Socialists."

Consuelo, feeling the pangs of guilt at being rich, yearning to study political economy, and finding that her religion does not help her solve her problems, says to Stanley that to her "the question whether the upper classes are to renounce their position or to use it seems to her more important than those questions which are commonly called religious." To which the priest replies that she is right, and that "*Political economy, and the social conditions of labour, have become in our day indeed a branch of theology—its youngest branch*. . . . Every age has its riddle, and this riddle is ours." Since, however, "the talents which produce money . . . would never be developed at all if it were not in the nature of things" that the few who have them should also have the riches that result, the Church does not enjoin the extinction of the desire for wealth, but only its regulation. Of course *all* the men who make industry work will not voluntarily hand over their profits to the general good; but, as Consuelo suggests, *some* of them might do so. "They might extend commerce . . . develop manufactures, as if they were doing so under some monastic vow—some vow of poverty with a modern meaning to it."

This thought of Consuelo's is developed into a full-fledged project. "Men who are housed like pigs can hardly pray like Christians," says Consuelo, "and where life is a long flight from starvation, it is not a flight that takes the fugitives to heaven." So "sanitary and social work . . . is a necessary part of modern religious propagandism," and what is planned is precisely the "modern monastic vow," a renunciation of profits by a dedicated band of new Catholic capitalists, an industrial monastic order, factories where management and labor should in fact be monks and nuns and "the spire should rise side by side with the chimney." The profits would all go into "a fund to relieve distress" especially in moments of financial crisis. And by the shining example they set, Carew adds, the new monks and nuns will "form a moral leaven amongst the labouring classes at large" and enhance the dignity of factory labor. If factory labor became conventual, many who now would never think of such a thing would renounce their lives of ease and join the new Order.

In his sermon preached before the audience that includes the positivist and "Humbert Spender," Stanley accepts—and welcomes, as a Catholic priest—the premise of the modern scientific moralist that the virtue of an action is to be measured by the degree to which it diminishes human suffering and promotes the general welfare. Just as the mediaeval Church took the philosophical system of Aristotle, a heathen, and made its conclusions "bone of its bone, flesh of its sacred flesh," so in the course of time the modern Church is assimilating this very "modern theory of virtue by which its own authors conceive that the theory of the Church will be superseded." Not so. Only the Church can make the new theory practicable.

Man's natural impulses are not virtuous: only conscience can "justify virtue in a way which shall satisfy the demands of the intellect." (And here Stanley's triad of natural impulse, conscience, and intellect can be translated into Freudian terms of id, superego, and ego.) But the well-being of the human race as such—apart from any further beliefs about it—cannot so present itself in a way as to satisfy the heart and mind for very long. Without faith, and as science advances, the earth will seem less and less important, and men tinier and less significant: "No idea more depressing, more hopeless, more ludicrously miscalculated to evoke heroism, or to curb passion, can possibly be imagined than the human race as a whole, as it shows itself to the eye of reason, unaided by faith." But belief in God and the human soul as related to God changes all that, transforming contempt into reverence and firing the lukewarm soul. Duty to the human race "regarded as a new and more definite interpretation of our duty to God, is a conception which to us as Catholics is of the very highest importance."

Stanley's entire effort is an earnest attempt to assimilate the ethics of the scientific moralist to the Catholic religion, and to appeal to adherents of both systems to recognize the necessity of such a combination. It is Mallock's most serious effort to convince his readers—to convince himself—that such an amalgamation was possible, that it was, perhaps, even in process, and that it pointed the way to action and to salvation. Very little can be done for mankind generally by any individual, and the only way to comfort ourselves in the face of "this paralyzing, this insidious thought" is through the paradoxical "holy and saving teaching which the Church alone can give, which to the positivist is a stumbling-block and to men of science foolishness, that it is more important to every man that he should do his utmost for humanity, than it can be for humanity that any one man should do his utmost for it." Amidst the many frivolities of his long novel and the epigrammatic urbanities of its *fin-de-siècle* dialogue, Mallock—with the earnestness of any Arnold—wrestled with doubts and whistled in the dark.

Love and Religion

In *A Human Document* (1892, no. 85), the social and political themes disappear and the religious theme seems almost submerged, as love takes the center of the stage. Robert Grenville is a recognizable Mallock hero, in that great things are expected of him and he is prepared to renounce his career; but he alone among the heroes does so in order to pursue a love affair. Set largely in Hungary, the illicit romance between Grenville and Irma Schilizzi—unhappily married to a boorish Levantine who has ceased to care for her except as a domestic ornament—is made by Mallock to take on portentous significance. Irma wavers interminably between encouragement and rebuff, passion and renunciation. Grenville's whole religious faith is wrapped up in his all-too-human love for Irma; though she does not feel guilty at betraying her husband, Irma's conscience will not allow her to forget that she is breaking a divine law.

The reader may well be puzzled as to what Mallock had in mind, though the novel is interesting enough in itself. Mallock himself, in his *Memoirs* (1920), remarked that the book leads "although by a quite different route, to the same conclusion as that suggested" in his earlier novels, "that in all the higher forms of affection a religious belief is implicit, which connects the lovers with the All, and establishes between them and It some conscious and veritable communion." To which he added that "no affection is complete unless it is in harmony with the cosmic will, which takes cognizance of the doings of the individual and gives to them something of its own eternity; but that insofar as the two are at variance, the individual must pay the price." *A Human Document*, then, must be read in part as a novel of the substitution of love for faith and of the punishment that follows.

In *The Heart of Life* (1895, no. 86), Mallock is back in his best epigrammatic vein. Alone among Mallock's heroes, Reginald Pole is actually seen enjoying the successful career that the others might have had: indecision and passion led to Vernon's death; Carew's future still lay ahead of him at the end of Mallock's story; Grenville deliberately sacrificed his professional future; but Pole's long "Blue Book," a report on trades unions in Europe, leads at once to his receiving a safe seat in the House of Commons, to office under the Government, to a brilliant series of parliamentary debating triumphs, and to the eventual frustration of indignant efforts to deprive him of his well-earned professional rewards.

His serious love affairs—involving as they do three young women—are more complicated than those of any other Mallock hero, and they also, in the end, take a satisfactory turn. Duped and led on by his fascinating distant cousin, Countess Shimna—a girl who has much in common with Cynthia Walters, the siren of *A Romance of the Nineteenth Century*, and yet is original enough to exercise a new fascination of her own—Pole cannot bring either himself or Ethel deSouza, a rich banker's heiress and sympathetic friend, to fall deeply enough in love for marriage. A fortunate shipwreck, conveniently drowning an inconvenient husband, makes it possible for Pole to achieve what looks like genuine and permanent happiness with his true love, former mistress, and mother of his young son. Though she has often treated him as Irma Schilizzi did Grenville, alternating warmth and chill, their affair ends triumphantly. This is an affirmative Mallock novel, not a negative one. Indeed, to Pole, "the fidelity of a man to a woman . . . of a father to his helpless child" are "those concentrated affections which are the heart and the light of life." So he wins what he most cherishes and what gives the book its title.

The social theme, though far more in evidence than in *A Human Document*, is nonetheless far less so than in *The Old Order Changes*. But Pole does embark on personal charitable projects in his rural West Country district, helping individual poor families, making a systematic study of local needs, and planning an orphanage with an industrial school attached and "perhaps a lodging for widows," of a sort that had been successful in Belgium, where he had studied them. A man of moderate wealth, Pole is ready to commit the larger portion of his income to these good works. His opposition to socialism and to "radical" liberalism is as vigorous as Carew's. But instead of very large-scale undertakings such as the new monastic order planned by Consuelo and supported by Carew, Pole is able to make an emotional commitment to small-scale local charitable foundations of a sort that he can manage alone, with the help of his family and of those who know local conditions best.

Nor are Pole's social projects directly connected with religion. Like Carew, Pole has the entrée into the private, exclusive world of the old Catholic families of England, several of whose members make their appearance. But unlike Carew and the other Mallock heroes, Pole has no particular wish to become a Catholic. He can lead family prayers, and even observe with delight and reverence his own young son saying the Lord's Prayer, without experiencing gnawing pangs of doubt and yearnings to believe. When the baby has said its prayer, Pole wonders if he knows what the words mean: the child's mother replies, "Perhaps not . . . but he feels it," and

Pole answers, "So do I. . . . Which of us can say more? Let us at all events, do our best for his sake; and we perhaps—or his generation—shall one day again know." The agonizing torments of Vernon, Carew, even Grenville, are simply not felt by Pole in the same way. He can even joke about matters of faith without being mournful or wistfully resigned. "Young men of the present day," says the shrewd Lord Wargrave to him, "have . . . no religion. They . . . cease to say prayers at twenty." To which Pole responds, "we shall all of us pray again when a Royal Commission reports upon what to pray to." And "Religious belief in these days is a Penelope's web, which is woven by the soul in emotion, and which the mind unweaves in meditation."

The Heart of Life—with its hero saner, healthier, far less neurotic and introspective than any of his predecessors—is nonetheless a novel about religion. But this time, Mallock unmercifully satirizes the Anglican clergy. Canon Bulman, who has been Pole's tutor, is an Evangelical moralist, who founds a league of prurient enquiry into the morals of all public men: the league is out to ruin the career of any candidate for office whom it can discover straying from the path of strict sexual virtue. Pole's own career is briefly threatened by its activities, and Bulman is portrayed as a repulsive hypocrite, lavishing money on his own physical comforts, including good-looking housemaids: he has separated himself from his own wife after a brief marriage. So obsessed by sexual purity that he even wants to take down the portrait of an erring ancestress of Pole's, Bulman is of course an extreme Radical in politics, denouncing the rich at every turn, while pursuing them socially with a virulent snobbism. Dr. Clitheroe—another cleric, personally charming and modest—proves to be an embezzler and gambler who brings Pole himself almost to ruin. Even the Reverend Sutherland Godolphin—a thoroughly decent Tractarian Church of England parson—is intolerably pompous and is made the butt of some of Mallock's wittiest and most patronizing satire. As for Dr. Mogg—the only Dissenting minister in any of Mallock's novels—he is an associate of Bulman's nefarious league, but otherwise a pure figure of fun. For the first time since he had put Jowett into *The New Republic* almost twenty years before, Mallock turned his attention to clergymen, but only to draw a series of devastatingly unflattering sketches. None is fit to be mentioned in the same breath as Frederic Stanley, the learned and civilized Catholic priest of *A Romance of the Nineteenth Century* and *The Old Order Changes.* In *The Heart of Life* there is no Catholic priest and very little impulse towards Catholicism.

If it is to this extent a less serious novel than any of its predecessors, it is even more appealing and readable. Lighthearted, unfailingly witty, full of surprises (Parnell and Kitty O'Shea appear; so does the second Duke of Wellington, wonderfully sketched; so does the Earl of Lytton—now Viceroy), it shows us Mallock in a happier mood than we have ever seen him, a spinner of sparkling conversations that can make even the most loosely woven narrative hold one's lasting interest.

"Fantastic Tricks"

In the last of his nineteenth-century novels, *The Individualist* (1899, no. 84), Mallock gave his familiar mixture a final shake. There is Tristram Lacy, newly enriched and promising, the nephew of the Prime Minister (a nice combination of Disraeli, Gladstone, and Lord Rosebery, with a touch of Bulwer-Lytton thrown in), who suffers the familiar lassitude and has undergone the familiar flirtation with Rome (he once forgot a dinner party because he was reading "a German history of the growth of the early Church"). Now even his "romance of family pride is gone. It was but one form of faith. It has died with all the others." For Lacy "modern knowledge and science—if indeed they tell us the truth—have broken in like daylight on the stage at an afternoon performance, leaving the scenery, but quite destroying the illusion, and putting our faiths, the footlights of life, out." There is the handsome and earnest Catholic young woman (this time a widow), the utterly beautiful young girl who falls in love with Lacy, the London society woman and political hostess who makes illicit love at night, in mask and domino, in what amounts to an upper-class house of assignation. The chief subject of the novel, Mallock himself later wrote, was "still the relation of religion to life, but the subject was handled in a spirit less of emotion than of pure social comedy." The emphasis this time was upon "an exhibition of the 'fantastic tricks' which those who reject the supernatural are driven to play in their attempt to provide the world with a substitute."

In *The Individualist*, these fantastic tricks are played by a group of earnest positivists, humanists, socialists, altruists, atheists, and others who have founded Startfield Hall, a "new philanthropic institution intended to form . . . the headquarters of a band of social and intellectual missionaries." Lacy, who owns some real estate nearby, offers a large contribution to the cause on condition that—besides teaching the poor their "natural rights" and "political economy"—Startfield Hall teach them also their "legal rights" and "domestic economy." Lessons in cooking, household management, and home medical care, he argues, would be very useful, and he further proposes a kind of legal aid society: "a solicitor should attend here, at stated hours, who would give advice, free of charge, to the poor, who as lodgers, tenants, or otherwise, might happen to be in legal difficulties." But the doctrinaire do-gooders dismiss the idea as "a capitalist's dodge," and Lacy's plan is rejected.

When readers of *The Individualist* found that Startfield Hall was located in Bloomsbury, and that the leading spirit among the founders was a certain Mrs. Norham, a woman of extraordinary earnestness, who had written *The Disinherited*, a "novel with a purpose which, despite its length and its solemnity, had achieved an enormous circulation and had raised her to the ranks of a prophetess," they naturally thought that Startfield Hall was a caricature of Passmore Edwards Hall, and Mrs. Norham a caricature of Mrs. Humphry Ward. Not at all, said Mallock solemnly: in 1880, eight years before *Robert Elsmere* had made Mrs. Ward famous, he had published a satirical sketch in which "Mrs. Norham" had already appeared as the wife of a Broad-Church clergyman and the editor of a paper called the *Agnostic Moralist*. But no matter how early he had used the name, in *The Individualist* he was surely using it as a disguise for Mrs. Ward. In 1892, he had attacked *Robert Elsmere* and Mrs. Ward in an article called "Amateur Christianity." Even those who thought her novel any good, he said, would agree that its popularity was "mainly an expression of the prevalence of the devout idea that the essence of Christianity will somehow survive its doctrines." No, says Mallock, with that mixture of class feeling and would-be faith we have so often seen in him, "Persons like Mrs. Ward and the classes whose opinion she reflects"—and for Mallock these are "English-speaking middle-class dissenters"—are "curiously misled when they think they can get rid of dogma without ridding themselves of anything besides." They had better stop calling themselves Christians and, since they regard Christ as "merely man," stop appealing to him as if he were God. These were Mallock's views—propounded at length—on Mrs. Ward, and much of the enjoyment of *The Individualist* derives from the occasionally hilarious portrait (or at least partial portrait) of her as Mrs. Norham.

Some of the best scenes, for example, are those in which she is confronted by her rival novelist, the feminist Mrs. Delia Dickson, who is almost surely Mallock's idea—somewhat wide of the mark, perhaps—of Mrs. Lynn Linton: "whereas Mrs. Norham proposed to reform society by the comparatively simple process of civilizing the masses, who were the makers of civilisation already, Mrs. Dickson was persuaded that so important a miracle depended on a revolution in character of the human male . . . which she was persuaded would soon be accomplished by Woman. . . ." At one awful moment, a well-meaning lady compliments "Mrs. Norham" on the scene in her novel, "in which Constance . . . waits for the clergyman in the vestry, resolved to seek comfort by confessing to him the infidelities of her husband," a scene which, embarrassingly enough, comes not from "Mrs. Norham's" novel at all but from one of "Delia Dickson's," possibly *Under Which Lord.* Things are better for Mrs. Norham when the Prime Minister—himself of course a novelist—whose books were "part of the classical literature of the century"—tells her that "no Englishwoman, not even George Eliot, has ever written our language with such vigour and purity as yourself." Mallock, indeed, has a good deal of fun with Mrs. Norham, climaxed in a positivist religious service full of echoes of *The New Paul and Virginia.*

Yet the joke was partly on Mallock after all. In Langham, the Oxford don of *Robert Elsmere,* so paralyzed by doubt that everything in his life—his academic career and his relations with women—has turned sour, Mrs. Ward in 1888 had produced, without knowing it, a far more telling portrait of the dilemma of a Mallock hero, and of

Mallock himself, than eleven years later Mallock was able to produce of her. Where Mrs. Norham is satirized as a parlor radical who likes nothing so much as the company of the rich and powerful, and as a positivist like Paul of *The New Paul and Virginia* who derives his enjoyment from the wine that somebody else is drinking, these blows go wide of the mark. But just as Langham, despising himself all the time for seeming to toy with the affections of a young girl, makes love to Catherine Elsmere's younger sister, Rose, a determined young musician quite able to take care of herself, and eventually lacks the courage to marry her, so Mallock—making mischief like his own Vernon or, indeed, like Lacy of *The Individualist* himself—could never bring himself to establish a stable permanent relationship with a woman. His philandering—reflecting the lack of seriousness that doubt stimulated—kept him forever from what in his own words should have been "the heart of life." And Mrs. Ward, who knew the type, had drawn it in Langham as effectively as Mallock himself. For such Victorians, no matter how they proclaimed their emancipation and sought substitutes for faith, doubt was a disease that sapped their moral fibre and eroded their chances for effective and happy lives.

A Summing Up

It would serve little purpose to try to generalize once again about the varied symptoms manifested by the extraordinary collection of fictional sufferers from religious doubt. Although the symposiasts of *The New Republic* were exaggerating when they declared that during the thirty years between 1847 and 1877 atheism had supplanted Christianity, and that "four out of five of the more thoughtful and instructed men of the day" regarded the very idea of a personal God or personal immortality as absurd, their overstatement cannot blind us to the realization that the phenomenon was extremely widespread indeed. The debate of the members of the Metaphysical Society—believers and unbelievers—on the impact of increased doubt upon morality shows that all observers who did not willfully blind themselves to their surroundings were agreed that doubt and unbelief and apostasy were rampant. Nor—as we have seen—were they confined to the "thoughtful and instructed men of the day," but pervaded all ranks of society and all levels of education.

There are, of course, certain phenomena that appear and reappear in our novels of doubt. Many of the novels are autobiographical and reveal the close relationship—directly stated by Butler in *The Fair Haven*—between parental behavior towards children and the religious development of those children as they grow up. Would Froude, or Mrs. Lynn Linton, or Olive Schreiner, or Butler himself have lost their faith if their parents had treated them differently? Even in the novels that are not autobiographical, cruelty to a child—as in *Donovan*—often plays a major part in launching the victim on the path to atheism. Yet doubts crop up, of course, in children from happy and united households, like the Arnolds'.

But the current that flows most strongly through the novels of doubt, with all their bewildering diversity, is the current of Froude's "rivers of wretchedness that run below the surface of modern society." When childhood faith is impaired or disappears, it is replaced most often by the strong impulse towards social benevolence. So Mrs. Lynn Linton's Victorian Christ, Joshua Davidson, is not divine, but wholly human and, like Mark Rutherford and M'Kay in Drury Lane, devoted to the outcasts of society. Even Miss Jewsbury's Everhard works among the Welsh miners. Donovan is brought slowly back from atheism by *acting* like a Christian, and is inspired by Osmond, the liberal Broad-Church slum priest. Robert Elsmere's new sect has little reality, but his Elgood Street settlement house and his social work among the Rotherhithe poor save his sanity: even as a believer, he had performed the same functions among the peasantry. In each of Mallock's novels, the same note is sounded: from Vernon's efforts in *A Romance of the Nineteenth Century* to sublimate his doubts and neurasthenia by generosity, through the elaborate social and religious projects of *The Old Order Changes*, to the satirical treatment in *The Individualist* of such efforts when divorced from religion.

As Gosse so shrewdly noted in *Father and Son*, believing Christians of all types and sects had, during the latter part of the century, come to put their emphasis upon philanthropy, upon "strenuous labour for the good of others." We would now add: so did unbelievers. From the most devout Catholic to the most uncertain freethinker and the most blatant atheist, all those who expressed themselves upon the religious question in novels increasingly proclaimed the desperate need of persons neglected by society, and they portrayed fictional characters as fulfilling their aspirations by helping such persons. In the end, then, the believers and the unbelievers joined hands on the social issue. For believers it had become what Mallock's Father Stanley called it, "the youngest branch of theology"; for unbelievers, who rejected theology root and branch, it was nonetheless the overriding preoccupation. On this at least, there was no difference between faith, no matter how intense, and doubt, no matter how militant.

LIST OF BOOKS
IN THE GARLAND REPRINT SERIES
VICTORIAN FICTION
NOVELS OF FAITH AND DOUBT

SELECTED BY THE AUTHOR

CATHOLIC AND ANTI-CATHOLIC NOVELS

1. [Kennedy, Grace] Anon. *Father Clement.* 1823.
   Bound with
   [Anon.]. *Father Oswald. A Genuine Catholic Story.* 1842.
2. Sewell, William. *Hawkstone: A Tale of and for England in 184-.* 1845.
3. Edgar, A. H. *John Bull and the Papists; or, Passages in the Life of an Anglican Rector.* 1846.
4. Trollope, Mrs. Frances Milton. *Father Eustace: A Tale of the Jesuits.* 1847.
5. [Harris, Elizabeth Furlong Shipton] A Companion Traveller. *From Oxford to Rome, and How it Fared with Some Who Lately Made the Journey.* 1847.
   Bound with
   Rest in the Church. 1848.
6. [Newman, John Henry] Anon. *Loss and Gain: The Story of a Convert.* 1848.
   Bound with
   Callista: A Sketch of the Third Century. 1856.
7. Fullerton, Lady Georgiana. *Grantley Manor: A Tale.* 1847.
8. Sinclair, Catherine. *Beatrice; or, The Unknown Relatives.* 1852.
9. Wiseman, Nicholas Patrick Stephen. *Fabiola; or, The Church of the Catacombs.* 1854.
10. Fullerton, Lady Georgiana. *Mrs. Gerald's Niece. A Novel.* 1869.
11. Burnand, Francis C. *My Time and What I've Done With It. An Autobiography. Compiled from the diary, notes, and personal recollections of Cecil Colvin.* 1874.

12. Dering, Edward Heneage. *Sherborne; or, the House at the Four Ways.* 1875.
13. Douglas, Lady Gertrude. *Linked Lives.* 1876.
14. Longueville, Thomas de. *The Life of a Prig.* 1885.
15. Randolph, Edmund. *Mostly Fools. A Romance of Civilization.* 1886.
16. [Barry, Canon William Francis] Anon. *The New Antigone.* 1887.
17. [Craigie, Pearl Maria-Theresa] John Oliver Hobbes. *The School for Saints.* 1897.

    Bound with

    Robert Orange. 1900.
18. Moore, George. *Evelyn Innes.* 1898.

    Bound with

    Sister Teresa. 1901.
19. Ward, Mary Augusta [Mrs. Humphry Ward]. *Helbeck of Bannisdale.* 1898.
20. Barry, William Francis. *The Two Standards.* 1898.
21. Sheehan, Patrick Augustine. *The Triumph of Failure.* 1899.

    Bound with

    [Dennehy, Henry E.] Cyril. *A Flower of Asia.* 1901.

TRACTARIAN AND ANTI-TRACTARIAN NOVELS

22. Gresley, William. *Portrait of an English Churchman.* 1838.

    Bound with

    Charles Lever; or, The Man of the Nineteenth Century. 1841.

    Bound with

    Church Clavering; or, The Schoolmaster. 1843.
23. Paget, Francis E. *St. Antholin's; or, Old Churches and New. A Tale for the Times.* 1841.

    Bound with

    Milford Malvoisin; or Pews and Pew-Holders. 1842.
24. Yonge, Charlotte M. *Abbeychurch; or, Self-Control and Self-Conceit.* 1844.

    Bound with

    The Castle-Builders; or, The Deferred Confirmation. 1854.

25. Fullerton, Lady Georgiana. *Ellen Middleton. A Tale.* 1844.
26. Sewell, Elizabeth Missing. *Margaret Percival.* 1847.
    Bound with
    The Experience of Life; or, Aunt Sarah. 1853.
27. Heygate, William Edward. *William Blake; or, The English Farmer.* 1848.
28. Skene, Felicia. *Use and Abuse.* 1849.
    Bound with
    Hidden Depths. 1866.
29. [Ingelow, Jean] Anon. *Allerton and Dreux; or, The War of Opinion.* 1851.
30. Yonge, Charlotte M. *The Heir of Redclyffe.* 1853.
31. [Davies, Charles Maurice] An Ex-Puseyite. *Philip Paternoster. A Tractarian Love Story.* 1858.
32. Disraeli, Benjamin. *Lothair.* 1870.
    Bound with
    Harte, Bret. *Lothaw, or the Adventures of a Young Gentleman in Search of Religion.* 1871.
33. Shorthouse, Joseph H. *John Inglesant.* 1880.
34. Pater, Walter. *Marius the Epicurean.* 1885.
35. Linton, Mrs. Eliza Lynn. *Under Which Lord? A Novel.* 1879.
36. Buchanan, Robert. *Foxglove Manor.* 1884.
37. Corelli, Marie. *A Romance of Two Worlds.* 1886.
38. Adderley, Hon. James Granville. *Stephen Remarx. The Story of a Venture into Ethics.* 1893.
    Bound with
    Caine, [Thomas] Hall. *The Christian.* 1897.

EVANGELICAL AND ANTI-EVANGELICAL NOVELS

39. Trollope, Mrs. Frances Milton. *The Vicar of Wrexhill.* 1837.
40. [Tonna, Mrs.] Charlotte Elizabeth. *Falsehood and Truth.* 1841.
    Bound with
    Conformity. 1841.

41. Long, Lady Catherine. *Sir Roland Ashton. A Tale of the Times.* 1844.
    Bound with
    Howard, Anne. *Mary Spencer. A Tale for the Times.* 1844.
42. Tayler, Charles B. *Mark Wilton. The Merchant's Clerk.* 1848.
    Bound with
    Farrar, Frederick William. *Eric; or, Little by Little.* 1858.
43. Eliot, George. *Scenes of Clerical Life.* 1858.
44. Guyton, Mrs. Emma Jane Worboise. *The Wife's Trials; or, Lilian Grey.* 1858.
    Bound with
    Husbands and Wives. 1873.
45. [Smith, Sarah] Hesba Stretton. *Jessica's First Prayer.* 1867.
    Bound with
    Little Meg's Children. 1868.
    Bound with
    Alone in London. 1869.
    Bound with
    Pilgrim Street. 1872.
46. Charles, Elizabeth. *The Bertram Family.* 1876.

BROAD-CHURCH NOVELS

47. Kingsley, Charles. *Hypatia; or, New Foes with an Old Face.* 1853.
48. Conybeare, William John. *Perversion; or, the Causes and Consequences of Infidelity.* 1856.
49. [Robinson, Frederick William] Anon. *High Church.* 1860.
50. [Robinson, Frederick William] Author of *High Church. No Church.* 1861.
51. [Robinson, Frederick William]. *Church and Chapel.* 1863.
52. Robinson, Frederick William. *Beyond the Church.* 1866.
53. MacDonald, George. *David Elginbrod.* 1863.
54. Butler, Samuel. *The Fair Haven. A work in defence of the miraculous element in our Lord's ministry upon earth . . . By the late John Pickard Owen, edited by William Bickersteth Owen, with a memoir of the Author.* 1873.
55. Davies, Charles Maurice. *Broad Church.* 1875.

56. Davies, Charles Maurice. *'Verts; or, the Three Creeds.* 1876.

NOVELS OF DISSENT

57. Gaskell, Elizabeth Cleghorn. *Ruth.* 1853.
58. Oliphant, Margaret O. W. *Salem Chapel.* 1863.
59. MacDonald, George. *Alec Forbes of Howglen.* 1865.
60. MacDonald, George. *Robert Falconer.* 1868.
61. Howitt, William. *Woodburn Grange.* 1867.
62. MacDonald, George. *Paul Faber, Surgeon.* 1879.
63. [White, William Hale] Mark Rutherford. *The Autobiography of Mark Rutherford, Dissenting Minister.* 1881.

    Bound with

    Mark Rutherford's Deliverance. 1885.
64. [White, William Hale] Mark Rutherford. *The Revolution in Tanner's Lane.* 1887.

    Bound with

    Miriam's Schooling. 1890.
65. [White, William Hale] Mark Rutherford. *Catherine Furze.* 1893.

    Bound with

    Clara Hopgood. 1896.
66. [Smith, Frederick R.] John Ackworth. *The Minder: the story of the Courtship, Call and Conflicts of John Ledger, Minder and Minister.* 1900.

    Bound with

    The Coming of the Preachers: A Tale of the Rise of Methodism. 1901.

NOVELS OF DOUBT

67. Jewsbury, Geraldine Ensor. *Zoe: The History of Two Lives.* 1845.
68. Froude, James Anthony. *The Nemesis of Faith.* 1849.

    Bound with

    Shadows of the Clouds. 1847.
69. Craik, Dinah Maria Mulock. *Olive.* 1850.
70. Arnold, William Delafield. *Oakfield; or, Fellowship in the East.* Second edition. 1854.

71. Yonge, Charlotte M. *The Clever Woman of the Family.* 1865.
72. [Linton, Mrs. Eliza Lynn] Anon. *The True History of Joshua Davidson.* 1872.
73. Reade, William Winwood. *The Outcast.* 1875.
74. Yonge, Charlotte M. *Magnum Bonum; or, Mother Carey's Brood.* 1879.
75. Gissing, George. *Workers in the Dawn.* 1880.
76. Mallock, W. H. *A Romance of the Nineteenth Century.* 1881.
77. [Bayley, Ada Ellen] Edna Lyall. *Donovan. A Novel.* 1882.
78. [Schreiner, Olive] Ralph Iron. *The Story of an African Farm.* 1883.
79. Buchanan, Robert. *The New Abelard. A Romance.* 1884.
80. Linton, Mrs. Eliza Lynn. *The Autobiography of Christopher Kirkland.* 1885.
81. Mallock, W. H. *The Old Order Changes.* 1886.
82. Ward, Mary Augusta [Mrs. Humphry Ward]. *Robert Elsmere.* 1888.
83. [Humphreys, Mrs. Desmond] Rita. *Sheba. A Story of Girlhood.* 1889.
84. Gould, Frederick James. *The Agnostic Island: A Tale.* 1891.
    Bound with
    Mallock, W. H. *The Individualist.* 1899.
85. Mallock, W. H. *A Human Document.* 1892.
86. Mallock, W. H. *The Heart of Life.* 1895.
87. Butler, Samuel. *The Way of All Flesh.* 1903.

OTHER NOVELS

88. Besant, Walter. *In Deacon's Orders.* 1895.
    Bound with
    Cholmondely, Mary. *Red Pottage.* 1899.
89. [Oliphant, Margaret O. W.]. *The Rector and the Doctor's Family.* 1863.
90. Oliphant, Margaret O. W. *The Perpetual Curate.* 1864.
91. Oliphant, Margaret O. W. *Miss Marjoribanks.* 1866.
92. Oliphant, Margaret O. W. *Phoebe, Junior. A Last Chronicle of Carlingford.* 1876.

BIBLIOGRAPHICAL NOTE

The chief source for this book has been the novels themselves, primarily the 121 titles I selected for inclusion in the Garland reprint series, but also a good many others "not in series (NIS)" to which I refer when appropriate. But of course I have gratefully availed myself of the work of previous scholars in Victorian religious history in general and on individual novelists and novels. *Victorian Prose, A Guide to Research*, ed. David J. DeLaura (New York: Modern Language Association of America, 1973)—hereafter *VP: Guide*—includes sections of thorough bibliographical information and useful comment on John Henry Newman, Walter Pater, The Oxford Movement, The Victorian Churches, and The Unbelievers. Many of the individual novelists are listed in *The New Cambridge Bibliography of English Literature*, Vol. 3, ed. George Watson (Cambridge: University Press, 1969), with references to scholarly work about them down to about 1966. It is often inaccurate in detail. It would be pointless to list here the hundreds of valuable books and articles, already listed in these bibliographies, which I have consulted and found helpful. In the paragraphs that follow I therefore confine myself to basic works, or works too recent for inclusion in the bibliographies, or works that may not have been mentioned in the sparse footnotes to the text, but which call for special mention.

Three earlier full-length books have dealt with large aspects of our subject. Joseph Ellis Baker, *The Novel and the Oxford Movement* (Princeton: Princeton University Press, 1932) is a pioneering work on the Tractarian novel, still useful and interesting. Margaret Maison, *The Victorian Vision. Studies in the Religious Novel* (New York: Sheed and Ward, 1961, published in England as *Search Your Soul, Eustace*) is the only previous attempt at a discussion of all aspects of Victorian religious fiction. Written from the Catholic standpoint, and full of insight into many individual novels and novelists, it is lively and contains a useful, long (though designedly incomplete) list of novels. Miss Maison, however, was forced to treat many important novels rather superficially. There are many slips: for example, George Eliot's Mr. Gilfil is not Evangelical but "High-and-Dry"; Squire Wendover's book, *Idols of the Marketplace* (in Mrs. Humphry Ward's *Robert Elsmere*), is not a "monumental history of religion," but a study of historical evidence ("testimony"); in dealing with Winwood Reade's *The Outcast*, Miss Maison mistakes a short preliminary episode for the entire novel. She and I differ in our views of many novels and novelists. Finally, Raymond Chapman, *Faith and Revolt. Studies in the Literary Influence of the Oxford Movement* (London: Weidenfeld and Nicolson, 1970) returns to the narrower Tractarian subject of Professor Baker's study with the advantages of more than a generation of additional scholarship to draw upon, and widens his net to include poets as well as novelists. With these general studies belong two works somewhat narrower in scope. U. C. Knoepflmacher, *Religious Humanism and the Victorian Novel: George Eliot, Walter Pater, and Samuel Butler* (Princeton: Princeton University Press, 1965) has been particularly valuable to me in my treatment of Samuel Butler. I have ventured occasionally to disagree with Knoepflmacher's conclusions, however, about all three of his novelists. Four of the five novelists treated in Vineta Colby, *The Singular Anomaly: Women Novelists of the Nineteenth Century* (New York: New York University Press, 1970)—Mrs. Lynn Linton, Olive Schreiner, Pearl Maria-Theresa Craigie, and Mrs. Humphry Ward—are also dealt with in this book; I found the chapters on Olive Schreiner and Mrs. Craigie useful.

All students of the Victorian period are indebted to Owen Chadwick, *The Victorian Church,* Vols. VII and VIII of *An Ecclesiastical History of England,* ed. J. C. Dickinson (London: Adam and Charles Black, 1966, 1970), for a beautifully written and sophisticated study with fine bibliographies, High-Church in its point of view. Indispensable and providing the kind of theological commentary impossible to find elsewhere without great difficulty is E. J. Bicknell, *A Theological Introduction to the Thirty-nine Articles of the Church of England,* 3d edition, revised by H. J. Carpenter (London, New York, Toronto: Longmans, Green,

1955). Two selections of documents with valuable long introductions are Owen Chadwick, *The Mind of the Oxford Movement* (London: Adam and Charles Black, 1960), and E. R. Norman, *Anti-Catholicism in Victorian England* (London: George Allen and Unwin, 1968), Historical Problems: Studies and Documents, ed. G. R. Elton. Geoffrey Best, "Popular Protestantism in Nineteenth-Century Britain," *Ideas and Institutions of Victorian Britain. Essays in Honour of George Kitson Clark*, ed. Robert Robson (London: G. Bell and Sons, 1967), pp. 115-142, is a fine essay.

On Newman's novels, I have taken issue, though without openly saying so, with the views of George Levine (in writings listed in *VP: Guide*, pp. 146-147), and agree with Martin Svaglie's strictures there set down. David Newsome, *The Parting of Friends. A Study of the Wilberforces and Henry Manning* (London: John Murray, 1966) gives the reader a fine account of the personal relationships among the most brilliant of the young men affected by the Oxford movement, and of the complex play of forces within the Church of England before about 1850. Olive Brose, *Frederick Denison Maurice, Rebellious Conformist* (Ohio University Press, 1971) is a book for which scholars have longed: a lucid analysis of Maurice's ideas against the background of his turbulent career. Much less ambitious, but helpful, is Frank Mauldin McClain, *Maurice, Man and Moralist* (London: SPCK, 1972). Melvin Richter's splendid book, *The Politics of Conscience. T. H. Green and His Age* (Cambridge: Harvard University Press, 1964), enables one to understand the climate of the seventies and eighties and the ethical origins of the doubt that is the subject of *Robert Elsmere.* Susan Chitty, *The Beast and the Monk. A Life of Charles Kingsley* (New York: Mason/Charter, 1975) uses much source material previously unavailable, correcting and enlarging previous treatments of Kingsley's life; the new information hardly affects one's interpretation of *Hypatia* or *Yeast.* Readers of the present book may be interested in my article, "Some Erring Children in Children's Literature: The World of Victorian Religious Strife in Miniature," *The Worlds of Victorian Fiction, Harvard English Studies* 6 (1975): 295-318.

I regret that Valentine Cunningham, *Everywhere Spoken Against. Dissent in the Victorian Novel* (Oxford: Clarendon Press,

1975), appeared after my manuscript had gone to the printer. Cunningham's fine study does not confine itself, as the chapter on Dissenters in this book has had to do, to novels primarily about Dissenters. He not only sharpens our apprehension of the position of Dissenters in Victorian England but discusses their appearance in the novels of the Brontës, Mrs. Gaskell, George Eliot, and Dickens. It is in his chapters on Mrs. Oliphant and William Hale White that he to some degree overlaps with my treatment of these authors. Students of the subject will probably find, however, that both of us are worth reading.

INDEX